THE REHEARSAL
TRANSPROS'D

AND

THE REHEARSAL
TRANSPROS'D
THE SECOND PART

ANDREW MARVELL

THE REHEARSAL TRANSPROS'D

AND

THE REHEARSAL TRANSPROS'D
THE SECOND PART

EDITED BY D. I. B. SMITH

OXFORD

AT THE CLARENDON PRESS

1971

Oxford University Press, Ely House, London W. 1

GLASGOW NEW YORK TORONTO MELBOURNE WELLINGTON
CAPE TOWN SALISBURY IBADAN NAIROBI DAR ES SALAAM LUSAKA ADDIS ABABA
BOMBAY CALCUTTA MADRAS KARACHI LAHORE DACCA
KUALA LUMPUR SINGAPORE HONG KONG TOKYO

PRINTED IN GREAT BRITAIN

TO THE MEMORY OF

J. B. LEISHMAN

AND

HERBERT DAVIS

ACKNOWLEDGEMENTS

I AM grateful to many people for their help. J. B. Leishman and Herbert Davis assisted and encouraged me with great kindness from the time that I undertook this edition. Professor Pierre Legouis most generously made available his copy of *A Love Letter to the Author of the Rehearsal Transpros'd*—a manuscript reply to Marvell's work, remarkable in its scurrility. My deepest indebtedness is, however, to that gracious scholar Mrs. Elsie Duncan-Jones who allowed me the use of her files on *The Rehearsal Transpros'd*. Where her material has been directly used in the annotations I have initialled it thus [E.D.J.] but I have benefited as well from many hints and suggestions drawn from her deep knowledge of Marvell. Dr. A. B. Scott and Mrs. Carmel Young assisted with some classical references.

I am grateful to the Canada Council and the University of Toronto for grants in aid of research, and to the many libraries (listed in the textual notes) where I have examined copies.

My especial thanks to the Bodleian Staff for their forbearing and kindness over the years.

D. I. B. S.

University College
Toronto

CONTENTS

INTRODUCTION

I

IN September 1672 Andrew Marvell, Member of Parliament for Hull, author of some lyrics, a few poems in praise of Cromwell, and sundry lampoons, emerged from the 'modest retiredness' to which he had 'hitherto been addicted',[1] to cross swords with the newest star of Anglican polemic, Samuel Parker.

Parker was an energetic young divine, rapidly climbing the ladder of preferment, turning out works exalting the power of the King in ecclesiastical matters and pouring floods of 'odious reproaches' upon the dissenters. He had been puritanically educated and his father had been made a baron of the Exchequer by Cromwell.[2] At Wadham he belonged to a strict sect known as the Grewellers. However, after the warden of the college had convinced him of the error of his ways, he became an enthusiastic member of the Church of England and turned against his former companions. In 1664 he was ordained and in 1665 he published *Tentamina de Deo* and became a fellow of the Royal Society. In the following year he published *A Free and Impartial Censure of the Platonick Philosophie*, in which those characteristics which Marvell found so distasteful in his later works are already displayed—his hatred of 'enthusiasm' and his dislike of the 'common and mechanical sort of men'. This theme is continued in a work of the same year, *An Account of the Nature and Extent of the Divine Dominion and Goodnesse*, where he fears that if the common people be '. . . suffered to run without restraint, they will break down all the banks of Law and Government . . .'.[3] In 1667 he became chaplain to Archbishop Sheldon and was presented to the rectory of Chatham, Kent. In 1669 he wrote the first work to which Marvell takes exception in *The Rehearsal Transpros'd*: *A Discourse of Ecclesiastical Politie, wherein the authority of the Civil Magistrate over the Consciences of Subjects in matters of Religion is asserted; the Mischiefs and*

---

[1] Below, Part II, p. 169.   [2] John Parker (*fl.* 1655), see *D.N.B.*
[3] Samuel Parker, *An Account of the Nature and Extent of the Divine Dominion and Goodnesse*, 2nd edn., 1667, p. 219.

Inconveniences of Toleration are represented, and all Pretenses pleaded in behalf of Liberty of Conscience are fully answered. The argument of the work is well stated in the title. In June 1670 he was made archdeacon of Canterbury and in November of the same year he was installed prebendary of Canterbury. In 1671 he replied to his answerers with *A Defence and Continuation of the Ecclesiastical Politie*, the second work which Marvell deals with. In 1672 he received the rectory of Ickham in Kent and wrote *A Preface Shewing what grounds there are of Fears and Jealousies of Popery*, prefixed to Bishop Bramhall's *Vindication of himself and the Episcopal Clergy from the Presbyterian Charge of Popery*. This finally goaded Marvell to action, and there appeared *The Rehearsal Transpros'd: Or Animadversions upon a late Book intituled A Preface . . .*, Parker was stung into replying with *A Reproof to the Rehearsal Transpros'd*. Marvell countered with the second part of *The Rehearsal Transpros'd* and his opponent was laughed so completely out of countenance that he retired from the struggle.

In the *Discourse of Ecclesiastical Politie*, Parker argues that the beliefs of men are so wayward and various, that it is necessary for the peace and good government of the nation, that the governor have absolute power in matters of religion. His zeal in upbraiding enthusiasm would have amazed the most ardent dissenter. He could see no middle way between religious tyranny and religious anarchy. Although critical of Hobbes, his acceptance of the absolute supremacy of civil power brings him very close to that thinker. He maintained moreover (in common with most of his fellow divines), that obedience is the fundamental law of human societies. In his reply, *Truth and Innocence Vindicated* (1669), John Owen argued that the judgements of conscience are antecedent to any command of the magistrate. Parker vociferously abuses Owen in the *Defence and Continuation of the Ecclesiastical Politie*, citing his sermons against toleration, delivered during the Interregnum. He continues to gird at the dissenters, noting that they '. . . are meerly acted by giddy and Enthusiastick whimsies, and derive all their religious motions and phantasms from the present state and constitution of their Bodies. . . .'[1]

---

[1] S. Parker, *A Defence and Continuation of the Ecclesiastical Politie*, 1671, p. 339.

The note of religious absolutism is again present throughout the *Preface to Bishop Bramhall's Vindication*, and he renews the attack on Owen as 'the greatest Pest and Most Dangerous Enemy of the Commonwealth'.[1] He points out the dangers of toleration (the King had meanwhile issued the Declaration of Indulgence) and warns that the 'fanatick' party will work the ruin of the Church of England. Once more he urges that the 'common' people must be awed into fear and obedience.

The Rehearsal Transpros'd takes its name and much of its light-hearted technique from Buckingham's farce *The Rehearsal* (1672), first performed on 7 December 1671. In the play, Bayes (in whose character Dryden is satirized) describes his method of composition.

... I take a Book in my hand, either at home, or elsewhere, for that's all one, if there be any Wit in't, as there is no Book but has some, I Transverse it; that is, if it be Prose put it into Verse, (but that takes up some time), if it be Verse, put it into Prose.

Johns: Methinks, Mr. *Bayes*, that putting Verse into Prose should be call'd Transprosing.[2]

The constant stream of wit and scurrility with which Marvell enlivened a work nominally in the field of theological controversy, made *The Rehearsal Transpros'd* an instant success, and provoked numerous replies in a similar vein. Henry Stubbe wrote *Rosemary and Bayes* (1672) in which he is critical of both Parker and Marvell. He was disturbed that the former should be regarded as representative of the Church of England, and pointed out that the latter's discourses were 'indiscreet, incoherent, stuffed with falsities and impertinencies'.[3] The Author of *A Common Place-Book Out of the Rehearsal Transpros'd* (1673), casts a number of slurs on Marvell's character, and objects to Marvell's treatment of the Civil War. Richard Leigh's *The Transproser Rehears'd* (1673) is the most successful effort to rail at Marvell in his own manner, visualizing him as a 'Coffee House *virtuoso*'.[4] He also finds fault with Marvell's treatment of Bishop Laud and the causes of the Civil War. *S'too him Bayes*

[1] *Preface to Bishop Bramhall's Vindication*, 1672, CIV (unpaginated).
[2] George Villiers, Duke of Buckingham, *The Rehearsal*, 1672, I, i, p. 4.
[3] Henry Stubbe, *Rosemary and Bayes*, 1672, p. 5.
[4] Richard Leigh, *The Transproser Rehears'd*, 1673, pp. 34 ff.

(1673) moves laboriously from quibble to quibble on Marvell's text, and also endeavours to discredit Marvell's character. In *Gregory, Father-Greybeard, with his Vizard off* (1673), Edmund Hickeringill is critical of Marvell's attitude to the clergy, accuses him of countenancing rebellion, and repeats Parker's call for obedience to the magistrate. Parker's *Reproof* turns upon Marvell the violent abuse which had hitherto fallen on the dissenters:

Thou a Rat-Divine! thou hast not the Wit and Learning of a Mouse; when thou endeavour'st to bite, thou canst not so much as nibble. Thou talk of Government, of the Crowns and State of Princes! to School, Truant, mind your Push-pin, and con your eight parts of Speech. . . .[1]

He relates as many scandalous stories about Marvell and his background as he possibly can, and continues to urge his great thesis:

That it is absolutely necessary to the peace and government of the world, that the Supreme Magistrate of every Commonwealth should be vested with a Power to govern and conduct the Consciences of Subjects in affairs of Religion.[2]

The second part of *The Rehearsal Transpros'd* effectively closed the debate and Antony Wood summed up the struggle:

. . . wherein was represented a perfect trial of each others skill and parts in a jerking, flirting way of writing, entertaining the reader with a great variety of sport and mirth, in seeing two such right cocks of the game so keenly engaging with sharp and dangerous weapons. And it was generally thought, nay even by many of those who were otherwise favourers of Parker's cause, that he (Parker) thro' a too loose and unwary handling of the debate (tho' in a brave, flourishing and lofty stile) laid himself too open to the severe strokes of his snearing adversary, and that the odds and victory lay on Marvell's side: Howsoever it was, it wrought this good effect upon our author, that for ever after it took down somewhat of his high spirit, insomuch that tho' Marvell in a second part replied upon our author's reproof, yet he judged it more prudent rather to lay down the cudgels than to enter the lists again. . . .[3]

---

[1] S. Parker, *A Reproof to The Rehearsal Transprosed*, 1673, p. 5.
[2] Ibid., p. 3.
[3] A. Wood, *Athenae Oxonienses*, ed. Bliss, vol. iv, 1820, col. 231.

II

Marvell's purpose in writing *The Rehearsal Transpros'd* seems to have been threefold: he wished to woo Charles II away from the clutches of the Church of England 'politicians', to convince him of the rightness of his policy of indulgence for dissenters, and to silence Samuel Parker. His work is therefore directed to the King. Its appearance was a masterpiece of timing, since he was able throughout to pose as Charles's saviour. He praised the King's wisdom, called on men to trust him, and disposed of any fears as to religious toleration. For royal policy in 1672—the war against the Dutch, and the acts leading up to it (the Stop to the Exchequer, and the Declaration of Indulgence)—proved exceedingly unpopular.[1] The Declaration of Indulgence in particular provoked fierce opposition, especially in Parliament. Even noted dissenters like Alderman Love attacked it. '. . . He had much rather still go without their desired Liberty, than have it in a Way that would prove so detrimental to the Nation.'[2] Many Nonconformists regarded it as a step toward the re-introduction of Popery. The House of Commons looked on it as a despotic suspension of the nation's laws.

. . . your majesty's having claimed a power to suspend penal Statutes, in matters Ecclesiastical, and which your maj. does still seem to assert, in the said Answer, to be 'intrusted in the crown, and never questioned in the reigns of any of your ancestors;' wherein we humbly conceive, your maj. hath been very much mis-informed; since no such power was ever claimed, or exercised, by any of your maj's predecessors; and, if it should be admitted, might tend to the interrupting of the free course of the laws, and altering of the legislative power, which hath always been acknowledged to reside in your majesty, and your two houses of parliament.[3]

Members of the Church of England regarded the Declaration as a death blow to the Establishment. Such at least was the opinion of Sir John Reresby.

The King did issue out his proclamation for indulgence to tender

---

[1] See K. H. D. Haley, *William of Orange and the English Opposition 1672–4*, 1953.
[2] L. Eachard, *The History of England*, 3rd edn., 1720, p. 889, col. 2.
[3] The Commons' Second Address to the King, 26 Feb. 1672/3, *The Parliamentary History of England*, vol. iv, 1808, col. 551.

conciencys. This made a great noise not only in the succeding Parlaments (wher at last it was reversed) but throughout the kingdome, and was the greatest blowe that ever was given, since the Kings restoration, to the Church of England. . . .[1]

The Church, fearful of its position, began to agitate against the growth of Popery, and to criticize Charles's policy of indulgence.

But now the pulpits were full of a new strain. Popery was every where preached against, and the authority of laws was much magnified. The bishops, he of London in particular, charged the clergy to preach against popery, and to inform the people aright in the controversies between us and the church of Rome. This alarmed the court as well as the city and the whole nation. Clifford began to shew the heat of his temper, and seemed a sort of a [sic] enthusiast for popery. The king complained to Sheldon of this preaching on controversy, as done on purpose to inflame the people, and to alienate them from him and his government.[2]

With Church and Parliament hostile towards his Declaration, it was no wonder that Charles was anxious that the Nonconformists, the very people who stood so much to gain by it, should not reject it. Indeed, in order to gain their compliance, he was prepared to bribe the leaders of the dissenting faction.

When the declaration for toleration was published, great endeavours were used by the court to persuade the nonconformists to make addresses and compliments upon it. Few were so blind as not to see what was aimed at by it . . . yet the presbyterians came in a body, and Dr. Manton, in their name, thanked the king for it; which offended many of their best friends. There was also an order to pay the more eminent men among them a yearly pension, of fifty pounds to most of them, and of an hundred pounds a year to the chief of the party. Baxter sent back his pension, and would not touch it, but most of them took it.[3]

Henry Stubbe, who replied to *The Rehearsal Transpros'd* with *Rosemary and Bayes* (1672), also wrote a defence of Charles's policy in two works: *A Justification of the Present War against the United Netherlands*

[1] Sir J. Reresby, *Memoirs*, ed. Browning, 1936, p. 84.
[2] Gilbert Burnet, *History of my Own Time*, ed. Airy, vol. i, 1897, p. 555.
[3] Ibid., pp. 554–5.

(1672) and *A farther Justification of the present War against the United Netherlands* (1673). He was well rewarded for his pains.

For the compiling of these two last books, the author was allowed the use of the Paper Office at Whitehall, and when they were both finished he had given him 200 £. out of his majesty's Exchequer, and obtained a great deal of credit from all people, especially from the courtiers and all that belonged to the king's court.[1]

In these circumstances *The Rehearsal Transpros'd* might almost have come as an answer to the King's prayer. Not only was his policy defended, his character praised, but the most vigorous opponent of toleration in the age was, after the publication of the second part of Marvell's book, silenced. Marvell posed as a loyal defender of the King against the violent strictures of an unscrupulous preferment-seeking divine. He pointed out how the Church had organized a campaign against Popery, simply in order to thwart the King's policy of indulgence,[2] just as Charles had complained to Sheldon. He went on to argue that Parker's behaviour in raising the cry of popery was therefore treasonable.[3] Throughout *The Rehearsal Transpros'd* Marvell contrasted a wise and prudent King with the brutal and arbitrary tyrant who would emerge as a result of following the counsels of Parker. Nowhere did he question Charles's policy, while he continually urged his readers to 'trust the King'. He even suggested that the King led a better life, morally considered, than many of the clergy, and understood their function better than they did[4]—an outrageous reflection on the clergy, and an indication of how far Marvell was prepared to compromise with truth, in the interest of expediency. Moreover, he argued, kings are possessed of a more than ordinary magnanimity. '. . . For Princes, as they derive the Right of Succession from their Ancestors, so they inherit from that ancient and illustrious extraction, a Generosity that runs in the Blood above the allay of the rest of mankind.'[5] *The Rehearsal Transpros'd* presents a picture of the King, as he might well have visualized himself in a moment of complacency. This is the art of the courtier at its most insinuating.

[1] Wood, *Athenae Oxonienses*, ed. Bliss, vol. iii, 1817, col. 1082.
[2] Below, Part I, p. 119. [3] Ibid., p. 118. [4] Ibid., p. 52.
[5] Below, Part II, p. 233.

Not only did *The Rehearsal Transpros'd* appear when the King needed it most, flattering him and advising a policy of enlightened self-interest, but the very manner in which it was written must have commended it to Charles. He disliked religious controversy. He was not fond of serious discourse and he was averse to preachers treating the authority of sovereigns or speculating about 'election' or 'reprobation' or 'free will'. This he expressed in his letter to the Archbishops in 1662.

The extravagance of preachers has much heightened the disorders, and still continues so to do, by the diligence of factious spirits, who dispose them to Jealousy of the government. Young divines in ostentation of learning, handle the deep points of God's eternal counsel's, or wrangle about gestures and fruitless controversies. To put a timely stop to these abuses, he has, as done by former Kings, drawn up directions for preachers, which are to be communicated to every minister. . . . *None are in their sermons to bound the authority of sovereigns, or determine the differences between them and the people; nor to argue the deep points of election, reprobation, free will, &c.; they are to abstain as much as possible from controversies. . . .*[1]

Marvell might have written *The Rehearsal Transpros'd* with this advice before him. Although he is hardly abstaining from controversy, his work is not any ordinary controversial one. He takes hardly anything that Parker says seriously, and is continually relating outrageous stories to his opponent's discredit. He is certainly most careful in refusing to consider 'deep' questions, and it is very difficult to get a clear idea of what Marvell thought about the fundamental issues of religion, from *The Rehearsal Transpros'd*. In a work which is supposedly concerned with religious toleration, apart from indicating that he is in favour of the King's policy of indulgence, Marvell does not make it clear whether he favoured comprehension or toleration—an issue which divided most other men who considered the problem. Most of the arguments he adduced in support of indulgence were from considerations of prudence. In accordance it would seem with the King's letter, Marvell even apologizes for dealing with kings and princes.[2] Almost the only original sections of the work, and the most effective, are the brilliant comic inven-

[1] *C.S.P.D.*, 14 Oct. 1662, p. 517.   [2] Below, Part I, p. 49.

tions when Marvell is bantering Parker. Nothing could be objected
to the orthodoxy of the doctrine behind the glittering façade.

Moreover, in thus making his opponent a laughing-stock, pil-
lorying him with witty buffoonery, Marvell was making an additional claim to the King's attention. Charles's love of drollery and
light amusement was well known; the Duke of Ormond noted of
him: '. . . his majesty spent most of his time with confident young
men, who abhorred all discourse that was serious, and, in the liberty
they assumed in drollery and raillery, preserved no reverence towards God or man. . . .'[1] The same thing had not escaped the Earl
of Halifax, and he remarked how courtiers took advantage of this
predilection to retain the King's interest.

His *aversion to Formality* made him dislike a *serious Discourse*, if very
long, except it was mixed with something to *entertain* him. Some even
of the graver sort too, used to carry this very far, and rather than fail,
use the coarsest kind of youthful talk.[2]

The Rehearsal Transpros'd is a masterly example of how to clothe a
serious purpose in wit and entertainments. For there can be no
doubt that Marvell's purpose—to separate the King from the power-
seeking element of the Church—was one that he regarded with the
utmost seriousness. This is evident in his letter to his friend Sir
Edward Harley on 3 May 1673, where he affirms his resolution to
reply to Parker's *Reproof.*

However I will for mine own private satisfaction forthwith draw
up an answer that shall haue as much of spirit and solidity in it as my
ability will afford & the age we liue in will indure. I am (if I may say
it with reverence) drawn in, I hope by a good Providence, to intermeddle in a noble and high argument W^ch therefore by how much
it is above my capacity I shall use the more industry not to disparage
it.[3]

That the work succeeded in gaining the attention and approbation of the King we know from the fact that he acted to prevent

[1] W. Harris, *A Historical and Critical Account of the Life of Charles II*, vol. ii, 1766,
p. 39.
[2] George Savile, 'A Character of King Charles II', *Works*, ed. Raleigh, 1912, p. 197.
[3] *Poems & Letters*, ed. Margoliouth, vol. ii, p. 312.

its suppression,[1] and from Burnet's testimony. Burnet wrote of Parker:

His extravagant way of writing gave occasion to the wittiest books that have appeared in this age, for Mr. Marvell undertook him and treated him in ridicule in the severest but pleasantest manner possible, and by this one character one may judge how pleasant these books were; for the last King [Charles II], that was not a great reader of books, read them over and over again.[2]

III

The printing history of the first part of *The Rehearsal Transpros'd* is a curious one: it was printed clandestinely without licence, prevented from being sold after the distribution of the first impression, and allowed only after the King had intervened on its behalf.

Although the Statutes concerning the control of the press required the licensing of all books and the prohibition of seditious works ('Sedition' was interpreted as anything critical of Church or State), not more than half the pamphlet literature published between 1662 and 1679 was licensed.[3] This monumental inefficiency probably sprang from the jealousy of the two foremost powers in matters concerning the press—the Surveyor of the Press Sir Roger L'Estrange, and the Stationers Company. Sir Roger took bribes,[4] and the Stationers Company treated all except their favourites with arbitrary malice: 'It was become a frequent Custom to Seise from some, and connive at others to Print and vend the same.'[5]

The Nonconformists took advantage of this chaos to wage a substantial propaganda campaign for religious toleration. There were

[1] See below.

[2] Gilbert Burnet, *A Supplement to the History of My Own Time*, ed. Foxcroft, 1902, p. 216.

[3] F. S. Siebert, *Freedom of the Press in England 1476–1776*, 1952, p. 243.

[4] Marvell notes '. . . I hope he hath considered *Mr. L.* in private and payed his Fees.' Below, Part I, pp. 22–3.

[5] Francis Smith, *An Account of the Injurious Proceedings of Sir George Jeffreys . . . against Francis Smith Bookseller*, 1681, E1v (mispaginated). See also the Lords Libels Committee 1676–7 for the charges and counter charges by L'Estrange and the Company: H.M.C., *Report 9*, pp. 75–8.

willing printers and an efficient organization for distributing the works.[1]

The unlicensed *Rehearsal Transpros'd* experienced no difficulty at its first printing. It was probably the work of Anne Brewster[2]— widow of the printer for Cromwell's Council of State, and connected with the publication of a number of 'libellous' works including Marvell's later *Account of the Growth of Popery*. In 1678 L'Estrange found her lodging with a copyist who covered the tracks of 'seditious' authors:

> She is in the house of a former officer under Cromwell, that writes three or four very good hands, and owns to have been employed in transcribing things for a counsellor in the Temple; from which one may fairly presume that all those delicate copies, which Brewster carried to the press, were written by her landlord, and copied by him from the author. Besides, it is very probable that the late libels concerning the *Growth of Popery* and the *List of the Members of Parliament* passed through the same hands. . . . If she be questioned, probably she will cast the whole on Mr. Marvell, who is lately dead, and there the enquiry ends.[3]

In 1672 Sir Roger had been equally tardy in tracking down *The Rehearsal Transpros'd*:

> He did not know or hear of the book until the first impression was distributed, and that inquiring of one Brome, a bookseller, about it, he told Lestrange that it was printed for Pinder, who owned the thing, and said, if the book were questioned there were those would justify it and bring him off.[4]

Ponder[5] ('Pinder') was as good as his word, and when two sheets

---

[1] See the Lords Libels Committee, H.M.C., *Report 9*, p. 75 and G. Kitchin, *Sir Roger L'Estrange*, 1913.

[2] The title-page has 'printed by *A.B.*' For Brewster see H. R. Plomer, *Dictionary of Booksellers and Printers 1641–1667*, 1907.

[3] *C.S.P.D.*, 23 Aug. 1678, pp. 372–3.

[4] H.M.C., *Report 7*, pp. 517b–18a. The book may well have been brought to L'Estrange's notice by Parker, since Marvell complains of efforts to have his work suppressed (see below, Part II, p. 173). Baxter was prevented from replying to Parker's 'Preface', and threats were made upon his life (*Reliquiae Baxterianae*, 1696, pt. III, p. 102).

[5] Nathaniel Ponder, a Nonconformist bookseller who had published the works of Dr. Owen and was later to publish those of Bunyan. See F. M. Harrison, 'Nathaniel Ponder: the Publisher of Pilgrims Progress', *The Library*, vol. xv, no. 3, 1934.

of the second issue were seized at the press by Mr. Mearne, Warden
of the Stationers Company, he went to L'Estrange and told him
that the Earl of Anglesey[1] wished to see him.

Lestrange went to Lord Anglesey at his house in Drury Lane,
when the Earl spoke to him in the presence, and as he believes in
the hearing of Pinder to this effect: Look you, Mr. Lestrange, there
is a Book come out (The Rehearsal Transposed [*sic*]), I presume you
have seen it. I have spoken to his Majesty about it, and the King says
he will not have it suppressed; for Parker has done him wrong, and
this man has done him right, and I desired to speak with you to tell
you this; and since the King will have the book to pass, pray give
Mr. Pinder your license to it that it may not be printed from him.[2]

L'Estrange pointed out that:

. . . there were some things not fit to be licensed, viz., the Roman
Emperor receiving a dagger, p. 244; the Wisdom of the King and
Parliament Exposed, p. 310. The Earl took the book, and agreed with
Lestrange, and advised him to alter them, letting the body of the
work remain.[2]

L'Estrange then objected that he did not like to alter a work without the author's permission. 'The Earl said he could not say anything of the author, but those alterations might be made without
him.'[2] Having received this assurance, L'Estrange left with Ponder
and went over the book with him ('all but 2 or 3 sheets') indicating
further objectionable passages. 'Lestrange's first exception was to
the bottom of the title page, "Printed by the assigns of John Calvin,
&c." and he changed and struck out several sharp reflexions upon
Bishop Laud and Dr. Parker, and others also of a more general prospect. . . .'[2] This done, he agreed to license the work, but pointed
out to Ponder that it was not intended to authorize it, but only to
save his propriety. The book's troubles were not over, however, for
the Clerk of the Stationers' Company refused to enter it.

. . . then he give his license to the book, which being signed by a
Warden of the Company and delivered to the Clerk to enter it according to custom for the benefit of the proprietor, and he refusing,

---

[1] Arthur Annesley (1614–86), one of the great 'dissenting Lords'; see *D.N.B.*
[2] H.M.C., *Report 7*, p. 518a.

Lestrange wrote to him at the instance of Pinder to know why, saying he disliked the thing as much as anybody, but being over-ruled he expected the Company's officer should likewise conform.[1]

But *The Rehearsal Transpros'd* did not find its way into the Stationers' Register.

The first evidence we have of L'Estrange's intervention is the changed title-page of the second issue of the first edition. Instead of the offending:

> *LONDON*, Printed by *A.B.* for the Assigns of *John Calvin* and *Theodore Beza*, at the sign of the Kings Indulgence, on the South-side of the *Lake Leman*. 1672.

There is simply:

> *LONDON*, Printed in the Year, 1672.

The body of the work remains unchanged. In fact Bodley's copy of the first edition (8° C118 Linc.) has a censored title-page pasted over the original. Clearly this was not sufficient and *The Rehearsal Transpros'd* was prevented once again.

Lestrange says the book was not printed according to the corrections and emendations of the copy licensed by him, and so in equity not imputable to the licenser. And whãs the first licence being withdrawn a second was desired by Pinder upon another title page, the license was granted expressly under the limitations of the former, and with condition of applying that second title page to the former corrected copy, which Pinder promised should be done.[1]

As a result, the 'Second Impression with Additions and Amendments' appeared. The text incorporated L'Estrange's changes and omissions and some stylistic changes and additions presumably from the hand of Marvell. The title-page returned to a form similar to the first issue of the first edition.

> *London*, Printed by *J.D.*[2] for the Assigns of *John Calvin* and

---

[1] Ibid.

[2] J. D. is John Darby, a notorious printer of libels, known as the 'Religious Printer'. '. . . He printed that excellent Speech of My Lord *Russel*, and several Pieces of Colonel *Sydney* and is a *True Asserter of* English *Liberties*. . . .' (J. Dunton, *Life and Errors*, 1705, p. 328.) He also printed the *Advice to a Painter* series. In his evidence before the Lords Libels Committee he testified that 1,500 copies of *The Rehearsal*

Theodore Beza, at the sign of the *King's Indulgence*, on the South-side the Lake-*Lemane*; and sold by *N. Ponder* in *Chancery-Lane*, 1672.

The first example of L'Estrange's work is probably on p. 2, l. 4, where a reference to Parker as *lewd* is omitted. On p. 109, l. 5, we may probably trace L'Estrange's hand where the phrase 'to whom it belongs' has been inserted following a reference to the licensing of books by bishops. The deletion of a reference, p. 157, l. 20, to Parker's treating his answerer *basely* may well be by L'Estrange; as may the deletion of references to *Ordination* and *Excusation* dinners lines 21, 22–3 of p. 204. The omission of the reference to the Nonconformists being 'thrown out of the Temple'[1] also appears to be the result of censorship. L'Estrange certainly deleted the passage concerning the Roman Emperor, p. 244, ll. 1–5, and probably changed the reference to Archbishop Laud, p. 286, ll. 14–17. He was also undoubtedly responsible for the alteration of the passage concerning 'the Wisdom of his Majesty and the Parliament' on p. 310, ll. 12–15. However, not all of L'Estrange's alterations were carried out for Ponder gave evidence that 'He confesses that L'Estrange ordered several words to be altered, but says that he afterwards allowed some of them at the request of one Mr. Tomson and himself'.[2] The standard of printing of the 'Second Impression' is not as high as that of the first edition and the inaccuracies, particularly in the printing of quotations, suggest that although Marvell was responsible for some of the revisions in this edition, he did not see the proofs.[3] Meanwhile the book's absence from the stalls had been noticed, for in November 1672 we find Benjamin Woodroffe writing to Theophilus seventh Earl of Huntingdon: 'It hath been stopped from spreading, but is

Transpros'd were to be printed—presumably of the 'Second Impression'—H.M.C., *Report 4*, p. 234.

[1] p. 232, ll. 7–8.

[2] H.M.C., *Report on the MSS. of the late Allan George Finch*, vol. ii, 1922, pp. 10–11. This may explain the fact that only some copies of the 'Second Impression' have the passage concerning the 'Wisdom of his Majesty' etc. (see below). Mr. Tomson is perhaps one of the family of Thompsons with whom Marvell was friendly—see *Poems & Letters*, ed. Margoliouth, vol. ii, and C. Robbins, 'Six Letters by Andrew Marvell', *Études Anglaises*, I, janvier–mars, 1964.

[3] Ponder's evidence: 'Knows of nobody but Dr. Owen who had the proofs in his hands.' H.M.C., *Report on the MSS of the late Allan George Finch*, vol. ii, p. 10.

again allowed to be bought.'[1] No further difficulty was experienced, and Marvell seems to have had the second part published without trouble.

There are two other contemporary editions of the first part of *The Rehearsal Transpros'd* both deriving from the first edition, both in 12° and probably pirated, and neither with any textual authority. The first of these is the so called 'Second Edition corrected' of which Ponder complains in his 'Advertisement' to the 'Second Impression'. It includes the first edition *errata*, but as Ponder notes, frequently corrupts 'both the Sence and Words of the Coppy'. The second appeared in 1673 claiming to be the 'Second Impression with Additions and Amendments' printed by *J.X.* The text, however, follows the first edition (with a multitude of accidental variants). Although like the other pirated edition it contains the *errata* corrections, the two editions do not appear to be related.

IV

PART I

This edition is based on a copy of the first edition of *The Rehearsal Transpros'd* in the Houghton Library, Harvard University. The first edition has been followed because it was not printed under the shadow of censorship, has fewer errors (particularly in quotations) and in general seems to have been more reliably printed. Much was omitted as a result of L'Estrange's objections, and even the major addition which resurrects a traditional ecclesiastical joke at the expense of Thomas à Becket, at the same time suppresses a satirical reference to the habits of contemporary priests of the Church of England.[2]

All the substantive variants of the 'Second Impression' have been included in the collation, together with variants from the two 'pirated' editions: 'The Second Edition Corrected' and the edition of 1673. Obvious spelling errors have been corrected (in almost every case by means of the 'Second Impression') and occasional

---

[1] H.M.C., *Report on the MSS of R. R. Hastings*, vol. ii, 1930, p. 161. Marvell seems to have written *The Rehearsal Transpros'd* some time after the end of August 1672, for he notes the raising of the siege of Groningen by the Bishop of Münster (p. 11) an event which took place on 27 Aug. and is reported in the *London Gazette*, No. 707, 26–9 Aug. [2] Below, Part I, p. 92.

mistakes in page references have been emended. Where Marvell or a compositor has misread or misrepresented words in a quotation, the original reading has been given. I have included in the text the 'Additions and Amendments' of the 'Second Impression' where these seem to be Marvell's genuine revisions and not the work of the censor or the compositor. I have retained the punctuation of the first edition, altering it only where the 'Second Impression' reading gives greater clarity and consistency. The *apparatus* has not been overburdened with accidental variants, or variants arising from obvious literal errors.

THE EDITIONS

First Edition (first issue)

Title-page: THE / REHEARSAL / TRANSPROS'D: / Or, / Animadversions / Upon a late Book, Intituled, / A PREFACE / SHEWING / *What Grounds there are* / *of Fears and Jealousies* / *of Popery.* // *LONDON*, Printed by *A.B.* for the / Assigns of *John Calvin* and *Theodore* / *Beza*, at the sign of the Kings Indul- / gence, on the South-side of the *Lake* / *Leman*. 1672.

Collation: 8° [A]¹, B–X⁸, Y³ [[A] and Y1 separate leaves]. 164 leaves pp: [2] 1–189, 191, 192, 192–326 [= 326]

Sigs: $ (4) (–Y3 Y4)

Contents: [A]1r: T.P.; [A]1v: blank; B1r: Half title under a row of type ornaments: *Animadversions upon the* / *Preface to Bishop* Bram- / hall's *Vindication &c.* / Text; Y3v,: FINIS. // *ERRATA.* [with list]

Notes: Harvard's two copies differ slightly, the second [EC65 M3685.672ra] having the spelling *Lemane* on the title-page. The Chapin Library copy follows the title-page given above.

Copies Examined: *Harvard*: EC65.M3685.672r (Copy Text); *Harvard*: EC65.M3685.672ra; *Chapin Library Williams College.*

First Edition (second issue)

The text is unchanged but a new title-page has been inserted in which the comic printer's imprint has been deleted: THE / RE-HEARSAL / TRANSPROS'D: / Or, / Animadversions / Upon a late Book, Intituled, / A PREFACE / SHEWING / *What Grounds there are / of Fears and Jealousies / of* Popery. // *LONDON* / Printed in the Year, 1672.

The copies in the Library of the University of Illinois and in the Oxford English Faculty Library have this title-page. There is a variant title-page in my own copy and those copies at Harvard, Yale and Bodley (in the latter, pasted over the first issue T.P.): THE / REHEARSAL / TRANSPROS'D: / OR, / Animadversions / Upon a late BOOK, entituled, / A PREFACE, / SHEWING /*What Grounds there are / of Fears and Jealousies / of Popery.* // *LONDON* / Printed in the Year, 1672.

The collation, signatures, pagination, and contents follow the first issue.

Copies Examined: *Bodley*: 8° C118 Linc.; *Harvard*: EC65.M3685. 672raa; Editor's Copy; *Yale*: Ij M368.672; *Illinois University Library*; *Oxford English Faculty Library*: Rar. D.234.

Notes: There are two significant press variants in the first edition as a whole. The first, 'ye' for 'yet' on the uncorrected inner forme of Y (p. 323.27)[1] of Bodley 8° C118 Linc. is also found in the 'Second Edition Corrected', where it is 'corrected' to 'yea'. The second, the omission of 'his' on the uncorrected outer forme of Y (p. 324.7)[2] in Bodley 8° C118 Linc., Harvard EC65.M3685.672ra, and Harvard EC65.M3685.672raa, must have been present in the revised and corrected copy of the first edition used to set up the 'Second Impression with Additions and Amendments'.

'The Second Edition Corrected'

Title-page: THE / REHEARSAL / TRANSPROS'D: / Or, / Animadversions upon a / Late BOOK, Intituled, / A PREFACE / SHEWING / *What Grounds there are / of Fears and Jealousies* / of Popery. // *The Second Edition, Corrected.* // *LONDON*, Printed by *A.B.* for the / Assings of *John Calvin* and *Theodore* / *Beza*, at the Sign of the Kings Indul- / gence, on the South-side of the *Lake* / *Lemane*, 1672.

Collation: 12°: [A]², B–H¹², I⁶, K². 94 leaves pp. [4] 1–37, 39, 38,

---

[1] p. 141.1 of this edition. [2] p. 144.5 of this edition.

40–72, 71, 72, 73–152, 134, 154–9, 164, 161–3, 160, 153, 166–81 [= 184] (pp. 143–78 in round brackets the rest in square brackets).

Sigs: $ (5) (–B3 C4, D4 misprinted D3, –I5, K2, K3, K4, K5)

Contents: [A]1: blank; [A]2r; Title; [A]2v: blank; B1r: Half-title under a row of type ornaments: *Animadversions upon the | Preface to Bishop* Bram- | hall's *Vindication*, &c. | Text; K2r: *FINIS*.

Notes: The pirated edition referred to by Ponder in his 'Advertisement' to the 'Second Impression'. It incorporates the *errata* and 'normalizes' many spellings but at the same time introduces a multitude of literal errors. The two types of brackets in pagination may indicate two compositors, though both appear to have been equally prone to misunderstanding.

Copies Examined: *Yale*: Ij M368.672A; *Bodley*: Vet. A3. f. 755.

The Second Impression with Additions and Amendments

There are two different states of the title-page used indiscriminately: THE | REHEARSAL | TRANSPROS'D; | Or, | Animadversions | Upon a late Book, Intituled, | A PREFACE | SHEWING | *What Grounds there are* | *of Fears and Jealousies* | *of* Popery. // The second Impression, with Additions | and Amendments. // *London*, Printed by *J.D.* for the Assigns of | *John Calvin* and *Theodore Beza*, at the sign | of the *King's Indulgence*, on the South-side | the Lake–*Lemane*; and sold by *N. Ponder* in | *Chancery-Lane*, 1672. [Bodley Vet. A3. f. 531; Editor's Copy; Yale Ij M368.672b] THE | REHEARSAL | TRANSPROS'D; | OR, | Animadversions | Upon a late BOOK, | INTITULED, | *A* PREFACE, *shewing* | *what Grounds there are* | *of Fears and Jealousies of* | *Popery.* // The second Impression, with Additions | and Amendments. // *LONDON*, Printed by *J.D.* for the Assigns of | *John Calvin* and *Theodore Beza* at the sign of | the *King's Indulgence* on the South-side of | the *Lake Lemane*; and Sould by *N. Ponder* | in *Chancery Lane*, 1672. [Harvard: EC65.M3685.672rb(A), and (B); Bodley Vet. A3. f. 628, and Ashm. 1591; Oxford English Faculty Library: Rar. D.123.] The 'Advertisement' in the copies with this latter T.P. has slightly different type ornaments.

Collation: 8°: [A]², B–X⁸, Y⁴; 166 leaves pp. [4] 1–229, 214, 219, 232–264, 165, 266–326. [= 326] (pp. 161–240, and 257–272, in round, the rest in square brackets.)

Sigs: $ (4) (-Y3, Y4)

Contents: [A]1: Blank; [A]2r: Title; [A]2v: 'An Advertisement from / the Bookseller', signed 'N.P.' between rows of type ornaments: *This Book having wrought it self thorow | many difficulties, it hath newly incoun- | tred with that of a Counterfeit Impression in 12° | under the Title and pretence of the 2d Edition | Corrected. Whereas in truth that Impression | is so far from having been Corrected, that it doth | grosly and frequently corrupt both the Sence and |Words of the Coppy.*; B1r: Half-title, under a row of type ornaments: *Animadversions upon the | Preface to Bishop Bram- | hall's Vindication, &c.*, Text; Y3v: *FINIS*.

Notes: The censored edition; probably set up by two compositors: Sheets M–Q and S are paginated in round, rather than square brackets and use swash capitals (*B*, *A* and *M* for example) not found in the other gatherings. Not all the copies have been completely censored, and of those I have examined only Bodley: Vet A3. f. 628, Yale: Ij M368.672b, and Harvard: EC65.M3685.672rb(B) have the extensive alterations and corrections to the inner forme of X that carry out L'Estrange's directions. In Bodley Vet A3. f. 531 and Harvard EC65.M3685.672rb(B), M8[1] is a cancel. In the former copy the cancel is pasted to the stub of the original leaf, in the latter the cancel stub is visible between pp. 162–3. Although each page has been reset and altered there seems to be no political reason for the cancel—the alterations are minor ones: one reading returns to a less clear first edition reading: 'of opinion' for 'of the opinion' and another becomes nonsense by the omission of 'have been'.

Copies Examined: *Harvard*: EC65.M3685.672rb(A), *Harvard . . .* (B), *Bodley*: Vet. A3. f. 531, Vet. A3. f. 628, Ashm. 1591; Editor's Copy; *Yale*: Ij M368.672b; *Oxford English Faculty Library*: Rar. D.123.

The Edition of 1673

Title-page: THE / REHEARSAL / TRANSPROS'D; / OR, / ANIMADVERSIONS / Upon a late Book, Intituled, A / PREFACE / SHEWING / What Grounds there are / of Fears and Jealousies of / Popery. // The second Impression, with Additions / and Amendments. // *London*, Printed by *J. X.* for the Assigns of *John | Calvin*

---

[1] p. 79 of this edition.

and *Theodore Beza*, at the sign of the / *King's Indulgence*, on the South-side the Lake- / *Lemane*. 1673.

Collation: 12°: A–B¹², D–G¹², ²G–H¹², K–L¹², ²L–N¹², O⁶. 162 leaves pp. [2] 1–46, 49–96, 65, 98–144, 143–90, 193–208, 219, 210–40, 229–300, 311–13, 114, 315–18, 119, 320–2 [= 324] (pp. 49–144, 193–240, 315–18 in round, the rest in square brackets).

Sigs: \$(5) (–A1, G1, M1, O5).

Contents: A1r: Title; A2r: Half title: ANIMADVERSIONS / Upon the Preface to / *Bishop* BRAMHALL'S / *VINDICATION, &c.* // Text begins; O6v: *FINIS*.

Notes: The format, the carelessness of the printing, the unusual initials of the printer, and the fact that the title-page of the authorized 'Second Impression' was used with the unauthorized first edition text, seem to indicate that this is a pirated edition. A copy of the first edition appears to have been divided between two compositors who then set up the work independently with resulting confusion of pagination and signatures. Compositor C1 setting A, B, ²G, H, ²L, M, N, O (gatherings B–D, L–N, R–Y of the first edition) and Compositor C2 setting D, E, F, G, K, L (gatherings E–K, O–Q of the first edition). C1 set A–B and numbered the pages of text 1–46. He then set ²G–H, numbering the pages 143–190, assuming that C2 had set four gatherings: C–F, paginated 47–142. Continuing his assignment C1 then set ²L–M, on the assumption that I and K had been set by C2. C1's pagination of this stint: 229–300 is presumably an error for 239–300, for according to his calculations C2's pagination should have ended at 238. This error is corrected by C1 (or a third compositor following C1's calculation) in the final gathering O, which is paginated 311–22. C2 presumably imagined that C1 would follow the usual practice and sign the first two gatherings B–C, beginning the pagination on B1r and leaving the prelims for [A]. He therefore set his gatherings D–G and paginated them 49–144. Assuming H and I to have been set by C1 and paginated 145–92, C2 then set K–L, numbering the pages 193–240. At the same time C2 clearly set page for page from his copy of the first edition, for the pagination of his stints: 49–144, 193–240, follows exactly the first edition pagination for those sections of the work.

Copies Examined: Library of the University of Leicester; Library of the American Antiquarian Society.

PART II

The second part of *The Rehearsal Transpros'd* does not pose nearly as many problems as the first part. There are only two editions, both of which were published by the publisher of the authorized 'Second Impression' of the first part, Nathaniel Ponder. There were no official proceedings against this work, indeed Marvell was able to bring it out under his own name. It was, however, not entered in either the Stationers' Register or the *Term Catalogues*. No doubt the book was tacitly allowed, as the first part had been after the intervention of the king.

A number of substantive changes are introduced in the second edition, some of which are clearly Marvell's—those additions or modifications which underline or extend the attack on Parker. The criticism is made more obvious, the lines of the caricature are more deeply etched. One has the impression that Marvell is trying to finish off his opponent and leave no possibility of recourse. His intent and method may be gathered from the fact that two of the more notable additions (pp. 271, 413) raise yet again, the tediously iterated charge that Parker was afflicted with venereal disease. Unlike the first part, there are no omissions or changes which might be ascribed to political or ecclesiastical pressure. There does, however, appear to have been a hurried attempt to modernize and simplify Marvell's tortuous and often difficult prose. Words and clauses are omitted which, while appearing to clarify the immediate context, render the larger passage obscure (pp. 27, 177). More modern spellings are substituted occasionally, as are less archaic word orders —though these may be compositorial alterations.

Neither edition is well printed and typographical errors abound. The printing of italic is execrable and there is a continual confusing of *c* and *e*. Bad inking and offsets in the first edition are compounded in the second: a spot of ink near a full stop becomes a colon: Balsam. ·⟩ Balsam: (p. 45.15); a mark near the r′ turns *mireris* into *mineris* (p. 259.14); *Dolliis* becomes *Doltis* (p. 116.3); a badly inked he becomes h′, and so on. As a result, the text of the second edition often depends on the vagaries of inking in the particular 'corrected' copy of the first edition from which it was set up. This latter fact, together with the impression that a process of smoothing has been attempted on the second edition, has led me to take a copy of the first edition as my copy-text. I have included from the second edition all changes and additions which seem clearly authorial, and where it is necessary to rescue the sense, I have used the punctuation of the second edition. All substantive variants between the two editions are noted, as are the sources of all textual changes in the first edition, with the exception of the correction of turned type.

First Edition

   Title-page: THE / REHEARSALL / TRANSPROS'D: // The SECOND PART. // *Occasioned by Two Letters: The first* / *Printed, by a nameless Author,* / *Intituled,* A Reproof, *&c.* / *The Second Letter left for me at a* / *Friends House, Dated* Nov. 3. / 1673. *Subscribed* J. G. *and* / *concluding with these words*; If / thou darest to Print or Publish / any Lie or Libel against Doctor / *Parker,* By the Eternal God I / will cut thy Throat. // Answered by ANDREW MARVEL // *LONDON,* / *Printed for* Nathaniel Ponder *at the* Peacock *in* / Chancery Lane *near* Fleet-Street, 1673. /

   Collation: 8° [π]², A–Z⁸, Aa–Cc⁸. 210 leaves paginated: [4] 1–65, 56, 67–134, 125, 136–238, 139, 240–319, 292, 321–414 [2] [=420]
   Sigs: $(4)

   Contents: [π]1r: blank [π]1v: Between rows of type ornaments: *REPROOF* p. 67. / IF you have any thing to object / against it, do your worst. You / know the Press is open. /

Licensed the 1st	By the Author and /
of *May* 1673.	Licenser of the Ecclesi- /
	astical Polity. /

[π] 2r: T.P.; [π] 2v: blank; A1r: Half title under a double line: THE / REHEARSAL / TRANSPROS'D. // The Second Part. // Text begins; Cc7v: text ends. // *THE END.* // *ERRATA.* (with list); Cc8: blank.

   Notes: Most of the variants between the copies of the first edition appear to be the result of bad inking, however in two of the copies

I have examined (Bodley: 8° C558 Linc., and [MS] Ashm. 1585)
p. 120. 14–15¹ (H4v, the outer forme) 'not not' has been corrected
to 'not', while only Bodley Linc. 8° is uncorrected on p. 275.1.²
(S2r, inner forme) *Enthuasme* for *Enthusiasme*. More interesting is the
fact that in all the copies I have examined, E5 and E6 are cancels.
In most cases at least one stub is clearly visible. The general messi-
ness of the text leads one to suspect that the reason for the cancels
was simply bad printing. In most copies of the first edition I2
(pp. 131–2)³ is also a cancel. However, the original state is preserved
in Christ Church Oxford: W.H. 8.43, and Dr. Williams' Library:
1024.E.6. In the original form Parker's fellow-chaplain Tomkins is
made the author of a statement which, it appears from the cancel,
had in fact been made by his examining professor. Marvell must
have learnt of his mistake and the correction was presumably made
at his instance.

Copies Examined: Editor's Copy; *Bodley*: 8° C558 Linc., [MS] Ashm.
1585; *Oxford English Faculty Library*: Rar. D.235; *British Museum*:
G.19515, 1019e 13; *Dr. Williams' Library*: 5614G, 1024.E.6; *Christ
Church Oxford*: W.H.8.43; *Harvard*: EC65.M3685.673r; *Magdalen
College Oxford*: N. 18. 26; *Yale*: Ij M368.673.

Second Edition

Title-page: Within a border of double rule: THE / REHEAR-
SALL / TRANSPROS'D: // The SECOND PART. // *Occasioned by
Two Letters: The first Print— / ed, by a nameless Author, Intituled* A /
Reproof, *&c.* / *The Second Letter left for me at a Friends* / *House, Dated*
Nov. 3. 1673. *Subscri-* / *bed* J.G. *and concluding with these words,* / *If
thou darest to Print or Publish any* / *Lie or Libel against Doctor
Parker,* By / *the Eternal God I will cut thy Throat.* // *Answered by*
ANDREW MARVEL // *LONDON,* / *Printed for* Nathaniel Ponder
at the Peacock *in* / Chancery-Lane *near* Fleet-Street, 1674.

Collation: 12°: [π]², A–P¹², Q⁶. 188 leaves paginated: [4] 1–200,
221, 222, 203–57, 358–62, 263–351, 452, 353–72. [=376] (pp. 221–2
follow the pagination of the 1st edition).

Sigs: \$(5) [E3 printed Ǝ3, G3 mis-signed G5, –G5, –L5, +P6,
–Q4, –Q5].

¹ p. 200.22 of this edition.   ² p. 267.20 of this edition.
³ p. 205 of this edition.

Contents: [π]1r: blank; [π]1v: between rows of type ornaments: *REPROOF*. p. 67. / IF you have anything to ob- / ject against it, do your / vvorst. You knovv the Press is / open. / *By the Author and* / *Licenser of the* Eccle- / siastical Politie. / Licensed the 1st. / of *May* 1673. ;[π]2r: T.P.; [π]2v: blank; A1r: Half-title under a row of type ornaments: THE / REHEARSAL / TRANSPROS'D. // The Second Part. // Text begins; Q6v: Text ends: between rules: *THE END.*

Notes: As with the first edition bad inking is responsible for a number of variants between copies of the second edition. However, there appear to have been a few minor press corrections. In Bodley Vet. A3. f. 399, Christ Church: W.F.8.24, and Harvard: EC65. M3685.673rb(A) the inner forme of M has been reset and corrected: p. 279.14¹ (M8r) *unnaimating* to *unanimating* and p. 287.26² (M12r) 'heells' to 'heels'. The original readings are preserved in Worcester College Library: L.R.1.21. In this last copy and in Harvard EC65. M3685.673rb(A) the final sheet Q has corrections to both formes. On the inner forme of Q, p. 362.25³ (Q1v) *Armenian* is corrected to *Arminian* and p. 369.16⁴ (Q5r) 'designed' is corrected to 'deigned'. On the outer forme, p. 368.14⁵ (Q4v) *Stillingfleets* is corrected to '*Stillingfleet* his' and 'is' is omitted (l. 15) in an effort to bring clarity to a very obscure passage. Also on the outer forme is the correction on p. 371.14–15⁶ (Q6r) 'hap-once' to 'happen'd once'.

Copies Examined: *Bodley*: Vet. A3. f. 399; *Christ Church Oxford*: W.F. 8.24; *Worcester College Oxford*: L.R.1.21; *Harvard*: EC65.M3685. 673rb(A).

---

¹ p. 281.23 of this edition.   ² p. 285.32 of this edition.
³ p. 323.10 of this edition.   ⁴ p. 326.21 of this edition.
⁵ p. 326.2 of this edition.   ⁶ p. 327.19 of this edition.

SIGLA

74   *Second Edition*

B¹   Bodley: Vet. A3. f. 399
B²   Christ Church Oxford: W.F.8.24
B³   Worcester College Oxford: L.R.1.21
B⁴   Harvard: EC65.M3685.673rb(A)

Errata = Errata to the first edition.

Except where otherwise indicated, the readings of X and Z follow those of W.

THE
REHEARSAL
TRANSPROS'D:
Or,
Animadverſions
Upon a late Book, Intituled,
A PREFACE
SHEWING
What Grounds there are of Fears and Jealouſies of Popery.

LONDON, Printed by *A.B.* for the Aſſigns of *John Calvin* and *Theodore Beza*, at the ſign of the Kings Indulgence, on the South-ſide of the *Lake Leman e.* 1672.

Animadversions upon the Preface to Bishop Bramhall's Vindication, &c.

THe Author of this Preface had first writ a *Discourse of Ecclesiastical Policy*; after that, *A Defence and Continuation of the Ecclesiastical Policy*; and there he concludes his Epistle to the Reader in these words: *But if this be the Penance I must undergo for the wantonness of my Pen, to answer the impertinent and slender Exceptions* 5 *of every peevish and disingenuous Caviller; Reader, I am reformed from my incontinency of Scribling, and do here heartily bid thee an Eternal Farewell.* Now this Expression lyes open to his own *Dilemma* against the Nonconformists confessing in their prayers to God such heinous Enormities. For if he will not accept his own Charge, his Modesty is all 10 impudent and counterfeit: Or, if he will acknowledge it, why then he had been before, and did still remain upon Record, the same lewd, wanton, and incontinent Scribler.

But, however, I hop'd he had been a Clergy-man of Honour, and that when herein the World and he himself were now so fully 15 agreed in the censure of his Writings, he would have kept his Word; or at least that his Pen would not, so soon, have created us a disturbance of the same nature, and so far manifested how indifferent he is as to the business either of Truth or Eternity. But the Author, alas, instead of his own, was faln now into *Amaryllis*'s Dilemma: (I 20 perceive the Gentleman hath travelled by his remembring *Chi lava la testa al asino perde il sapone*, and therefore hope I may without Pedantry quote the words in her own *whining* Italian)

> *S'il peccar è si dolce e'l non peccar si necessario,*
> *O troppo imperfetta Natura che ripugni a la Legge.* 25
> *O troppo dura Legge che Natura offendi.*

6 *disingenuous*] *disingenious* Z.   7 *here om.* Z.   13 lewd *om.* Y.   25 *ripugni a* Errata; *ripugnia* W.

If to scribble be so sweet, and not to scribble be so necessary;
O too frail Inclination, that contradictest Obligation:
O too severe Obligation, that offendest Inclination.

For all his Promise to write no more, I durst alwayes have laid Ten
5 pound to a Crown on Natures side. And accordingly he hath now
blessed us with, as he calls it, *A Preface, shewing what Grounds there
are of Fears and Jealousies of Popery.*

It will not be unpleasant to hear him begin his Story. *The ensuing
Treatise of Bishop* Bramhall's *being somewhat superannuated, the* Book-
10 seller *was very sollicitous to have it set off with some Preface that might
recommend it to the Genius of the Age, and reconcile it to the present juncture
of Affairs.* A pretty task indeed: That is as much as to say, To trick
up the good old Bishop in a yellow Coif and a Bulls-head, that he
may be fit for the Publick, and appear in Fashion. In the mean time
15 'tis what I alwayes presaged: From a Writer of Books, our Author
is already dwinled to a Preface-monger, and from Prefaces I am confident he may in a short time be improved to endite Tickets for the
Bear-Garden. But the Bookseller I see was a cunning Fellow, and
knew his Man. For who so proper as a young Priest to sacrifice to
20 the Genius of the Age; yea, though his Conscience were the Offering? And none more ready to nick a juncture of Affairs than a malapert Chaplain; though not one indeed of a hundred but dislocates
them in the handling. And yet our Author is very maidenly, and
condescends to his Bookseller not without some reluctance, as
25 being, forsooth, first of all *none of the most zealous Patrons of the Press.*

Though he hath so lately forfeited his Credit, yet herein I dare
believe him: For the Press hath ought him a shame a long time, and
is but now beginning to pay off the Debt. The Press (that *villanous
Engine*) invented much about the same time with the Reformation,
30 that hath done more mischief to the Discipline of our Church, than
all the Doctrine can make amends for. 'Twas an happy time when
all Learning was in Manuscript, and some little Officer, like our
Author, did keep the Keys of the Library. When the Clergy needed
no more knowledg then to read the Liturgy, and the Laity no more
35 Clerkship than to save them from Hanging. But now, since Print-

2 *contradictest* Y; *contradicteth* W.   4 write] waite X.   8 *The*] *This*
Parker.   28 off] of X.   34 then] than X, Y.

ing came into the World, such is the mischief, that a Man cannot write a Book but presently he is answered. Could the Press but once be conjured to obey only an *Imprimatur*, our Author might not disdain *perhaps* to be one of its most zealous Patrons. There have been wayes found out to banish Ministers, to fine not only the 5 People, but even the Grounds and Fields where they assembled in Conventicles: But no Art yet could prevent these seditious meetings of Letters. Two or three brawny Fellows in a Corner, with meer Ink and Elbow-grease, do more harm than an *hundred Systematical Divines* with their *sweaty Preaching*. And, which is a strange 10 thing, the very Spunges, which one would think should rather deface and blot out the whole Book, and were anciently used to that purpose, are become now the Instruments to make things legible. Their ugly Printing-Letters, that look but like so many rotten-Teeth, How oft have they been pull'd out by B. and L. the Publick- 15 Tooth-drawers! and yet these rascally Operators of the Press have got a trick to fasten them again in a few minutes, that they grow as firm a Set, and as biting and talkative as ever. *O Printing!* how hast thou disturb'd the Peace of Mankind! that Lead, when moulded into Bullets, is not so mortal as when founded into Letters! There 20 was a mistake sure in the Story of *Cadmus*; and the Serpents Teeth which he sowed, were nothing else but the Letters which he invented. The first Essay that was made towards this Art, was in single Characters upon Iron, wherewith of old they stigmatized Slaves and remarkable Offenders; and it was of good use sometimes 25 to brand a Schismatick. But a *bulky* Dutchman diverted it quite from its first Institution, and contriving those innumerable *Syntagmes* of Alphabets, hath pestred the World ever since with the *gross Bodies of their German Divinity.* One would have thought in Reason that a Dutchman at least might have contented himself only 30 with the Wine-press.

But, next of all, our Author, beside his aversion from the Press, alledges, that *he is as much concerned as* De-Wit, *or any of the High and Mighty Burgomasters, in matters of a closer and more comfortable importance to himself and his own Affairs.* And yet who ever shall take the 35 pains to read over his Preface, will find that it intermeddles with the

9–10 *Systematical Errata; Schismatical* W.

King, the Succession, the Privy-Council, Popery, Atheism, Bishops, Ecclesiastical Government, and above all with Nonconformity, and *J. O.* A man would wonder what this thing should be of a *closer importance*; But being *more comfortable* too, I conclude it must be one
5 of these three things; either his Salvation, or a Benefice, or a Female. Now as to Salvation he could not be so much concern'd: for that care was over; there hath been a course taken to insure all that are on his bottom. And he is yet surer of a Benefice; or else his Patrons must be very ungrateful. He can not have deserved less than a
10 Prebend for his first Book, a *Sine-cure* for his second, and for this third a Rectorship, although it were that of *Malmsbury*. Why, then of necessity it must be a Female. For that I confess might have been a sufficient excuse from writing of Prefaces, and against the importunity of the Book-seller. 'Twas fit that all business should have
15 given place to the work of Propagation. Nor was there any thing that could more closely import him, than that the Race and Family of the Railers should be perpetuated among Mankind. Who could in Reason expect that a Man should in the same moments undertake the labour of an Author and a Father? *Nevertheless, he saith, he could*
20 *not but yeeld so far as to improve every fragment of time that he could get into his own disposal, to gratifie the Importunity of the Bookseller.* Was ever Civility graduated up and inhanc'd to such a value! His Mistris herself could not have endeared a Favour so nicely, nor granted it with more sweetness.
25 *Was the Bookseller more Importunate, or the Author more Courteous?*
The Author was the Pink of Courtesie, the Bookseller the Bur of Importunity.
And so, not being able to shake him off, *this*, he saith, *hath brought forth this Preface, such an one as it is; for how it will prove, he himself*
30 *neither is, nor (till 'tis too late) ever shall be a competent Judge, in that it must be ravish'd out of his hands before his thoughts can possibly be cool enough to review or correct the Indecencies either of its stile or contrivance.* He is now growing a very Enthusiast himself. No Nonconformist-Minister, as it seems, could have spoke more *extempore.* I see he is
35 not so civil to his Readers as he was to his Bookseller: and so *A. C.*

---

3 what] that Z.   4 *importance*; Y; ∼, W.   32 *review* Parker; *revive* W, etc.

and *James Collins* be gratified, he cares not how much the rest of the World be disobliged. Some Man that had less right to be fastidious and confident, would, before he exposed himself in publick, both have cool'd his Thoughts, and corrected his Indecencies: or would have considered whether it were necessary or wholsom that he 5 should write at all. Forasmuch as one of the Ancient *Sophists* (they were a kind of Orators of his Form) kill'd himself with declaming while he had a Bone in his Throat, and *J.O.* was still in being. *Put up your Trumpery good noble Marquess.* But there was no holding him. Thus it must be, and no better, when a man's Phancy is up, and his 10 Breeches are down; when the Mind and the Body make contrary Assignations, and he hath both a Bookseller at once and a Mistris to satisfie: Like *Archimedes*, into the Street he runs out naked with his Invention. And truly, if at any time, we might now pardon this Extravagance and Rapture of our Author; when he was 15 pearch'd upon the highest Pinacle of Ecclesiastical Felicity, being ready at once to asswage his Concupiscence, and wreck his Malice.

But yet he knows not which way his Mind will work it self and its thoughts. This is *Bayes* the Second. —'*Tis no matter for the Plot—The* 20 *Intrigo was out of his head—But you'l apprehend it better when you see't.* Or rather, he is like *Bayes* his Actors, *that could not guess what humour they were to be in: whether angry, melancholly, merry, or in Love.* Nay, insomuch that he saith, *he is neither Prophet nor Astrologer enough to foretel.* Never Man certainly was so unacquainted with himself. 25 And, indeed, 'tis part of his discretion to avoid his acquaintance and tell him as little of his mind as may be: for he is a dangerous fellow. But I must ask his pardon if I treat him too homely. It is his own fault that misled me at first, by concealing his quality under such vulgar comparisons as *De-wit* and the *Burgomasters*. I now see it all 30 along; This can be no less a man then Prince *Volscius* himself, in dispute betwixt his Boots which way his mind will *work it self*; whether Love shall detain him with his *closer Importance*, Parthenope, *whose Mother, Sir, sells Ale by the Town-Wall*: or Honour shall carry him *to head the Army that lies concealed for him at Knightsbridge*, and to 35 incounter *J. O.*

4 would] should X.   7 of his] in his Z.   21 *head*] *dead* X.

Go on cryes Honour: tender Love saith Nay.
Honour aloud commands, Pluck both Boots on.
But safer Love doth whisper, Put on none.

And so now when it comes that he is *not Prophet nor Astrologer enough*
5 *to foretel* what he will do, 'tis just,

> *For as bright Day, with black approach of Night,*
> *Contending, makes a doubtful puzzling Light;*
> *So does my Honour and my Love together,*
> *Puzzle me so, I am resolv'd on neither.*

10 Yet no Astrologer could possibly have more advantage and opportunity to make a Judgment. For he knew the very minute of the
Conception of his Preface, which was immediately upon his Majesties issuing his Declaration of Indulgence to Tender Consciences.
Nor could he be ignorant of the moment when it was brought forth.
15 And I can so far refresh his memory, that it came out in the Dog-
dayes,

> *—the Season hot, and She too near:*
> *O mighty Love!* J. O. *will be undone.*

According to the Rule in *Davenant's Ephemerides; But the heads which*
20 *at this moment, and under the present Schemes and Aspects of the Heavens he*
intends to treat of (pure Sidrophel) *are these two: First, Something of the*
Treatise it self. Secondly, of the seasonableness of its publication: and this,
unless his Humour jade him ('tis come to a Dog-trot already) *will lead*
him further into the Argument as it relates to the present state of things, and
25 *from thence 'tis odds but he shall take occasion to bestow some Animadver-*
sions upon one J. O. There's no trusting him. He doubtless knew
from the beginning what he intended. And so too all his story of
the Bookseller, and all the *Volo Nola's,* and *shall-I shall-I's* betwixt
them, was nothing but fooling: And he now all along owns himself
30 to be the Publisher, and alledges the slighter and the main reasons
that induced him. Would he had told us so at first; for then he had
saved me thus much of my labour. Though, as it chances, it lights
not amiss on our Author, whose delicate stomach could not brook
that *J.O.* should say, *he had prevailed with himself, much against his*

3 *safer*] softer Buckingham.   9 *am resolv'd on*] *can resolve for* Buckingham.

inclination, to bestow a few (and those idle) hours upon examining his Book: and yet he himself stumbles so notoriously upon the very same fault at his own threshold.

But now from this Preamble he falls into his Preface to Bishop *Bramhall:* though indeed like *Bayes* his Prologue, that would have serv'd as well for an Epilogue, I do not see but the Preface might have past as wel for a Postscript, or the Headstal for a Crooper. And our Authors *Divinity* might have gone to *Push-Pin* with the Bishop, which of their two Treatises was the *Procatarctical Cause* of both their Edition. For, as they are coupled together, to say the truth, 'tis not discernable, as in some Animals, whether their motion begin at the head or the tail; whether the Author made his Preface for Bishop *Bramhal's dear sake*, or whether he published the Bishop's Treatise for sake of his *own dear Preface*. For my own part I think it reasonable that the Bishop and our Author, should (like fair Gamsters at Leap-frog) stand and skip in their turns; and however our Author got it for once, yet, if the Bookseller should ever be follicitous for a Second Edition, that then the Bishops Book should have the Precedence.

But before I commit my self to the dangerous depths of his Discourse, which I am now upon the brink of, I would with his leave make a motion: that, instead of Author, I may henceforth indifferently call him *Mr. Bayes* as oft as I shall see occasion. And that, first, because he hath no Name or at least will not own it, though he himself writes under the greatest security, and gives us the first Letters of other Mens Names before he be asked them. Secondly, because he is I perceive a lover of Elegancy of Stile, and can endure no mans Tautologies but his own, and therefore I would not distaste him with too frequent repetition of one word. But chiefly, because *Mr. Bayes* and he do very much Symbolize; in their understandings, in their expressions, in their humour, in their contempt and quarrelling of all others, though of their own Profession. Because, our Divine, the Author, manages his contest with the same prudence and civility, which the Players and Poets have practised of late in their several Divisions. And, lastly, because both their Talents do

---

1 *(and those idle) om.* Owen.   24 will not] would Z.   29 chiefly Y; cheifly W.

peculiarly lie in exposing and personating the Nonconformists. I would therefore give our Author a Name, the memory of which may perpetually excite him to the exercise and highest improvement of that Virtue. For, our *Cicero* doth not yet equal our *Roscius*, and one turn of *Lacy's face* hath more *Ecclesiastical Policy* in it, than all the Books of our Author put together. Besides, to say Mr. *Bayes* is more *civil* than to say *Villain* and *Caitiff*, though these indeed are more *tuant*. And, to conclude; The Irrefragable Doctor of School-Divinity, pag. 460 of his *Defence*; determining concerning Symbolical Ceremonies, hath warranted me that not only Governours, but any thing else, may have power to appropriate new names to things, without having absolute authority over the things themselves. And therefore henceforward, seeing I am on such sure ground, *Author*, or Mr. *Bayes*, whether I please. Now, having had our Dance, let us advance to our more serious Counsels.

And first, Our Author begins with a Panegyrick upon Bishop *Bramhal*; a Person whom my age had not given me leave to be acquainted with, nor my good fortune led me to converse with his Writings: but for whom I had collected a deep Reverence from the general Reputation he carried, beside the Veneration due to the Place he filled in the Church of *England*. So that our Author having a mind to shew us some proof of his Good Nature, and that his Eloquence lay'd not all in Satyr and Invectives, could not, in my opinion, have fixed upon a fitter subject of commendation. And therefore, I could have wished for my own sake, that I had missed this occasion of being more fully informed of some of the Bishop's Principles, whereby I have lost part of that pleasure which I had so long enjoyed in thinking well of so considerable a Person. But however, I recreate my self with believing that my simple judgment cannot, beyond my intention, abate any thing of his just value with others. And seeing he is long since dead, which I knew but lately, and now learn it with regret, I am the more obliged to repair in my self whatsoever breaches of his Credit, by that additional Civility which consecrates the Ashes of the Deceased. But by this means I am come to discern how it was possible for our Author to speak a good word of any man. The Bishop was expired, and his Writings

26 of the *om.* X.   36 of Y; for W.

jump much with our Author. So that if you have a mind to die, or
to be of his Party, (there are but these two Conditions) you may
perhaps be rendred capable of his Charity. And then write what
you will, he will make you a Preface that shall recommend you and
it to the *Genius* of the Age, and reconcile it to the Juncture of 5
Affairs. But truly he hath acquitted himself herein so ill-favourdly
to the Bishop, that I do not think it so much worth to gain his approbation; and I had rather live and enjoy mine own Opinion, than
be so treated. For, beside his reflexion on the Bishop, and the whole
Age he lived in; that *he was, as far as the prejudice of the Age would per-* 10
mit him, an acute Philosopher (which is a sufficient taste of Mr. *Bayes*
his Arrogance, that no Man, no Agĕ can be so perfect but must
abide his Censure, and of the officious virulence of his Humour,
which infuses it self, by a malignant remark, that (but for this
acuter Philosopher) no man else would have thought of, into the 15
Praises of him whom he most intended to celebrate). If, I say, beside
this, you consider the most elaborate and studious Periods of his
Commendation, you find it at best very ridiculous. By the Language he seems to transcribe out of the *Grand-Cyrus* and *Cassandra*,
but the Exploits to have borrowed out of the *Knight of the Sun*, and 20
King Arthur. For in a luscious and effeminate Stile he gives him
such a *Termagant* Character, as must either fright or turn the
stomach of any Reader; *Being of a brave and enterprising temper, of an*
active and sprightly mind, he was alwayes busied either in contriving or per-
forming great Designs. Well, *Mr. Bayes*, I suppose by this, that he 25
might have been an over-match to the Bishop of *Cullen* and the
Bishop of *Strasburg*. In another place, *He finished all the glorious De-*
signs that he undertook. This might have become the Bishop of *Mun-*
ster before he had rais'd the Siege from *Groningen*. *As he was able to*
accomplish the most gallant attempts, so he was always ready not only to 30
justifie their Innocence, but to make good their Bravery. I was too prodigal
of my Bishops at first, and now have never another left in the
Gazette, which is too our Authors Magazin. *His Reputation and In-*
nocence were both Armor of Proof against Toryes and Presbyterians. But
me-thinks Mr. *Bayes* having to do with such dangerous Enemies, 35

---

10 *prejudice*] *Prejudices* Parker.   12 no Age] nor Age Z.   23 *Being of a*]
Being a Z.   24 *in*] *it* Y.   33 too] to X; *om.* Y.   35 Mr.] ~, Y.

you should have furnished him too with some weapon of Offence,
a good old Fox, like that of another Heroe, his Contemporary in
Action upon the Scene of Ireland, of whom it was sung,

> *Down by his side he wore a Sword of price,*
> *Keen as a Frost, glaz'd like a new made Ice:*
> *That cracks men shell'd in Steel in a less trice,*
> *Than Squirrels Nuts, or the Highlanders Lice.*

Then he saith; '*Tis true, the Church of* Ireland *was the largest Scene of his*
Actions; but yet there, in a little time, he wrought out such wondrous
Alterations, and so exceeding all belief, as may convince us that he had a
mind large and active enough to have managed the Roman Empire at its
greatest extent. This indeed of our Author's is *Great:* and yet it reach-
eth not a strain of his fellow-*Pendets* in the History of the *Mogol*;
where he tells *Dancehment Kan, When you put your foot in the Stirrop,*
and when you march upon Horseback in the front of the Cavalry, the Earth
trembles under your feet, the eight Elephants that hold it on their heads not
being able to support it. But enough of this Trash.

Beside that it is the highest *Indecorum* for a Divine to write in such
a stile as this [part Play-book and part-Romance] concerning a
Reverend Bishop; these improbable *Elogies* too are of the greatest
disservice to their own design, and do in effect diminish alwayes the
Person whom they pretend to magnifie. Any worthy Man may
pass through the World unquestion'd and safe with a moderate
Recommendation; but when he is thus set off, and bedawb'd with
Rhetorick, and embroder'd so thick that you cannot discern the
Ground, it awakens naturally (and not altogether unjustly) Interest, Curiosity, and Envy. For all men pretend a share in Reputation, and love not to see it ingross'd and monopolized, and are
subject to enquire, (as of great Estates suddenly got) whether he
came by all this honestly, or of what credit the Person is that tells
the Story? And the same hath happened as to this Bishop, while our
Author attributes to him such Atchievements, which to one that
could believe the Legend of Captain *Jones*, might not be incredible.
I have heard that there was indeed such a Captain, an honest brave

6 cracks X; craeks W etc.   9 wondrous] wonderful Parker.   13 not a] not
to a Z.   14 Kan, When] Kan, That when Y.   you] he Y.   your] his Y.
15 you march] he march'd Y.   16 trembles] trembled Y.   your] his Y.

fellow: but a Wag that had a mind to be merry with him, hath quite spoil'd his History. Had our Author epitomized the Legend of sixty six Books *de Virtutibus Sancti Patricii* (I mean not the Ingenious Writer of the *Friendly Debates*, but St. *Patrick* the Irish Bishop) he could not have promis'd us greater Miracles. And 'tis well for him that he hath escaped the fate of *Secundinus*, who (as *Josselin* relates it) acquainting *Patrick* that he was inspired to compose something in his Commendation, the Bishop foretold the Author should die as soon as 'twas perfected. Which so done, so happened. I am sure our Author had died no other death but of this his own *Preface*, and a surfeit upon Bishop B*ramhall*, if the swelling of Truth could have choak'd him. He tells us, I remember somewhere, that this same Bishop of *Derry* said, the *Scots* had a civil expression for these *Improvers of Verity*, that they are *good Company*; and I shall say nothing severer, than that our Author speaks the language of a Lover, and so may claim some pardon, if the habit and excess of his Courtship do as yet give a tincture to his discourse upon more ordinary Subjects. For I would not by any means be mistaken, as if I thought our Author so sharp set, or so necessitated that he should make a dead Bishop his Mistress; so far from that, that he hath taken such a course, that if the Bishop were alive, he would be out of love with himself. He hath, like those frightful Looking-glasses, made for sport, represented him in such bloated lineaments, as, I am confident, if he could see his face in it, he would break the Glass. For, hence it falls out too, that men seeing the Bishop furbish'd up in so martial accoutrements, like another *Odo* Bishop of B*aieux*, and having never before heard of his prowess, begin to reflect what *Giants* he defeated and what *Damsells* he rescued. Serious Men consider whether he were ingaged in the conduct of the *Irish* Army, and to have brought it over upon *England*, for the Imputation of which the Earl of *Strafford* his Patron so undeservedly suffered. But none knows any thing of it. Others think it is not to be taken literally, but the wonderfull and unheard-of Alterations that he wrought out in *Ireland*, are meant of some Reformation that he made there in things of his own Function. But then men ask again, how he comes to have all the honour of it, and whether all the while that great

10 no other] nother Z.   11 Bishop Y; Biship W.   14 are] had Y.

Bishop *Usher*, his Metropolitane, were unconcerned? For even in Ecclesiastical Combates, how instrumental soever the Captain hath been, the General usually carries away the honour of the Action. But the good *Primate* was engaged in Designs of lesser moment, and
5 was writing his *de Primordiis Ecclesiæ Britanicæ*, and the Story of *Pelagius* our Countryman. He, honest man, was deep gone in *Grubstreet* and *Polemical Divinity*, and troubled with fits of *Modern Orthodoxy*. He satisfied himself with being *admired by the blue and white Aprons*, and *pointed at by the more judicious Tankard-bearers*. Nay,
10 which is worst of all, he undertook to abate of our Episcopal *Grandeur*, and condescended indeed to reduce the Ceremonious Discipline in these Nations to the Primitive Simplicity. What then was this that Bishop *Bramhal* did? Did he, like a Protestant Apostle, in one day convert thousands of the *Irish* Papists? The contrary is evi-
15 dent by the Irish Rebellion and Massacre, which, notwithstanding his *Publick Employment and great Abilities*, happened in his time. So that after all our Authors bombast, when we have search'd all over, we find our selves bilk'd in our expectation: and he hath erected him, like a *St. Christopher* in the Popish Churches, as big as ten Por-
20 ters, and yet only imploy'd to sweat under the burden of an *Infant*.

All that appears of him is, first, that he busied himself about a *Catholick Agreement among the Churches of Christendom*. But as to this, our Author himself saith, that he was not *so vain, or so presuming as to hope to see it effected in his dayes*. And yet but two pages before he
25 told us, that *the Bishop finish'd all the glorious Designs which he undertook*. But this Design of his he draws out in such a circuit of words, that 'tis better taking it from the Bishop himself, who speaks more plainly alwayes, and much more to the purpose. And he saith, pag. 87 of his Vindication, *My design is rather to reconcile the* Popish
30 Party *to the* Church of England, *than the Church of* England *to the* Pope. And how he manages it, I had rather any man would learn by reading over his own Book, than that I should be thought to misrepresent him, which I might, unless I transcribed the whole. But in summe it seems to me that he is upon his own single judgment
35 too liberal of the Publick, and that he retrenches both on our part

---

24 *effected*] *affected* X.   yet *om.* Z.   31 how] now Y.   32 thought] taught Z.   33 transcribed] transcribe Z.   35 retrenches] trenches Z.

more than he hath Authority for, and grants more to the Popish than they can of right pretend to. It is however indeed a most glorious Design, to reconcile all the Churches to one Doctrine and Communion (though some that meddle in it do it chiefly in order to fetter men straiter under the formal bondage of fictitious Disci- 5 pline); but it is a thing rather to be wished and prayed for, than to be expected from these kind of endeavours. It is so large a Field, that no man can see to the end of it; and all that have adventured to travel it, have been bewildred. That Man must have a vast opinion of his own sufficiency, that can think he may by his Oratory 10 or Reason, either in his own time, or at any of our Author's *more happy Junctures of Affairs*, so far perswade and fascinate the *Roman*-Church, having by a regular contexture of continued Policy for so many Ages interwoven it self with the Secular Interest, and made it self necessary to most Princes, and having at last erected a Throne 15 of Infallibility over their Consciences, as to prevail with her to submit a Power and Empire so acquired and established in Compromise to the Arbitration of an humble Proposer. God only in his own time, and by the inscrutable methods of his Providence is able to effect that *Alteration:* though I think too he hath signified in part 20 by what means he intends to accomplish it, and to range so considerable a Church, and once so exemplary, into Primitive Unity and Christian Order. In the mean time such Projects are fit for pregnant Scholars that have nothing else to do, to go big with for forty years, and may qualifie them to discourse with Princes and 25 States-men at their hours of leisure; but I never saw that they came to Use or Possibility: No more than that of *Alexanders* Architect, who proposed to make him a Statue of the Mountain *Athos* (and that was no Molehill); and among other things, that Statue to carry in its hand a great habitable City. But the Surveyor was gravell'd, 30 being asked whence that City should be supplied with Water. I would only have ask'd the Bishop, when he had carv'd and hammer'd the Romists and Protestants into one *Colossian* Church, how we should have done as to matter of Bibles. For the Bishop, p. 117.

complains that unqualified people should have a promiscuous Licence to reade the Scriptures: and you may guess thence, if he had moreover the Pope to friend, how the Laity should have been used. There have been attempts in former Ages to dig through the Separating *Istmos* of *Peloponnesus*; and another to make communication between the *Red-Sea* and the *Mediterranean:* both more easie than to cut this *Ecclesiastick* Canal, and yet both laid by, partly upon the difficulty of doing it, and partly upon the inconveniences if it had been effected. I must confess freely, yet I ask pardon for the presumption, that I cannot look upon these undertaking Church-men, however otherwise of excellent Prudence and Learning, but as men struck with a Notion, and craz'd on that side of their head. And so I think even the Bishop had much better have busied himself in Preaching in his own Diocess, and disarming the Papists of their Arguments, instead of rebating our weapons; than in taking an *Oecumenical* care upon him, which none called him to, and, as appears by the sequel, none conn'd him thanks for. But if he were so great a Politician as I have heard, and indeed believe him to have been, me-thinks he should in the first place have contrived how we might live well with our Protestant Neighbours, and to have united us in one Body under the King of *England*, as Head of the Protestant Interest, which might have rendred us more considerable, and put us into a more likely posture to have reduced the Church of *Rome* to Reason. For the most leading Party of the *English* Clergy in his time retained such a Pontifical stiffness towards the Foreign Divines, that it puts me in mind of *Austin* the Monk, when he came into *Kent*, not deigning to rise up to the *British* or give them the hand, and could scarce afford their Churches either Communion or Charity, or common Civility. So that it is not to be wondred if they also on their parts look'd upon our Models of Accommodation with the same jealousie that the *British* Christians had of *Austin*'s Design, to unite them first to (that is, under) the *Saxons*, and then deliver them both over bound to the Papal Government and Ceremonies. But seeing hereby our hands were weakened, and there was no probability of arriving so near the end of the work, as to a consent

6 Red] *Read* Z.   18 Politician Y; Politicion W.   31 of] *as* X.   34 hereby] thereby Z.

among Protestants abroad; had the Bishop but gone that step, to have reconciled the Ecclesiastical Differences in our own Nations, and that we might have stood firm at home before we had taken such a Jump beyond-Sea, it would have been a Performance worthy of his Wisdom. For at that time the Ecclesiastical Rigours here 5 were in the highest ferment, and the Church in being arrayed it self against the peaceable Dissenters only in some points of Worship. And what great Undertaking could we be ripe for abroad, while so divided at home? or what fruit expected from the labour of those Mediating Divines in weighty matters, who were not yet 10 past the Sucking-bottle; but seem'd to place all the business of Christianity in persecuting men for their Consciences, differing from them in smaller matters? How ridiculous must we be to the Church of *Rome* to interpose in her Affairs, and force our Mediation upon her; when, besides our ill correspondence with the Foreign 15 Protestants, she must observe our weakness within our selves, that we could not, or would not step over a straw, though for the perpetual settlement and security of our Church and Nation? She might well look upon us as those that probably might be forced at some time by our folly to call her in to our assistance (for with no 20 Weapons or Arguments but what are fetch'd out of her Arsenals can the Ceremonial-Controversie be rightly defended) but never could she consider us as of such Authority or Wisdom, as to give Ballance to her Counsels. But this was far from Bishop *Bramhall's* thoughts: who, so he might (like *Cæsar*) *manage the Roman Empire at its utmost* 25 *extent*, had quite forgot what would conduce to the Peace of his own Province & Country. For, p. 57. he settles this Maxime as a Truth, *That second Reformations are commonly like Metal upon Metal, which is false Heraldry.* Where, by the way, it is a wonder that our Author in enumerating the Bishop's perfections in Divinity, Law, History, 30 and Philosophy, neglected this peculiar gift he had in Heraldry; and omitted to tell us that his Mind was large enough to have animated the Kingdoms of *Garter* and *Clarencieux* at their greatest dimensions. But, beside what I have said already in relation to this Project upon *Rome*, there is this more, which I confess was below Bishop *Bram-* 35 *hall's* reflexion, and was indeed fit only for some vulgar Politician,

11 past the] past X.

or the Commissioners of *Scotland* about the late Union: Whether it would not have succeeded, as in the consolidation of Kingdoms, where the Greatest swallows down the Less; so also in Church-Coalition, that though the Pope had condescended (which the
5 Bishop owns to be his Right) to be only a Patriarch, yet he would have swoop'd up the Patriarchate of *Lambeth* to his Mornings-draught, like an Egg in Muscadine. And then there is another Danger always when things come once to a Treaty, that, beside the debates of Reason, there is a better way of tampering to bring Men
10 over that have a Power to conclude. And so who knows in such a Treaty with *Rome*, if the *Alps* (as it is probable) would not have come over to *England*, as the Bishop designed it, *England* might not have been obliged, lying so commodious for Navigation, to under-take a Voyage to *Civita Vechia?* But what though we should have
15 made all the Advances imaginable, it would have been to no pur-pose: and nothing less than an intire and total resignation of the Protestant Cause would have *contented* her. For the Church of *Rome* is so well satisfied of her own sufficiency, and hath so much more wit than we had in Bishop *Bramhall's* days, or seem to have yet
20 learn'd; that it would have succeeded just as at the Council of *Trent.* For there, though many Divines of the greatest Sincerity and Learning, endeavoured a Reformation, yet no more could be ob-tained of Her than the Nonconformists got of those of the Church of *England* at the Conference of *Worcester-House.* But on the contrary,
25 all her Excesses and Errors were further rivited and confirmed, and that great Machine of her Ecclesiastical Policy there perfected.

So that this Enterprise of Bishop *Bramhalls*, being so ill laid and so unseasonable, deserves rather an Excuse than a Commendation. And all that can be gathered besides out of our Author concerning
30 him is of little better value; for he saith indeed, that *he was a zealous and resolute Assertor of the Publick Rites and Solemnities of the Church.* But those things, being only matters of external neatness, could never merit the Trophies that our Author erects him. For neither can a Justice of Peace for his severity about Dirt-baskets deserve a
35 Statue. And as for *his expunging some dear and darling Articles from the Protestant Cause,* it is, as far as I can perceive, onely his substituting

15 Advances] Advantages Z.

some *Arminian* Tenets (which I name so, not for reproach, but for difference) instead of the *Calvinian* Doctrines. But this too could not challenge all these Triumphal Ornaments in which he installs him: For, I suppose these were but meer *mistakes on either side, for want of being* (as the Bishop saith pag. 134.) *scholastically stated; and that he,* 5 *with a distinction of School-Theologie, could have smoothed over and plained away these knots though they had been much harder.*

For the rest, which he leaves us to seek for, and I meet casually with in the Bishop's own Book; I find him to have been doubtless a very good-natur'd Gentleman. Pag. 160. *He hath much respect for* 10 *poor Readers;* and pag. 161. He judges *that if they come short of Preachers in point of Efficacy, yet they have the advantage of Preachers as to point of Security.* And pag. 163. He commends the care taken by *the Canons that the meanest Cure of Souls should have formal Sermons at least four times every year.* Pag. 155. He *maintains the Publick Sports on the Lords-* 15 *day by the Proclamation to that purpose, and the Example of the Reformed Churches beyond-Sea*: and *for the Publick Dances of our Youth upon Country-Greens on Sundayes, after the duties of the day, he sees nothing in them but innocent, and agreeable to that under-sort of people.* And pag. 117. (which I quoted before) he *takes the promiscuous Licence to unqualified* 20 *persons to reade the Scriptures, far more prejudicial, nay, more pernitious, than the over-rigorous restraint of the Romanists.* And indeed, all along he complies much for peace-sake, and judiciously shews us wherein our separation from the Church of *Rome* is not warrantable. But although I cannot warrant any man who hence took occasion to 25 traduce him of Popery, the contrary of which is evident, yet neither is it to be wondred, if he did hereby lye under some imputation, which he might otherwise have avoided. Neither can I be so hard-hearted as our Author in the Nonconformists case of Discipline, to think it were better that *he, or a hundred more Divines of his temper* 30 *should suffer, though innocent, in their Reputation, than that we should come under a possibility of losing our Religion.* For as they (the Bishop, and I hope most of his Party) did not intend it so, neither could they have effected it. But he could not expect to enjoy his Imagination without the annoyances incident to such as dwell in the middle 35

story: the Pots from above, and the Smoak from below. And those
Churches which are seated nearer upon the Frontire of Popery, did
naturally and well if they took Alarm at the March. For, in fact,
that incomparable Person *Grotius* did yet make a Bridge for the
5 Enemy to come over; or at least laid some of our most considerable
Passes open to them and unguarded: a crime something like what
his Son *De Groot* (here's Gazette again for you) and his Son-in-law
Mombas have been charged with. And, as to the Bishop himself, his
Friend; an Accusatory Spirit would desire no better play than he
10 gives in his own Vindication. But that's neither my business nor
humour: and whatsoever may have glanced upon him, was directed
only to our Author; for publishing that Book, which the Bishop
himself had thought fit to conceal, and for his impertinent efflores-
cence of Rhetorick upon so mean Topicks, in so choice and copious
15 a Subject as Bishop *Bramhal*.

Yet though the Bishop prudently undertook a Design, which he
hoped not to accomplish in his own dayes, our Author, however,
was something wiser, and hath made sure to obtain his end. For
the Bishop's Honour was the furthest thing from his thoughts, and
20 he hath managed that part so, that I have accounted it a work of
some Piety to vindicate his Memory from so scurvy a commendation. But the Author's end was only railing. He could never have
induc'd himself to praise one man but in order to rail on another.
He never oyls his Hone but that he may whet his Razor; and that
25 not to shave, but to cut mens throats. And whoever will take the
pains to compare, will find, that as it is his only end; so his best, nay
his only talent is railing. So that he hath, while he pretends so much
for the good Bishop, used him but for a Stalking-horse till he might
come within shot of the Forreign Divines and the Nonconformists.
30 The other was only a copy of his countenance: But look to your
selves, my Masters; for in so venomous a Malice, Courtesie is
always fatal. Under colour of some mens having taxed the Bishop,
he flyes out into a furious Debauch, and breaks the Windows, if he
could, would raze the foundations of all the Protestant Churches
35 beyond Sea: but for all men at home of their perswasion, if he meet

them in the dark he runs them thorow. He usurps to himself the
Authority of the Church of *England*, who is so well bred, that if he
would have allowed her to speak, she would doubtless have treated
more civilly those over whom she pretends no Jurisdiction: and
under the names of *Germany* and *Geneva*, he rallies and rails at the   5
whole Protestancy of *Europe*. For you are mistaken in our Author
(but I have worn him thread-bare) if you think he designs to enter
the Lists where he hath but one man to combate. Mr. *Bayes*, ye
know, *prefers that one quality of fighting single with whole Armies, before
all the moral Virtues put together.* And yet I assure you, he hath several   10
times obliged moral Virtue so highly, that she ows him a good turn
whensoever she can meet him. But it is a brave thing to be the
Ecclesiastical *Draw-Can-Sir*; He kills whole Nations, he kills Friend
and Foe; *Hungary, Transylvania, Bohemia, Poland, Savoy, France*, the
Netherlands, Denmark, Sweden, and a great part of the Church of *Eng-*   15
land, and all *Scotland* (for these, beside many more, he mocks under
the title of *Germany* and *Geneva*) may perhaps rouse our Mastiff, and
make up a Danger worthy of his Courage. A man would guess that
this Giant had promised his *Comfortable Importance*, a Simarre of the
beards of all the *Orthodox Theologues* in Christendom. But I wonder   20
how he comes to be Prolocutor of the Church of *England*! For he
talks at that rate as if he were a *Synodical Individuum*; nay if he had
a fifth Council in his belly he could not dictate more dogmatically.
There had been indeed, as I have heard, about the dayes of Bishop
Bramhal, a fort of Divines here of that Leaven, who being dead, I   25
cover their names, if not for healths sake, yet for decency, who
never could speak of the first Reformers with any patience; who
pruned themselves in the peculiar Virulency of their Pens, and so
they might say a tart thing concerning the Foreign Churches, cared
not what obloquy they cast upon the history or the profession of   30
Religion. And those men undertook likewise to vent their Wit and
their Choler under the stile of the Church of *England*; and were indeed so far owned by her, that what preferments were in her own
disposal, she rather conferr'd upon them. And now when they were
gone off the Stage, there is risen up this Spiritual Mr. *Bayes*; who   35
having assumed to himself an incongruous Plurality of Ecclesiastical
Offices, one the most severe, of Penitentiary-Universal to the

Reformed-Churches; the other most ridiculous, of Buffoon-General
to the Church of *England*, may be henceforth capable of any other
Promotion. And not being content to enjoy his own folly, he has
taken two others into Partnership; as fit for his design, as those two
5 that clubb'd with *Mahomet* in making the *Alchoran:* who by a perverse Wit and Representation might travesteere the Scripture, and
render all the carefull and serious part of Religion odious and contemptible. But, lest I might be mistaken as to the Persons I mention, I will assure the Reader that I intend not *Huddibras:* For he is
10 a man of the other Robe, and his excellent Wit hath taken a flight
far above these Whiflers: that whoever dislikes the choice of his Subject, cannot but commend his Performance, and calculate if on so
barren a Theme he were so copious, what admirable sport he would
have made with an Ecclesiastical Politician. But for a *Daw-Divine*
15 not only to foul his own Nest in *England,* but to pull in pieces the
Nests of those beyond Sea, 'tis that which I think undecent and of
very ill example. There is not indeed much danger, his Book, his
Letter, and his Preface being writ in English, that they should pass
abroad: but, if they be printed upon incombustible Paper, or by
20 reason of the many Avocations of our Church they may escape a
Censure, yet 'tis likely they may dye at home the common fate of
such Treatises amongst the more judicious Oylmen and Grocers.
Unless *Mr. Bayes* be so far in love with his own Whelp, that, as a
Modern Lady, he will be at the charge of translating his Works into
25 *Latin,* transmitting them to the Universities, and dedicating them
in the *Vaticane*. But, should they unhappily get vent abroad (as I
hear some are already sent over for curiosity) what scandal, what
heart-burning and animosity must it raise against our Church:
unless they chance to take it right at first, and limit the Provocation
30 within the Author. And then, what can he expect in return of his
Civility, but that the Complement which passed betwixt *Arminius*
and *Baudius* should concenter upon him, that he is both *Opprobrium
Academiæ,* and *Pestis Ecclesiæ*. For they will see at the first that his
Books come not out under Publick Authority, or recommendation:
35 but only as things of Buffoonery do commonly, they carry with
them their own *Imprimatur*; (But I hope he hath considered *Mr. L.*

5 a *om.* X.   18 writ] write Z.   27 hear] here Y.

in private, and payed his Fees.) Neither will the Gravity therefore
of their Judgments take the measures, I hope, either of the Education at our Universities, or of the Spirit of our Divines, or of the
Prudence, Piety, and Doctrine of the Church of *England,* from such
an Interloper. Those Gardens of ours use to bear much better fruit. 5
There may happen sometimes an ill Year, or there may be such a
Crab-stock as cannot by all ingrafting be corrected. But generally
it proves otherwise. Once perhaps in a hundred years there may
arise such a Prodigy in the University (where all Men else learn better Arts and better Manners) and from thence may creep into the 10
Church (where the Teachers at least ought to be well instructed in
the knowledge and practice of Christianity) so prodigious a Person
I say may even there be hatch'd, as shall neither know or care how
to behave himself to God or Man; and who having never seen the
receptacle of Grace or Conscience at an Anatomical Dissection, may 15
conclude therefore that there is no such matter, or no such obligation among Christians; who shall persecute the Scripture it self,
unless it will conform to his Interpretation; who shall strive to put
the World into Blood, and animate Princes to be the Executioners
of their own Subjects for well-doing. All this is possible; but comes 20
to pass as rarely and at as long periods in our Climate, as the birth
of a false Prophet. But unluckily, in this fatal Year of Seventy two,
among all the Calamities that Astrologers foretel, this also hath
befaln us. I would not hereby confirm his vanity, as if I also believed that any Scheme of Heaven did influence his actions, or that 25
he were so considerable as that the Comet under which they say
we yet labour, had fore-boded the appearance of his Preface. No,
no: though he be a creature most noxious, yet he is more despicable.
A Comet is of far higher quality, and hath other kind of imployment.
Although we call it an Hairy-Star, it affords no prognostick of what 30
breeds there: but the Astrologer that would discern our Author and
his business, must lay by his Telescope, and use a Microscope. You
may find him still in Mr. *Calvin's* head. Poor Mr. *Calvin* and Bishop
Bramhal, what crime did you dye guilty of, that you cannot lye
quiet in your Graves, but must be conjured up on the Stage as oft 35
as *Mr. Bayes* will ferret you? And which of you two are most

3 Spirit X, Y; Spitit W.   33 in Mr.]~ Master Y.

unfortunate I cannot determine; whether the Bishop in being always courted, or the Presbyter in being always rail'd at. But in good earnest I think Mr. *Calvin* hath the better of it. For, though an ill man cannot by praising confer honour, nor by reproaching fix an
5 ignominy, and so they may seem on equal terms; yet there is more in it: for at the same time that we may imagine what is said by such an Author to be false, we conceive the contrary to be true. What he saith of him indeed in this place did not come very well in: for *Calvin* writ nothing against Bishop *Bramhal*, and therefore here it
10 amounts to no more than that his Spirit forsooth had propagated an original *Waspishness* and false *Orthodoxy* amongst all his Followers. But if you look in other pages of his Book, and particularly pag. 663 of his *Defence*, you never saw such a Scarcrow as he makes him. *There sprang up a mighty Bramble on the South side the* Lake Lemane, *that*
15 *(such is the rankness of the soil) spread and flourished with such a sudden growth, that partly by the industry of his Agents abroad, and partly by its own indefatigable pains and pragmaticalness it quite over-ran the whole Reformation.*—You must conceive that *Mr. Bayes* was all this while in an Extasy in *Dodona's Grove*; or else here is strange work worse
20 than *explicating a Post*, or *examining a Pillar*. A *Bramble* that had *Agents abroad*, & it self an *indefatigable Bramble*. But straight our Bramble is transformed to a Man, and he *makes a Chair of Infallibility for himself*, out of his own Bramble Timber. Yet all this while we know not his Name. One would suspect it might be a Bp *Bramble*.
25 But then *he made himself both Pope and Emperor too of the greatest part of the Reformed World.* How near does this come to his Commendation of Bishop *Bramhall* before? For our Author seems copious, but is indeed very poor of Expression: and, as smiling and frowning are performed in the face with the same muscles very little altered; so
30 the changing of a line or two in Mr. *Bayes* at any time, will make the same thing serve for a Panegyrick or a Philippick. But what do you think of this Man? Could Mistris *Mopsa* her self have furnished you with a more pleasant or worshipful Tale? It wants nothing of perfection, but that it doth not begin with *Once upon a time*? Which
35 Master *Bayes*, according to his Accuracy, if he had thought on't, would never have omitted. Yet some Critical People, who will

8 saith] said Y.   33 or Y; and W.   It] In Z.   35 Master] Mr. Y.

exact Truth in Falshood, and tax up an old-wife's fable to the punc-
tuality of History, were blaming him t'other day for placing this
Bramble on the South-side of the *Lake Lemane*. I said, it was well
and wisely done that he chose a South Sun for the better and more
sudden growth of such a Fruit-tree. Ay, said they, but he means 5
Calvin by the Bramble; and the *rank soyl on the South-side the Lake
Lemane* is the City of *Geneva*, situate (as he would have it) on the
South-side of that Lake. Now it is strange that he, having travell'd
so well, should not have observed that the Lake lies East and West,
and that *Geneva* is built at the West end of it. Pish, said I, that's no 10
such great matter, and, as *Mr. Bayes* hath it upon another occasion,
*Whether it be so or no, the fortunes of Cæsar and the Roman Empire are not
concerned in't*. One of the Company would not let that pass, but told
us if we look'd in *Cæsar's* Commentaries, we should find their fortunes were concern'd, for it was the *Helvetian* Passage, and many 15
mistakes might have risen in the marching of the Army. Why then,
replied I again, Whether it be East, West, North, or South, there is
neither *Vice* nor *Idolatry* in it, and the Ecclesiastical Politician may
command you to believe it, and you are bound to *acquiesce* in his
Judgment, whatsoever may be *your private Opinion*. Another, to con- 20
tinue the mirth, answered, That yet there might be some Religious
Consideration in building a Town East and West, or North and
South, and 'twas not a thing so indifferent as men thought it: but
because in the Church of *England*, where the Table is set Altar-wise,
the Minister is nevertheless obliged to stand at the North-side 25
(though it be the North-end of the Table) it was fit to place the
Geneva Presbyter in diametrical-opposition to him upon the *South-
side of the Lake*. But this we all took for a cold conceit, and not
enough matured. I, that was still upon the doubtful and excusing
part, said, That to give the right situation of a Town, it was neces- 30
sary first to know in what position the Gentleman's head then was
when he made his Observation, and that might cause a great diver-
sity, as much as this came to. Yes, replyed my next Neighbour: or,
perhaps some roguing Boy that managed the Puppets, turned the
City wrong, and so disoccidented our Geographer. It was grown 35
almost as good as a Play among us: and at last they all concluded

1 up an] upon an Y.   2 were] where X.   11 *Mr.*] Master X.

that *Geneva* had *sold Mr. Bayes a Bargain,* as the *Moon* serv'd the
Earth in the *Rehearsal,* and in good sooth had *turn'd her breech on him.*
But this, I doubt not, Mr. *Bayes* will bring himself off with Honour:
but that which sticks with me is, that our Author having under-
5 taken to make *Calvin* and *Geneva* ridicule, hath not pursued it to so
high a point as the Subject would have afforded. First, he might
have taken the name of the beast *Calvinus,* and of that have given
the Anagram, *Lucianus.* Next, I would have turn'd him inside outward, and have made him *Usinulca.* That was a good Hobgoblin
10 name to have frighted Children with. Then he should have been
a *Bramble* still, ay, an *indefatigable Bramble* too: but after that he
should have continued (for in such a Book a passage in a Play is
clear gain, and a great loss if omitted) and upon that Bramble
Reasons grew as plentiful as Blackberries, but both unwholsome, and
15 they stain'd all the *white Aprons so* that there was no getting of it out.
And then, to make a fuller description of the place, he should have
added; That near to the City of *roaring Lions* there was a Lake, and
that Lake was all of Brimstone, but stored with over-grown Trouts,
which Trouts *spawned Presbyterians,* and those *spawned* the *Millecan-*
20 *tons* of all other Fanaticks. That this Shoal of *Presbyterians landed at
Geneva* and devoured all the Bishop of *Geneva's* Capons, which are
of the greatest size of any in the Reformed-World. And ever since
their mouths have been so in relish that the Presbyterians are in all
parts the very Canibals of Capons: in so much that if Princes do not
25 take care, the race of Capons is in danger to be totally extinquished.
But that the River *Rhosne* was so *sober* and *intelligent,* that its Waters
would not mix with this *Lake perillous,* but ran sheere thorow without ever touching it: nay, such is its apprehension lest the Lake
should overtake it, that the River dives it self under ground till the
30 Lake hath lost the scent: and yet when it rises again, imagining that
the Lake is still at its heels, it runs on so impetuously that it chuseth
rather to pass through the *roaring Lions,* and never thinks it self safe
till it hath taken sanctuary at the Popes Town of *Avinion.* He might
too have proved that *Calvin* made himself *Pope and Emperour,* because
35 the City of *Geneva* stamps upon its Coyn the two-headed Imperial

2 *Earth* Errata; *Sun* W, Y³˒⁵.   breech] breach Z.   13 loss] less Y.   20
this] the Y.

Eagle. And, to have given us the utmost Terror, he might have considered the Alliance and Vicinity of *Geneva* to the *Canton* of *Bern*, the Arms of which City is the Bear, (and an Argument in Heraldry, even Bishop *Bramhal* himself being Judge, might have also held in Divinity) and therefore they keep under the Town-house con- 5 stantly a whole den of Bears. So that there was never a more dangerous situation, nor any thing so carefully to be avoided by all Travellers in their wits, as *Geneva:* the *Lions* on one side, and the *Bears* on the other. This Story would have been Nuts to Mother Midnight, and was fit to have been imbellished with Mr. *Bayes* his 10 Allegorical Eloquence. And all that he saith either by fits and girds of *Calvin*, or in his justest Narratives, hath less foundation in Nature: and is indeed twice incredible, first in the matter related, and then because Mr. *Bayes* it comes from: or, to express it shorter, because of the Tale and the Tales-man. He is not yet come to that Authority 15 but that his Dogmatical *Ipse Dixits* may rather be a reason why we should not believe him. If Mr. *Bayes* will speak of Controversy; let him enter into a regular Disputation concerning these *Calvinian* Tenets, and not write an History. Or, if he will give us the History of *Calvin*, let him at the same time produce his Authors. And 20 whether History or Controversy, let him be pleas'd so long to abate of the exuberancy of his Fancy and Wit; to dispense with his Ornaments and superfluencies of Invention and Satyre, and then a man may consider whether he may believe his Story, and submit to his Argument. But in the mean time (for all he pleads in pag. 97. of his 25 *Defence*) it looks all so like subterfuge and inveagling; it is so nauseating and teadious a task, that no man thinks he ows the Author so much service as to find out the reason of his own *Categoricalness* for him. One may beat the Bush a whole day; but after so much labour shall, for all game, only spring a Butterfly, or start 30 an Hedghog. Insomuch that I am ever and anon disputing with my self whether Mr. *Bayes* be indeed so ill-natured a person as some would have him, and do not rather innocently write things (as he professes pag. 4. of his *Preface*) so *exceeding all belief*, that he may make himself and the company merry. I sometimes could think 35 that he intends no harm either to Publick or Private, but only rails

33 write things] write these things X.

contentedly to himself and his Muses; That he seeks onely his own
diversion, and chargeth his Gun with Wind but to shoot at the Air.
Or that, like Boyes, so he may make a great Paper-Kite of his own
Letter of 850 pages, and his *Preface* of an hundred, he hath no further
5 design upon the Poultry of the Village. But he takes care that I
shall never be long deceiv'd with that pleasing imagination: and
though his Hyperboles and Impossibilities can have only a ridiculous effect, he will be sure to manifest that he had a felonious
intention. He would take it ill if we should not value him as an
10 Enemy of Mankind: and like a raging *Indian* (for in *Europe* it was
never before practised) he runs a *Mucke* (as they cal it there) stabbing every man he meets, till himself be knockt on the head. This
here is the least pernicious of all his mischiefs: though it be no less
in this & all his other Books, than to make the *German Protestancy* a
15 reproachful Proverb, and to turn *Geneva* and *Calvin* into a Common-
Place of Railing. I had alwayes heard that *Calvin* was a good
Scholar, and an honest Divine. I have indeed read that he spoke
something contemptuously of our Liturgy: *Sunt in illo Libro quædam
tolerabiles ineptiæ.* But that was a sin which we may charitably sup-
20 pose he repented of on his death-bed. And if Mr. B*ayes* had some
just quarrel to him on that or other account, yet for *Divinity's Sake*
he needed not thus have made a constant Pissing-place of his Grave.
And as for *Geneva* I never perceived before but that it was a very
laudable City, that there grew an excellent Grape on the South-side
25 of the Lake *Lemane*, that a man might make good chear there, and
there was a *Pall-mall*, and one might shoot with the *Arbalet*, or play
at *Court-boule* on Sundayes. What was here to inrage our Author so
that he must raze the Fort of St. *Katherine*, and attempt with the
same success a second *Escalade?* But the difficulty of the Enterprize
30 doubtless provoked his courage, and the honour he might win made
the justice of his Quarrel. He knew that not only the Common-
wealth of *Switzerland*, but the King of *France*, the King of *Spain*, and
the Duke of *Savoy* would enter the lists for the common preservation
of the place: and therefore though it be otherwise but a petty
35 Town, he disdained not where the Race was to be run by Monarchs,
to exercise his footmanship. But is it not a great pity to see a man
in the flower of his age, and the vigor of his studies, to fall into such

a distraction, That his head runs upon nothing but Romane
Empire and Ecclesiastical Policy? This happens by his growing too
early acquainted with *Don Quixot*, and reading the Bible too late:
so that the first impressions being most strong, and mixing with
the last, as more novel, have made such a medly in his brain-pan   5
that he is become a mad Priest, which of all the sorts is the most
incurable. Hence it is that you shall hear him anon instructing
Princes, like *Sancho*, how to govern his *Island*: as he is busied at
present in vanquishing the *Calvinists* of *Germany* and *Geneva*. Had he
no Friends to have given him good counsel before his Understand-   10
ing were quite unsettled? or if there were none near, why did not
men call in the neighbours and send for the Parson of the Parish to
perswade with him in time, but let it run on thus till he is fit for
nothing but B*edlam, or Hogsdon*? However though it be a particular
damage, it may tend to a general advantage: and young students   15
will I hope by his example learn to beware henceforward of over-
weening Presumption and preposterous Ambition. For this Gentleman, as I have heard, after he had read *Don Quixot* and the Bible,
besides such School-Books as were necessary for his age, was sent
early to the *University*: and there studied hard, and in a short time   20
became a competent Rhetorician, and no ill Disputant. He had
learnt how to erect a *Thesis*, and to defend it *Pro* or *Con* with a serviceable distinction: while the Truth (as his Camarade Mr. *Bayes*
hath it on another occasion.)

> *Before a full Pot of Ale you can swallow,*   25
> *Was here with a Whoop and gone with a Hollow.*

And so thinking himself now ripe and qualified for the greatest
Undertakings, and highest Fortune, he therefore exchanged the
narrowness of the University for the *Town*; But coming out of the
confinment of the Square-cap and the Quadrangle into the open   30
Air, the World began to turn round with him: which he imagined,
though it were his own giddiness, to be nothing less then the *Quadrature* of the *Circle*. This accident concurring so happily to increase

17–18 Gentleman X, Y; Gentelman W.   23 Truth (as] Truth is (as Y.
24 occasion.) Y; ~. W.   26 *Hollow*] *hallow* X, *Holla* Y.   31 World] Wold Y.
33 *Circle*] *Circler* X.

the good opinion which he naturally had of himself, he thenceforward apply'd to gain a-like reputation with others. He follow'd
the Town life, haunted the best companies; and, to polish himself
from any Pedantick roughness, he read and saw the Playes, with
5 much care and more proficiency than most of the Auditory. But all
this while he forgot not the main chance, but hearing of a vacancy
with a Noble man, he clapp'd in, and easily obtained to be his
Chaplain. From that day you may take the date of his Preferments
and his Ruine. For having soon wrought himself dexterously into
10 his Patrons favour, by short Graces and Sermons, and a mimical way
of drolling upon the *Puritans*, which he knew would take both at
Chappel and Table; he gained a great Authority likewise among all
the domesticks. They all listened to him as an Oracle: and they
allow'd him by common consent, to have not only all the *Divinity*,
15 but more wit too than all the rest of the family put together. This
thing alone elevated him exceedingly in his own conceit, and raised
his *Hypocondria* into the Region of the Brain: that his head swell'd
like any Bladder with wind and vapour. But after he was stretch'd
to such an height in his own fancy, that he could not look down
20 from top to toe but his Eyes dazled at the Precipice of his Stature;
there fell out, or in, another natural chance which push'd him headlong. For being of an amorous Complexion, and finding himself (as
I told you) the *Cock-Divine* and the *Cock Wit* of the Family, he took
the priviledge to walk among the Hens: and thought it was not im-
25 politick to establish his new-acquired Reputation upon the Gentlewomens side. And they that perceived he was a Rising-Man, and
of pleasant Conversation, dividing his Day among them into Canonical hours, of reading now the Common-prayer, and now the Romances; were very much taken with him. The Sympathy of Silk
30 began to stir and attract the Tippet to the Pettycoat and the Petti-
coat toward the Tippet. The innocent Ladies found a strange un-
quietness in their minds, and could not distinguish whether it were
Love or Devotion. Neither was he wanting on his part to carry on
the Work; but shifted himself every day with a clean Surplice, and,
35 as oft as he had occasion to bow, he directed his Reverence towards
the Gentlewomens Pew. Till, having before had enough of the

15 rest] test Y.   19 an] a X.

Libertine, and undertaken his Calling only for Preferment; he was transported now with the Sanctity of his Office, even to extasy: and like the Bishop over *Maudlin Colledge* Altar, or like *Maudlin de la Croix*, he was seen in his Prayers to be lifted up sometimes in the Air, and once particularly so high that he crack'd his Scul against 5 the Chappel Ceiling. I do not hear for all this that he had ever practised upon the Honour of the Ladies, but that he preserved alwayes the Civility of a *Platonick Knight-Errant*. For all this Courtship had no other operation than to make him stil more in love with himself: and if he frequented their company, it was only to speculate his own 10 Baby in their Eyes. But being thus, without Competitor or Rival, the Darling of both Sexes in the Family and his own Minion; he grew beyond all measure elated, and that crack of his Scull, as in broken Looking-Glasses, multipli'd him in self-conceit and imagination.   15

Having fixed his Center in this Nobleman's House, he thought he could now move and govern the whole Earth with the same facility. Nothing now would serve him but he must be a madman in print, and write a Book of *Ecclesiastical Policy*. There he distributes all the *Territories of Conscience* into the Princes Province, and 20 makes the *Hierarchy* to be but Bishops of the Air: and talks at such an extravagant rate in things of higher concernment, that the Reader will avow that in the whole discourse he had not one *lucid interval*. This Book he was so bent upon, that he sate up late at nights, and wanting sleep, and drinking sometimes Wine to animate 25 his Fancy, it increas'd his Distemper. Beside that too he had the misfortune to have two Friends, who being both also out of their wits, and of the same though something a calmer phrensy, spurr'd him on perpetually with commendation. But when his Book was once come out, and he saw himself an Author; that some of the 30 Galants of the Town layd by the new Tune and the *Tay, tay, tarry,* to quote some of his impertinencies; that his Title page was posted and pasted up at every avenue next under the Play for that afternoon at the Kings or the Dukes House: the Vain-Glory of this totally confounded him. He lost all the little remains of his understanding, 35

13 elated] elevated Z.   21 Air:] *Air*; Y.   22 concernment] concernments Y.   26 his *Errata*; h W¹, ³, ⁶, ⁷, ⁹; h e W², ⁴, ⁵, ⁸.

and his *Cerebellum* was so dryed up that there was more brains in a Walnut and both their Shells were alike thin and brittle. The King of *France* that lost his wits, had not near so many unlucky circumstances to occasion it: and in the last of all there is some Similitude. For, as a negligent Page that rode behind and carried the Kings Lance, let it fall on his head, the King being in Armour, and the day hot, which so disordered him that he never recovered it: so this Gentleman, in the Dog-dayes, stragling by *Temple-bar*, in a massy Cassock and Surcingle, and taking the opportunity at once to piss and admire the Title-page of his Book; a tall Servant of his, one *J. O.* that was not so careful as he should be, or whether he did it of purpose, lets another Book of four hundred leaves fall upon his head; which meeting with the former fracture in his *Cranium*, and all the concurrent Accidents already mentioned, has utterly undone him. And so in conclusion his Madness hath formed it self into a perfect *Lycanthropy*. He doth so verily believe himself to be a Wolf, that his speech is all turn'd into howling, yelling, and barking: and if there were any Sheep here, you should see him pull out their throats and suck the blood. Alas, that a sweet Gentleman, and so hopeful, should miscarry! For want of Cattel here, you find him raving now against all the *Calvinists* of *England*, and worrying the whole Flock of them. For how can they hope to escape his chaps and his paws better than those of *Germany* and *Geneva*; of which he is so hungry, that he hath scratch'd up even their dead bodies out of their Graves to prey upon? And yet this is nothing if you saw him in the height of his fits: but he hath so beaten and spent himself before, that he is out of breath at present; and though you may discover the same fury, yet it wants of the same vigor. But however you see enough of him, my Masters, to make you beware, I hope, of valuing too high, and trusting too far to your own Abilities.

It were a wild thing for me to *Squire* it after this *Knight*, and accompany him here through all his Extravagancies against our *Calvinists*. You find nothing but *Orthodoxy*, *Systems*, and *Syntagms*, *Polemical Theology*, *Subtilties* and *Distinctions*. *Demosthenes*; *Tankard-bearers*; *Pragmatical*; *Controversial*: General terms without foundation or reason assigned. That they seem like words of Cabal, & have no

2 thin] thine Y[2, 5].   16 verily] severely X.

significance till they be decipher'd. Or, you would think he were playing at *Substantives* and *Adjectives*. All that rationally can be gathered from what he saith, is, that the Man is mad. But if you would supply his meaning with your imagination, as if he spoke sense and to some determinate purpose; it is very strange that, conceiving himself to be the Champion of the Church of *England*, he should bid such a general defiance to the *Calvinists*. For, he knows, or perhaps I may better say he did know before this Phrensy had subverted both his Understanding and Memory, that most of our ancient, and many of the later Bishops nearer our times, did both hold and maintaine those Doctrines which he traduces under that by-word. And the contrary Opinions were even in Bishop *Prideaux*'s time accounted so novel, that, being then publick Professor of *Divinity*, he thought fit to tax Doctor *Heylin* at the Commencement for his new-fangled Divinity: *Cujus*, saith he, in the very words of promotion, *te Doctorem creo*. He knew likewise that of our present Bishops, though one had leisure formerly to write a *Rationale* of the *Ceremonies* and *Liturgie*, and another a Treatise of the *Holiness of Lent*; yet that most of them, and 'tis to be supposed all, have studied other Controversies, and at another rate than Mr. *Bayes* his Lead can fathom. And as I know none of them that hath published any Treatise against the *Calvinian* tenets, so I have the Honour to be acquainted with some of them who are intirely of that judgment, and differ nothing, but (as of good reason) in the point of *Episcopacy*. And as for that, Bishop *Bramhal* page 61. hath proved that *Calvin* himselfe was of the *Episcopal* perswasion. So that I see no reason why Mr. *Bayes* should here and every where be such an enemy to *Controversial skill*, or the *Calvinists*. But I perceive 'tis for Bishop *Bramhall*'s sake here that all the Tribe must suffer. This *Bayes* is not a good Dog: for he runs at a whole flock of Sheep, when Mr. *B.* was the Deer whom he had in view from the beginning. However, having foil'd himself so long with every thing he meets, after him now he goes, and will never leave till he hath run him down. Poor Mr. *B.* I find that when he was a Boy he pluck'd Bishop *Bramhall's Sloes*, and *eat his Bullice*; and now, when he is as superannuated as the

2 *Adjectives.* All] *Adjectives.* And all X.   24 nothing, but (as . . . reason) Y;
~ ~, ~ . . . ~, W.   32 foil'd Y; foild W.   35 *eat*] ate Y.

Bishop's book, he must be whipp'd for't, there is no remedy. And yet I have heard, and Mr. B*ayes* himself seems to intimate as much, that how-ever he might in his younger years have mistaken, yet that even as early as Bishop *Bramhall's* Discourse, he began to re-
5 tract: and that as for all his sins against the Church of *England*, he hath in some late Treatises cryed *Peccavi* with a Witness. But, Mr. B*ayes*, doth not this now look like *Sorcery* and *Extortion*, which of all crimes you purge your self from so often without an Accuser? For first; whereas the old Bishop was at rest, and had under his last
10 Pillow laid by all cares and contests of this lower World; you by your *Necromancy* have disturb'd him, and rais'd his Ghost to persecute and haunt Mr. *B.* whom doubtless at his death he had pardoned. But if you called him up to ask some Questions too con-cerning your Ecclesiastical Policy, as I am apt to suppose, I doubt
15 you had no better Answer than in the Song:

> *Art thou forlorn of God, and com'st to me?*
> *What can I tell thee then but miserie?*

And then, as for Extortion; who but such an *Hebrew Jew* as you, would, after an honest man had made so full and voluntary Resti-
20 tution, not yet have been satisfied without so many pounds of his flesh over into the bargain? Though *J. O.* be in a desperate condi-tion, yet methinks Mr. *B.* not *being past Grace*, should not neither *have been past Mercy.* Are there no terms of Pardon, Mr. *Bayes?* is there no time for Expiation? but, after so ample a Confession as he
25 hath made, must he now be hang'd too to make good the Proverb? It puts me in mind of a Story in the time of the *Guelphs* and *Ghibilines*, whom I perceive Mr. *Bayes* hath heard of: They were two Factions in *Italy*, of which the *Guelphs* were for the Pope, and the *Ghibilines* for the Emperour; and these were for many years carried on
30 and fomented with much animosity, to the great disturbance of Christendom. Which of these two were the *Nonconformists* in those dayes I can no more determine, than which of our Parties here at home is now *schismatical.* But so *nonconformable* they were to one another, that the Historian said they took care to differ in the least
35 circumstances of any humane action: and, as those that have the

24 Expiation? Y, Z; ∼; W.   28 Italy, Y; ∼ W.

Masons Word, secretly discern one another; so in the peeling or cutting but of an Onion, a *Guelph* and *vice versa* would at first sight have distinguish'd a *Ghibiline*. Now one of this latter sort coming at *Rome* to Confession upon *Ash-wednesday*, the Pope or the Penitentiary sprinkling Ashes on the Man's head with the usual ceremony, instead of pronouncing *Memento homo quod Cinis es & in Cinerem reverteris*, changed it to *Memento homo quod Ghibilinus es, &c.* And even thus it fares with Mr. B. who though he should creep on his knees up the whole Stairs of *Scholastick Penitence*, I am confident neither he, nor any of his Party, shall by Mr. *Bayes* his good will ever be absolved. And therefore truly if I were in Mr. B's case, if I could not have my Confession back again, yet it should be a warning unto me not without better grounds to be so coming and so good natured for the future. But whatever he do, I hope others will consider what usage they are like to find at Mr. *Bayes*'s hand, and not suffer themselves by the touch of his *Penitential Rod* to be transformed into Beasts, even into *Rats*, as here he hath done with Mr. B. I have indeed wondred often at this *Bayes* his insolence, who summons in all the World, and *preacheth* up only this *Repentance:* and so frequently in his Books he calls for *Testimonies, Signal Marks, Publick Acknowledgment, Satisfaction, Recantation*, and I know not what. He that hath made the passage to Heaven so easie that one may fly thither without Grace (as *Gonzales* to the Moon only by the help of his *Gansas*) he that hath *disintricated* its narrow paths from those *Labyrinths* which *J. O.* and Mr. B. have planted; this Overseer of God's Highwayes (if I may with reverence speak it) who hath paved a broad Causway with Moral Virtue thorow his Kingdom; he me-thinks should not have made the *process of Loyalty* more difficult than that of *Salvation*. What *Signal Marks*, what *Testimonies* would he have of this Conversion? Every man cannot, as he hath done, write an *Ecclesiastical Policy*, a *Defence*, a *Preface:* and some, if they could, would not do it after his manner; lest in stead of obliging thereby the King and the Church, it should be a Testimony to the contrary. Neither, unless men have better Principles of Allegiance at home, are they likely to be reduced by Mr. *Bayes* his way of perswasion.

4 *wednesday* Y; *weduesday* W.   4–5 Penitentiary Y; Peniteniary W.   15 *Bayes's* Y; *Bayes* W.

He is the first Minister of the Gospel that ever had it in his Commission *to rail at all Nations*. And, though it hath been long practised, I never observed any great success by reviling men into *Conformity*. I have heard that *Charms* may even invite the Moon out
5 of Heaven, but I never could see her moved by the *Rhetorick* of *barking*. I think it ought to be highly penal for any man to impose other conditions upon his Majesties good Subjects than the King expects, or the Law requires. When you have done all, you must yet appear before Mr. B*ayes* his Tribunal, and he hath a new Test
10 yet to put you to. I must confess at this rate the *Nonconformists* deserve some Compassion: that after they have done or suffered legally and to the utmost, they must still be subjected to the *Wand* of a *Verger*, or to the wanton lash of every *Pedant*; that they must run the *Ganteloop*, or down with their breeches as oft as he wants the
15 prospect of a more pleasing *Nudity*. But I think they may chuse whether they will submit or no to his Jurisdiction. Let them but (as I hope they do) fear God, honour the King, preserve their Consciences, follow their Trades, and look to their Chimnies; and they need not fear Mr. B*ayes* and all his Malice. But after he hath suffi-
20 ciently insulted over Mr. B's ignorance and vanity, with other Complements of the like nature, in recompence of that *candor and civility* which he acknowledges *him to have now learnt towards the Church of England*, Mr. B*ayes* (forgetting what had past long since betwixt him and the Bookseller) saith, in excuse of his severity, that
25 *this Treatise was not published to impair Mr. B's esteem in the least, but for a correction of his scribling humour, and to warn their Rat-Divines that are perpetually nibling and gnawing other mens Writings.* Now I must confess Mr. *Bayes* this is a very handsom Welcome to Mr. B. that was come so far to see you, and doubtless upon this encouragement he
30 will visit you often. This is an admirable dexterity our Author hath (I wish I could learn it) *to correct a man's scribling humour without impairing in the least his reputation*. He is as courteous as Lightning, and can melt the Sword without ever hurting the Scabbard. But as for their *Rat-Divines*, I wonder they are not all poysoned with nibling
35 at his Writings, he hath strewed so much *Arsenick* in every leaf. But

---

19 Mr.] Master Y.   and all Y; and and all W.   25 *impair*] *impart* Z.
27 perpetually] perpetuall Z.

however, methinks he should not have grudged them so slender a sustenance. For though there was a Sow in *Arcadia* so fat and insensible that she suffered a Rats nest in her buttock, and they had both Dyet and Lodging in the same Gammon; yet it is not every *Rats* good fortune to be so well provided. And for *Pushpin-Divinity*, I confess it is a new term of Art, and I shall henceforward take notice of it, but I am afraid in general it doth not tend much to the reputation of the Faculty.

And now, though he told us at the beginning, that the Bookseller was the main reason of publishing this Book of the Bishop and his own Preface, he tels us that the main reason of its publication was to give some check to their present disingenuity, that is to say to that of *J. O.* And *J. O.* be it at present. He is come so much nearer however to the Truth, though we shall find ere we have done that there is still a mainer reason.

When I first took notice of this misunderstanding betwixt Mr. B*ayes* and *J. O.* I considered whether it were not Execution-day with the whole *Latine Alphabet:* whether all the Letters were not to suffer in the same manner, except *C* only, which (having been the mark of Condemnation) might have a pardon to serve for the Executioner. I began to repent of my Undertaking, being afraid that the Quarrel was with the whole *Cris-cross-Row*, and that we must fight it out through all the Squadrons of the *Vowels*, the *Mutes*, the *Semi-vowels*, and the *Liquids*. I foresaw a sore and endless labour, and a battel the longest that ever was read of; being probable to continue as long as one Letter was left alive, or there were any use of Reading. Therefore, to spare mine own pains, and prevent *Ink-shed*, I was advising the Letters to go before Mr. *Bales*, or any other his Majesties Justices of Peace, to swear that they were in danger of their Lives, and desire that Mr. *Bayes* might be bound to the *Good-behaviour*. But after this I had another Phancy, and that not altogether unreasonable; that Mr. *Bayes* had, onely for health and exercise-sake, drawn *J. O.* by chance out of the number of the rest, to try how he could rail at a Letter, and that he might be well in breath upon any occasion of greater consequence. For, how perfect soever a man may have been in any Science, yet without continual

7 of *om.* X.   18 whole *om.* X.

practice he will find a sensible decay of his faculty. Hence also, and upon the same natural ground, it is the wisdom of Cats to whet their Claws against the Chairs and Hangings, in meditation of the next *Rat* they are to encounter. And I am confident that Mr. *Bayes* by this way hath brought himself into so good railing case, that pick what Letter you will out of the Alphabet, he is able to write an Epistle upon it of 723 pages (I have now told them right) to the Author of the *Friendly Debates*.

Now though this had very much of probability, I had yet a further Conjecture; that this *J. O.* was a *Talisman*, signed under some peculiar influence of the heavenly bodies, and that the Fate of Mr. *Bayes* was bound up within it. Whether it be so or no I know not: but this I am assured of, without the help either of *Syderal Magick* or *Judicial Astrologie*, that when *J* and *O* are in *Conjunction* they do more certainly than any of the *Planets* forebode that a great *Ecclesiastical Politician* shall that Year run mad. I confess after all this, when I was come to the dregs of my phansie (for we all have our infirmities, and Mr. *Bayes* his *Defence* was but the *blew-John* of his *Ecclesiastical Policy*, and this *Preface* the Tap-droppings of his *Defence*) I reflected whether Mr. *Bayes* having no particular cause of indignation against the Letters, there might not have been a mistake of the Printer, and that they were to be read in one word *Io* that uses to go before *Pæan*: that is in English a Triumph before the Victory. Or whether it alluded to *Io* that we read of at School, the Daughter of *Inachus*; and that as *Juno* persecuted the Heifer, so this was an *He-Cow*, that is to say a *Bull* to be baited by Mr. *Bayes* the *Thunderer*. But these being Conceits too trivial, though a *Ragoust* fit enough for Mr. *Bayes* his palate, I was forced moreover to quit them, remarking that it was an *J* Consonant. And I plainly at last perceived that this *J. O.* was a very Man as any of us are, and had a Head, and a Mouth with Tongue and Teeth in it, and Hands with Fingers and Nails upon them: nay, that he could read and write, and speak as well as I or Mr. *Bayes*, either of us. When I once found this, the business appeared more serious, and I was willing to see

---

3 meditation] mediation X.   5 that Y; thar W.   7 them *Errata*; him W.   23 uses] use X.   27 *Ragoust Errata*; *Ragouse* W.   30 perceived] perceive Z.   33 Mr.] Master X.

what was the matter that so much exasperated Mr. *Bays*, who is a
Person, as he saith himself, *of such a tame and softly humour, and so cold
a complexion, that he thinks himself scarce capable of hot and passionate
impressions.* I concluded that necessarily there must be some extraordinary Accident and Occasion that could alter so good a Nature.   5
For I saw that he pursued *J. O.* if not from *Post to Pillar*, yet from
Pillar to Post, and I discerned all along the footsteps of a most
inveterate and implacable Malice. As oft as he does but name
those two first Letters, he is, like the Island of *Fayal*, on fire in
three-score and ten places.   10

You see, Mr. *Bayes*, that I too have improved my wit with reading the *Gazettes*. Were you of that Fellows diet here about Town,
that epicurizes upon burning Coals, drinks healths in scalding
Brimstone, scraunches the Glasses for his *Dessert*, and draws his
breath through glowing Tobacco-pipes. Nay, to say a thing yet   15
greater; had you never tasted other sustenance than the Focus of
burning Glasses, you could not shew more *flame* than you do alwayes
upon that subject. And yet one would think that even from the
little sports, with your *comfortable importance* after Supper, you should
have learnt when *J. O.* came into play, to *love your Love* with an J,   20
because he is *Judicious*, though you *hate your Love with an* J, because
he is *jealous*: and then to *love your Love with an O*, because he is *Oracu-
lous*, though you *hate your Love with an O*, because he is *Obscure:* Is it
not strange, that in those most benign minutes of a Man's life, when
the Stars smile, the Birds sing, the Winds whisper, the Fountains 25
warble, the Trees blossom, and universal Nature seems to invite it
self to the B*ridal*; When the Lion pulls in his Claws, and the Aspick
layes by its Poyson, and all the most noxious Creatures grow
amorously innocent: that even then, Mr. *Bayes* alone should not be
able to refrain his Malignity? As you love your self, *Madam*, let him   30
not come near you. He hath been fed all his life with Vipers instead
of Lampreys, and Scorpions for Crayfish: and if at any time he eat
Chickens they had been cramb'd with Spiders, till he hath so
invenomed his whole substance that 'tis much safer to bed with a
Mountebank before he hath taken his Antidote. But it cannot be   35

4 concluded] conclude Y²⁻⁷.   14 *Dessert Errata; Desart* W; *Desert* X.
25 smile] simile Y.   33 cramb'd] cramb Z.

any vulgar furnace that hath chafed so *cool* a Salamander. 'Tis not
the strewing of *Cowitch* in his *Genial-bed* that could thus disquiet him
the first night. And therefore let's take the Candle and see whether
there be not some body underneath that hath cut the Bed-Cords.
5 There was a worthy Divine, not many years dead, who in his
younger time being of a facetious and unlucky humour, was commonly known by the name of *Tom Triplet*. He was brought up at
Pauls School, under a severe Master, Dr. *Gill*, and from thence he
went to the University. There he took liberty (as 'tis usual with
10 those that are emancipated from School) to tel Tales, and make the
Discipline ridiculous under which he was bred. But, not suspecting
the Doctor's intelligence, comming once to Town, he went in full
School to give him a Visit, and expected no less than to get a *Play-
day* for his former acquaintance. But, instead of that, he found him-
15 self hors'd up in a trice; though he appeal'd in vain to the Priviledges
of the University, pleaded *Adultus*, and invoked the mercy of the
Spectators. Nor was he let down till the Master had planted a
Grove of Birch in his back-side, for the Terrour and publick Example
of all Waggs that divulge the Secrets of *Priscian*, and make merry
20 with their Teachers. This stuck so with *Triplet*, that all his life-time
he never forgave the Doctor, but sent him every New-years-tide an
Anniversary Ballad to a new Tune, and so in his turn avenged himself of his jerking Pedagogue.

Now when I observed that of late years Mr. *Bayes* had regularly
25 *spawned* his Books; in 1670 the *Ecclesiastical Policy*; in 1671 the *Defence of the Ecclesiastical Policy*; and now in 1672 this *Preface* to Bishop
Bramhal, and that they were writ in a stile so vindictive and poynant,
that they wanted nothing but rime to be right *Tom Triplet*; and that
their edge bore alwayes upon *J. O.* either in broad meanings or
30 in plain terms; I began to suspect that where there was so great
resemblance in the Effects, there might be some parallel in their
Causes. For though the Peeks of Players among themselves, or of
Poet against Poet, or of a Conformist-Divine against a Nonconformist, are dangerous, and of late times have caused great disturbance;
35 yet I never remarked so irreconcileable and implacable a spirit as

18 publick] puplick X.   31 the *om.* X.   Effects, there] Effects, there might
be some parallel in Effects, there X.   35 and implacable *om.* X.

that of Boyes against their Schoolmasters or Tutors. The quarrels
of their Education have an influence upon their Memories and
Understandings for ever after. They cannot speak of their Teachers
with any patience or civility: and their discourse is never so flippant, nor their Wits so fluent as when you put them upon that 5
Theme. Nay, I have heard old Men, otherwise, sober, peaceable and
good-natured, who never could forgive *Osbolston*, as the younger are
still inveighing against Dr. *Busby.* It were well that both old and
young would reform this vice, and consider how easie a thing it is
upon particular grudges, and as they conceive out of a just censure, 10
to slip either into juvenile petulancy or inveterate uncharitableness.
And had there not been something of this in his own case, I am confident Mr. *Bayes* in his *Ecclesiastical Policy*, in order to the publick
Peace and security of the Government, could not have failed to admonish Princes to beware of this growing Evil, and to brandish the 15
Publick Rods if not *the Axes* against the Boyes, to teach them better
manners. And he would have assured them that they might have
done it with all safety, notwithstanding that there were in proportion an hundred Boyes against one *Preceptor.* But therefore is it not
possible that *J. O.* and Mr. *Bayes* have known one another formerly 20
in the University; and that (as in Seniority there is a kind of Magistracy) *Bayes* being yet young, *J. O.* conceiv'd himself in those dayes
to be his Superior, and exercised an Academical Jurisdiction or
Dominion over him? Now whether *J. O.* might not be too severe
upon him there (for all men are prone to be cogent and supercilious 25
when they are in Office) or whether Mr. *Bayes* might not make some
little escapes and excursions there (as young men are apt to do when
they are got together) that I know not, and rather believe the contrary. But that is certain that the young Wits in the Universities
have alwayes an animosity against the Doctors, and take a peculiar 30
felicity in having a lucky hit at any of them. I rather suppose that
after Mr. *Bayes* had changed the place, and his condition, to be the
Noblemans Chaplain, that he might commit some exorbitance in
J. O's opinion, or preach or write something to *J. O*'s reproach, and
published the Secrets of the *Holy Brotherhood:* and that *J. O.* having 35
got him within his reach, did therefore (figuratively speaking)

10 conceive] conceived X.   11 or] of X.   24 him? Y; ∼. W.

—Instead of Maid Jillian
Take up his Malepillian,
And whipt him like a baggage—

as *Tom Triplet* expresses it. This might well raise Mr. *Bayes* his
5 Choler, who, considering himself to be now in Holy Orders, and
conceiving that he had been as safe as in a Sanctuary under his
Patrons protection, must needs take it ill to be handled so irreverently. If it were thus in Fact, and that *J. O.* might presume too
much upon his former Authority to give him Correction; yet it is
10 the more excusable, if Mr. *Bayes* had on his part been guilty of so
much disingenuity. For though a man may be allowed once in his
life to change his Party, and the whole Scene of his Affairs, either for
his Safety or Preferment; nay, though every man be obliged to
change an hundred times backward and forward, if his Judgement
15 be so weak & variable; yet there are some drudgeries that no man
of Honour would put himself upon, and but few submit to if they
were imposed. As suppose one had thought fit to pass over from
one Perswasion of the Christian Religion unto another; he would
not chuse to spit thrice at every Article that he relinquished, to
20 curse solemnly his Father and Mother for having educated him in
those Opinions, to animate his new Acquaintances to the massa-
cring of his former Camarades. These are businesses that can only be
expected from a Renegade of *Argier* or *Tunis*; to over-doe in expiation, and gain better credence of being a sincere *Musulman*. And
25 truly, though I can scarcely believe that Mr. *Bayes* hath so mean
and desperate intentions, which yet his words seem too often to
manifest; the Offices however which he undertakes are almost as
dishonourable. For he hath so studied and improved their *Jargon* as
he calls it, heard their Sermons and Prayers so attentively, searched
30 the Scriptures so narrowly, that a man may justly suspect he had
formerly set up of *J. O*'s Profession, and having the language so
perfectly, hath upon *this juncture of affairs* betaken himself to turn
Spy and *Intelligencer*; and 'tis evident that he hath travell'd the
Country for that purpose. So that I cannot resemble him better
35 than to that Politick Engine who about two years ago was employed

1 *Maid Errata*; *Dame* W.   12 Scene] Scence Z.   15 yet] ye X.

by some of *Oxford* as a *Missionary* amongst the Nonconformists of the adjacent Counties; and, upon design, either gathered a Congregation of his own, or preach'd amongst others, till having got all their Names, he threw off the Vizard, and appear'd in his own Colours, an honest *Informer*. But I would not have any man take Mr. *Bayes* his *Fanatical Geography* for authentick, lest he should be as far misled, as in the situation of *Geneva*. It suffices that Mr. *Bayes* hath done therein as much as served to his purpose, and mixed probability enough for such as know not better, and whose ears are of a just bore for his fable.

But *I. O.* being of age and parts sufficient either to manage or to neglect this Quarrel, I shall as far as possible decline the mentioning of him, seeing I have too upon further intelligence and consideration found that he was not the person whom Mr. *Bayes* principally intended. For the truth of it is, the King was the Person concerned from the beginning.

His Majesty before his most happy and miraculous Restauration, had sent over a Declaration of his Indulgence to tender Consciences in Ecclesiastical matters. Which, as it was doubtless the real Result of the last Advice left Him by his glorious Father, and of his own consummate Prudence and natural Benignity; so at his Return he religiously observed and promoted it as far as the Passions and Influences of the contrary Party would give leave. For, whereas among all the decent Circumstances of his welcom Return, the Providence of God had so cooperated with the duty of his Subjects, that so glorious an Action should neither be soiled with the blood of Victory, nor lessened by any capitulations of Treaty, so not to be wanting on his part in courtesy, as I may say, to so happy a conjuncture, He imposed upon himself an Oblivion of former offences, and this Indulgence in Ecclesiastical affairs. And to royal and generous minds no stipulations are so binding as their own voluntary promises: not is it to be wondred if they hold those Conditions that they put upon themselves the most inviolable. He therefore carried the Act of Oblivion and Indempnity thorow: that Party who had

3 amongst] among X.   4 own *om.* X.   13–14 further . . . consideration
Y; *In parentheses* W.   15 For Y; ~, W.   30 this] his X.   31 no]
do X.

suffered so vastly in the late Combustions not refusing to imitate his
Generosity, but throwing all their particular Losses & Resentments
into the Publick Reckoning. But when it came to the Ecclesiastical
Part, the accomplishment of which onely remain'd behind to have
5 perfected his Majesty's felicity, the business I warrant you would
not go so, (as I shall have occasion to say more particularly.) For,
though I am sorry to speak it, yet it is a sad truth, that the Animosities and Obstinacy of some of the Clergy have in all Ages been
the greatest Obstacle to the Clemency, Prudence and good Inten-
10 tions of Princes, and the Establishment of their Affairs. His Majesty
therefore expected a better season, and having at last rid himself of
a great Minister of State who had headed this Interest, he now proceeded plainly to recommend to his Parliament effectually and with
repeated instances, the Consideration of tender Consciences. After
15 the Kings last representing of this matter to the Parliament, Mr.
Bayes took so much time as was necessary for the maturing of so
accurate a Book which was to be the standard of Government for all
future Ages, and he was happily delivered in 1670 of his Ecclesiastical Policy. And, though he thought fit in this first Book to treat
20 his Majesty more tenderly than in those that followed, yet even in
this he doth all along use great liberty and presumption. Nor can
what he objects, page 282, to weak Consciences, take place so justly
upon them as upon himself: who, while his Prince might expect his
Compliance, doth give him Counsel, advises him how to governe
25 the Kingdom, blames and corrects the Laws, and tells him how this
and the other might be mended. But that I may not involve the
thing in generals, but represent undeniably Mr. *Bayes* his performance in this undertaking, I shall without Art write down his own
words and his own *quod Scripsi Scripsi*, as they ly naked to the view
30 of every Reader.

The grand Thesis upon which he stakes not onely all his own
Divinity and Policy, his Reputation, Preferment and Conscience
(of most of which he hath no reason to be prodigal) but even
the Crowns and Fate of Princes, and the Liberties, Lives and
35 Estates, and, which is more, the Consciences of their Subjects,

(which are too valuable to be trusted in his disposal,) is this, pag. 10. *That it is absolutely necessary to the peace and government of the World, that the supream Magistrate of every Commonwealth should be vested with a Power to govern and conduct the Consciences of Subjects in affairs of Religion.* And pag. 12. he explains himself more fully: that *Unless Princes have* 5 *Power to bind their Subjects to that Religion that they apprehend most advantagious to publick peace and tranquillity, and restrain these religious mistakes that tend to its subversion, they are no better than Statues and Images of Authority.* Pag. 13. *A Prince is endued with a Power to conduct Religion, and that must be subject to his Dominion as well as all other Affairs of State.* 10 P. 27. *If Princes should forgoe their Soveraignty over mens Consciences in matters of Religion, they leave themselves less power than is absolutely necessary, &c.* And in brief: *The Supream Government of every Commonwealth, where-ever it is lodged, must of necessity be universal, absolute, and uncontroulable in all affairs whatsoever that concern the Interests of Man-* 15 *kind and the ends of Government.* P. 32. *He in whom the Supream Power resides, having Authority to assign to every Subject his proper function, and among others these of the Priesthood; the exercise thereof as he has power to transfer upon others, so he may if he please reserve it to himself.* P. 33. *Our Saviour came not to unsettle the Foundations of Government, but left the* 20 *Government of the World in the same condition he found it.* P. 34. *The Government of Religion was vested in Princes by an antecedent right to Christ.*— This being the Magisterial and main Point that he maintains, the rest of his Assertions may be reckoned as Corollaries to this *Thesis,* and without which indeed such an unlimited Maxime 25 can never be justified. Therefore, to make a Conscience fit for the nonse, he sayes, p. 89. *Men may think of things according to their own perswasions, and assert the freedom of their judgments against all the Powers of the Earth. This is the Prerogative of the Mind of Man within its own Dominions, its Kingdom is intellectual, &c. Whilst Conscience acts within its* 30 *proper sphere, the Cicil Power is so far from doing it violence, that it never can.* P. 92. *Mankind have the same natural right to Liberty of Conscience in matters of Religious Worship as in Affairs of Justice and Honesty; that is to say, a Liberty of Judgment, but not of Practice.* And in the same page

---

1 (which . . . disposal,) Y; ~ . . . ~, W.   12 *matters*] *matter* X.   13 *&c om.* X.   18 *these*] *those* Z; *this* Parker.   *thereof*] whereof Parker.   19 *upon others*] to another Parker.

he determines *Christian Liberty* to be *founded upon the Reasonableness of this Principle. P.* 308. *In cases and disputes of Publick concernment, Private men are not properly* sui Juris, *They have no power over their own actions: they are not to be directed by their own judgments, or determined by their own wills, but by the commands and determinations of the publick Conscience; and if there be any sin in the Command, he that imposed it shall answer for it, and not I whose whole duty it is to obey. The Commands of Authority will warrant my Obedience, my Obedience will hallow, or at least excuse my action, and so secure me from sin, if not from error: and in all doubtful and disputable cases, 'tis better to err with Authority than to be in the right against it: not only because the danger of a little error (and so it is if it be disputable) is outweighed by the importance of the great duty of Obedience, &c.*

Another of his Corollaries is, *That God hath appointed* (p. 80.) *the Magistrates to be his Trustees upon Earth, and his Officials to act and determine in Moral Virtues and Pious Devotions according to all accidents and emergencies of affairs: to assign new particulars of the Divine Law; to declare new bounds of right and wrong, which the Law of God neither doth nor can limit. P.* 69. *Moral Virtue being the most material and useful part of all Religion, is also the utmost end of all its other duties. P.* 76. *All Religion must of necessity be resolved into Enthusiasm or Morality. The former is meer Imposture; and therefore all that is true must be reduced to the latter.* Having thus enabled the Prince, dispensed with Conscience, and fitted up a Moral Religion for that Conscience; to show how much those Moral Virtues are to be valued, P. 53. of the Preface to his *Ecclesiastical Policy* he affirms that *'tis absolutely necessary to the peace and happiness of Kingdoms, that there be set up a more severe Government over Mens Consciences and Religious Perswasions, than over their Vices and Immoralities.* And, pag. 55. of the same, that *Princes may with less hazard give liberty to mens Vices and Debaucheries than their Consciences.* But for what belongs particularly to the use of their Power in Religion; he first (p. 56. of his Book) saith, that *the Protestant Reformation hath not been able to resettle Princes in their full and natural rights in reference to its concerns:* & 58. *most Protestant Princes have been frighted, not to say hector'd out of the exercise of their Ecclesiastical jurisdiction. P.* 271.

If Princes will be resolute (and if they wil govern so they must be) they may
easily make the most stuborn Conscience bend to their resolutions. P. 21.
Princes must be sure to bind on at first their Ecclesiastical Laws with the
straitest knot, and afterward keep them in force by the severity of their execu-
tion. 223. speaking of honest and well meaning men: *So easy is it for*   5
men to deserve to be punished for their Consciences, that there is no Nation in
the World, in which were Government rightly understood and duly managed,
mistakes and abuses of Religion would not supply the Galleys with vastly
greater numbers than Villany. Pag. 54. of the Preface to Ecclesiast.
Policy. *Of all Villains the well-meaning Zealot is the most dangerous.*   10
P. 49. *The Fanatick-Party in Country Towns and Villages ariseth not (to*
speak within compass) above the proportion of one to twenty. Whilst the pub-
lick peace and settlement is so unluckily defeated by quarrels and mutinies of
Religion, to erect and create new Trading Combinations, is only to build so
many Nests of Faction and Sedition, &c. For it is notorious that there is not   15
any sort of people so inclinable to seditious practices as the Trading part of
a Nation. And now though many as material passages might be
heap'd up out of his Book on all these and other as tender Subjects,
I shall conclude this imperfect enumeration with one Corollary
more, to which indeed his grand Thesis and all the superstructures   20
are subordinate and accommodated. P. 166. *Princes cannot pluck a*
pin out of the Church, but the State immediately shakes and totters. This is
the *Syntagm* of Mr. *Bayes* his Divinity, and *System* of his Policy: The
Principles of which confine upon the *Territories* of *Malmsbury*, and
the stile, as far as his Wit would give him leave, imitates that Lan-   25
guage: But the Arrogance and Dictature with which he imposes it
on the world, surpasses by far the presumption either of *Gondibert*
or *Leviathan*. For he had indeed a very Politick fetch or two that
might have made a much wiser man then he, more confident. For
he imagined first of all, that he had perfectly secured himself from   30
any mans answering him: not so much upon the true reason, that
is, because indeed so paltry a Book did not deserve an Answer; as
because he had so confounded the Question with differing terms
and contradictory expressions, that he might upon occasion affirm

2 *resolutions*] Commands Parker.   P. 21. *Ed*; P. 221. W etc.   4 *straitest*]
straightest X.   5 223. Y; ~ W.   8 *Galleys*] Galles X.   14 *create*
new] encourage Parker.   18 these] those X.   19 imperfect] perfect Z.

whatsoever he denyed, or deny whatsoever he affirmed. And then besides, because he had so intangled the matter of Conscience with the Magistrates Power, that he supposed no man could handle it thorowly without bringing himself within the Statute of treason-
5 able words, and at least a *Premunire*. But last of all, because he thought that whosoever answered him must for certain be of a contrary Judgment, and he that was of a contrary Judgment should be a Fanatick; and if one of them presumed to be medling, then Mr. *Bayes* (as all Divines have a *Non-obstante* to the *Jejunium Cecilianum*,
10 and to the *Act of Oblivion* and *Indempnity*) would either burn that, or tear it in pieces. Being so well fortified on this side, upon the other he took himself to be impregnable. His Majesty must needs take it kindly that he gave him so great an accession of *Territory*: and, lest he should not be thought rightly to understand Govern-
15 ment, nay lest Mr. *Bayes* by virtue of P. 271. should not think him fit to govern, he could not in prudence and safety but submit to his Admonition and Instructions. But if he would not, Mr. Bayes knew, ay that he did, how to be even with him, and would write another Book that should do his business. For, the same Power that had
20 given the Prince that Authority, could also revoke it.

But let us see therefore what success the whole Contrivance met with, or what it deserved. For, after things have been laid with all the depth of humane Policy, there happens lightly some ugly little contrary accident from some quarter or other of Heaven, that frus-
25 trates and renders all ridiculous.

And here, for brevity and distinction sake, I must make use of the same priviledge by which I call him Mr. *Bayes*, to denominate also his several Aphorisms or Hypotheses: and let him take care whether or no they be significant.
30   First, The *Unlimited Magistrate*.
        Secondly, *The Publick Conscience*.
        Thirdly, *Moral Grace*.
        Fourthly, *Debauchery Tolerated*.
        Fifthly, *Persecution recommended*.
35   And lastly, *Pushpin-Divinity*.

3 Magistrates Y; Majestrates W.   6 for certain] needs Z.   15 271]
171 X.   18 ay] nay Z.   22 laid] aid X.   23 depth] depths Z.

And now, though I intend not to be longer than the nature of *Animadversions* requires, (this also being but collateral to my work of examining the Preface, and having been so abundantly performed already) yet neither can I proceed well without some Preface. For, as I am obliged to ask pardon if I speak of serious things ridiculously; so I must now beg excuse if I should hap to discourse of ridiculous things seriously. But I shall, so far as possible, observe *decorum*, and, whatever I talk of, not commit such an Absurdity, as to be grave with a Buffoon. But the principal cause of my Apology is, because I see I am drawn in to mention Kings and Princes, and even our own; whom, as I think of with all duty and reverence, so I avoid speaking of either in jest or earnest, lest by reason of my private condition & breeding, I should, though most unwillingly, trip in a word, or fail in the mannerliness of an expression. But Mr. B*ayes*, because Princes sometimes hear men of his quality play their Part, or preach a Sermon, grows so insolent that he thinks himself fit to be their Governour. So dangerous it is to let such creatures be too familiar. They know not their distance, and like the Ass in the Fable, because they see the Spaniel play with their Masters Leggs, they think themselves priviledged to paw and ramp upon his Shoulders. Yet though I must follow his track now I am in, I hope I shall not write after his Copy.

As for his first Hypothesis of the *Unlimited Magistrate*, I must for this once do him right, that after I had read in his 12th page, that *Princes have power to bind their Subjects to that Religion they apprehend most advantagious to publick Peace and Tranquillity*; a long time after, not as I remember till pag. 82. when he bethought himself better, he saith, *No Rites nor Ceremonies can be esteemed unlawful in the Worship of God, unless they tend to debauch men either in their practices or their conceptions of the Deity*. But no man is in Ingenuity obliged to do him that service for the future; neither yet doth that limitation bind up or interpret what he before so loosly affirmed. However, take all along the Power of the Magistrate as he hath stated it; I am confident if Bishop *Bramhall* were alive (who could no more forbear *Grotius*, than Mr. *Bayes* could the Bishop, notwithstanding their

---

10 drawn in *om.* Z.   11 of *om.* X.   13 & breeding *om.* Z.   28 *nor*]
or Parker.   32 he before] before he Z.

friendship) he would bestow the same Censure upon him that he
doth upon *Grotius*, p. 18. *When I read his Book of the Right of the
Sovereign Magistrate in Sacred things, he seem'd to me to come too near an
Erastian, and to lessen the power of the Keys too much, which Christ left as
a Legacy to his Church. It may be he did write that before he was come to
full maturity of judgment: and some other things, I do not say after he was
superannuated, but without that due deliberation which he useth at other
times;* (wherein a man may desire Mr. B*ayes* in Mr. *Bayes*) *Or it may
be some things have been changed in his* Book, *as I have been told by one of
his nearest friends, and that we shall shortly see a more Authentick Edition
of all his Works. This is certain, that some of those things which I dislike,
were not his own judgment after he was come to maturity in Theological
matters.* And had Mr. *Bayes* (as he ought to have done) carried his
Book to any of the present Bishops, or their Chaplains, for a Licence
to print it, I cannot conceive that he could have obtained it in better terms than what I have collected out of the 108 page of his
Answerer: *Notwithstanding the old Pleas of the* Jus Divinum *of Episcopacy, of Example and Direction Apostolical, of a Parity of Reason between
the condition of the Church whilst under Extraordinary Officers, and whilst
under Ordinary, of the power of the Church to appoint Ceremonies for
Decency and Order, of the pattern of the Churches of old;* (all which under
Protestation are reserved till the first opportunity;) I have upon
reading of this Book, found that it may be of use for the *present
Juncture of Affairs,* and therefore let it be printed. And, as I think,
he hath disobliged the Clergy of *England* in this matter; so I believe
the favour that he doth his Majesty is not equivalent to that
damage. For that I may, with Mr. *Bays* his leave, prophane *Ben.
Johnson,* though the gravest Divines should be his Flatterers; he
hath a very quick sense, and (shall I prophane *Horace* too in the same
period?)

>   *Hunc male si palpere recalcitrat undique tutus.*

If one stroke him ilfavouredly, he hath a terrible way of kicking, and
will fling you to the Stable-door; but is himself safe on every side.

8 desire] discern W3, 4, 7, 8.   Mr. Bayes . . . Mr. Bayes] Grotius . . . Grotius
Bramhall.   9 *have been*] *may be* X.   *his* Book] some of his Works Bramhall.
14 present *om.* Y.   Bishops, or] Bishops, to whom it belongs, or Y.   22 opportunity; Y; ~. W.   29 and *om.* X.

He knows it's all but that you may get into the Saddle again; and that the Priest may ride him, though it be to a Precipice. He therefore contents Himself with the Power that He hath inherited from his Royal Progenitors Kings and Queens of *England*, and as it is declared by Parliament: and is not to be trepann'd into another 5 kind of Tenure of Dominion to be held at Mr. *Bayes* his pleasure, and depend upon the strength only of his Argument. But (that I may not offend in Latin too frequently) he considers that by not assuming a Deity to himself, he becomes secure and worthy of his Government. There are lightly about the Courts of Princes a sort of 10 Projectors for Concealed Lands, to which they entitle the King, to begg them for themselves: and yet generally they get not much by it, but are exceeding vexatious to the Subject. And even such an one is this Mr. *Bayes* with his Project of a *Concealed Power*, that most Princes, as he saith, *have not yet rightly understood*; but whereof the 15 King is so little enamour'd, that I am confident, were it not for prolling and molesting the People, his Majesty would give Mr. *Bayes* the Patent for it, and let him make his best on't, after he hath paid the Fees to my Lord Keeper.

But one thing I must confess is very pleasant, and he hath past an 20 high Complement upon his Majesty in it: that he may, if he please, reserve the Priesthood and the Exercise of it to himself. Now this indeed is surprising; but this onely troubles me, how his Majesty would look in all the Sacerdotal habiliments, and the Pontifical Wardrobe. I am afraid the King would find himself incommoded 25 with all that furniture upon his back, and would scarce reconcile himself to wear even the Lawn-sleeves and the Surplice. But what? even *Charles the fifth*, as I have read, was at his Inauguration by the Pope, content to be vested, according to the Romane Ceremonial, in the habit of a Deacon: and a man would not scruple too much the 30 formality of the dress in order to Empire.

But one thing I doubt Mr. *Bayes* did not well consider; that, if the King may discharge the Function of the Priesthood, he may too (and 'tis all the reason in the world) assume the Revenue. It would be the best Subsidy that ever was voluntarily given by the Clergy. 35

2 Precipice Y; Precipiece W.   12 they] them Y.   13 an] a Z.   14 Mr.
om. X   15 saith] said Y.

But truly otherwise, I do not see but that the King does lead a more unblamable Conversation, and takes more care of Souls than many of them, and understands their Office much better, and deserves something already for the pains he hath taken.

5   The next is *Publick Conscience*. For as to mens private Consciences he hath made them very inconsiderable, and, reading what he saith of them with some attention, I only found this new and important Discovery and great Priviledge of Christian Liberty, that *Thought is free*. We are however obliged to him for that, seing by conse-
10 quence we may think of him what we please. And this he saith a man may assert against all the Powers of the Earth: And indeed with much reason and to great purpose; seeing, as he also alledges, the Civil Power is so far from doing violence to that liberty, that it never can. But yet if the freedom of thoughts be in not lying open
15 to discovery, there have been wayes of compelling men to discover them; or, if the freedom consist in retaining their judgments when so manifested, that also hath been made penal. And I doubt not but beside *Oaths* and *Renunciations*, and *Assents* and *Consents*, Mr. *Bayes*, if he were searched, hath twenty other tests and picklocks in his
20 pocket. Would Mr. *Bays* then perswade men to assert this against all the Powers of the Earth? I would ask in what manner? To say the truth I do not like him, and would with the Nonconformists to be upon their guard, lest he trepan them first by this means into a Plot, and then peach, & so hang them: If Mr. *Bayes* meant otherwise
25 in this matter, I confess my stupidity, and the fault is most his own who should have writ to the capacity of vulgar Readers. He cuts indeed and faulters in this discourse, which is no good sign, perswading men that they may, and ought to practise against their Consciences, where the Commands of the Magistrate intervenes.
30 None of them denies that it is their duty, where their Judgements or Consciences cannot comply with what is injoyned, that they ought in obedience patiently to suffer; but further they have not learned. I dare say that the Casual Divinity of the Jesuites is all thorow as Orthodox as this Maxime of our Authors: and, as the
35 Opinion is brutish, so the Consequences are devilish. To make it

therefore go down more glibly, he saith, that *'tis better to err with Authority, than to be in the right against it in all doubtful and disputable cases: because the great duty of Obedience outweighs the danger of a little error, (and little it is if it be disputable.)* I cannot understand the truth of this reasoning; that whatsoever is disputable is little; for even the most important matters are subject to controversie: And besides, things are little or great according to the Eyes or Understandings of several men; and however, a man would suffer something rather than commit that little error against his Conscience, which must render him an Hypocrite to God, and a Knave amongst Men. *The Commands* (he saith) *and Determinations of the publick Conscience ought to carry it; and if there be any sin in the Command, he that imposed shall answer for it, and not I whose duty it is to obey;* (And mark) *the Commands of Authority will warrant my Obedience, my Obedience will hallow, or at least excuse my action, and so secure me from sin if not from error*; and so you are welcome Gentlemen. Truly a very fair and conscionable Reckoning! So far is this from hallowing the Action, that I dare say it wil, if followed home, lead only to all that *sanctified Villany*, for the invention of which we are beholden to the Author. But let him have the honour of it: for he is the first Divine that ever taught Christians how another man's sin could confer an *Imputative Righteousness* upon all Mankind that shall follow and comply with it. Though the Subject made me serious, yet I could not reade the expression without laughter: *My Obedience will hallow, or at least excuse my Action.* So inconsiderable a difference he seems to make betwixt those terms, That if ever our Author come for his merits to be a Bishop, a man might almost adventure instead of *Consecrated* to say that he was *Excused.*

The third is *Moral Grace.* And whoever is not satisfied with those passages of his concerning it, before quoted, may find enough where he discourseth it at large, even to surfeit. I cannot make either less or more of it than that he overturns the whole fabrick of Christianity, and Power of Religion. For my part, if Grace be resolv'd into Morality, I think a man may almost as well make God too to be only a Notional and Moral Existence.

12–13 *imposed shall*] *imposed it shall* Parker, X, Z.   26 those terms,] those two terms. Z.   merits to be] merits in election for to be Y.   27 to] o X.

And white-apron'd *Amaryllis* was of that opinion:

> *Ma tu Sanctissima Honestà che sola sei*
> *D'alma ben nata inviolabil Nume.*

But thou most holy Honesty, that only art the inviolable Deity of the well-
5 *born Soul.*

And so too was the Moral Poet: (for why may not I too bring out my Latin shreds as well as he his,

> *Quæsitum ad fontem solos deducere verpos)*
> *Nullum Numen abest si sit Prudentia---*

10 There is no need of a Deity where there is Prudence; or, if you will, where there is *Ecclesiastical Policy.*

But so far I must do Mr. *Bayes* right, that, to my best observation, if Prudence had been God, *Bayes* had been a most damnable Atheist. Or, perhaps only an Idolater of their number, concerning whom he
15 adds in the next line

> *—sed te*
> *Nos facimus Fortuna Deam Cæloque locamus.*

But we make thee Fortune a Goddess, and place thee in Heaven.

However I cannot but be sorry that he hath undertaken this des-
20 perate vocation, when there are twenty other honest and painful wayes wherein he might have got a *Living*, and made Fortune pro- pitious. But he cares not upon what Argument or how dangerous he runns to shew his ambitious Activity: whereas those that wil dance upon Ropes, do lightly some time or other break their necks.
25 And I have heard that even the *Turk*, every day he was to mount the High-Rope, took leave of his *Comfortable Importance* as if he should never see her more. But this is a matter forreign to my Judi- cature, and therefore I leave him to be tryed by any Jury of Divines: and, that he may have all right done him, let half of them be *School-*
30 *Divines* and the other moity *Systematical*, and let him except against as many as the Law allows, and so God send him a good deliverance. But I am afraid he will never come off.

The fourth is *Debauchery tolerated.* For supposing, as he does, that 'tis better and *safer to give a Toleration to mens Debaucheries than to*

6 Moral] Mortal X.   7 his] is X.   28 be tryed] be trayed X.

their Religious Perswasions, it amounts to the same reckoning. This is a very ill way of discoursing; and that a *greater severity ought to be exercised over mens Consciences than over their Vices and Immoralities.* For it argues too much indiscretion, by avoiding one evil to run up into the contrary extream. And Debauch'd Persons will be ready hence to conclude, although it be a perverse way of reasoning, That where the Severity ought to be less, the Crime is less also: nay, even that the more they are debauch'd, it is just that the Punishment should still abate in proportion; but however, that it were very imprudent and unadvisable to reform and erre on the Religious hand, lest they should thereby incur the greater penalties. Mr. *Bayes* would have done much better had he singled out the Theme of Religion. He might have loaded it with all the truth which that subject would bear; I would allow him that *Rebellion is as the sin of Witch-craft,* though that text of Scripture will scarce admit his interpretation. He could not have declamed more sharply than I, or any honest man else, would upon occasion against all those who under pretence of Conscience raise War, or create publick Disturbances. But Comparisons of Vice are dangerous, and though he should do this without design, yet, while he aggravates upon Religion, and puts it in ballance, he doth so far alleviate and encourage Debauchery. And moreover (which to be sure is against his design) he doth hereby more confirm the austerer sort of Sinners, and furnishes them with a more specious Colour and stronger Argument. It had been better Policy to instruct the Magistrate that there is no readier way to shame these out of their Religious Niceties than by improving Mens Morals. But, as he handles it, never was there any Point more unseasonably exposed; at such a time, when there is so general a depravation of Manners, that even those who contribute towards it do yet complain of it; and though they cannot reform their practice, yet feel the effects, and tremble under the apprehension of the Consequences. It were easie here to shew a man's reading, and to discourse out of History the causes of the decay and ruine of Mr. *Bayes* his *Roman Empire,* when-as the Moralist has it,

—*sævior armis*

Luxuria incubuit, Victumque ulciscitur Orbem.

21 encourage] discourage Z.   26 these] those Z.   out] our Y.

And descending to those Times since Christianity was in the
Throne, 'tis demonstrable that for one War upon a Fanatical or
Religious account, there have been an hundred occasioned by the
thirst of Glory and Empire that hath inflamed some great Prince to
5 invade his Neighbours. And more have sprung from the Contentiousness and Ambition of some of the Clergy; But the most of all
from the Corruption of Manners, and alwayes fatal Debauchery. It
exhausts the Estates of private persons, and makes them fit for
nothing but the High-way or an Army. It debases the spirits and
10 weakens the vigor of any Nation; at once indisposing them for War,
and rendring them uncapable of Peace. For, if they escape intestine
troubles, which would certainly follow when they had left themselves by their prodigality or intemperance, no other means of subsistence but by preying upon one another; then must they either,
15 to get a maintenance, pick a quarrel with some other Nation, wherein they are sure to be worsted; or else (which more frequently
happens) some neighbouring Prince that understands Government
takes them at the advantage, and, if they do not like ripe Fruit fall
into his lap, 'tis but shaking the Tree once or twice, and he is sure
20 of them. Where the Horses are, like those of the *Sybarites*, taught
to dance, the Enemy need only learn the Tune and bring the
Fiddles. But therefore (as far as I understand) his Majesty to obviate
and prevent these inconveniencies in his Kingdoms, hath on the one
hand never refused a just Warre; that so he might take down our
25 Grease and Luxury, and keep the *English* Courage in breath and
exercise: and on the other, (though himself most constantly addicted
to the Church of *England*) hath thought fit to grant some liberty to
all other Sober People, (and longer than they are so God forbid they
should have it) thereby to give more temper and allay to the com-
30 mon and notorious Debauchery.

But Mr. *Bayes* nevertheless is for his fifth; *Persecution recommended:*
and he does it to the purpose. *Julian* himself, who I think was first
a Reader, and held forth in the Christian Churches before he turned
Apostate and then Persecutor, could not have outdone him either
35 in Irony or Cruelty. Only it is God's mercy that Mr. *Bayes* is not
Emperour. You have seen how he inveighs against Trade: *That*

21 learn the] learn thy Z.

whilst mens Consciences are acted by such peevish and ungovernable Prin-
ciples, to erect Trading-Combinations is but to build so many Nests of Fac-
tion and Sedition. Lay up your Ships, my Masters, set Bills on your
Shop-doors, shut up the Custom-house; and why not adjourn the
Term, mure up *Westminster*-hall, leave Plowing and Sowing, and 5
keep a dismal Holy-day through the Nation; for Mr. *Bayes* is out of
humour. But I assure you it is no jesting matter. For he hath in one
place taken a List of the Fanatick Ministers, whom he reckons to
be but about an hundred *Systematical Divines:* though I believe the
Bartlemew-Register or the *March*-Licences would make them about 10
an hundred and three or an hundred and four, or so: But this is but
for rounder number and breaks no square. And then for their
People, either *they live in greater Societies of men* (he means the City
of *London* and the other Cities and Towns-Corporate, but expresses
it so to prevent some inconvenience that might betide him) *but* 15
there their noise is greater than their number. Or else in *Country-Towns*
and Villages, where they arise not above the proportion of one to twenty. It
were not unwisely done indeed if he could perswade the Magistrate
that all the Fanaticks have but one neck, so that he might cut off
Nonconformity at one blow. I suppose the Nonconformists value 20
themselves tho upon their Conscience and not their Numbers: but
they would do well to be watchful, lest he have taken a List of their
Names as well as their Number, and have set Crosses upon all their
Doors against there should be occasion. But till that *happy juncture,*
when Mr. *Bayes shall be fully avenged of his new Enemies the wealthy* 25
Fanaticks (which is soon done too, for he saith *there are but few of them*
men of Estates or Interest) he is contented that they should only be
exposed (they are his own expressions) to the *Pillories, Whipping-*
posts, Galleys, Rods, and *Axes*; and moreover and above, to all other
Punishments whatsoever, provided they be of a severer nature than 30
those that are inflicted on men for their immoralities. O more then
humane Clemency! I suppose the Division betwixt Immoralities
and Conscience is universal, and whatsoever is wicked or penal is
comprehended within their *Territories.* So that although a man
should be guilty of all those heinous enormities which are not to be 35

9 an] a X.   15 him *Errata*; them W.   23 Number] Numbers Z.
27 contented] content Z.   30 be] he Z.   31 inflicted] afflicted Z.

named among Christians, beside all lesser Peccadillo's expressly
against the ten Commandments, or such other part of the Divine
Law as shall be of the Magistrates making, he shall be in a better
condition and more gently handled, then a *well-meaning Zelot*; For
5 this is the man that Mr. *Bayes* saith *is of all Villains the most dangerous*:
(even more dangerous it seems then a malicious and ill-meaning
Zelot) this is he whom in *all Kingdoms where Government is rightly
understood*, he would have condemned *to the Galleys for his mistakes and
abuses of Religion*. Although the other punishments are more severe,
10 yet this being more new and unacquainted, I cannot pass it by without some reflexion. For I considered what Princes make use of
Gallyes. The first that occurred to me was the *Turk*, who according to *Bayes* his maxim, hath established Mahometism among his
subjects, as the *Religion that he apprehends most advantagious to publick
15 peace and settlement*. Now in his Empire the Christians only are
guilty of those *Religious Mistakes that tend to the subversion of Mahometism*: So that he understands Government rightly in chaining the
Christians to the Oar. But then in Christendom, all that I could
think of were the King of *France*, the King of *Spain*, the Knights of
20 *Malta*, the *Pope*, and the rest of the *Italian* Princes. And these all
have bound their Subjects to the Romish Religion as most advantagious. But these people their Galleys, with Immoral Fellows and
Debauchees: whereas the *Protestants*, being their Fanaticks and mis-
takers in Religion, should have been their *Ciurma*. But 'tis to be
25 hoped these Princes will take advice and understand it better for
the future. And then at last I remembered that his Majesty too
hath one Gally latly built, but I dare say it is not with that intention: and our Fanaticks, though few, are so many, that one will not
serve. But therefore if Mr. *Bayes* and his partners would be at the
30 charge to build the King a whole Squadron for this use, I know not
but it might do very well (for we delight in Novelties) and it would
be a singular obligation to *Sir John Baptist Dutel*, who might have
some pretence to be General of his Majesties Gallies. But so much
for that. Yet in the mean time I cannot but admire at Mr. *Bayes* his
35 courage; who knowing how dangerous a Villain a well-meaning
Zelot is, and having calculated to a man how many of them there

1 beside] besides Z.

are in the whole Nation, yet dares thus openly stimulate the Magistrate against them, and talk of nothing less, but much more, than *Pillories*, *Whipping-Posts*, *Galleys*, and *Axes* in this manner. It is sure some sign (and if he knew not so much he would scarce adventure) of the peaceableness of their Principles, and of that restraint under which their tender Consciences hold them, when nevertheless he may walk night and day in safety; though it were so easie a thing to deifie the Divine after the ancient manner, and no man be the wiser. But that which I confess would vex me most, were I either an ill or a well-meaning Zealot, would be, after all to hear him (as he frequently does) sneering at me in an ironical harangue, to perswade me, forsooth, to take all patiently for Conscience-sake, and the good example of Mankind: Nay, to wheedle one almost to make himself away to save the Hangman a labour. It was indeed near that pass in the Primitive times, and the tyred Magistrates ask'd them, whether they had not Halters and Rivers and Precipices, if they were so greedy of Suffering? But, by the good leave of your Insolence, we are not come to that yet. *Non tibi sed Petro:* or rather, *sed Regi*. The Nonconformists have suffered as well as any men in the World, and could do so still if it were his Majesty's pleasure. Their *Duty to God hath hallowed*, and their *Duty to the Magistrate hath excused* both their Pain and Ignominy. To dye by a Noble hand is some satisfaction: But when his Majesty, for Reasons best known to Himself, hath been graciously pleased to abate of your Rigors, I hope Mr. *Bayes* that we shall not see when you have a mind to junket with your *Comfortable Importance* that the *Entremeses* shall be of a Fanaticks Giblets: nor that a Nonconformists head must be wip'd off as oft as your nose drivles. 'Tis sufficient, Sir, we know your Inclination, we know your Abilities, and we know your Lodging: And when there is any further occasion you will doubtless be sent for. For, to say the truth, this *Bayes* is an excellent Tool, and more useful than ten other men. I will undertake that he shall rather than fail, be the Trepanner, the Informer, the Witness, the Atturney, the Judge; and, if the Nonconformist need the benefit of his Book, he shall be Ordinary too, and say he is an ignorant fellow, *non legit:* and then, to do him the last Christian office, he would be

7 and] and and X.   24 known] know Y.   28 wip'd] whip'd X.

his Hangman. In the mean time, let him enjoy it in speculation, secure of all the Imployments when they shall fall. For I know no Gentleman that will take any of them out of his hands, although it be an age wherein men cannot well support their quality, without
5 some accession from the publick: and for the ordinary sort of People, they are I know not by what disaster besotted and abandon'd to Fanaticism. So that Mr. *Bayes* must either do it himself in person, or constitute the chief Magistrate to be his Deputy. But Princes do indeed understand themselves better most of 'm, and do neither
10 think it so safe to intrust a Clergy-man with their Authority, nor decent for themselves to do the drudgery of the Clergy. That would have past in the Dayes of Saint *Dominick*: but when even the Inquisition hath lost its edge in the Popish Countryes, there is little appearance it should be set up in *England*. It were a worthy Spec-
15 tacle, were it not? to see his Majesty like the Governor in *Synesius*, busied in his Cabinet among those Engines whose very names are so hard that it is some torture to name them; the *Podostrabæ*, the *Dactylethræ*, the *Otagræ*, the *Rhinolabides*, the *Cheilostrophia*, devising, as they say there are particular Diseases, so a peculiar Rack for every
20 Limb and Member of a Christians Body. Or, would he (with all Reverence be it spoken) exchange his Kingdom of *England* for that of *Macassar*? where the great *Arcanum* of Government is the culti-vating of a Garden of venimous Plants, and preparing thence a Poy-son, in which the Prince dips a Dart that where it does but draw
25 blood, rots the person immediately to pieces; and his Office is with that to be the Executioner of his Subjects. God be prais'd his Majesty is far of another temper: and he is wise, though some men be malicious.

But Mr. *Bayes* his fixt, is that which I call his *Push-pin Divinity*.
30 For he would perswade Princes that *there cannot a Pin be pull'd out of the Church but the State immediately totters*. That is strange. And yet I have seen many a Pin pull'd out upon occasion, and yet not so much as the Church it self hath wagg'd. It is true indeed, and we have had sad experiments of it, that some Clergy-men have been so

---

8 chief X; cheif W etc.   15 it Y; in W.   17 *Podostrabæ Errata; Podo-strabee* W.   18 *Dactylethræ Errata; Dactylethree* W; *Dactylethreæ* Y.   *Otagræ Errata; Otagree* W.   23 venimous Y; Poysonous W.   24 dips] keeps Z.

opiniastre that they have rather exposed the State to ruine than they would part with a Pin, I will not say out of their Church, but out of their Sleeve. There is nothing more natural then for the Ivy to be of opinion that the Oak cannot stand without it support: or, seeing we are got into Ivy, that the Church cannot hold up longer 5 than It underprops the Walls: whereas it is a sneaking insinuating Imp, scarce better than Bindweed, that sucks the Tree dry, and moulders the building where it catches. But what, pray Mr. *Bayes*, is this Pinne in *Pallas's* buckler? Why 'tis some Ceremony or other, that is *indifferent in its own nature*, that *hath no antecedent necessity* but 10 *only as commanded*, that *signifies nothing in it self but what the Commander pleases*, that even by the Church which commands it, is *declared to have nothing of Religion in it, and that is in it self of no great moment or consequence, only it is absolutely necessary that Governours should enjoyn it to avoid the evils that would follow if it were not determined.* Very well, 15 Mr. *Bayes*. This I see will keep cold: anon perhaps I may have a stomach. But I must take care lest I swallow your Pin.

Here we have had the Titles, and some short Rehearsal of Mr. *Bayes* his six Playes. Not but that, should we disvalise him, he hath to my knowledg a hundred more as good in his budget: but really 20 I consult mine own repose. But now among friends, was there ever any thing so monstrous? You see what a man may come to with Divinity and High-feeding. There is a scurvy disease, which though some derive from *America*, others tell a story that the *Genoueses* in their Warrs with *Venice* took some of their Noblemen, whom they 25 cut to pieces and barrel'd up like Tunny, and so maliciously vented it to the *Venetians*, who eating it ignorantly, broke out in those nasty botches and ugly symptoms, that are not curable but by Mercury. What I relate it for is out of no further intention, nor is there any more similitude than that the Mind too hath its Nodes sometimes, 30 and the Stile its Buboes, and that I doubt before Mr. *Bayes* can be rid of 'm, he must pass through the Grand Cure and a dry Diet.

And now it is high time that I resume the thread of my former History concerning Mr. *Bayes* his Books in relation to his Majesty. I do not find that the *Ecclesiastical Policy* found more acceptance than 35 could be expected from so judicious a Prince: nor do I perceive that

14 necessary X, Y; neccssary W.　　22 You] Yet Y².　　32 the] a Z.

he was ever considered of at a Promotion of Bishops, nor that he hath the reversion of the Arch-Bishoprick of *Canterbury*. But if he have not by Marriage barr'd his way; and it should ever fall to his lot, I am resolved instead of *his Grace* to call him alwayes *his Morality*. But as he got no Preferment that I know of at Court (though his Patron doubtless having many things in his gift, did abundantly recompence him) so he mist no less of his aim as to the Reformation of Ecclesiastical-Government upon his Principles. But still, what he complains of pag. 20. *the Ecclesiastical Laws were either weakened through want of Execution, or in a manner cancell'd by the opposition of Civil Constitutions.* For, beside what in *England*, where all things went on at the same rate, in the neighbouring Kingdom of *Scotland* there were I know not how many *Mas Johns* restored in one day to the work of their Ministry, and a door opened whereby all the rest might come in for the future, and all this by his Majesty's Commission. Nay, I think there was (a thing of very ill example) an Arch-Bishop turn'd out of his See for some Misdemeanour or other. I have not been curious after his name nor his crime, because as much as possible I would not expose the nakedness of any person so eminent formerly in the Church. But henceforward the King fell into disgrace with Mr. *Bayes*, and any one that had eyes might discern that our Author did not afford his Majesty that Countenance and Favour which he had formerly enjoy'd. So that a Book too of *J. O*'s happening mischievously to come out at the same season, Upon pretence of answering that, he resolved to make his Majesty feel the effects of his displeasure. He therefore set pen to paper again, and having kept his Midwife of the *Friendly Debate* by him all the time of his pregnancy for fear of miscarrying, he was at last happily delivered of his second Child, the *Defence of the Ecclesiastical Policy*, in the year 1671. It was a very lusty Baby, and twice as big as the former, and (which some observed as an ill sign, and that if it lived it would prove a great Tyrant) it had, when born, all the Teeth, as perfect as ever you saw in any mans Head. But I do not reckon much upon those ominous criticismes. For there was partly a natural cause in it, Mr. *Bayes* having gone so many months, more than the Civil Law allowes for the utmost term of legitimation, that it was no wonder if the Brat were at its birth more forward than others usually are. And indeed Mr. *Bayes* was so provident against abortion, & careful for some reasons that the Child should cry, that the only question in Town (though without much cause, for truly 'twas 5 very like him) was, whether it was not spurious or supposititious. But Allegories and Raillery and Hard Words apart: In this his second Book, what I quoted before out of Bishop *Bramhal*, p. 18. with allusion to our Author, is here faln out as exactly true as if it had been expresly calculated for *Bayes* his Meridian. He finds him- 10 self to have come too near, nay to have far out-gone an *Erastian*, That he had writ his Ecclesiastical Policy before he was come to maturity of Judgement, that one might desire Mr. *Bays* in Mr. *Bays*, that something had been changed in his Book. That a more authentick Edition was necessary, that some things which he had said before, 15 were not his Judgment after he was come to maturity in Theological matters.

I will not herein too much insist upon his Reply, where his Answerer asks him pertinently enough to his grand Thesis, what was then become of their old plea of *Jus Divinum*? Why, saith he, 20 must you prescribe me what I shall write? Perhaps my next Book shall be of that Subject. For, perhaps he said so only for evasion, being old excellent at parrying and fencing. Though I have good reason to believe that we may shortly see some Piece of his upon that Theme, and in defence of an Aphorism of a great Prelate in the 25 last King's time, *That the King had no more to do in Ecclesiastical Matters, than Jack that rubb'd his Horses heels.* For Mr. *Bayes* is so enterprising you know, *Look too't, Ile doo't.* He has face enough to say or unsay any thing, and 'tis his priviledge, what the School-Divines deny to be even within the power of the Almighty, to make Con- 30 tradictions true. An evidence of which (though I reserve the further instances to another occasion that draws near) does plainly appear in what I now principally urge, to show how dangerous a thing it is for his Majesty and all other Princes to lose Mr. *Bayes* his

favour. For whereas he had all along in his first Book treated them
like a company of Ignorants, and that did not understand Government, (but that is pardonable in Mr. *Bayes*) in this his second, now
that they will not do as he would have them, when he had given
5 them Power and Instructions how to be wiser for the future, He
casts them quite off like men that were desperate. He had, you
know, p. 35. of his first Book and in other places, vested them with
an universal and unlimited Power, and uncontroulable in the Government of Religion (that is, over mens Consciences) but now in
10 his second, to make them an example to all incorrigible and ungrateful persons, he strips and disrobes them again of all those Regal
Ornaments that he had superinduced upon them, and leaves them
good Princes in *querpo* as he found 'm, to shift for themselves in the
wide World as well as they can. Do but read his own words, p. 237.
15 of his *Defence*, parag. 5. and sure you will be of my mind. *To vest the*
Supreme Magistrate in an unlimited and uncontroulable Power, is clearly to
defeat the Efficacy and Obligatory force of all his Laws, that cannot possibly
have any binding virtue upon the minds of men, when they have no other
inducement to obedience but only to avoid the penalty. But if the Supreme
20 *Power be absolute and unlimited, it doth for that very reason remove and*
evacuate all other Obligations, for otherwise it is restrained and conditional;
and if men lye under no other impulsion than of the Law it self, they lye under
no other obligation than that of prudence and self-interest, and it remains
intirely in the choice of their own discretion whether they shall or shall not
25 *obey, and then there is neither Government nor Obligation to Obedience; and*
the Principle of mens Complyance with the mind of their Superiours, is not the
declaration of their will and pleasure, but purely the determination of their
own judgments; and therefore 'tis necessary for the security of Government,
though for nothing else, to set bounds to its jurisdiction; Otherwise, like the
30 *Roman Empire, &c.* I know it would be difficult to quote twenty
lines in Mr. *Bayes* but we should encounter with the *Romane Empire*.
But observe how laboriously here he hath asserted and proved that
all he had said in his first Book was a meer mistake before he were
come to years of discretion. For as in Law a Man is not accounted

14 237. Y; ~ W.   16 *uncontroulable*] unaccountable Parker.   17 *bis*] *the* Z.
19 *obedience*] obedients Y.   *but only*] than barely Parker.   *if*] *of* Y.   22 im-
pulsion] *Impulsive* Parker.   23 *other om.* Parker.   24 17 *in*] at Parker.
26 *of men's*] *o mens* X.   *their om.* Parker.   30 to] te Y².   33 were] was Z.

so till he hath compleated 21, and 'tis but the last minute of that
time that makes him his own Man, (as to all things but Conscience
I mean, for as to that he saith men are never *sui Juris*) so though the
distance of *Bayes* his Books was but betwixt 1670 and 1671, yet a
year, nay an instant at any time of a man's life may make him wiser, 5
and he hath, like all other fruits, his annual maturity. It was so long
since as 1670 p. 33. that this *Universal Unlimited and Uncontroulable
Power was the natural right of Princes antecedent to Christ, firmly established by the unalterable Dictates of Natural Reason, Universal Practice,
and Consent of Nations, that the Scripture rather supposes than asserts the* 10
Ecclesiastical (and so the Civil) *Jurisdiction of Princes.* 'Twas in 1670,
p. 10. That it was *absolutely necessary;* and p. 12. *that Princes have that
power to bind their Subjects to that Religion that they apprehend most
advantagious to Publick Peace, &c.* So that they derive their title from
Eternal Necessity, which the Moralists say the Gods themselves 15
can not impeach. His Majesty may lay by his *Dieu* and make use
onely of his *Mon Droit:* He hath a Patent for his Kingdom under the
Broad-Seal of Nature, and next under that, and immediately *before*
Christ, is over all Persons and in all Causes as wel Ecclesiastical as
Civil (and over all mens Consciences) within his Majesty's Realms 20
and Dominions Supream Head and Governour. 'Tis true, the
Author sometimes for fashion-sake speaks in that Book of Religion
and of a Deity, but his Principles do necessarily, if not in terms,
make the Princes Power *Paramount* to both those, and if he may by
his uncontroulable and unlimited universal Authority introduce 25
what Religion, he may of consequence what Deity also he pleases.
Or, if there were no Deity, yet there must be some Religion, that
being an Engine most advantagious for Publick Peace and Tranquillity. This was in 1670. But by 1671 you see the case is altered.
Even one night hath made some men gray. And now p. 238 of his 30
second Book, besides what before p. 237. he hath made Princes
accountable, ay and to so severe an Auditor as God himself. *The
Thrones of Princes are established upon the Dominion of God.* And p. 241.
'Tis no part of the Princes concernment to institute rules of Moral Good and

---

3 he saith men *Errata*; many W.   4 *Bayes om.* Z.   betwixt *om.* Z.
12 p. 10] p. 19 Y².   12–13 *that power*] tha⁓ Z; *power* Parker.   31 besides what
before p. 237. Y; *om.* W.

F

Evil, that is the care and the Prerogative of a Superiour Law-giver. And p. 260. he owns that if the Subjects can plead a clear and undoubted preingagement to that higher Authority, they have a liberty to *remonstrate* to the equity of their Laws. I do not like this Remon-
5 strating nor these Remonstrants. I wish again that Mr. *Bayes* would tell us what he means by the term, and where it will end, whether he would have the Fanaticks remonstrate: but they are wary, and ashamed of what they have done in former times of that nature: or whether he himself hath a mind to remonstrate, because the Fana-
10 ticks are tolerated. That is the thing, that is the business of this whole Book: and knowing that there is a clear and undoubted pre-ingagement to the higher Authority of Nature and Necessity, if the King will persist in tolerating these people, who knows after remon-strating, what Mr. *Bayes* will do next? But now in summe what
15 shall we say of this man, and how had the King been served if he had followed *Bayes's* advice, and assumed the power of his first Book? He had run himself into a fine *Premunire*, when now after all he comes to be made accountable to God, nay even to his Subjects. And by this means it happens, though it were beyond Mr. *Bayes* his
20 forcast, and I dare say he would rather have given the Prince again a power antecedent to Christ, and to bring in what Religion he please; he hath obliged him to as tender a Conscience as any of his Christian subjects, and then goodnight to *Ecclesiastical Policy.* I have herein indeavoured the utmost ingenuity toward Mr. *Bayes,*
25 for he hath laid himself open but to too many disadvantages already, so that I need not, I would not press him beyond measure, but to my best understanding, and if I faile I even ask him pardon, I do him right. 'Tis true, that being distracted betwixt his desire that the Consciences of men should be persecuted, and his anger at
30 Princes that will not be advised, he confounds himself every where in his reasonings, that you can hardly distinguish which is the *Whoop* and which is the *Holla,* and he makes Indentures on each side of the way wheresoever he goes. But no man that is sober will fol-low him, lest some Justice of Peace should make him pay his five
35 shillings, beside the scandal; and it is apparent to every one what he drives at. But were this otherwise, I can spare it, and 'tis suffi-

2 clear] clean Y.   35 beside] Besides Y.

cient to my purpose that I do thus historically deduce the reason
of his setting forth his Books, and shew that it was plainly to *remon-*
strate against the power of his Prince, and the measures that he hath
taken of governing; to set his Majesty at variance not only with his
Subjects, but with himself, and to raise a Civil-War in his *Intellectual* 5
Kingdom, betwixt his controulable & his uncontroulable Jurisdiction.
And because, having to do with a wise man, as Mr. *Bayes* is, one
may often gather more of his mind out of a word that drops casually,
than out of his whole watchful and serious discourse, when he is
talking of matters of Policy and that require caution; I cannot slight 10
one passage of Mr. *Bayes*, page 656. Where raging bitterly against
all the Presbyterians and other Sects, and as much against the
allowing them any Tenderness, Liberty, Toleration or Indulgence,
he concludes thus, *Tenderness and Indulgence to such men, were to nourish*
Vipers in our own Bowels, and the most sottish neglect of our own quiet and 15
security, and we should deserve to perish with the dishonour of Sardanapalus.
Now this of *Sardanapalus* I remember some little thing ever since I
read, I think it was my *Justine*; and I would not willingly be such
a Fool as to make a dangerous Similitude that has no foundation.
For if Mr. *Bayes* in the Preface of his *Defence*, to excuse his long 20
teeming before it were brought forth, places it partly upon his
recreations: I know not why much more a Prince should not *be will-*
ing to enjoy the innocent comforts of this life, as well as to do the common
drugeries. But I am thinking what Mr. B*ayes* meant by it; for every
Similitude must have, though not all, yet some likeness: Now I am 25
sure there were no Nonconformists and Presbyterians in *Sardana-*
palus his dayes, I am sure also that *Sardanapalus* was no Clergyman,
that he was no subject; but he was one of the *Uncontroulable* Creatures, that instead of exercising his Ecclesiastical Power delighted
in spinning; till some body come in on the sudden, and catching 30
him at it, cut his thred. Come 'tis better we left this Argument and
the Company too, for you see the Crime, you see the Sentence: and
who ever it be, there is some Prince or other whom Mr. *Bayes* will
have to perish. That p. 641. is indeed not so severe, but 'tis pretty
well; where, on the same kind of Subject, whetting the Prince 35

2 to] Y; ro W.   3 measures] measure X.   23 do] *endure* Parker.
24 *drugeries*] drudgeries X.

against those People, he saith, *That Prince that hath felt the pounces of these ravening Vultures, if after that he shall be perswaded to regard their fair speeches at such time as they want power, without other evident and unquestionable tokens of their conversion, deserves to be King of the Night.* Now for this matter, I believe Mr. *Bayes* knows that his Majesty hath received such evident and unquestionable tokens of Loyalty from the Nonconformists; otherwise his own Loyalty would have hindred him from daring to use that expression.

And now I should continue my History to his third Book in hand, the Preface to Bishop *Bramhal*. But having his second Book stil before me, I could not but look a little further into it, to see how he hath left matters standing betwixt himself and his Answerer. And first I lighted on that place where he strives to disintangle himself from what he had said about Trade in his former Book. Here therefore he defies the whole Fanatick world to discover one Syllable that tends to its discouragement. Let us put it upon that issue, and by this one example take the patern of his ingenuity in all his other contests. *Whoop*, Mr. *Bayes*, pag. 49. *with what conscience does the Answerer tell the people that I have represented all Tradesmen as seditious, when 'tis so notorious I only suppose that some of them may be tainted with Seditious Principles? If I should affirm that when the Nobility or Clergie are possest with Principles that incline to Rebellion and disloyal Practices, they are of all Rebels the most dangerous, should I be thought to impeach them of Treason and Rebellion?* Holla, Mr. *Bayes!* But in the 49th page of your first Book you say expresly, *For 'tis notorious that there is not any sort of people so inclinable to Seditious Practices as the Trading part of a Nation.* Is this the same thing now? and how does this Defence take off the Objection? And yet he tears and insults and declaims as if he had the Truth on his side. At last he strives to bring himself off and salve the matter in the same page 49. With, *In brief it is not the rich Citizen, but the Wealthy Fanatick that I have branded for an ungovernable Beast, and that not as Wealthy but as Fanatick.* Subtle Distinguisher! I see if we give him but Rope enough what he will come to. Mr. *Bayes*, many as prosper a man as your self hath march'd up *Holborn* for distinguishing betwixt the Wealth and the

---

4 *conversion*] *conversation* Y.   24 *Rebellion*] Disloyalty Parker.   28 tears] tares Z.

Fanatick: and moreover let me tell you, Fanatick Money hath no Ear-mark.

So concerning the Magistrates power in Religion, wherein his Answerer had remark'd some unsafe passages: *Whoop* Mr. *Bayes!* P. 12. of his first Book before quoted: *Unless Princes have power to bind* 5 *their Subjects to what Religion they apprehend most advantagious, &c. they are no better than Statues of Authority.* Holla Bayes. Pag. 467. of the second Book: *This bold Calumny I have already I hope competently enough discovered and detested. Yet he repeats this fundamental Forgery in all places, so that his whole Book is but one huge Lye* 400 *pages long.* Judge 10 now who is the Forger; And yet he roars too here as if he would mix Heaven and Earth together. But you may spare your raving, you will never claw it off as long as your name is *Bayes.*

So his Answerer it seems having *p.* 85. said, that *Bayes* confines the whole Duty of Conscience to the inward thoughts and perswa- 15 sions of the mind, over which the Magistrate hath no power at all: *Whoop Bayes,* page 89. of his first Book, *Let all matters of mere Conscience, whether purely moral or religious, be subject to Conscience only, i.e. Let men think of things according to their own perswasions, and assert the Freedom of their Judgments against all the Powers of the Earth. This is the* 20 *Prerogative of the mind of man within its own Dominions, its Kingdom is intellectual, &c.* P. 91. *Liberty of Conscience is internal and invisible, and confined to the minds and judgements of men; and while Conscience acts within its proper sphere, the Civil power is so far from doing it Violence, that it never can.* Holla Bayes. *p.* 229. of his Second Book, *This in down right Eng-* 25 *lish is a shameless Lye. Sir, you must pardon my rudeness, for I will assure you, after long Meditation, I could not devise a more pertinent answer to so bold an one as this.* I believe you Mr. *Bayes:* You meditated long, some twelve months at least; and you could not devise any other answer, and in good earnest he hath not attempted to give any other answer. 30 *I confess 'tis no extraordinary Conceit, but tis the best Repartee my barren Fancy was able to suggest to me upon so rude an occasion.* Well, Mr. *Bayes!* I see it must come to a quarrel; for thus the Hectors use to do, and to give the Lye at adventure, when they have a minde to try a mans Courage. But I have often known them dye on the spot. 35

So his Answerer *p.* 134. having taxed him for his speaking against

11 here] hear Z.

an expression in the Act of Parliament of *5to Eliz.* concerning the Wednesday Fast. *Whoop, Bayes, pag.* 59. of his first Book. *The Act for the Wednesday Fast the Jejunium Cecilianum* (our Ecclesiastical Politician is the better States-man of the two by far, and may make
5 sport with *Cecill* when he pleases) *was injoyned with this clause of Exception, That if any person should affirm it to be imposed with an intention to bind the Conscience, he should be punished as spreader of false News.* So careful was the supreme Magistrate in those dayes not to impose upon the Conscience; and the Wisdom of it is confirmed by the
10 experience of our time: When so eminent a Divine, as I mentioned before, thought fit to write a whole Volumne concerning the Holiness of LENT; though, if I be not deceived, this Doctrine too is prohibited by Act of Parliament, under the same Penalty. But, saith *Bayes* there, *The matter indeed of this Law was not of any great moment,*
15 *but this Declaration annexed to it proved of a fatal and mischievous Consequence.* 'Tis very well worth reading at large: but in short the Consequence (or the occasion 'tis no matter when I have to do with *Bayes*) was, that "Princes how peremptory soever they have been in asserting the Rights of their Supreme Power, in Civil Affairs,
20 they have been forced to seem modest and dissident in the exercise of their Ecclesiastical Supremacy." Now, *Holla, Bayes. p.* 298. of his Second Book. "To what purpose does he so briskly taunt me for thwarting mine own principles, because I have censured the impertinency of a needless Provision in an Act of Parliament?" Observe,
25 these are not the Answerers but *Bayes* his own Words; whereby you may see with what Reverence and Duty he uses to speak of his Superiours and their Actions, when they are not so happy as to please him. "I may obey the Law, though I may be of a different Perswasion from the Law-givers in an Opinion remote and imper-
30 tinent to the matter of the Law it self: nay, I may condemne the wisdom of enacting it, and yet at the same time think my self to lie under an indispensable Obligation to obey it: for the formal reason of its obligatory power (as any Casuist will inform him) is not the Judgment and Opinion of the Law-giver, but the Declaration of his

Will and Pleasure." Very good and sound Mr. *Bayes*: but here you have opened a passage; and this is as impertinent in you and more dangerous than what you blamed in that Act, that the Nonconformists may speak against your Ecclesiastical Laws; for their Casuists then tell them that, they lying under an indispensable obligation 5 not to conform to some of them, do fulfil and satisfy their Obedience in submitting to the penalty.

I looked further into what he saith in defence of the Magistrates assuming the Priesthood; what for his Scheme of moral Grace; what to palliate his irreverent expressions concerning our Blessed Saviour 10 and the Holy Spirit; what of all other matters objected by his Answerer: and if you will believe me; but I had much rather the Reader would take the pains to examine all himself, there is scarce any thing but slender trifling unworthy of a Logician, and beastly railing unbecoming any man, much more a Divine. At last, having 15 read it all through with some attention, I resolved, having failed so of any thing material, to try my fortune whether it might be more lucky, and to open the Book in several places as it chanced. But, whereas they say that in the *Sortes Virgilianæ*, wheresoever you light you will find somthing that will hit and is proper to your intention; 20 on the contrary here, there was not any leaf that I met with but had something impertinent, so that I resolved to give it over. This only I observed upon the whole, that he does treat his Answerer the most basely and ingratefully that ever man did. For, whereas in his whole first Book there was not one sound Principle, and scarce any 25 thing in his second, but what the Answerer had given him occasion to amend and rectifie if he had understanding; after so great an obligation he handles him with more rudeness than is imaginable. I know it may be said in Mr. *Bayes* his defence, that in this his second Book he hath made his matters in many places much worse 30 then they were before. But I say that was *Bayes* his want of understanding, and that he knew not how to take hold of so charitable an opportunity as was offered him, and 'twas none of the Answerers fault. There are amongst men some that do not study always the true Rules of Wisdom and Honesty, but delight in a perverse kind 35 of Cunning, which sometimes may take for a while and attain their

12 believe X, Y; beleive W.   24 basely and *om*. Y.   26 his] the X.

design, but most usually it fails in the end and hath a foul farewell. And such are all Mr. *Bayes* his Plots. In all his Writings he doth so confound terms, he leaps cross, he hath more doubles (nay triples and quadruples) than any Hare, so that he thinks himself secure of 5 the Hunters. And in this second Book, even the length of it was some Policy. For you must know it is all but an Epistle to the Author of the *Friendly Debate*; and thought he with himself, who hath so much leisure from his own affairs that he will read a Letter of another mans business of eight hundred pages? But yet, thought 10 he again, (and I could be content they did read it) in all matters of Argument I will so muddle my self in Ink, that there shall be no catching no finding me; and besides I will speak alwayes with so Magisterial a Confidence, that no modest man (and most ingenious persons are so) shall so much as quetch at me, but be beat out of 15 Countenance: and plain men shall think that I durst not talk at such a rate but that I have a Commission. I will first, said he in his heart, like a stout Vagrant, beg, and, if that will not do, I will command the Question and as soon as I have got it I will so alter the property and put on another Periweg that I defie them all for discovering me 20 or ever finding it again. This, beside all the lock and advantage that I have the Nonconformists upon since the late times; and though they were born since, and have taken more sober Principles, it shall be all one for that matter. And then for Oratory and Railing, let B*ayes* alone. This contrivance is indeed all the strength of Mr. 25 *Bayes* his Argument, and, as he said, (how properly let the Reader judge) *p.* 69. before quoted, *that Moral Virtue is not onely the most material and useful part of all Religion, but the ultimate end of all its other Duties:* So, Railing is not onely the most material and useful part of his Religion, his Reason, his Oratory, and his Practise; but the ulti- 30 mate end of this and all his other Books. Otherwise he is neither so strongly fortified nor so well guarded, but that without any Ceremony of Trenches or Approaches, you may at the very first march up to his Counters-scarp without danger. He puts me in minde of the incorrigible Scold, that though she was duck'd over 35 head and ears under water, yet stretched up her hands with her two thumb-nails in the Nit-cracking posture, or with two fingers

33 Counters-scarp] Counterscrap Y, Z.

divaricated, to call the man still in that Language Lousy Rascal and Cuckold. But indeed, when I consider how miserable a Wretch his Answerer has rendred him, and yet how he persists still, and more to rail and revile him; I can liken it to nothing better betwixt them, than to what I have seen with some pleasure the Hawking at the 5 Magpy. The poor bird understands very well the terrible pounces of that Vulture: but therefore she chatters amain most rufully, and spreads and cocks her tail, so that one that first saw and heard the sport would think that she insulted over the Hawk in that chatter, and she huff'd her train in token of courage and Victory: when, alas, 10 'tis her fear all, and another way of crying the Hawk mercy, and to the end that the Hawk finding nothing but tail and feather to strike at, she may so perhaps shelter her body.

Therefore I think there is nothing in my way that hinders me, but that I may now go on to the History of this Mr. *Bayes* his Third 15 Book, the Preface to Bishop *Bramhall*, and to what *Juncture of Affairs* it was reconciled. His Majesty (perhaps upon Mr. *Bayes* his frequent Admonitions both in his first and second Book, that Princes should be more attentive and confident in exercising their Ecclesiastical Jurisdiction, though, I rather believe, he never deign'd to read a line 20 in him, but what he did herein, was onely the result of his own good understanding) resolved to make some clear tryal how the Nonconformists could bear themselves under some Liberty of Conscience. And accordingly he issued, on *March* the 15th 1671, His Gracious *Declaration of Indulgence*, of which I with His Majesty and the King- 25 dom much joy, and, as far as my slender judgment can divine, dare augurate and presage mutual Felicity, and that what ever humane Accident may happen (I fear not what *Bayes* foresees) they will, they can never have cause to repent this Action or its Consequences. But hereupon *Bayes* finding that the King had so vigorously exerted 30 his Ecclesiastical Power, but to a purpose quite contrary to what Mr. *Bayes* had alwayes intended, he grew terribly angry at the King and his Privy Council: so that hereupon *he started*, as himself saies, *into many warm and glowing Meditations: his heart burnt and the fire kindled, and that heated him into all this wild and rambling talk* (as some 35

9 sport] sporr Y[2, 4, 6]. 15 Mr.] M. X. 20 deign'd *Errata*; design'd W.
32 terribly Y; terrible W.

will be forward enough to call it) *though he hopes it is not altogether
idle, and whether it be or be not, he hath now neither leisure nor patience to
examine.* This he confesses upon his best recollection, in the last
page of this Preface: Whereupon I cannot but animadvert, as in my
5 first page, that this too lies open to his *Dilemma* against the Nonconformists Prayers: For if he will not accept his own Charge, his
Modesty is all impudent & counterfeit: If he does acknowledge it,
he is an hot-headed Incendiary; and a wild rambling talker, and in
part, if not altogether, an idle Fellow. Really I cannot but pity him,
10 and look upon him as under some great disturbance and dispondency of mind: that this with some other scattering passages here
and there, argues him to be in as ill a case as *Tiberius* was in his distracted Letter to the Senate: There wants nothing of it but the *Dii
Deæque me perdant* wishing, Let the Gods and the Goddesses confound
15 him worse than he finds himself to be every day confounded. But
that I may not lose my thred. Upon occasion of this his Majesties
Gracious Declaration, and against it, he writes this his third Book the
Preface to Bishop Bramhall, and accordingly was unhappily delivered
of it in *June* (I have forgot) or *July*, in 1672. For he did not goe his
20 full time of it, but miscarried; partly by a new fright from *J. O.* and
partly by a fall he had upon a *Closer Importance.* But of all his three
Bolts this was the soonest shot, and therefore tis no wonder if he
miss'd his mark, and took no care where his arrow glanced. But
what he saith of his Majesty and his Council, being toward the lat-
25 ter end of his Discourse, I am forced to defer that a little, because,
there being no method at all in his wild rambling talk; I must either
tread just on in his footsteps, or else I shall be in a perpetual maze,
and never know when I am come to my journeyes end.

And here I cannot altogether escape the mentioning of *J. O.*
30 again, whom (though I have shown that he was not the main cause
of publishing *Bayes* his Books) yet he singles out, and on his pretence
runs down all the Nonconformists; this being, as he imagined, the
safest way by which he might proceed first to undermine and then
blow up his Majesties gracious Declaration. And this indeed is

10–11 and dispondency *om.* Y.   11 some *om.* Y.   14 *Deæque*] *Diæque* Z.
19 have] had X.   20 new Y; *om.* W.   24–5 latter] later Z.   27 maze]
amaze Z.

the least immethodical part of the whole Discourse. For first he
undertakes to defend, that Railing is not onely lawful, but expedient. Secondly, that though he had Railed, the person he spoke of
ought not to have taken notice of it. And Thirdly, that he did not
Rail. As to these things I do not much trouble my self, nor interest   5
my self in the least in *J. O.*'s Quarrel: no otherwise than if he were
John a Nokes and I heard him rail'd at by *John a Stiles:* Nor yet would
I concern my self unnecessarily in any mans behalf; Knowing that
'tis better being at the beginning of a Feast, than to come in at the
latter end of a Fray. For if so I should, as often it happens in such   10
Rencounters, not onely draw Mr. *Bayes*, but *J. O.* too upon my
back, I should have made a sweet business on't for my self.

   Now as to the Lawfulness and Expedience of Railing; were it not
that I do really make Conscience of using Scripture with such a
drolling Companion as Mr. *Bayes*, I could overload him thence both   15
with Authority and Example. Nor is it worth ones while to teach
him out of other Authors, and the best precedents of the kind, how
he, being a Christian and a Divine, ought to have carried himself.
But I cannot but remark his Insolence and how bold he makes upon
this Argument, p. 88. of his Second Book, with the Memories of   20
those great Persons there enumerated, several of whom, and particularly my Lord *Verulam*, I could quote to his confusion, upon a
contrary and much better account. *So far am I from repenting my*
severity towards them, that I am tempted rather to applaud it by the Glorious
examples of the greatest Wits of our Nation, King James, Arch-Bishop   25
Whitgift, Arch-Bishop Bancroft, Bishop Andrews, Bishop Bilson, Bishop
Mountegue, Bishop Bramhal, Sir Walter Rawleigh, Lord Bacon &c. and
he might have added Mr. *Tarlton* with as good pretence to this
honour as himself. The *Niches* are yet empty in the Old Exchange;
pray let us speak to the Statuary that, next to King *James's*, we may   30
have *Bayes* his Effigies. For such great Wits are Princes fellows, at
least when dead. At this rate there is not a Scold at *Billingsgate* but
may defend her self by the patern of King *James* and *Arch-Bishop*
Whitgift, &c. Yet this is passable, if you consider our man. But that
is most intolerable p. 7. of the Preface to his first Book, where he   35

   19 remark] mark Z.   23 *repenting*] recanting Parker.   28 this] his Y.
30 *James's*] *Jame's* Y.   35 p. 7 *Ed*; p. 17 W etc.

justifies his debauched way of writing by paralel to our Blessed
Saviour. And I cannot but with some aw reflect how near the punishment was to the offence; when having undertaken so profane an
Argument, he was in the very instant so infatuated as to say that
5 Christ was not only *in an hot fit of Zeal, but in a seeming Fury too and
transport of Passion.* But however, seeing he hath brought us so good
Vouchers, let us suppose what is not to be suppos'd, that Railing is
lawful. Whether it be expedient or no, will yet be a new question.
And I think Mr. *Bayes,* when he hath had time *to cool his thoughts,*
10 may be trusted yet with that consideration, and to compute whether
the good that he hath done by Railing do countervaile the damage
which both he in particular and the Cause he labours, have suffered
by it. For in my observation, if we meet with an Argument in the
Streets, both Men, Women and Boys, that are the Auditory, do
15 usually give it on the modester side, and conclude, that she that
rails most has the least reason.

For the second, Where he would prove that though he had railed,
yet his Answerer *J. O.* ought not to have taken notice of it, nor
those of the Party who are under the same condemnation, but that
20 he should have abstracted and kept close to the Argument, I must
confess it is a very secure and wholsom way of railing. And allowing
this, he hath good reason to find fault with his Answerer, as he does,
for turning over his Book, though without turning it over I know
not how he could have answered him, but with his Hat, or with
25 Mum. But for ought I can see in that only answer which is to his
first Book, he hath been obedient and abstracted the Argument
sufficiently; and if he hath been any where severe upon him, he hath
done it more cleanly and much more like a Gentleman, and it hath
been only in showing the necessary inferences that must follow
30 upon the Authors Maximes, and unfound Principles. But as to any
answer to *Bayes* his second Book or this third, for ought I can see
J. O. sleeps upon both Ears.

To this third undertaking, to show that he hath not Rail'd; I
shall not say any thing more, but let it be judg'd by the Company,

5 *of Zeal,* X, Y; ∼, ∼ W.   *too om.* Parker.   8 no, Y; ∼ W.
11 Railing Y; Raillieg W; Railling X.   15 she *Errata*; he W.   22 hath]
had Y.   33 this X, Y; his W.

and to them let it be refer'd. But in my poor opinion I never saw a man thorow all his three Books in so high a Salivation.

And therefore, till I meet with something more serious, I will take a walk in the Garden and gather some of Mr. *Bayes* his Flowers. Or I might more properly have said I will go see *Bedlam* and pick straws with our Mad-man. First he saith, that some that pretend a great interest in the holy Brother-hood, upon every slight accident are beating up the Drums against the Pope and Popish Plots; they discry Popery in every common and usual chance, and a Chimny cannot take fire in the City or Suburbs but they are immediately crying Jesuites and Firebals. I understand you, Sir. This, Mr. *Bayes*, is your Prologue, that is to be spoke by *Thunder* and *Lightning*. *I am loud Thunder, brisk Lightning I. I strike men down. I fire the Town*—*Look too't. Wee'l doot*. Mr. *Bayes*, it is something dangerous medling with those matters. As innocent persons as your self, have felt the fury of the wild multitude, when such a Calamity hath disordered them. And after your late Severity against Tradesmen, it had been better you had not touched the fire. Take heed lest the Reasons which sparkle, forsooth, in your Discourse have not set their Chimnyes on fire. None accuses you, what you make sport with, of burning the Ships at *Chatham*, much less of blowing up the *Thames*. But you ought to be careful, lest having so newly distinguished betwixt the Fanatick and his Wealth, they should say, That you are distinguishing now betwixt the Fanaticks and their Houses. These things are too edged to be jested with: if you did but consider that not onely the *Holy Brother-hood*, but the *Sober and intelligent Citizens* are equally involved in these sad Accidents. And in that lamentable Conflagration (which was so terrible, that though so many years agoe, it is yet fresh in mens memories, and besides, is yearly by Act of *Parliament* observed with due Humiliation and Solemnity.) It was not Trade onely and Merchandise suffered, which you call their *Diana*, and was not so much to be considered; But Saint *Pauls* too was burnt, which the Historians tell us was *Diana's* Temple.

The next thing is more directly levell'd at *J. O.* for having in some later Book used those words, *We cannot conform to Arminianism*

19 have] hath Y.   36 later] latter X.

or *Socinianisme on the one hand, or Popery on the other*. What the Answerer meant by those words, I concern not my self. Onely I cannot but say, That there is a very great neglect somewhere, wheresoever the Inspection of Books is lodged, that at least the
5 *Socinian* Books are tolerated and sell as openly as the Bible. But *Bayes* turns all into Mirth; *He might as well have added all the -isms in the Old Testament, Perizzitism, Hivitism, Jebuzitism, Hittitism, &c.*

No, Mr. *Bayes*, that need not; and though this indeed is a very pretty Conceit, and 'twere pity it should have been lost; yet I can
10 tell you a better way. For, if rhiming be the business, and you are so good at *tagging of points in a Garret*, there is another word that will do it better, and for which, I know not how truly, you tax your Answerer too here, as if he said, *The Church of England were desperately Schismatical, because the Independents are resolved one and all, to continue*
15 *separate from her Communion*. Therefore let *Schism*, if you please, rhime to *-ism*. And though no man is obliged to produce the Authority of the greatest Wits of the Nation to justify a Rhime, yet for your *dear sake*, Mr. *Bayes*, I will this once supererogate. The first shall be your good friend Bishop *Bramhall*, who among many other memorable
20 Passages, which I believe were the reason that he never thought fit to print his own Book; p. 101. teaches us, not absurdly, that *It was not the erroneous Opinions of the Church of Rome, but the obtruding them by Laws upon other Churches, which warranted a Separation*. But if this will not doe, *Vous avez* Doctor *Thorndikes* Deposition in print, for he,
25 I hear, is lately dead. *The Church of* England *in separating from the Church of* Rome, *is guilty of Schism before God*. I have not the Book by me, but I am sure 'tis candidly recited as I have read it. Then (to show too that there is a King on this side) his present Majesty's Father in his Declaration 4*to Caroli*, 1628. affirms that a Book, en-
30 tituled, *Appello Cæsarem* or *an Appeal to Cæsar*, and *published in the year* 1625. *by Richard Montague then Batcheler of Divinity, and now Bishop of* Chichester, *had opened the way to those Schisms and Divisions which have since ensued in the Church, and that therefore for the redress and remedy thereof, and for the satisfaction of the Consciences of his good People, he had*
35 *not only by publick Proclamation called in that Book, which ministred matter of offence, but to prevent the like danger for the future, reprinted the Articles*

7 *Hittitism* Errata; *Hivitism* W.   11 so] also Y.

of Religion, established in the time of Queen Elizabeth *of Famous Memory:*
and by a Declaration, before those Articles, did restrain all Opinions to the
Sense of those Articles, that nothing might be left for private Fancies and
Innovations, &c. And if this will not amount fully, I shall conclude
with a Villanous *Pamphlet* that I met with t'other day; but of which   5
a *great Wit* indeed was the Author. And, whereas Mr. *Bayes* is
alwayes defying the Nonconformists with Mr. *Hookers Ecclesiastical*
Polity, and the Friendly Debate; I am of opinion, though I have a great
Reverence for Mr. *Hooker,* who in some things did answer himself,
That this little Book, of not full eight leaves, hath shut that *Ecclesi-*   10
astical Polity, and Mr. *Bayes's* too, out of doors: But for the *Friendly*
Debate, I must confess, that is unanswerable. 'Tis one Mr. *Hales of*
Eaton; a most learned Divine, and one of the Church of *England,*
and most remarkable for his Sufferings in the late times, and his
Christian Patience under them. And I reckon it not one of the least   15
Ignominies of that Age, that so eminent a Person should have been
by the Iniquity of the times reduced to those necessities under which
he lived; as I account it no small honour to have grown up into some
part of his Acquaintance, and convers'd a while with the living
remains of one of the clearest heads and best prepared brests in   20
Christendom. That which I speak of is his little *Treatise of Schism,*
which though I had read many years ago, was quite out of my mind,
till I occasionally light upon't at a Book-seller's stall. I hope it will
not be tedious, though I write of some few (and yet whatsoever I
omit I shall have left behind more) material Passages. "Schism is   25
one of those Theological Scarcrows with which they who use to uphold a party in Religion, use to fright away such, as making inquiry
into it are ready to relinquish and oppose it, if it appear either erroneous or suspicious. Schism is, if we would define it, an unnecessary
separation of Christians from that part of the Visible Church of   30
which they were once members. Some reverencing Antiquity more
than needs, have suffered themselves to be scared with imputation
of Schism more than needs. Nothing absolves men from the guilt of
Schism, but true and unpretended Conscience. But the Judgments

8 of opinion] of the opinion Y[2, 3, 5-7].   12 that is] that it is Y[1, 4].
16 have been *om.* Y[1, 4].   22 had] have Y[1, 4].   23 till] rill Y.   29 would]
should Y[1, 4].   31-2 more than needs] above due measure Hales.

of the Ancients many times (to speak most gently) are justly to
be suspected. Where the cause of Schism is necessary, there not
he that separates, but he that is the cause of Separation is the Schismatick. Where the occasion of Separation is unnecessary, neither
5 side can be excused from guilt of Schism. But who shall be the
Judg? That is a point of great difficulty, because it carries fire in the
Tail of it: for it brings with it a piece of Doctrine which is seldom
pleasing to Superiours. You shall find that all Schisms have crept
into the Church by one of these three waies, either upon matter of
10 Fact, or upon matter of Opinion, or point of Ambition. For the first,
I call that matter of Fact, when something is required to be done
by us, which either we know or strongly suspect to be unlawful."
Where he instances in the old great Controversy about EASTER,
"For it being upon error taken for necessary that an Easter must be
15 kept, and upon worse than error (for it was no less than a point of
Judaism forc'd upon the Church) thought further necessary that the
ground of the time for the Feast, must be the Rule left by *Moses* to
the Jews: there arose a stout Question, Whether 'twas to be celebrated with the Jews on the fourteenth Moon, or the Sunday fol-
20 lowing. This caused as great a Combustion as ever was; the West
separating and refusing Communion with the East for many years
together. Here I cannot see but all the World were Schismaticks,
excepting only that we charitably suppose to excuse them from it,
that all parties did what they did out of Conscience. A thing which
25 befell them by the ignorance, for I will not say the malice, of their
guides; and that through the just judgment of God, because,
through sloth and blind obedience, men examined not the things
they were taught, but like beasts of burthen patiently couched
down, and indifferently underwent all whatsoever their Superiours
30 laid upon them. If the discretion of the chiefest guides of the
Church did, in a point so trivial, so inconsiderable, so mainly fail
them: Can we without the imputation of great grossness and folly,
think so poor-spirited persons competent Judges of the Questions
now on foot betwixt the Churches? Where, or among whom, or
35 how many the Church shall be, it is a thing indifferent: What if

4 occasion Y; cccasion W.   23 to excuse them from it *om*. Hales.
25 by] through Hales.

those to whom the Execution of the publick Service is committed, do something, either unseemly or suspicious, or peradventure unlawful; what if the Garments they wear be censured, nay, indeed be suspicious. What if the gesture or adoration to be used to the Altars, as now we have learned to speak? What if the Homilist have preached or delivered any Doctrine, of the truth of which we are not well perswaded, (a thing which very often falls out) yet, for all this, we may not separate, except we be constrained personally to bear a part in it our selves. Nothing can be a just cause of refusing Communion in Schism, that concerns Fact, but only to require the execution of some unlawful or suspected Act. For, not only in Reason, but in Religion too, that Maxim admits of no release, *Cautissimi cujusque præceptum, quod dubitas ne feceris:* That whatsoever you doubt of, that you in no case do." He instances then in the Second Council of *Nice*, where, saith he, the *"Synod* it self was the Schismatical party in the point of using the Images, which, saith he, all acknowledge unnecessary, most do suspect, and many hold utterly unlawful: Can then the injoyning of such a thing be ought else but an abuse? Can the refusal of Communion here be thought any other thing than Duty? Here, or upon the like occasion to separate, may peradventure bring personal trouble or danger, against which it concerns any honest man to have *Pectus preparatum.*" Then of Schism from Opinion; "Prayer, Confession, Thanksgiving, Reading of Scripture, Administration of Sacraments in the plainest and the simplest manner, were matter enough to furnish out a sufficient Liturgy, though nothing either of private Opinion or of Church Pomp, of Garments, of prescribed Gestures, of Imagery, of Musick, of matter concerning the Dead, of many Superfluities which creep into the Church, under the name of Order and Decency, did interpose it self. To charge Churches and Liturgies with things unnecessary was the first beginning of Superstition. If the Fathers and special Guides of the Church would be a little sparing in incumbring Churches with Superfluities, or not over-rigid either in reviving obsolete customs, or imposing new: there would be far less

---

2 something Y; somethimg W.   7 perswaded] W[2, 3, 5, 7, 8], X, Y; perswaaded W[1, 4, 6, 9].   24 Scripture] Scriptures Hales.   29 Decency, Y; ∼ W.
32 in] of Hales.   33 over-rigid X, Y; over-ridged W.

cause of Schism or Superstition; and all the inconvenience likely to
ensue, would be but this, They should in so doing yield a little to
the imbecility of their inferiours; a thing which Saint *Paul* would
never have refused to do. It is alike unlawful to make profession of
5 known or suspected falshood, as to put in practice unlawful or suspected Actions. The third thing I named for matter of Schism was
Ambition, I mean Episcopal Ambition; One head of which, is one
Bishops claiming Supremacy over another, which, as it hath been
from time to time a great Trespass against the Churches Peace, so
10 it is now the final ruine of it. For they do but abuse themselves and
others, who would perswade us that Bishops by Christs Institution
have any Superiority over other men further than that of Reverence, or that any Bishop is superiour to another further than positive Order agreed upon among Christians hath prescribed. Time
15 hath taken leave, sometimes, to fix this name of CONVENTICLES
upon good and honest Meetings. Though open Assemblies are
required, yet, at all times while men are really pious, all Meetings
of men for mutual help of Piety and Devotion, wheresoever, and
by whomsoever celebrated, were permitted without exception. In
20 times of manifest Corruption and Persecution, wherein Religious
Assembling is dangerous, Private Meetings, howsoever besides
Publick Order, are not only lawful, but they are of Necessity and
Duty. All pious Assemblies, in times of Persecution and Corruption,
howsoever practised, are indeed, or rather alone, the Lawful Con-
25 gregations: and Publick Assemblies, though according to form of
Law, are, indeed, nothing else but RIOTS and CONVENTICLES,
if they be stained with Corruption and Superstition." Do you not
see now, Mr. *Bayes*, that you needed not to have gone so far for a
word, when you might have had it in the Neighbourhood? If there
30 be any Coherence left in your Scull, you cannot but perceive that I
have brought you Authority enough to prove that *Schism* (for the
Reason we may discourse another time) do's at least rhime to *Ism*.
But you have a peculiar delight and felicity, (which no man envies
you) in Scripture-Drollery, nothing less will taste to your Palate:

10 abuse] abase Hales.   12–13 than...further *om*. X.   12 that of] thar of Y.
17 really] truely Hales.   19 were] where X.   20 Corruption] corruptions
Hales.   Persecution] persecutions Hales.   24 howsoever X, Y; howoever W.
28 to have gone so far Y; have gone so for W.

whereas otherwise you have travelled so far in *Italy*, that you could not escape the Titles of some Books which would have served your turn as well, *Cardinalism, Nepotism, Putanism,* if you were in a *Paroxism* of the *Ism's*.

When I had writ this, and undergon so grateful a Penance for no less than that I had transcribed before out of our Author; I could not upon comparing them both together but reflect most seriously upon the difference of their two wayes of Discoursing. I could not but admire that Majesty and Beauty which sits upon the forehead of masculine Truth and generous Honesty: but no less detest the Deformity of Falshood disguised in all its Ornaments. How much another thing it is to hear him speak, that hath cleared himself from froth and growns, and who suffers neither Sloth nor Fear, nor Ambition, nor any other tempting Spirit of that nature to abuse him, from one, who as Mr. *Hales* expresseth it, makes Christianity Laquey to Ambition; How wretchedly, the one to uphold his *Fiction*, must incite Princes to Persecution and Tyranny, degrade Grace to Morality, debauch Conscience against its own Principles, distort and mis-interpret the Scripture, fill the World with Blood, Execution, and Massacre; while the other needs and requires no more but a peaceable and unprejudicate Soul and the native Simplicity of a Christian-spirit! And me-thinks, if our Author had any spark of Vertue unextinguished, he should, upon considering these together, retire into his Closet, and there lament and pine away for his desperate follie; for the disgrace he hath, as far as in him is, brought upon the *Church of England* by such an undertaking, and for the eternal shame to which he has hereby condemn'd his own Memory.

I ask you heartily pardon, Mr. *Bayes*, for treating you against *Decorum* here, with so much gravity. 'Tis possible I may not trouble you above once or twice more in the like nature; but so often at least, I hope, one may in the writing of a whole Book, have leave to be serious. Your next Flower, and that indeed is a sweet one, *Dear Heart, how could I hug and kiss thee for all this Love and Sweetness?* Fy, fy, Mr. *Bayes*, Is this the Language of a Divine, and to be used, as you sometimes express it, in the face of the Sun? Who can escape from thinking that you are adream'd of your *Comfortable Importance*?

16 Laquey *Errata*; Lacquey Y; lackque W.

These are (as the *Moral Satyrist* calls them in the cleanliest manner the thing would bear) *Words left betwixt the Sheets:* Somebody might take it ill that you should misapply your Courtship to an Enemy. But in the *Roman Empire* it was the priviledg of the Hangman to
5 deflour a Virgin before Execution. But, sweet Mr. *Bayes*, (for I know you do nothing without a precedent of some of the greatest Wits of the Nation) Whose example had you for this *seeming Transport* of a gentler *Passion?*

Then comes, *Wellfare poor Macedo for a modest Fool.* This I know
10 is matter of *Gazette*, which is as Canonical as *Ecclesiastical Policy.* Therefore I have the less to say to't. Only, I could wish that there were some severer Laws against such Villains who raise so false and scandalous reports of worthy Gentlemen; and that those Laws were put in execution: And that men might not be suffered to walk the
15 streets in so confident a garb, who commit those Assassinates upon the reputation of deserving persons.

Here follows a sore Charge: that the Answerer had *without any provocation, in a publick and solemn way, undertaken the Defence of the Fanatick Cause.* Here, indeed, Mr. *Bayes*, You have Reason, And you
20 might have had as just a quarrel against whosoever had undertaken it. For, your design and hope was from the beginning, that no man would have answered you in a publick and solemn way; and, nothing would vex **a** wise man, as you are, more than to have his Intention and Counsel frustrated. When you have rang'd all your
25 forces in battel, when you have plac'd your Canon, when you have sounded a charge, and given the Word to fall on upon the whole Party; if you could then perswade every particular person of 'm, that you gave him no Provocation, I confess, Mr. B*ayes*, this were an excellent and a new way of your inventing, to conquer single,
30 ('tis your Moral Vertue) whole Armies. And so the *admiring Drove* might stand gaping, till one by one, you had cut all their throats. But, Mr. *Bayes*, I cannot discern but that you gave him as much Provocation in your first Book, as he has you in his *Evangelical Love, Church-Peace and Unity,* which is the pretence of your issuing this
35 Preface.

2 bear Y; bare W.   8 *Passion?* Y; ~. W.   10 *Policy*] *Polity* Z.
13–14 and . . . execution: *om.* X.

For, having for your *Dear Sake* (beside many other troubles that I have undertaken, without your giving me any Provocation) sought out and perused that Book too, I do not find you any where personally concern'd, but as you have, it seems upon some conviction, assumed to your self some vices or errours against which he speaks only in general, and with some modesty. But for the rest, you say upon full perusal, *you finde not one Syllable to the purpose, beside a perpetual Repetition of the old out-worn Story of Unscriptural Ceremonies, and some frequent whinings, and sometimes ravings,* &c. Now to see the Dulness of some mens Capacities above others. I upon this occasion, begun, I know not how it came, at p. 127. And thence read on to the end of his Book. And from thence I turn'd to the beginning and continued to p. 127. and could not all along, observe any thing but what was very pertinent to the matter in hand. But this is your way of excusing your self from replying to things that yet you will be medling with, and nibling at: and 'tis besides a pretty knack (the Nonconformists have it not alone) of frighting or discouraging sober people from reading those dangerous Treatises, which might contribute to their better information. I cannot but observe, Mr. *Bayes,* this admirable way (like fat *Sir John Falstaffe's* singular dexterity in sinking) that you have of answering whole Books or Discourses, how pithy and knotty soever, in a line or two, nay sometimes with a word. So it fares with this Book of the Answerers. So with a Book or Discourse of his, I know not, of the *Morality of the Lords Day*; which is answered by a *Septenary Portion in the Hebdomadal Revolution.* So, whether Book or Discourse I also know not of the *Self-evidencing light of the Scripture,* where *Bayes* offers (and it seems strange) to produce as good proofs for it out of the *Alcoran.* So I show'd you where he answers Demonstration with the Lye. And one thing more comes into my mind; where, after he has blunder'd a great while to bring himself off the Magistrates exercising the Priesthood in his own person, he concludes with an irresistible defence against his Answerer, *This is suitable to the Genius of his ingenuity, and betraies him as much as the word INTANGLMENT, which is the Shiboleth of all his Writings.* So he defeats all the *gross bodies of*

2 without Y; withour W.   6 only *om.* X.   7 perusal Y; per-perusal W.
21 or] and Y.   32 Priesthood Y; Pristhood W.

Orthodoxy with calling them *Systemes and Syntagmes*. So you know he answers all the Controversial Books of the Calvinists that ever have been written, with the Tale of *Robin Hood,* and the *mighty Bramble on the South side of the Lake Leman*. Mr. *Bayes,* You cannot enough
5 esteem and cherish this Faculty. For, next to your single beating whole Armies, I do not know any Virtue that you have need of so often, or that will upon trial be found more useful.

And to this succeeds another Flower, I am sure, though I can scarce smell out the Sense of it. But it is printed in a distinct
10 Character, and that is always a certain sign of a Flower. For our Book-sellers have many Arts to make us *yield to their importunity*: and among the rest, they promise us, that it shall be printed in fine Paper, and in a very large and fair letter; that it shall be very well examined that there be no Errata; that wheresoever there is a pretty
15 Conceit, it shall be marked out in another Character; that the Sentences shall be boxed up in several paragraphs, and more Drawers than in any Cabinet; that the Books shall all be bound up in Calves Leather. But my greatest care was that when I quoted any Sentence or word of our Author's, it might be so discernable, lest I should go
20 for a Plagiary. And I am much offended to see that in several places he hath not kept touch with me. The Word of Mr. *Bayes's* that he has here made more notorious, is *Categoricalness*: and I observe that wheresoever there comes a word of that termination he shows it the same honour; as if he had a mind to make *Bayes* a Collar of *Nesses*.
25 What the mystery is, I cannot so easily imagine; no more than of *Shiboleth* and *Intanglement*. But I doubt Mr. *Bayes* is sick of many complicated Diseases; or to keep to our rhime, *Sicknesses*. He is troubled not only with the *Ismes* but the *Nesses*. He might, if he had pleased, here too to have shown his wit, as he did in the others, and
30 have told us of *Sheerness, Dongioness, Inverness* and *Cathness*. But he omitted it perhaps in this place, knowing how well he had acquitted himself in another, and out of the Scripture too, which gives his Wit the highest relish. 'Tis p. 72. of his first Book, where, to prove that the fruits of the Spirit are no more than Morality, he quotes

15 Character; Y; ~. W.   15–18 that the Sentences...Leather. Y; *om*. W.
22 more Y; *om*. W.   29 shown Y; show'd W.   30 *Inverness Ed; Innerness*
W etc.   30–1 But...perhaps] Y; But he might very well have omitted it W.

Saint *Paul*, Gal. 5. 22. Where the Apostle enumerates them; *Love*, *Joy*, *Peace*, *Patience*, *Gentleness*, *Goodness*, *Faith*, *Meekness* and *Temperance*: but our Author translates Joy to *Chearfulness*, Peace to *Peaceableness*, and Faith to *Faithfulness*: What Ignorance, or rather, what Forgery is this of Scripture and Religion? Who is there of the *Systematical*, *German*, *Geneva*, *Orthodox Divines*, but could have taught him better? Who is there of the *Sober*, *Intelligent*, *Episcopal Divines* of the Church of *England* but would abhor this Interpretation? Yet, when his Answerer, I see, objects this to him, *p.* 220. *Bayes*, like a dexterous Scholastical Disputant, it being told him, That Joy is not Chearfulness, but that *Spiritual Joy which is unspeakable*; that Peace is not Peaceableness in his Sense, but *that Peace of God which through Jesus Christ is wrought in the hearts of Believers by the Holy Ghost*; and that Faith in God is there intended, not faithfulness in our Duties, Trusts or Offices: What does he do? *p.* 337. He very ingenuously and wisely, when he is to answer, quite forgets that Faith was once named: and, having supprest that, as to the rest he wipes his Mouth, and rubs his Forehead, and saith the *Cavil is but a little one, and the Fortune of* Cæsar *and the Roman Empire depend not upon it, and therefore he will not trouble the Reader with a Critical Account of the reason of his Translation.* No, don't Mr. *Bayes*, 'Tis very well; let it alone. But, though not the Fortunes of *Cæsar* and the Roman Empire, I doubt there is something more depends upon it, if it be matter of Salvation. And I am afraid besides, that there may a curse too belong to him who shall knowingly add or diminish in the Scripture. Do you think Bishop *Bramhall* himself, if he had seen this, could have abstained (p. 117. before quoted,) from telling our Author *That the promiscuous Licence given to people qualified or unqualified, not only to read but to interpret the Scriptures according to their private spirits or particular fancies, without regard either to the Analogy of Faith, which they understand not, or to the Interpretation of the Doctors of former Ages, is more prejudicial (I might better say) pernicious both to particular Christians, and to whole Societies, than the over-rigorous restraint of the Romanists.*

The next is a piece of Mirth, on occasion of some discourse of the Answerers, about the Morality of the Lords-day: Where it seems,

3 translates X, Y; tanslates W.   4 and *om.* X.   9 220] 200 X.   15 does . . . do Y; dos . . . doe W.   19 *Fortune*] Fortunes Parker.   *depend*] *depends* Y.

he useth some hard words, which I am naturally an enemy to; but might be done of purpose to keep the Controversy from the white-Aprons, within the white Surplices, to be more learnedly debated. But this fares no better than all the rest. There is no kind of
5 *Morality*, I see, but *Bayes* will try to debauch it: *Oh, what edifying Doctrine, saith he, is this to the White-Aprons! and doubtless they would with the Jews, sooner roast themselves, than a small joint of Mutton upon the Sacred day of Rest.* Now, I do not, neither, I believe, does *Bayes* himself know any of them that are thus superstitious. So that Mr.
10 *Bayes* might, if he had pleased, have spared his jibing at that day, which hath more sacredness in it by far than many, nay than any of those things he pleads for. But when men are once *Adepti* and have attain'd *Bayes* his height, and Divinity at least *is rightly understood*, they have a Priviledge, it seems, not onely to play and make
15 merry *on* the Sabbath day, but *with* it.

After this I walked a great way through bushes and brambles before I could find another Flower: but then I met with two upon one stalk; on occasion of his Answerers having said something of the day of Judgment when men should be accountable. *Oh*, saith he,
20 *We shall be sure to be accounted with at the day of Judgment*; and again, *Ah sweet day, when these people of God shall once for all, to their unspeakable Comfort and Support, wreak their eternal Revenge upon their reprobat Enemies.* This puts me in mind of another expression of our Authors alluding too this way. *'Tis an easie matter by this dancing and capering*
25 *humour to perpetuate all the Controversies in the world, how plainly soever determinable, to the coming of* Elias: *and after this rate shall the Barbers bason remain* Mambrino's *helmet; and the Asses Pannel a furniture for the Great Horse, till the day of Judgment.* Now, good Mr. *Bayes*, I am one that desire to be very well resolved in these things; and though not
30 much indeed, yet I attribute something to your judgment. Pray tell us in good earnest, what you think of these things, that we may know how to take our measures of living accordingly. For, if indeed there be no Judgment, no account for what is done here below, I have lost a great deal of precious time, that I might have injoyed in
35 one of the fruits of your spirit, that is *Chearfulness*. How many good

8 *Sacred day of Rest*] *Day of Sacred Rest* Parker.   12 pleads] pleaded Y.
20 the] *that* Y.

jests have I balk'd, even in writing this book, lest I should be
brought to answer for every profane and idle word! How frequent
opportunities have I mist in my life of geniality and pleasure,
and fulfilling Nature in all its ends! How have you frighted the
Magistrate in vain, from exercising his uncontrolable Ecclesiastical 5
Power, with the fear of an after-reckoning to God Almighty! And
how have you, p. 238. defeated the obligatory force of all his Laws,
and set his Subjects at liberty from all obligations to the duty of
Obedience: for they lye under no Obligation, you say then, but of
Prudence and Self-interest. But unless there hath been some errour 10
in our education, and we have been seasoned with ill Books at first,
so that we can never lose the impression, there is some such matter,
and the Governour had reason, when he trembled to hear Saint *Paul*
discoursing of that Subject. The Fanatical *Book of Martyrs* (for we
will not with some call the Bible so) tells us some old Stories of per- 15
sons that have been cited by some of them to appear at such a day,
and that by dying at the time prefixed, they have saved their
Reconnoissances. And in the *Scotch* History we read of a great Cardinal that was so summoned by poor Mr. *Guichard*, and yet could
not help it, but he must take that long and sad journey of Death to 20
answer at the Grand Assizes. If therefore there be such a thing, I
would not for fear, and if there be not, yet I would not for good luck
sake, set that terrible day at defiance, or make too merry with it.
'Tis possible that the Nonconformists many of them may be too
censorious of others, and too confident of their own Integrity. 25
Others of them are more temperate, and perhaps destitute of all
humane redress against their sufferings: Some of those make rash
Challenges, and the other just Appeals to appear at that dreadful
Tribunal. In the mean time, 'tis not for you to be both the *Enemy*
and their Judg. Much less do's it befit you, because perhaps they 30
speak too sillily or demurely of it, or too braving and confidently,
therefore to make a mere mockery of the whole business of that
supreme Judge and Judicature. And one thing I will say more,
though slighter; that, though I am not so far gone as *Campanella*
was in the efficacy of words, and the magick of the face, and 35

14 *Martyrs* Y; ~. W.   18 Reconnoissances] Recognissances Z.   22 for
good] fear good X.

pronunciation, Yet I marked how your Answerer look'd when he spoke of the day of Judgment. Very gravely, I assure you, and yet without any dressing or adorning his *Supercilium*'s: And I have most often observed that serious words have produced serious Effects.

5   I have, by this time me-thinks, gather'd enow: nor are there many more left, unless I should goe for a Flower to the *Dunghill*, which, he saith, *is his only Magazin*. And this being an expression which he has several times used (for no Nonconformist repeats so often) I cannot but remark, that besides his natural Talent, Mr.
10 *Bayes* hath been very industrious, and neglected no opportunity of acquiring a perfection of railing. For this is a phrase borrowed from a modern Author lately dead, and I suppose *Bayes* had given him a Bond for repayment at the day that he spoke of so lately.

There are indeed several others at which I am forc'd to stop my
15 nose. For by the smell, any man may discern they grew upon a ranker soil, than that on the South-side of the *Lake Lemane*, even upon the bank of the *Thames* in the Meadow of *Billingsgate*: as that of the Lye, which, he saith, no Gentleman, much less a Divine, ought to put up. Now if this were to be tryed by a Court-Martial
20 of the Brothers of the Blade, 'Tis to be considered whether it were the down-right Lye, or whether it were the Lye by Interpretation. For in the disputes of the Schools there is nothing more usual, than *Hoc est Verum. Hoc est falsum.* But this passes without any blemish of Honour on either side, and so far it is from any obligation to a
25 Challenge or a Duel, that it never comes to be decided, so much as by the Study-door key. But *quod restat probandum* do's the business without demanding other satisfaction. Then, if it were the down-right Lye; it is to be examined who gave the Lye first: for that alters the case. And last of all (but which is indeed upon a quarrel the
30 least material point, yet, it too comes under some consideration) which of the two was in the right, and which of them spoke truth, and which lyed. These are all things to be discussed in their proper places. For I do not observe that the Answerer gave *Bayes* the down-right Lye. But I find that *Bayes* gave him the Lye first in terms.
35 And as to the Truth of the things controverted and alledged, there

---

3 dressing or adorning Y; depressing or exalting W.   21 were the Y; were only the W.

needs no more than the depositions that I formerly transcribed concerning *Bayes* his own words. But all this is only a Scene out of
Bayes his *Rehearsal*.

> *Villain, thou liest,—*
> *—Arm, arm, Valerio arm,*   5
> *The Lie no flesh can bear I trow.*

And then as to the Success of the Combate,

> *—They fly, they fly*
> *Who first did give the Lye.*

For that of Caitife, and other Provocations that are proper for the   10
same Court, I will not meddle further. And for the being *past Grace
and so past Mercy*; I shall only observe that the Church of *England* is
much obliged to Mr. *Bayes* for having proved that Nonconformity
is the Sin against the Holy Ghost.

There remains but one Flower more that I have a mind to. But   15
that indeed is a Rapper. 'Tis a *Flower of the Sun*, and might alone
serve both for a Staff and a Nose-gay for any Noble-man's Porter.
*Symbolicalness is the very Essence of Paganism, Superstition and Idolatry.
They will and ought sooner to broyl in Smithfield than submit to such
Abominations of the Strumpet and the Beast.* '*Tis the very Potion wherewith*   20
the Scarlet-Whore made drunk the Kings of the Earth. Heliogabalus *and*
Bishop Bonner *lov'd it like Clary and Eggs, and alwayes made it their
mornings-draught upon burning days; and it is not to be doubted but the
seven Vials of Wrath that were to be poured out upon the Nations of the
Earth under the Reign of Antichrist were filled with Symbolical Extracts*   25
and Spirits: with more such stuff which I omit. This is I confess a
pretty Posy for the Nose of such a Divine. Doctor *Baily*'s Romance
of the *Wall-Flower* had nothing comparable to't. And I question,
whether, as well as Mr. *Bayes* loves preferment, yet though he had
lived in the Primitive-Church, he would not as *Heliodorus* Bishop of   30
Trissa, I take it, that renounced his Bishoprick rather than his title

---

2 own *om.* Y.   5 *Valerio*] Gonsalvo Buckingham.   5–6 arm, / *The*]
arm; what ho? / The Buckingham.   8 *They fly, they fly*] they fly Buckingham.
19 *than submit*] *than to submit* Y.   20 *Abominations*] *Abomination* Y.   26 with
more such stuff which I omit *om.* Y.

to the History of *Theagenes* and *Chariclia,* have done in like manner: nay, and have delivered up his Bible too into the bargain, before he would quit the honour of so excellent a piece of Drollery. This is surely the Bill of Fare, not at the *Ordination--Dinner* at the *Nags-head,*

5 but of the *Excusation-Dinner* at the *Cock*; and never did Divine make so good Chear of *Owens* Peas-porridge and Scripture. I know no Dainty wanting, or that could have pleased his Tooth so well, except the Leg of a Pheasant at the *Dog* and *Partridge*; for he is of *Thomas a Becket's* Dyet; who eat, he said, *Phaesianum sicut alij Mulu-*

10 *ellum,* and can mortifie himself upon Pheasant, as well as others with Salt-fish. Good Mr. *Bayes,* or Mr. *Thunder,* or Mr. *Cartwright* (not the Nonconformist *Cartwright,* that was you say (as some others too of your acquaintance) converted: but the Player in the Rehearsal) this *Divinity* I doubt was the *Bacchus* of your Thigh, and not the

15 *Pallas* of your Brain.

Here it is that after so great an excess of Wit, he thinks fit to take a Julep and resettle his Brain, and the Government. He grows as serious as 'tis possible for a madman, and pretends to sum up the whole state of the Controversie with the Nonconformists. And to

20 be sure he will make the story as plausible for himself as he may: But therefore it was that I have before so particularly quoted and bound him up with his own Words as fast as such a *Proteus* could be pinion'd. For he is as waxen as the first matter, and no Form comes amiss to him. Every change of Posture does either alter his opinion

25 or vary the expression by which we should judg of it: and sitting he is of one mind, and standing of another. Therefore I take my self the less concerned, to fight with a Wind-mill like *Don Quixote*: or to whip a Gig as boyes do, or with the Lacqueys at *Charing-cross* or *Lincolns-Inne*-fields to play at the *Wheel of Fortune,* lest I should fall

30 into the hands of my Lord Chief Justice, or Sir *Edmond Godfrey.* The truth is in short and let *Bayes* make more or less of it if he can; *Bayes* had at first built up such a stupendious Magistrate, as never was of God's making. He had put all Princes upon the Rack to stretch them to his dimension. And, as a streight line continued grows a

35 Circle, he had given them so infinite a Power that it was extended

4 *Ordination--Dinner* at the *om.* Y.   5 of the *Excusation-Dinner om.* Y.
6–11 I know . . . Salt-fish. Y; *om.* W.   12 *Cartwright,* Y; ~ W.

unto Impotency. For though he found it not, till it was too late
in the Cause; yet he felt it all along (which is the understanding of
Brutes) in the Effect. For, hence it is that he so often complains,
that Princes knew not aright that Supremacy over Conscience, to
which they were so lately, since their deserting the Church of
Rome, restored. That in most Nations Government was not rightly
understood, and many expressions of that Nature: Whereas indeed
the matter is that Princes have always found that uncontrolable
Government over CONSCIENCE to be both unsafe and impracticable. He had run himself here to a stand, and perceiv'd that there
was a God, there was Scripture; the Magistrate himself had a Conscience, and must *take care that he did not injoyn things apparently evil.*
Being at a stop here, he would therefore try how he could play the
Broker on the Subjects side: and no Pimp did ever enter into a more
serious disputation to vitiate an innocent Virgin, than he to debauch their Consciences. And to harden their unpractis'd modesty,
he imboldens them by his own example, showing them the experiment upon his own Conscience first. But after all, he finds himself
again at the same stand here and is run up to the Wall by an Angel.
God, and Scripture, and Conscience will not let him go further: but
he owns, that if the Magistrate injoyns things apparently evil, the
Subject may have liberty to remonstrate. What shall he do then?
for it is too glorious an enterprize to be abandon'd at the first
rebuffe. Why he gives us a new Translation of the Bible, and a new
Commentary. He saith that Tenderness of Conscience might be
allowed in a Church to be constituted, not in a Church constituted
already. That tenderness of Conscience and Scandal are Ignorance,
Pride and Obstinacy. He saith, the Nonconformists should com-
municate with him till they have clear evidence that it is evil. This
is a civil way indeed of gaining the question, to perswade men that
are unsatisfyed, to be satisfied till they be dissatisfied. He threatens,
he rails, he jeers them, if it were possible, out of all their Consciences
and Honesty; and finding that will not doe, he calls out the Magistrate, tells him, these men are not fit to live, there can be no security
of Government while they are in being: bring out the Pillories,

---

4 Conscience] Consciences X.   14-15 a more serious Y; seriouser W.
19 Angel. Y; ∼: W.

Whipping-posts, Gallies, Rods, and Axes, (which are *Ratio ultima Cleri*, a Clergy-mans last Argument, ay and his first too): and pull in pieces all the Trading Corporations those Nests of Faction and Sedition. This is a faithful account of the summ and intention of all his undertaking, for which I confess, he was as pick'd a man as could have been employ'd or found out in a whole Kingdome: but it is so much too hard a Task for any man to atchieve, that no Goose but would grow giddy with it.

For whereas he reduces the whole Controversy to a matter of two or three Symbolical Ceremonies (and if there be nothing else, more the shame of those that keep such a pudder for them) it is very well worth observing how he hath behaved himself, and how come off in this Dispute. It seems that the Conformists define a Sacrament to be an Outward visible sign of an Inward Spiritual Grace. It seems that the Sacraments are usually called in the Greek *Symbola*. It seems further that some of the Nonconformists, under the name therefore of Symbolical Ceremonies, dispute the lawfulness of those that are by our Church injoyned, whereby the Nonconformists can onely intend that these Ceremonies are so applyed, as if they were of a Sacramental nature and institution, and that therefore they are unlawful. Our Authors Answerer handling this Argument, does among other things make use of a pertinent Passage in Saint *Austin*, *Signa quum ad res divinas pertinent Sacramenta appellantur.* What does Mr. *Bayes* in this case? for it went hard with him. Why, as good luck would have it, not being willing that so great a Politician, to the irreparable damage of the Church, should yet be destroyed, *J. O.* had forgot to quote the Book and the Page. Now though you send a man the length of your Weapon, and name your Second; Yet Mr. *Bayes* being, as you see often, admirably read in the Laws of Duelling, knew that unless the Time and Place be appointed, there is no danger. He saith therefore, p. 452. of his second Book, that he *should have advantage on his side, if he should lay odds with him, that there is no such passage in all the Volumns of Saint* Austin.—But however, that it is neither civil nor ingenuous to trouble him with such Objections, as he cannot answer without reading over eight or ten large Volumns in Folio. It was too much to expect from one of so much business, good *Augustulus:*

> *Quum tot sustineas & tanta negotia solus;*
> *Res Sacras Armis tuteris, Moribus ornes,*
> *Legibus emendes —* 5

Which may be thus translated: When you alone have the Ceremonies to defend with Whipping-posts, Rods and Axes; when you have Grace to turn into Morality; when you have the Act of Oblivion and Indemnity and the Ecclesiastical Declaration of *March* to tear in pieces; it were unreasonable and too much to the dammage 10 of the publick to put you on such an imployment. I ask your Pardon, Mr. *Bayes,* for this Paraphrase and Digression: for I perceive I am even hardned in my Latine, and am prone to use it without fear or reverence. But Mr. *Bayes,* there might have been a remedy for this, had you pleased. Where then were all your *Leaf-turners?* a 15 sort of poor Readers *that you, as well as Bishop* Bramhal, *ought to have some Reverence for,* having made so much use of them to gather materials for your Structures and Superstructures. I cannot be perswaded, for all this, but that he knows it well enough, the passage being so remarkable in it self, and so dirtyed with the Nonconfor- 20 mists thumbs, that he could not possibly miss it: and I doubt he does but laugh at me now, when, to save him a labour, I tell him in the simplicity of my heart, that even I my self met with it in *Ep. 5ta ad Marcellinum,* and the words these, *Nimis autem longum est convenienter disputare de varietate signorum quæ cum ad res divinas pertinent* 25 *Sacramenta appellantur.* But whether there be such a place or no, he hath no mind that his Answerer should make use of it: nor of the Schoolmen, whom before he had owned for the Authors of the Church of *England*'s Divinity; but would bind up the Answerer to the Law onely and the Gospel. And now Mr. *Bayes* saith he will be 30 of the School-mens opinion *as long as they speak Sense* and no longer, (and so I believe of Saint *Austin*'s) that is to say, so long as they will serve his turn: for all Politicians shake men off when they have no more use of 'm, or find them to thwart the design. But, Mr. *Bayes,* why may not your Answerer or any man else quote St. *Austin,* as 35

4 *Sacras*] Italas Horace.

well as you may the Scripture? I am sure there is less danger of perverting the place, or of mis-interpretation. And though perhaps a
Nonconformist may value the Authority of the Bible above that of
the Fathers, yet the *Welch* have a Proverb; that the Bible and a
5 Stone do well together: meaning perhaps, that if the one miss the
other will hit. You, that are a Duellist, know how great a bravery
'tis to gain an enemies Sword, and that there is no more home-
thrust in disputation, than the *Argumentum ad hominem.* So that if
your Adversary fell upon you with one of your own Fathers, it was
10 gallantly done on his part; and no less wisely on yours to fence in
this manner, and use all your shifts to put it by. For you too, Mr.
Bayes, do know, no man better, that it is not at all times safe nor
honourable to be of a *Fathers* opinion.

Having escaped this danger he grows, nor can I blame him,
15 exceeding merry: and insults heavily over *Symbolical* wheresoever
he meets with it, for in his Answerer I find it not. But wheresoever
'twas it serves to good purpose. For no man would imagine that he
could have received so universal a Defeat, and appear in so good
humour. A terrible Disputant he is, when he has set up an hard
20 word to be his Opponent; 'Tis a very wholesome thing he knows,
and prolongs life: for all the while he can keep up this ball, he may
decline the Question. But the poor word is sure to be mumbled and
mowsled to purpose, and to be made an example. But let us, with
Mr. *Bayes* his leave, examine the thing for once a little closer. The
25 Nonconformists, as I took notice before, do object to some of the
Rites of the Church of *England* under the name of Symbolical or significant Ceremonies. They observe the Church of *England* does in
the discourse of Ceremonies printed before the Common Prayer
Book, declare that the retaining of those Ceremonies, is not onely
30 *as they serve for decent Order and godly Discipline; but as they are apt to stir
up the dull mind of man to the remembrance of his duty to God, by some
special and notable significancy whereby he may be edified.* They further
observe the Church of *England's* definition of a Sacrament: That it
is *an outward visible sign of an inward spiritual Grace.* They find these
35 Ceremonies, so constituted, impos'd upon them by Authority; and

5 the one Y; one Z; one one W.   7 an Y; your W.   32 *significancy*]
signification *Common Prayer.*

moreover, according to our Authors principle, made a new part of the Divine Law. They therefore quarrel and except against these under the notion of Sacraments, and insist that the Church is not impowred to institute such Ceremonies under such obligations and penalties as they are imposed. Or, if you will, in stead of Church you may say rather the Magistrate: for as much as our Author hath *pro hac vice* delivered the Keyes and the whole power of the House into his hands.

Now the Author having got them at this lock, crys Victory. Nothing less will serve him than a three dayes triumph, as if he had conquered *Europe*, *Asia* and *Africa*, and let him have a fourth day added, if he please, over the *Terra Incognita* of *Geneva*. There is no end of his Ostentation and Pageantry: and the dejected Nonconformists follow the wheels of his Chariot, to be led afterwards to the Prison and there executed. He had said p. 446. of his Second Book, *Here* Cartwright *begun his Objection, and here he was immediately check'd in his Carrear by* Whitgift (you might Mr. Author, for respect's sake have called him at least Mr. if not Archbishop *Whitgift*) *who told him plainly, he could not be ignorant that to the making of a Sacrament, besides the external Element, there is required a Commandment of God in his Word that it should be done, and a promise annexed to it, whereof the Sacrament is a Seal.* And in pursuance hereof, p. 447. our Author saith, *Here then I fix my foot, and dare him to his teeth, to prove that any thing can be capable of the nature or office of Sacraments that is not established by Divine Institution and upon Promise of Divine Acceptance.* Upon the confidence of this Argument 'tis that he *Hectors* and *Achillizes* all the Nonconformists out of the pit in this Preface. This is the sword that was consecrated first upon the Altar, and thence presented to the Champions of the Church in all Ages. This is that with which Archbishop *Whitgift* gave *Cartwright his death's wound: and laid the Puritan Reformation a gasping.* This is the weapon wherewith Master *Hooker gained those lasting and eternal Trophies over that baffled Cause.* This is that with which Bp. *Bramhall wrought those wonderful things that exceeded all belief.* This hath been transmitted successively to the Writer of the *Friendly Debate*, and to this our Author. It is in conclusion the *Curtana* of our Church. 'Tis *Sir Salomon's* sword, Cock

17 respect's Y; respect W.   32 *Trophies*] Trophy of Success Parker.

of as many men as it hath been drawn against. Wo worth the man
that comes in the way of so dead-doing a tool, and when wielded
with the arm of such a *Scanderbag* as our Author. The Nonconformists had need desire a Truce to bury their dead. Nay there are
5 none left alive to desire it: but they are slain every mother's Son of
them. Yet perhaps they are but stounded and may revive again.
For I do not see all this while, that any of them have written, as a
great Prelate of ours, a Book of *Seven Sacraments*: or attempted to
prove that these *Symbolical* Ceremonies are indeed Sacraments.
10 Nothing less. 'Tis that which they most labour against, and they
complain that these things should be imposed on them with so high
Penalty, as want nothing of a Sacramental nature but Divine Institution. And because an Humane Institution is herein made of equal
force to a Divine Institution, therefore it is that they are agrieved.
15 All that they mean, or could mean, as far as I or any man can perceive, is only that these Ceremonies are a kind of *Anti-Sacraments*,
and so obtruded upon the Church, that without condescending to
these additional Inventions, no man is to be admitted to partake of
the true Sacraments which were of Christ's appointing. For, with-
20 out the Sign of the Cross, our Church will not receive any one to
Baptism, as also without kneeling no man is suffered to come to the
Communion. So that methinks, our Author and his partners have
wounded themselves only with this Argument: and have had as
little occasion here to sing their *Te Deum*'s, as the *Roman* Emperour
25 had to triumph over the Ocean, because he had gathered Peri-
winkles and Scallop shells on the Beach. For the Author may trans-
form their reasonings as oft as he pleases (even as oft as he doth his
own, or the Scriptures): but this is indeed their Fort out of which
I do not see they are likely to be beat with all our Authors Canon:
30 that no such new Conditions ought to be imposed upon Christians
by a less than Divine Authority, and unto which if they do not
submit, though against their Consciences, they shall therefore be
deprived of Communion with the Church. And I wonder that our
Author *could not observe any thing in the Discourse of Evangelical love, that*
35 *was to the purpose, beside a perpetual repetition,* of the outworn story of

2 tool Y; tooll W.   wielded Y; weilded W.   21 as *om.* Y.   29 Canon]
Cannon Y.

unscriptural Ceremonies, and a peculiar uncouthness and obscurity of stile; when as this Plea is there for so many pages distinctly and vigorously insisted on. For it is a childish thing (how high soever our Author magnifies himself in this way of reasoning) either to demand from the Nonconformists a patern of their Worship from the Scripture, who affect therein a Simplicity free from all exterior circumstances, but such as are natural or customary: or else to require of them some particular command against the Cross, or kneeling, and such like Ceremonies, which in the time of the Apostles and many Ages after were never thought of. But therefore general and applicable Rules of Scripture they urge as directions to the Conscience; unto which our Author gives no satisfactory Solution, but by superseding and extinguishing the Conscience, or exposing it to the severest penalties. But here I say then is their main exception, that things indifferent, and that have no proper signature, or significancy to that purpose, should by command be made necessary conditions of Church-Communion. I have many times wished for peaceableness-sake that they had a greater latitude; but if unless they should stretch their Consciences till they tear again, they cannot conform, what remedy? For I must confess that Christians have a better Right and Title to the Church, and to the Ordinances of God there, than the Author had to his Surplice. And that Right is so undoubted and ancient, that it is not to be innovated upon by humane restrictions and capitulations.

Bishop *Bramhall* p. 141. saith, *I do profess to all the World, that the transforming of indifferent Opinions into necessary Articles of Faith, hath been that* Infana Laurus, *or cursed Bay-tree, the cause of all our brawling and contention.* That which he saw in matter of Doctrine he would not discern in Discipline, whereas this among us, the transforming of things, at best indifferent, into necessary points of practice, hath been of as ill consequence. And (to reform a little my seriousness) I shall not let this pass without taking notice that you Mr. *Bayes,* being the most extravagant person in this matter that ever I heard of, as I have shown, you are mad, and so the *Infana laurus*; so I wish you may not prove *that cursed Bay-tree too,* as the Bishop translates it. If you had thought of this, perhaps we might have missed both

10 never] not Y.   22 had Y; hath W.   30 of practice] practice Z.

the Bishops Book and your Preface; for you see that sometimes no
Man hath a worse friend than he brings from home.

It is true, and very piously done, that our Church does declare
that the kneeling at the Lords Supper is not injoyned for adoration
5 of those Elements, and concerning the other Ceremonies as before.
But the *Romanists* (from whom we have them, and who said of old,
we would come to feed on their Meat, as well as eat of their Porridge)
do offer us here many a fair declaration, and distinction in very
weighty matters, to which nevertheless the Conscience of our
10 Church hath not complyed. But in this particular matter of kneeling, which came in first with the Doctrine of Transubstantiation,
the *Romish Church* do reproach us with flat Idolatry, in that we not
believing the real presence in the Bread and Wine, do yet pay to
something or other the same adoration. Suppose the Antient
15 *Pagans* had declared to the Primitive Christians, that the offering
of some grains of Incense was only to perfume the room, or that the
delivering up of their Bibles, was but for preserving the Book more
carefully. Do you think the Christians would have palliated so far,
and colluded with their Consciences? Men are too prone to err on
20 that hand. In the last King's time, some eminent Persons of our
Clergy made an open defection to the Church of *Rome*. One, and he
yet certainly a Protestant, and that hath deserved well of that cause,
writ the Book of *Seven Sacraments*. One in the Church at present,
though certainly no less a Protestant, could not abstain from argu-
25 ing the *Holiness of Lent:* Doctor *Thorndike* lately dead, left for his
Epitaph, *Hic jacet corpus Herberti Thorndike Prœbendarij hujus Ecclesiœ
qui vivus veram Reformatœ Ecclesiœ rationem & modum precibus studiisq;
prosequibatur*, and nevertheless he adds; *Tu Lector requiem ei & beatam
in Christo resurrectionem precare.* Which things I do thus sparingly set
30 down, only to shew the danger of inventive piety; and if Men once
come to add new devices to the Scripture, how easily they slide on
into Superstition. Therefore, although the Church do consider her
self so much as not to alter her Mode unto the fancy of others, yet
I cannot see why she ought to exclude those from Communion,
35 whose weaker consciences cannot for fear of scandal step further.
For the Non-conformists, as to these Declarations of our Church

29 things Y; thing W.   30-1 once come Y; come once W.   36 these] those Y.

against the Reverence to the Creatures of Bread and Wine; and concerning the other Ceremonies as before, will be ready to think they
have as good a plea as that so much commended by our Author
against the clause, *that whosoever should affirm the Wednesday Fast to be
imposed with an intention to bind the Conscience,* should be punished *like* 5
the spreaders of false news; which is, saith *a Learned Prelate plainly to
them that understand it, to evacuate the whole Law. For all humane power
being derived from God, and bound upon our Consciences by his power, not
by Man, he that saith it shall not bind the Conscience, saith it shall be no
Law, it shall have no authority from God, and then it hath none at all; and* 10
*if it be not tyed upon the Conscience, then to break it is no sin, and then to
keep it is no duty. So that a Law without such an intention is a contradiction.
It is a Law only which binds if we please, and we may obey when we have
a mind to it, and to so much we are tyed before the Constitution. But then
if by such a Declaration it was meant, that to keep such Fasting-days was no* 15
*part of a direct Commandment from God, that is, God had not required them
by himself immediately, & so it was abstracting from that Law no duty
Evangelical, it had been below the wisdom of the Contrivers of it, for no man
pretends it, no man saith it, no man thinks it, and they might as well have
declared that that Law was none of the ten Commandments,* p. 59. of his 20
first Book. So much pains does that learned Prelate of his take (who
ever he was) to prove a whole Parliament of *England* Coxcombs.
Now I say that those Ecclesiastical Laws, with such Declarations
concerning the Ceremonies by them injoyned, might, *mutatis mutan-*
dis, be taxed upon the same '*Topick.* But I love not that task, and 25
shall rather leave it to Mr. *Bayes* to paraphrase his learned Prelate.
For he is very good at correcting the impertinence of Laws and
Lawgivers: and though this work indeed be not for his turn at
present, yet it may be for the future. And I have heard a good
Engineer say, That he never fortified any place so, but that he 30
reserved a feeble point, whereby he knew how to take it, if there
were occasion.

   I know a medicine for Mr. *Bayes* his Hiccough (it is but naming
J. O.) but I cannot tell certainly, though I have a shrew'd guess
what is the cause of it. For indeed all his Arguments here are so 35
abrupt and short, that I cannot liken them better, considering too

6 *Prelate* Y; *Pelate* W.   31 whereby Y; by which W.

that frequent and perpetual repetition. Such as this, *Why may not the Soveraign Power bestow this Priviledge upon Ceremony, as well as Use and Custom, by virtue of its prerogative? What greater Immortality is there in them when determined by the Command and Institution of the Prince, than*
5 *when by the consent and institution of the people?* This is the Tap-lash of what he said, p. 110. "When the Civil Magistrate takes upon him to determine any particular Forms of outward Worship, 'tis of no worse Consequence than if he should go about to define the signification of all words used in the Worship of God." And p. 108. of his
10 first Book: "So that all the Magistrates power of instituting significant Ceremonies, &c. can be no more Usurpation upon the CONSCIENCES of Men, than if the Sovereign Authority should take upon it self, as some Princes have done, to define the signification of words." And afterwards: "The same gesture, and actions are
15 indifferently capable of signifying either honour or contumely: and so words; and therefore 'tis necessary their signification should be determined," &c. 'Tis all very well worth reading. P. 441. of his Second Book. " 'Tis no other usurpation upon their Subjects Consciences than if he should take upon him to refine their Language,
20 and determine the proper signification of all phrases imployed in Divine Worship, as well as in Trades, Arts and Sciences." P. 461. of the same; "Once we will so far gratify the tenderness of their Consciences and curiosity of their Fancies, as to promise never to ascribe any other significancy to things than what himself is here
25 content to bestow upon words." And 462. of the same. "So that you see, my Comparison between the signification of Words and Ceremonies stands firm as the Pillars of the Earth, and the Foundations of our Faith. Mr. *Bayes* might, I see, have spared Sir *Salomon's* Sword of the Divine Institution of the Sacraments. Here is the
30 terriblest weapon in all his Armory; and therefore I perceive, reserved by our Duellist for the last onset. And, I who am a great well-wisher to the Pillars of the Earth, or the eight Elephants, lest we should have an Earth-quake; and much more a Servant to the

---

3 *Immortality*] *Immorality* Parker.   5 This is Y; This the W.   6 110]
100 X.   7 'tis] *it is* Y.   9 all words] *all the words* Y.   10 Book: Y;
~. W.   So] *Shewing* Y^{1-4, 6, 7}.   14 gesture] Gestures Parker.   16 'tis] *it is* Y.
17 'Tis] This is Y.   18 'Tis] *It is* Y.   their] his Parker.   21 in Trades]
in all Trades Y.   P. 461 X; P. 1461 W etc.   28 *Salomon's*] *Solomon's* Z.

King's Prerogative, lest we should all fall into confusion; and perfectly devoted to the Foundations of our Faith, lest we should run
out into Popery or Paganism; have no heart to this incounter: lest
if I should prove that the Magistrates absolute unlimited and
uncontrolable Power doth not extend to define the signification of 5
all words, I should thereby not only be the occasion of all those
mischiefs mentioned, but, which is of far more dismal Importance,
the loss of two or three so significant Ceremonies. But though I therefore will not dispute against that Flower of the Princes Crown, yet,
I hope that without doing much harm, I may observe that for the 10
most part they left it to the People, and seldom themselves exercised it. And even *Augustus Cæsar*, though he was so great an Emperour, and so valiant a man in his own person, was used to fly from
a new word though it were single, as studiously as a Mariner would
avoid a Rock for fear of splitting. The difference of one Syllable in 15
the same word hath made as considerable a Controversy as most
have been in the Church, betwixt the *Homousians* and the *Homoiousians*. One letter in the name of Beans in *Languedoc*, one party calling
them *Faves*, and the other *Haves*; as the transposition only of a letter
a, another time in the name of a Goat, by some call'd *Crabe*, and by 20
others *Cabre*, was the loss of more men's lives than the distinguishing but by an Aspiration in *Shiboleth* upon the like occasion. So that
if a man would be learnedly impertinent, he might enlarge here to
show that 'tis as dangerous to take a man by the tongue, as a Bear
by the tooth. And had I a mind to play the Politician, like Mr. 25
Bayes, upon so pleasant and copious a Subject, I would demonstrate
that though the imposition of Ceremonies hath bred much mischief
in the world, yet (shall I not venture too on a word once for tryal)
such a Penetration or Transubstantiation of Language would throw
all into Rebellion and Anarchy, would shake the Crowns of all 30
Princes, and reduce the World into a second *Babel*. Therefore Mr.
Bayes I doubt you were not well advised to make so close an Analogy
betwixt imposing of significant words and significant Ceremonies:
for I fear the Argument may be improved against you, and that

1 all *om.* Y.   9 that] the Y.   13 was] who Y.   15 difference]
differences X.   19–20 letter a, Y; ∼ ∼ W; a *om.* X.   21 *Cabre*] *Crabre* Y.
23 learnedly] learned Z.   28 on a] upon one X.   for tryal] for a tryal X.

Princes finding that of words so impracticable, and of ill consequence, will conclude that of Ceremonies to be no less pernicious.
And the Nonconformists (who are great Traders, you know, in
Scripture, and therefore thrown out of the Temple) will be certainly
on your back. For they will appropriate your pregnant Text of *Let
all things be done decently and in order*, to preaching or praying in an
unknown Tongue, which such an imposition of words would be:
and then, to keep you to your Similitude, they will say too that
your are all Latine Ceremonies, and the Congregation does not
understand them. But were not this Dominion of words so dangerous, (for how many millions of men did it cost your *Roman* Empire
to attain it!) Yet it was very unmannerly in you to assign to
Princes, who have enough beside, so mean a trouble. When you
gave them leave to exercise the Priesthood in person, that was something to the purpose; That was both Honorable, and something
belongs to it that would have help'd to bear the charge. But this
Mint of words will never quit cost, nor pay for the coynage. This
is such a drudgery; that, rather than undergo it, I dare say, there
is no Prince but would resign to you so Pedantical a Soveraignty.
I cannot but think how full that Princes head must be of Proclama-
tions. For, if he published but once a Proclamation to that purpose,
he must forthwith set out another to stamp and declare the signification of all the words contained in it, and then another to appoint
the meaning of all the words in this, and so on: that here is work
cut out in one Paper of State for the whole Privy Council, both
Secretaries of State, and all the Clerks of the Council, for one Kings
Reign, and *in infinitum*. But, I cannot but wonder, knowing how
ambitious Mr. *Bayes* is of the power over words, and jealous of his
own Prerogative of refining Language, how he came to be so liberal
of it to the Prince: Why, the same thing that induced him to give
the Prince a power antecedent and independent to *Christ*, and to
establish what Religion he pleased, &c. Nothing but his spight
against the Non-conformists. I know not that thing in the world,
except a Jest, that he would not part with to be satisfied in that
particular. He hoped doubtless by holding up this Maxim, to obtain that the words of the Declaration of the 15th *March* should be

4 and ... Temple *om*. Y.   14 the *om*. Y.

understood by contraries. You may well think he expected no less
an equivalent, he would never else have permitted the Prince even
to define the signification of all words used in the Worship of God,
and to determine the proper signification of all Phrases imploy'd in
Divine Worship. Nay Mr. *Bayes*, if it be come to that, and you will
surrender your Liturgy to the Prince, I know not what you mean;
for 'tis bound up with your Bible. Was it ever heard that that Book
so sacred, and in which there could not one errour be found by all
the *Presbyterians* at the *Worster-House*-Conference, should, upon so
uncertain a prospect, be now abandon'd so far, as that every word
and Phrase in it may receive a new and contrary signification! But
the King for ought I see likes it well enough as it is (and therefore
I do so too). Yet in case His Majesty should ever think fit to reform
it, and because such kind of work is usually referr'd back to some
of the Clergy; I would gladly put in a *Caveat*, that our Author may
in no case be one of them. For 'tis known that Mr. *Bays* is subject
to a distemper; and who knows but when he is in a fit, as he made
such mad alterations of the fruit of the Spirit in the Epistle for the
day, he may as well insert in some other part of the *Service, Wellfare
poor Macedo for a modest Fool*; and then, *Oh how I hug thee, Dear Heart,
for this!* and pretend that the Supreme Magistrate should stamp
upon it a signification sacred and serious. I would not have spoken
so severely of him, but that his *more laboured periods*, as he calls them,
are so often fill'd with much bolder and more unwholesome trans-
lations. But however that he may not at his better intervals be
wholly unemployed in the work of Uniformity, I should recommend
to him rather to turn the *Liturgy* and the *Rationale* into the Universal Language, and so in time the whole World might come to be of
his Parish.

When he was drawn thus low, did not he, think you, stand need
of tilting? He had done much more service to the Cause, had he
laid by all those cheating Argumentations, and dealt candidly, like
the good Arch Deacon not long since dead; who went about both
Court and Countrey, preaching upon the *Cloke left at Troas, and the
Books, but especially the Parchments*. The honest Man had found out
there the whole Liturgy, the Canonical Habits, and all the Equipage

34 preaching X, Y; preacing W.

of a Conformist. This was something to the matter in hand, to produce Apostolical Example and Authority: And much more to the purpose than that beaten Text of *doing all things decently and in order*.

5　One Argument I confess remains still behind, and that will justifie any thing. 'Tis that which I call'd lately *Rationem ultimam Cleri;* Force, Law, Execution, or what you will have it. I would not be mistaken, as though I hereby meant the body of the *English* Clergy, who have been ever since the Reformation (I say it without dis-
10　paragement to the Foraign Churches) of the most Eminent for Divinity and Piety in all Christendom. And as far am I from cen-suring, under this title, the Bishops of *England*, for whose Function, their Learning, their Persons I have too deep a veneration to speak any thing of them irreverently. But those that I intend only, are a
15　particular bran of persons, who will in spight of Fate be accounted the Church of *England*, and to shew they are Pluralists, never write in a modester Stile than *We*, *We*; nay, even these, several of them, are Men of parts sufficient to deserve a Rank among the Teachers and Governors of the Church. Only what Bishop *Bramhal* saith of
20　*Grotius* his defect in School Divinity;

> *Unum hoc maceror & doleo tibi deesse.*

I may apply to their excess and rigour in matter of Discipline. They want all consideration, all moderation in those things; and I never heard of any of them at any time, who, if they got into Power or
25　Office, did ever make the least experiment or overture towards the peace of the Church and Nation they lived in. They are the *Politick Would-be's* of the Clergy. Not Bishops, but Men that have a mind to be Bishops, and that will do any thing in the World to compass it. And, though Princes have always a particular mark upon these
30　Men, and value them no more than they deserve, yet I know not very well, or perhaps I do know, how it oftentimes happens that they come to be advanced. They are Men of a fiery nature that must always be uppermost, and so they may increase their own Splendor, care not though they set all on flame about them. You

would think the same day that they took up Divinity they divested
themselves of Humanity, & so they may procure & execute a Law
against the Nonconformists, that they had forgot the Gospel.
They cannot endure that Humility, that Meekness, that strictness
of Manners and Conversation, which is the true way of gaining 5
Reputation and Authority to the Clergy; much less can they content themselves with the ordinary and comfortable provision that
is made for the Ministry: But, having wholly calculated themselves
for Preferment, and Grandeur, know or practise no other means to
make themselves venerable but by Ceremony and Severity. Where- 10
as the highest advantage of promotion is the opportunity of condescention, and the greatest dignity in our Church can but raise
them to the Title of *Your Grace*, which is in the Latine *Vestra
Clementia*. But of all these, none are so eager & virulent, as some,
who having had relation to the late times, have got access to 15
Ecclesiastical Fortune, and are resolved to make their best of her. For
so, of all Beasts, none are so fierce and cruel as those that have been
taught once by hunger to prey upon their own kind; as of all Men,
none are so inhumane as the *Canibals*. But whether this be the true
way of ingratiating themselves with a generous and discerning 20
Prince, I meddle not; nor whether it be an ingenuous practice towards those whom they have been formerly acquainted with: but
whatsoever they think themselves obliged to for the approving of
their new Loyalty; I rather commend. That which astonishes me,
and only raises my indignation is, that of all sorts of Men, this kind 25
of Clergy should always be, and have been for the most precipitate,
brutish, and sanguinary Counsels. The former Civil War cannot
make them wise, nor his Majesties Happy Return, good natured;
but they are still for running things up unto the same extreams.
The softness of the Universities where they have been bred, the 30
gentleness of Christianity in which they have been nurtured, hath
but exasperated their nature; and they seem to have contracted no
Idea of wisdom, but what they learnt at School, the Pedantry of
Whipping. They take themselves qualified to Preach the Gospel,
and no less to intermeddle in affairs of State: Though the reach of 35

3 Nonconformists Y; Nonconformists W.   16 *Fortune*] *Fortunes* Y.   21
ingenuous] ingenious Y¹⁻⁴, ⁶, ⁷.   27 brutish X, Y; bruitish W.

their Divinity is but to persecution, and an Inquisition is the height of their Policy.

   And you Mr. *Bayes*, had you lived in the days of *Augustus Cæsar* (be not scandalized, for why may you not bring sixteen hundred
5 years, as well as five hours into one of your Playes?) would not you have made, think you, an excellent Privy Counsellour? His Father too was murdered. Or (to come nearer both to our times, and your resemblance of the late War, which you trumpet always in the Ear of his Majesty) had you happen'd in the time of *Henry* the *fourth* of
10 *France*, should not you have done well in the Cabinet? His Predecessor too was assassinated. No, Mr. *Bayes*, you would not have been for their purpose: They took other measures of Government, and accordingly it succeeded with them. And His Majesty, whose Genius hath much of both those Princes, and who derives half of the
15 Blood in his Veins from the latter, will in all probability not be so forward to hearken to your advice as to follow their Example. For these Kings, Mr. *Bayes*, how negligent soever or ignorant you take 'em to be, have I doubt, a shrewd understanding with them. 'Tis a Trade, that God be thanked, neither you nor I are of, and there-
20 fore we are not so competent Judges of their Actions. I my self have often times seen them, some of them, do strange things, and unreasonable in my opinion, & yet a little while, or sometimes many years after, I have found that all the men in the world could not have contrived any thing better. 'Tis not with them as with you.
25 You have but one Cure of Souls, or perhaps two, as being a Noble-mans Chaplain, to look after: And if you make Conscience of discharging them as you ought, you would find you had work sufficient, without writing your *Ecclesiastical Policies*. But they are the Incumbents of whole Kingdoms, and the Rectorship of the Common
30 people, the Nobility, and even of the Clergy, whom you are prone to *affirm when possest with principles that incline to rebellion and disloyal practices, to be of all Rebels the most dangerous, p.* 49. the care I say of all these, rests upon them. So that they are fain to condescend to many things for peace-sake, and the quiet of Mankind, that your
35 proud heart would break before it would bend to. They do not

think fit to require any thing that is impossible, unnecessary, or wanton, of their people; but are fain to consider the very temper of the Climate in which they live, the Constitution and Laws under which they have been formerly bred, and upon ill occasions to give them good words, and humour them like Children. They reflect 5 upon the Histories of former times, and the present Transactions to regulate themselves by in every circumstance. They have heard that one of your *Roman* Emperours, when his Captain of the Life-Guard came for the Word, by giving it unhandsomely, received a Dagger. They observe how the Parliament of *Poland* will be their 10 Kings Taylor, and among other reasons, because he would not wear their Mode, have suffer'd the *Turk* to enter, as coming nearer their Fashion. Nay, that even *Alexander* the *Great* had almost lost all he had conquered by forcing his Subjects to conform to the *Persian* habit. That the King of *Spain,* when upon a Progress he enters 15 *Biscai,* is pleased to ride with one Leg naked, and above all to take care that there be not any Bishop in his Retinue. So their poeple will pay their Taxes in good Gold and Silver, they demand no Subsidy of so many bushel of Fleas, lest they should receive the same answer with the Tyrant, that the Subject could not furnish that 20 quantity, and besides they would be leaping out still before they could be measured; and should they fine the people for non-payment, they reckon there would be little got by distraining. They have been told that a certain Queen being desired to give a Town-Seal to one of her Cities, lighting from Horse, sate down 25 naked on the Snow, and left them that Impression, and though it caused no disturbance, but all the Town-Leases are Letters-Pattents; Kings do not approve the Example. That the late Queen of *Sweden* did her self no good with saying, *Io non voglio governar le Bestie,* but afterwards resigned. That the occasion of the revolt of *Swizzerland* 30 from the Emperour and its turning Commonwealth, was only the imposing of a Civil Ceremony by a Capricious Governour, who set up a Pole in the high-way with a Cap upon the top of it, to which he would have all Passengers be uncover'd, and do obeyance. One

2 are] as Y.   7–10 They...Dagger *om.* Y.   17 any] a X.   22 measured; Y; ~, W.   fine] finde Y.   24 certain X, Y; cerain W.   34 and do] and to do Y.

sturdy *Swiss*, that would not conform, thereupon overturn'd the Government, as 'tis at large in History. That the King of *Spain* lost *Flanders* chiefly upon introducing the Inquisition. And you now Mr. *Bayes* will think these, and an hundred more that I could tell
5 you, but idle stories, and yet Kings can tell how to make use of 'm. And hence 'tis that in stead of assuming your unhoopable jurisdiction, they are so satisfied with the abundance of their power, that they rather think meet to abate of its exercise by their discretion. The greater their fortune is, they are content to use the less
10 extravagancy. But because I see, Mr. *Bayes*, you are a little deaf on this ear, I will talk somewhat closer to you. In this very matter of Ceremonies, which you are so bent upon, that your mind is always running on't when you should be hearkning to the Sermon; do not you think that the King knows every word you said, although he
15 never gave your Book the reading? That you say, that the Clause 5° *Eliz.* of the *Wednesday*-Fast has been the original of all the Puritan-Disorders. That the Controversy is now reduced onely to two or three Symbolical Ceremonies. That these Ceremonies are things indifferent in their own nature, and have no antecedent necessity,
20 but onely bind as they are commanded. That they signify nothing in themselves but what the Commander pleases. That the Church it self declares that there is nothing of Religion or adoration in them. That they are no parts of Religious Worship. That they are onely Circumstances. That the imposing of a significant Ceremony,
25 is no more than to impose significancy upon a word. That there is not a word of any of these Ceremonies in the Scriptures. That they are in themselves of no great moment and consequence, but 'tis absolutely necessary that Government should injoyn them, to avoid the evil that would follow if they were not determined: and that
30 there cannot be a Pin pull'd out of the Church, but the State immediately totters. Do not you think that the King has considered all these things? I believe he has; and perhaps, as you have minced the matter, he may well think the Nonconformists have very nice Stomachs, that they cannot digest such chopp'd hay: But on the
35 other side, he must needs take you to be very strange men, to cram these in spite down the throats of any Christian. If a man have an

16 5°] 50 X.   22 there] their Z.

Antipathy against any thing, the Company is generally so civil, as to refrain the use of it, however not to press it upon the person. If a man be sick or weak the Pope grants a Dispensation from *Lent*, or Fasting dayes: ay, and from many a thing that strikes deeper in his Religion. If one have got a cold, their betters will force them to be 5 covered. There is no end of Similitudes: but I am led into them by your calling these Ceremonies Pins of the Church. It would almost tempt a Prince that is curious, and that is setled (God be praised) pretty fast in his Throne, to try for experiment, whether the pulling out of one of these Pins would make the State totter. But, Mr. 10 *Bayes*, there is more in it. 'Tis matter of Conscience: and if Kings do, out of discretion, connive at the other infirmities of their People; If great persons do out of civility condescend to their inferiours; and if all men out of common humanity do yield to the weaker; Will your Clergy only be the men, who, in an affair of 15 Conscience, and where perhaps 'tis you are in the wrong, be the onely hard-hearted and inflexible Tyrants; and not only so, but instigate and provoke Princes to be the ministers of your cruelty? But, I say, Princes, so far as I can take the height of things so far above me, must needs have other thoughts, and are past such 20 boyes-play to stake their Crowns against your Pins. They do not think fit to command things unnecessary, and where the profit cannot countervail the hazard. But above all they consider, that God has instated them in the Government of Mankind, with that incumbrance (if it may so be called) of Reason, and that incumbrance 25 upon Reason of Conscience. That he might have given them as large an extent of ground and other kind of cattle for their Subjects: but it had been a melancholy Empire to have been only Supreme Grasiers and Soveraign Shepherds. And therefore, though the laziness of that brutal magistracy might have been more secure, yet the 30 difficulty of this does make it more honourable. That men therefore are to be dealt with reasonably: and conscientious men by Conscience. That even Law is force, and the execution of that Law a greater Violence; and therefore with rational creatures not to be used but upon the utmost extremity. That the Body is in the power 35 of the mind; so that corporal punishments do never reach the

19 so far Y; as far W.   34 rational creatures] a rational creature X.

offender, but the innocent suffers for the guilty. That the Mind is in the hand of God, and cannot correct those perswasions which upon the best of its natural capacity it hath collected: So that it too, though erroneous, is so farr innocent. That the Prince therefore, by how much God hath indued him with a clearer reason, and by consequence with a more enlightned judgment, ought the rather to take heed lest by punishing Conscience, he violate not only his own, but the Divine Majesty. But as to that Mr. *Bayes*, which you still inculcate of the late War, and its horrid Catastrophe, which you will needs have to be upon a religious account: 'Tis four and twenty years ago, and after an *Act of Oblivion*; and for ought I can see, it had been as seasonable to have shown *Cæsars* bloody Coat, or *Thomas a Beckets* bloody Rochet. The chief of the offenders have long since made satisfaction to Justice; and the whole Nation hath been swept sufficiently of late years by those terrible scourges of Heaven: So that methinks you might in all this while have satiated your mischievous appetite. Whatsoever you suffered in those times, his Majesty who had much the greater loss, knowing that the memory of his Glorious Father will always be preserved, is the best Judge how long the revenge ought to be pursued. But if indeed out of your superlative care of his Maiesty and your *Living*, you are afraid of some new disturbance of the same nature, let me so far satisfie you as I am satisfied. The Nonconformists say that they are bound in Conscience to act as far as they can, and for the rest to suffer to the utmost. But because though they do mean honestly, 'tis so hard a Chapter for one that thinks himself in the right to suffer extremities patiently, that some think it impossible; I say next, that it's very seldom seen that in the same age, a Civil War, after such an interval, has been rais'd again upon the same pretences: But Men are all so weary, that he would be knock'd on the head that should raise the first disturbance of the same nature. A new War must have, like a Book that would sell, a new Title. I am asham'd Mr. *Bayes* that you put me on talking thus impertinently (for Policy in us is so). Therefore to be short, the King hath so indulged and obliged the Non-conformists by his late mercy, that if there were any such Knave, there can be no such Fool among them, that

3 its] it X.   30 all so *Errata*; also W.

would ever lift up an ill thought against him. And for you Mr. *Bayes* he is assured of your Loyalty, so that I think you may enjoy your *Living* very peaceably, which I know is all your business. 'Twas well replyed of the *English* man in *Edward* the *fourths* time, to the *French* man that ask'd him insulting, When they should see us there again? *When your sins are greater than ours.* There are as many occasions of War, as there are Vices in a Nation: And therefore it concerns a Prince to be watchful on all hands. But should Kings remember an injury as long as you implacable Divines do, or should we take up Arms upon your Peeks, because your Ecclesiastical Policy is answered, to revenge your quarrel, the World would never be at quiet. Therefore Mr. *Bayes* let all those things of former times alone, and mind your own business; for Kings, believe me, as they have Royal understandings, so have Gentlemens memories.

And now Mr. *Bayes* I think it is time to take my leave, having troubled you with so long a visit. Only before I quit this matter, because I do not love to be accounted singular in my opinion, I will add the judgment of one Author, and that as pertinent as I could pick out to our purpose. I have observed that not only other Princes, but Queen *Elizabeth* too hath the misfortune to be much out of your favour. But for what reason I cannot possibly imagine; for none ever deserved better as to the thing of Uniformity, unless it be the ill luck she had to pass that *impertinent Clause* in the Act 5° *Eliz.* of the *Jejunium Cecilianum.* You cannot, for her sake, indure the Wit or Learning of her times, but say, p. 94. of your second Book, *Though this trifling Artifice of sprinkling little fragments of Wit and Poetry might have passed for Wit and Learning in the days of Queen* Elizabeth, *yet to men of Learning, Reading and Ingenuity, their vulgar use has sullied their lustre, and abated their value.* This is indeed, Mr. *Bayes,* a very labour'd period, and prepared by you, I believe, on purpose as a model of the Wit and Eloquence of your days. But not only so; but p. 483. of the same Book, I think you call her in derision and most spightfully and unmannerly, plain *Old Elsibeth.* And those that knew her humour, think you could not have disobliged her more than in stiling her so; both as a Woman, which Sex never love to

---

10 Peeks *Errata*; Becks W; Pecks Z.   15 Mr.] Master X.   23 5°] of the fifth of X.   32 her] Her Z.

be thought old, and as a Queen, who was jealous lest Men should therefore talk of the succession. Besides the irreverent nick-name you give her, that you might as well have presumed to call her *Queen Bess*, or *Bold Bettrice*. Now to the end that that Queen of
5 famous Memory may have a little female revenge upon you, & to give you a tast of the Wit and Learning even of her times; I will *sprinkle* here one *Fragment*, which not being a *Scholar-like saying of antient Poet or Philosopher*, but of a Reverend Divine, I hope, Mr. *Bayes*, may be less displeasing to you. The Man is *Parker*. Not
10 *Robert Parker*, who writ another Treatise of Ecclesiastical Policy, and the Book *de Cruce*, for which if they had catch'd him, he had possibly gone to the Gallows, or at least the Gallyes. For he was one of those well-meaning Zealots, that are of all Villains the most dangerous. But it is the Arch-Bishop of *Canterbury*, *Parker* (For if I named him
15 before without addition, 'twas what I learnt of you speaking of *Whitgift*) He in his Book *de Antiquitatibus Ecclesiæ Britannicæ*, p. 47. speaking of the slaughter of the Monks of *Bangor*, and so many Christians more, upon the instigation of *Austin* the Monk, who stirred up *Ethilbert* King of *Kent* against them, because they would
20 not receive the Romish Ceremonies; useth these words, *Et sanè illa prima de Romanis Ritibus inducendis per Augustinum tunc excitata contentio, quæ non nisi clade & sanguine innocentium Britannorum poterat extingui; ad nostra recentiora tempora, cum simili pernicie cædeque Christianorum pervenit. Cum enim illis gloriosis ceremoniis à purâ Primitivæ Ecclesiæ sim-*
25 *plicitate recesserunt, non de vitæ sanctitate, de Evangelij prædicatione, de spiritus sancti vi & consolatione multum laborabãt; sed novas indies alter-cationes de novis ritibus per Papas singulos additis, qui neminem tam excelso gradu dignum qui aliquid, ceremoniosi non dicam, monstrosi inauditi & inusitati non adjecisset; instituebant. Suggestaque & scholas fabulis rixisque*
30 *suis implebant. Nam prima Ecclesiæ species simplicior & integro & interno Dei cultu, ab ipso Verbo præscripto, nec vestibus splendidis, nec magnificis structuris decorata, nec auro, argento, gemmisque fulgens fuit: Etsi liceat his exterioribus uti modo animum ab illo interiori & integro Dei cultu non*

---

8 Mr.] Master X.   9 *Parker*. Not Y; ~, not W.   12 least the] least
to the Z.   20 *sanè*] *sunt* Z.   22–3 *extingui*] *sedari* M. Parker.   28 *dignum
qui*] dignum iudicabant, qui M. Parker.   30 *integro &*] integro ac M. Parker.
31 *præscripto, nec*] præscripto candida, nec M. Parker.   *splendidis*] splendida
M. Parker.   33 *illo*] illa M. Parker.

abducant; Curiosis & morosis ritibus ab illâ primævâ & rectâ simplicitate
Evangelicâ degeneravit. Illa autem in Romanâ Ecclesiâ rituum multitudo
ad immensum illius magni Augustini Hipponensis Episcopi temporibus crev-
erat: ut questus sit Christianorum in Ceremoniis & ritibus duriorem tunc
fuisse conditionem quam Judæorum, qui etiamsi tempus Libertatis non ag- 5
noverint, Legalibus tamen sarcinis non humanis præsumptionibus subjicieban-
tur; nam paucioribus in divino cultu quam Christiani Ceremoniis utebantur.
Qui si sensisset quantus deinde per singulos Papas coacervatus cumulus acces-
sit, modum Christianum credo ipse statuisset; qui hoc malum tunc in
Ecclesiâ viderat. Videmus enim ab illâ ceremoniarum contentione nedum 10
Ecclesiam esse vacuam; quin homines alioquin docti atque pii de vestibus &
hujusmodi nugis ad huc, rixoso magis & militari, quam aut philosophico aut
Christiano more inter se digladiantur. These words do run so direct
against the Genius of some men that contributed not a little to the
late Rebellion, and, though so long since writ, do so exactly de- 15
scribe that evil spirit with which some men are even in these times
possest, who seem desirous upon the same grounds to put all things
in combustion, that I think them very well worth the labour of
translating. [And indeed, that first contention then raised by *Augus-*
tine about the introducing of the Romish Ceremonies, which could 20
not be quenched but by the blood & slaughter of the innocent
Britains; hath been continued e'n to our later times, with the like
mischief & murder of Christians. For when once by those glorious
Ceremonies they forsook the pure simplicity of the Primitive
Church, they did not much trouble themselves about Holiness of 25
Life, the preaching of the Gospel, the efficacy and comfort of the
Holy Spirit: but they fell every day into new squabbles about
new-fangled Ceremonies added by every Pope, who reckoned no
man worthy of so high a degree but such as invented somewhat, I
will not say Ceremonious, but monstrous, unheard of, and before 30
unpractised; and they fill'd the Schools and the Pulpits with their
Fables and brawling of such matters. For the first beauty of the

---

1 *abducant*] abducunt M. Parker.   *et*] ac M. Parker.   2 *degeneravit*] degene-
rasse M. Parker.   3 *Hipponensis Episcopi*] Hipponensis in Africa Episcopi
M. Parker.   3–4 *temporibus creverat*] temporibus, ita creverat M. Parker.
4 *&*] ac M. Parker.   *ritibus duriorem*] ritibus ob multitudem duriorem M. Parker.
4–5 *tunc fuisse conditionem om.* X.   8 *si sensisset*] si se sensisset M. Parker.
12 *militari*] militare Y.   26 *and comfort*] and the comfort Y.

Church had more of simplicity and plainness; and was neither adorned with splendid vestments, nor magnificent structures, nor shin'd with gold, silver and precious stones; but with the intire and inward worship of God, as it was by Christ himself prescribed.
5 Although it may be lawful to use these external things, so they do not lead the mind astray from that more inward and intire Worship of God; by those curious and crabbed Rites it degenerated from that antient and right Evangelical Simplicity. But that multitude of Rites in the Romish Church had unmeasurably increased in the
10 times of that great *Augustine* the Bishop of *Hippo*, in so much that he complained that the Condition of Christians, as to Rites and Ceremonies, was then harder than that of the Jews; who although they did not discern the time of their Liberty, yet were onely subjected to Legal burthens, instituted first by God himself, not to
15 humane Presumptions. For they used fewer Ceremonies in the Worship of God than Christians. Who, if he could have foreseen how great a heap of them was afterwards piled up, and added by the several Popes, he himself doubtless would have restrained it within Christian measure, having already perceived this growing evil in
20 the Church. For we see, that even yet the Church is not free from that contention: but men, otherwise learned and pious, do still cut and slash about Vestments and such kind of trifles, rather in a swashbuckler and Hectoring way, than either like Philosophers or like Christians.]

25 Now Mr. *Bayes*, I doubt you must be put to the trouble of writing another Preface against this Arch-bishop. For nothing in your Answerer's Treatise of *Evangelical Love* does so gird or aim at you, for ought I can see, or at those whom you call the Church of *England*, as this Passage. But the last period does so plainly delineate
30 you to the life, that what St. *Austine* did not presage, the Bishop seems to have foreseen most distinctly. 'Tis just your way of writing all along in this matter. You bring nothing sound or solid. Only you think you have got the *Great Secret*, or the *Philosophers Stone* of Railing, and I believe it, you have so multiplied it in *Projection:* and
35 as they into Gold, so you turn every thing you meet with into

11 of Christians] of the Christians Y.   26 another] an; ther Z.   this]
the Z.

Railing. And yet the Secret is not great, nor the *Process* long or difficult, if a man would study it, and make a trade on't. Every Scold hath it naturally. It is but crying Whore first, and having the last word, and whatsoever t'other sayes, cry, Oh. these are your Nonconformist's tricks, Oh you have learnt this of the Puritans in *Grubstreet*. Oh you white-aprond Gossip. For indeed, I never saw so provident a fetch: you have taken in before hand all the Posts of railing, and so beset all the Topicks of just crimination, foreseeing where you are feeble, that if this trick would pass, it were impossible to open ones mouth to finde the least fault with you. For in your first Chapter of your Second Book, beside what you do alwaies in an hundred places when you are at a loss, you have spent almost an hundred pages upon *a Character of the Fanatick deportment toward all Adversaries*. And then on the other side, you have so ingrossed and bought up all the ammunition of Railing, search'd every corner in the Bible, and *Don Quixot* for Powder, that you thought, not unreasonably, that there was not one shot left for a Fanatick. But truth, you see, cannot want words: and she will laugh too sometimes when she speaks, and rather than all fail too, be serious. But what will you say to that of the Arch-bishops, *than either like Philosophers or like Christians?* For the excellency of your Logick, Philosophy and Christianity in all your Books, is either, as in Conscience, to take away the subject of the question: or, as in the Magistrate, having gotten one absurdity, to raise a thousand more from it. So that, except the manufacture and labour of your periods, you have done no more than any School-boy could have done on the same terms. And so, Mr. *Bayes*, Good night.

And now Good-morrow, Mr. *Bayes*; For though it seems so little a time and that you are but now gone to bed, it hath been a whole live-long night, and you have toss'd up and down in many a troublesom dream, and are but just now awaked at the Title page of your book: *A Preface shewing what grounds there are of fears and jealousies of Popery*. It is something artificially couch'd, but looks, as if it did allow, that there are some grounds of fears and jealousies of that nature. But here he words it, *a Consideration what likelihood, or*

---

4 t'other sayes] others say Z. 7 so *om*. X. 13 *toward*] *towards* Y.
15 bought *Errata*; brought W. 26 any] my Z.

how much danger there is of the return of Popery into this Nation. Had he not come to this at last, I should have thought I had been all this while reading a Chapter in *Mountagne's Essayes*; where you finde sometimes scarce one word in the discourse of the matter held forth
5 in the Title. But now indeed he takes up this Argument and debates it to purpose. For I had before begun to show that he had writ not only his two former Books, but especially too this Preface, with an evil eye and aim at his Majesty, and the measures he had taken of Government. And whoever will take the pains to read
10 here, will soon be of my mind. His Majesty had I said, the 15*th* of *March* 1671. issued his Declaration of Indulgence to tender Consciences. He, on the contrary, issues out thereupon, all in haste and as fast as he could write, this his Remonstrance or Manifesto against Indulgence to tender Consciences: and to make his Majesties
15 proceedings more odious, stirs up this seditious matter, of what probability there is of Popery.

And this he discourses, to be sure, in his own imagination very cunningly. For he knows that there was an Act of Parliament in this Kings Reign with a greater penalty than that of 5° *Eliz.* of
20 spreading false News, against reports of this nature. And therefore, he resolves to handle it so warily, that he himself might escape, but might draw others that should answer him, within the danger of that Act, and that he might lay the crime at their doors. But, notwithstanding all his slights and *Legerdemain*, it doth enough detect
25 his malice and ill intention to his Majesties Government, that he should take this occasion, altogether foreign and unseasonable, to raise a publick and solemn discourse through the whole Nation, concerning a matter the most odious and dangerous that could be exposed. So that now, no man can look at the wall, no man can pass
30 by a Book-sellers stall, but he must see *A Preface showing what GROUNDS there are for* FEARS *and* JEALOUSIES *of POPERY.*

It had been something a safer and more dutiful way of writing, A Preface showing the CAUSELESNESS of the Fears and Jealousies of POPERY. For I do not think it will excuse a Witch, to say, That
35 she conjur'd up a Spirit only that she might lay it: nor can there be

a more dexterous and malicious way of calumny, than by making a needless Apology for another, in a criminal Subject. As, suppose I should write a Preface showing what Grounds there are of Fears and Jealousies of *Bayes* his being an Atheist. But this is exactly our Authors method and way of contrivance, whereby, more effectually by far than by any flying Coffee-house tattle, he traduces the State, and by printing so pernicious a question, fills all mens mouths, and beats out all mens eyes with the probability of the return of POPERY. Had he heard any that malignly and officiously talk'd to such a purpose, it had been the part of one so prudent as he is, not to have continued the Discourse. Had he (as he hath a great gift that way) pick'd up out of any mans talk or writing, matter whereof to make an ill story; there was a better and more regular way of proceeding, had he meant honestly to his Majesties Government, to have prevented the evil, and to have brought the offender to punishment. He should have gone to one of the Secretaries of State, or to some other of his Majesties Privy Council, and have given them Information. But, in stead of that, I am afraid that in the survey of this business, we shall find, that even some of them are either accused, or shrowdly mark'd out with a character of our Authors displeasure. Therefore, I will now come nearer to his matter in hand, although it concerns me to be careful of coming too near, nor shall I dwell too long upon so jealous and impertinent a subject.

To consider what likelihood or how much danger there is of the return of Popery into this Nation. The very first word is; *For my part, I know none.* Very well considered. Why then, Mr. *Bayes*, I must tell you, that if I had printed a Book or Preface upon that Argument, I should have thought my self, at least a Fool for my labour. The next considerer is mine Enemy; I mean he is an Enemy to the State, whoever shall foment such discourses without any likelyhood or danger. Yet, Mr. *Bayes*, you know, I have for a good while had no great opinion of your Integrity; neither here. I doubt you prevaricate a little with some body. For, I suppose you cannot be ignorant that some of your superiours of your Robe did, upon the publishing that Declaration, give the Word, and deliver Orders through their Ecclesiastical Camp, to beat up the Pulpit-drums against Popery. Nay,

4 an] and X.

even so much that there was care taken too for arming the *poor
Readers, that though they came short of Preachers in point of efficacy, yet
they might be inabled* to do something *in point of* common *Security*. So
that, though for so many years, some of your Superiours had forgot
there was any such thing in the Nation as a Popish Recusant,
though *Polemical* and *Controversial Divinity* had for so long been hung
up in the Halls, like the rusty obsolete Armour of our Ancestors,
for monuments of Antiquity; and for derision rather than service;
all on a sudden (as if the 15th of *March* had been the 5th of *November*)
happy was he that could climb up first to get down one of the old
Cuirasses, or an Habergeon that had been worn in the dayes of
Queen *Elizabeth*. Great variety there was, and an heavy doo. Some
clapp'd it on all rusty as it was, others fell of oyling and furbishing
their armour: Some piss'd in their Barrels, others spit in their pans,
to scowr them. Here you might see one put on his Helmet the
wrong way: there one buckle on a Back in place of a Breast. Some
by mistake catched up a Socinian or Arminian Argument, and some
a Popish to fight a Papist. Here a Dwarf lost in the accoutrements
of a Giant: there a *Don-Quixot* in an equipage of differing pieces, and
of several Parishes. Never was there such Incongruity and Non-
conformity in their furniture. One ran to borrow a Sword of *Calvin*.
This man for a Musket from *Beza*: that for a Bandeleers even from
Keckerman. But when they came to seek for Match, and Bullet, and
Powder, there was none to be had. The Fanaticks had bought it
all up, and made them pay for it most unconscionably, and through
the nose. And no less sport was it to see their Leaders. Few could
tell how to give the word of Command, nor understood to drill a
Company: They were as unexpert as their Soldiers aukward: and
the whole was as pleasant a spectacle, as the exercising of the
Train'd-bands in —*shire*. But Mr. *Bayes* (for I believe you do nothing
but upon common advice) either this was all intended but for a
false alarum, and was onely for a pretence to take arms against the
Fanaticks (which you might have done without raising all this din
and obloquy against the State, and disquieting his Majesties good
Subjects): or else you did really think (and who can help misappre-

hensions?) that you did know some likelihood or danger of the return of Popery. I crave you mercy Mr. *Bayes*, I took you a little short. *For my part I know none*, you say, *but the Nonconformists boysterous and unreasonable opposition to the Church of England.*

This I confess hath some weight in it. For truly before *I knew none* 5 too. I was of your Opinion Mr. *Bayes*, and believed that Popery could never return into *England* again, but by some very sinister accident. This expression of mine is something uncouth, and therefore because I love to give you satisfaction in all things, Mr. *Bayes*, I will acquaint you with my reason of using it. *Henry* the *fourth* of 10 *France*, his Majesties Grandfather, lived (you know) in the dayes of Queen *Elizabeth*. Now the wit of *France* and *England*, as you may have observed, is much of the same mode, and hath at all times gone much after the same current Rate and Standard; only there hath been some little difference in the alloy, and advantage or disad- 15 vantage in the exchange according to mens occasions. Now *Henry the fourth*, was (you know too) a Prince like Bishop *Bramhall*, *of a brave and enterprising temper, and had a mind large and active enough to have managed the Roman Empire at its utmost extent; and* particularly *as) far as the prejudice of the age (Old Elsibeths Age) would permit him)* he was 20 very wittie and facetious, and the Courtiers strove to humor him alwaies in it, and increase the mirth. So one night after supper he gave them a Subject (which recreation did well enough in those times, but were now insipid) upon which, like Boyes at *Westminster*, they should make a *French* Verse extempore. The Subject was, *Un* 25 *Accident sinistre*. Straight answers, I know not whether 'twas *Bassompierre* or *Aubignè*:

> *Un sinistre Accident & un Accident sinistre;*
> *De veoir un Pere Capuchin chevaucher un Ministre.*

For when I said, to see Popery return here, would be a very sinister 30 accident; I was just thinking upon that story; the Verses, to humour them in translation, being only this,

> *O what a trick unlucky, and how unlucky a trick,*
> *To see friend Doctor Patrick, bestrid by Father Patrick!*

---

19 *utmost*] *greatest* Parker.   particularly X, Y; particulary W.   27 *Aubignè*:
Ed.; *Aubigne*. Y; *Obignè*: W.   31 story; the] story of the Y.

Which seem'd to me would be the most improbable and preposterous spectacle that ever was seen; and more ridiculous for a sight,
than the *Friendly Debate is* for a Book. And yet if Popery come in,
this must be and worse.

5   But now I see there is some danger by the Nonconformists opposition to the Church of *England*. And now your business is all fixed.
The Fanaticks are ready at hand to bear the blame of all things.
Many a good job have I seen done in my time upon pretence of the
Fanaticks. I do not think Mr. *Bayes* ever breaks his shins, but it is
10   by stumbling upon a Fanatick. And how shall they bring in Popery?
why thus, three wayes. *First, By creating disorders and disturbances in
the State. Secondly, By the assistance of Atheism and Irreligion. Thirdly,
By joyning with crafty and Sacrilegious Statesmen in confederacy.* Now
here I remark two things. One, that however you do not find that
15   the Fanaticks are inclinable to Popery, only they may accommodate
it by creating disturbances in the State. Another is, that I see these
Gentlemen, the Phanaticks, the Atheists, and the Sacrilegious
Statesmen are not yet acquainted; but you have appointed them a
meeting (I believe it must be at your Lodgings or no where;) and
20   I hope you will treat them handsomly. But I think it was not so
wisely done, nor very honestly, Mr. *Bayes*, to lay so dangerous a
Plot as this; and instruct men that are strangers yet to one another,
how to contrive together such a Conspiracy. But first to your first.
     The *Fanaticks you say may probably raise disturbance in the State.* For
25   they *are so little friends to the present Government, that their enmity to that
is one of the main grounds of their quarrel to the Church.* But now, though
I must confess it is very much to your purpose, if you could perswade men so, I think you are clear out, and misrepresent here the
whole matter. For I know of no enmity they have to the Church
30   it self, but what it was in her power always to have remedied, and
so it is still. But such as you it is that have always strove by your
leasings to keep up a strangeness and misunderstanding betwixt the
King and his people; and all the mischief hath come on't does lye
much at your door. Whereas they, as all the rest of Man-kind, are

2–3 and . . . Book. *om.* Y.   3 *Friendly* X, Z; *Frienly* W etc.   9 breaks]
brake Y.   32 leasings] leasing Y.   33 mischief hath] mischief that
hath X.   33–4 lye much] much lye Y.

men for their own ends too: And no sooner hath the King shown
them this late favour, but you Mr. *Bayes*, and your partners reproach them for being too much friends to the Prerogative. And
no less would they be to the Church, had they ever at any age in
any time found her in a treatable temper. I know nothing they 5
demand, but what is so far from doing you any harm, that it would
only make you better. But that indeed is the harm, that is the thing
you are afraid of. Here our Author divides the discourse into a
great Elogy of the Church of *England*; that if he were making her
Funeral Sermon, he could not say more in her commendation; and 10
a contrary invective against the Nonconformists, upon whom (as
if all he had said before had been nothing) he unloads his whole
Leystall, and dresseth them up all in *Sambenitas*, painted with all the
flames & Devils in hell, to be led to the place of Execution, & there
burnt to ashes. Nevertheless I find on either side only the natural 15
effect of such Hyperboles and Oratory, that is, not to be believed.
The Church of *England* (I mean as it is by Law established, lest you
should think I equivocate) hath such a stock of solid and deserved
reputation, that it is more than you (Mr. *Bayes*) can spoil or deface
by all the Pedantry of your commendation. Only there is that 20
partie of the Clergy, that I not long ago described, and who will
alwaies presume to be the only Church of *England*, who have been
a perpetual Eye-sore, that I may not say a Canker and Gangreen in
so perfect a beauty. And, as it joyes my heart to hear any thing
well said of her; so, I must confess, it stirs my choler, when I hear 25
those men pride and boast themselves under the Mask of her
Authority. Neither did I therefore approve of an expression you
here use: *The Power of Princes would be a very precarious thing without
the assistance of Ecclesiasticks, and all Government do's & must ow its quiet
and continuance to the Churches Patronage.* That is as much as to say, 30
That but for the assistance of your *Ecclesiastical Policy*, Princes might
go a begging: and that the Church, that is you, have the *Jus patro-
natus* of the Kingdom, and may present whom you think fitting to
the Crown of *England*. This is indeed something like the return of
Popery; and right 35

Petra dedit Petro, Petrus Diadema Rudolpho.

1 King] Ling Y.   2 this] his Y.

The Crown were surely well help'd up, if it were to be held at your convenience, and the Emperour must lead the Patriarchs Ass all his life-time. And little better do I like your *We may rest satisfied in the present Security of the Church of* England, *under the Protection of a wise and gracious Prince: especially when besides the impregnable confidence that we have from his own Inclination, it is so manifest, that he never can forsake it either in Honour or Interest.* This is a prety way of cokesing indeed, while you are all this while cutting the grass under his feet, and animating the people against the exercise of his Ecclesiastical Supremacy. Men are not so plain-hearted, but they can see through this oblique Rhetorication and Sophistry. If there be no danger in his time of taking a *Pin out of the Church* (for that it is you intend) why do you then speak of it in his time, but that you mean mischief? but here you do not only mow the grass under his feet, but you take the pillow from under his head. *But should it ever happen that any King of* England *should be prevail'd with to deliver up the Church, he had as good at the same time resign up his Crown.* This is prety plain dealing, and you have doubtless secur'd hereby that Princes Favour: I should have thought it better Courtship in a Divine, to have said, O King, Live for ever. But I see Mr. *Bayes*, that you and your Partners are very necessary men, and it were dangerous disobliging you. But as in this imprudent and nauseous discourse, you have all along appropriated or impropriated all the Loyalty from the Nobility, the Gentry and the Commonalty, and dedicated it to the Church; So, I doubt, you are a little too immoderate against the body of the Nonconformists. You represent them, to a man, to be all of them of Republican Principles, most pestilent, and, *eo nomine*, enemies to Monarchy; Traytors and Rebells; such miscreants as never was in the world before, and fit to be pack'd out of it with the first Convenience. And, I observe, that all the Argument of your Books is but very frivolous and trivial: onely the memory of the late War serves for demonstration, and the detestable sentence & execution, of his late Majesty is represented again upon the Scaffold; and you having been, I suspect, better acquainted with

---

1 help'd *Errata*; held W.   6 *Inclination*] *Inclinations* Parker.   12 intend] intended X.   14 but] bus Y.   22 as *om.* X.   29 was] were Z. 31 Books] Book Y.

Parliament Declarations formerly upon another account, do now apply and turn them all over to prove that the late War was wholly upon a Fanatical Cause, and the dissenting party do still goe big with the same Monster. I grew hereupon much displeased with my own ignorance of the occasion of those Troubles so near our own times, and betook my self to get the best Information concerning them, to the end that I might, if it appear'd so, decline the dangerous acquaintance of the Nonconformists, some of whom I had taken for honest men, nor therefore avoided their Company. But I took care nevertheless, not to receive Impressions from any of their party; but to gather my lights from the most impartial Authorities that I could meet with. And I think I am now partly prepared to give you, Mr. *Bayes*, some better satisfaction in this matter. And because you are a dangerous person, I shall as little as possible, say any thing of my own, but speak too before good Witnesses. First of all therefore, I will without farther Ceremony, fall upon you with the but-end of another Arch-bishop. 'Tis the Arch-bishop of *Canterbury*, *Abbot*, in the Narrative under his own hand concerning his disgrace at Court in the time of his late Majesty. I shall onely in the way demand excuse, if, contrary to my fashion, the names of some eminent persons in our Church long since dead, be reviv'd here under no very good character; and most particularly that of Archbishop *Laud*, who, if for nothing else, yet for his learned Book against *Fisher*, deserved far another Fate than he met with, and ought not now to be mentioned without due honour. But those names having so many years since escaped the Press, it is not in my power to conceal them; and I believe Archbishop *Abbot* did not write but upon good Consideration.

This I have premised for mine own Satisfaction, and I will add one thing more, Mr. *Bayes*, for yours. That whereas the things now to be alledged relate much to some Impositions of Money in the late King's time, that were carryed on by the Clergy; I know you will presently be ready to carp at that, as if the Nonconformists had, and would be alwaies enemies to the Kings supply. Whereas, Mr. *Bayes*, if I can do the Nonconformists no good, I am resolv'd I will do them no harm, nor desire that they should ly under any imputation on

23 if *om.* Z.

my account. For I write by mine own advice, and what I shall
alledge concerning the Clergies intermedling with supplies, is upon
a particular aversion, that I have upon good reason, against their
disposing of our Money. And, Mr. *Bayes*, I will acquaint you with
the Reason, which is this. 'Tis not very many years ago that I used
to play at *Picket*; And there was a Gentleman of your robe a *Dig-*
nitary of Lincoln, very well known and remembred in the Ordinaries,
but being not long since dead, I will save his name. Now I used to
play *Pieces*, and this Gentleman would always go half a Crown
with me, and so all the while he sat on my hand he very honestly
gave the Sign, so that I was alwaies sure to lose. I afterwards discovered it, but of all the money that ever I was cheated of in my
life, none ever vexed me so, as what I lost by his occasion. And ever
since, I have born a great grudge against their fingring of any thing
that belongs to me. And I have been told, and show'd the place
where the man dwelt in the late King's time near *Hampton Court*,
that there was one that used to rob on the highway, in the habit
of a Bishop, and all his fellows rid too in Canonical Coats. And I can
but fansy how it madded those, that would have perhaps been content to relieve an honest Gentleman in distress, or however would
have been less griev'd to be robb'd by such an one, to see themselves so *Episcopally* pillaged. Neither must it be less displeasing
alwaies to the Gentry and Commonalty of *England*, that the Clergy
(as you do Mr. *Bayes*) should tell them that they are never *sui Juris*,
not only as to their Consciences, but even as to their Purses; and
you should pretend to have this *power of the Keyes* too, where they
lock their Money. Nay, I dare almost aver upon my best observation, that there never was, nor ever will be a Parliament in *England*,
that could or can refuse the King supplies proportionable to his
occasions, without any need of recourse to extraordinary wayes; but
for the pickthankness of the Clergy, who will alwaies presume to
have the thanks and honour of it, nay, and are ready always to
obstruct the Parliamentary Aids, unless they may have their own
little project pass too into the bargain, and they may be gratified
with some new *Ecclesiastical Power*, or some new Law against the
Fanaticks. This is the naked truth of the matter. Whereas *English*

1 mine] my Y.   21 robb'd] rob'd Y.   31 for] to Z.

men alwayes love to see how their money goes, and if there be any interest or profit to be got by it, to receive it themselves. Therefore Mr. *Bayes* I will go on with my business, not fearing all the mischief that you can make of it.

'There was, *saith he*, one *Sibthorp*, who not being so much as 5 Batchelor of Arts, by the means of Doctor *Pierce* Vice-Chancelor of *Oxford*, got to be confer'd upon him the title of Doctor. This Man was Vicar of *Brackley* in *Northamptonshire*, and hath another Benefice. This Man preaching at *Northampton*, had taught, that Princes had power to put Poll-money upon their Subjects heads. His being a 10 Man of a low fortune, conceiv'd the putting his Sermon in Print might gain favour at Court, and raise his fortune higher.' It was at the same time that the business of the Loan was on foot. In the same Sermon 'he called that Loan a Tribute, Taught that the Kings dutie is first to direct and make Laws. That nothing may excuse 15 the subject from active obedience, but what is against the Law of God or Nature, or impossible; that all Antiquity was absolutely for absolute obedience in all civil and temporal things.' And the imposing of Poll-monie by Princes, he justifi'd *out of* St. *Matthew*: And in the matter of the *Loan*, *What a Speech is this*, saith the Bishop, *he* 20 *observes the forwardness of the Papists to offer double*. For this Sermon was sent to the Bishop from Court, and he required to Licence it, not under his Chaplin, but his own hand. But he, not being satisfi'd of the Doctrine delivered, sent back his reasons why he thought not fit to give his approbation, and unto these Bishop *Laud*, who was 25 in this whole business, and a rising Man at Court, *undertook an answer*. 'His life in *Oxford*, saith Arch-bishop *Abbot*, was to pick quarrels in the Lectures of publick Readers, and to advertise them to the Bishop of *Durham* that he might fill the Ears of King *James* with discontent against the honest men that took pains in their 30 places, and setled the Truth (which he call'd Puritanism) in their Auditors. He made it his work to see what Books were in the Press, and to look over Epistles Dedicatory, and Prefaces to the Reader, to see what faults might be found. 'Twas an observation what a

sweet Man this was like to be, that the first observable act he did, was the marrying of the Earl of *D.* to the Lady *R.* when she had another Husband a Nobleman, and divers Children by him.' Here he tells how, for this very cause, King *James* would not a great while
5 endure him, 'till he yielded at last to Bishop *Williams* his importunity, whom notwithstanding he straight strove to undermine, and did it at last to purpose: for, saith the Archbishop, 'Verily, such is his undermining nature, that he will under-work any Man in the World, so he may gain by it. *He call'd in the Bishop of* Durham,
10 Rochester, *and* Oxford, tryed men for such a purpose, to the answering of my Reasons, and the whole stile of the Speech, runs We, We. In my memory, Doctor *Harsnet* then Bishop of *Chichester,* and now of *Norwich (as he came afterward to be Arch-bishop of* York) preached at White-Hall upon, *Give unto Cæsar the things that are Cæsars*; a Ser-
15 mon that was afterwards burned, teaching that Goods and Money were Cæsars, and so the Kings: Whereupon King *James* told the Lords and Commons that he had failed in not adding According to the Laws and Customs of the Countrey wherein they did live. But *Sibthorp* was for absolutely absolute. So that if the King had sent to
20 me for all my Money and Goods, and so to the Clergy. I must by *Sibthorps* proportion send him all. If the King should send to the City of *London* to command all their wealth, they were bound to do it. I know the King is so gracious he will attempt no such matter; but if he do it not, the defect is not in these flattering Divines.' Then
25 he saith, reflecting again upon the Loan which *Sibthorp* called a Tribute. 'I am sorry at heart, the King's Gracious Majesty should rest so great a Building on so weak a Foundation, the Treatise being so slender, and without substance, but that proceeded from an hungry Man.' Then he speaks of his own case as to the licensing
30 this Book, in parallel to the Earl of *Essex* his divorce, which to give it more authority, *was to be ratified judicially by the Arch-bishop.* He concludes how finally he refused his approbation to this Sermon,

6 strove] drove Z.   7 it *om.* Y.   8 undermining] aspiring Abbot.
9 so he] so that he Z.   13 *afterward] afterwards* Y.   *be Arch-bishop] be the Arch-bishop* Z.   15 afterwards Y; afterwrds W.   17 According Y; according W.   21 send X, Y; sent W; have sent Abbot.   24 these] their Abbot.
26 King's Gracious Majesty] King, my gracious Master Abbot.   28 that proceeded] that it proceeded Abbot.   30 this] of his Z.   31 *judicially] judiciously* Z.

and saith, 'it was thereupon carried to the Bishop of *London*, who
gave a great and stately allowance of it, the good Man not being
willing that any thing should stick with him that came from Court,
as appears by a Book commonly called the seven Sacraments, which
was allowed by his Lordship with all the errours, which have been   5
since expunged.' And he adds a pretty story of one Doctor *Woral*,
the *Bishop of* London's *Chaplain, Scholar good enough, but a free fellow-
like man, and of no very tender Conscience*, who before it was Licensed
by the Bishop, *Sibthorps* Sermon being brought to him, *hand over head
approved it, and subscribed his name*. But afterwards hearing more of it,   10
went to a Counsel at the *Temple*, who told him, that by that Book
there was no Meum nor Tuum left in England, *and if ever the Tide turn'd
he might come to be hang'd for it*, and thereupon *Woral scraped out his
name again*, and left it to his Lord to License. Then the Arch-Bishop
takes notice of the *instructions for that Loan*. 'Those that refused, to   15
be sent for Souldiers to the King of *Denmark*. Oaths to be administred with whom they had conference; and who disswaded them,
such persons to be sent to prison, &c. He saith that he had complain'd thrice of *Mountagues* Arminian Book, to no purpose: *Cosins*
put out his Book of seven Sacraments (strange things) but I knew   20
nothing of it, but as it pleased my Ld of *Durham* and the Bp of *Bath*,
so it went.' In conclusion, the good Arch-bishop for refusing this
License of *Sibthorps* Sermons, was, by the underworking of his adversaries, first commanded from *Lambeth*, and confined to his house
in *Kent*, and afterwards sequestred, and a Commission passed to   25
exercise the Archiepiscopall Jurisdiction to the Bishops of *London*,
Durham, Rochester, Oxford, and Bishop *Laud* (who from thence arose
in time to be the Arch-bishop.) If I had leisure, how easy a thing
it were for to extract out of this Narrative a just parallel of our
Author, even almost upon all points: but I am now upon a more   30
serious subject, and therefore shall leave the Application to his own
ingenuity, and the good intelligence of the Reader.

About the same time (for I am speaking within the circle of 2°
3°, and 4°. *Caroli*) that this Book of *Sibthorps*, called *Apostolical*

18 such . . . prison] divers were to be imprisoned Abbot.   19 Book]
Y; -∽ W.   22 *so it went*] So the World did read Abbot.   29 this Y; the W.
30 points: Y; ∼? W.   33–4 2° 3°, and 4°] 20, 30 and 40 Z.

8124228   K

Obedience, was printed, there came out another of the same stamp, intitled *Religion and Allegiance*, by one Doctor *Manwaring*. It was the substance of two Sermons preached by him at *Whitehall*, beside what of the same nature at his own Parish of Saint *Giles*. Therein

5 he delivered for truth, 'That the King is not bound to observe the Laws of the Realm concerning the Subjects rights and liberties, but that his Royal word and command in imposing Loans and Taxes without common consent in Parliament, does oblige the Subjects Conscience upon pain of eternal Damnation. That those who

10 refused to pay this Loan offended against the Law of God, and the Kings supream Authority, and became guilty of Impiety, Disloyalty, and Rebellion. That the Authority of Parliament was not necessary for the raising of Aids and Subsidies, and the slow proceedings of such great Assemblies were not fitted for the supply of the States

15 urgent necessities, but would rather produce sundry impediments to the just designs of Princes.' And after he had been questioned for this doctrine, nevertheless he preached again, 'That the King had right to order all as to him should seem good, without any mans consent. That the King might, in time of necessity demand Aid,

20 and if the Subjects did not supply him, the King might justly avenge it. That the Propriety of Estate and Goods was ordinarily in the Subject, but extraordinarily in the King: that in case of the King's need, he hath right to dispose them.' He had besides, entring into comparison, called the refusers of the Loan 'temporal Recu-

25 sants, and said, the same disobedience that they (the Papists as they then called them) practise in spirituals, that or worse, some of our side, if ours they be, dare to practise in temporals.' And he aggravated further upon them under the resemblance of *Turks*, *Jews*, *Corah*, *Dathan* and *Abiram*. 'Which last, said he, might as well liken

30 themselves to the three Children; or *Theudas* and *Judas*, the two Incendiaries in the daies of *Cæsar*'s tribute, might as well pretend their Cause to be like that of the *Maccabees*, as what the Refusers alledged in their own defence.'

I should not have been so large in these particulars, had they been

35 onely single and volatile Sermons, but because this was then the

9 That those] That that those Z.   13 the *om*. X.

Doctrine of those persons that pretended to be the Church of *England*. The whole Quire sung that Tune, and in stead of the Common Law of *England*, and the Statutes of Parliament, that part of the Clergy had invented these *Ecclesiastical Laws*, which according to their predominancy, were sure to be put in execution. So that 5 between their own Revenue, which must be held *Jure Divino*, as every thing else that belong'd to them, and the Prince's that was *Jure Regio*, they had not left an inch of propriety for the Subject. It seem'd that they had granted themselves *Letters of Reprisal* against the Laity, for the losses of the Church under *Henry the Eighth*, and 10 that they would make a greater havock upon their Temporalties in retaliation. And indeed, having many times since ponder'd with my greatest and earnest impartiality, what could be the true reason of the spleen that they manifested in those daies, on the one hand against the *Puritans*, and on the other against the *Gentry*, (for it was 15 come, they tell me, to *Jack Gentleman*) I could not devise any cause, but that the Puritans had ever since the Reformation, obstructed that laziness and splendor which they injoyed under the Popes Supremacy, and the Gentry had (sacrilegiously) divided the *Abby-Lands*, and other fat morsels of the Church at the Dissolution, and 20 now was the time to be revenged on them.

While therefore the Kingdom was turned into a Prison, upon occasion of this *Ecclesiastical Loan*, and many of the eminentest of the Gentry of *England* were under restraint, they thought it seasonable to recover once again their antient Glory, and to *Magnificate* 25 the Church with triumphal Pomp and Ceremony. The three Ceremonies that have the Countenance of Law, would not suffice, but they were all upon new Inventions, and happy was he that was endued with that capacity, for he was sure before all others to be preferrd. There was a *Second* Service, the *Table* set *Altar-wise*, and 30 to be called the *Altar*; *Candles, Crucifixes, Paintings, Images, Copes, bowing to the East, bowing to the Altar*, and so many several Cringes & Genuflexions, that a man unpractised stood in need to entertain both a Danceing Master and a Remembrancer. And though these things were very uncouth to *English* Protestants, who naturally 35

10 *Eighth* Y; *Eight* W.   16 *Gentleman* Y; ~. W.   26 triumphal] triumphant X.   31 *Altar*; Y; ~, W.   *Images* Y; *Imagery* W.

affect a plainness of fashion, especially in sacred things; yet, if those Gentlemen could have contented themselves with their own Forma-litie, the Innovation had been more excusable. But many of these Additions, and to be sure, all that had any colour of Law, were so
5 imposed and prest upon others, that a great part of the Nation was e'n put as it were to fine and ransom upon this account. What Censures, what Excommunications, what Deprivations, what Im-prisonments? I cannot represent the misery and desolation, as it hath been represented to me. But wearied out at home, many
10 thousands of his Majesties Subjects, to his and the Nations great loss, thought themselves constrained to seek another habitation, and every Country, even though it were among Savages and Cani-balls, appear'd more hospitable to them than their own.

    And, although I have been told by those that have seen both,
15 that our Church did even *then* exceed the *Romish* in Ceremonies and Decorations; and indeed, several of our Church did thereby fre-quently mistake their way, and from a *Popish* kind of Worship, fell into the *Roman Religion*; yet I cannot upon my best judgment believe, that that party had generally a design to alter the Religion
20 so far, but rather to set up a new kind of *Papacy* of their own, here in *England*. And it seemed they had, to that purpose, provided themselves of a new Religion in *Holland*. It was *Arminianism*, which though it were the *Republican* Opinion there, and so odious to King *James*, that it helped on the death of *Barnevelt*, yet now they under-
25 took to accommodate it to Monarchy and Episcopacy. And the choice seemed not imprudent. For on the one hand, it was removed at so moderate a distance from *Popery*, that they should not dis-oblige the *Papists* more than formerly, neither yet could the *Puri-tans*, with justice reproach these men, as *Romish Catholicks*; and yet,
30 on the other hand, they knew it was so contrary to the antient reformed Doctrine of the Church of *England*, that the *Puritans* would never imbrace it, and so they should gain this pretence further to keep up that convenient and necessary Quarrel against Non-conformity. And accordingly it happened, so that here again was
35 a new *Shiboleth*. And the *Calvinists* were all studiously discounten-anced, and none but an *Arminian* was judg'd capable and qualified

    1 affect]▮affects X.

for imployment in the Church. And though the King did declare, as I have before mentioned, that *Mountague's Arminian* Book had been the occasion of the Schisms in the Church; yet care was immediately taken, by those of the same robe and party, that he should be the more rewarded and advanced. As also it was in *Man-* 5 *warings* Case: who though by Censure in Parliament made incapable of any Ecclesiastical preferment, was straight made Rector of *Stamford-Rivers* in *Essex*, with a Dispensation to hold too his Living in St. *Giles's*. And all dexterity was practised to propagate the same Opinions, and to suppress all Writings or Discourses to the con- 10 trary.

So that those who were of understanding in those dayes tell me, that a man would wonder to have heard their kind of preachings. How in stead of the practical Doctrine which tends to the reforming of Mens Lives and Manners, all their Sermons were a very Mash of 15 *Arminian* Subtilties, of Ceremonies, and Decency, and of *Man-waring*, and *Sibthorpianism* brew'd together; besides that in their conversation they thought fit to take some more licence the better to *dis-Ghibelene* themselves from the *Puritans*. And though there needed nothing more to make them unacceptable to the sober part 20 of the Nation, yet moreover they were so exceeding *pragmatical*, so intolerably ambitious, and so desperately proud, that scarce any Gentleman might come near the Tayle of their Mules. And many things I perceive of that nature do even yet stick upon the stomacks of the *Old Gentlemen* of those times. For the *English* have been always 25 very tender of their Religion, their Liberty, their Propriety, and (I was going to say) no less of their Reputation. Neither yet do I speak of these things with passion, considering at more distance how natural it is for men to desire to be in Office, and no less natural to grow proud and intractable in Office; and the less a Clergyman 30 is so, the more he deserves to be commended. But these things before mentioned, grew yet higher, after that Bishop *Laud* was once not only exalted to the See of *Canterbury*, but to be chief Minister. Happy had it been for the King, happy for the Nation, and happy for himself, had he never climbed that Pinacle. For whether it be 35

2 *Arminian* Y; *In parentheses* W.   13 preachings] preaching Y.   15 Mash Errata; Mask W.

or no, that the Clergy are not so well fitted by Education, as others for Political Affairs, I know not; though I should rather think they have advantage above others, and even if they would but keep to their *Bibles*, might make the best Ministers of State in the world; yet it is generally observed that things miscarry under their Government. If there be any Counsel more precipitate, more violent, more rigorous, more extreme than other, that is theirs. Truly I think the reason that God does not bless them in Affairs of State, is, because he never intended them for that imployment. Or if Government, and the preaching of the Gospel, may well concur in the same person, God therefore frustrates him, because though knowing better, he seeks and manages his greatness by the lesser and meaner *Maxims*. I am confident the Bishop studied to do both God and his Majesty good service, but alas how utterly was he mistaken. Though so learned, so pious, so wise a Man, he seem'd to know nothing beyond *Ceremonies, Arminianism,* and *Manwaring.* With that he begun, and with that ended, and thereby deform'd the whole reign of the best Prince that ever wielded the *English* Scepter.

For his late Majesty being a Prince truly Pious and Religious, was thereby the more inclined to esteem and favour the Clergy. And thence, though himself of a most exquisite understanding, yet thought he could not trust it better than in their keeping. Whereas every man is best in his own Post, and so the Preacher in the Pulpit. But he that will do the Clergyes drudgery, must look for his reward in another World. For they having gained this Ascendent upon him, resolv'd whatever became on't to make their best of him; and having made the whole business of State their *Arminian* Jangles, and the persecution for Ceremonies, did for recompence assign him that imaginary absolute Government, upon which Rock we all ruined.

For now was come the last part of the *Archbishops* indiscretion; who having strained those strings so high here, and all at the same time, which no wise man ever did; he moreover had a mind to try the same dangerous Experiment in *Scotland,* and sent thither the Book of the *English Liturgy,* to be imposed upon them. What followed thereupon, is yet within the compass of most Mens

6 there] their X.   18 wielded Y; weilded W.   22 thought *om.* X.
24 drudgery] druggery X.

memories. And how the War broke out, and then to be sure Hell's
broke loose. Whether it were a War of Religion, or of Liberty, is
not worth the labour to enquire. Which-soever was at the top,
the other was at the bottom; but upon considering all, I think the
Cause was too good to have been fought for. Men ought to have 5
trusted God; they ought and might have trusted the King with
that whole matter. The *Arms of the Church are Prayers and Tears*, the
Arms of the Subjects are Patience and Petitions. The King himself
being of so accurate and piercing a judgment, would soon have felt
where it stuck. For men may spare their pains where Nature is at 10
work, and the world will not go the faster for our driving. Even as
his present Majesties happy Restauration did it self, so all things
else happen in their best and proper time, without any need of our
officiousness.

But after all the fatal consequences of that Rebellion, which can 15
only serve as Sea-marks unto wise Princes to avoid the Causes, shall
this sort of Men still vindicate themselves as the most zealous
Assertors of the Rights of Princes? They are but at the best *well-
meaning Zealots*. Shall, to decline so pernicious Counsels, and to
provide better for the quiet of Government, be traduced as the 20
Author does here, under these odious terms of *forsaking the Church,
and delivering up the Church*? Shall these Men always presume to
usurp to themselves that venerable stile of the *Church of England*?
God forbid. The *Independents* at that rate would not have so many
distinct Congregations as they. There would be *Sibthorps*-Church, 25
and *Manwarings*-Church, and *Mountagues*-Church, and a whole Bed-
roll more, whom for decencies-sake I abstain from naming. And
every Man that could invent a new Opinion, or a new Ceremony,
or a new Tax, should be a new Church of *England*.

Neither, as far as I can discern, have this sort of the Clergy since 30
his Majesties return, given him better incouragement to steer by
their Compass. I am told, that preparatory to that, they had frequent meetings in the City, I know not whether in *Grubstret*, with
the Divines of the other party, and that there in their Feasts of
Love, they promised to forget all former Offences, to lay by all 35

Animosities, that there should be a new Heaven, and a new Earth, all Meekness, Charity, and Condescention. His Majesty I am sure sent over his Gracious Declaration of *Liberty to tender Consciences,* and upon his coming over, seconded it with his Commission under the

5 broad Seal, for a Conference betwixt the two parties, to prepare things for an Accommodation, that he might confirm it by his Royal Authority. Hereupon what do they? Notwithstanding this happy Conjuncture of his Ma^stie's Restauration, which had put all Men into so good a humour, that upon a little moderation & temper of

10 things, the Nonconforminsts could not have stuck out; some of these Men so contriv'd it, that there should not be the least abatement to bring them off with Conscience, and (which insinuates into all men) some little Reputation. But to the contrary; several unnecessary additions were made, only because they knew they

15 would be more ingrateful & *stigmatical* to the Nonconformists. I remember one in the *Letany,* where to *False Doctrine and Heresie,* they added *Schism,* though it were to spoil the *Musick* and cadence of the period; but these things were the best. To show that they were Men like others, even cunning Men, revengeful Men, they drill'd

20 things on, till they might procure a Law, wherein besides all the Conformity that had been of former-times enacted, there might be some new Conditions imposed on those that should have, or hold any Church-Livings, such as they assur'd themselves, that rather than swallow, the Nonconformists would disgorge all their Bene-

25 fices. And accordingly it succeeded; several thousands of those Ministers being upon one memorable day outed of their subsistence. His Majesty in the meantime, although they had thus far prevailed to frustrate his Royal Intentions, had reinstated the Church in all its former Revenues, Dignities, and Advantages, so far from the

30 Authors mischievous aspersion of ever thinking of converting them to his own use, that he restored them free from what was due to him by Law upon their first admission. So careful was he, *because all Government must owe its quiet and continuance to the Churches Patronage,* to pay them, even what they ought. But I have observed, that

35 if a Man be in the Churches debt once, 'tis very hard to get an

---

9 & *om.* X.   13 to] on Y³⁻⁵.   14 only because *om.* Y³⁻⁵.   knew they]
knew which Y³⁻⁵.   29 and *om.* X.   34 ought] ow'd Z.

acquittance: And these men never think they have their full Rights, unless they Reign. What would they have had more? They rowl'd on a flood of wealth, and yet in matter of a Lease, would make no difference betwixt a Nonconformist, and one of their own fellow sufferers, who had ventur'd his life, and spent his Estate for the King's service. They were restor'd to Parliament, and to take their places with the King and the Nobility. They had a new *Liturgy* to their own hearts desire; And to cumulate all this happiness, they had this new Law against the *Fanaticks*. All they had that could be devised in the World to make a Clergy-man good natur'd.

Nevertheless after all their former sufferings, and after all these new enjoyments and acquisitions, they have proceeded still in the same track. The matter of Ceremonies, to be sure, hath not only exercised their ancient rigour & severity, but hath been a main ingredient of their publick Discourses, of their Sermons, of their Writings. I could not (though I do not make it my work after a great example, to look over *Epistles Dedicatory*) but observe by chance the Title page of a Book 'tother day, as an *Emblem* how much some of them do neglect the Scripture in respect to their darling Ceremonies. A *Rationale upon the Book of Common-Prayer of the Church of England by* A. Sparrow, *D. D. Bishop of* Exon. *With the Form of Consecration of a Church or Chapel, and of the place of Christian Burial. By* Lancelot Andrews *late Lord Bishop of Winchester. Sold by Robert Pawlet at the Sign of the Bible in Chancery Lane.* These surely are worthy cares for the Fathers of the Church.

But to let these things alone; How have they of late years demean'd themselves to his Majesty, although our Author urges their immediate dependance on the King to be a great obligation he hath upon their Loyalty and Fidelity? I have heard that some of them, when a great Minister of State grew burdensome to his Majesty and the Nation, stood almost in defiance of his Majesties good pleasure, and fought it out to the uttermost in his defence. I have been told that some of them in a matter of *Divorce*, wherein his Majesty desired that Justice might be done to the party agriev'd, opposed him vigorously, though they made bold too with a point

1 acquittance] acquaintance X.   7 and the] and Z.   17 *Epistles* X, Y; *Epistles* W.   20 Ceremonies X; Ceremonis W etc.

of Conscience in the case, and went against the Judgment of the best Divines of all parties. It hath been observed, that whensoever his Majesty hath had the most urgent occasions for supply, others of them have made it their business to trinkle with the *Members of*
5 *Parliament*, for obstructing it, unless the King would buy it with a new Law against the Fanaticks. And hence it is that the Wisdom of his Majesty and the Parliament must be exposed to after ages for such a *Superfœtation of Acts* in his Reign about the same business. And no sooner can his Majesty upon his own best Reasons try
10 to obviate this inconvenience, but our Author, who had before outshot *Sibthorp* and *Manwaring* in their own Bows, is now for retrenching his Authority, and moreover calumniates the State with a likelyhood, and the reasons thereof of *the return of Popery* into this Nation. And this hath been his first Method by the *Fanaticks raising*
15 *disturbance:* whereupon, if I have raked farther into things than I would have done, the Author's Indiscretion will, I hope, excuse me, and gather all the blame for reviving those things which were to be buried in Oblivion. But, by what appears, I cannot see that there is any probability of disturbance in the State, but by men of his
20 spirit and principles.

The Second way whereby the Fanatick party, he saith, may at last work the ruine of the Church, is *by combining with the Atheists, for their Union is like the mixture of Nitre and Charcoal, it carries all before it without mercy or resistance.* So it seems, when you have made Gun-
25 powder of the Atheists and Fanaticks, we are like to be blown up with Popery. And so will the Larks too. But his zeal spends it self most against the *Atheists*, because they use to *jear* the Parsons. That they may do, and no Atheists neither. For really, while Clergy men will, having so serious an office, play the *Drols* and the Boon-
30 companions, and make merry with the Scriptures, not onely among themselves, but in Gentlemen's company, 'tis impossible but that they should meet with, at least, an unlucky Repartee sometimes, and grow by degrees to be a tayle, and contempt to the people. Nay, even that which our Author always magnifies, the Reputa-

---

6–7 And . . . for] And this is that which of late years hath caused Y³⁻⁵.
8 *Superfœtation* Z; *Superfetation* Y; *Superfœ ation* W; Supœrfeation X.   in his Reign
om. Y³⁻⁵.   34 Author *Ed.*; Athour W etc.

tion, the Interest, the secular grandure of the Church, is indeed the
very thing which renders them ridiculous to many, and looks as
improper and buffoonish, as to have seen the Porter lately in the
good *Doctors Cassock* and Girdle. For, so they tell me, that there are
no where more Atheists than at *Rome*, because men seeing that 5
Princely garb and Pomp of the Clergy, and observing their life and
manners, think therefore the meaner of Religion. For certainly, the
Reputation and Interest of the Clergy, was first gained by abstracting themselves from the world, attending their Callings, Humility,
strictness of Doctrine, and the same strictness in Conversation; and 10
things are best preserved by the same means they were at first
attained. But if our Author had been as concern'd against Atheisme,
as he is against their disrespect of his function, he should have been
content that the Fanatick Preachers might have spent some of their
Pulpit-sweat upon the Atheists, and made a noise in their ears, about 15
Faith, Communion with God, attendance upon Ordinances, which he himself jears at so pleasantly. Neither do I like upon the same reasons
his manner of Discourse with the Atheists, where he complains that
ours are not like those good Atheists of former times, who never
did thrust themselves into publick cares and concerns, 'minding 20
nothing but Love, Wine, and Poetry.' Nor in another place, 'Put the
case the Clergy were Cheats and Juglers, yet it must be allowed
they are necessary Instruments of State to aw the Common People
into fear and obedience, because nothing else can so effectually in-
slave them ('tis this it seems our Author would be at) as the fear 25
of invisible powers, and the dismall apprehensions of the world to
come: and for this very reason, though there were no other, it is fit
they should be allowed the same honour and respect, as would be
acknowledged their due, if they were sincere and honest men.' No
Atheist could have said better. How mendicant a cause has he here 30
made of it; they will say, They see where the shoo wrings him, and
that though this be some ingenuity in him, yet it is but little Policy.
Nay, perhaps they will say, That they are no Atheists neither, but
only, I know not by what Fate, every day, one or other of the
Clergy does, or saith, some so ridiculous and foolish thing, or some 35

1 secular] singular Z.   6 their] the X.   23 of] *in the* Parker.   25 fear]
dread Parker.

so prity accident befalls them, that in our Authors words, a *man must be very splenetick that can refrain from laughter*. I would have quoted the page here, but that the Author has, I think for evasion sake, omitted to number them in his whole Preface. But whether
5 there be any Atheists or no, which I question more than Witches, I do not for all this take our Author to be one, though some would conclude it out of his Principles, others out of his Expressions. Yet really, I think he hath done that sort of men so much service in his Books, by his ill handling, and while he personates one party,
10 making all Religion ridiculous, that they will never be able to requite him but in the same manner. He hath opened them a whole Treasury of words and sentences, universally applicable; where they may rifle or chuse things, which their pitiful wit, as he calls it, would never have been able to invent and flourish. But truly, as
15 the simple *Parliament* 5° *Eliz.* never imagined what consequence that clause in the *Wednesday Fast* would have to *Puritanism*, neither did he what his *Periods* would have to Atheism; and yet though he is so more excusable, I hope, I may have the same leave on him, as he on that *Parliament*, to censure his Impertinence. To close this;
20 I know a Lady that chid her Master of the Horse for correcting the *Page* that had sworn a great Oath. For, saith she, *The Boy did therein show only the Generosity of his Courage, and his acknowledgement of a Deity,* And indeed, he hath approv'd his Religion, and justified himself from Atheism much after the same manner.
25   The third way and last (which I being tired, am very glad of) by which the Fanaticks may raise Disturbances, and so *introduce Popery*, is by joyning crafty and sacrilegious States-men into the Con-federacy. But really here he doth speak concerning King, and Counsellors, at such a rate, and describe and characterize some
30 men so, whomsoever he intends, that though I know there are no such, I dare not touch, it is too hazardous. 'Tis true he passes his Complement ill-favouredly enough. 'The Church has at present an impregnable affiance in the wisdom, &c. of so gracious a Prince, that is not capable of such Counsels, should they be suggested to

2 *laughter*] laughing   Parker.   4 his Y³⁻⁵; this W etc.   6 to be X,
Y³⁻⁵, Z; to to be W etc.   33 so gracious a] *a Gracious* Parker.   34 of such]
of attending to such Parker.

him: though certainly no man that is worthy to be admitted to his
Majesties Favour or Privacy; can be supposed so fool-hardy or pre-
sumptuous as to offer such weak and dishonourable Advice to so
wise and able a Prince; Yet Princes are mortal, and if ever hereafter,
(and some time or other it must happen) the Crown should chance ₅
to settle upon a young and unexperienced head, this is usually the
first thing in which such Princes are abused by their Keepers and
Guardians, &c.' But this Complement is no better at best, than if
discoursing with a man of another, I should take him by the Beard.
Upon such occasions in company, we use to ask, Sir, *Whom do you* ₁₀
mean? I am sure our Author takes it alwayes for granted, that his
Answerer intends him upon more indefinite and less direct provocations. But our Author does even personate some men as speaking
at present against the Church, 'They will intangle your affairs,
indanger your safety, hazard your Crown. All the reward you shall ₁₅
have to compensate your misfortunes, by following Church Counsels, shall be that a few Church-men, or such like people, shall cry
you up for a Saint or a Martyr.' Still *your, your,* as if it were a close
discourse unto His Majesty himself. Though if this were the worst
that they said, or that the Author fathers upon them, I wish the ₂₀
King might never have better Counsellors about him. But if the
Author be secure, for the present, in his Majesties Reign, fears not
Popery, not forsaking the Church, not assuming the Church Revenues, why is he so provident? why put things in men's heads they
never thought of? why stir such an odious, seditious, impertinent, ₂₅
unseasonable discourse? why take this very minute of time, but
that he hath mischief, to say no worse, in his heart? He had no such
remote conceit (for all his talk) of an *Infant* coming to the Crown.
He is not so weak but knows too much, and is too well instructed,
to speak to so little purpose. That would have been like a set of ₃₀
Elsibeth Players, that in the Country having worn out and over-acted
all the Playes they brought with them from *London,* laid their wits
together to make a new one of their own. No less man than *Julius*
Cæsar was the Argument; and one of the chief parts was *Moses,*

---

9 another W², ⁷, X, Y; onother W¹, ⁴⁻⁶, ⁸, ⁹.   16 misfortunes] *Misfortune*
Parker.   18 or] *and* Parker.   19 this] these X.   31 the *om.* Z.
33 together X, Y³⁻⁵;toget ther W etc.

perswading *Julius Cæsar* not to make War against his own Countrey, nor pass *Rubicon*. If our Author did not speak of our present times (to do which nevertheless had been sufficiently false and absurd) but writ all this meerly out of his Providence for after ages, I shall no more call him *Bayes*, for he is just such a *second Moses*. I ask pardon, if I have said too much, but I shall deserve none, if I meddle any further with so improbable and dangerous a business.

To conclude, the Author gives us one ground more, and perhaps more *Seditiously* insinuated than any of the former; that is, if *it should so prove, that is, if the Fanaticks by their wanton and unreasonable opposition to the ingenious and moderate Discipline of the Church of* England, *shall give their Governours too much reason to suspect that they are never to be kept in order by a milder, & more gentle Government than that of the Church of* Rome, *and force them at last to scourge them into better manners, with the Briars and Thorns of their Discipline.* It seems then that the Discipline contended about, is worth such an alteration. It seems that he knows something more than I did believe of the Design in the late times before the War. Whom doth he mean by *our Governours?* the King; No, for he is a single person. The Parliament, or the Bishops.

I have now done, after I have (which is I think due) given the Reader, and the Authour, a short account how I came to write this Book, and in this manner. First of all, I was offended at the presumption and arrogance of his stile; whereas there is nothing either of Wit, or Eloquence in all his Books, worthy of a Readers, and more unfit for his own, taking notice of. Then his infinite *Tautology* was burdensome, which seem'd like marching a Company round a Hill upon a pay-day so often, till if the Muster-master were not attentive, they might receive the pay of a Regiment. All the variety of his Treat is *Pork* (he knows the story) but so little disguised by good Cookery, that it discovers the miserableness, or rather the penury of the Host. When I observed how he inveighs against the *Trading-part* of the Nation, I thought he deserved to be within the *five mile Act*, and not to come within that distance of any Corporation. I could not patiently see how irreverently he treated Kings

10–11 *opposition*] *peevishness* Parker.   11 *ingenious*] *ingenuous* Parker.   13 *gentle*] Parker; *genle* W etc.; *gentler* Y³⁻⁵.   14 last] *least* Y³⁻⁵.

and Princes, as if they had been no better then *King Phys*, and *King Ush* of *Branford*. I thought his profanation of the Scripture intolerable; For though he alledges that 'tis only in order to shew how it was misapplyed by the Fanaticks, he might have done that too, and yet preserved the Dignity and Reverence of those Sacred Writings, which he hath not done; but on the contrary, he hath in what is properly his own, taken the most of all his Ornaments, and Imbellishments thence in a scurrilous and sacrilegious stile; insomuch that were it honest, I will undertake out of him to make a better, that is a more ridiculous and profaner Book, than *all the Friendly Debates* bound up together. Methought I never saw a more bold and wicked attempt, than that of reducing *Grace*, and making it a meer *Fable*, of which he gives us *the Moral*. I was sorry to see that even Prayer could not be admitted to be a Virtue, having thought hitherto it had been a *Grace*, and a peculiar gift of the Spirit; But I considered, that that Prayer ought to be discouraged, in order to prefer the *Liturgy*. He seem'd to speak so little like a Divine in all those matters, that the *Poet* might as well have pretended to be the *Bishop Davenant*, and that description of the Poets of *Prayer* and *Praise* was better than our Authors on the same Subject. *Canto* the 6th, where he likens Prayer to the Ocean;

> *For Prayer the Ocean is where diversly*
> *Men steer their course each to a several coast,*
> *Where all our interests so discordant lye,*
> *That half beg winds, by which the rest are lost.*

And Praise he compares to the Union of Fanaticks and Atheists, *&c.* that is *Gunpowder*; *Praise is Devotion fit for mighty minds*, &c.

> *Its utmost force, like Powder, is unknown.*
> *And though weak Kings excess of praise may fear,*
> *Yet when 'tis here, like Powder, dangerous grown,*
> *Heavens vault receives, what would the Palace tear.*

Indeed all *Astragon* appear'd to me the better *Scheme of Religion*. But it is unnecessary here to recapitulate all, one by one, what I have in the former Discourse taken notice of. I shall only add, what gave,

9 that were it] that it were Z.   14 thought] though X.   22 *Ocean*] *O'can* X.
24 *lye*] be Davenant.   28 *Powder*] Powder's Davenant.   34 of.] cf. X.

if not the greatest, yet the *last* impulse to my writing. I had
observed in his first Book, p. 57. that he had said 'Some pert and
pragmatical Divines, had filled the world with a Buzze and Noise
of the Divine Spirit; which seemed to me so horribly irreverent, as
5 if he had taken his similitude from the *Hum and Buz* of the *Humble-
Bee* in the *Rehearsal*.

In the same Book, I have before mentioned that most unsafe
passage, of our *Saviour being not only in an hot fit of zeal, but in a seeming
fury and transport of Passion.* And striving to unhook himself hence.
10 p. 152. of his Second Book, Swallows it deeper, saying, *Our blessed
Saviour did in that action take upon him the* Person *and* Priviledge *of a* Jewish Zealot. Take upon him the Person, that is *Personam induere.* And
what part did he play? Of a *Jewish Zealot.*

The Second Person of the Trinity (may I repeat these things
15 without offence) to take upon him the Person of a Jewish Zealot,
that is, of a notorious Rogue and Cut-throat.

This seemed to proceed from too slight an Apprehension and
Knowledge of the duty we ow to our Saviour. And last of all, in
this Preface, as before quoted, he saith, the *Nonconformist Preachers
20 do spend most of their Pulpit-sweat in making a noise about Communion with
God.* So that there is not one Person of the Trinity that he hath not
done despight to: and lest he should have distinct Communion with
the Father, the Son and the Holy Ghost, for which he mocks his
Answerer; he hath spoken evil distinctly of the Father, distinctly
25 of the Son, and distinctly of the Holy Ghost. That only remain'd
behinde, wherein our Author might surpass the Character given to
Aretine, a famous man of this faculty,

> *Qui giace il Aretino*
> *Chi de tutti mal disse fuor d' Iddio*
30 *Ma di questo si scusa perche no'l conobbe.*
> *Here lies Aretine,*
> *Who spoke evil of all, except God only,*
> *But of this he beggs excuse, because he did not know him.*

1 greatest Y; greattest W   yet] ye W4; yea X.   4 to me] to to me Y.
5 his *om.* W2, 4, 5, Y.   8 of *om.* Y1, 2, 4, 6, 7.   10 Book, Swallows] Book, he
swallows Y.   11–12 *a* Jewish Zealot] the Jewish Zealots Parker.   20 *about
Communion*] about Faith, Communion Parker.   27 this faculty, Y; his Faculty. W.
29 Iddio Y; Addio W; Adido X.   30 scusa Y; seusa W; sensa X.

And now I have done. And shall think my self largely recompensed for this trouble, if any one that hath been formerly of another mind, shall learn by this Example, that it is not impossible to be merry and angry as long time as I have been writing, without profaning and violating those things which are and ought to be most sacred.

FINIS.

---

1 And shall Y; And I shall W.

REPROOF p. 67.

IF you have any thing to object against it, do your worst. You know the Press is open.

Licensed the 1*st.*
of *May*, 1673.

By the Author and Licenser of the Ecclesiastical Polity.

THE
REHEARSALL
TRANSPROS'D:

The SECOND PART.

*Occasioned by Two Letters : The first
Printed ,   by a nameless Author,
Intituled,* A Reproof, *&c.*
*The Second Letter left for me at a
Friends House , Dated* Nov. 3.
1 6 7 3. *Subscribed* J. G. *and
concluding with these words* ; If
thou darest to Print or Publish
any Lie or Libel against Doctor
Parker , By the Eternal God I
will cut thy Throat.

Answered by ANDREW MARVEL

LONDON,
Printed for Nathaniel Ponder *at the* Peacock *in*
Chancery Lane *near* Fleet-Street, 1673.

REHEARSAL TRANSPROS'D

The Second Part

THe *Author of the Ecclesiastical Polity* (why not Doctor *Sermon*?) doubts, with some reason, whether he has not in that Study *lost his Understanding*. To convince himself therefore and others of the contrary, he attempts to shew here at the beginning, that he not only knows as yet what he does, but remembers still the very circumstances of his actions. He tells me: *I had heard from him sooner had he not, immediately after he undertook my Correction, been prevented by a dull and lazy distemper; but being now recruited*, &c. Sooner or later imports not, it comes much to the same account. No Naturalist has determin'd the certain time of a Mountains pregnancy, how long it goes before it be deliver'd: but one has told us what kind of Child it always produces. And as for his dull and lazy Distemper, the Courtesie was no less superfluous to inform me of what most men have been long since fully satisfyed upon undeniable Testimony. What is the World concern'd in the Revolutions of his health, or the courses of Physick that he runs through at Spring and Fall? *Plutarch* indeed gives us the Minutes of *Alexander* the *Great's* sickness after his last debauch; and the *Dutch* Historian *Aytzema* is so punctual in the late *Prince of Oranges* malady, as even to Chronicle in Folio what days he did *excernere Dura*, when *Fætida*, and when *Fæces laudabiles*. What then? Must it therefore follow that this *Orange* Doctor by having commenced in this Princes Train, is grown so considerable, that the *Temper of his mind*, the *Juncture of his Affairs*, and the *State of his Body* should be transmitted to posterity? That after Ages must read in what Moon his invention was fluent, and in what *Epocha*, costive? That as in his late Preface he enter'd his

closer Importance upon Record, so in this voluminous Pamphlet his close Stool too should be Register'd? But suppose he were of such Moment, he is too hard put to it, and but ill befriended, that he must do himself that Office. Was there not one true *English* Man
5 left to help him? Ungrateful World, that when he has *lost his Labour and Understanding* in writing them an *Ecclesiastical Polity*, would not afford him some other Pen for his own Ecclesiastical History. But he is so self-sufficient, and an *At-all* of so many capacities, that he would Excommunicate any Man who should have presumed to
10 intermeddle so far within his Province. Has he been an Author? he is too the Licenser. Has he been a Father? he will stand too for God father. Is he then to be marryed? he asks his own Banes in Print. And now after he thinks himself cured, and in Wedding and Writing case, he cannot forbear nevertheless but he must be pub-
15 lishing his diseases. Had he Acted *Pyramus* he would have been *Moon-shine* too, and the *Hole in the Wall*. That first *Author of Ecclesiastical Polity*, *Nero* was of the same temper. He could not be contented with the *Roman Empire* unless he were too his own *Præcentor*; and he in the same manner, out of meer Charity, when he appre-
20 hended death, lamented only the detriment that Mankind must sustain in losing so considerable a Fidler. When a Man is once possess'd with this Fanatick kind of Spirit, he imagines, if a Shoulder do but itch, that the World has gall'd it with leaning on't so long and therefore he wisely shrugs to remove the Globe to the other.
25 If he chance but to sneeze, he salutes himself, and courteously prays that the *Foundations of the Earth* be not shaken. And even so *the Author of the Ecclesiastical Polity*, ever since he crept up to be but the Weather-cock of a Steeple, he trembles and creaks at every puff of Wind that blows him about, as if the *Church of* England *were falling,*
30 *and the State totter'd*. And then after Men are once come to mistake themselves as so necessary, it is no wonder if they inpute it for a great Obligation, as oft as they condescend to give the Publick an account of their Privacies. There is not any so undecent Circumstance of their life but they think it worthy to be committed to
35 Paper, and, foul as it is, yet they forthwith send it away to the Printer. And now all Christendom doubtless has taken notice that

12 marryed? 74; ~: 73.

the Author of the Ecclesiastical Polity has lain in of a dull and lazy distemper, and to be sure the Ecclesiasticks of his faculty have deeply Sympathized with his condition. The News will, after the rebound of some Months, reach *Constantinople* and *Agra*; and as soon as they hear of his recovery, the *Mufti* and the *Mulla* will certainly send to 5 congratulate him. But however he has methinks not dealt so kindly herein with his native Country, as their universal concernment for him might have deserved. For though indeed there must needs be a mighty profit upon the exportation of his Book, and those especially beyond the Line will think it a great advantage to buy the 10 account of his health at any rate with so large a Volume into the bargain; yet he might out of gratitude to our curiosity have advertis'd us at home the cheaper way, by the same Gazette of the 15*th*. of *May*, 1673. in which he cries his Book to make it Vendible. Whereas the inserting it thus in so thick an *Octavo*, is a most palpable project upon Mens affections, and next to imposing his Book 15 upon the Church wardens of every Parish, and the Chapters of all the Cathedrals. As well as Men love him, yet they desire not that his Sickness should be as chargeable to the Countrey as a Visitation. Nay, even the Clergy of his own Province scruple at the Price, and 20 take it ill that as oft as their Arch-deacon comes abroad again in Print, they should be oblig'd in this manner to pay Procurations and Synodals. But of all Men it falls most severely upon the Non-conformists, who having been exhausted with so many other penalties formerly, cannot so well afford to buy their Penance so dear, and 25 take off his Books every Year in Commutation. 'Tis true, he has been kind to them, and to such a degree, that he hath done more service to their Cause by writing against it, than all their own Authors that ever writ for them. But that therefore being so contrary to his intention, the Accident diminishes the Courtesie. And if 30 yet for *old acquaintance* sake they could be content to give somewhat for *a Book in some places erroneous, in some places scarce sense, and of ill Consequence*; they compute that if *the Reproof to the Rehearsal Transpros'd in a Discourse to its Author by the Author of the Ecclesiastical Polity* be of the same Nature, and at the same price, it is however better of the 35

13–14 of the 15*th*. of *May*, 1673. 74; *om*. 73.   20 of his own Province 74;
om. 73.   34 *Polity* 74; *Policy* 73.

two to buy an *English* Bible with all its faults. He is return'd to be a *Precious Man* indeed, more precious than ever heretofore at the University; if since he arose to be *the Author of the Ecclesiastical Polity*, a poor Fanatick that has been of his intimacy cannot be inform'd how he does under the prodigal expence of Five Shillings.

He cannot sure take it unkindly if I enter into a further consultation of the Nature of his indisposition, and the remedies; seeing he has so voluntarily interested me therein, and his Readers. For the Officious always spring game to the Curious. The Disease being as he relates so dull and lazy, I should think at first that it might have been a Lethargy, and whereas he imagines himself recruited, that he has only in order to a Cure (as is usual in that case) been cast into a Feaver. For he has forgot himself most extreamly, and his whole discourse, as proceeding from a Man in the confines of two so contrary distempers, partakes all thorow equally of Stupidity and Raving.

But when I reflect further upon the Symptoms, and his description, it seems more probably to be the *Abelteria*, a Greek discomposure, and to which those of his constitution are generally subject. The malignity of this affects the Mind rather than the Body, and therefore lies further beyond the reach of Physick. When once it takes a Man he is desperate, and there is no more possibility of his recovery; nor is that strange, it being the property of those that have it by how much they grow worse to conceive always that they are in a better Condition.

Some indeed will have it, that under those Terms of a dull and lazy distemper he calumniates a more active and stirring Disease, (as the Spleen and the Scurvy do oftentimes bear the blame of another infirmity) and that it is no *Grecian* malady but derives its name from a Countrey much nearer. But that *Distemper is so unsuitable to the Civility of his Education, and the Gravity of his Profession*, that I question much whether it could be *so Clownish and Licentious* (bold though it be) *to accost* a Personage of his Figure and Character. Yet who knows after that new *Alliance* in the Year 1665. betwixt Nature and Divinity, that amorous season of his *Tentamina Physico-Theologica*, (if he were the Author) whether his Nature may not have given his Divinity the slip, and running its own random have

5 Shillings] Shilling 74.

met with some misadventure? For even then he had learnt how
Aristotle Worshiped his Wench under show of Sacrificing to a
Goddess. He inform'd us so early how *Stilpo* disputing before the
Areopagites, that *Minerva* could not be a God, because she was a
Woman, and therefore a Goddess; *Theodorus* somewhat smuttily ₅
ask'd him, whether he had seen her without her Shift. And this
reparty of *Theodorus* he recommends there for so ingenious, that he
ranks it among his Colours, why that Philosopher, who call'd himself God, should not be counted an Atheist; Though I can scarce
discern any more Wit or Theology in it then in his own Argument ₁₀
lately among a Knot of eminent Divines, the Women being present;
that the rest of the Clergy-Mens Wives were but Dish-clouts, his
own a Goddess; and they had been perfectly quit, had but *Stilpo* now
cap'd *Theodorus*, by telling him that they were all however no more
then needed to scowre his Mouth after so slovenly a comparison. ₁₅
In the same Book he demonstrates at large how impossible it was
(though *Epicurus* his Opinion) for Mankind to be produced at first
from certain Vesicles or Pimples of the Earth. You would wonder
to see how solidly and elaborately, with what *dint* of *Reason* he con-
futes so dangerous an Heresy, to the great instruction doubtless, ₂₀
and advantage of Sir *John Hinton*, and Doctor *Chamberlain*. Then he
takes their Office out of their Hands, and proceeds immediately to
read a publick Lecture of the Figure and Use of the Vessels of
Generation, and more especially those of the Female. Like a forward
Chick he pecks through Doctor *Harvyes* Egg-shell, and tells us that ₂₅
most famous Physician was not so cunning as he should have been
in the chief Mystery of the seminal business. At last this blushing
Gentleman, this very Picture of modesty, in open terms undertakes
to explain the pleasure annex'd to the Act of Procreation, and is so
tickled with the imagination [presaging too perhaps, that it might ₃₀
ere long be his fortune to dine with a God, (so he stiles the Arch-
bishop) and bed a Goddess, (so he calls his Mistress)] that although
he censures *Lucretius* for speaking so broad, yet he cannot refrain
from using his own Words, *that 'twas so excessively sweet, as to be the
solace not only of Mankind, but the Deities.* And all this stir is there ₃₅

4 *Areopagites* 74; *Arcopagites* 73.   28 very *om.* 74.   30 [presaging *Ed.*;
)~ 73; 74.   32)] *Ed.*;) 73, 74.

made by the present *Author of the Ecclesiastical Polity*, in order forsooth to prove Gods providence, as if that could not be, or were not
sufficiently evidenced without his *Gossiping* collections of naked
Midwifery. Insomuch that one who understood not beyond his
5 Latine, might justly doubt, whether by the *Tentamina Physico-Theo-*
logica he meant indeed the Essays of his Divinity, or the Tempta-
tions of his Nature. Neither can it in Reason seem strange if the
vigorous and frequent contemplation of such Objects transported
him further, and her too as well as other Creatures might (to use
10 his own Phrase) *out of that vehement and unbridled concupiscence rush in*
furias ignemque thorow Fire and Water upon a dangerous experiment
against the *Pimples of the Earth and Paracelsus* his Limbeck. For he
himself in a succeeding Book (said to be his) *the censure of the Platon-*
ick Philosophy confesses; *that if in any respect Virtue and Religion intrench*
15 *upon the liberty of our Natures, 'tis in the instances of sensuality, and that*
when the man is divided from the Beast, and his Reason separated from the
inferiour and bruitish appetites, then arise irregular and unreasonable desires,
&c. so that by his own acknowledgment, it is not impossible but
the Man in him may at some time have been obliged to carry the
20 brute a *pick a pack*. Only there is this difference betwixt his Beast
and others, that his mind, it seems, is more subject to irregular and
unreasonable desires when abstracted within it self whereas the
Reason of other Men suffers most in conjunction with the inferiour
and brutish appetites. So that although in the same Book he mag-
25 nifies those spruce Gentlemen the *Platonists, as being professedly the*
most generous contemners of Women in the World; and affirms, *that their*
amours (for they were accus'd of Sodomy) *were not kindled by lust and*
petulancy, but were pure and cleanly enough to become Angels, and separated
Souls; though in the usual pompous explication of his own perfec-
30 tions he glories; *that he hath tasted less of sensual delights than he thinks*
any one placed in the said circumstances and capacities; for he hath hitherto
scarce imploy'd any of his Senses but that of seeing; notwithstanding all
those preventive insinuations, I see no reason to trust him further
then I would his own Curate of *Ikham*, with his Maid Mary *Parker*.
35 But I rather suspect that where he stops short in the carreer of a

17 *and* 74; *und* 73.   31 *said*] *same* Parker.   34 his own 74; the 73.
35 that *om*. 74.

Sentence, *that he thinks nothing concerns him so much as those designs that aspire to serve his dearest - - -* the rest was Bawdy. For though he were on the Rode to *Canterbury*, let any Female but cross his Way, 'tis odds that his Beast will stumble, and throw his Arch-deaconship in the Cart-rut, with his whole *Tridentine* Portmantle of Polity and Theology. Yet though I speak these things with some certainty, to evidence them to others would require a more difficult scrutiny. For whatsoever 'twas that befell him, he has been so concern'd of late to stop all Avenues, and every Cranny of Intelligence, that were he to pass through the discipline of sweating, there could not have been more strictness about the Doors and the Windows. And then his Physicians on the other side are shut up as close by the Obligation of their Faculty, having all of them sworn secrecy to *Hippocrates*. Neither is it indeed at first sight probable that if he were so obnoxious to them, one of *so sweet a Nature* should so openly declare himself against the Non-conformists. Had he been cured by a *Jew*, so great a Prince as the *Author of the Ecclesiastical Polity* would surely, either out of his Clemency or his Wisdom, have been gracious to the whole Tribe, and for his Doctors sake have at least conniv'd at their Synagogue. He is not the first that *Phys.* has whisper'd out of his Kingdom: And yet if he thought the matter once secured from discovery, I question much whether any other tie could hold him. For I know none so loose from all the restrictions of Humanity as some within his Girdle, and were there a Court of Faculties for that purpose he could not take out more ample dispensations from common Ingenuity and Gratitude. So that there could not have been more conformity betwixt the Person and the Disease, and an *Implacable Divine* could never be better fitted than with that distemper which his *Italian* Author can tell him does sometimes make Truce, but never admits a Pacification. But he is I perceive a very *Secret one*, in another sense then formerly, and perhaps did only publish his malady, the better to disguise it: So that I will not out of respect press this Point further. If he should by giving so partial an account fail of a Cure, he is the more excusable; for it will have been the first time that his Modesty did him prejudice. Yet this caution for humanity's sake I would leave with him;

11 the *om.* 74.

that he trust not too much to the Asses Milk in his *Hicringills Dispensatory*; for every one knows that if he have no better Specifick, he will ever and anon be troubled with the Reliques.

But whatever old mischief may possibly lurk in his Body; I am told by one, who pretends to the best intelligence, that this was a new Disease, which spred much through the Nation about last Autumn. I hear not that any dyed of it, and therefore its name is not yet read of in the Bills of Mortality. To be short, as I am certainly inform'd, he was sick of *the Rehearsal Transpros'd.* Then indeed the *Rehearsal Transpros'd* deserv'd a *Reproof*, for exceeding its Commission, I am sorry if that should occasion a distemper, which I ordered as Physick; the *Rehearsal Transpros'd* being too only a particular prescription in his case, and not to be applyed to others without special direction. But some curious persons would be licking at it, and most Men finding it not distastful to the Palate, it grew in a short time to be of common use in the Shops. I perceive that it wrought a sensible alteration in all that took it; but varying in some for the better, in others for the worse, according to the difference of their Complexions. Some were swoln up to the Throat, some their Heads turn'd round, and others it made their Hearts ake; but all these were but a few in number; most Men found only a little tingling in their Ears, and after its greatest violence it discharged it self in an innocent fit of uncessant laughter. But the greatest harm it did was to the *Author of the Ecclesiastical Polity*, for whose good it was principally intended: For before he had half taken it, his spirits began to fail him, and it put him past not only *the common drudgeries* of Preaching and reading Prayers; but those other things too which he stiles *the innocent comforts of Humane life.* So that he laid it by for a considerable time, and was resolv'd to have taken no more of it; finding it so contrary to his Nature. In that interval, his Humours being stir'd, the pre-domineering Choler in a short time diffus'd it self so through his Body Ecclesiastick, that it struck him into a deep Jaundice; and his Soul seem'd to have set up a guilt Vehicle of the new Lacker. The great little Animal was on a sudden turn'd so Yellow, and grown withall so unwieldy, that he might have past currant for the Elephant upon a Guinny. For

11 which I] which 74.

as he had long since foretold, *having been so inconsiderate as to write Books, and faln so lately under the severe lash of one that knew him not,* it was his concurring misfortune to be now *exposed to the severer commands of those that knew him.* The cause was at present much altered from what in his Preface to Bishop *Bramhall,* and over and above the 5 importunity of the Bookseller, he was now obliged to write in Canonical obedience. But his Yellow Coife rendred him very unfit to appear in publick, and being troubled thus with the Jaundice, and under a necessity of exercising at the same time all the remainders yet left him of Reason, Wit or Invention, 'tis probable that he 10 found indeed cause to complain of a dull and lazy distemper, and now too late repented, *that he had sold himself into so great a slavery.* However having driven himself into that Condition he must now needs go through with his task; and therefore the time too being limited, he hastened to bring himself in plight by such common 15 remedies as were next to hand, writing too all the while by girds and snatches hand over head. His other self *Hicringill* (who seems very well informed of all his distempers, and of this particularly) had told him that a Louse was good against the Jaundice, and the *Author of the Ecclesiastical Polity* himself had for all Events the *Sacrament of* 20 *Lousiness* by him of his own preparation: So that this being much easier to be procured then the Tribute of Fleas was to be collected, there is no doubt to be made, but that he tryed the Vertue of this Medicine. And as the *Tartars* cracking the same Vermine with their Teeth, are used to wish solemnly, that they had their Enemies 25 at the like advantage; so methinks I see how he snapp'd them e're they got down, and ever anon prayed betwixt the teeth for the Non-conformists. But he had heard how his old acquaintance Doctor *Rabelais,* upon examination for his degree, answer'd, that if his *Gargantua* were sick, he would prescribe him *Pilulas Evangelicas, ex* 30 *centum libris Aloes & Myrrhæ.* He computed thence, that in his own case the Dose must be proportionable betwixt the Civil and the Ecclesiastical Giant. And if so, that though all Prisons should be depopulated, though *Beggars-bush* pillag'd, though the *Phthiriases* of all former persecutors revived, yet the quantity would not be 35

---

1 *write] print* Parker.   2 *severe]* severer Parker.   3 misfortune 74; misforrune 73.   *severer]* severe · Parker.   20 *Polity* 74; *Policy* 73.

sufficient; but as once the Incense of all *Arabia* was spent on one Funerall, so the Lice of all the World must be consumed upon his malady: But what he most consider'd was, that this must necessarily end in an utter dissolution of the Government of the *Phthiro-*
5 *phagi*, and that contrary to all good Ecclesiastical Polity, the *Presidents of the sacred Rites* (for the other orders of Men 'twas less matter) should in reference to his cure be depriv'd of that *lean and slender subsistence* which was yet left them. This would have been a Sacrilege greater, because more universal than to have rifled the Louse out
10 of St. *Francis* his Bosom. So that upon this *Algebra* and prospect, he desisted at last from the Lousy Diet, part out of his good Nature, part out of his Conscience, and partly out of Impossibility. And had he at the same time betaken himself in good earnest to the *Extractum Apostoli* of Faith, Hope, and Charity, as a *Succedaneum*, (for
15 even his second *Rabelais*, Doctor *Hicringill* renders them equivalent to a Louse) he had been certainly cured both Mind and Body. But some doubt there is that his *Shop-Divines* have not the right Composition of that medicine. However he was not now in case or disposition to take it; and the *Rehearsal Transpros'd*, which after many
20 a grimasse he had now at last gulp'd down, had so terribly disorder'd him, that he had quite forgot there was any such remedy in the ancient *Praxis* of Christianity. But this Gentleman of *So tame*, if you will believe him, *and softly an Humour of so cold a Complexion, that he Scarse thinks himself capable of hot and passionate impressions*; he that is
25 only offended at *them who will not suffer themselves to be embraced by those whose unbounded embraces would comprehend all*, and *quanquam alias præmitis sit indolis*, was altered beyond all imagination. I cannot determine whether I being but a new unlicensed Practitioner, and the *Rehearsal Transpros'd* my first experiment, there might be some
30 errour in the preparation, and it were too *strong of the Minerall*, or whether indeed it were the extraordinary foulness of his Stomack. But it hath brought up such ulcerous stuff as never was seen; and whereas I intended it only for a *Diaphoretick* to cast him into a breathing sweat, it hath had upon him all the effects of a Vomit.
35 Turnep-tops, Frogs, rotten Eggs, Brass-coppers, Grashoppers, Pins,

Mushromes, &c. wrapt up together in such balls of Slime and
Choler, that they would have burst the Dragon, and in good earnest seem to have something supernatural. Insomuch that he seems
not to sit at present for the Arch-deacons Seat as to take his place
below in the Church among the *Energumeni*. But it is possible that
after so notorious an evacuation, he may do better for the future;
and it is more then visible that either his Disease or his Nature cannot hold out much longer. Therefore I shall not grudge from time
to time to lend him my best assistance, though I hope that this
Iteration will do his business, and carry off all the dregs of his distemper. And now from what I have said hitherto, and that I may
begin so far an accommodation betwixt us, I shall if he please recant
and yield that the *asswaging his Concupiscense, and wreaking his malice,
has been the highest Pinacle of his Ecclesiastical in-felicity*.

Having treated him in as short a method as so Chronical a malady
would admit, I shall now be inforced to remove some dirt, that I
may make my way cleaner to come at him: for otherwise there is
no passing, but then I shall quickly have dispatch'd with him. He
saith, *I have cowardly and dishonourably accosted him in such a clownish
and licentious a way of writing as I knew to be unsuitable both to the Civility
of his Education, and the Gravity of his Profession.* I thought I had in the
close of my former book, and all thorow sufficiently satisfy'd him
of the reasons and way of my proceeding with him: but seeing he
hath it seems so soon forgot them (as men willingly do, what it is
grievous to remember) I shall now at more leisure refresh his memory, and deduce the order of my thoughts upon that and this
occasion.

Those that take upon themselves to be Writers, are moved to it
either by Ambition or Charity: imagining that they shall do therein
something to make themselves famous, or that they can communi-
cate something that may be delightful and profitable to mankind.
But therefore it is either way an envious and dangerous imployment. For, how well soever it be intended, the World will have
some pretence to suspect, that the Author hath both too good a
conceit of his own sufficiency, and that by undertaking to teach
them, he implicitly accuses their ignorance. So that not to Write

5

10

15

20

25

30

35

24 SO *om*. 74.

at all is much the safer course of life: but if a mans Fate or *Genius* prompt him otherwise, 'tis necessary that he be copious in matter, solid in reason, methodical in the order of his work; and that the subject be well chosen, the season well fix'd, and, to be short, that

5 his whole production be matur'd to see the light by a just course of time, and judicious deliberation. Otherwise, though with some of these conditions he may perhaps attain commendation; yet without them all he cannot deserve pardon. For indeed whosoever he be that comes in Print whereas he might have sate at home in quiet,

10 does either make a Treat, or send a Chalenge to all Readers; in which cases, the first, it concerns him to have no scarcity of Provisions, and in the other to be compleatly Arm'd: for if any thing be amiss on either part, men are subject to scorn the weakness of the Attaque, or laugh at the meanness of the Entertainment. In con-

15 clusion, the Author of the *Ecclesiastical Polity* hath in his own particular very fully stated and comprehended this whole matter. For he saith here in his Preface to the Reader, that *if his Book have any effect* (I suppose he means any good effect) *he hath a double reward*; (that is both the publick and his private satisfaction) *but if it have*

20 *none* (that is impossible) *that then he hath his own reward*; (that is sure to be accounted none of the wisest) and indeed this Reward too is double; for if he fails of his design, he saith *he must confess that he has lost both his Labour and his Understanding.* This is the common condition to which every man that will Write a Book must be content

25 with patience to submit.

But, among all the differences of writing, he that does publish an Invective, does it at his utmost peril, and 'tis but just that it should be so. For a mans Credit is of so natural and high concernment to him, that the preserving of it better, was perhaps none of the least

30 inducements at first to enter into the bonds of Society, and Civil Government; as that Government too must at one time or other be dissolved where mens Reputation cannot be under Security. 'Tis dearer than life it self, and (to use a thought something perhaps too delicate, yet not altogether unreasonable) if beside the Laws of

17 here *om.* 74.   19 (that is both the publick and his private satisfaction) *but if it have none om.* 74.   satisfaction) *Ed.*; ∼; 73.   22 *has*] *hath* 74.   23 *both om.* 74.   34 Laws] Law 74.

Murther men have thought fit, out of respect to humane nature, that whatsoever else moves to the death of man should be forfeit to pious uses, why should there not as well be Deodands for Reputation? And this I intend not only of those who publish ignominious falshoods, to whom no Quarter ought to be granted, but even of such partly who by a truth too officious shall procure any mans infamy. For 'tis better that evil men should be left in an undisturbed possession of their repute, how unjustly soever they may have acquired it, then that the Exchange and Credit of mankind should be universally shaken, wherein the best too will suffer and be involved. It is one thing to do that which is justifiable, but another that which is commendable, and I suppose every prudent Writer aims at both: but how can the Author of an Invective, though never so truely founded, expect approbation (unless from such as love to see mischief at other mens expence) who, in a world all furnished with subjects of praise, instruction and learned inquiry, shall studiously chuse and set himself apart to comment upon the blemishes and imperfections of some particular person? Such men do seldom miss too of *their own reward:* for whereas those that treat of innocent and benign argument are represented by the *Muses,* they that make it their business to set out others ill-favouredly do pass for *Satyres,* and themselves are sure to be personated with prick-ears, wrinkled horns, and cloven feet.

Yet if for once to write in that stile may be lawful, discreet or necessary, to do it a second time is lyable to greater Censure. Not so much because the After-meath seldom or never equals the first Herbage; (a Caution not unfit however for all Authors) as that by-standers will begin then to suspect, that what they look'd on first as an accident with some divertisement, do's rather proceed from a natural malignity of temper. For few Readers are so ill natured but that they are quickly tired with personal and passionate discourses; and when the contest comes to be continued and repeated, if they interess themselves at all, they usually incline and think that the justice lies on the weaker side. But whether the last appeal of Writers lie to the Readers or to a Mans own ultimate Recollection, this Invective way cannot be truly satisfactory either

23 and *om.* 74.   34 and 74; *om.* 73.

to themselves or others. For it is a prædatory course of life, and indeed but a privateering upon reputation; wherein all that stock of Credit, which an honest Man perhaps hath all his age been toyling for, is in an hour or two's reading plunder'd from him by a Free-booter. So that whatsoever be the success, he that chances in these Contests to be Superiour, can at best (for that too is disputable) be accounted of the two the less unfortunate. And certainly (as it was usual of old for any Man who had but casually acted in an unlucky rencounter) he that hath had his Pen once in the Reputation of another, ought to withdraw, and disappear for some time till he has undergone and past through all the Ceremonies of Expiation.

But if the Credit of all Men whatsoever be, and ought to be so well guarded both by Nature, Law, and Discretion, the Clergy certainly of all others ought to be kept and preserv'd sacred in their Reputation. For they being Men of the same Spirit with others, and no less subject to Humane Passions, but confined within the regularity of their Function; It is indeed unmanly, whatsoever scuffle others may make among themselves, to vilifie or treat them with those affronts which nothing but the respect of Decency or Conscience could hinder them from resenting as well as others. But (which is more considerable) whoever too shall fix upon them an ill report, do's thereby frustrate the very effect of their ministry in proportion. For though Baptism is not to be vacated by the contrary intention of him that officiates, yet few Men will or can be perswaded by his Doctrine, whose practice they conceive to be opposite. A conversation differing from Doctrine is Spiritual Nonsense: Neither will Men believe by the Ear, when their Eye informs them otherwise. If an Artificer indeed make his Work fit for Mens wearing, 'tis sufficient: Or if he that Sells have good of the kind, Men inquire no further. No Mans Shooe wrings him the more because of the Heterodoxy, or the tipling of his Shooe-maker: And a Billet burns as well though bought of whatsoever Wood-monger: But the Clergy being Men dedicate by their Vocation to teach what is Truth, what Falshood, to deter men from vice, and lead them unto all virtue; 'tis expected from them, and with good reason, that

6 too is] is too 74.   7 the less] less 74.

they should define their opinion by their manners. And therefore men ought to be chary of aspersing them on either account, but even reflect upon their failings with some reverence. A Clergy-man ought to have treble damages both for his Tithes and his Credit: and it were to be wish'd that with the same ease that their main- 5 tenance comes in from the fruits of mens labour, they had too no less proportion out of the yearly increase of every mans Reputation: the rest would thrive the better for it. Their virtues are to be cele-brated with all incouragement: and, if their vices be not notoriously palpable, let the Eye as it defends its Organ, so conceal the Object 10 by Connivence.

And yet nevertheless, and all that has been said before being granted, it may so chance that to write, and that Satyrically, and that a second time and a third; and this too even against a Clergy-man, may be not only excusable but necessary. That I may spare 15 a tedious recapitulation, I shall prove all the rest upon the strongest instance, that is in the case of a Clergy-man. For it is not impos-sible that a man by evil arts may have crept into the Church, thorow the Belfry or at the Windows. 'Tis not improbable that having so got in he should foul the Pulpit, and afterwards the Press 20 with opinions destructive to Humane Society and the Christian Religion. That he should illustrate so corrupt Doctrines with as ill a conversation, and adorn the lasciviousness of his life with an equal petulancy of stile and language. In such a concurrence of misdemeanours what is to be done? Why certainly, how pernicious 25 soever this must be in the example and consequence, yet, before any private man undertake to obviate it, he ought to expect the judg-ment of the Diocesan and the method of the Ecclesiastical Disci-pline. There was in the ancient times of Christianity a wholsome usage, but now obsolete, which went very far in preventing all these 30 occasions. For whosoever was to receive Ordination, his name was first published to the Congregation in the same way as the Banes of those that enter into Matrimony: and if any could object a sufficient cause against him that was proposed, he was not to be admitted to the Ministry. He that would be a Preacher was to be first 35 himself commented upon by the People, and in the stile of those ages was said *Prædicari*. But since that circumspection has been devolved into the single oversight of the later Bishops, it cannot be otherwise, but some one or other may sometimes escape into the Church, who were much fitter to be shut out of Doors. Yet then if our great Pastors should but exercise the Wisdom of common Shepheards, by parting with one to stop the infection of the whole Flock, when his rottenness grew notorious; or if our Clergy would but use the instinct of other creatures, and chase the blown Deer out of their Heard; such mischiefs might quickly be remedied. But on the contrary it happens not seldome that this necessary duty (which is so great a part of true *Ecclesiastical Politie*) is not only neglected, but that persons so dangerous are rather incouraged by their Superiors, and he that, upon their omission, shall but single out one of them, yet shall be exposed to the general out-cry of the Faculty, and be pursued with Bell, Book, and Candle, as a declared and publick enemy of the Clergy. Whereas they ought to consider that by this way of proceeding, they themselves do render that universal which was but individual, and affix a personal crime upon their whole Order, and, for want of separating from one obnoxious, do contribute to the causes of separation, justifying so far that Schism which they condemn. In this Case, and supposing such a failer of justice in those whose Province it is to prevent or punish, I ask again what is to be done? Why certainly the next thing had been to admonish him in particular as a Friend does his Friend, or one Christian another. But he that hath once Printed an ill book has thereby condens'd his words on purpose lest they should be carried away by the wind; he has diffused his poyson so publickly in design that it might be beyond his own recollection; and put himself deliberately past the reach of any private admonition. In this Case it is that I think a Clergy-man is laid open to the Pen of any one that knows how to manage it; and that every person who has either Wit, Learning or Sobriety is licensed, if debauch'd to curb him, if erroneous to catechize him, and if foul-mouth'd and biting, to muzzle him. For they do but abuse themselves who shall any longer consider or reverence such an one as a Clergy-man, who as oft as he undresses degrades himself and would never have come into the Church but to take Sanctuary. Rather, wheresoever men

1 later] latter 74.   2 sometimes *om*. 74.   24 hath *om*. 74.

shall find the footing of so wanton a Satyr out of his own bounds, the neighbourhood ought, notwithstanding all his pretended capering Divinity, to hunt him thorow the woods with hounds and horn home to his harbour.

How far and whether at all the *Author of the Ecclesiastical Politie* is culpable on these accounts, I must refer to the Readers judgment upon perusal of my first and this my second book, though I could much rather wish that men would be at leisure to take the length of him out of his own discourses. But, had he not appear'd so to me, I should never have molested him, adventur'd my self, or interessed the Publick by writing in this manner. For I am too conscious of mine own imperfections to rake into and dilate upon the failings of other men; and though I carry always some ill Nature about me, yet it is I hope no more than is in this world necessary for a Preservative; but as for the Clergy, the memory of mine own extraction, and much more my sense of the Sanctity of their function ingage me peculiarly to esteem and honour them. Insomuch that for their sakes I bear much respect even to their *poor* wives, of whom I may say (as Bishop *Bramhall* comparing the Readers with the Preachers, and who understood both) that *if they come short* of other Women *in point of Efficacy, yet they have the advantage* of other Women *in point of Security.* And though I am not so inamour'd of them as to worship 'em for *Goddesses*; yet I am so far from rejecting them as *Dish-clouts*, that what the *Author of Eccles. Politie* affirms of the Clergy of the Church of *England, I dare averre* concerning their Wives, *that taking them under all their disadvantages they are at this very time vastly the furthest off from being justly contemptible (to mention no other Order or Profession of Women) of any Clergy-mens Wives in the world. The pre-eminence is so evident that it clears the comparison from all possible suspicion of being proud or odious.*

Being of this temper there could be no great appearance of my being overforward to come out in Print in such a Stile against one of his cloath, unless upon some very extraordinary occasion. And such this occasion seemed to me, and so urgent and justifiable that it might absolve me in any Readers opinion. For this sharpness of Stile does indeed for the most part naturally flow from the humour

27 *justly contemptible*] *justly* c*only contemptible* 74.

of the Writer: and therefore tis observable that few are guilty of it but either those that write too young (when it resembles the acidity of juices strain'd from the fruits before they be matured) or else those that write too old (and then 'tis like the sowrness of liquors which being near corrupting turn eager) And both these are generally disrellish'd: or if men do admit them for sawce, yet he must be very thirsty that will take a draught of 'm; whereas the generousest wine drops from the grape naturally without pressing, and though piquant hath its sweetness. And though I cannot arrogate so much as even the similitude of those good qualities to my Writing, yet I dare say that never was there a more pregnant ripeness in the causes. For having read one, two, three, and now four books of the same Author, and of the same subject, which was no less then that weighty matter of *Ecclesiastical Politie* and all its dependances, I observed first, that there was no name to them; a thing of very ill example. For every one that will treat of so nice and tender argument ought to affix his name, thereby to make himself responsible to the publick for any dammage that may arise by his undertaking. Otherwise though he has a License in his pocket, or he perhaps himself the Licenser, it is but a more authoriz'd way of libelling; and it looks too like a man that shall lay a train of Gun powder, and then retire to some obscure place from whence after he has applyed his match, he may solace himself with the mischief; or though it be not so design'd, yet the effect is not more probably to stop a flame than to propagate it, and in stead of preserving, to subvert and blow up the Government: Whereas if men were obliged to leave that anonymous and sculking method both of Writing and Licensing, they would certainly grow more careful what opinions they vented, what expressions they used, and we might have miss'd many books that have of late come out by the same authority contrary to all good manners, and even to the Doctrine of our Church under which they take protection. Had there been no other cause but this, it might have sufficed, and when *Ecclesiastical Politie* march'd *Incognito*, and Theology went on mumming, it was no less allowable for any one to use the license of Mascarade to show him, and the rest of 'm the consequence of such practice.

7 that] who 74.   23 match 74; mach 73.

But beside this, when I perused his books, and others of the same patern, I saw that they plainly incroached upon other mens vocations, and that a sort of Divines, among whom he alwayes acted the highest parts, had clann'd together to set up above those of the King and Duke a new Company of Comedians. Such was their 5 Dramatick and Scenical way of scribling, and they did so teem with new Plays perpetually, that there was no Post nor Pillar so sacred that was exempt, no not even the walls of *Pauls* it self much less the *Temple-gate*, from the pasting up of the Titles. Insomuch that I have seen a Lacquey that could not read, having been sent 10 to take down the Play for the afternoon, has by mistake brought away the Title of a new book of Theology. Yet if they did it well, they might perhaps in time get some custom; but alas those great men in the Pulpit how ridiculous do they appear on a Stage, and he that has all his life been cramp'd in a Reading pew at what a loss 15 must he be when he comes to tread in whatsoever Theater! They are so unfit to bear a part among any Civil and Judicious Company, that, whatsoever place they may hold in the Church, I am confident they must make all their friends to be but receiv'd into the *Nursery*. And had not Mr. *Killegrew* foreseen that they must of course within 20 a little time fall to dirt of themselves, he would ere this to be sure have trounced the *Author of the Ecclesiastical Politie*, for intrenching upon his Patent. But he knew they were below his neglect and the *Pit* would quickly do their business, and not only hiss but palt them off the Stage. And I, that had sate so long more quiet than all the 25 rest of the Spectators, could not at last restrain my self from using also the liberty of the House and revenging the expense of my time and money, by representing the *Author of the* Comedy call'd the *Ecclesiastical Politie* in that Farse of mine own the *Rehearsal Transpros'd*. 30

Neither yet was this all that deserved reprehension in his Writings, He useth such a Ruffian-like stile, and upon which, to my knowledge, he peculiarly values himself, that any one would suspect he had travell'd and convers'd all his life time either among the Nation of the *Bravo's* and *Filoux*, or else been educated in the 35 Academy of the *Venetian* Galleys which he himself was in his second

1 beside] besides 74.

book so apprehensive of, that he never rested until he had found in his third how to supply them with Slaves out of the Non-conformists. But I perceive since that men of his parts can arrive at those perfections sitting but in their Closets and over-hearing the Watermen which others after long Voyages and observation neither would nor could ever attain to. Then the Arrogance which runs through all his books is insupportable, boasting proudly of himself, vilifying and censuring others to such a degree that as I never heard any thing equal, so neither any thing like it but the Mountebanks abroad, who after a deal of Scaffold Pageantry to draw audience, entertain them by decrying all others with a Panegyrick of their own Balsam. There is scarce any sort and rank of men ancient or modern, scarce any particular person though of the most established and just reputation, but he does if he meet them not hale them into his way to invey against them and trample upon them, nay even such as have but a book, or two, or three before (perhaps a page, perhaps a line) been happy in his good opinion. And this he does for the most part in the most bitter manner that is possible: I know not whether I may properly call it Satyrical, but let it go so for once, for what he wants in wit he supplyes however in good will, and where the Conceit is deficient, he makes it out always with railing. He scarce ever opens his mouth, but that he may bite, nor bites, but that from the *Vesicles* of his Gums he may infuse a venom. Had he been but innocently dull, he might have been sure no man would have medled with him: but when there was no end of his buttering one book upon another, and he still writ worse and worse, with less vigour always, but more virulence, that perpetual grating did indeed set my teeth on edge, and I thought that even the most candid Readers would out of their equity not take it amiss if at last he did by hearing ill himself, lose part of that pleasure which he had so frequently taken in traducing and speaking hitherto ill of others. For no man needs Letters of Mart against one that is an open Pirate of other mens Credit: and I remember within our time one *Simons*, who rob'd alwayes upon the *Bricolle*, that is to say, never interrupted the Passengers but still set upon the Thieves themselves after, like Sir *John Falstaff*, they were gorged with a booty; and by

35 Thieves] Thieve 74.   36 after, like] after that, like 74.

this way, so ingenious, that it was scarce criminal, he lived secure and unmolested all his dayes with the reputation of a Judge rather than an High-way man. But my greatest incentive was, as I told him in my former Pamphlet, the perniciousness of the whole design of his books; tending, in my opinion, to the disturbance of all 5 Government, the misrepresenting of the generous and prudent Counsels of His Majesty, and raising a mis-intelligence betwixt Him and His People; beside his calumniating the whole foraign Protestancy, his stirring up of persecution against those at home, and his mangling even of Religion it self and Christianity: And to 10 this purpose he suited befitting Principles, and to those a Language as harmonious: seeming to have forgot not only all Scripture rules, but even all Scripture expressions; unless where he either distorts them to his own interpretation, or attempts to make them ridiculous to others; Insomuch, that, of all the books that ever I read, I 15 must needs say I never saw a Divine guilty of so much ribaldry and prophaneness, Which though it was a matter of such Decency to his undertaking that I account it to have been even Necessary, yet in the whole I look'd upon as so uncanonical and impious, that it would bear an higher and more deserved accusation than that of *Onias* the 20 Son of *Simeon* the *Just*, for officiating in a Womans Zone instead of the Priestly girdle, and for the sacred Pectoral wearing his Mistresses Stomacher. I must confess that when all these things centred together upon my imagination, and I saw that none of his Superiors offer'd to interpose against an evil so great in it self, and 25 as to me appear'd so publick in the consequence and mischief, I could hold no longer, and I, though the most unfit of many, assumed upon him the Priviledge (if any such Priviledge there be) of an English *Zelote*.

Otherwise I indeed look'd upon him whosoever he were, as a per- 30 son in parts much my Superior, until the Cause as he took and handled it, had depress'd and levell'd his understanding: neither could I ever discover before such an exuberance in mine own, either abilities, which I am sensible how mean, or yet in my inclination, that should tempt me from that modest retiredness to which I 35 had all my life time hitherto been addicted. And truly after I had

22 Mistresses 74; Mistress 73.

written, I had so slender an opinion of mine own performance, that I can attribute the acceptance which it found only to his favour, who had so handled the matter, that nothing could have come out at that time against him but must be assured of welcom. And that among the other more weighty causes by reason of his unspeakable arrogance before mention'd: a Vice so generally odious, that to repress it is no less grateful; so that *Lucretius* might better have said that to be — *hominum Divumque voluptas*; there being scarce any spectacle more pleasing to God and Man than to see the proud humbled. But could I have imagined that my book could have had either so good or so ill a reception as it diversly met with, I have so much respect to those whom he calls the vulgar, and to whom he bids alwayes Universal contempt and defiance as a rout of Wolves and Tigres, Apes and Baboons, that I should however have bestow'd more pains upon it, I know not whether with better success. Yet the errours of that not being now revocable but by asking pardon of whosoever may have innocently mistaken my book, and declaring, which I do, that if any thing therein do tend to the disparagement of the Church of *England*, I wish it unsaid as it was unthought, and do hereby utterly disclaim it; I took it to be part of my gratitude to go no more to Sea, having been sufficiently toss'd for one man upon the billows of applause and obloquy to put me in mind of a Shipwrack, which when the waves go high may either way happen. And as to the *Author of the Ecclesiastical Polity* himself, whose person I was so far ignorant of, that I could only take aim at his errours, and much less could intend any other of that function, but those few who might assume to themselves his Character; I found nevertheless after the writing of that book, that natural relenting of mind which most men feel after they have done an harsh though necessary action. Insomuch that had it been in my power to have set him right again in mens opinions as it was in his to set himself wrong, I should have certainly done it. But for that he and every one else may please to believe as they shall see occasion. But this however must be evident which follows.

Whereas I had in that book, as is in that stile usual, intermixed things apparently fabulous, with others probably true, and that partly out of my uncertainty of the Author, and partly that if he pleas'd he might continue so; it seems however that I chanced to come so near his Form that it started him, and he thought fit to discover himself. Hereupon and having understood what he was about, I thought it my duty if possible to break off this ruder inter- course for the future, and reduce the matter unto a more manly 5 way of argument. I therefore took care to advertise him that I heard from several hands, that if in the answer intended there were any unjust and personal reflections, it would tend much to the disrepu- tation of himself and some persons whom he most esteemed, and that there was preparation made to that purpose. Upon this he 10 sent me word, that if any Answer were intended; 'twas more than he was acquainted with, or would concern himself about; and assured me my private reputation nor no mans else should ever be injur'd in publick by his consent. I do not by quoting this answer of his pretend to sue his Word, to which he is no more a Slave than 15 to the *Venetian* Galleys (such men being at liberty to comment upon their own as well as other Texts at their pleasure) Nevertheless be- fore this, and at that present time as well as ever since, I understood that he had sent out a general *Siquis* thorow his own Province and the other to make Inquisition concerning me. He voiced my book 20 all over as a most pernicious engine bent against the whole body of the Clergy. And upon that pretence he summon'd in all that ow'd suit and service to his Court, or the Church of *England*. The whole *Posse Archidiaconatus* was raised to repress me, and great riding there was and sending post every way to pick out the ablest Ecclesiastical 25 Droles to prepare an Answer. Some came in daily as Voluntiers, and others were more mercenary. For certainly there was never such an hubbub made about a sorry book, and, since the day of St. *Bar- tholomew*, there has not appear'd so great an expectation of an uni- versal Donative. Some one flatter'd himself with being at least a 30 Surrogate; another was so modest as to set up with being but a Paritor; while the most generous hoped only to be graciously smiled upon and well treated at a good Dinner: but the more hungry starvelings generally look'd upon it as an immediate Call to a Bene- fice, and he that could but write an Answer, whatsoever it were, 35 took it for the most dexterous cheap, and legal way of Simony. So

17 at] at at 74.　　28 St. *om.* 74.　　33 good *om.* 74.

that, as is usual upon those occasions, there arose no small com-
petition and mutiny among the Pretenders; and, it being impossible
to satisfie them all, many an one departed with a sad heart and
dejected countenance, when their Answers would not pass muster.
5 For it was not every book that could now be admitted. 'Twas
requir'd upon this occasion to gain a License, that there should be
some Wit more than ordinary, which most of them could not be at
the expense of; some measure of Impudence, which few of them
would pretend to; and above all such a proportion of Falshood as
10 might alone have supply'd the other defects and made their books
current; but scarce any of them would do it out of good Conscience.
For that indeed was now the principal business and the only argument that, as he had handled it, remain'd to this Cause; and therefore the *Author of the Ecclesiastical Polity* had alter'd his lodgings to
15 a Calumny Office, and kept open chamber for all comers that he
might be supplyed himself, or supply others as there was occasion.
But, though he had been a little choice at first, the Informations
came in so slenderly, that he was glad to make use of any thing
rather than sit out: and there was at last nothing so slight but it
20 grew material, nothing so false but he resolved it should go for
truth, and what wanted in matter he would make out with invention and artifice. So that he and his remaining Camarades seem'd
to have set up a Glass-house, the Model of which he had observed
from the height of his window in the Neighbourhood, and the Art
25 he had been initiated into ever since from the Manufacture (he will
criticize because not Orifacture) of *Soape-bubbles*, he improved by
degrees to the mysterie of making *Glass-drops*, and thence in running
leaps mounted by these virtues to be Fellow of the Royal Society,
Doctor of Divinity, Parson, Prebend, and Arch-deacon. The Fur-
30 nace was so hot of it self that there needed no coals, much less any
one to blow them. One burnt the Weed, another calcined the Flint,
a third melted down that mixture; but he himself fashion'd all with
his breath, and polished with his stile till out of a meer jelly of Sand
and Ashes, he had furnish'd a whole Cupboard of things so brittle
35 and incoherent that the least touch would break them again in
pieces, so transparent that every man might see thorow them.

32 fashion'd] rashioned 74.

In the mean time such care was used that the License of my book was recall'd, and the *Rehearsal Transprosed* was dubb'd a Theological Book, only to bring it under the verge of that Jurisdiction, on purpose that it might be prohibited. It hath indeed been usual to degrade a Priest, or scrape a shaven crown to deface his character before he were deliver'd over to secular justice: but this was a strange and contrary method to force a poor book into Holy Orders, that so it might be subjected to censure and execution by the Ordinary. This was an honour which to my knowledge the poor book neither affected nor deserved; though indeed it might have deserved it as well as the *Preface to Bishop Bramhall*, which occasion'd its Writing, and that 'tis true came out in state under the Title of a Theological Book in the Printed Catalogue of that year, as several others do of the same nature. When he had thus provided that my book should not speak for it self, and moreover used means, which having proved ineffectual I shall not particularize, to obstruct me from liberty of ever vindicating it for the future; it seem'd to him the most favourable season that ever was or could have been invented to keep his promise, and to publish his Answers to preserve *my private reputation*. For one Answer would not suffice; but therefore, to fit his ware for the purse and fancies of all Chapmen, and to *ingratiate* not only the *Booksellers*, but the Pedlers; he order'd the matter so and digested it into several Volumes, that a man might buy a Groat, Sixpence, a Shilling, Eighteen pence, Half a crown, or Five Shillings-worth of Theological Wit and Verity, as he saw occasion. The rest issued promiscuously; only before that which was to bear his own character, and the other which was to be call'd *Hicringills* were divulged, he procured that I should be asked by good Authority whether the *Rehearsal Transpros'd* were of my doing, which I under my hand avowed. By this means he had gained however three points, as he imagined. The first, that he should thereby have some months time more to mature two such excellent pieces, which he intended as the *Hercules* Pillars, and *Ne-plus-ultras* of the Reason, Wit, Sobriety, Good-breeding and Orthodoxy of the Clergy of the Church of *England*. The next that he should now be able to take such certain aim at me, that he might every shot he

7 contrary method] ccontary to method 74.

made hit me in the eye, or at least (for I have to do with a very critical adversary) in its Cavity, for I suppose his first arrow must have struck the eye out. And the last doubtless; that having let me know *that he would not concern himself,* and *assur'd me that my private* *reputation, nor any mans else should ever by him be injur'd in publick,* he might, now be understood I was the professed Author, give by these books so ample testimonial of his own Veracity. Though for some other reasons beside this last I rather conceive it might have been more expedient for him not to have been so inquisitive of the Author, or at least after he had learnt it not to have taken that notice of me. Not that I assume to my self any of those lineaments wherewith he describes me; but however after I had own'd the *Rehearsal Transpros'd,* whatsoever in either of his books he reflects upon the Author he must acknowledge as said by himself of me and directed to me. At last when all other plots and clancular contrivances against me had failed him, these two books also which he had kept in reserve, were in some hast Printed off; his day of Marriage too drawing fast on, which he intended to calender by a victory, and would perhaps have been deferr'd longer by the Friends, had he not first signaliz'd his prowess. So that now there were no less than half a dozen Answers out against me (not to mention several other Pamphlets wherein the Authors or Booksellers by drawing in but by head and shoulders one line perhaps concerning the *Rehearsal Transpros'd,* or by only naming it hoped to procure vent or better their livelyhood) He had thus got a *Sixiesme du valet* in his hand already, and if he can but show three more of the same Honour to make a *Quatorze,* I am repiqued inevitably and spoyl'd for a Gamster by a Dignitary much Superior to him of *Lincoln.* There were no less than six *Scaramuccios* together upon the Stage, all of them of the same gravity and behaviour, the same tone, the same habit, that it was impossible to discern which was the true *Author* *of the Ecclesiastical Politie.* I believe he imitated the Wisdom of some other Princes, who have sometimes been perswaded by their Servants to disguise several others in the Regal garb, that the enemy might not know in the battel whom to single. But for my part

15 plots and *om.* 74.   15–16 contrivances] contrivance 74.   24 *Rehearsal* 74; *Rehearsal* 73.   29 true *om.* 74.

though I know that several Gentlemen, and some of them Divines, are commonly named as the Authors of those books, yet they are persons for the most part of more Candor, Learning, and good Judgement than that I should suspect the truth of it, or that they could possibly descend to so mean and contrary an undertaking. 5 And even that *Gregory Greybeard*, which alone of all the six pretends to a Father, and to be writ by one that hath not only a Sir-name, but a Christen-name also, it sounds so strangely and unlike the name of any humane creature, that rather than so, it seems to me a word of Cipher, like the *Smectymnuus* formerly of the Presbyterians, 10 and so *Hicringill* to denote the Club of this whole party. But it is more probably by much the issue of the very same *Author of the Ecclesiastical Politie*. If it should be any other, 'tis a thing more remarkable than what is reported of the two learned brothers of St. *Marthe*, who being Twins and living to a great age were so like one 15 another, that they were not to be distinguish'd, but that one wore a Plain-band and the other a Ruff: nay, their minds had no less similitude; insomuch that, having with-drawn all day to study at any time on the same subject, when they came to compare at night they should find that they had light for the most part upon the 20 same conceptions. For he that shall read the *Reproof to the Rehearsal Transpros'd*, and then this *Hicringill*, will discern so little difference in their expressions, humour and thoughts (such as no man else could have hit upon) as he must necessarily infer and conclude that they are the works of one and the same Artificer, and so much I can 25 prove; that, if any one were not of his penning, yet all of them pass'd under his Inspection, Approbation, or License. So that upon perusal of all those books that have appear'd in so many several shapes against me, first *Rosemary and Bayes*, then the *Common Places*, next the *Transproser Rehears'd*, fourthly *S'too him Bays*, afterwards the *Reproof*, 30 and in fine, *Gregory Gray-beard*; I find plainly that 'tis but the same Ghost that hath haunted me in those differing dresses and Vehicles. Insomuch that upon consideration of so various an identity, methinks after so many years I begin to understand Doctor *Donn's*

3 persons 74; petsons 73.   8 sounds 74; souunds 73.   9 creature] creatures 74.   19 came] come 74.   21 *Hicringill* 74; *Hieringill* 73. 32 Vehicles] Vehicle 74.   33–34 methinks 74; methings 73.

Progress of the Soul, which pass'd through no fewer revolutions, and had hitherto puzzled all its Readers.

> For—*This Great Soul, which here amongst us now*
> *Does dwell,* and—*to which* Luther *and* Mahomet *were*
> *Prisons of flesh, this Soul which oft did tear*
> *And mend the wracks of th' Empire and late* Rome,
> *And liv'd when every great Change did come.*

did nevertheless fix it self at first in so mean a condition as is scarce credible, in a chast and innocent Apple. But that being soon pluck'd, it betook it self into a Mandrake, and

> *To show that in Loves business he should still*
> *A dealer be and be us'd well or ill,*
> *His Apples kindle, his Leaves force of Conception kill.*

('Tis pity that his Curate of *Ickham* was not acquainted with its virtues.) From this it took its flight into a Sparrow, and lived a chirping life, as is there described,

> *Already this hot Cock, in bush and tree,*
> *In Field and Tent, o'reflutters its next Hen,* &c.

From thence it drop'd, I know not how, into a little Fish: after that, into another little Fish: and there learnt the Art of Tipling, which it practis'd for some time in that moderate proportion. But next, in its third swimming leap it pitch'd into a Whale, and grew up to be the great Leviathan—*Now drinks he up Seas,—*

> *—and ever as he went,*
> *He spouted rivers up—*

Immediately after this, the Soul by some misadventure dwindled into a Mouse, but a very busie Mouse, and of great design: So that

> *—being late taught that great things might by less*
> *Be slain, to gallant mischief it doth it self address:*

and pick'd out no less opposite than an Elephant to buckle with,

> *Who foe to none, suspects no enemies,* &c.

---

3 *This*] the   Donne 1633.   4 *Does*] Doth   Donne 1633.   *which*] whom
Donne 1633.   13 *kindle*] kinde   Donne 1633.   18 *its*] his   Donne 1633.   28 *being*] om.
Donne 1633.   29 *it doth itself*] doth herselfe   Donne 1633.   31 *Who*] And
Donne 1633.

and having crept up thorow his Trunk was gnawing his Brain-strings asunder, but suddenly was crush'd under the ruines of so great an adversary. In process of time it enter'd into a Wolf, and infested *Abel*'s flock;

> Abel *as white and mild as his sheep were,*   5
> *who, in that Trade of Church and Kingdom's, there*
> *was the first type—*

but being hindred by a vigilant Bitch, the Wolf corrupted her to his purpose; yet at last was taken in a trap and kill'd. But straight it enter'd into the young *Lycisca*, that was new knotted, and the 10 whelp growing up was imploy'd by *Abel* in keeping the same Flock, but the Mungrel was not to be trusted: for partaking of both natures,

> *He as his Damme from Sheep drove Wolves away,*
> *And as his Sire he made them his own prey.*   15
> *Five years he liv'd, and cozened with his Trade:*

and then coming at last to be discovered,

> *From Dogs a Wolf, from Wolves a Dog he fled:*
> *And like a Spy, to both sides false, he perished.*

The Soul being then at a loss, got admittance into an Ape, which 20 being very facetious and full of Gambolls, grew into great favour with Madam *Siphatecia*: but for some ugly tricks, and making too bold with his Mistresses *Apron*, he was with a great stone knock'd dead by *Thelemite* her Brother. After this Soul had passed thorow so many Brutes, & been hunted from post to pillar, its last recep- 25 tacle was in the humane nature, and it housed it self in a female Con-ception, which after it came to years of consent, was Married to *Cain* by the name of *Themech*. This was the sum of that witty fable of Doctor *Donne*'s, which if it do not perfectly suit with all the transmigrations of mine Answerer, the *Author of the Ecclesiastical* 30 *Politie*, nor equal the Progress of so great a Prince, yet whoever will be so curious as himself to read that Poem, may follow the parallel much further than I have done, lest I should be tedious to the Reader by too long and exact a similitude. But if it do not quadrate

18 *he*] *he he* 74.

here, the resemblance will perhaps be more visible upon the examination of what remains to be consider'd next to the *Gravity of his
Profession*, that is the *Civility of his Education*, which he charges me
by my former book to have discomposed. For it is the interest of
the Publick, especially he appealing to it upon this particular, that
it should remain upon Record how Syllogistical a life his hath been
to the Stile and Principles that he has manag'd and prosecuted.

Whoever shall go back to trace his Original, will quickly be at a
stand & find themselves so soon involved in the Fabulous Age, that
they will run astray and be benighted in his History before noon.
They will find his *Saturn* to have reign'd much later than *William*
the *Conquerour*; or if, like a true born *Arcadian*, he derive himself
from before the Moon, it must be understood concerning the last
Change. I cannot yet learn, though he hath imployed me long
about it, who was his Grand-father: but, as modern as he must have
been, 'tis the certainer Heraldry to extract him from a *Vesicle of the
Earth*, and let him go for the Grand-son of a *Pimple*. For no Prince
how great soever begets his Predecessors, and the noblest Rivers
are not Navigable to the Fountain. Even the Parentage of the *Nile*
is yet in obscurity, and 'tis a dispute among Authors whether *Snow*
be not the head of his Pedigree. I read indeed as long ago as in the
Reign of *Edward* the 4*th*. concerning one *Henry Parker*, a Carmelite
Friar, who having preach'd against the secular grandeur and pomp
of the Clergy in those times, was forced to make a publick Recantation at *Pauls-Cross*. But this is too obsolete: and though otherwise
the Analogy might easily be propagated, yet I suppose the honest
Monk kept to his vow of Continence: and besides, should the
Author of the Ecclesiastical Politie, descend from that Line, it would
make too great a Solecism in his Scutcheon. There was also in the
latter end of Queen *Elizabeth*, and beginning of King *James*, one
Robert Parker, the Author of another kind of *Ecclesiastical Politie*, a
Learned, but severe Non-conformist, who writ also the book *de
Cruce*, for which he was forced to cross the Seas. But neither can I
find him to come within the proportion of time or Scale of his
Genealogy. Therefore to come nearer, I find in the Reign of the late
King *Charles* one *Humfrey Parker*, Yeoman, who together with Mr.
Chancey, for opposing the Rails about the Communion Table at

Ware was sentenced to make a solemn submission and acknowledgment of his fault, as he did accordingly. There are several Arguments that might incline me to think the *Author of the Ecclesiastical
Politie* is com'd of his Succession, and one particularly, because in
the Record I read that this *Humfrey* took a Journey upon this occa- 5
sion into *Northampton-shire*, the seat of the Answerers Family. But
that which seems to come nearest home to him and the Chronology
of his Grandfather, is in the year 1640. in a Petition from the City
of *London* and several Counties to the then Parliament; complaining
among other things of *Martin Parkers* Ballads, in disgrace of Reli- 10
gion, to the increase of all vice, and withdrawing of people from
reading, studying and hearing the Word of God and other good
books. 'Tis not at all unlikely that this, as an hereditary provocation, hath stuck upon him ever since, and that he swore at the
Altar, when he was but nine years old, to be aveng'd for this affront 15
to his lineage. We see often that the signature of the Grand-father
revives upon the child, and, as some Rivers diving for a while under
ground, makes a Bridge of the Parents to spring up again at that
interval. Hence doubtless hath proceeded all his peek against the
Nonconformists; hence that unquenchable *Nemesis* against the City; 20
hence it is that he hath taken upon him to defend in gross at this
time the whole mass of enormityes, right or wrong, then complain'd of in that Petition: all this mischief for a Ballad-makers sake
of the kindred. The Duke of *Muscovy* indeed declared War against
Poland, because he and his Nation had been vilifyed by a *Polish* Poet: 25
but the *Author of the Ecclesiastical Politie* would it seems disturb the
peace of Christendom for the good old cause of a superannuated
Chanter of *Saffron-hill* and *Pye-corner*. But though indeed he doth
not write his books in the *Smithfield* Meetre, yet they are all Blank
Ballad, and the subject and consequence *to the disgrace of Religion,* 30
*the increase of all vice, and with-drawing people from reading, studying, and
hearing the Word of God, and other good books is exactly the same.* So that
he may when he will put in for Letters of Administration in the
Prerogative Court, and enter his Claim too with the Heralds: for
every one will yield him to be the next of kin to that Author; or let 35
him but produce his own Writings, 'tis Evidence sufficient. If it

31 *with-drawing*] *wish-drawing* 74.

should prove otherwise, the fault is in his own obscurity, that hath
left all the Neighbourhood and me in the dark; and let him make
what shift he will to procure himself a Grand-father, for I have taken
pains enough, I am sure, to help him to one.

5   But however for that matter, let the worst come to the worst, he
had a Mother undeniably and probably a Father: Otherwise he
would be shrowdly disappointed, and in a worse case then *Prince
Prettyman* lamenting,

> *What Oracle this Secret can evince,*
> *Sometimes a Fishers Son, sometimes a Prince:*
> *It is a secret great, as is the world,*
> *In which I like the Soul am toss'd and hurl'd:*

And he might with good reason exclaim more pathetically—*Bring
in my Father, why d'ye keep him from me? Although a Fisherman, he is my
Father.*

> *Was ever Son yet brought to this distress,*
> *To be for being a Son made fatherless?*
> *Oh you just Heavens! rob me not of a Father:*
> *The being of a Son take from me rather.*

His Mother is said to have been an honest Yeoman's Daughter, and
to have been his Fathers Servant, with whom she lived with good
reputation and so ever since her marriage; except what disgrace may
have reflected from her issue, which being her grief and misfortune
ought not to be her scandal. But though he came of a good Mother,
he had a very ill Sire. He was a man bred toward the Law, and betook himself, as his best practice, to be a Sub Committee man, or,
as the stile ran, one of the Assistant Committee in *Northampton-shire.*
In the rapine of that employment, and what he got by picking the
teeth of his Masters he sustain'd himself, till he had raked together
some little estate. And then being a man for the purpose, and that
had begun his fortune out of the sequestration of the Estates of the
Kings party, he to perfect it the more, proceeded to take away their
Lives; not in the hot and Military way (which diminishes always
the offence) but in the cooler blood and sedentary execution of an

High Court of Justice. Accordingly he was preferr'd to be one
of that number that gave Sentence against the three Lords, *Capel*,
Holland, and *Hamilton*, who were beheaded. By this Learning in the
Law he became worthy of the degree of a Serjeant, and sometimes
to go the Circuit till for misdemeanor he was Petition'd against. 5
But for a taste of his abilities, and the more to re-ingratiate himself,
he printed in the year 1650, a very remarkable book called *The
Government of the People of* England, *precedent and present the same. Ad
subscribentes confirmandum, Dubitantes informandum, Opponentes convincendum*; and underneath, *Multa videntur quæ non sunt, Multa sunt quæ* 10
non videntur. Under that ingraven, two Hands joyn'd with the
Motto, *Ut uniamur*, and beneath a Sheaf of Arrows with this Device,
Vis unita fortior; and to conclude, *Concordia parvæ res crescunt Discordia
dilabuntur*. A most Hieroglyphical Title and sufficient to have supplyed the Mantlings and Atchievements of the Family! By these 15
Parents he was sent to *Oxford*, with intention to breed him up to
the Ministry. There in a short time he enter'd himself into the
Company of some young Students who were used to Fast and Pray
weekly together, but for their refection fed sometimes on a Broth
from whence they were commonly call'd *Grewellers:* only it was 20
observed that he was wont still to put more *Graves* than all the rest in
his Porrige. And after that he pick'd acquaintance not only with the
Brotherhood at *Wadham Colledge*, but with the *Sisterhood* too at
another old *Elsibeths*, one *Elizabeth Hampton's*, a plain devout Woman,
where he train'd himself up in hearing their Sermons and Prayers, 25
receiving also the Sacrament in the House, till he had gain'd such
proficience that he too began to exercise in that Meeting, and was
esteem'd one of the *preciousest* young men in the University. But
when thus, after several years approbation, he was even ready to
have taken the charge not of an *admiring drove* or *heard*, as he now 30
calls them, but of a Flock upon him, by great misfortune, the King
came in by the miraculous providence of God influencing the dis-
tractions of some, the good affections of others, and the weariness
of all towards that happy Restauration after so many sufferings to
his Regal Crown and Dignity. Nevertheless, he broke not off yet 35
from his former habitudes, and though it were now too late to

5 to go] go to 74.

obviate this inconvenience, yet he persisted, as far as in him was, that is by praying, caballing, and discoursing to obstruct the restoring of the Episcopal Government, Revenues, and Authority. Insomuch that finding himself discountenanced on those accounts by the then
5 Warden of *Wadham*, he shifted Colledges to *Trinity*, and, when there, went away without his Degree, scrupling forsooth the Subscription then required. From thence he came to *London*, where he spent a considerable time in creeping into all Corners and Companies, Horoscoping up and down concerning the duration of the
10 Government: not considering any thing as best, but as most lasting and most profitable. And after having many times cast a figure, he at last satisfyed himself that the Episcopal Government would indure as long as this King lived, and from thence forward cast about how to be admitted into the Church of *England*, and find the High-
15 way to her preferments. In order to this he daily inlarged, not only his Conversation but his Conscience, and was made free of some of the Town-vices: imagining like *Muleasses* King of *Tunes* (for I take witness that on all occasions I treat him rather above his quality than otherwise) that by hiding himself among the Onyons, he
20 should escape being traced by his Perfumes. Ignorant and mistaken man, that thought it necessary to part with any virtue to get a Living; or that the Church of *England* did not require and incourage more sobriety, than he could ever be guilty of: whereas it hath alwayes been fruitful of men, who, together with obedience to that
25 Discipline, have lived to the envy of the Non-conformists in their conversation, and without such could never either have been preserved so long or after so long a dissipation have ever recover'd. But neither was this yet in his opinion sufficient: and therefore he resolved to try a shorter path which some few men have trode not
30 unsuccessfully: that is, to print a book, if that would not do, a second, if not that, a third of an higher extraction and so forward, to give experiment against their former party of a keen stile and a Ductile judgement. His first Proof-piece was in the year 1665, the *Tentamina Physico theologica*: a tedious transcript of his Common
35 place book, wherein there is very little of his own, but the arrogance and the unparallel'd censoriousness that he exercises over all other

8 spent 74; spnnt 73 .

Writers, beside his undutiful inveying even then against the *Vesicles of the Earth* for meer bubbles, as he did shortly after against his Fathers Memory, and in his Mothers presence before several witnesses, for a couple of *whining Phanaticks*. However he accounted it a safe book, on all sides, it being of so trite and confessed an argu- 5 ment that few judicious men would read it to examine the errours: and in so rough and scabbed a *Latine*, that a man must have long nails, and those sharper than ordinary, to distinguish betwixt the Skin and the Disease, the Faults and the Grammar. To omit his usual volume and circumference of periods; which though he takes 10 alwayes to be his chiefest strength, yet indeed, like too great a Line, weakens the defense, and requires too many men to make it good. But the Cause being against Atheism, he was secure that none would attaque him. For whether there be any Atheists is some controversie, and he is Compurgator for most of 'm: or if there be 15 such, yet they know the Bastions are all undermined and they should be blown up as soon as enter'd. But let him shew me any Atheist that he hath reduced by his book, unless he may pretend to have converted some (as in the old *Florentine* Wars) by meer tyring them out, and perfect weariness. In this Treatise however it 20 was difficult for him to have hedged in the Non-conformists: only here and there he sprinkles a glittering ore, to give hopes of a vein underneath of such metal as might by a skilful hand be founded into any figure; and having shown as he thought sufficiently that he believ'd there was a God, he imagin'd that thenceforward, write 25 what, and against whom he would, it might pass as indisputably; that all would be current which past his Touch-stone; that as his Predecessor *Midas* turn'd into Gold whatsoever he touched, so every thing by his handling should be transmuted to Orthodoxy. When he had Cook'd up these musty Collections, he makes his first 30 invitation to his *old Acquaintance* my Lord Arch-bishop of *Canterbury*, who had never seen before nor heard of him. But I must confess he furbishes up his Grace in so glorious an Epistle, that, had not my Lord been long since proof against the most Spiritual Flattery, the Dedication only without ever reading the book, might have served 35 to have fix'd him from that instant as his Favourite. Yet all this I

1 then] then then 74.

perceive did not his work, but his Grace was so unmindful, or
rather so prudent, that the Gentleman thought it necessary to spur
up again the next year with another new book to show more plainly
what he would be at. This he dedicates to Doctor *Bathurst* and to
5 evidence from the very Epistle that he was ready to renounce that
very Education the Civility of which he is so tender of as to blame
me for disordering it, he picks occasion to tell him: *to your prevailing
advise, Sir, do I owe my first rescue from the Chains and Fetters of an unhappy Education.* But in the book which he calls, a *free and impartial
10 Censure of the Platonick Philosophy,* (censure 'tis sure to be whatsoever
he writes) he speaks out, and demonstrates himself ready and
equipp'd to surrender not only the Cause, but betray his party
without making any Conditions for them, and to appear forthwith
himself in the head of the contrary Interest. Which supposing the
15 dispute to be just, yet in him was so mercenary, that none would
have descended to act his part but a Divine of Fortune. And even
Lawyers take themselves excused from being of Counsel for the
King himself, in a Cause where they have been entertain'd and instructed by their Client. But so flippant he was, and forward in this
20 book, that, in despight of all Chronology, he could introduce *Plato*
to invey against *Calvin,* and from the Platoniques he could miracu-
lously hook in a Discourse against the Non-conformists. After this
feat of activity he was ready to leap over the Moon: no scruple of
Conscience could stand in his way, and no preferment seemed too
25 high for him; For about this time, I find that having taken a turn
at *Cambridge,* to qualifie himself, he was received within doors to be
my Lord Arch-bishops other Chaplain, and into some degree of
favour: which, considering the difference of their humours and ages,
was somewhat surprizing. But, whether indeed in times of heat and
30 faction the most temperate Spirits may sometimes chance to take
delight in one that is spightful, and make some use of him; or
whether it be that even the most grave and serious persons do for
relaxation divert themselves willingly by whiles with a Creature
that is unlucky, mimical and gamesome; so it was. And thencefor-
35 ward the nimble Gentleman danced upon Bell-ropes, vaulted from
Steeple to Steeple, and cut Capers out of one Dignity to another.
Having thus dexterously stuck his Groat in *Lambeth* Wainscot it

may easily be conceived he would be unwilling to lose it, and therefore he concern'd himself highly, and even to jealousie in upholding
now that Palace, which if falling, he would out of instinct be the
first should leave it. His Majesty about that time labouring to
effect his constant promises of Indulgence to his people, the Author 5
therefore walking with his own shadow in the evening took a great
fright lest all were agoe. And in this conceit being resolv'd to make
good his Figure, and that one Government should not last any
longer than the other, he set himself to write those dangerous Books
which I have now to do with: wherein, he first makes all that he 10
will to be Law, and then: whatsoever is Law to be Divinity. And
I shall appeal to all Readers, and I hope make it good, that never in
any age, by any man (that I may not say any Church-man) have
there been published Discourses either so erroneously founded, or
so foully managed, or of so pernicious consequence. In conclusion, 15
this is that man who insists so much and stirrops himself upon the
Gravity of his Profession, and the Civility of his Education: which
if he had in the least observed in respect either to himself or others,
I should, I could never have made so bold with him. And nevertheless, it being so necessary to represent him in his own likeness that 20
it may appear what he is to others, and to himself, if possibly he
might at last correct his indecencies, I have not committed any fault
of stile, nor even this tediousness, but in his imitation. I have not
used any harsh expressions but what were suitable to that Civility
of Education which he practises, and that Gravity of Profession 25
which he hath set up of: and even therein I have taken care, beside
what my nature hath taken care for, to shoot below the mark, and
not to retaliate to the same degree; being willing, as I must yield
him the preference for many good qualities, so in his worst however
to give him the precedence. And yet withall that it hath been thus 30
far the odiousest task that ever I undertook, and has look'd to me
all the while like the cruelty of a Living Dissection, which, however
it may tend to publick instruction, and though I have pick'd out
the most noxious Creature to be anatomiz'd, yet doth scarce excuse
or recompence the offensiveness of the scent and fouling of my 35
fingers. Therefore I will here break off abruptly, leaving many a

36 here] hear 74.

vein not laid open, and many a passage not search'd into; nor read
any further upon this Soul of the World, or prosecute afresh its
allegory from the Apple, the Mandrake, the Sparrow, the Fishes,
the Mouse, the Mungrel, the Ape, unto the day of Marriage, but
5 leave the Moral to the judicious. And I could here take advantage
perhaps plausibly enough to put a final conclusion to this whole
book, for if a man hath taken off his railing, he hath therein answered
his Argument. But if I have undergone the drudgery of the more
loathsome part already, I will not defraud my self of what is more
10 truly pleasant, & remains behind the lighter burthen, the conflict
with, if it may be so call'd his Reason. For his whole book is,
according to his usual Address, a Letter to me, & it concerns my
Civility to return an Answer to every part of it. He hath ask'd me
many questions, and I take my self obliged to resolve them. And
15 he hath promis'd me the Press shall be open; neither would I therefore be behind hand with him in courtesie. So that I have now only
three things of which he hath made it necessary that I caution the
Reader. The first is not to be misled by a pestilent way that he
has of Youing me, and so making me an Epidemical person, affixing
20 thereby what hath ever, he pretends to have been said or done by
any in the Cause of Non-conformity at any time to my account:
although it hath never enter'd into my Book or Imagination, and
he had been more kind, if, as sometimes he does out of civility he
had Thou'd me to the end of the Chapter. The second is not on
25 the other part to impute any errors or weakness of mine to the Non-
conformists, nor mistake me for one of them, (not that I fly it as a
reproach, but rather honour the most scrupulous:) for I write only
what I think befits all men in Humanity, Christianity and Prudence
toward Dissenters. The last is not to think that I am any such old
30 Acquaintance as he claims, to insinuate me of dis-ingenuity, for of
our acquaintance I shall give account hereafter.

THat which gave me the first occasion of Writing was, as I have
said formerly, his third *Crambe*, of the same purulent matter, and
virulent stile, the *Preface to Bishop* Bramhall: and against that and

its incomparable extravagancies was my whole Discourse bent and levell'd. Only about the middle of mine I touch'd in passing upon some points of his other Treatises, that is, the *Power of the Magistrate, Conscience, Morality, Debauchery, Persecution,* &c. But he, whether by mistake or on purpose, turns my method quite backward, and, avoiding that which was direct for what is but collateral, begins in his second page, in his usual Military Metaphors of *Attack, Front and Rear,* &c. with the Ninety seventh of my Book. This however, is an accident that hath befaln other great Commanders as well as himself. For his Ancient Friend, *William the Conqueror,* at the battel of *Hastings,* had in the same manner the back of his Cuirasses placed before, by the error of him that put them on. The thing is ominous I doubt to the *Author of the Ecclesiastical Politie,* and assuredly (as the Duke then said) *This day his Fortune will turn, and he will be a King or nothing before night.* Yet I will not decline the pursuit, but plod on after him in his own way, thorow thick and thin, hill or dale, over hedge and ditch wherever he leads; till I have laid hand on him, and deliver'd him bound either to Reason or Laughter, to Justice or Pity. If at any turn he gives me the least opportunity to be serious I shall gladly take it: but where he prevaricates or is scurrilous (and where is he not?) I shall treat him betwixt Jest and Earnest. That which is solid and sharp, being imp'd by something more light and airy, may carry further and pierce deeper, and therefore I shall look to it as well as I can, that mine Arrows be well pointed, and of mine own whetting; but for the Feathers, I must borrow them out of his Wing. Neither yet would I have this similitude improv'd to his disparagement: for he is a Bird of Prey, and an High-flyer, and, though he hath lessen'd himself by the Height of his Place, he cannot certainly be other than an Eagle, and perhaps the same fate may attend him.

First therefore, as to the Power of the Magistrate, he saith in gross: that *the Supream Government of every Common-wealth must of Necessity be Universal, Uncontroulable, Indispensable, Unlimited, and Absolute in all affairs whatsoever that concern the Interests of Mankind and the ends of Government; as well in matters of Religion as in all other Civil concerns.* This is I confess pretty strongly worded, and drawn up doubtless by the advice of his Counsel Learned: But if these be terms

unknown yet in our Law, we must refer it to the Supream Government *to define their signification.* However, if it be not Law, 'tis pity
but it were so. 'Tis the very *Elixir Potestatis* and *Magisterium
Dominii:* So fine a thing that no man living but would be inamour'd
5 with it: For, wot ye well, it is *a Power* he saith *establish'd* of yore, at
or before the beginning of the World, e're there was any such thing
known or thought of, as Periwigs or Glass-Coaches *by the unalterable
dictates of Natural Reason and Universal Practice and Consent of Nations.*
Only in *the Jewish Common wealth for some peculiar Reasons of State,*
10 (which he knows but will not tell us) 'twas for some time otherwise.
But this Power was *antecedent to Christ* himself, and it was so well
founded, that there was none, or very little need of the Authority
of the Scripture in the Case, and therefore *the Scripture rather supposes
than asserts this Jurisdiction.* Yet in our Saviours time, and for some
15 while after there was such *a Posture of Affairs,* and *such an unhappy
Juncture of Affairs* (how mechanically he expresses it?) that, while
the Heathen Princes enjoy'd this Power by the Antecedent Right
of Soveraignty, and accordingly exercised it over Christians, 'twas
also necessary to supply it among them *by Miracles of Severity.* But
20 *when once Christianity became the Imperial Religion, this Power began to
resettle where Nature had placed it,* and so the world jog'd on, and *its
Affairs were competently well Govern'd (though better or worse, according
to the wisdom and vigilance of the several Emperors*) till the Bishop of
Rome, seeing this Power to be so rich and beautiful a Creature began
25 to cast a sweet Eye on her, and, by the address of his constant sollicitation and courtship carried her sheer away from all the Princes
of Christendom. So this Jewel of the Crown was for several hundred
of years imbezel'd till *Henry* the 8*th.* and other Princes found it again
by chance in the ruines of an old Monastery at the Reformation.
30 But though the *Wisdom of the elder Ages had alwayes practised this
Power,* yet since that *Governors have not been thorowly instructed in its
Nature and Extent. Government hath not been rightly understood nor duly
managed,* the Reformation *hath not been able to resettle Princes in their
full and Natural rights.* What will not the man deserve that can

4 *Dominii* Errata *Domini* 73.   5 of] cf. 74.   9 *Jewish . . . State*] Reasons
peculiar to that State Parker.   15 there 74; rhere 73.   31 since that *Ed.*;
(in italics 73). The words are not Parker's.

show them better and teach Governors a Receipt against so
Chronical Negligence and Ignorance? *So little have Princes understood
their own Interests. So fatal has been their miscarriage.* Send for a Physician e're they be all out of hope, and while there is yet some life in
'm. But he will do well to make sure of his Fee beforehand, as those 5
that sold the *Jcterus*, a Bird good against the Jaundise, hid it till
they were pay'd lest the buyer at first sight be cur'd. The Great
Secret after all is, that *the Prince may and hath Power to transfer the
Exercise of the Preisthood upon another, and that he may if he please reserve
it to himself.* Is this all? The notion is something new indeed; but 10
he hath deduced it very well, and 'tis pretty probable: though I
have known the time, and many others may remember it when it
would not have been granted. I make account the *Author of the
Ecclesiastical Politie* is sufficiently impowred by the whole Clergy, at
least of *England:* and doubtless therefore his Majesty, among other 15
Princes, will if he find it good and for his service accept the Donation, not much inferiour to that of *Constantine.* 'Tis a great piece of
gratitude now in them, and 'twould have done well and more
seasonably, had his late Majesty before the War been informed by
them in this particular and the dependances. But I have some 20
reason to be jealous that the *Author of the Ecclesiastical Politie* is not
thus liberal without some design; that he hath some job or other to
be done, and how Unlimited and Absolute soever he hath made and
declared the Magistrate, there is some condition annex'd upon
failure of which this Fiefe shall Reincamerate. For he was of another 25
opinion in his *Preface to Bishop* Bramhall, when he said *all Government
does and must owe its quiet and continuance to the Churches Patronage.* Yes:
there is another *Croisade* to be undertaken, and he hath a project in
his head to ingage all Princes in a war against Non-conformity, a
second *Bellum Archidiaconale.* For though he was resolved, even in 30
his first book, to run his head against a wall, and very ingenuously
professes there too, that *if he had spoke reason he had without any more
adoe carry'd the Cause, if he had not he was content to lose his labour;* he
intended not it should go so easily. But in that very first Book,
while he was in the sweetest temper, in his natural serenity, and 35

30–1 even in his first book, 74; *om.* 73.   31 ingenuously] ingeniously 74.
32 *had om.* 74.

most benign inclinations, not heated or provok'd by any Adversary; and before he had expected one minute what so strong a Reason, what so perswasive eloquence might have effected with the Non-conformists, joyn'd with that interest which he had so many years
5 been creating amongst them, even then at the same time he sounds another *Trumpet* then that in *Sheere-lane*, to Horse, and hem in his Auditory. He proclaims them, for meer dissenting upon tenderness of Conscience, *Villains, Hypocrites, Rebels, Schismaticks, and the greatest and most notorious Hereticks*. He summons therefore the Magistrate
10 to do his Office that is to impose Ceremonies, which he owns to be indifferent, upon those that hold the contrary, with the severest Penalties, and the strictest Execution. What is this but to put Governors upon the Tenters, to invent how possibly they may run their Subjects into Disobedience, and then to invent and apply the
15 Tortures for their Disobeying? As for the poor Subjects there is no help for them, but he gives them very excellent and Ghostly coun-sel to *abide their sad Fate* with patience and Resignation; but in stead of them he layes his Imposition now upon the Magistrate and leaves him not so much as the Power to will nor chuse; but he must govern
20 by the Laws of *the Author of the Ecclesiastical Politie.* He *must scourge them into order. He must Chastise them out of their peevishness, and Lash them into obedience, There is no remedy but the Rod and Correction. He must restrain them with more rigor than unsanctifyed Villains. He must expose them to the Correction of the publick Rods and Axes.* Is this at last
25 all the business why he hath been building up all this while that Necessary, Universal, Uncontroulable, Indispensable, Unlimited, Absolute Power of Governors; only to gratifie the humour and arro-gance of an Unnecessary, Universal, Uncontroulable, Dispensable, Unlimited and Absolute, Arch-deacon? Still *must, must, must*: But
30 what if the Supream Magistrate won't? Why, *must* again, eight times at least in litle more than one page, and thorow his whole book proportionably. This is (and let him make a Quibble on't if he please) like *Doctor Rabelais* his setting *Julius Cæsar* to beat *Mus-tard*: and just as worshipful an imployment, as if he should prefer
35 his Majesty from his Kingdom and *Whitehall* to the Government of his Ancient Palace of *Bridewell.* But Laws and Impositions he saith

4 had so] had been so 74.

signifie nothing without Penalties, nor these without acting up roundly by rigorous Executions. Therefore that he might be true to his own principles, if the Supream Magistrate be disobedient, he hath provided against him too pretty severely. He hath denounced that in that case men deserve *to perish like* Sardanapalus. That such a Prince *deserves to be King of the Night,* and to conclude, he affirms that *Princes unless they will be resolute,* that is to do what he would have them, *they must not Govern.* 'Tis come to *Noli igitur regnare*: They had need to take heed of him it seems, and how they behave themselves. But they may very well take all this kindly of him, and as an honour, for it is no less Authority than he exercises over God Almighty. For he will have it that God too *must of necessity have vested Princes in at least as much Power as was absolutely necessary to the Nature and Ends of Government.* And what the Authors ends are we have and shall take occasion more particularly to examine hereafter.

What needs there further for evidence in this matter, or if men would out of love to justice be more exactly inform'd, let them but read, if their patience will not last longer, the Contents at least of the several Chapters of his *Ecclesiastical Politie,* in this and the other matters. It is sufficient punishment for some Offenders to be placed in publick with their book, or its Title affix'd before them. But because he will not be satisfy'd with that, I shall presume so far on my Readers as to trace him thorow the Maze of what in the *Reproof* he would answer. He insults first because he saith I expose an innocent and undeniable Proposition of his, that the Magistrate hath such a Power as is before described to govern and conduct the Consciences of his Subjects in affairs of Religion; and yet I say not a word in its confutation: but he forgets that where I quote that, I in the very next line subjoyn thus, *And* pag. 22. *he explains himself more fully*: *That unless Princes have Power to bind their Subjects to that Religion that they apprehend most advantageous to publick peace and tranquillity and restrain those religious mistakes that tend to its Subversion they are no better than Statues and Images of Authority.* And this I several times inculcated into him; but of this he takes not the least notice I warrant you: 'tis all hush'd. Is not this now a candid Reprover? But because I know he will hereupon be wriggling, I will shew him

7 resolute 74; resolutt 73.   12 too *must*] must too 74.

that these words cannot be interpreted otherwise by him than according to their first appearance and full latitude. He cannot mean it in matters of Ceremony, which indeed he ought to have kept to, but that the subject it seems turn'd into an argument, and
5 led him further to confess and speak out what was in the bottom. For concerning Ceremonies he saith indeed, *That 'tis absolutely necessary that Governors injoyn matters of no great moment and consequence in themselves, thereby to avoid the evil that would naturally attend upon their being not injoyn'd: so that when they are determin'd, though perhaps they are*
10 *of no great use to the Common wealth in themselves, yet they have at least this considerable usefulness as to prevent many great mischiefs that would probably follow if they were not determined*: A most memorable passage, and that deserves to be recorded as the full sum and state of the controversie. Yet he most ingenuously professes that *All that concerns Religious*
15 *Worship is no part of Religion itself, but only an Instrument, &c. and therefore though the Christians Laws command us by some exterior signs to express our interior Piety, yet they have no where set down any particular expressions of worship and adoration.* So also *All Rituals and Ceremonies and Postures and manners of performing the outward expressions of Devotion are*
20 *not in their own Nature capable of being Parts of Religion.* And thus in many other places: So that he hath gained nothing by the first objection which he hath raised but a Proposition not so undeniable, nor very innocent, that the Prince hath Power to bind his Subjects to that Religion which he apprehends most advantageous, *&c.* His
25 next exception against me is very material, that I have quoted so many passages out of his book. It has I believe indeed anger'd him as it has been no small trouble to me: but how can I help it? I wish he would be pleas'd to teach me an Art (for if any man in the world, he hath it) to answer a book without, *turning over the Leaves* (for that
30 in a former Answer offended him) or without citing the passages: In the mean time if to transcribe so much out of him must render a man as he therefore stiles me a *Scandalous Plagiary* I must plead Guilty: but by the same Law whoever shall either be Witness or Prosecutor, in behalf of the King, for Treasonable words, may be
35 *indited* for an High-way-man. After this he asks me roundly whether

8 *evil*] evils Parker.   14 *ingenuously*] ingeniously 74.   *Religious*] External Parker.
16 *Christians*] Christian Parker.   19 *outward* 74; *eutward* 73.

I do seriously believe that his Majesty has no Power in matters of Religion. Let him first make good his own Assertions, which I have charged him with and then I will tell him more of my mind; yet because he questions me of my Belief (which I believe he never yet did to any man in his own Parsonages, or either at *Ickham* or *Chart-* 5 *ham*) I do however count my self obliged to give him some answer, as much as he can chalenge of me; that is, I do most certainly believe that the Supream Magistrate hath some Power, but not all Power in matters of Religion. And particularly, to advance so much further to our *Author of the Ecclesiastical Politie*, I do not believe that 10 Princes have Power to bind their Subjects to that Religion that they apprehend most advantageous. And I will give him a Reason too of this my Belief. He himself saith (and it is worthy to be taken good notice of) *that the Fanaticks of late have so imbroiled Christendom, that Christian Princes begin to be of a perswasion, that Christianity is an* 15 *enemy to Government.* Now it is therefore to be presumed, that he is very conversant and intimate with all the Princes of Christendom. But I suppose that they reveal'd this secret of State to him only in confidence, for I never before heard of it in publick: and it is not so ingenuously or prudently done of him to proclaim in Print the sub- 20 ject of a familiar discourse, and private conference with them. This sure will make Princes more cautelous for the future, whom they chuse for their Ministers, and to believe that even he, unless he be better at keeping a secret, is not so fit to be of their Privy-Counsel: no not in Affairs Ecclesiastical. But if it be so (as who dare contro- 25 vert it after so authentical authority as the Author's of the *Ecclesi-astical Politie*) that Princes are indeed perswaded that Christianity is an Enemy to Government, it is not so safe to acknowledge that they have Power to bind to what Religion they apprehend most advantageous. Especially if it should chance that so pliable a Gen- 30 tleman should be at their elbow, who, out of excess of Conformity indulges the greatest Non-conformity imaginable. *We condemn,* saith he, *neither Turks nor Papists for their forms and Postures of Adoration (unless they fall under one or both of the obliquities aforesaid.) Let them but address the same worship to its proper object, and we will never stand stifly* 35 *with them about their outward Rites and Ceremonies of its expression, but will*

13 worthy 74; worty 73.   20 ingenuously] ingeniously 74.

freely allow them to conform to the significant Customs of their Countrey, as we do to those of ours. 'Tis most graciously done that his *We-ship* will allow them it: Will he not sound a Trumpet too when he has done to give 'm leave to go to dinner? I due time sure there will be an
5 Hat for him to make him in requital the Cardinal-Deacon. But why will he not carry the good humour thorow, and be as merciful to his Neighbours? All abroad and nothing at home? There have been and are several Rites and Customs too in the Countries of *England*, which do neither countenance Vice, nor disgrace the Deity, and
10 these dissenting people do address the same Worship to its due and proper Object. But (not to prevent my self) should he now, that is so clear as to matter of Ceremonies, be back'd at the same time with another Fellow-Prebend of his no less Frank in Religion, who should tell the Princes that he abhors being a Papist as much as being a Pres-
15 byterian, and will as soon be a Turk, as he will be either: what might become of us, if the Princes were satisfy'd of their own Power, and of these mens Discretion? It might breed no small alteration in the *affairs* of Christendom. For whatsoever the Papists be, there are many things to be said why the Turks is a very advantageous Religion.
20   Then he quotes his Majesties Declaration to make good his— *making use of that Supream Power in Ecclesiastical Matters, which is not only inherent in the Crown, but has been declared and recognized to be so by several Statutes and Acts of Parliament.* I honour the Quotation, and am come not long since from swearing religiously to own that
25 Supremacy. And it is surely the more valid for having received from the *Author of the Ecclesiastical Politie* this Confirmation. Only it might have been wish'd that all his Books had not been writ directly counter to it, and under pretence of gratifying him with Titles he had not cut him out of the Exercise and Liberty of his
30 Jurisdiction. But having in his *Ecclesiastical Politie* created himself Perpetual Dictator, *Nequid Res-clerica detrimenti capiat*, and marching every where with four and twenty *Rods and Axes* before him, he deputes the *Consul* to be indeed both his *Magister Equitum* and his *Pontifex Maximus:* but all along speaks in the *Us* and the *We* of him-
35 self, and treats the good Civil Uncontrolable Magistrate with the *Must, Must,* to evidence his own rigorous Superiority. And in that

34 the *We*] *We* 74.

only place where he seems to give the Magistrate some little License, he doth it with so ill a grace and stigmatizes both the Magistrate and the People with such a mark and Character, that 'twould put a generous Prince upon some deliberation whether he were best to make use of an authority so ignominiously granted. For all that 5 is to be obtained is this and in these terms. *Should any Prince through unhappy miscarriages in the State be brought into such straits and exigences of affairs as that he cannot restrain the headlong inclinations of his Subjects without the hazard of raising such commotions and disturbances as perhaps he can never be able to allay, and so should be forced in spight of himself to* 10 *indulge them their liberty in their fancies and perswasions about Religion; yet, unless he will devest himself of a more material and more necessary part of his authority, than if he should grant away his power of the* Militia, *or his Prerogative of ratifying Civil Laws; unless I say, he will thus hazard his Crown and make himself too weak for Government by renouncing the best* 15 *part of his Supremacy, he* Must *lay an obligation upon all persons to whom he grants this religious freedom, to profess that 'tis matter of meer favour and indulgence, and that he has as much power to govern all the publick affairs of Religion as any other matters that are either conducive or prejudicial to the publick peace and quiet of the Common-wealth. And if they be brought* 20 *to this Declaration they will but confess themselves (to say no worse) turbulent and Seditious persons, by acknowledging that they refuse their obedience to those Laws which the Supream Authority has just Power to impose.* I know not whether all these Solemnities were duely observed in the late Declaration; or whether the failing in some of these Rituals 25 may have render'd it less sacred. But our Authors concession here looks something like the Cardinal *Antonio's* suffrage, when he could not have his man chosen; *Sia dunque Pamfilio Papa al nome del Diavolo.* However this, such as it is, joyn'd with the former quotation does amount to some kind of Sanction, and the Parties concern'd may do 30 well to consider of it.

He inquires next *whether I have never read or heard of any publick disturbances, under pretence of Religion.* Yes I have and whosoever shall do so deserves to be severely punish'd. *Whether I have not heard of the merry pranks of* John *of* Leyden *and the Anabaptists of* Germany. 35

---

3 that *om.* 74.   8 *Subjects* 74; *Subjicts* 73.   18 *has*] *hath* 74.   23 *Authority* 74; *Authorioy* 73.

Yes, and they were handled as they deserved. Nay, moreover I have heard of the Anabaptists too of *New-England*, in a Book Printed in the year 1673, intituled *Mr.* Baxter *baptiz'd in Blood*, which came out under the License of *the Author of the Ecclesiastical Politie*; being therefore as is to be supposed a Book of Theological nature. It was indeed a piece of Ecclesiastical History, which he thought it seems very fit *to reconcile to the present Juncture of Affairs, and recommend to the Genius of the Age: faithfully relating the Cruel Barbarous and Bloody Murther of Mr.* Baxter *an Orthodox Minister, who was kill'd by the Anabaptists and his Skin most cruelly flea'd off from his Body.* And yet from beginning to end there never was a compleater falshood invented. But after the *Author of the Ecclesiastical Politie* had in so many books of his own indeavour'd to harangue up the Nation into Fury against Tender Consciences, there could not have been contrived by the wit of Man, any thing more hopeful to have blooded them upon the Non-conformists than such a Spectacle, and at the end of his Orations to flourish the Skin of an Orthodox Minister in this manner flea'd off by the Anabaptists. So that *Se non era vero fu ben trovato.* And in good earnest I dare not swear but it was *the Author of the Ecclesiastical Polities* own handy-work. Several words I observe that he frequently and peculiarly makes use of in his other books, *Concerns, Villains, Villanies, Booby*, &c. but, as for his *brisk and laboured periods*, they may be traced every where. What say you to this for Example? *As the Profession of the Gospel is a most sacred thing, the Doctrine of the Gospel a most holy rule, the Author of our Religion an exemplar and patern of meekness: So when Christians renounce this Sacred Profession, lay aside this Holy Gospel, and abrenunciate Christ the patern of meekness, they soon become the most desperate Villains in the World.* (Ay: very truly said were it but rightly applyed) Never in my life did I read any thing that more lively expresses and nicks the Energy of our Authors sense, or the rotundity and cadence of his Numbers: and so in many places more too long to be instanced. And indeed what reason could there be, what likelyhood that any other man should go so far out of the way with such a book to him who was the most improper Licenser of things of that Nature? Unless he may have therefore been thought the most proper Licenser, because he had

4 *Ecclesiastical* 74; *Ecclesiasticæl* 73.   36 thought *om.* 74.

given so many Testimonies as books of his good inclination to such matters; and that (not only in History, but even in Doctrine too) he did not so nearly consider the Truth as the Interest. And therefore if perhaps he were not the Author, yet I dare undertake that when he came to the Licensing of that Pamphlet, he felt such an 5 expansion of heart, such an adlubescence of mind, and such an exaltation of spirit, that betwixt Joy & Love he could scarcely refrain from kissing it. And this no man living can deny, that either if he thought there were any fault in it, he took care to correct and fit it for the Press with that advantage that it came out, or else he 10 found it so satisfactory that it past his approbation without any amendment, and so transporting that he forgot to keep a Copy for his own justification. And truly had it not chanced that there was present and immediate proof upon the place to convict the Forgery as soon as published, it might probably have had the effect for 15 which it was designed. However no thanks to the Licenser, who either was also the Author, or the more criminal of the two; by how much the Licenser is alwayes presumed to have the stricter inspection, the better judgment, and more honesty, and is therefore intrusted by my Lord Arch-bishop to give the stamp of publick 20 authority. So that whereas this Author saith that, *had we but an Act of Parliament to abridge Preachers the use of fulsom and lushious Metaphors, it might perhaps be an effectual Cure of all our Distempers,* (what of the dull and lazy one too?) *Let not the Reader smile at the odness of the Proposal* (Neither? Is not that lawful before it come to be 25 enacted, as certainly it will upon his recommendation?) I must rather say, that had we but an Act of Parliament to abridge Licensers from publishing falshoods, how sweet soever and luscious, and to command and inable them to authorize truth, there would be a sensible amendment in our modern History, Polity, and Theology. 30 I know he will take it unkindly that this should be revived after, he will say, he hath given so ample satisfaction since for it in his testimonial to the contrary. But he may please to consider that this was since the late Act of General Pardon; that it all happen'd since the writing of the Reproof; that he hath only given a Masterly 35

7 scarcely] scarce 74.   15 have] have have 74.   28 and 74; end 73.
33 But *Ed.*; Bus 73; Bnt 74.

Certificate as it were from a Justice of Peace, instead of making an humble Recantation as an Offender; that it is but the same Law which he every where would exact of the Non-conformists, and the same right which he does Mr. *B.* in the Preface to Bishop *Bramhall.*

5 Had he but, as they say indeed, he complemented the Anabaptists on this occasion, so Printed it too, *that he esteem'd them to be the nearest to Truth of all the Dissenters from the Church of* England, it had been some sign of Penitence and Integrity, and amounted to some degree of Restitution.

10   From this of the Anabaptists, he falls as severely upon the word *Unhoopable*, which I it seems used in representing his *Unlimited*, &c. But whereas I only threw it out like empty Cask to amuze him, knowing that I had a *Whale* to deal with, and least he should over-set me; he runs away with it as a very serious business, and so

15 moyles himself with tumbling and tossing it, that he is in danger of melting his *Sperma Ceti.* A Cork I see will serve without an Hook, and in stead of an Harping Iron, this grave and ponderous Creature may like Eeles be taken and pull'd up only with bobbing. What adoe he makes with Tubs, Kinderkins, Hogsheads, and their dimen-

20 sions! that you might suspect him first to have served as Gager of the *Lambeth* brewing? I wonder that he should descend to so low imployment: but even that prudent Emperor *Claudius* publish'd an Edict *de bene Picandis Doliis.* And I perceive that a person of con-siderable Ecclesiastical Tunnage, did very lately *resemble the Church*

25 *of* England *with its Ceremonies to a Vessel which* must *of* necessity *be composed of Staves, Hoops, Withs and Pins: but if the Pins were pull'd out, then of consequence the Withs slacken, the Hoops ungird, and the Staves fall all asunder into confusion,* so that you see the Trope of an Hoop is not so Apocryphal. And I should have thought that, if not out of

30 respect to the Church of *England*; yet had it been only out of rev-erence to *Cornelius* his Tub among the rest, it might have becom'd the *Author of the Ecclesiastical Politie* upon this occasion to have been something more serious.

    And no less does he intangle himself in another line of mine, weak

35 enough I confess, yet though of but a single hair strong enough to

---

11 *Unlimited* 74; *Untimited* 73.   23 *Doliis*] *Doltis* 74.   27 *consequence* 74; *consequenee* 73.

land him. 'Tis where I chanc'd to say, that *he hath given here the Magistrate so infinite a power that it is extended to impotency as a streight Line continued grows a Circle.* Here indeed I am hard put to it, and I begin too late to be sensible of my rashness in provoking so terrible an Adversary. But in good earnest I thought it enough when I wrote 5 it, that in any small Segment of a great Circle the curvature is not perceptible, but rectifies more by how much the Figure is extended. And at the same time I reflected, that if mine Author should carp at it (for I foresaw very well all the way where he would take hold, and where he would as soon eat his fingers) I would refer him as being 10 an Ecclesiastical Mathematician to Cardinal *Cusanus* his Treatise *de Docta Ignorantia.* p. 10. c. 14. where he might see in the Diagram: *Quod Infinita Linea sit Triangulus,* and p. 17. c. 15. *Quod ille Triangulus sit Circulus.* But if this will not satisfie him, let him try conclusions with his own Girdle, which circumscribes somthing that is Infinite. 15

And no less considerable is that which he undertakes to *maintain that all Figures are Hoopable:* and I on the contrary will defend that if he can make that good, he hath found out the Circle of the Quadrature.

From hence he runs out into Plays *designing,* as he told us his 20 Friend did of the *Friendly Debate, to set off his Reasonings with a Comical humour and pleasantness.* I must here acknowledge the defect of my reading. For *Du Foy* I have not heard of, and it might better have become him to have quoted in stead of the *Conquest,* the Archbishop of *Granada.* But for what he recites out of the *Rehearsal* and 25 the Kings of *Branford,* I understand it better, and seeing he is pleas'd to alter the Scene, I shall joyn with him, and try whether the humour of *Bayes* be so worn out that it may not give the Auditory a second dayes diversion. For indeed, 'tis too ceremonious and tiresome to repeat so often upon all occasions the *Author of the* 30 *Ecclesiastical Politie,* and though I bear him great respect, yet I had rather of the two offend him than my Readers. He does indeed complain of it something pathetically that I should have fix'd that name upon him, and in good earnest could I have yet in all this while have invented any name more consonant and agreeable to his 35 Character, I would have chang'd for it. Neither did I at first make

1 *here om.* 74.   3 *Line* 74; *Ljne* 73.   7 perceptible] preceptible 74.   15 Infinite. 74; ~ 73.

use of the *Rehearsal* so much in order to make merry with him as for
a more publick and serious advantage. For having observed that
he and others of his Coat did, for want either of Reading, Wit, or
Piety, as oft as they would be facetious, make bold with the Scrip-
5 ture; thinking too perhaps that being so long acquainted they might
be more familiar with it; I had a mind to show them by this
example, that there was not so much need of Prophaneness to be
ridiculous, or to take the Sacred Writings in vain; but that if they
did but take up at adventure any book that was commonly read,
10 known or approved of, they had the same and better opportunity
than out of the Bible, to gather thence variety, allusion, and matter
sufficient to make the people merry: and I hope I have attain'd my
end in some measure. But beside this, I have now one Reason more
and his own Authority to treat him under this Title, he having been
15 since so far in love with the name, as even to send to *Colchester* to
procure him as much *Bayes* as would serve for a Facing. One thing
indeed he objects with some fading colour that there is an errour
in Chronology, the Play of the *Rehearsal*, not having been made
publick til after his first Book came out which yet is something
20 excusable, seeing it was publish'd before his second or third, and
to be sure however before mine. But you know Mr. *Bayes*, that you
wanted not the opportunity to see it long before it was Printed, and
that Comedy, as all judicious and lasting things ought, was long
consider'd of e're it was thought fit to come abroad. Had you fol-
25 low'd the same example; and not divulged and promulgated your
Preface to Bishop Bramhall, as you confess *before your thoughts were
cool enough, or could possibly be so, to review or correct the indecencies either
of its stile or contrivance,* had you *but had either leisure or patience to
examine it,* all this labour might have been spared betwixt you and
30 me, and I for mine own part should never have *tired either your self
or the Reader.* But that I may be quit with you for so weighty an
Emendatio temporum; have you not observed that your *Hickringil* or
Gregory, though not published till after your *Reproof* foretells of it
nevertheless, threatning what a vengeance Book was impending
35 over me? *That I must shortly be disciplin'd by another hand, advising me*

to say my Prayers, and tremble at the Rod that was coming upon me, except I thought it the wisest way to save the Hang-man *a labour.* It is a title so honourable that I should scarce have adventur'd to give it him, but seeing he thinks fit to assume it, you may shift and divide it as you can betwixt you. This was I confess the most authentick way of Prophecy imaginable, it being fulfill'd before hand, but the worst piece of Chronology that ever I heard of. Indeed, Mr. *Bayes*, it appears to me very evident, that as I told you before this *Hicringill*, was your own book, and it was Licens'd too by your self, as certainly as *Baxter baptiz'd in blood.* The Strains and Recherches are all along exactly the same with those of the *Reproof.* Read but for example in the very same page in answer to what I say of the King of *Polands* being obliged to wear that Countrey habit. *For which unsufferable affront to His Majesties our Gracious Soveraign his Crown and Dignity Hereditary and not Elective, and at the good will either of People or Parliament, I leave him to be chastiz'd for this bold intrenchment and invasion of our Kings Prerogative and Title to his Crown.* Then read your *Reproof. This is an impudent intrenchment upon his Majesties Crown and Prerogative, for the* Polish *Kingdom being Hereditary and not Elective, the Parliament deals with their Kings as,* &c. *Friend by your Politick Lectures you indanger your head,* &c. Was there ever such a double Picklock of the Law, to find out such a dangerous *innuendo?* But thus those twin-books sympathize all thorow, although the *Reproof* was brought forth a considerable time before the other. Only, Mr. *Bayes*, as when in the *Rehearsal* you once resolv'd that for your *first Prologue you would come out in a long black veil with an huge Hangman behind you with a furr'd cap, and his Sword drawn;* you could not for a long time determine whether the *Reproof* or *Hicringill* should be *the Prologue for the Epilogue, or the Epilogue for the Prologue;* whether your first or your second self should come foremost. But having several things in your two books, some fit as you thought to be said in anothers person, and others in your own, you stood a great while thumming the Busk of your *Comfortable Importance*, whether, whether, to divine which of these two should first be hatched, and *which leg should go first.* And from this irresolution and controversie arose this most gross and yet most subtle errour in your Chronology, which would require another *Scaliger* to reform it. The Case is parallel, and you were even so puzzled betwixt those two books as you were at *Canterbury* betwixt your two Capacities, how you should take place not only of others, but even of your self; whether as you were Arch-deacon, or as you were youngest Prebend: and, though an alternative had been more advisable, you determined that in all Enterviews with your self (which are not so frequent except in your Looking-glass) and in all publick Solemnities among others, the Arch-deacon should both in Place and Time have the Precedence.

Having I hope thus far done you right in matter of Chronology, I shall indeavour no less to satisfie you in point of Comedy, and your politick argument concerning the danger of a distinct jurisdiction in Civil affairs, and those of Conscience which you very weightily fetch from the two Kings of *Branford*. And therefore be pleas'd to accept as serious a Reply from the same Author *to conclude Sir, the Place you fill has more than amply exacted the Talents of a wary Pilot, and all these threatning storms, which like impregnant clouds do hover o'r our heads (when they once are grasp'd but by the eye of reason) melt into fruitful showres of blessings on the people.* Or if you have something to object against this, take your Answer from the Kings themselves at their restauration. *Now Mortals that hear how we tilt and carreer, With wonder will fear The event of such things as shall never appear.* For no less causeless are the apprehensions which you raise up, Mr. *Bayes*, concerning Consciencious people under an equal Government.

I cannot now but take some notice of another argument, your threatning me here and in several other places with the loss of mine Ears, which however are yet in good plight, and apprehend no other danger, Mr. *Bayes* but to be of your Auditory. But it is no less than you have projected against all the Non-conformists, to the great prejudice of the Nation, in wasting so unseasonably so much good Timber to make *Whipping-Posts* for them and *Pillories*. This hath been a considerable part indeed of the Ecclesiastical Politie, and doubtless a most effectual means of Conversion, and bringing

14 distinct 74; dihinct 73.   15 Conscience 74; Gonscience 73   25 *Bayes* Ed.; *Eayes* 73; *Baye* 74.   30 *Bayes* 74; *Baycs* 73.   34 Ecclesiastical Politie] *Italic* 74.

men over to the Church of *England*. I cannot tell where you have
learnt it, unless from the Wisdom and Piety of the *Tartars*, who in
the year 1240. though they left upon every mans head one ear
standing, yet fill'd no less than Nine huge Sacks with the ears that
they cut off of the Christians. But there is no perill as far as I per-   5
ceive to either of us; for my Ears Mr. *Bayes* do not so much as glow
for all your talking of them, and I will secure yours at least upon
one account for you are so far from running away like *Evagrius* for
fear of a Bishoprick, that much less will you like *Ammonius* cut off
one of your own Ears to render your self uncapable of that Office.   10
  There follows one thing more which I know is personally intended to me, but you have couch'd it so darkly, that at first I could
my self scarce understand it. You tell of an Antique Medal.

> *On the Reverse whereof was graved*
> *Th' alliance betwixt Christ and* David.   15

and desire me to tell you in what Emperors time it was coyned.
Why, it was as I remember in the year 1650. and of *the Government
of the People of* England *precedent and present the same.* But if you would
hereby insinuate any thing either concerning my self or my Father,
I shall once for all unriddle in two or three lines the mysterie of this   20
your quotation, because otherwise such nodding reflexions impress
the Reader more effectually than your more *brisk and laboured*
Calumnies which at other times you word more plainly, and vent
more openly against us. This therefore is a greater errour in Chronology than your former; for as to my self, I never had any, not the   25
remotest relation to publick matters, nor correspondence with the
persons then predominant, until the year 1657. when indeed I enter'd into an imployment, for which I was not altogether improper,
and which I consider'd to be the most innocent and inoffensive
toward his Majesties affairs of any in that usurped and irregular   30
Government, to which all men were then exposed. And this I
accordingly discharg'd without disobliging any one person, there
having been opportunity and indeavours since his Majesties happy
return to have discover'd had it been otherwise. But as to my
Father, he dyed before ever the War broke out, having lived with   35
some measure of reputation, both for Piety and Learning: and he

was moreover a Conformist to the established Rites of the Church of *England*, though I confess none of the most over-running or eager in them. I desire you, Mr. *Bayes*, to make my excuse to the Readers for having troubled them so far with my private affairs, by your 5 occasion. But whether they will so easily admit my excuse, for you I know not, you having by the servility of your performances since manifested, that, had you then been of age sufficient, you would not have declined a more homely imployment, which as you may read in *Philip de Comines*, another *Oliver*, a Barber, discharged under *Lewis* 10 the Eleventh. For the rest as to the Distich you have here quoted, whosoever was its Author, it might better have become your Divinity to have supprest so profane an allusion; but that, as I have told you before, and shall often have occasion, you have a singular snickering after Scripture Drollery. It may seem to some by the manner 15 of your expression as if you had a mind to ascribe it to me: but I resign all my interest in it to you and most men that are conversant about Town know very well who was the Author, who dyed some years since: and it may concern you, for some reasons not out of respect to be named, to take heed that you come not to resemble 20 him in two of his Capacities.

There remain still behind some Figures of Brass which you bestow upon me, as *Colossus of brass*, in requital to which I can onely return you *Colosseros*. *Brass upon Brass is false Heraldry*: but Salt upon Salt is not. *Brazen Brow*. *Out-brazen*. *Brass-copper*, and I know not 25 how many more of the same Metal and Statuary. I cannot possibly learn or imagine where you have improved your talent to such proficience, unless perhaps you have practised with a Modern Divine who is said to have appear'd not many years ago, and Preached in the Copper-Mines of *Sweden*. And indeed such is your performance 30 here all along, and much more hereafter when you treat concerning the most sacred arguments, that I suspect it is not all your own; but (though I shall not therefore call you *a Scandalous Plagiary*) that you have attracted by force of Phantasy some extraordinary Spirit to your assistance. As *Cicero* said on another occasion

35 ——*Multa quidem Ipse,*
Multa sed & Dæmon tibi suggerit.

15 ascribe] subscribe 74.   31 it *om.* 74.   32 therefore *om.* 74.

So that I hope the Readers will in so unequal a contest assist me also, at lest with their good wishes; and should I be worsted in such discourse or rather absolutely decline it, that yet they will not think the worse of me. Had he but wrote like a Man only, I might possibly have answer'd him: but where there appears something more than Humane in the business, I may well be excused.

But though in his Railing he is more than Man, he hath as moderate and reasonable a Reasoning as other Mortals: and that being therefore more proportionable to my weakness, I shall deal with as soon as I can find it; for it hath that advantage, that it is for the most part Invisible. But in the mean time I shall, to shew him how justly I might have declined all this trouble, quote him two Authors, the one Civil, the other Ecclesiastical, so nearly related to himself, and this Controversie that till he has answer'd them, I account my self under no obligation. The first is his fellow-Chaplain Doctor *Tomkins*, who in the last Act at *Oxford*, the Question being, *An summæ Potestates Civiles gaudjant Potestate Clavium*: held it in the Negative, and being urged with all the testimonies and arguments to the contrary out of the *Ecclesiastical Politie*, the Professor was fain to help him out at a dead lift, disavowing his authority in the face of the whole Country and University in plain terms: *Non stamus hujus Authoritati*. Now where two persons so eminent and equal in Learning, the two Say-masters of Orthodoxy, and of whom all Theology must ask License, are of so contrary opinion in the very Fundamentals of Ecclesiastical Government, is it not time to have a general Vacation, and that all private Process should be respited till so dangerous a division betwixt the two *Pins of the Church of* England, be again cimented? The other is the supposed Father of the *Author of the Ecclesiastical Politie* (for as long as his Book is nameless, I can always speak of him only at random) in that Tract before mentioned *the Government of the People of* England *precedent and present the same*. It was writ to spirit men to subscribe to the Ingagement *to be true and faithful to the Common-wealth as then established without a King or the House of Lords*: and there he asserts

that, *Populus suo Magistratu prior est tempore, natura & dignitate: quia Populus Magistratum constituit & quia Populus sine Magistratu esse potest sed Magistratus sine Populo non potest esse.* Also out of another classical Author, *Vindiciæ contra Tyrannos,* he affirms: *Reges sunt a*
5 *Populo & sunt constituti causa Populi.* More he undertakes to prove that the Kings of *England* had no Negative voice rightfully and by Law, but that it was contrary to the Law and their Oath at Coronation. And then *a fortiori,* that the Lords neither can have any Negative upon the People. That Acts of Parliament may pass and be
10 valid without consent of the Lords Spiritual: and many other passages of an higher nature, if higher could be, which I cite not, least the very reading of them should prejudice the publick, that Book being the very Quintessence of a Sub-Committee-man turn'd Sergeant at Law, and of the High-Court of Justice. It befitted our
15 Author to have wash'd off the blood from his own Threshold before he had accused others: and no man is ingaged to answer his Necessary, Universal, Uncontroulable, Unappealable, Indispensable, Unlimited, Absolute Magistrate, as long as his own Father stands upon Record against him, and he *spends not so much as one Quible in his*
20 *confutation.* Nevertheless I will super errogate and use all the means possible to find some more cleanly spot in him: though indeed he does all over so wallow and coat himself in dirt, that he is almost impenetrable, and, unless his Skin were flea'd off like *Baxters,* there is no touching him without pollution.
25   He expostulates with me for *perverting the whole Design of his Book.* What do I know the Designs that are managed betwixt him and his Book when they are together in Private? But when any discourse is made publick, it must abide the common interpretation: and *Sit Liber Reus Testis & Iudex.* You know very well that, though no man
30 ever spoke more perspicuously and fully then *Calvin* concerning the Obedience due to Magistrates, yet for one particular passage *De Privatis hominibus semper loquor Nam si qui nunc sint populares Magistratus,* &c. he is upon all occasions dress'd up by your self and others of your make as the bug-bear of Princes. Therefore, Mr.
35 *Bayes,* you should have done well to admonish your book, if it would

needs be treating of Government, yet by his example to have learn't discretion and to weigh every word; for you cannot imagine what hurt a silly well-meaning book may do in the world far from its intention: but if it have on the contrary a felonious intention, and not having the fear of God before its Eyes, as I doubt yours has not, you know then that it may do more mischief than you can ever make amends for. And this is all the matter depending betwixt your Book and me, for ought I can perceive by you. The contest is rather of the Truth of Fact than the Truth of Opinion; and a dispute rather of the Eye than the Understanding. Your Book hath said so and so concerning the Magistrate as you have seen in my former quotations. And now you come and would bear me down with more then ordinary confidence that your Book said no such thing, or else you understand its sense better than it self. Therefore pray let us see, Mr. *Bayes*, what you have to alledge: but in the mean time what have my Readers and I to do but to pity one another? I must quote all over again, and they read it all and you will affirm and deny; deny and affirm, without any regard to Truth or Honesty; and yet all this and more we must indure out of Love to Justice. But I hope at least, Mr. *Bayes*, that if I do convince you that the quotations are right on my part, you will be so ingenuous as to put me upon no further trouble, but confess your Book misunderstood you and was in an errour. For if there be no fault in the Matter, why should you deny it?

You say that what you affirm'd of the Magistrates Authority to take upon him the exercise of the Priesthood, was only *as things stood in the bare state of Nature*: and, though you said the Magistrates Power was antecedent to Christ, *yet its continuance depends meerly upon his Confirmation, in that* (very politically said) *whatever Prince does not reverse a former grant confirms it.* Let us see how it is possible that these should either be your words or meaning. *The Priestly and the Royal Office in the first ages of the world, and for well nigh 2500 years descended together and upon the same person.* Then *this* same *Power because it must be seated somewhere can only properly belong to him in whom the Supream Power resides.* Then: *For he alone having authority to assign to every Subject his proper function, and among others this of the Priesthood, as*

20 you *om.* 74.   27 *Nature* 74; *Mature* 73.   36 *this* 74; *thts* 73.

he may transfer the exercise thereof to another so may he if he please reserve it to himself. And therefore *this the Wisdom of the elder ages always practised.* Can there be any thing more plain under Heaven, then that you distinguish the elder times against these, and having done so,
5 then assert that what was constant in those former times remains still the same, and that of necessity? But go on: *this* same *Power was firmly establish'd in the World by the unalterable dictates of* Natural *Reason and Universal Practice and Consent of Nations.* And then: *though in the* Jewish *Common-wealth for peculiar reasons of State, the two Offices*
10 *of King and Priest were separated, yet the Power of the Priest remain'd subject to the other.* But this was only a present interruption. For then: *our Saviour at his birth came not to diminish the* Natural *rights of Princes,* so that all of them (for the *Jewish* Common-wealth was already dissolved by the *Romane* power, and by his coming;) were reinstated
15 certainly in the Royal and Priestly Office as before, *for he came not to set up any new Models of Polity.* But however: *when Christianity had prevail'd long after to be the Imperial Religion, then its Government began to resettle where* Nature *had placed it,* nay so far it went that *therefore the Divine Providence did begin to withdraw, the miraculous power of the*
20 *Church* (and you can tell us why too here, though the Jewish reasons of State for some peculiar reason you thought fit should be private;) *For the necessity ceased, the Power of Miracles being now as well supplyed by the* Natural *and ordinary power of the Prince.* And then came the *Pope,* as you told us before, and then came the *Reformation* which
25 was almost as bad it seems, for *though it wrought wonderful alterations in the Christian world, yet it has not been able* (but you it seems have been able) *to resettle Princes in their full and* Natural *rights in reference to the Concerns of Religion.* Now, Mr. *Bayes,* what is become of your Excuse, that you *affirm'd this Power in the bare state of Nature, but not*
30 *under the guidance of Revelation, nor indifferently to all ages and periods of the Church under whatsoever positive Laws and different Institutions?* whereas your whole business has been to prove that Princes and mankind are herein still under the bare state of Nature, though your Book perhaps did not intend it. But pray therefore Reprove your
35 Book, Reprove even your *Reproof,* and if that will not serve, *take it under Correction;* but if it prove incorrigible, I know not what course

30 guidance 74; guidanee 73.

I should advise you to take with such a Rascal. For it hath said beside, *To what purpose should Christ grant Princes a new Commission, when this Power, was already so firmly establish'd in the World by the unalterable dictates of Natural reason, &c?* And this perhaps, out of your Natural indulgence to your own book, you took no notice of. But by this means what becomes of that Confirmation of *Christs* which you speak of? For, as your book argues very strongly, it must have been either an Usurpation or impertinent. And whereas you say; *That though the Magistrates were vested with an Ancient and Antecedent Right, yet its Continuance, ever since our Saviour commenced this Empire, depends meerly upon his Confirmation: in that whatsoever Prince does not Reverse a former Grant Confirms it*; howsoever the Truth prove to be in Fact, yet it is not much obliged to your Argument. For that *who does not reverse a former Grant confirms it*, Supposes that the Power of Nature was equal, if not Superior, to that of our Saviour. For where a New and Superior Power is introduced all former Grants are null, unless they be expressly Confirmed. And so, if the Power of *Christ* were Superior to that of Nature, and he hath not positively Confirmed that Authority of the Civil Magistrate, it is absolutely extinguished, & the Magistrate hath no Power at all left him, but runs into a *Præmunire* by exercising it. Beside you call the Original of the Magistrates Authority, the *Unalterable dictate of Natural Reason*: so *Christs* Confirmation could have signifyed nothing. For what is unalterable is unconfirmable; and yet this too was in the state of depraved Nature. Nevertheless such is your inconsistence, that you own our Saviours Authority to be Superior. And it befitted you so to do, for, if you will believe him, *All Power was given him in Heaven and Earth.* And he did not confirm it, and therefore he did confirm it. For the *Scripture*, you say, *rather supposes then asserts it*, and *Every Prince not reversing a former Grant confirms it.* This is your Argument. Nay, but further if you read *p.* 40. There is a solemn Renunciation, as full as could be drawn up by Counsel, of any Power of *Christ* in the whole matter, *We derive not therefore the Magistrates Ecclesiastical Jurisdiction from any grant of our Saviours; but from an antecedent right wherewith all Soveraign Power was indued before*

10 *this*] his Parker.   22 Magistrates 74; Mrgistrates 73.   28–9 And ... it. *om.* 74.   30–1 This ... Argument *om.* 74.

8124228   P

ever he was born into the World. Here is an Ingagement with a witness, beyond that of 1650. Fathers nown Son. And *will you be true
and faithful to the Government establish'd, without Christ,* &c? And is the
Reproof then writ to prove *that the Government of* England *precedent
to* Christ *and present is the same?* and *Ad subscribentes Confirmandum,
Dubitantes Informandum, Opponentes Convincendum?* For in this I suppose 'twas not your Books fault only, but you and it were both of
the same opinion; which is the reason that you say, *we derive it not:*
that is sure you and your Book. For if you meant it otherwise, you
should have done well to shew your Plenipotence from all those
that authorized you. However methinks, betwixt You and your
Book, you might have had more wit than to have excluded any
Grant of our Saviours, whatsoever, unless (as indeed you treat him
like other Princes and *Crown'd heads,* only allowing him a Power
something less than to others and more moderate) you confine his
everlasting Kingdom to the day of his Birth, and date his Dominion
that is infinite from *Anno Domini & Anno Regni nostri primo.* And
now after all this, I leave it to the most candid or severest Reader
to judge, whether for one in your case to affirm *that you spoke of the
Magistrates exercising the Priesthood in his own person, only in the bare
state of nature;* and *that you did not make the Magistrates Power independent herein from Christ;* be not a flat contradiction to your self, and so
outfacing to all ingenuity, that had you not first wash'd your face
in Stygian water, it were impossible for you to persist without
blushing. And what detriment the Church of *England* might suffer
upon this occasion, I leave it to themselves to consider. But I perceive some are wiser then some, and, though you were so forward
as to undertake this side of the Argument, yet it was so order'd
betwixt you or somewhere else, that Doctor *Tomkins* should defend
the contrary. For the Church of *England* is so intelligent, as not to
trust all in one Doctors bottom: but knows that it is good having
two Strings to the Ecclesiastical Bow, that if one break the other
may hold.

Neither, considering what you have thrown out upon this occasion, was it at all improperly said by me that if the King might
exercise the Priesthood in his own person it was all the reason of
the world that he should too assume the Revenue. This, though

it were the only passage in my whole book that could possibly be
perverted to an ill sense in this matter, is by you and the rest of
your *Scaramuccios* invidiously applyed and aggravated both here and
in many other places at large, as if it had been seriously intended
by me for his Majesties assuming the Church Revenue. Whereas 5
it appears to have been meant quite contrary, and only to represent
your Malice in defaming the Government, or those persons emi-
nently instrumental under his Majesty both in Church and State,
as if there were some such counsel or design on foot; and to show
you how ridiculous your fear was (if it were not counterfeit) of any 10
such matter, and to fright you somthing the more with your own
argument. For indeed though you acuse me as if I put his Majesty
in mind to violate his Coronation Oath for preserving the Rights
of the Church, it was all that I said only to put you in mind, that,
if the Magistrate may exercise the Priesthood in his own person, 15
any such Coronation Oath was in it self invalid; as being contrary
to *the unalterable Dictates of Natural Reason*: and that, if he did exercise the Priesthood himself, he was by that Oath perjured, unless he
himself also assumed the Revenue. For though you are pleasant,
and say that by the same reason he may as well, because he is the 20
Supream Civil Magistrate, assume the Revenues of the Laity; the
argument holds not: forasmuch as the Ecclesiastical Maintenance
is annex'd to the Function, and, this being extinguished, that de-
volves naturally upon the King; or, the King exercising the Function himself, the Revenue is so much the more due to him and such 25
other Lay-persons as he shall depute under him in stead of the
Clergy. But this being a thing so dissonant to mine own and other
mens ordinary conceptions, (though I shall show you in a fitter
place hereafter why you ought still to continue in the same opinion). I left you to be responsible for your own consequences; For 30
that you may understand, Mr. *Bayes*, that I am none of those that,
were I in capacity, could give any so pernicious advice, I tell you
and desire you henceforward to take notice of it; that I am so far
from thinking enviously of the Revenue of the Church of *England*,
that (though I will not as you do call that *Sacriledge* which makes 35
up the estates of so many of the Nobility and Gentry of *England*, and
of which the Church too hath its part, if it be Sacriledge,) that I

think in my Conscience it is all but too little, and wish with all my heart that there could be some way found out to augment it. But in the mean time, (to tell you my heart, for what needs dissembling among friends?) I am inclinable to think, as the Revenue now
5 stands, there is sometimes an errour in the Distribution. And for example, I think it is a shame that such an one as you should for writing of Political, flattering, persecuting, scandalous Books, be recompens'd with more preferment, then would comfortably maintain ten Godly Orthodox and Conformable Ministers, who take
10 care of the peoples Souls committed to their charge and reside among them. Whereas you, as being too great for your Sacred imployment, must be exercising it by your Spiritual Deputy or Deputies, and one of them so notorious, that, though married, it was his usual practice, under pretence of studying late at night for his Ser-
15 mons, to lye with his Maid *Mary Parker* before-mentioned, and in stead of instructing your Parish in the *Fruits of the Spirit*, he gave them an example of the *Works of the Flesh*, which *are these, Adultery, Fornication, Uncleanness, Lasciviousness,* &c. so far indeed excusable, if, as 'tis said, after he had finished the work, he attempted to ad-
20 minister something to undoe it again, and make the fruit abortive. You in the mean time, as if you were an Exempt of the Clergy, and as Parson can transmit over the Cure of Souls to your Curate, saunter about City and Countrey whither your gilt Coach and extravagance will carry you, starving your People and pampring your
25 Horses, so that a poor man cannot approach *their heels* without dying for't. I speak not of stale Achronismes, but of things that really happen'd all since the writing of your *Reproof*, and which deserve one better. For what reason can you alledge why you should gluttonize and devour, as much as would honestly suffice so many of
30 your Brethren that take pains in the word, like the great Eater of *Kent* when you are either so unable or so *dull and lazy* that you do not one mans labour? This is the great bane and scandal of the Church, that such Livings as more immediately belong to it should be the worst supplyed, and that you and some few Ingrossers like
35 you should represent your selves by so ignorant and vicious Curates, men not fit to be mention'd in the same Collect, and upon

3 (to 74; ~ 73.

whom indeed *the Spirit of Grace* cannot descend but by *Miracle*: and
while things are no better order'd, it is not strange at all if Non
conformity take root and spred further among Conscientious persons, nor that the Revenue of the Church, though in it self too
slender, should nevertheless appear too great and envious by the 5
manner of Distribution. This is more then I should have said, had
not you by your unseasonable discourses drawn it out of me, but
however is intended principally to your self: though as long as the
Church shall not think fit to repress such Writers it is unavoidable,
but that some faults already too visible should be mention'd. 10

But to proceed: You say, *that I have upbraided you with ascribing an
infinite jurisdiction to Princes without any regard to the Divine Laws, and
that you give an Ecclesiastical authority to the Civil Magistrate absolutely
Paramount to any other Jurisdiction whereas you meant it,* you say, *only
in defiance to the claim of any other Humane Power.* What shall I answer 15
in this case? Will you not remember that you say your *Power of the
Prince is antecedent to* Christ; that *it was established such by the
unalterable dictates of Natural reason?* That *God of Necessity must have
given them such power?* If it be antecedent to *Christ,* how is it accountable to him? If established by natural reason, does it not result only 20
from man as a loose and free agent however produced, and though
from the *Vesicles of the Earth* yet acting by Nature? and if God of
necessity must give the Magistrate this Power, do you not make
God accountable rather to him; and may not the Magistrate bring
his action against the Deity *de Potestate imminuta,* or accuse him 25
Læsæ Majestatis? So that hereby the sum of your Doctrine appears
to be (if without offence I may name it) that your Priestly and Uncontroulable Power of the Civil Magistrate is Antecedent to *Christ,*
Contemporary to the World, nay at least Co-eternal, if not Pre-
eternal, to God himself. And this is the more strongly confirm'd 30
by your asserting, which I told you of, that the *Magistrate hath
Power to bind his Subjects to that Religion that he apprehends most advantageous to publick Peace and Tranquillity:* So that he may if he chuse
his Religion chuse his God too, unto whose Jurisdiction he will be
accountable, and if he begin to think as you say he does, *that* 35
Christianity is an enemy to Government, he may make use of Paganism.

22 *Vesicles* 74; *Vesisicles* 73.

But still you clamour *that when you asserted the Soveraign Power to be Absolute, Uncontroulable, 'twas not to be understood so in regard to God.* (Why then pray do not brave it and justifie you self at this rate, but make your submission humbly, and acknowledge your offence as an honest man should do). And that, *when you said 'twas Absolute and Unlimited, no man, unless he would give his mind to misunderstanding, could understand it in any other sense, than that it was not confined to matters purely Civil, but extended its jurisdiction to matters of Ecclesiastical Importance,* (that is the word it seems in all senses, *Comfortable, Close, Ecclesiastical*) *upon which account alone you determin'd it to be Absolute, Universal and Uncontroulable.* Why I perceive you did not, or would not observe what I had all the while been driving at and of what I was all along jealous; that the thing would not end there, but that, as you had given to certain Uses, and for certain Valuable Considerations an Universal and Absolute Power to the Prince in Ecclesiasticals, so you would, if it were but out of Revenge, bestow the same upon him in Civils.

But you say: *there was never a man of such immodesty in the world to charge you with these things, whereas you know no Writer ancient or Modern that hath so vehemently and industriously asserted the contrary, spending two whole Chapters in your first Book, to prove, that the Opinion of the Unlimited humane Authority was no less than rank Atheism and Blasphemy, and subverts the Power of all Government, and safety of all Societies.* Ay a very good man are you: hold you there. But I hinted to you once before, Mr. *Bayes*, that this writing forsooth against Atheism from the first hath stood you in very good stead, and under pretence of confuting Mr. *Hobbs* (who I believe could explain himself as innocently as you have done) you have usher'd in whatsoever Principles men lay to his charge, only disguised under another Notion to make them more venerable. Nay, in good earnest, I do not see but your *Behemoth* exceeds his *Leviathan* some foot long, in whatsoever he saith of the Power of the Magistrate in matters of Religion and Civils; save that you have levyed the *Invisible Powers* to your assistance, the better to fright men out of their Wits, their Consciences and their Proprieties. I have told you in my former Book that I do

3 pray *om.* 74.   5). 74; ~ 73.   6 *misunderstanding,* 74; ~. 73.
28 you have] you should have 74.   29 disguised 74; dishuised 73.

really believe you are no Atheist, and however I know you have so much wit as to keep it to your self, though not perhaps to avoid some opinions, which if followed home, might in due time lead to it. But to what purpose is it, Atheism, or not Atheism, and what difference in the matter, if under pretext of Divinity an Uncontroulable Principle be insinuated and obtruded to the invasion of all the Rights of Mankind and Priviledges of Reason: if an Unlimited and Absolute Power be challenged in things of Ecclesiastical as well as Civil, and of Civil as well as those of Ecclesiastical Consideration? and I think under one or other of these all are comprehended.

I have something a troublesome and unnecessary task herein if I were to deal with a person of ordinary ingenuity; for his Book is in Print, and I have also in Print charged this upon him, and nevertheless by this last Book he puts me again upon this double-drudgery, to prove first that he said it, and afterwards to prove that he meant what he said. But, though I know this is only a piece of his Art, hoping to tire out the Auditory, not out of any belief of his own Innocence, yet a Guilty person ought not to be debarr'd from making the best of his own Case, and I hope the Readers will, by his tedious evasions and tergiversations in a thing so evident, be the rather provoked to do him Justice. Having therefore sufficiently witness'd his words, I shall now proceed to manifest his Intention. And to that purpose I shall alledge one or two material passages; the first in his first Book, *the Ecclesiastical Politie.*

He saith, '*Tis better to submit to the unreasonable Impositions of* Nero *and* Caligula, *then to hazard the Dissolution of the State.* What he means here by Dissolution of the State, he might have done well to have expressed: but what the unreasonable Impositions are, cannot be understood otherwise then either in matters of Religion or of Propriety, and how both those Emperors acquitted themselves on those two accounts, appears in their History. For as to *Nero*, beside his personal vices, which can scarce be imitated or parallel'd but by *Caligula*, I will but succinctly mention how he behav'd himself to the Publick in the course of his Government. If men bequeath'd nothing to him by their last Wills and Testaments in token of

33 but] out 74.

gratitude to the Prince, he confiscated the whole estate, and fined all Lawyers whatsoever by whose advice such Wills had been drawn. He decreed, that, though there were but one Informer, it should suffice to convict men of Treason, either for Words or Actions. Whensoever he bestow'd an Office, he did it with these Instructions: *You understand what I have need of, and therefore let us make it our business, that no man may have any thing which he can call his own.* Beside so many particular instances of Savage cruelty, he design'd to cut off the heads of all the Governors of Provinces. To poyson the whole Senate at a Dinner. To burn the City, and at the same time to turn out Wild beasts among the People to terrifie them from quenching the Fire. A blazing Star appearing, he resolv'd to divert the *Omen* from his own head, by the Massacre of all the Nobility, and the most considerable persons in *Rome.* He did cause the City of *Rome* to be set on fire, and so carelesly, that divers of his Officers, being taken with fire and flax in their hands, and in the very act, yet were let go for fear of offending him, and some houses not being so easily burnt he took care to have them beaten down with Engines. And, though it was manifest how it was designed and acted, he derived the crime of all this upon the innocent Christians. He Sacrilegiously took the Donatives from the Temples and melted down the Images of the very Tutelar Gods of *Rome* to make money. He contemned all Religions, and particularly is reckon'd to have been the first Persecutor of Christianity. He affirmed publickly, that *none of his Predecessors had known their own Power:* the very same words in a manner, and spoke in the same sense as those of our Author, that *Governors have not been throughly instructed in the Nature and Extent of their Power:* and the other; *that no Nation hath rightly understood and duely managed Government because they have not chain'd their Non-conformists to the Oare, and condemn'd them to the Galleys.* The Conclusion of this Tragedy is common; how *Nero* was by the Senate proclaim'd an Enemy to the State, and Sentenced to be punish'd after the Ancient manner; that is to be stripp'd naked, and his head held up with a Fork, till he were whipp'd unto Death; but this by another death he prevented. This is I suppose one, Mr. *Bayes,* of your *Uncontroulable Magistrates,* these his *Unreasonable Impositions,* and

20 Christians] Christian 74.   34 were] where 74.

this your *Dissolution of the Government*; and you think 'twas better that this *Nero* had still reign'd then that *Galba* should have succeeded. I would all of you that are of that mind had such Governors. And thus much concerning *Nero*.

But now as to *Caligula* and his *Impositions*, What disposition he was of he manifested by his *wishing that all the People of* Rome *had but one Neck*: beside that, he was used to *lament the unhappiness of his time, because it was not signaliz'd by any publick Calamity*; (as if there needed any other Calamity but his Government, and he himself had not abundantly supply'd the defect of any other misfortune) *whereas, said he, the Reign of* Augustus *was felicitated by the defeat of* Varus *and his Legions, as* Tiberius *his was memorable for the fall of the Amphitheatre at* Fidence (in the ruines of which Twenty thousand men perish'd) *but my unfortunate prosperity will leave me in danger of being inglorious after death and forgotten*. But he took good and effectual care to the contrary. He was often heard to say, that he *would certainly reduce things into such a condition, that the Lawyers should not have any thing to say or do, but what he thought just and equitable:* and he was as good as his word. The things may be seen in particular in his History: his whole Reign having been a Pandect of Rapine and Tyranny, and his rule by which he proceeded, *that he might do what he pleas'd with whom he pleas'd:* As to the *Sacred Rites and their Presidents*, take one instance. The Priest being ready to offer a Sacrifice at the Altar, he took upon himself, *according to the unalterable dictates of Natural Reason, to exercise the Priesthood in person*, and having vested himself as in the Power, so too in the Sacerdotal habit, he took up the Mallet, and feigning to knock the Beast down, in stead thereof struck down the Officer who stood by with the Knife. Which should methinks be a sufficient caution unto Church-men hereafter how they trust the Civil Magistrate with exercising the tooles of the Priesthood. But this is nothing in respect of what follows. He commanded that the Statue of *Jupiter Olympius* among many others should be brought over from *Greece*, and their heads taken off to place his in the room of 'm. He seated himself often in the middle betwixt *Castor* and *Pollux* to be adored by the People. He built a Temple to himself, and appointed Priests to his own Divinity: and even then there

5

10

15

20

25

30

35

33 place his] his place 74.

wanted not ambitious men, who by favour aspired to that Office, or purchased it by Simony; upon any Ecclesiastical vacancy. The Sacrifices appointed for his own Worship, were Peacocks, Pheasants, and all other the delicatest Fowl, and of greatest rarity. He took upon him the Ensigns of all the Gods: the Lion from *Hercules*, the Caps from the *Castors*, the Ivy and Thyrsis from *Liber*, the Caduceus from *Mercury*, the Sword Helmet and Buckler from *Mars*, the Crown Bow, Arrows and Graces from *Apollo*. He made love to the *Moon*, and pretended to her imbraces. But more then this he commanded that his Image should be set up in the Temple at *Jerusalem*, and that the Temple should be dedicated only to him, and he there to be worship'd under the name of the *New Jupiter*. He caused his Statues moreover to be placed in the *Jews* Synagogues to be there adored. Insomuch, that the great *Grotius* does most accurately deduce and expound the 2 *Thessalonians*, 2 c. 3 and 4 verses concerning him (though differing therein from other Interpreters) and that St. *Paul* adventur'd to call him the *Son of Perdition, that is worthy to dye in the most miserable manner*, as he did afterwards, *and the Adversary that is the Enemy of God*: and that *his sitting as God in the Temple of God was to be meant of his command to erect his Image there, though it were not effected, yet however seeing he did his best to have it done.* And this, Mr. *Bayes*, is your other Magistrate, who *understood it seems the Nature and Extent of his Power*; and, as you would have Princes do, *made inflexible Laws under the severest Penalties, and acted up roundly to them.* But when all people were weary of him, one *Cassius Charea*, a Tribune of one of the Prætorian Cohorts, for many affronts receiv'd from him, and among others that of giving *Priapus* and *Venus* for the Word, undertook his death, and so happen'd the Dissolution of his Government. Nevertheless I shall not decide here what submission was to be made either to *Nero's* or his Impositions; but only remember what your Doctor *Heylin* said concerning King *Edward* the sixth. *It shall be left to the Readers Judgment, whether the King was either better studyed in his own Concernments, or seem'd to be worse principled in matters which concern'd the Church.* And in another place, *King* Edwards *death I cannot reckon for an infelicity to the Church of* England, *he being ill principled in himself, and easily inclined to embrace such Counsells.* Neither will you I hope

35 *infelicity* 74; *infelicity* 73.

affirm that the loss of these two Emperors was any grievous Judgment upon the *Roman* Commonwealth, or a very sad affliction to the State of Christianity. This same *Caligula* was he that took so great affection to *Incitatus*, a fleet and metall'd Courser, that beside a Stable of Marble, a Manger of Ivory, Housing-cloaths of Purple, and 5 a Poictrell of precious stones, he furnish'd him an house very nobly, and appointed him a family to entertain those who render'd visits to his *Equinity* and his *Hinnibility* (words of yours on another occasion) and to treat such Guests as were invited, with the more magnificence. Nay, so far did he carry on this humour, that 'tis said, 10 had he not been prevented, he design'd to have made this racehorse Consul; as fit however for that Office, as his Master to be Emperor. What pity 'tis, Mr. *Bayes*, that you did not live in that fortunate age, when desert was so well rewarded and understood, when preferments were so current! Certainly one of your Heels and 15 Mettle would quickly have arrived to be somthing more then an Arch-Deacon. If an Horse had so great a Court, and so rich Furniture, and stood so fair for Election, what might not such an one as you have expected! Give me leave, Mr. *Bayes*, having been so long in your debt to requite and cap you with an *Ancient Distich*: but if 20 I Thou you this once, it is not out of disrespect but only to repeat it the more faithfully. Had you then lived,

> *Thou shouldst have had a Silver Stye,*
> *And she her self have pigg'd thee by.*

So that there would have been no occasion for you to have coveted, 25 as you do, your Neighbour Prebends House, but you should have begun at last, as *Nero* said, to dwell like your self and have been installed in a Palace suitable to your Dignity. But though those happy dayes are past and gone, you need not grumble; unless nothing will suffice you, and you are so ambitious of a fortune, that 30 you cannot be content with the Spirituals of *Simon Magus* and the Temporalls of *Caligula*.

Hactenus, saith *Grotius* upon the same place; *Impium Principem descripsit, nunc venit ad Impium Doctorem*; So that the field lies open (were it not against good Huntmanship to course two Hares at 35

11 prevented 74; prevenred 73.   27 begun] began 74.

once) to run your Doctoral similitude here through your *Prote En-noia*, showing her self at so many windows; your Doctrines and deceits, tending *ut homines ad flagitia impelleres aut in flagitiis detineres*; your attempting to fly with the assistance of two other Spirits. But
5 I will let all these things rest till another occasion shall offer, nor am I at present in humour to be too severe upon you. Only pray let me show you, Mr. *Bayes*, with how much reason you have recommended to the publick the Civil Magistrate *Caligula*, seeing you do so particularly resemble him. Who that shall but cast his eye upon
10 you in your writings, can take any other representation of you, then that you have not only usurped the winged Bonnet from *Mercury*, the Thyrses and Ivy from *Bacchus*, the Bow and Arrows and the Graces from *Apollo*, the Lion from *Hercules*, the Sword, Buckler, and Head-piece from *Mars*; but that you have even stoln the *Cerberus*
15 from *Pluto*, and the Snakes and Torches from the *Furies?* And though I will not strain it so high as that *you exalt your self above all that is called God in the Temple*, yet it is notorious that you pretend to more *Worship* then belongs you in the Cathedrall. Nor does it look otherwise when men see you crowd your self in between the
20 Dean and the Senior Prebend, then like *Caligula*'s taking the middle between *Castor* and *Pollux*. 'Tis the same Imperial Spirit that makes you justle so for place, that out of your seeking for Preeminence, you have almost made a Schism in the Church of *Canterbury:* and it concerns Christian Princes to take care how you rise higher, lest the
25 ancient Ecclesiastical Controversies be revived, to the *disturbance of the publick Tranquillity, and the Ends of Government.* Then as *Caligula* had his Images in the Synagogues, so have you your Curates at *Ickham* and *Chartham*, for they *having no Power*, you know, *are no better then Statues and Images of Authority.* But Mr. *Lee* of *Ickham* in par-
30 ticular is so like you, that if both your heads were cut off and *Trans-pros'd* on each others shoulders, no man living but would take you one for the other. But to omit these, I shall, as in the case of *Don Sebastian*, show by some more private marks of your body and mind, that though you might have imposed upon the *Parthians* for
35 a *Pseudo-Nero*, iti s impossible you should be a *Perkin Caligula*, but the very Original. First, he had a singular quality for which he

12 Bow] Bows 74.

admired himself, and gave it a peculiar name of *Adiatrepsia*, which was his unmoved constancy in assisting at, and looking upon the most horrid executions: and no less is your unrelenting and undaunted resolution in first condemning the Non-conformists to *the Galleys*, *the Pillories*, *the Whipping-Posts*, *the Publick Rods and Axes*, and afterwards beholding the Execution with an extraordinary sedateness and judicial temper of Spirit. He had beside this a peculiar Antipathy which was the reason that it was made an hainous and capital offence in his reign to name but a Goat upon whatsoever occasion. And the same aversion have you, if not to a greater height; insomuch that, I having but mention'd a Goat in my former Book, and under the disguised names too of *Crabe* and *Cabre*, you do as good as accuse me of animating therefore the Subjects to Rebellion. He was moreover, as I told you, ingaged in a great intrigue of Courtship with the *Moon*, like that of your Camarade *Bayes*: *Where shall I thy true Love know, Thou pretty pretty* Moon? *To morrow soon, ere it be noon, On Mount* Vesuvio. And you in like manner boast your self to be Married to a Goddess: but which of them 'tis I know not, for *Selene* was adored under the figure of *Minerva*: but 'tis most probably *Luna*, for you courted her in the language of *Bayes* his Eclipse, but something more smutty, as I could rehearse to you from a good hand, were it not too broad for any mans mouth but yours, and that I would not have you blame me again for *betraying publickly the mirth and freedom of private conversation*. The last token of your *Caligulism* shall be the Sacrifices which he appointed of Pheasants and Peacocks to his Deity: & accordingly your Friend the *Author of the Friendly Debate* hath sacrificed a *Pheasant*, and I have sacrificed a *Peacock* to your Divinity; and I hope it will be therefore henceforth and for ever to me propitious and favourable. Now that I have thus far represented in the persons of *Caligula* and *Nero* what it was that you meant in your former argument, and what those Impositions are which you instruct Princes to practise and their people to submit to, I shall dismiss this Testimony, after I have mentioned one Imposition more of *Caligula*'s, and indeed very laudable, which if you also will submit to, I would recommend to your graver consideration. He condemned those Authors, whose Writings gave no satisfaction to the publick, either to blur them over with a Spunge,

or lick them out with their tongues; unless they rather chose to be disciplin'd with Ferulaes, in Commutation of Penance, or to be duck'd over head and ears in the next River: a Punishment, which were it but for your incorrigible faculty of railing and scolding, you
5 could scarce under so gentle a Government have avoided.

But to pass over, Mr. *Bayes*, from your *Roman Empire*, and come nearer home, the second Testimony that I shall produce out of your own Book of the same Nature, shall be what you reply upon me concerning the Vicar of *Brackley* in *Northampton-shire*, your Country-
10 man Doctor *Sibthorpe*, and who commenced Doctor much after the same manner that you did. His Sermon is extant in the History, and some *Heads* and *Points* of it I gave you in my first book as a *Pinne-paper* of your modern Orthodoxy, and the very *Flower* of your *Brann* (not of the Church of *England*, as you would suggest) in the
15 Doctrine of some men in the late times concerning Impositions, and I shall here sift it after your grinding. Here in the *Reproof* you undertake to tell the story of that Doctors Sermon, which needed not for the Sermon is yet extant beside what is legible in Arch-bishop *Abbots* Narrative: but you adventure besides to justifie it and
20 *Manwarings* case also, which you allow to be the same with *Sibthorpes*. But whereas you limit the matter to the indiscretion only of a single Country Vicar or so, I gave you those particular relations for an example of what was then the Doctrine *a la mode* at that time in most of your pulpits, and which you here attempt to bring again
25 in fashion. You defend that Loan and the carrying of it on in that manner, and if there were any illegal design of absolute Government promoted, you ascribe it to *the Impudence of the Members of Parliament*, to the *Assaults they then made upon the Royal Power by their bold and unreasonable demands*; to their *bringing things to that pass, that*
30 *nothing must be done unless the King would either grant away all his power to them, or keep it all to himself*; to the *rudeness and insolence of their demands, so that the King must sometimes govern without them or not at all.* And as to those persons and Members that were imprison'd for refusing the Loan; you say *they had forgot the respect they ought to their*
35 *Prince, and the duty they ought to God*; that the *King was forced on those courses by the stubbornness of Presbyterian Parliaments*; (No, Sir, it was

19 adventure besides 74; also adventure 73.   24 again *om.* 74.

by the Flattery of Archidiaconal Preachers) that as things then
stood betwixt him and his Parliaments, *Punctilios of Law were super-
seded; Their demands were disloyal and unreasonable:* all *good and ingenuous
Subjects ought not to have stood then so curiously upon Precedents and
Nicetyes of old Custom.* And in conclusion you determine *ex Tripode*   5
that *whatever that Parliament or the Refusers of the Loan were by the Laws
of the Land, they were even then most notorious Rebels by all the Laws of
the Gospel.* It is worth taking notice more particularly that the Parliament which you have thus qualifyed was the Parliament 3°
Caroli, which I have heard by unprejudiced men to have been an   10
Assembly of the most Loyal, Prudent, and Upright *English* Spirits
that any age could have produced. Their actions are upon Record,
and by them not by your perishing and false glosses and relations,
will posterity judge concerning them. And if we had no other
effects and Laws from them but *the Petition of Right,* it were suffi-   15
cient to eternize their memory among all men that wear an *English*
heart in their bosome. But it is too much for you to make their
Process however, and to arraign a Parliament as Traytors by an
Ecclesiastical Bill of Attaindor. *You dare,* you say, *determine them so.*
'Tis indeed like your fellow *Bayes* his *Draw-can-Sir*—   20

> *You huff, you strut; look big and Stare,*
> *And all this you can do because you dare:*

But I assure you, notwithstanding your complaint *of Ecclesiastical
Laws, being in a manner cancell'd by the oppositions of Civil Constitutions,*
'twill never be well in *England* as long as that Doctrine holds that   25
men though Loyal by the Laws of the Land, yet are most notorious
Rebells by all the Laws of the Gospel. Here is Divinity indeed, not
on Gods name I am sure, nor the Kings; whose then, you may consider. *You say indeed if Doctor* Sibthorpe *intermedled with the Kings
Absolute Power of imposing Taxes without Consent in Parliament, he went*   30
beyond his own Commission. But why might he not, Sir, as well as you?
Where is your Commission, unless what he might not Preach, you
have License to Print, and that alters the case? 'Tis it seems no
matter for *Manwaring,* you say, for *his Zeal in the Cause of Loyalty was
punish'd with Preferments to defie the Pragmaticalness of that Parliament,*   35

7 *then most*] *then the most* 74.

and so was *Sibthorpe*, and so you doubtless expect to be if you be not already sufficiently punish'd with Preferments for the same merit. You will do well to Register your name in some Office of Address, or rather with the Clerks of both Houses; that if any new occasion 5 of Preferment should start, they may not escape you, nor you according to your deserts be forgotten. In conclusion, these kind of Sermons were not the least inducement of that Petition wherein I told you *Martin Parkers* Ballads were complain'd of; the very next Article but one being against *such as Preach'd that Subjects have no* 10 *Propriety in their Estates, but that the King may take from them what he pleaseth, and that all is the Kings, and he is bound by no Law.* In this Petition, though I find sundry things intermix'd which had better been omitted, yet it is no wonder, if having this just cause of complaint, their pen being in their hand they dash'd out further then 15 was fitting against the Clergy. And now I hope I have pretty well evidenced that your Book hath said what it did say, and that you meant what you said, and it was but the self same design which both of you managed together. And yet, Mr. *Bayes*, you think this is hard dealing, when you betwixt ranting and whining affirm this 20 your Grand Thesis of the Unlimited and Absolute Magistrate, *to be so granted and undoubted a truth that it is plainly ratifyed by the unanimous consent of all mankind. Nay* (inhumane!) *when a man has demonstrated its certainty from that unavoidable influence that Religion alwayes has upon the Peace of Kingdomes. But when beside you have drawn up a brief and plain* 25 *account of the parts, the coherence; and the design; when you have provided with equal care and caution* too *against the inconveniences of both extreams; Unlimited Power on the one hand, and unbounded License on the other: when the bounds you have proposed are so easie to be observed, and so unnecessary to be transgressed by all parties concern'd. That Governers only take care not* 30 *to impose things certainly and apparently evil, and that subjects be not allow'd to plead Conscience for disobedience in any other case: and when you have so carefully avoided all kind of severity more then is absolutely necessary.* Alas good Sir have you so, and nevertheless do they misuse you? Where is your Witness? But pray what are indeed these bounds that you 35 have set? Let us consider; though when you had made the Magis-

---

9 *that* 74; *thæt* 73.   12–13 had better been] had been better 74.   18 Mr. 74; Mt. 73.   24 *of*] *of the* 74.

trate once Unlimited, I know not whether he gave you leave again
to set Bounds to him. But indeed they are as you say very easie.
Only that he take care not to impose things certainly and apparently
evil. But what things are so, you take not so much care to inform
him. Oh! I have it: *He may command any thing in the worship of God* 5
that does not tend to debauch mens Practices, or their Conceptions of the
Deity. But I was of opinion that the Magistrate would think fit not
only to refrain from imposing things certainly and apparently evil,
but that he would even have shun'd the Appearance of evil: I am
sure, if he won't, his Subjects for their part ought both as men, and 10
more as Christians, to follow that Maxime. But therefore in such
weighty cases who shall be the Expositor, who the Judge betwixt
People and Magistrate, one would have thought the Scripture
should for good reason have decided a Case of Conscience. No it
may as to matter of Obedience to the Magistrate; but as to the 15
Magistrates Ecclesiastical Power of commanding, it has rather supposed it and Christ himself, being as you make him but Natures
Successor, thought not fit to meddle with it. Why then we must
have something else, *a Guardian of humane Nature*, (you know whence
the word comes) to decide the business. In conclusion (though it 20
be unusual, yet some precedents there are in the *Roman* Empire) you
declare your self the Magistrate and Judge of all Controversies,
without expecting the suffrages of the Prince or People. We are like
to be well-govern'd then, Mr. *Bayes*, are we not think you all well
taught and edifyed. Pray tell me first whether you be a Lawful 25
Prince. But that is not so much matter neither: for some Usurpers
because of the tenderness of their Title, have thought fit to carry
with the greatest Clemency and equality to the people, and to make
very good and wholsome Laws for the Publick. What yours are, I
must intreat the Readers to see at least in the Contents of the 30
seventh and eighth Chapters of your *Ecclesiastical Politie*: where you
tell them strange Stories, and argue at a wild rate, and, knowing
they were such Dunces as that they would not comprehend your
reasoning, you fall out upon your poor distressed Subjects, and
Rogue and Rascal them in the most significant terms of Rebells, 35
Traytors, Villains, Schismaticks, and the most notorious Hereticks,

9 but . . . evil *om.* 74.   36 Villains, *om.* 74.

and, which you avow from the beginning of the Book to have been
your design, you muster up all Christian Princes to *Neronize* and
Caligulize them, unless they themselves the Princes will chuse for
their omission to be *Uilenspiegled* and *Sardanapalized* by you. But the
5 Bounds which you boast your self to have so wisely and equally
determined betwixt the Magistrate and the People are so inconsiderable and low, that any man may without weights leap plum
over them. If any Subject do take that which is commanded to be
apparently evil he needs but, as I quoted you in my former Book,
10 consider that *if there be any Sin in the Command, he that imposes it shall*
answer for it, not the man whose duty it is to obey; for the Commands of
Authority (mark but here the gradation of his capering Divinity)
will warrant my Obedience, my Obedience will hallow or at least excuse my
action, and so secure me from Sin, if not from Errour. And in another
15 place which I have since taken more notice of. *Publick Peace and*
Tranquillity is a thing in it self so good and necessary, that there are very
few actions that it will not render virtuous, whatever they are in themselves,
wherever they happen to be useful and instrumental to its attainment. Was
there ever any man that writ of things of so high consequence, as
20 to concern mens Reason, Honesty, and Salvation, at so profligate
and loose a rate! I will not be tedious, but those whole Chapters
are such Stuff. You should have told us which actions were excused,
and which were hallow'd, that we might have known how to shew
them respect according to their several qualities. You should have
25 caused the Magistrate to enter into good and sufficient security,
and be bound in a round sum to save the Subject harmless. And the
Penalty of the Bonds should have differ'd, what in case he run the
Subject only into Errour, and what in case of Sin, And the day too
should have been expressed, although it had been but the Day of
30 Judgment. And in the other place; if there be so few Actions that
the Publick Peace will not render virtuous whatever they are in
themselves, it had been kindly done of you, Mr. *Bayes*, to enumerate
them, and to have gratifyed our curiosity with shewing us the
whole process and manner of the Transmutation. And no less arbi-
35 trary and conjectural is that expression concerning the Magistrates

---

12 mark . . . the 74; *Italic* 73.   13–14 *will . . . Errour* 74; *not Italic* 73.
16 that 74; thnt 73.   18 *wherever*] whenever Parker.

Power: *The same Providence that intrusted Princes with the Government of humane affairs, must of necessity have vested them with at least as much Power as was absolutely Necessary to the Nature and ends of Government.* You should have done well to have given us the Date when Providence intrusted the several Princes, and by what means it was brought about. You should have prescibed just how much power was intrusted, for if it were a *Depositum*, it is fit that there should be great exactness in order to account for it. But suppose Providence should have intrusted them with a little more Power then were absolutely necessary, whether or no would it have been absolutely destructive? A small errour in the quantity leads on to great absurdities. Neither will the same Proportion agree with all Politick Bodies. The *Turk*, the *Pope*, the *Emperour*, the King of *France*, the King of *Poland*, and so on, are not all intrusted with the same Power: but some of 'm have more and some perhaps less then is absolutely necessary. 'Tis pity that you were not at the Admensuration, and that you like *Apollo* did not order the Balance of Government, or fill the Cartridges and distribute them to each Magistrate according to his *Calibre*. Then whereas you say that Providence must of necessity have intrusted the Magistrate with at least as much Power as was absolutely necessary, you ought to have consider'd whether, according to your usual Exactness, Necessity upon Necessity *be not false Heraldry*: and when you add to the Nature and Ends of Government you should have exprest what those were; for Authors are very much divided about it: you say, Publick Peace and Tranquillity. Why but some, for the attainment of that, hold it to be Necessary that Subjects should have no Arms, others that they should have no Wealth, no Propriety, and a third that they should have no Understanding, no Learning, nor Letters. You have indeed exprest your self in another place of the same Book that *there is no Creature so ungovernable as a wealthy Fanatick*: Now you that say, *Princes must have at least as much Power as is necessary to the ends of Government*, should also have weigh'd how much Wealth at least, and how much Religion at least was Necessary to make a man a *Wealthy Fanatick*, that Princes might have calculated better how to govern them. Whether a Dram of Wealth mix'd with a Pound of Conscience, or whether a

7 that *om.* 74.   12 all] a 74.

Scruple of Conscience infused in a thousand Pounds a year do compound a Wealthy Fanatick. For otherwise there may be a great errour in the Dose of Government: and you may, even during your dull and lazy distemper, have had experience how Necessary it is
5 to be exact in the preparation and quantity, though it were but of *Callimelanos.* The word Fanatick is of a large acceptation. The Papists are Fanaticks; The Presbyterians, the Independents, the Anabaptists of *New England,* and I know not how many more are Fanaticks. The Parliament 3° *Caroli,* that drew up the Petition of
10 Right, and others that you mention, excluding that of Forty, were Presbyterian, Fanatical, Puritanical, and Rebellious Parliaments. Who knows at this rate where Fanaticism will end, and whether, according to your notion, every man who has an estate or who asserts propriety, may not in a short time be deemed a Fanatick;
15 nay, whether you your self, that were formerly a Fanatick in point of Religion, may not now you are grown so wealthy, upon that account at least, turn Presbyterian? Moreover in your *Censure* too *of Platonick Philosophy,* when you first made courtship to *Ecclesiastical Politie,* but the Intrigue was not so avowed and publick, you have
20 said: *Governours must keep their Subjects from sinking into too much Ignorance or rising to too much Knowledge in matters of*—(I wonder what this—should mean: it is not sure *of those designs that aspire to serve your dearest*—) *for the former renders them salvage, which is apparently destructive to Government; the latter makes them proud, conceited, and zealous, that*
25 *breeds contempt of Governours and sets them upon headless plots and designs of Reformation, that usually proceed to Rebellion,* &c. I see now that it is to be supplyed *or rising to too much knowledge in matters of*—Religion. You that do, as if it were in Rogation week, perambulate the Bounds of Government, and leave them *so easie to be understood, and*
30 *so unnecessary to be transgressed,* why would you here have conceal'd them, or was it that in this manner you drew a Line betwixt the Prince and the Subject to serve ever after for their Boundary? Will you believe me? seeing you had blam'd me for saying that *you have extended the Princes Power to Impotency as a streight Line continued grows*
35 *a Circle;* when I saw this streight Line of yours, I took my Compasses and *divaricating* them for experiment, I drew the Circular

Line all along thorow it, that you could not see what was become of it, and without the least offence to the Figure upon either account. But here again, Mr. *Bayes*, or to use a *Chaucer*'s word for change, Mr. *Limitour*, you are much out and too indefinite. You should if you would have said any thing to the purpose, have read a Lecture here to Princes upon the Centers of Knowledge and Ignorance, and how and when they Gravitate, and Levitate. But as you failed in the matter of Wealth and Fanaticisme, and you did not instruct them how to know when their Subjects were fat or lean enough, when they were honest or dishonest enough; so you have here disappointed Governours extremely, who would have been glad to have behaved themselves well, and to have ruled with good reputation, that they are at an absolute loss to know how to diet their Subjects and to distinguish when their people are fools enough, and when wise enough, or how much ignorance would suffice a Reasonable man. But however upon this Survey, if the rule hold good that an Indefinite is equipollent to an Universal, I collect from these two passages of yours last quoted, that you are pretty well satisfyed that Providence having of necessity intrusted Princes with at least as much Power as is absolutely necessary to the Nature and Ends of Government, they ought for Peace and Tranquilities sake (for 'tis *Must* too in this out of your *Platonick Philosophy*) to keep their Subjects from Arms, from Letters, and from Propriety. For as you said formerly *there are few actions* (whether of the Governour or of the People) *which that Nobler end of Publick Tranquillity will not render virtuous, whatsoever the actions be in their own nature.* How others will judge of it I know not, or how far Princes will think that Expedient which you affirm necessary: but certainly if this course were once effectually taken, the whole year would consist of Halcyon Holy-dayes, and the whole world free from Storms and Tempests would be lull'd and dandled into a Brumall Quiet.

Neither are you more distinct in the matter of Necessity, wherein, it being the Original from which you first derive all this Absolute and Unlimited Government, it behoved you if ever to have *shown your Heraldry*. For though Necessity be a very honourable Name of

28 that *om*. 74.   36 *your* 74; *you* 73.

good extraction and alliance, yet there are several Families of the
Necessities, as in yours of *Bayes*, and though some of 'm are Patrician,
yet others are Plebeian. There is first of all a necessity; that some
have talk'd of, and which I mention'd you in my former Book, that
5 was pre-eternal to all things, and exercised dominion not only over
all humane things, but over *Jupiter* himself and the rest of the
Deities and drove the great Iron nail thorough the Axle-tree of
Nature. I have some suspicion that you would have men understand it of your self, and that you are that Necessity. For what can
10 you be less or other who have given an Absolute and Unlimited
Power to Princes, who have made Nature preexistent to our Saviour,
and preeminent, and have therefore forced him to subscribe to its
dictates, and confirm its grants though to his own derogation and
prejudice, who have obliged Providence to dispense Power to the
15 Magistrate according to your good pleasure, and herein have claim'd
to your self that Universal Dictatorship of Necessity over God and
Man, though it were but *Clavi figendi causa,* and to strike thorow all
Government, Humane and Divine with the great Hammer? There
is another which may be named the Necessity of the Neck, or
20 *Caligula's* Necessity before spoke of; that is that the whole body of
the People should have but one Neck. Do you mean this? for it is
very useful and virtuous toward the attainment of *Publick Tranquillity and the ends of Government.* A third is the Necessity of the
Calf, which in this Case would be very considerable to the Magis-
25 trate. For the Calves of the Legs being placed behind where they
are altogether unuseful, it were necessary in some mens opinion, to
place the Calf rather before for defense, lest men should break their
Shins by making more hast then good speed. You may then reckon
Necessity of State, to which in former times 'twas usual to oppose
30 Impossibility: and of kin to these is Necessity that has no Law, and
that Necessity where the King loses his Right, that is when nothing
is to be had. And lastly, there is one sort of men for whose sake
there is a common Maxime establish'd, that there is an Absolute
Necessity they should have good Memories. I have thus far grati-
35 fied your indifiniteness by this enumeration that you may henceforward pick and chuse a Necessity as you shall see occasion. And

7 Deities 74; Deitiess 73.   22 toward] towards 74.

in the mean time, that I may furnish you with a Christen-name as well as a Sir-name, and set you up for an Author, you may please henceforward to write your self Mr. *Necessity Bayes*. But though the Necessity you speak of does more or less partake of all or most of those I have mention'd, it seems to me rather reducible to that of 5 the Calf. That is to say, You do hereby seem to imagine, that Providence should have contrived all things according to the utmost perfection, or that which you conceive would have been most to your purpose. Whereas in the shape of Mans body, and in the frame of the world, there are many things indeed lyable to Objec- 10 tion, and which might have been better if we should give ear to proud and curious Spirits. But we must nevertheless be content with such bodies, and to inhabit such an Earth as it has pleased God to allot us. And so also in the Government of the World, it were desirable that men might live in perpetual Peace, in a state of good 15 Nature, without Law or Magistrate, because by the universal equity and rectitude of manners they would be superfluous. And had God intended it so, it would so have succeeded, and he would have sway'd and temper'd the Minds and Affections of Mankind so that their Innocence should have expressed that 20 of the Angels, and the Tranquility of his Dominion here below should have resembled that in Heaven. But alas! that state of perfection was dissolv'd in the first Instance, and was shorter liv'd than Anarchy, scarce of one days continuance. And ever since the first Brother Sacrificed the other to Revenge, because 25 his Offering was better accepted, Slaughter and War has made up half the business in the World, and oftentimes upon the same quarrel, and with like success. So that as God has hitherto, in stead of an Eternal Spring, a standing Serenity, and perpetual Sun-shine, subjected Mankind to the dismal influence of Comets 30 from above, to Thunder, and Lightning, and Tempests from the middle Region, and from the lower Surface, to the raging of the Seas, and the tottering of Earth quakes, beside all other the innumerable calamities to which humane life is exposed, he has in like manner distinguish'd the Government of the World by the 35

10 things 74; thrngs 73.   15 might 74; migh 73.   19 Minds 74; Mind 73.
29 perpetual 74; peerpetual 73.   32 Surface, 74; ∼. 73.

intermitting seasons of Discord, War, and publick Disturbance.
Neither has he so order'd it only (as men endeavour to express it) by
meer permission, but sometimes out of Complacency. For though it
may happen that both the Parties may be guilty of War, as both
5 of Schisme, yet there are many cases in which War is just, and few
however where there is not more Justice on one side then the other.
To repell an Invasion from abroad, or extinguish an Usurpation at
home would not require a long consultation with Conscience. The
Jews themselves learnt at last that 'twas lawful to fight a battel on
10 the Sabbath day, rather then submit their throats to the Enemy:
And had all Sectaries been of the opinion of some Anabaptists and
others, that all War is unlawful, they would have afforded matter
rather of derision then disturbance. Nevertheless it is most certain,
that Tranquillity in Government is by all just means to be sought
15 after, and it might easily be attain'd and preserved, did those that
most pretend to it sincerely labour it. But Men have oftentimes, as
I have partly show'd you in your own Doctrine, other Ends of
Government, and that to compass them require other Means then
will consist with so specious a Title. How should such persons
20 arrive at their design'd port, but by disturbance? for if there were
a dead calm always, and the Wind blew from no corner, there would
be no Navigation. You will object perhaps, and I stand corrected,
that though there should not be a breath of air, it might be performed by Galleys: and 'tis indeed the very thing proposed in your
25 *Ecclesiastical Politie*, that you might be row'd in state over the Ocean
of Publick Tranquillity by the publick Slavery. But because you
are subject to misconstrue even true *English*, I will explain my self
as distinctly as I can, and as close as possible what is mine own
opinion in this matter of the Magistrate and Government; that see-
30 ing I have blamed you where I thought you blame-worthy, you
may have as fair hold of me too, if you can find where to fix your
Accusation.

The Power of the Magistrate does most certainly issue from the
Divine Authority. The Obedience due to that Power is by Divine
35 Command; and Subjects are bound both as Men and as Christians

---

1 Disturbance. 74; ~, 73.   6 side *om.* 74.   8 not] no- 74.   16 most
om. 74.

to obey the Magistrate Actively in all things where their Duty to
God intercedes not, and however Passively, that is either by leaving
their Countrey, or if they cannot do that (the Magistrate or the
reason of their own occasions hindring them) then by suffering
patiently at home, without giving the least publick disturbance. 5
But the Dispute concerning the Magistrates Power ought to be
superfluous: for that it is certainly founded upon his Commission
from God, and for the most part sufficiently fortified with all humane advantages. There are few Soveraign Princes so abridged, but
that, if they be not contented, they may envy their own Fortune. 10
But the modester Question (if men will needs be medling with
matters above them) would be how far it is advisable for a Prince
to exert and push the rigour of that Power which no man can deny
him; For Princes, as they derive the Right of Succession from their
Ancestors, so they inherit from that ancient and illustrious extrac- 15
tion, a Generosity that runs in the Blood above the allay of the rest
of mankind. And being moreover at so much ease of Honour and
Fortune, that they are free from the Gripes of Avarice and Twinges
of Ambition, they are the more disposed to an universal Benignity
toward their Subjects. What Prince that sees so many millions of 20
men, either labouring industriously toward his Revenue, or adven-
turing their Lives in his Service, and all of them performing his
Commands with a religious obedience, but conceives at the same
time a relenting tenderness over them, whereof others out of the
narrowness of their Minds cannot be capable? But if this gracious 25
Temper be inconsistent with *the Nature and Ends of Government*, it
behoves them to be aware, and by the rougher methods to provide
for their own and the Peoples security. For though Princes are not,
as in some barbarous parts of the world, sworn as 'twere upon the
Almanack, and violate their Coronation Oath, unless the seasons of 30
the Year be very punctual, yet (abating only for any extraordinary
accident from Heaven) they are responsible to him that gave them
their Commission for the happiness or infelicity of their Subjects
during the term of their Government. It is within their Power,
depends upon their Counsels, and they cannot fail of a prosperous 35
Reign, but by a mistaken choice betwixt Rigour or Moderation.

20 toward] towards 74.

But whoever shall cast his eye thorow the History of all Ages, will
find that nothing has always succeeded better with Princes then
the Clemency of Government: and that those, on the contrary, who
have taken the sanguinary course, have been unfortunate to themselves and the people, the consequences not being separable. For
whether that Royal and Magnanimous gentleness spring from a
propensity of their Nature, or be acquired and confirmed by good
and prudent consideration, it draws along with it all the effects of
Policy. The wealth of a Shepheard depends upon the multitude of
his flock, the goodness of their Pasture, and the Quietness of their
feeding: and Princes, whose dominion over mankind resembles in
some measure that of man over other creatures, cannot expect any
considerable increase to themselves, if by continual terrour they
amaze, shatter, and hare their People, driving them into Woods, &
running them upon Precipices. Nay even if this similitude were
pursued to the uttermost, and *the Absolute and Unlimited Power* over
rational beings were so desirable as some, for their own sinister ends,
will alwayes be suggesting to Governors, there is not any so proper
and certain way of attaining it, as by this softness of handling. If
men do but compute how charming an efficacy one Word, and more
one good Action has from a Superior upon those under him, it can
scarce be reckon'd how Powerful a Magick there is in a Prince who
shall by a constant tenour of humanity in Government go on daily
gaining upon the affections of his People. There is not any Priviledge so dear, but it may be extorted from Subjects by good usage,
and by keeping them alwayes up in their good humour. I will not
say what one Prince may compass within his own time, or what a
second, though surely much may be done: but it is enough if a great
and durable design be accomplished in the third Life, and, supposing an hereditary succession of any three taking up still where the
other left, and dealing still in that fair and tender way of manage-
ment, it is impossible but that even without reach or intention upon
the Princes part, all should fall into his hand, and in so short a time
the very memory or thoughts of any such thing as Publick liberty
would, as it were by consent, expire and be for ever extinguish'd.
So that, whatever the Power of the Magistrate be in the Institution,

10 goodness] good 74.   25 usage] usages 74.

it is much safer for them not to do that with the Left hand which they may do with the Right, nor by an Extraordinary what they may effect by the Ordinary way of Government. A Prince that goes to the Top of his Power is like him that shall go to the Bottom of his Treasure. And therefore it is very unadvisable however to put a great stress upon little things, and where the Obedience will not countervail the Experiment. It is like a man that knits all his force to throw an inconsiderable weight: he both strains his arm with it, falls short and makes no impression; whereas he that chuses a just weight, does neither find himself the weaker after he has deliver'd it, and reaches the length he aim'd at. And this I doubt has been the case in laying on so much load upon account of things at best only indifferent and ceremonious. But as it is the Wisdom and Vir-tue of a Prince to rule in this manner, so he hath that advantage that his safety herein is fortified by his Duty, and as being a Christian Magistrate, he has the stronger obligation upon him to govern his Subjects in this Christian manner. Even during the Law under the Mosaical dispensation, in that regall Chapter of the 17th. of *Deuter-onomy*, it is solemnly commanded that *when the King sits upon the Throne of his Kingdome, he shall write him a Copy of the Law in a Book out of that which is before the Priests the Levites, and it shall be with him, and he shall read therein all the dayes of his life, that he may learn to fear the Lord his God, to keep all the words of the Law, and these Statutes to do them: that his heart be not lifted up above his brethren, and that he turn not aside from the commandment to the right hand or to the left, to the end he may prolong his dayes in the Kingdom, he and his children.* And though our Saviour came to abrogate the Ceremonial part of the Law, yet this was so essential to the Magistrates duty, that he confirmed and establish'd it stronger by his Doctrine. He declares indeed, that those Christians *are Blessed who are persecuted for Righteousness sake, and when men shall revile, persecute and say all manner of evil against them*: but it does not therefore follow that the Magistrate by fulfilling that Prediction does gain any of the Beatitudes. Rather he is invited to the contrary course, for as much as the Merciful are blessed, for they

5

10

15

20

25

30

4 shall go] goes 74.   19–26 *when . . . children* 74; *not Italic* 73.   20 *the*] this Deut. 17: 18.   23 *the Law*]this ~ Ibid., 17: 19.   24 *above* 74; over 73. 30–1 *are . . . them* 74; *not Italic* 73.

shall obtain mercy, and blessed are the Meek for they shall inherit the earth. And so, in the 13 to the *Romans*, where the duty of the Subject is so fully and excellently described, 'tis nevertheless as to the Magistrate said that *he is not*, (which is to say, he ought not to
5 be) *a terrour to good works, but to the evil*. Neither is it fair for any man to speak as though our Saviour had in a manner balked the whole business of the Magistrates duty intermixed with his jurisdiction. For whatsoever *Christ* did generally dictate, unless where he speaks to men under the express capacity and notion of Subjects,
10 is equally bound upon the Magistrate as well as the People. And where he denounces, *Woe to them that shall offend one of his little ones that believe in him, and whoso doth it, that it were better for him that a Milstone were hang'd about his neck, and that he were drown'd in the Sea*, is said without reservation either to Prince or Subject. Neither
15 where the Apostle *Paul* speaks of the *tribulation which God recompences to the troublers of Christianity*, is there any exempt Jurisdiction to be pleaded. The Power of Princes is not improperly resembled and derived down by Paternal Authority, and that which a Master hath in his Family: and in the *6th.* to the *Ephesians* where the rules are
20 given of domestick obedience, yet both *Parents* are forbid too from *provoking their children to wrath*, and *Masters* that they *do not threaten their Servants*. Indeed although *Christ* did not assume an earthly and visible Kingdome, yet he by the Gospel gave Law to Princes and Subjects, obliging all mankind to such a peaceable and gentle frame
25 of Spirit as would be the greatest and most lasting security to Government, rendring the People tractable to Superiors, and the Magistrate not grievous in the exercise of his Dominion: And he knew very well that without dethroning the Princes of the World at present, yet by the constant preaching of that benevolous and
30 amiable Doctrine, by the assimilating and charitable Love of the first Christians, and by their signal patience under all their sufferings and torments, all opposition would be worn out, and all Princes should make place for a Christian Empire. Neither therefore did he, or the Apostles, or the Primitive Christians that trode on in

their steps, notwithstanding their obedience to the Magistrate, in-
termit the declaring and propagating the whole Christian Doctrine
in the doing of which, if I can express it so with decency, they did
an act of the most direct and highest contumacy and disobedience
to those that then Governed. And so it did and always will happen, 5
that whereas Christianity is indeed most certainly the greatest
Friend to Government, and takes the greatest care, makes the best
provision of any Doctrine whatsoever for the preserving of its
authority; yet where the Magistrate does clash with the rules and
ends of Christianity, he does of consequence subvert his own power, 10
and undermine his own Foundation; not by any malignity that
there is in the Religion, but by a distinct efficacy that it has in
maintaining it self thorow all opposition. But when once Christianity had in this regular and direct way obtained the Soveraignty,
Ecclesiastical persons in whose keeping the Counterparts of Chris- 15
tian Doctrine, and example are most properly deposited, began
exceedingly to degenerate. For the former sincerity and devotion
of the Teachers, joyned with their abstinence from riches or secular
honours and imployments, had, as it will do always, render'd them
in the opinion of others worthy of that which they most contemn'd 20
and avoided, and by how much they fled they were the more follow'd by a devout Liberality: And good reason it was that as the
people did partake of their Spirituals, so should they too of the
Peoples Temporals: neither could any plenty then seem envious,
when the Donors saw them to be so good Stewards of what they 25
gave them, converting little to their own profit, but dispensing the
most part to pious and charitable uses. But in those dayes *Venenum*,
as 'twas said, *infusum est Ecclesiæ*, and Religion having brought forth
Riches, the Daughter devoured the Mother. Not that I think any
reward can be too great for one that is faithful in the discharge of 30
so sacred an Office, but those that can go upright under the load of
wealth, make up the lesser number of mankind, and for the most
part they that seek it more earnestly do the worst deserve it. Too
many of that order did then begin to sleight their own Function,
although of all others the most eligible and worthy: consisting in 35
the sweetness of a contemplative life, the inestimable care of mens

23 should they] they should 74.   34 sleight] slight 74.

Souls, a freedom from the common occasions of vice, and from the Mechanical drudgery of raking together a fortune. That which was an Office before, was now turn'd into a Benefice, and one would not suffice the Appetite, but they introduced the Polygamy of Plurali-
5 ties. Non-residence was so legal, that it was almost grown to a Science, and a man might have compil'd a Systeme of its several terms of Art and Distinctions. They follow'd the Courts of Princes, and intangled themselves in secular affairs, beyond what is lawful or convenient to the Sanctity of their Vocation: and from that un-
10 natural Copulation of Ecclesiastical and Temporal together, have those Monsters of Practice and Opinion been begotten, with which the World has been ever since infested; They incumbred Christianity (that is the most short and plain Religion) with an innumerable rabble of Rites and Ceremonies; neglecting the sincere and
15 solid for a *Mosaical* rubbish, that tends nothing to Edification, and which our Saviour had swept out of his Temple. They affected pre-eminence, and ruled their flock by constraint, Lording it over Gods inheritance. They rent the Universal Church in pieces, sometimes about the observation of a Festival, otherwhiles about their scuffles
20 for precedence. By degrees they bearded Princes themselves, and chalenged so exempt a Jurisdiction, that it was resolved even the Concubines of Priests were not within the cognizance of the Civil Magistrate. In conclusion, they let the reins loose to their own Covetousness, Ambition, Pride, Ignorance, Formality, and Conten-
25 tions: and could never take up again. Insomuch that well-nigh ever since it has been more then half the business of Princes to regulate the brabbles and quarrels that have been unnecessarily sow'd by some of the Clergy; and they have brought the World to that pass that indeed it cannot longer subsist then Kings shall have and exer-
30 cise an Ecclesiastical Supremacy as far as it can be stretched. And when the best Function was by these means the worst corrupted, so far have they been from returning to the good and ancient wayes of Christianity, that all their indevours have bent to the establishing of their iniquity by Laws, and propagating it by the most indirect
35 methods of humane Policy. They have strove constantly to make all Reformation, not only ridiculous but impossible; and to draw

19 scuffles 74; scufflles 73.

Princes into their Confederacy. Unto which end although they had accumulated the wealth of most Kingdoms into their own Coffers, and grasped at all Jurisdiction, as oft as there was any fear of a Reformation, they have been very liberal again of Power and Treasure to dispose and inable the Magistrate to War and Violence. There have never been wanting among them such as would set the Magistrate upon the Pinnacle of the Temple, and showing him all the Power, Wealth, and Glory of the Kingdoms of the Earth, have proffer'd the Prince all so he would be tempted to fall down and worship them. So that the Ecclesiastical Wisdom has resembled that after the Deluge, which having once wash'd the World clean from that filth of Luxury and Impiety that it had in so long a time been contracting men thought it wonderful Politick, instead of trusting to Gods promise, and following Righteousness the only security against Gods judgments, to erect an impregnable *Babel* of Power, that should reach to Heaven. But all such vain attempts are still by the Divine Providence turn'd into confusion. In the mean time Nations, it is true, have by this means been run up into Schismes, Heresies, and Rebellions, which are indeed crimes of the highest nature, and of the most pernicious consequence; but do not in the least diminish, yea rather aggravate the guilt of those men who have alwayes design'd to secure their own misdemeanors by publick oppression. For all Governments and Societies of men, and so the Ecclesiastical, do in process of long time gather an irregularity, and wear away much of their primitive institution. And therefore the true wisdom of all Ages hath been to review at fit periods those errours, defects or excesses, that have insensibly crept on into the Publick Administration; to brush the dust off the Wheels, and oyl them again, or if it be found advisable to chuse a set of new ones. And this Reformation is most easily and with least disturbance to be effected by the Society it self, no single men being forbidden by any Magistrate to amend their own manners, and much more all Societies having the liberty to bring themselves within compass. But if men themselves shall omit their duty in this matter, the only just and lawful way remains by the Magistrate, who, having the greatest trust and interest in preserving the publick wellfare, had

9 he 74; he he 73.   28 off 74; of 73.   29 found *om.* 74.

need take care to redress in good season whatsoever corruptions that may indanger and infect the Government. Otherwise, if the Society it self shall be so far from correcting its own exorbitances, as to defend them even to the offence and invasion of the Univer-
5 sality; and if Princes shall not take the advantage of their errours to reduce them to reason; this work, being on both sides neglected, falls to the Peoples share, from which God defend every good Government. For though all Commotions be unlawful, yet by this means they prove unavoidable. In all things that are insensible
10 there is nevertheless a natural force alwayes operating to expel and reject whatsoever is contrary to their subsistence. And the sensible but brutish creatures heard together as if it were in counsel against their common inconveniences, and imbolden'd by their multitude, rebel even against Man their Lord and Master. And the Common
15 People in all places partake so much of Sense and Nature, that, could they be imagined and contrived to be irrational, yet they would ferment and tumultuate at last for their own preservation. Yet neither do they want the use of Reason, and perhaps their aggregated Judgment discerns most truly the errours of Govern-
20 ment, forasmuch as they are the first to be sure that smart under them. In this only they come to be short-sighted, that though they know the Diseases, they understand not the Remedies, and though good Patients, they are ill Physicians. The Magistrate only is authorized, qualified, and capable to make a just and effectual
25 Reformation, and especially among the Ecclesiasticks. For in all experience, as far as I can remember, they have never been forward to save the Prince that labour. If they had, there would have been no *Wickliffe*, no *Husse*, no *Luther* in History. Or at least, upon so notable an emergency as the last, the Church of *Rome* would then
30 in the Council of *Trent* have thought of rectifying it self in good earnest, that it might have recover'd its ancient character: whereas it left the same divisions much wider, and the Christian People of the world to suffer, Protestants under Popish Governors, Popish under Protestants, rather then let go any point of interessed
35 Ambition. The instances made by the Emperour, and by the King of *France*, with their Proposals for Reformation, the indevours of

1 take *om.* 74.   14 against 74; again 73.   31 ancient] ancients 74.

sundry great and religious Prelates, and among the rest the Arch-
bishop of *Granada*, whom I named on a former occasion, all came to
nothing: and I wish our later times did not furnish us with parallels
of the same nature. What I have said thus far concerning the
Ecclesiasticks, I have said with great regret; and it would be yet 5
greater did not the imputation upon such particular persons as are
culpable on these accounts set off the multitude of those that are
commendable for the contrary with a fuller lustre. But as to our
Church, as I wish that none therein could come within this reflexion,
yet truly there are not so many notorious defects in its Govern- 10
ment, that any can suspect me to have directed this discourse to
those Reverend persons that are the Guides of it; and who, if they
would but add a little more moderation to their great prudence,
might quickly mend what is to be mended, to the great quiet of
themselves, and edification of the People. In this one matter only 15
of the Ceremonial Controversie (as it is managed) in our Church,
I must confess my want of capacity, which I have reason in all other
things to acknowledge; and though indeed our Ecclesiastical Governours have the Law herein upon their side, it befitted them however to have seen that the dispute should have been managed even 20
on their part with more humanity: which having been otherwise,
has drawn me as it might any man else beyond mine own diffidence
to say what I thought expedient. Even the Church of *Rome*, which
cannot be thought the most negligent of things that concern her
interest, does not, that I know of, lay any great stress upon Rituals 25
and Ceremonials, so men agree in Doctrine: nor do I remember that
they have persecuted any upon that account, but left the several
Churches in the Priviledge of their own fashion. Insomuch that in
the very Ritual of the Mass, the most religious part of their Worship, the *Mosarabe* Ceremonies are allow'd where formerly practised, 30
in which Horses and Fencings are introduced after the manner of
the *Moores*, which *Antonius* of *Valtellina* affirmed to have a great
Mysterie and Signification in them, but that thereby that Mass so
differ'd from the *Roman* that no *Italian* would think it were a Mass,
should he see it celebrated. I have as much as possible disingaged 35

7 off 74; of 73.   11 discourse to 74; discourse to to 73.   16 (as it is
managed) 74; *om*. 73.

my mind from all Bias and Partiality, to think how or what prudence men of so great Piety and Learning as the Guides of our Church could find out all along, it being now near an Hundred and fifty years, to press on and continue still impositions in these mat-
5 ters. On the Non-conformists part it is plain that they have per-sisted in this dispute, because they have, or think they have the direct authority of Scripture on their side, and to keep themselves as remote as might be from the return of that Religion, from which they had reformed: whereas on the other side, in the former times
10 Rigour was heighten'd with Rigour, and Innovation multiplyed by Innovation, that no man can conjecture where it would have ended. But whatever design the Ecclesiastical Instruments managed, it is yet to me the greatest mysterie in the world how the Civil Magis-trate could be perswaded to interess himself with all the severity
15 of his power in a matter so unnecessary, so trivial, and so pernicious to the publick quiet. For had things been left in their own state of Indifferency, it is well known that the *English* Nation is generally neither so void of Understanding, Civility, Obedience, or Devotion, but that they would long ago have voluntarily closed and faln
20 naturally into those reverent manners of Worship which would sufficiently have exprest and suited with their Religion. And when things were carried on to an extraordinary height by the Rulers of the Church, they suffered long, and even to extremity; which is as much as could by any Magistrate be expected, unless that too were
25 made a Crime, and they must suffer for suffering. It is true at last men proceeded beyond the bounds of Christian Moderation and Patience; and there fell out those dismal effects, which, if they can-not be forgotten, ought to be always deplored, always avoided. To conclude this matter thus far, there is no Command in Scrip-
30 ture that injoyns the Christian Magistrate to lay any such Imposi-tions: and that Promise, *that Kings shall be nursing-fathers to the Church,* is so far from warranting any such thing, that it rather implyes the contrary; neither that they should so pamper the Clergy and humour their weaknesses, as to forget that in our Church the
35 National multitude is more properly included, and that as Nursing Fathers they ought to be careful lest they overlay any of their

19 voluntarily 74; voluntary 73.

Children. Those therefore that ascribe an Absolute and Unlimited Power to the Magistrate, will not I hope deny them, peremptorily, to proceed within the Bounds of their own Discretion. And if our Saviour has reserved some cases to his own Jurisdiction, as I shall treat hereafter, no Prince I hope will think it a diminution, but that rather he is thereby discharged, and eased of that part of Government wherein there would have been the most trouble, and can be the least advantage.

And that can be only in Case of *Conscience*, which is the second thing that in your pleasant and droling manner you have chose to insist upon. I have in some measure shown you, Mr. *Necessity Bayes*, how many absurdities you have incurred in managing the Absolute and Unlimited Ecclesiastical Power of the Magistrate as well as Civil. That you may the more exalt that, you continue as in your former Books to revile and debase Conscience, so that you may put it out of Countenance, and out of all good conceit with it self. *Most mens minds or Consciences*, you have said, *are weak, silly and ignorant things, acted by fond and absurd Principles.* You say, men talk of it as of *some distinct Puppet within them, or as if it were a Pope in their Bellies*; whereas *Conscience*, you say, is *an indeterminate thing, and has no more certain a signification then the clinking of a Bell, that is as every man fancies.* I understand Sir, what you mean; *As the fool thinks, so the Conscience tinks.* Commend me to you, Mr. *Bayes*, for a good Conscience-maker. Who that were in his wits would trouble himself with a thing so inconsiderable? And yet the mischief is, that this is that by which every man must be excused or accused. But the good again of that mischief is, that this will have no effect till the Day of Judgment. In the mean time I take it I assure you to be as serious a thing, as you would make it ridiculous; and what I fancy by it, is Humane Reason guided by the Scripture in order to Salvation. What you determine it to be, is to be seen more particularly in the third Chapter of your *Ecclesiastical Politie*, and summarily in the Contents: and you reproach me for representing it as if you there *confined the whole duty of Conscience to the inward thoughts of the Mind and its perswasions*; and this (to avoid tediousness, and that I may not return your immodest answer) I shall refer to the Reader. If as there you say: *the Inward Actions of the Mind, and Matters of meer Conscience* be made terms Convertible, if *Mankind have a Liberty of Conscience as far as concerns their Judgments, but not their Practices*; if *the Nature of Christian Liberty relate to our Thoughts, and not to our Actions*; if *Christian Liberty consist in the Restauration of the Mind of Man to its natural Liberty from the Yoke of the Ceremonial Law*; I durst almost trust your self, though I have no great inducement to confide in you, with the arbitration betwixt us. For if the Inward Actions of the Mind only be the Matters of meer Conscience, do you not confine the whole duty of Conscience to the inward thought and perswasions of the Mind? Or if a Man would help you over the Stile, and allow somthing to be Conscience that is not meer Conscience, do not you evacuate it again in saying, that men have a Liberty of Conscience as far as concerns their Judgments, but not their Practises? So that here is a second Commitment, and you have confined Conscience back again to the Inward Thoughts only and perswasions of the Mind. Nay even, if Christian Liberty consist in the Restauration of the Mind of Man to its Natural Liberty from the *Mosaical* Law, does not that too according to your Doctrine here dispense only with our Judgments, but our Practice is still, or may be bound up to the Observance of all the *Mosaical* Institutions. So that if you please you may keep the Lye to your self of which you are so liberal, or let it remain in the middle till it be decided whom it of right belongs to, and let him take it and make his best on't. But in this of the *Jewish* Law you are indeed very distinct, and as dogmatical as a man would wish. For you say, that *if the Proconsul of* Judæa *should publish an Edict that all Christians shall submit to Circumcision out of regard to the eternal Obligation to the Law of* Moses, *that were a manifest violence to the freedom of the Gospel: but whatever else he may command, so he pretend not to any warrant of Divine Authority; whatever abuse it may be of his own power, it is no abuse of Christian Liberty.* So that you do not determine that it would be so much as an abuse of his own power, but you do determine, that, if he do command not only Circumcision, but whatsoever else, (how strangely comprehensive are those words!) it is no abuse of Christian Liberty. But you are so far in love with this Notion, that you say the *Mosaical dispensation being*

Cancell'd by the Gospel, those indifferent things that had been made necessary by a Divine positive command return'd to their own nature, to be used or omitted only as occasion should direct. So that here you plainly assert what you left disputable in the former passage, that the Magistrate may if he please lawfully introduce and set up the *Jewish* Religion again among Christians. 'Tis a sad case in the mean time, and truly if our Saviours Cancelling the *Mosaical* Law do but render the same indifferent, I am afraid that his Confirming of the Magistrates Ecclesiastical Power, that you told us of, is not much better, and had no great validity. But I do not now wonder that you said it was in the Power of the Magistrate to establish what Religion he took to be most advantageous: for I see you are an honest man of your word, and meant it in good earnest. He may command whatsoever he pleases. He may set up the whole Jewish Religion as occasion shall direct. Whither on Gods name will these Ceremonies of ours lead us at last, what shall we come to? I see there is nothing Divine or Humane so unalterable or so Sacred, no Liberty that belongs to Men or to Christians that you are not ready to violate and prostitute to your own end; and you will turn any thing Jew or Heathen, and preach up others to it rather then lose a Speculation, or be foyl'd in an argument. Whereas no man hath devested himself of any Natural Liberty as he is a Man, by professing himself a Christian, but one liberty operates within the other more effectually, & strengthen themselves better by that double Title. Especially if your rule hold, in this case; *that our Saviour hath Confirmed what he hath not Reversed.* For as to this particular of the *Mosaical* Law, *Christ* has abrogated it for ever in perpetuity; and it must sure be a very pretty Doctrine this of yours, that so the Antecedent Necessity be taken away, the Magistrate may erect it again by a Subsequent. So in conclusion our Saviour has done just nothing, neither indeed could he by your argument: and the Christian Subject being only at Liberty in his judgment, is notwithstanding obliged in Obedience to conform to the whole Jewish Ceremonial, as oft as the Magistrate may think it expedient. But I say you ought to know and acknowledge that our Saviour has establish'd Christianity to indure till his second coming; and hath in the Institution of that

10 that 74; thar 73.   15 Whither 74; Whether 73.

Religion condescended, though he might have exacted both, to be himself treated without Ceremony, so that were supplyed by Reality. For Christianity has obliged men to very hard duty, and ransacks their very thoughts, not being contented with an un-
5 blameableness as to the Law, nor with an external Righteousness: it aims all at that which is sincere and solid and having laid that weight upon the Conscience, which will be found sufficient for any honest man to walk under, it hath not pressed and loaded men further with the burthen of Ritual and Ceremonial traditions and
10 Impositions. For whether indeed they be so heavy as they appear to the Scrupulous, yet they are not so light to be sure as you would perswade men: and most Creatures know when they have their just load, nor can you make them go if you add more. In conclusion it is most certain that as our Saviour has exacted those duties which
15 are necessary with more declarative strictness from Christians, then was under any other Religion, and thereby bound the Conscience to a severer scrutiny within it self over all our performances; so hath he gratified them on the other part with larger exemptions and Priviledges from things Indifferent and Unnecessary. And it is a
20 gross abuse whosoever strives to limit Christian Liberty only from the *Jewish* Ceremonial Law, which you too will hardly grant us. But whatsoever general Rules, Laws and Precepts are given in Scripture, and more particularly in the New Testament, to direct the Magistrate in the moderation of his Power in things of this
25 nature, do make up the great Charter of Christian Liberty, and they may justly plead it. 'Tis true that the decision and punishment of those that shall transgress therein if they be Supreme Magistrates is reserved to Gods Tribunal, and the Appeal thither, which you almost laugh at, is the most proper: but the Law by which those
30 that offend their weak Brother, will then be proceeded upon, is very legible, both having been dictated by our Saviour himself and by his Apostles. Yet though the Supreme Magistrate cannot be questioned, I am not at all doubtful but that he may punish any such transgression in his Subalterns and Substitutes: and if it would
35 please God to inspire the hearts of Princes to curb that sanguinary and unchristian Spirit of those that for their own corrupt ends make

31 having 74; haeing 73.

Government so uneasie to Princes; so that we might once come to the experiment how happy a Prince and people might be under a plain and true Christian administration, I believe all men, and especially Princes would be so satisfy'd, and in love with it, that they would make it Treason to give them any contrary counsel. 5

But the occasion of all this medly and Hoch-poch that you make in matters of meer Conscience, and of Mixt Conscience, in the Liberty of Christians as to their Judgment, but not to their Practice, of the Magistrates Power to impose things by a subsequent, so he do it not by an Antecedent Necessity; is from your Ignorance 10 of Divine and Humane things which makes you jumble them so together that you cannot distinguish of their several Obligations. Or else it is your voluntary and affected perverting of your own knowledge, is the same manner as in *Turky* they turn themselves so long giddy, till they can neither think nor see what is before them, and 15 fall down in an extasie fit for Inspiration. Or it is that you may thus contribute to your own Maxime, and, seeing *Governors must keep their People from sinking into too much Ignorance, or rising to too much knowledge in matters of,*—to do your part in muffling them up to play before you at the Blind-man-buff of Conscience. For whereas you 20 quote out of the first of *Peter* 2. 13. and 15. *Submit to every Ordinance of man for the Lords sake, for so is the will of God, that with well doing you may put to silence the Ignorance of foolish men,* it appears as if you had on purpose omitted what comes between in the latter end of the 13*th.* and the whole 14*th* verse: *Whether it be to the King, as Supreme,* 25 *or unto Governors as unto them that are sent by him for the punishment of evil doers, and for the praise of them that do well*: and you neglect in the 16*th* verse, *As free, and not using your liberty as a cloak of maliciousness,* the conclusion; *but as the Servants of God*: and *as Free* you Print in the common character that men may not unless they look in the Bible, 30 discern that it is part of the Text. These are pretty little contrivances. But if this be consider'd in the whole, it seems to me that by *every Ordinance of man* is not meant every Law of man, but the Governors themselves, whether Supreme or Substitute. And that submission not to be intended singly concerning an Active Obedi- 35 ence: For few men will offer to say that if Ordinances should be

23 *the* 74; *ihe* 73.   29 *as Free*] You are free   Parker.

interpreted by Laws, men ought so to obey *every* Law; for their duty is described *as free*, and *as the Servants of God*; so that whensoever those come to be contradistinguished, not Man but God is to be obey'd. And therefore this Apostle, and so all the rest did actively
5 disobey by Preaching the Gospel, and in particular Saint *Paul* perceiv'd another kind of *Necessity* then yours; *Necessity was laid upon him to preach the Gospel.* And you may find in the 9*th* to the *Hebrews* that those *Ordinances* which you contend still to be lawful, are absolutely voided. For *the first Covenant also had Ordinances of Divine Ser-*
10 *vice, and a worldly Sanctuary.* And v. 10. *it stood only in meats and drinks and divers washings and Carnal Ordinances Imposed on them until the time of Reformation.* And you cannot unless you shut your eyes but discern *Col.* 2. 14. that our *Saviour has blotted out the hand-writing of Ordinances, and taken it out of the way nailing it to his Cross.* Neither in
15 the 13*th* to the *Romans*, does it appear to me otherwise then that therefore men ought not to contemn, contradict, resist the Magistrate, who indeed is the *Ordinance of God* according to that Text and others; but in the same place it is evident, that, as to active obedience to Governours in particular cases, the matter must be decided
20 betwixt God and every mans Conscience. And I must still desire you to remember that by Conscience I understand Humane reason acting by the Rule of Scripture, in order to obedience to God and a Mans own Salvation. But you not content to have said that the *Magistrate hath Power to make that a particular of the Divine Law which*
25 *God hath not made so*, do avowedly and plainly make all Humane Laws that do not Countenance Vice, or Disgrace the Deity to be particulars of the Divine Law, and that to break any other Law then such, is a sin, And that *all laws Civil as well as Ecclesiastical equally oblige the Conscience*, and upon pain of Damnation. So that hereby whatsoever
30 is enacted on Earth is at the same time enacted in Heaven. Every Law carries along with it the pain of Excommunication. Whatsoever the Magistrate binds on Earth is bound in Heaven: and he delivers every man who transgresses in Cartwheels, and the number of Horses in his Team, or that buries not in Flannel over to
35 Satan. There is no Christian Magistrate, but, if he thought the matter went so high, he would be very tender how he made Laws

8 *Ordinances* 74; *Ordinanees* 73.   9 *Ordinances* 74; *Orbinances* 73.

and rather then multiply them to the Damnation of his good Subjects, he would bear with many a Publick inconvenience. But this
desperate Maxime (though what I am going to say is unavoidable,
yet I do it with reverence) does impose upon Gods Conscience, that
he must make that a Sin which was not so before the Magistrate 5
commanded the Duty; it makes God to be the Magistrates Minister;
and, whereas the Law-giver contents himself with the Penalty that
the Law exacts in case of failure, nevertheless at the same time he
obliges God to execute damnation upon the Offender. I am almost
confident that the Divine Justice would never have been thus far at 10
the Magistrates beck, but that you have told God, that *he must of
necessity grant him at least thus much Power*; and therefore I must confess there is no help for it. Will you never be ashamed of this
damning and damned Doctrine? It were better that all Uniformity
had never been invented, then that it should be upheld by such 15
Theology. But I will not fall into a further transport, seeing some
allowance is to be given you, by reason of your ancient acquaintance, and your present friendship with the Non-conformists; which
obliges you to do them all good offices, and therefore, like that
Italian, you would not do them an half-Courtesie, but contrive to 20
kill their Bodies and damn their Souls with one labour. Are there
not many Customs that have gained the Force of Laws? Are there
not many Persons that are ignorant of several Laws that are made?
Are there not many Laws that by disuse are grown obsolete and
stand yet Un-repealed? What would you in this case advise God to 25
do with poor Sinners? Will nothing serve but Hell-fire, or will you
agree that there may be some gentler *Limbo* prepared for them,
where they may sweat out their guiltiness? It is impossible in such
gross absurdities, but that a man should speak to the quick, though
never so desirous to treat of sacred things with due reverence. But 30
moreover whatsoever Obligations may be put upon Mankind, they
are to be expounded by that great and fundamental Law of Mercy.
And therefore it was that our Saviour, even in the case of a Divine
Positive Law, declared accordingly and interpreted the meaning of,
I will have Mercy and not Sacrifice, as a general dispensation in all 35
things that come within that respect and consideration. But to

23 Persons that 74; ~ thar 73.   27 *Limbo* 74; *not Italic* 73.

proceed further, I say, with submission still to better judgements, and especially to Superiors, that I conceive the Magistrate, as in Scripture described, is the Ordinance of God constituting him, and the Ordinance of Man assenting to his Dominion. For there is not
5 now any express Revelation, no Inspiration of a Prophet, nor Unction of that Nature as to the declaring of that particular person that is to Govern. Only God hath in general commanded and disposed men to be Governed. And the particular person reigns according to that right, more or less, respectively, which under Gods provi-
10 dence he or his Predecessors have lawfully acquired over the Subject. Therefore I take the Magistrates Power to be from God, only in a Providential constitution; and the nature of which is very well and reverently expressed by Princes themselves, *By the Grace of God King of,* &c. but I do not understand that God has thereby imparted
15 and devolved to the Magistrate his Divine Jurisdiction. God that sees into the thoughts of mens hearts, and to whom both Prince and Subjects are accountable, sees not as man sees, nor judges as he judges; but is his own Measure and the first Rectitude. But for the Magistrate it is surely sufficient that God has fortify'd him with a
20 Divine Law that he may not be resisted: but his Administration is humane, neither is it possible either for him to exact or men to pay him more then a Civil obedience in those Laws which he constituteth. Otherwise it were in his Power not only, as some and *Caligula* for example, to decree that he is God, but even to be so. God
25 surely, although it does for the most part or ought to fall out that the same action is a sin against God, and a disobedience to the humane Law, punishes the Fact so far as he sees and knows in himself that it is sinful and contrary to the Eternal rule of Justice: but an humane Law can create only an humane obligation; and unless
30 the breach chance likewise to be against some express Divine Law, I cannot see but that the offendor is guilty not to God, but onely to the Magistrate, and hath expiated his Offence by undergoing the Penalty.

I should be very sory to disseminate in a matter so weighty,
35 any Errour, nay even an unseasonable or dangerous Truth; none being more desirous or more sensible of the Necessity of Publick

28 it *om.* 74.

Obedience. And therefore as I have consulted none to make them conscious or culpable of what mistake I may run into, so if any shall convince me of one herein, I shall ingenuously retract it. But if this appear to be sufficient in reason for the preserving of Government, 'tis probable that it will prove to be so likewise in fact, and that 5 there is no further provision made for the Magistrate. I do suppose therefore that the true stress and force of Laws lyes in their aptitude and convenience for the general good of the People; and no Magistrate is so wanton as to make Laws meerly out of the pleasure of Legislation, but out of the prospect of some utility to the Publick. 10 Few Subjects are so capable as to imagine any further Obligation: neither does that opinion lean towards Atheism, but proceeds rather from an honorable apprehension concerning God; that he could not institute Government to the prejudice of mankind, or exact obedience to Laws that are destructive to the Society. There- 15 fore, as long as the Magistrate shall provide Laws that appear useful in the experiment, the whole people will stand by him to exact obedience from the refractary, and pursue them like a Common Enemy. But if it fall out otherwise, that the Laws are inconvenient in the practice, men are so sensible of that, and so dull in Divinity, 20 that, should the Legislator persist never so much, he would danger to be left in the field very single; and should you, Mr. *Necessity Bayes*, inculcate your heart out, the Auditory would scarce be converted. Indeed how is it possible to imagine, and to what purpose, that ever any Magistrate should make Laws but for a general ad- 25 vantage? and who again but would be glad to abrogate them when he finds them pernicious to his Government? And therefore it is very usual to make at first Probationary Laws, and for some term of years only; that both the Law-giver and the Subject may see at leisure how proper they are and suitable to the effect for which they 30 were intended. And indeed all Laws however are but Probationers of time; and, though meant for perpetuity, yet, when unprofitable, do as they were made by common consent, so expire by universal neglect, and without Repeal grow Obsolete. There is again beside the Convenience of a Law, another security in the Penalty. For 35 because few Laws are so perfect or convenient, but that some man

34 neglect 74; negrect 73.

will out of a vicious temper or interest transgress them; the Penalties too of Pecuniary Mulcts, or of Life, or Limme, or Liberty and
whatsoever else are necessary, and doubtless the Magistrate does
therein hold the ballance of Justice, and weigh the punishment as
5 near as may be, that it should be proportionable to the offence. And
out of that care it is, that Governors make the same fault sometimes
capital, otherwhiles Pecuniary, other, Imprisonment, *&c.* but that,
whatsoever it is, being once undergone, all men reckon that the
Magistrate and Justice are satisfied. For indeed how can Humane
10 Laws bind beyond the declared intention of the Magistrate in them?
They who obey them find therein their Convenience and Reward
they who break them the Punishment: and upon those two wheels
all Government hath turned. But to make all Obedience matter of
Salvation, is a Note that I believe no Tyrant ever thought of: and
15 it would be some trouble to calculate, when a Law is alter'd here
upon Earth, and the same offence shall one year be Capital, and the
next year perhaps thought fit to be Finable; how far the Judicature
of Heaven takes the same measures, as it is a sin, in the Damnation:
Or suppose the Crime be pardon'd here, why should not the
20 Malefactor plead it too in Heaven? Or how came it that *the Parliament* 3° *Caroli, whatsoever they were by the Laws of the Land, were
notorious Rebels by all the Laws of the Gospel?* You say they are no Laws
unless they oblige the Conscience. It is no great matter however:
For if they be not Laws they are at least Halters; and the Obliga-
25 tion of that without Conscience will be sufficiently effectual. It
was, you know, an Order in one Government that he that proposed
a new Law should appear with an halter about his neck in the
Assemby; it being thought reasonable that he should know his own
neck would be concerned as well as others in the inconvenience.
30 But for such an Ecclesiastical Law-giver as you, I know not what
Memento were competent; who bring in a Law that whosoever shall
disobey any Statute, nay any By-Law, though he deserves not to
be hang'd, nor to be fined ten pounds, yet shall in a trice and
the very same moment be damned. You should before you thus
35 confounded all humane and divine things together, have at least

---

7 fault 74; sault 73.   10 declared] declarest 74.   them? 74; ~ 73.
20 Or 74; or 73.   35 confounded] confound 74.

reflected upon affairs nearer your understanding; To what purpose then have all those former Contests been managed, whether Episcopacy were *Jure Divino* or *Jure Humano?* Whether Residence in a mans Living were by Divine or by Canon Law? In which last Controversie the Arch-bishop, whom I minded you of at your Siege 5 of *Granada*, determined it to be of Divine Obligation. But the Pope said that to declare that the Non-resident should incur the Deprivation of the Benefice, would be a readier way and much more effectual. And that is indeed too experienced a Truth that humane Penalties do more powerfully affect mens obedience then Divine 10 Obligations. But therefore as it is unlawful to palliate with God and enervate his Laws into an humane only and Politick consideration; so is it on the other side unlawful and unnecessary, to give to Common and Civil constitutions a Divine Sanction, and it is so far from an owning of Gods Jurisdiction, that it is an Invasion upon it. 15 Now that I may more manifestly and further evidence, that, how horrid soever this opinion be which I object to you, yet I have not in the least aggravated your sense or words; it may be necessary, knowing what manner of man I have to deal with, to press you and instance a little closer in that one particular of the *Jejunium Cecili-* 20 *anum,* or the *Wednesday* Fast, in the 5° *Elizabethæ,* to which purpose it is material that the original Clause be cited. 'Tis thus, *And because no manner of person shall misjudge of the intent of this Statute containing orders to eat fish, and forbear eating of flesh, but that the same is properly intended and meant Politickly, for the increase of Fishermen and Mariners,* 25 *and repairing of Port-Towns and Navigation, and not for superstition to be maintained in choice of Meats; Be it enacted, that whosoever shall by teaching, writing, or open speech notifie that any eating of Fish or forbidding of Flesh, mentioned in this Act, is of any Necessity for the saving of the Soul of man, or that it is the Service of God, otherwise then as other Politick Laws* 30 *are and be, then that such persons shall be punish'd as spreaders of false News. This Act to last for ten years,* &c. Now upon consideration of what you maintain and quote out of a late Learned Prelate, whom you

---

1 understanding; 74; ~, 73.   4 In 74; in 73.   13 is it] it is 74.
18 necessary, 74; ~; 73.   21 *Elizabethæ* 74; *Elizabethee* 73.   23-4 *containing*]
limiting Rastell.   24 *properly*] purposely Rastell.   27 *in* 74; *in in* 73.
27-8 *by teaching*] by preaching, teaching Rastell.   28 *forbidding*] forbearing
Rastell.

leave nameless, that you might have the honour of it; *Then the Law is no Law at all, and if it be not tyed upon the Conscience, it is no Sin to break it and to keep it is no duty*: and adding hereunto what you say in the *Reproof*; upon this occasion; *I will chalenge you and all your party of mankind to maintain that whoever enacts a Law with this Proviso, that it shall not bind in Conscience, enacts no Law; whether therefore the Clause were added by* Cecil *or by the Parliament, I am not concerned and though you should throw in the Queen, and Convocation, and all, I care not, I will declare that they were all miserably out in their Divinity*: I say, considering this, I am very jealous that neither your late Learned Prelate, nor you ever read the Clause, but took it up at adventure. For there is not a word of Conscience in the whole Clause, and if you would mount what is said to mean Conscience, the Clause does not however exclude it, for it runs you see thus: *or that it is the Service of God otherwise then as all other Politick Laws are and be.* Indeed at this rate you may say and make what you please. But it is plain that this Clause which is a part of the Act, and you call impertinent, was inserted with most exemplary and Christian prudence, to avoid not only apparent manifest evil, but the very appearance of evil, and to show the perswasion of those times, though it prove so contrary to yours, that the Ordinances of Meats and Drinks were so abolish'd by our Saviour, that this Act could not concern men in their Salvation: and therefore too they made it but a Probationer, that the Subject also might have time to try the convenience or inconvenience. Therefore, Sir, I would advise you to go to your Statute book, and see whether the Act be continued or repealed; least at any time you have incurr'd not only the Penalty of False news, *by teaching, writing and open Speech*, but least you have unwittingly run your self into Damnation, according to your own doctrine, by disobeying the Act. But as to your *throwing in the Queen and Convocation too, and that they were all wretchedly out in Divinity*; you might have consider'd whether Arch-bishop *Parker* were not there among them, who methinks how light soever all the rest were, might have weigh'd something in your balance. This however is according to your wonted bravery, Mr. *Bayes*, and, as your Camarade said of the Crit-

---

5 *whoever* Parker; *whatever* 73, 74.   24 have 74; have have 73.   33 were, 74; ~ 73.

icks, so Queen, Parliament, Convocation, when they are not of your mind, *have no more wit in them then so many Hobby-horses*: and as Mr. *Johnson* replyed thereupon, *you have said enough of them in Conscience.* You are it seems your self the man you mention in your Platonick Philosophy, 5

Celsa qui mentis ab arce Despicis Errantes, humana Senacula *ridens.*—

And you look down upon these *odde* passages of Humane Laws, at the same time you make them divine, as very despicable. Since you are come to be the *Cardinal* Deacon, you look, as you say the Cardinals of *Rome* express it, upon all secular affairs as the *Undershrieval-* 10 *ties of that life*, with great *Sossiego* and calmness. From what I have alledg'd of yours in this Clause I hope it is evident, that you do maintain not only that Statute, but all others to bind under pain of damnation. What need I trouble my self in proving it out on you? 'Tis what you contend avowedly to make us believe. *God has* 15 *annexed*, you say, *the same Penalties to disobedience to Mans Laws as his own.* Henceforth I pray do not criticize so severely upon *Calvine*, nor upbraid him with his *Horrendum Decretum* of Divine Predestination: for at this rate you will make every Humane Law as horrible and terrible. Take heed of hooking things up to Heaven in this manner; 20 for, though you look for some advantage from it, you may chance to raise them above your reach, and if you do not fasten and rivet them very well when you have them there, they will come down again with such a swinge, that if you stand not out of the way, they may bear you down further then you thought of. I assure you I 25 am sore afraid and very sory for it, that not only you but all your Clergy of *England* are in a way to be damned. For there is a Law that hath all the Force and validity that any Ecclesiastical or Civil Constitution can carry among us, and something more to boot, which was perhaps the reason that you said the Anabaptists were 30 so much in the right: That is in the order of Publick Baptism in the Common-Prayer Book. For the Words are these, *The Priest, if they shall certifie him that the Child may well indure it, shall dip it in the water discreetly and warily, but if they do certifie that the Child is weak, it shall*

2 as 74; ~, 73.   6 *Despicis*] Despicit Parker.   *humana* Senacula *ridens*] humanaque gaudia ridet Parker.   11 *that*] *this* 74.   15 believe. 74; ~ 73. 24 swinge] swing 74.

suffice to pour water upon it. This is in a matter of no less moment then the Sacrament of initiation into Christianity: and you know very well what is nevertheless the Practice, and you have in your Doctrine informed us of the Consequence. Therefore, in my humble
5 opinion, it were better for you, Mr. *Bayes*, to speak civilly of Princes, whensoever like Nursing-Fathers or Nursing-Mothers they speak tenderly of things relating to the Conscience and Salvation of their Subjects: though indeed either it seems they must themselves learn a new Divinity, or teach you better manners. And you would do
10 well and wisely not to stretch, Gold-beat, and Wyer-draw Humane Laws thus to Heaven: least they grow thereby too slender to hold, and lose in strength what they gain by extension and rarefaction. Reverend Mr. *Hooker* ought to have serv'd you for a better example, who though he was willing to drive this nail as far as it would go,
15 yet having spent his whole eighth book in sifting the Obligation of humane Laws concludes his whole *Ecclesiastical Politie* with these Words, *Disobedience therefore unto Laws which are made by the* Magistrate *is not a thing of so small account as some would make it. However too rigorous it were, that the breach of every humane Law should be held a deadly*
20 *sin. A mean there is between those Extremities if so be we can find it out.* You might have done wisely to have imitated his Modesty. And no less pernicious is all that you say further in this matter which I named *publick Conscience.* Forasmuch as you said, that, *in cases of Publick Concern mens wills and judgments are to be directed and determined*
25 *by the Commands and Determinations of the Publick Conscience.* She is a Lady doubtless of great Quality and Virtue, I should be glad to know her lodging and be better acquainted with her: though often it happens that there is little difference betwixt Publick and Prostitute. But she being very generous, *if there be any sin in her Commands*
30 *will her self answer for it,* and discharge you of all danger *she will warrant your Obedience, and hallow, or at least excuse your Action.* Do what you will with her, *She will secure you from Sin, if not from Errour.* She *will render your Actions virtuous, whatever they are in themselves.* 'Tis the best Woman that ever was born. And further: *a Doubting*

---

6 Nursing-Fathers 74;   Nursing-fathers 73.   Nursing-Mothers 74;   Nursing Mothers 73.   16 with 74; with with 73.   17-18 *the* Magistrate] men Hooker.   18 *some* 74; *somc* 73.   19 *held*] made   Hooker.

*Conscience must alwayes at least as much fright us from disobeying, as from
obeying any humane Law.* Ay, Private Conscience is a meer Trollop
to her, an old Beldam superannuate, and a Bulbegger fit to fright
Children. These *at-leasts* are the very Spirit and flame of Casual
Theology. Frighted at least as much on this side, and frighted at   5
least as much on that side. What will become at this rate of the
poor simple Doubter? He will be in as bad a Case as you when you
were distracted betwixt your Book-seller and your *Comfortable
Importance:* or like a Horse, he may stand and starve between two
equal Hay-cocks; or hang in an *at-least* betwixt Heaven and Hell till   10
the Day of Judgment. Nay, but to avoid that inconvenience, *if we
would speak properly, the Commands of Authority perfectly determine and
evacuate all doubtfulness and irresolution of Conscience*: So that now instead of what the Apostle said, *He that doubts is damned if he eat*, the
business is sheer alter'd, and if he doubts, he is therefore damned.   15
And all your seventh and eighth Chapters of *Ecclesiastical Politie*
swarm with such affirmative and Imperative Divinity. So that you
need not have astonish'd your self, when you find it ought after
long consideration, *that my Book was rather a Censure then a Confutation,*
(yet that too others will judge of:) neither ought you to have   20
taken it so ill though I had only *squirted*, as you call it at your *Thesis*
and Corollaries, unless you knew that Syringing had been, *if we
would speak properly*, more suitable to your *Distemper*. But to conclude
this Matter. Whatsoever *Villany* you say *there is in those mens Religion
who distinguish betwixt Grace and Morality*, and how *Modern* soever   25
that *Orthodoxy*, I am sure these opinions of yours are of an higher
tincture: but because it is a Theology of your own begetting, 'tis
reason to let you too have the naming of it. But 'tis likely to prove
a very wicked wretch, and, should it grow up as in *Probability* at
this rate, under your Instruction and Education, its Malice would   30
soon supply its Age, and 'twill take very desperate courses: and what
End it will come to you may easily imagine. I hope nevertheless
that this Doctrine is yet an Alien in our Church, and therefore, if
for some notorious offence it come to its twelve God-fathers, let it
have however its Priviledge, and be tryed *per Medietatem Conscien-*   35
tiæ. There is one thing more in your discussion of Christian Liberty

16 eighth] eight 74.   20 too 74; (too 73.   28 too] to 74.

8124228   S

concerning the *Gnosticks*, whom you very frequently parallel to the Non-conformists; which, would I seek for new matter of mirth or stir up fresh controversies, does administer me abundant occasion. But I shall defer that till your Diagnosticks be better. For I am
5 afraid you take that as you do many things else upon trust, and should you, upon further consultation with your Chronologers, discern that their Heresie began not till after the death of the Apostles, you would be shrewdly disappointed to find your self guilty of the *Pseudonymos Gnosis*, in that particular. That which in my former
10 Book I call'd your third Play, of *Morall Grace*, you here act over again; but with so trivial levity that indeed I perceive I did you injury in calling it so, for I see it is but an old Farse new vamp'd. And truly here especially, but thorow your whole *Reproof*, it seems that you do not trouble your self so much about the weight of the
15 matter, as disquiet your mind with an Emulation of Wit, of which you ought to be a good Husband, for you come by it very hardly. Whether I have any at all I know not, neither, further then it is not fit for me to reject any good quality wherewith God may have indued me, do I much care: but would be glad to part with it very
20 easily for any thing intellectual, that is solid and useful. Neither therefore do I at all complain or trouble my self, though I see you borrow or steal it before my face, and that you *turn* (with what felicity let others judge) *three parts of my own Book*, as you say you could, *upon me*. Much good do you with it, I will never question
25 you for't. But therefore when you should have been treating here with due gravity concerning the most serious Subject perhaps in all Christianity, you fall a mousing about the definition of a Quibble. You need not upbraid me with that which is the best of your Science, and I foresee within a few Pages that I shall discover you
30 to be much better at it than I am, and that you (if it be a Quibble it befits you) are a meer Word-pecker. You have contrary to all Architecture and good œconomy made a Snow-house in your upper Roome, which indeed was Philosophically done of you, seeing you bear your head so high as if it were in or above the middle Region,
35 and so you thought it secure from melting. But you did not at the same time consider that your Brain is so hot, that the Wit is dis-

1 to 74; *om.* 73.   22 (with 74; ((~ 73.   30 you 74; you are 73.

solv'd by it, and is always dripping away at the Icicles of your Nose. But it Freezes again I confess as soon as it falls down, and hence it proceeds that there is no passage in my Book, deep or shallow, but with a chill and key-cold conceit you can ice it in a moment, and slide shere over it without scatches. But, having done that, you shew your self mightily offended that I have upon this subject of Grace told you, that *if it be resolved into Morality, I think a man may almost as well make God too to be only a Notional and Moral Existence.* I have told you that I foresaw every where at what you would be carping, so I did here, and nevertheless thought fit to express it so upon good deliberation: And could you now have held your Tongue you had heard no more of it, whereas now I am obliged frankly to satisfie you of my severall Reasons. And 'tis first upon occasion of your *Tentamina Physico-Theologica* before mentioned, which you Dedicated to my Lord Arch-bishop; it being your first Address to Ecclesiastical Fortune, and an Essay by writing against Atheisme, to gain Authority to whatsoever Doctrine you should afterwards disseminate. I should not say what follows did I think I could thereby offend my Lord Arch-bishop who having the oversight of this whole Church upon him; does, of course and conscientiously doubtless, transmit such applicatory discourses to his Chaplains. So I suppose you bespoke Doctor *Grigg* to make a favourable Report in your behalf, and give you as he did, a Cast of his Office in the License. I must deduce the thing to make it clear to you. As soon as I open'd the Book at the Title, and saw the Authors name, if you be the same person, I met with *Typis A. M.* but we two not being then acquainted, surely you could not prophesie that I should be the man that should Print you in so legible a Character in a first, and now this second Edition. Next after that *Venales*; which I could not reconcile either in Gender or Number but concerning you and your Book, that henceforwards you were both alike Venall; you indeed, as in an Auction, to be Sold by Inch of Candle. Where? *apud Jo. Sherley.* Ay, there it was where you and your Book both lodged at one anothers expense. For whatever others are, you were then a meer *Shop divine*, and did so nibble all his Library, and dirty them with your Thumbs, that the poor man had not one new Book left,

35 *divine*, Ed.; ∼. 73, 74.

but was fain to Sell them all at second hand. But where was his
Shop? *Ad insigne Pelicani.* A very Emblematical sign where you
digged and pick'd your very Heart-blood and Brains out to nourish
your young *Tentamina.* Where was this? *in parva Britannia.* You
5 should have done well to have Printed us the Map of it; for I find
it not in your *Heylin,* who mis-led you *on the South side of the* Lake
Leman. But, wherever you live, you will take a course to make it
little Britaine. This is not all: *Et apud Sam. Thompson,* to direct men
further; and you were to be had at as many places as *Buckworths*
10 *Lozengis. In Cæmeterio Divi Pauli:* Bury him out of the way 'tis no
matter: But, *ad Insigne Capitis Episcopi,* at the Sign of the Bishops-
head, there you are sure to be heard of. And, to convince men that
this was not all pure Chance, but there was something of Design
and Wit in't, turne but over the Leaf and you meet full bob; *Reve-*
15 *rendissimo in Christo Patri & Domino, Domino* Gilberto *Providentia Divina,*
Archiepiscopo Cantuariensi, *totius* Angliæ *Primati & Metropolitana; &*
Augustissimo Principi, Carolo *Secundo, Magna* Britanniæ, Franciæ *&*
Hiberniæ *Regi, a Secretioribus Consilijs.* So here you *apud Jo.* Sherley
in Parva Britannia, and my Lord Arch-bishop, *totius* Angliæ *Primas,*
20 and Carolus *Secundus Magnæ* Britanniæ *Rex* are brought to an Enter-
view, and to set up a Triumvirate together. But I was at first surprized by your Marshalling and Commaes, not being able readily to
distinguish whether it were not Dedicated also to the King, and
which of the two was the others Privy-Counsellor. Well to pro-
25 ceed; *Nullus dubito quin mireris pedibus tuis provolvi Recentem quendam*
Ignotæ Frontis Clientulum, and well he might, for he knew not yet the
height and bredth of your Forehead: had he, to remark it the better,
it being so unknown, set a Brand upon it, it had been some courtesie
to the Publick. *Et forsan obstupescis.* 'Tis an uncivil supposition, did
30 you not since lessen it by affirming in your *Hicringill; Clerus Britan-*
nicus stupor mundi: Suppose, Mr. *Bayes, you may suppose it seems what you*
please; I have nothing to do with your suppose: suppose quoth a!—but you
intend to make him amends: *hominis fiduciam.* This salves it indeed
a little: For truly; if any thing in the world could rebate the vigour
35 of so acute and solid a judgment, it must have stounded him to
reflect upon your Confidence, then in that Address, but much more

7 live, Ed.; ~. 73, 74.   8 *Thompson,* 74; ~. 73.   25 *Mireris*] *Mineris* 74

in your latter writings. But *Qui fælicius litaturas sperarem studiorum Primitias quam si in Summi Pontificis dextram libandas submitterem?* Prity well. *Tum quod animæ germinantis impetum represserint quorum potius intererat tenella Conaminum germina radijs maturantibus inspirasse.* The inspiring with beams is a new Invention. But sweet germinating soul what was it did betide thee? Was it changed in the Cradle? Alas for't. You were whimpring I doubt already, as you did afterwards to Doctor *Bathurst,* about *the Chains and Fetters of an unhappy* (yet civil) *Education. Si vero jubare vestro afflentur*; do you mean Sunburning or Blasting? *fiet sorte* (suppose again though it were *quod non est supponendum*) *ut indies maturescant, dum tandem studia nostra ad meliorem frugem pervenerint.* You found *Ecclesiastical Polities, Defenses, Prefaces, Reproofs* even now stirring within you, *Ut plerumque solent Adolescentium partus minus vigoris & maturitatis adipisci.* Do you mean it literally? you do to be sure where you speak in the next Line of enjoying *fælici Genio & sorte,* which was all you cared for, and which you promised your self *tanti syderis aspectu:* take heed you become not *syderatus,* for that is worse, than a Fanatick, *Sibi postulat Immensa Numinis Magistas sacratissimos & prorsus Augustos* Mecænates. Nay then I see you did indeed Dedicate the Book both to my Lord Archbishop and the King, and in that precedence; or otherwise you have given my Lord a Title which he would not have thank'd you for: But the whole expression, had any one but you, Mr. *Bayes,* used it, is very Pedanticall, for though you were scraping about for a *Mecænas,* God to be sure stands not in need of one, or however not of your chusing. But now your Theology thickens upon us: *Cum pro Aris dimicaverim cujus potius auxilia implorarens quam vestra, Venerande Antistes, qui ijs tanquam numen Tutelare præsideas.* Here however you make my Lord indeed but a *Tanquam* Deity; but expect a little. *Non vide cujus tantundem intersit ut Victor evadam, quantam summi Pontificis: Nempe si optimo numini imperium abrogetur quid sequitur nisi prosinus Maximo Pontifici abrogandum essee?* Really, Mr. *Bayes,* very closely argued, and from an efficacious Topick. But here you have made my Lord *Summus Pontifex* and *Pontifex Maximus,* to the great

6 Was 74; was 73.   11 *supponendum* 74; *supponenduv* 73.   17 heed you] heed that you 74.   20 my 74; by 73.   27–8 *Venerande* Parker; *Vencerande* 73, 74.   31 *imperium* Parker; *mipercum* 73; *impericum Errata,* 74.

disparagement of the other *Old Gentleman* you speak of; but, which is more, the pegging out of the Prince, who might otherwise by your latter Law have pretended a title to the place, and exercised it in person. Beside that you have curtal'd *Optimus Maximus* from the Deity, and made him glad to go half with the Bishop, lest he should leave him nothing. But at last it comes in plain terms: *Adeo res eadem sit de numine bene mereri atque de vestra Clementia*; which I can English no otherwise but thus, Insomuch that it is the very same thing to deserve well of God as of your Grace. That afterwards is prity concerning your self: *Hosce Gigantum fraterculos non sat duxi expugnare nisi ut fabulantur superos,* &c. making that what had been but fabled of the Gods, you had atchiev'd in good earnest. Had my Lord seen't, or had but Sir *Francis Vere*, he would for certain have spit in your Mouth. But your last Collect is something strange, praying for him; *ut sero tandem in Triumphantis Ecclesiæ Gloriam & dignitatem* (that *dignitatem* comes off at last very poorly) *cooptetur.* 'Tis true better late than never; But to pray that it may be very late before a man get to Heaven; hath I confess been done in the case of a secular Prince once by a Heathen Poet; but was not so decent a piece of Chaplainship towards my Lord Arch-bishop. I see you writ, Mr. *Bayes*, here after the Copy of Mr. *Croxton*, and others in the former times; *sanctissime Pater* and *sanctitas vestra, spiritus sancti effusissime plenus; optimus Maximusque in terris; Quo rectior non stat Regula & quo prior est corrigenda Religio.* These were fine Complements to be bandyed among Ecclesiasticks. But what was in your mind, Mr. *Bayes*, to write this Letter, when a year after you appeal to Doctor *Bathurst, that it was he knew one of your greatest designs in this World to be one of the most unconcerned men in 't?* You did it out of the meere abstracted generosity of your heart, and writ only your Letters Testimonial, in this manner, on my Lord Arch-bishops behalf. For what I perceive you had by this breath only cool'd your own Porridge, and things were not as they should be, till upon further sollicitation you began to foresee and tell your friends *that you were exceedingly straitned in time;* and then a little after were all Cock a

---

4 *Maximus* 74; *Maxomus* 73.   14 But 74; but 73.   21 writ] write 74.
23 *Maximusque*] *Maximus qui* 74.   31 you 74; yon 73.   34 *exceedingly* 74;
execdingly 73.   little 74; litttle 73.

Hoop, *upon the very point of your departure to* London. *My dearest Coz.* (*where you before us in the Sun-beams buz.*) *From Trin. Col. Oxon May* 2. Though you are so fertil that when a man hath once begun, he can scarcely give over laughing, I have not forgotten that my occasion of quoting this your Epistle, was, to shew you might take 5 it well I express'd your Notion of God so modestly; when, in the very Treatise where you confound Atheism from *Pelion* to *Ossa* from top to bottom, yet you would at the same time for your own ends Deify a Person you had never seen, and worship an Unknown God. But you were so hungry at that time, that you would have ador'd 10 an Onion, so it had cryed Come eat me.

Another reason why I said to you that to resolve Grace into Morality was almost the same as to make God a notional and Moral Existence, was from a Passage I met with in your *Platonick Philosophy. From all which Premises we see that Gods benignity, goodness, and* 15 *beneficence, consist in a gracious propensity to let forth the Communication of his fulness to his Creatures, which being lodged in the Divine will, does not only suppose its freedom, but is also Subject to its determinations; so that though it may incline yet it cannot either command or destroy its liberty: because if it should, it would not only interfiere*—Here is indeed material 20 intellectual Puff-past; *Pinners hall* has nothing like it. This is to show how excellent you are at quoiting a Pea to stick upon the Point of a Needle. But what would, I know not what, not only interfiere with? Why, *not only with Gods Moral accomplishments, but it would withall be inconsistent with it self.* Gods Morall accomplishments! If 25 it were an Oath I should not think it binds me: but in the mean time methinks it has somthing in it bordering upon Blasphemy: But we Laymen do not distinguish well when the Clergy blaspheme, and when they speak reverently. You perhaps, Mr. *Bayes,* intended it very well and honourably, but you had talked your self round, 30 and wanted a better word only: for I must confess 'twere proper enough to speak of the *Moral Accomplishments* of some young Gentleman at the Inns of Court that were upon his Preferment; but I do not remember to have heard it used at any time upon this Occasion.

2 *where . . . us*] Or else before you Buckingham.   *where*] *were* 74.   3 *May* 2] *May* 1 Parker.   16 *Communication*] Communications Parker.   18 *determinations*] *Determination* 74.   20 *because* 74; *bccause* 73.   25 *inconsistent* 74; *ineonsistent* 73.   34 *at*] *om.* 74.

I hope you see by this time that a man might at your rate of talking
have made God as well only a notional and Moral existence. And
to make the preaching of any other doctrine ridiculous you fall into
such a desperate fit of blasphemy as I never heard any man but your
5 self; you indeed have it often. *The Non-conformist Preachers, you say,
make a grievous noise of the Lord Christ, talk loud of getting an interest in
the Lord Christ, tell fine Romances of the secret Amours between the Believing Soul and the Lord Christ, and prodigious Stories of the miraculous
feats of Faith in the Lord Christ.* Did ever Divine rattle out such pro-
10 fane Balderdash! I cannot refrain, Sir, to tell you that you are not
fit to have Christ in your mouth. You talk like a Mountebanke, and
seem to know so little of our Saviour as if you had never convers'd
but with *Salvator Winter.* Is this our great Champion against
Atheisme? Is this he that tells young Gentlemen; *They are not
15 acquainted with any Histories, unless that perhaps of the Follies and Amours
of the French Court? Alas young Gentlemen you are too rash and forward:
Your Confidence swells above your understandings. 'Tis not for you to pretend to Atheism. 'Tis too great a Priviledge for Boys and Novices. 'Tis
sawciness for you to be profane, and to Censure, Religion, Impudence and ill
20 Manners.* It were so indeed in the presence of so great an Artist.
They ought to expect till you have instructed them better in't, and
set up an Academy and a publick Lecture to that purpose. What
Distinction do you make betwixt the Amours of the French Court,
and the secret Amours betwixt the believing Soul and the Lord
25 Christ? What betwixt the Feats of Faith in the 11*th.* to the *Hebrews,*
and the Chivalry of *Don Belianis* or *Don Quixote?* What between
the Romances of the Lord Christ, and those of the *Grand Cyrus* or
Cleopatra? None at all. *Tell me truly* as you are wont to conjure me,
and by the tyes of ancient Friendship, was it not here that, as you told
30 Doctor *Bathurst, the Recreation you took to frame your Thoughts and
Conceptions into Words, did almost equal the Ravishing delight you derive
from their first Births and Discoveries?*

It is an uncomely thing to pass immediately from such foul
expressions into any discourse of so serious a subject without some

14 Atheisme? Is 74; ~; is 73.   15 *Histories*]
History Parker.   18 *Atheism* 74; *Athisme* 73.   30 *to* 74; *om.* 73.   33 It 74;
it (*no new paragraph*) 73.

more cleanly transition; and a man had need wash himself first before he handles any place of Scripture after you have so bemired the Argument. 'Tis the fifth to the *Galatians* where you had before expounded the Fruits of the Spirit to be meer Moral virtues, and the *Joy*, *Peace*, and *Faith* there spoken of to be only *Peaceableness*, *Chear-* 5 *fulness* and *Faithfulness*, as if they had been no more than the three Homileticall conversable Virtues, *Veritas*, *Comitas*, and *Urbanitas*. And truly you do so face me out in justifying this your interpretation, that I was almost ready to have yielded it up and confess my self in the wrong. Neither did I think it any thing extraordinary 10 if you had chanced once in your life to have understood a thing rightly, or for my self to have been more than once mistaken. But you do so insult and vociferate upon it, like one of your *bulky* Princes who had the Trumpet ready to sound whensoever he hit the Ball at Tennis, that I have a mind to try a little further whether 15 you were not in the Errour. In that of Faith you say *that whatsoever other acceptations it has in Scripture, 'tis to be expounded here of Faithfulness in opposition to the Perfidiousness* of the *Gnosticks*, Peace of *Peaceableness in opposition to the Contentiousness of the Gnosticks*. 'Tis great pity that you could not invent too how Joy should mean Chearfulness, 20 in opposition to the Melancholy of the *Gnosticks*. And you say that *Faith here is reckoned up as one of the Fruits of the Christian Faith, and therefore must be something distinct from it, and therefore can be nothing but the virtue of Fidelity.* Whereas it is plainly enumerated as a Fruit of the Spirit of God here in the 22d. Verse, and 'tis strange 25 you should be so sleepy as not have seen in the 5th. Verse: *For we through the Spirit wait for the hope of Righteousness by Faith*: but you had indeed a particular reason to wink at that in this Controversy. And in the 6th. Verse, *in Jesus Christ Faith only availeth which worketh by Love.* So that you have mis-interpreted the place 30 only out of love to your notion, and by this pretence to enervate the Grace and Work of Gods Spirit; indeed to make a meer Play of Faith, that you seem to have nothing of a Divine, but from hence to deserve the name of that *Du-Foy*, whom you in *p.* 11. of

1 a 74; a a 73.   8 And 74; and 73.   12 mistaken. 74; ~, 73.
16 *whatsoever* 74; *whensoever* 73.   17 *has*] *hath* 74.   18 *Perfidiousness*
74; *Prefidiousness* 73.   19 great 74; *om.* 73.   26 Verse: 74; ~. 73.
32–1 [p. 265]; indeed . . . quoted 74; *om.* 73.

your *Reproof* have quoted. For even *Grotius* too, who is of great reputation with all men, and ought with you to have more authority than ordinary; does in his Annotation on this Text expound Faith to be here *Aperta Professio veræ Fidei*, an open profession of the true
5 Faith, *& opponitur Hæresibus*. So that, if I might advise you as a friend, 'twere convenient for you to quit your Comment, though being your own it must needs be dear to you; and observe rather the Apostles rule in the last Verse of the same Chapter, *Let us not be desirous of Vain-glory, provoking one another, envying one another.* But
10 of all that you say in this business nothing is more pleasant then where arguing this matter you say to me; *If you have credit enough to borrow a Bible in the neighbourhood, you will quickly find (if you can find the Epistle) that St.* Paul *is there describing the opposite effects between the Flesh and the Spirit, and therefore as all the Fruits of the Flesh there reckoned*
15 *up are Immoral Vices, so must all the Fruits of the Spirit there opposed to them be Moral Virtues.* It follows not. For those that speak distinguishingly of Grace understand thereby an extraordinary Work of Gods Spirit, subduing their Wills, and heightning mens performances beyond the possibility of our endeavours. But no Fanatick,
20 nor Un-fanatick ever doubted but that men have pravity enough to be wicked, without any extraordinary assistance of some other Spirit. So that you argue; Men have sufficient Power of their own to do that which is Evil, therefore they have sufficient Power also of themselves by an ordinary influence to do that which is Good and
25 Adequate to Salvation. I deny not nevertheless that some sins are so desperate and of so high Malice and Contrivance, that no man could invent them out of his own Ingenuity, or practice them in his own Confidence, but must be strengthned thereto by supernatural Auxiliaries, and then indeed the Opposition you speak of betwixt
30 Immoral Vices and Moral Virtues or, as others, betwixt Sin and Grace, is more full and runs parallel. And seeing you are talking of *Gnosticks* (but I have lately given you a caution about them, and I cannot find in History how the *Gnosticks* had already made an inrode upon the *Galatians*.) *Simon Magus*, that goes for one of them with
35 you, is one that mounted above the humane pitch in his performances, and men *tell us prodigious stories of the miraculous feats that he*

3 Annotation] Annotations 74.   11 to] to to 74.   23 they 74; the 73.

did, but it was by the extraordinary assistance of two Devils, one
it seems not having been sufficient. But, as to the main Controversie of the Non-conformists distinguishing betwixt Grace and
Morality, you only shew therein the Malice of your Wit: Whereas
there is none of them but acknowledges Morality to be absolutely 5
necessary, and that without it Christianity is nothing; but however
that to render men capable of Salvation there is a more extraordinary influence of Gods Spirit required and promised. You in the
mean time make merry with it, and as in your *Reproof* (to shew your
skill in Anatomy) you will have Conscience to be seated in the 10
Glandula Pinealis ('twas civily done however that you placed it not
in some other *Glandule*.) So in your *Defence*, you say, *It were an easie
task for a man that understands the Anatomy of the Brain, the structure of
the Spleen and Hypochondria, the Divarications of the Nerves, their twist-
ings about the Veins and Arteries, and the Sympathy of the Parts, to give as* 15
*certain and Mechanical an account of all its Fanatick streaks and phrensies,
as of any Vital or Animal function in the body. The Philosophy of a Fanatick being as intelligible by the Laws of Mechanisme, as the Motion of the
Heart and Circulation of the Blood: And there are some Treatises that give
a more exact and consistent Hypothesis of Enthusiasme than any* Des Cartes 20
has given of the natural results of matter and motion. 'Tis very well said,
and what was to be expected from such a one as you, of whose
Philosophy and Religion the Mechanisme is so visible in the *Tentamina,* concerning that *Sophisme of Nature,* and the *vehemens & eff-
ranata venerei coitus cupiditas & exquisitissima voluptas,* though there is 25
a Maxime on the othe side, *Omne Animal triste est post coitum, præter
Gallum Gallinaceum, & Sacellanum gratis fornicantem.* But this Hypothesis of yours, confounding the extraordinary influx of Gods Spirit
for the Power of Nature, seems to arise from your being ill principled, and not well read in the Doctrine of the Church of *England* 30
concerning Original sin, which you make *not be a Crime but an in-
felicity inflicted by God himself upon Mankind, as a Punishment of* Adams
Sin, and what is an Act of his (that was Gods) *will, can be no fault of ours.*
We should be all engaged to you would you carry this point thorow
and make it good. And another reason of your opinion is your too 35

high conceit of mens good Works; as if, contrary to the stream of the Scripture, we could be thereby justified. For though you would make all the Party of *English* Non-conformists answer for one passage in *Flacius Illyricus*; *Bona Opera sunt perniciosa ad Salutem*, 'tis falsly 5 imposed upon them by you; and 'twere well that you understood *Flacius* himself rightly; for whosoever shall to the prejudice of our Saviours merit, and debasing the operation of the Holy Ghost, attribute too much to his own natural vigour and performances, will be in some danger of finding his *Bona Opera perniciosa ad Salutem*. For 10 mine own part I have, I confess, some reason, perhaps particular to my self, to be diffident of mine own *Moral Accomplishments*, & therefore may be the more inclinable to think I have a necessity of some extraordinary assistance to sway the weakness of my belief, and to strengthen me in good duties. If you be stronger I am glad of it; 15 and let every man after he has read and consider'd what we have of it in the Scripture, and what even in our Common Prayer book, take what course and opinion he thinks the safest. But this Controversie is of so high a nature that it overthrows your Maxime, that *all things disputable are little:* and the matter is so serious that it 20 is not fit for you and me to treat of it in such a mixed and perfunctory Stile. You have already been answer'd upon this Subject by one, who at least rivals you in the Knowledge and Practice either of Grace or Morality. And as to your *chalenge* to all the world *to produce any ancient writer that has understood this matter otherwise then you* 25 *have done*, if you will but have a little patience, I am told that it will be accepted and complyed with. Therefore I shall not at present oblige my self further to this dispute: and indeed, though what I could say might perhaps add not much weight or moment to the better understanding of it, yet neither on the other side do I think 30 you a fit man to be discoursed with of such matters. For to what purpose should I make a secret of that which you make it your business to divulge and propagate among all, but especially female, Companies? Are not you the same person that say; *of all things in the world you would not make your Son a Preacher?* 'Twas seasonably 35 and timely consider'd. *For 'tis better being drunk twice then making one*

24 *has . . . otherwise*] gives any other account of them Parker.   33 say;] says, 74.

Sermon. Do not you *invey against the drudgery of that Sacred Office,* to which nevertheless you have so many titles? But yet you say, *you can indure it pretty well, and it goes pleasantly off, when you have a company of handsom young Women for your Auditory? but the old Jades do quite disgust you, and they are mobled up like so many Judges.* Are not you 5 he that think it below your Dignity to step down to the Private Prayers in the family; and that, an honest Gentleman of your old acquaintance lodging with you in your chamber, left him to his Devotions, and told him you had in the mean while spent your time to as good purpose in reading of *Plutarch?* Do not you jeer the 10 Women when they are serious and tell them; *you are troubled with Sin I warrant you: tis nothing but some fond scruple the Minister has put into your head; let them learn of you, for you your self have not sinn'd this quarter of a year.* Is it not you that entertain them with a leading Narrative, of *a certain Lady that stray'd up into your Chamber, where you* 15 *drunk her up to such an height till you had drunk her down, and lay'd her upon your bed till you had recover'd her?* You told a Lady of better quality; that, *in case Popery were introduced, you would be one of the first to comply with it.* What must others then do, think you, after your so illustrious example? Is not this, think you, *very edifying Doctrine* 20 *for the White aprons?* Yet, I assure you, I would not have told you of it, but that I have very good Authority for't. In the mean time therefore, if you will take my advice, do not you intermeddle further in this dispute, but make friends as soon as you can both with Grace and Virtue: for, how inconsiderable soever you may imagine 25 them at present, you may at some time or other stand in need of both their assistance. You draw into this brangle too reverend Mr. *Hooker,* though he is unconcern'd in it, and you use his name continually as a piece of Inchantment only, that you understand not. For I have Commission to tell you that you said in good Company, 30 *Hang Mr.* Hooker's *Ecclesiastical Politie; it was a long winded book, and you never had the patience to read it, but it was no matter you would alwayes upbraid the Non-conformists with him, for you knew the Rogues had not read it neither.* And truly this is your usual practice and ingenuity as to other Authors. 35

The fourth thing, which I transiently objected to you, was your asserting that it was necessary to punish men more severely for their Errours in Religious Perswasions, then for their Immoralities and Debaucheries: and upon this therefore you greedily fix, pretend-
5 ing to some advantage. You say, *that I have exhibited so foul a charge against you, without referring so much as to one passage of yours to make it good, and that therefore I prove nothing at all, but that I have a bold face and a foul mouth; For We all know,* you say, (what *We* are you? I doubt you stand single and no man else will vouch for you) *that you are not*
10 *unskilful in improving the smallest and most inconsiderable advantages, that had you been furnish'd with any shadow of proof, you would have smother'd it,* &c. Really I began upon this your confidence to misdoubt my self, being very willing to believe that you had some reliques of Honesty, especially in a matter that would be manifest and evident
15 to all men that would have recourse to my former book. Hereupon I went to it my self. There I found: *Having thus inabled the Prince, dispensed with Conscience, and fitted up a Moral Religion for that Conscience, to show how much those Moral Virtues are to be valued,* p. 53. *of his Preface to the Ecclesiastical Politie, he affirms that it is absolutely necessary to the*
20 *peace and happiness of Kingdoms, that there be set up a more severe Government over mens Consciences, and religious perswasions then over their Vices and Immoralities:* and p. 55. *of the same, that Princes may with less hazard give liberty to mens Vices and Debaucheries then their Consciences.* Then again I find that I have quoted you, speaking of honest and well-
25 meaning men, to have said; *So easie is it for men to deserve to be punished for their Consciences, that there is no Nation in the world in which were government rightly understood and duly managed, mistakes and abuses of Religion would not supply the Galleys with vastly greater numbers then Villany,* For that I cited your *p.* 223. And I immediately add *p.* 54. *of the*
30 *Ecclesiastical Politie he saith of all Villains the well-meaning zelote is the most dangerous.* Do I not by all this so much as refer to one passage of yours? And again, under the title of *Debauchery Tolerated,* (forasmuch as you advise in that *p.* 55. rather to tolerate that than Conscience) I refer in my *p.* 119. which is no great distance, to the very

---

8 *mouth;* 74; ~, 73.   11 *would have*] would not have 74.   19 *the*] his part I.
20 *severe* 74; *sevore* 73.   29 54 part I; 44 73, 74.   29–30 *the Ecclesiastical Politie*] the Preface to Ecclesiast. Policy part I.

same passages. And it had been needless to cite any more, your book being full and crawling all over with such expressions. And further (for having been desirous you should take notice of it I have reminded you in several places) I find I have objected the same to you, *and that you are contented the Non-conformists should be exposed to the* 5 *Pillories, Whipping-Posts, Galleys, Rods and Axes; and moreover and above to all other punishments whatsoever, provided they be of a severer nature then those that are inflicted on men for their Immoralities, &c. So that although a man should be guilty of all those heinous enormities, not to be named among Christians, beside all lesser Peccadillos expressly against the ten Command-* 10 *ments, or such other part of the Divine Law as shall be of the Magistrates making, he shall be in a better condition, and more gently handled then a well-meaning Zelot.* Is here again no Reference so much as to one passage no shadow of proof? Gentle Reader, what shall we do with this man, that puts us continually upon such tedious tasks in things so 15 notorious? And you, Mr. *Bayes,* in what a miserable case are you, so distracted that you know neither what to do, nor what you do! Whereas I told you there was a Maxime establish'd for one sort of men, that 'tis necessary they should have good memories. Yet such is my fate to have to do with such a man all along and thorow; 20 insomuch that, though I am no forward Undertaker, I think I can manifest to you when you are at leisure, that in the Reproof (a book but of 528 pages) you are guilty of at least a thousand Falshoods: therefore I hope men will not be too forward to be imposed upon by you. But for my self, I am therefore so little moved with all the 25 aspersions and ill language wherewith you have fraught your discourse, that I can only say your Tongue is not made of Bone: or that, whatever other Slave you be, which your self owned, you are not, (that I may suit you with a Cardinals phrase) a Slave of your word. Whereas, next after this *Tentamen* of your veracity you tax 30 me for saying, *'Tis demonstrable that for one War upon a Fanatick or Religious account, there have been an hundred occasioned by the thirst and glory of Empire; and more have sprung from the contentiousness and ambition of some of the Clergy:* to give no less Essay of your Candor, you fall on turning and wresting that, quite forgetting what follows, 35

6 *Axes;* 74; ~, 73.   7 *punishments* 74; *punishmenss* 73.   15 tasks 74;
task 73.   30 tax] taxt 74.   35 wresting] resting 74.

and was direct to the matter in hand; *but the most of all from the corruption of manners, and alwayes fatal Debauchery*. But however, you say *if this were true, 'tis lamentable impertinent; for all the Wars that do concern our present debate, are Rebellions and not Invasions*. Who told
5 you that? But 'tis probable Rebellions as well as Invasions have sprung from the same turbulence. I for my part left it applicable either way, and therefore, if it will do you any service, you may if you please add Rebellions too into the Scale, and I will submit it to be weigh'd by the Reader. And whereas you would confound my
10 terms, as if it were all one, a War upon a Fanatick or Religious account, and a War from the Contentiousness and ambition of the Clergy; I suppose few that read it, beside you self, but will perceive that the Religious or Fanaticks are directly opposed there and distinguish'd from the predominant Clergy. But as to your business
15 of *Algebra*, and your computation of an hundred Wars, or an hundred and one, it is I confess very ingenious: 'tis worth my quoting; *if an hundred have been occasioned by thirst and glory of Empire, then if more by the ambition and contentiousness of the Clergy, there have been at least an hundred and one of the last*. As to this, be pleas'd to read that
20 passage in your *Ecclesiastical Politie*, where you say; *'tis easie for one Commonwealth that has gain'd by Rebellion to produce an hundred that it has hazarded, if not utterly ruined*. If you will first name me an hundred Common-wealths, I will joyn issue with you: and I will drop Clergy against Common-wealth, till one of us come at the end of
25 our reckoning. You then cite me for having said on occasion of your greater rigour against Non-conformity then Debauchery, *that comparisons of Vice are dangerous*; which *jumps*, you say, *with as wise a Paradox of the Stoicks, that all Crimes are equal*: This of yours is a very strong consequence, and if it will hold I ask your pardon, for I assure
30 you I did not intend it so. But, however you can wring this against my known meaning, that of the Stoicks suits much better with a passage of your own formerly quoted; *that all Laws Civil as well as Ecclesiastical equally oblige the Conscience*. If they equally oblige the Conscience, a common understanding would think that all Crimes
35 are Equall. But as to the Hinge of the Controversie; that is the

danger to the publick, you affirming that; *Debauchery or Immorality rarely proves so dangerous, as either serious or affected pretenses of Religion*: (pity it were that serious pretenses should prove so.) Take but out at adventure any one Kingdom for instance, and work your Question upon it, I suppose you will find the contrary: But I know upon 5 what ground and reason principally you maintain this Maxime. It is from your hatred and fear of Reformation; wherein you tread in the very foot-steps of Doctor *Heylin* and some others, who have deliberately applyed themselves to vilifie, and make odious the Foreign, and even the *English* Reformation, than which they could 10 not have invented any thing more obliging to the *Romish* Church and meritorious. For the Foreign Reformation was indeed wrought out of the Fire, and increased in those other Countries either by the Wars and Persecutions stirred up against it, or else did it self draw the Sword in defence of the just Civil Liberties (for it seldome can 15 happen but that Tyranny in Religion introduces it self by an Invasion of Propriety.) And therefore it was that our severall Princes, and particularly King *James* (who was Conscientious and knowing as any man in that point) have ingaged both their Swords and Pens, both Reason of State and of Religion, not only their Publick but 20 their Private Conscience in that quarrel: And, if there must always be Wars, I know no Cause more justifiable, nor any Design which were in Prudence more fitting to be still prosecuted and continued. Divers also of our Bishops and eminentest men in our *Church* have appear'd in the justifying of the Foreign Reformation. For other- 25 wise, though Ours was indeed brought about something more peaceably, the Church of *Rome*, if we should single out our selves from other Protestants, would have found us more weak, if not more pliable, and might urge the same if not stronger and more efficacious Arguments against us. But you may at this rate of *the danger* 30 *of serious pretenses of Religion*, say in your usual confidence that; whosoever our Princes were, and throw in King *James* too, and King *Charles*, and Parliaments, Bishops and Convocations and all, you must and will declare that *They were miserably out in their Divinity*. And upon the same Reason and Apprehension it is that you would 35

3 so.) Take 74; so) take 73.   11 *Romish* 74; *Rimish* 73.   17 it 74; ir 73.
19 Swords] Sword 74.   34 *They* . . . *Divinity* 74; *not Italic* 73.
8124228   T

be thus severe at home; and do raise this out-cry against Non-
conformity in balance to Debauchery; that you may thereby quench
the good inclination of my Lords the Bishops either as to a revisal
of themselves, or moderation toward others; incense his Majesty
5 against so estimable a part of his people; infuriate and inviperate
the Nation against peaceable Dissenters; and all to amuse men from
observing, or to perswade them into the protecting of your own
irregularities. Hence it is that you say; *tender Consciences, instead of
being complyed with,* must *be restrained with more peremptory and un-*
10 *yielding rigour then naked and unsanctified Villany.* Hence; *if Governours
would consider seriously into what exorbitances peevish and untoward
principles about Religion naturally improve themselves, they could not but
perceive it to be as much their Concernment to punish them with the severest
inflictions as any whatsoever Principles of Rebellion in the State.* Nay once
15 you appeal to Governours themselves (which is an extraordinary
piece of Civility in you) *to judge whether it does not concern them with as
much vigilance and severity either to prevent their rise, or suppress their
growth, as to punish any the foulest Crimes of Immorality.* 'Tis something
like the Story of *Gondomar* this, who from the example of a Mother
20 that whip'd her Girle beforehand least she should break the Pitcher,
argued that Sir *Walter Rawleighs* head should be cut off before he
went to *Guiana.* Indeed it is the very wisdom of *Herod,* who, lest
there should a King be born among them, Massacred all the Children at *Bethlehem.* So they must be prevented, or so suppressed. As
25 (and more then) any the foulest Immorality, as (and more then) any
Principles of Rebellion. So here is a Law, that not to kneel at the
Lords Supper shall be more Penall than Murther; not to wear a Surplice more Criminall than Adultery; and to omit the Cross in Baptisme less Pardonable than Perjury. If this were once, as you would
30 have it, enacted and, that the whole Conventicle should forfeit their
Lives and Estates as in other cases of Treason, do you think that
God has annexed the same Penalties too here *to Disobedience to Mans Laws
as his own?* You have already thrown in *Queen and Convocation and all;*
but, if you will maintain this Maxime, you must too throw in our
35 Saviour and Apostles and all, and *declare that they are no less miserably
out in their Divinity.* But you imagine doubtless, and do not a little

19 a 74; n 73.   22 to 74; too 73.

applaud your self for the invention; that by the Doctrine of punishing Non-conformity more severely than the foulest Immorality, you
have made your self the Head of a Party, and a World of People
will clutter henceforward to shelter themselves under the Wing of
your Patronage. I confess it is a great and brave undertaking, and 5
which, I believe, none ever managed before, nor will be so hardy as
to take it up again for the future. Let it be Ingraven on your Tomb.
But perhaps nevertheless you may fail in your account, and, though
you reckon your Function to be a Drudgery, & do in your Printed
books debase, as much as you dare, the value of the Bible under the 10
scornful name of *the English Bible*; and not only Satyrize the Non-
conformists Sermons, but traduce all Preaching, and make it seem
unnecessary, that so the Liturgy might be sufficient for Salvation;
I believe you will find very few that will come up to you. For
whether it be the Laity, there are not many of them such Liber- 15
tines but they would be glad to learn better, and once a Week to be
told of their faults by an exemplary Teacher. And though you
brave it like a Landlord, and that the *Clergy are possess'd by as good
right of their revenue as any Seculars* (only it were to be wish'd that
Benefices were hereditary) they have a Rustick kind of opinion that 20
you ought to do somthing for't, and that, whereas you have the
Tythe of their labour, they should have the whole of yours. This
perhaps you think unreasonable: but they think too, worse, that
you may well abide to give them good example; forasmuch as you
are pay'd for living soberly and honestly among them, whereas they 25
must be good at their own expence. And this is and hath been
always their Clownish humour that they may see somthing for
their Money: neither are any almost so debauch'd that they will
grudge their dues to a grave learned and pious Minister; but most
think for such an one nothing is too much, and for the contrary 30
nothing too little. This you think hard dealing here in your *Reproof*, and yet I assure you there it pinches. And moreover, though
you would pretend never so much to be the Landlord of your Living, if you do not behave your self there as you should do, I think
there is a very legal way to devest you of your Propriety, and there 35

5 your 74; you 73.   7 Tomb. 74; ~ 73.   19 *right* 74; *rigbt* 73.
35 Propriety 74; Propriery 73.

is a Trust reposed in some Persons to look to your manners. Neither on the other side are the Clergy so generally depraved that they need fly to you for Sanctuary: and I know many of them that conne you little thank for so scandalous a Doctrine. For those of them
5 indeed that are among them debauch'd and immoral, there could not any thing more inveagling or more seasonable have been calculated. You have gained your self immortal renown, and how they chuckle and hug themselves and you for the invention. *It is a Crime in a Clergyman to be happy, nay to be a man. And if he will but be unkind*
10 *and uncivil to himself, they will love him for that if for nothing else.* There spoke an Arch-Deacon! But you should not serve your self in such occasions of so equivocal and applicable expressions, lest ill use should be made of them beyond your intention. Who can tell whether the good Doctor at *York* last *Shrove-Tuesday* were unkind
15 and uncivil to himself? Your Curate of *Ickham*, when he laid with his Maid, whether was not he kind to himself? And even you when you dissolved that precious Lady in good Sack at your Chamber, were not you kind to your self? And when you first got your *Dull and lazy Distemper*, were not you unkind to your self? Men are too
20 prone to expound such passages to their own Inclinations: and some *Wag* may chance to write an History of the Clergies Kindnesses to themselves, and their Unkindnesses. Therefore let me request you, Mr. *Bayes*, the next time to define how that Word *unkind to himself,* or *uncivil to himself* is to be understood properly for the future. But
25 in good earnest, were it not for some that are unkind to themselves, you and your fellows would soon forfeit all the Clergies Reputation. But of all your Freaks upon this Subject of punishing Non-conformity beyond the foulest Immorality, there is none so capricious as the Declaration which you have without any occasion administred
30 on my part, and with a boldness beyond all precedent drawn up in his Majesties name. Yet seeing you are here so obligingly courteous to me as to promise me your License and the Liberty of the Press in these words *p.* 67. of your *Reproof*, thus: *If you, or he, or any Body else have ought to object against* it, *you know the Press is open,* do your
35 worst: I accept the favour, and seeing your Declaration, I doubt,

hath not so well been taken notice of for want of the Character in which such Publick matters ought to be promulged, I have in return of your Civility prevail'd with my Printer to do you a cast of his Office.

By the Arch-Deacon.

A DECLARATION

For the Tolerating of

DEBAUCHERY.

BAYES R.

Whereas ever since our happy Restauration, we have, out of our special zeal and care for the interest and security of the Church of England, executed with all severity all penal Laws against whatsoever sort of Non-conformists and Recusants; but yet finding by the sad experience of 12 years, how ineffectual all forcible courses are either to reduce or restrain dissenters, We think our self obliged to make use of that unhoopable Power, that is naturally inherent in us, not granted by Christ, but belonging to us and our Predecessors under the broad Seal of Nature next and immediately before him. By vertue whereof we have and claim an absolute dominion not only over the consciences of all our subjects, but over all the Laws of God and Man, so as to repeal or dispense with their obligation, as shall from time to time seem good to our Royal Will and Pleasure. And therefore that we may obviate and prevent those mischiefs that are likely to befal our Kingdom from the sobriety and demureness of the Non-conformists, our Will and Plea-sure is to give a free and uncontroulable Licence to all manner of Vice and Debauchery; and of our Princely Grace and Favour we release to all our Loving Subjects the Obligation of the Ten Commandments, and all Laws of God, and Statutes of this Realm whatsoever contrary to the contents of this our Declaration: And we require of all Judges, Justices and other Officers, whatsoever, that the execution of all manner of penalties, annexed to the Laws aforesaid, whether by Pillories, Whipping-posts, Gallies, Rods or Axes, &c. be immediately suspended, and they are hereby suspended. From whence we hope by the Blessing of God to give some check and allay to the insolence of Fanatick Spirits, and by debauching our good people out of all tenderness of Conscience to free our 𝕶ingdoms from those great and grievous annoyances, wherewith they perpetually disturb our Government, and at last bring back all the advantages of peace and good fellowship, both to our Self and all our loving Subjects, &c.

5   Given at Our Archi-Diaconal Court,
           the First day of *May*, 1673.
           GOD SAVE THE KING.
           And————the Inventor.

_____

                    LONDON,
10   Printed for *James Collins* at the Kings Arms
                in *Ludgate-street,* 1673.

The thing, Mr. *Bayes,* is very Judiciously drawn up by you: only I am surprized thus to see it conclude with an, *&c.* For it is true that I have heard in the former times of the *Etcætera* Oath, and there 15 was another Dignitary, who like you penn'd Declarations; yet I never saw before an *Et-cætera* Declaration. But I cannot compre hend by what License from his Majesty, or upon what occasion from me you have publish'd so daringly this Paper. For if you have any conceal'd criticism upon those words, *Debauchery Tolerated,* I 20 explain'd what I meant by what I quoted out of you, and accused you no further then what those words signified and Imported. And the Fact stood thus. His Majesty before his happy return trans- mitted hither a Gracious Declaration concerning Liberty to Tender Consciences, and hath ever since pursued it. You, on the contrary, 25 declare *p.* 55. before quoted, and in many passages the same, *That Princes may with less hazard give Liberty to mens Vices and Debaucheries then to their Consciences.* But a Toleration or Indulgence to Con- science has been thought advisable. Do not you then maintain that a Liberty to Vice and Debauchery was the more advisable of the 30 two? And was not this enough to charge you in the terms of *De- bauchery tolerated?* But as for his Majesty, he had sufficiently mani- fested his judgment both of the one and the other by a Declaration

13 surprized 74; surpized 73.

of Indulgence to tender Consciences, and by a Proclamation against Debauchery: so that you had little reason to raise so malapert an allusion, and profane his name in a Mock-declaration, which indeed is your own and no mans else, and is not unsuitable to your Principles and Practise. Yet whatsoever mischief you intended by it, (for some you intend always) I am perswaded you were partly transported by the Ornament that you thought it would be to your Book. Nay, I do not think but you took it for a great piece of Wit, so great, that for its sake and two or three Speeches that you make for the Parliament men, you writ the whole Book; or else I had scaped both *Reproof* and *Correction*. But because I have observed how careful you are to find out, before you attempt a great jump of wit, some convenient Rise, and you would not doubtless have penn'd so notable a Declaration without some Precedent, I cast about where to meet with it, and after a little searching, I found this in the *Cæsares Juliani*, where that Emperour having undertaken to Marshal his Predecessors under the Patronage of some proper Deity, when he comes to *Constantine* does thus Satyrically represent him. *But* Constantine *not being able among all the Gods to find a Patern of his own life, casting his eye about saw the Goddess of Luxury near him, and streight ran to her. She hereupon receiving him delicately and embracing him, trick'd him up in Womans cloaths, and conducted him to the Goddess of Intemperance. Finding his Son returned, and making to all men this publick* Proclamation.

Let all men take notice, of whatsoever condition and quality, whether they be Adulterers, or Murtherers, or guilty of any other Immorality, Vice, or Debauchery, *that hereby they are warranted and invited to continue boldly and confidently in the same, and I declare that, upon dipping themselves only in this Water, they are, and shall be so reputed, pure and blameless to all intents and purposes. And moreover, as oft as they shall renew and frequent such other* Vices, Immoralities or Debaucheries. *I do hereby give and grant to them and every one of them, respectively, that by thumping his Breast, or giving but himself a pat on the Forehead, he shall thereupon be immediately discharged and absolved of all guilt and penalty therefore incurred: any Law or Statute to the contrary notwithstanding.*

This is in the 99*th*. Page of that Book, Printed at *Paris* 1583. to
prevent any such accident for the future as that of the Epistle to
Marcellinus; for I am sensible of the great trouble I thereby gave you,
though you have it recompensed by the great reputation you have
5 acquired by your learned criticismes upon it. But good, Mr. *Bayes*,
surely you were hard set, that you had no body here to go to but
Julian the Apostate for an Invention. Or however, if you had contracted some acquaintance or similitude with him, you could not
have pick'd out a more unhappy instance for your imitation then
10 this present. For, as he in this Proclamation ingratefully derides
Constantine, so do you traduce his Majesty by your Declaration, which
deserves to perish with your Book: whereas he by his Proclamation against Debauchery hath sufficiently testified his judgement,
and, as he hath resembled *Constantine* in his patience and industry
15 toward composing (howsoever obstructed) the Ecclesiastical
differences among us, so in his Largess and Munificence to the
Church hath far exceeded him.

And this leads me directly to your fifth Play, Mr. *Bayes*, of *Persecution recommended*: though I might perhaps more properly have
20 call'd it a *Spectacle*, and exceeding whatsoever was exhibited at any
time among the *Romans*, for cruelty. I had hereupon said, that,
Julian *himself who was first a Reader and held forth in the Christian Churches,*
before he turn'd Apostate, and then Persecutor, could not have out-done you
either in Irony or Cruelty: and for the truth of that I refer to your whole
25 *Ecclesiastical Politie*. You return me in answer to this passage; (for
in my whole Book I have but this once mention'd him) *you bring the*
Emperour Julian *upon the Stage, as a more cruel and execrable Monster of*
Persecution then Antichrist or the Dragon himself, and you throw your slaver
upon him with so much scorn and rudeness that the People take him for as very
30 *a rake-shame as Bishop* Bonner, *or Pope* Hildebrand. You are very
gentle, Mr. *Bayes*, and good natured to extremity; which makes me
the more wonder at this transport, for in your whole Book there are
not above one or two like instances, and you have imbraced no mans
quarrel with more concernment and vehemency. There must be
35 something extraordinary in it. Had I then known that he was so
old an acquaintance of yours as I since find in your *Platonick Philo-*

21 that 74: rhat 73.

sophy, or had I imagined that he was so near of kin to you, and one of your *Dearest Cuzzes*, I should perhaps, according to the rules of conversation, have spoke of him with more respect, but however I am cautioned sufficiently for the future. Especially seeing he has so ample Testimonial from you, *that he was a very civil Person, a great* 5 *Virtuoso, and though somewhat heathenishly inclined, yet he had nothing of a persecuting Spirit in him against Christians as may be seen at large in* Ammianus Marcel. l. 22. And you add immediately; *unless you will suppose, as he did, that there is no such effectual way of persecuting an establish'd Church, as by suspending all Ecclesiastical proceedings against Schis-* 10 *maticks and Hereticks and granting an unlimited Universal Toleration.* I do not suppose it, but you do; and it is one of the greatest arguments in your *Ecclesiastical Politie* against Toleration or Indulgence, Therefore let us see what your *Ammianus* saith, *But when* Julian *observed that he was now free to do what he would, he reveal'd his secret design,* 15 *and by plain and absolute Edicts commanded that the Temples should be open'd, sacrifices offer'd, and the Worship of the Gods restored: and to strengthen the effect of what he had proposed to himself, he therefore called the Christian Bishops that were at odds with one another, and their divided people together into his Palace, admonishing them that laying aside their intestine* 20 *quarels, every one should boldly exercise without all disturbance his own Religion; which he therefore did, that this Liberty increasing their dissentions, he might be secured thenceforward against the unanimating of the Christian people. For he had found by experience, that no Beasts were so cruel against man, as Christians for the most part are inveterate against one* 25 *another.* So it was then, and so you would still have it. But what have you yet gain'd by this Author? Under his Toleration they grew to a better understanding and Union; under his Persecution they cimented still closer; and so it will always probably succeed: whereas, in the former flourishing times, the Church was so miser- 30 ably rent by the factions and contests of the then Bishops; and so was *Julian's* experiment, and so I hope will all others of that kind be frustrated. But further, does not your *Ammianus* tell you of *a most inhumane Edict, and in respect to* Julian*'s memory fit to be buried in*

12–13 arguments 74; argumenrs 73.   17 sacrifices 74; saerifices 73.   21 disturbance 74; distuebance 73.   22 therefore 74; thercfore 73.   did, that 74; ∼ ∼ 73. 24 For 74; for 73.

*perpetual silence, that no Grammarian or Rhetorician should presume to teach
any Christian.* This he twice mentions with the same remark. Does
he not tell you that *Apollo's Temple at* Antiochia *being burnt down,*
whether by chance and *Asclepiades* the Heathen Philosophers candle,
or otherwise, *he upon meer suspicion caus'd the Christians to be question'd
and tormented more severely then usual, and commanded their great Church
at* Antioch *to be shut up thenceforward.* He saith too *that* Julian *left
behind him there a turbulent and cruel Governour on purpose, affirming that
he was not worthy of the Place, but the People deserved to be so handled;* So
that this Author makes as much herein against your *great Virtuoso,*
as could be expected from one that was no Christian, and in *Julian's*
Service. Let this therefore serve as a return to you for my 5ª *ad
Marcellinum,* on which you spend so many pages: for this is your
Fifth Play, you know, and this is your *Marcellinus:* Only you have
made him but *Marcel:* and have, out of a certain instinct nibbled off
the end of him, least he should at any time fly in your face. But if
upon occasion of this *Marcellinus* you had here too remember'd St.
Austin 18° *de Civitate Dei,* you might have been better informed concerning your *Julian.* Or if you will not admit him, would you but
have given as much credit to *Gregory Nazianzen,* or to *Chrysostome,*
and *Nectarius,* and all the Ecclesiastical Writers of that time, as to
Ammianus Marcellinus an Heathen Soldier, you could not sure have
had so good an opinion of him. I have upon this occasion from you,
made a Collection whereby to manifest that during his short raign,
there was by his means and under his Authority as great, if not
greater, ravage and cruelty exercised then in any of the former
Persecutions: but I will not so far gratifie your ignorance or your
falshood. You perhaps, because his is not reckoned among the ten
Persecutions, thought there had been no more, neither in his time,
nor Pope *Hildebrands,* nor Bishop *Bonners,* nor since. But I have truly
a better esteem of your reading, and that all this comes from that
good inclination you have to such matters; so that you either sneer
them off at the end of your nose as old impertinent Stories, to jeer
out our credulity, or do openly aver a known falshood in defence of
Julian, for whom you have so great a friendship, and whose actions
you approve of. But no man will think the better of your cause, for

9 *handled;* 74; ⁓, 73.

your justifying it by Panegyricks of *Julian the Apostate* and Cardinal *Granvell*. The ripping up of Bellies, and tearing of mens Bowels, the whipping of Virgins, digging out their Eyes, pulling forth their Teeth, cutting off Hands and Tongues, breaking of Legs, boyling of men in Caldrons, grilling them on Grid-irons, roasting them on 5 Spits, fricassing them in Frying-pans, were but a small part of the Felicities of *Julians* Empire, *that* Virtuoso, *and who had nothing of a persecuting Spirit against Christians.* He was I see an excellent Cook for your Palate: and what Ragousts had here been for you to have furnish'd the *Mazarines* on your Table! you that can relish nothing 10 less then Pillories, Whipping-posts, Galleys, Rods and Axes! 'Tis true nevertheless that I find not any Edict of his against Christians: for his Malice solaced it self in a more subtle way, by interpreting an old Statute about the violating of Temples; and under colour of that he proceeded against them, and caus'd them either to abjure 15 their faith, or quit their Estates, and if they chose the last, he subjected them notwithstanding to death, and the most exquisite torments. Truly, Mr. *Bayes,* you have a very notable face, and many men I meet very like you. *Caligula* before, how great a resemblance was there betwixt you? And now *Julian,* one would almost swear 20 you were spit out of his Mouth. He set up a Nick-name for the Christians, to mark them out to be knock'd o'th' head: So do you give the Non-conformists the name of Fanaticks, as he them of *Galileans*; but the great *Galilean* was too hard for him. Pray Sir, who are these Fanaticks? Most of 'm, I assure you, better men then your 25 self, of truer principles then you are, and more conformable to the Doctrine of the Church of *England:* only you by the advantage of some Knick-knacks have got the ascendent over them, and left them in the lurch, so that now you have the priviledge to miscall, abuse and triumph over them at your pleasure. And above all the Pesti- 30 lence of *Julians* wit and yours is incomparable, but betwixt you. There is not any more visible Token of a mean Spirit then to taunt and scoff at those in affliction, and for a man by virulent jeers to exasperate and impoyson the wounds of his own giving. Such words are like chaw'd Bullets; and as if it were not sufficient to 35 shoot thorow, you invenom them with your Spittle. Neither is any

1 *the* 74; *she* 73.   6 Frying 74; Frving 73.   20 And 74; and 73.

torment to an ingenuous mind so sensible as to be so insulted over, and for him that undertakes to be their Judge to pelt them with such expressions of malice, as the condemned themselves *in Curiæ egressu* would not have used though it were their priviledge. There
5 is a certain Civility due to such as suffer, and to bruise a broken Reed is inhumane. Nevertheless such was *Julians* practice, and when he seized the Estates of the Christians, it was, he said, but to discharge them of this worldly pelf, that being quit of such baggage they might march on to Heaven with better expedition. When
10 he tormented them he was not only a Reader, but a Preacher, and instructed them that it was their part only to be Patient under Affliction, for so *Christ* their King had commanded them. And you in like manner point out the wealthy Fanaticks to the Magistrate as ungovernable Creatures; mark forth an hundred *Systematical-*
15 *Rat-Pushpin-Shop-Divines* for the publick vengeance; laugh at the calamities of the City when in ashes; interdict and embargue all Traffick till the Ceremonies be complyed with; and smile at *some that would be thought wonderfully grave and solemn States-men, who labour with mighty projects of Trade and Manufacture, while those things which*
20 *you your self allow to be perhaps of no great use to the Commonwealth, are not submitted to.* You tell a man that if *he has not a good Conscience, yet he has a brazen wall*; That *there is little difference betwixt a soft head and a Tender Conscience*; That *weakness of Conscience alwayes proceeds in some measure from want of Wit*; therefore that men should actively obey
25 at all adventures, because *they have the Publick wisdom to warrant them and their own Folly to excuse them*; You call the Scrupulous Dissenters so many *Old Boyes*, and would *have them lash'd out of their peevishness.* But why do I reproach you with these things which I am perswaded, nay certain, that you take for an honour? I oblige you by
30 the very repetition, and you clap and crow at the Wit and Malice of your expressions. So some men find a second entertainment in the savoryness of their own Belches. Therefore I will not further gratifie you herein or nauseate the Reader: your whole Book of *Ecclesiastical Politie* having been Writ not with a Pen but a Stilletto,
35 and with an intention so un-Theological, that the Writer might not unjustly be tryed upon the Statute for stabbing. Methinks I

discern now what secret impulse directed you in your learned Exercitations concerning *Tintinnabulum* and *Clangor*; though you knew it not, but your Bell like that in *Spain*, which forebodes no good, tinkled of its own accord, and rung it self backward. You are indeed a meer *Tintinnabulum* your self, and, if with your leave I may 5 transfer the expression, though *you spoke with the tongues of men and Angels, not having charity you are become as sounding Brass, or a tinkling Cymbal*. But whereas you are of a dimension small enough to hang in the Ear of an Hobby-horse, yet you raise a noise and *Clangor* like the *Stentoro-Phonick*; sounding the Trumpet of War, and ringing the 10 *Tocsain* of Persecution. Insomuch, that, not content to have Press'd and Muster'd up all the Princes of Christendom in your Service, you raise too the Ecclesiastical *Militia*, and the Train-bands of the Church in your quarrel. *When mens Consciences, you say, are so squeamish or so humorsome, as that they will rise against the Customs and* 15 *Injunctions of the Church they live in* She Must *scourge them into order, and chastise them, not so much for their fond perswasion as for their troublesome peevishness*. You will teach her to be a very Shrew if she will take your counsel. Was it not enough that *He must* and *They must*, but *She Must* too? Suppose she has not a mind, and that She will not 20 suffer you to wear the Britches. You could have said no more to her had She been your *Comfortable Importance*. Really, if you be so masterful in the Church, I doubt you will learn to play reaks at home. But if She find her self not well or not well used, I would advise her to appeal to *Julian:* for he made a Law that Women 25 Married should have liberty to divorce themselves from their Husbands.

I have thus far instanced that though you are not so great a Conjurer as *Julian*, yet it is not your fault if you have not been as severe a Persecutor. I come now to your sixth and last Play of *Push-pin* 30 *Divinity*. For, as in all other things, so in this too you tread on Mr. *Bayes* his heels; *who, whereas every one makes five Acts to one Play, what does Me he, but make five Playes to one Plot; by which means the Auditors have every day a new thing, and then upon* Saturday *to make a close of all* (*for he ever begins upon a* Monday) *he makes you up a sixth Play that sums* 35 *up the whole matter to them, and all that for fear they should have forgot it;*

---

18 *peevishness* 74; *peevishnesss* 73.   30 *Push-pin* 74; *Push pin* 73.

only you too have a seventh Play for Sunday. So do you here recapitulate all your former profaneness, with some additions, pretending to represent the Non-conformists Divinity. The Expressions are your own, *Whether Conversion be perform'd in an instant, or whether it be* 5 *divided into several Acts and Scenes. As first the Work of Vocation is the Prologue. Secondly, this Vocation infuseth faith, only say some, but Faith and Repentance say others, and then, Thirdly, this Faith must be Acted, so that it seems believers may have Faith before they act it,* i. e. *they may believe before they believe. Fourthly, by this Act we apprehend Christs person,* 10 *and by this apprehension we are united to him. Fifthly, from this Union proceed the Benefits, first of Justification, then of Sanctification,* &c. These are I perceive what you call *the Scholastick nothings of Faith and Justification.* You understand nothing but the Union of Benefices: these other things you laugh at as so many, ten real differences in the 15 same thing. And yet, if one would call over the Muster-role of your self, he should find near as many differences; and you would have been sory that any of them should be omitted; Fellow of the Royal Society; Doctor of Divinity, Chaplain to my Lord Arch-bishop, Parson of *Ickham,* Parson of *Chartham,* Prebend of *Canterbury,* Arch- 20 deacon of *Canterbury,* &c. Yet methinks, if you be so delicate and scrupulous in a Tautology of Religion as you pretend this to be, you ought to be eased in this Tautology of Livings and Dignities. Had you been well catechized in Bishop *Usher's Body of Divinity,* or, because you will slight him as a *Systematical* Bishop, would you but 25 once read Mr. *Hooker's* Life, *p.* 17. or his Sermon of Justification, *p.* 520. you might for his sake, if not for the Apostles, speak at least, if not think, more reverently concerning these Doctrines or Speculation. Then you go on, *Whether the Word and Sacrament have only a Moral operation in the Conversion of a Sinner, as a man draws in an Horse to* 30 *him by the sight of Provender, or a Hog after him by the ratling of beans,* and so on till you come to, *Blessed Apostle, shouldst thou but make a visit to the Christian World, how wouldst thou stand aghast to see such a vast body of Modern Orthodox Faith framed out of thy writings,* &c. *How would it recover to thy memory all that gibberish in which thou wert so idely* 35 *busie while thou satest at the feet of Rabbi* Gamaliel? How came Saint

Paul and you so well acquainted? I doubt you are not in a fit pickle
to speak with him, and if he saw what you write, it would recover
to his memory his fighting with beasts at *Ephesus*. What do you tell
him of *Gamaliel*? 'tis a wonder you tell him not too, that *much Learning has made him mad.* Blessed Mr. *Bayes*, that were brought up at 5
the feet of *Elizabeth Hampton*, should she but make a visit to *Holywell*, and read those scandalous Volumes that you have written and
published, she would go near, although she were bed-rid, to kick
you: did she but see that so *precious* a young man, of her own Education, should in this manner stir up persecution, trample under 10
foot the Graces of Gods Spirit, cry down the observation of the
Lords Day, vilifie and mock the *English* Bible; *as not in every particular
the Word of God, nor in any one thing the Words of the Prophets, nor of*
Christ *nor the Apostles; as a Book in some places erroneous, in some scarce
sense, and of dangerous consequences,* &c. that you should lead men off 15
from searching the Scriptures, dispute against the work of Preaching, and sum up the whole duty of Man (which an excellent though
unknown Writer of our Church has done at another kind of rate,)
in six Burlesque lines of Rhime-doggrel:

> 𝕭𝖞 𝖙𝖍𝖊 𝕷𝖎𝖙𝖚𝖗𝖌𝖞 𝖉𝖆𝖎𝖑𝖞 𝖕𝖗𝖆𝖞,　　　　　20
> 𝕾𝖔 𝖕𝖗𝖆𝖞 𝖆𝖓𝖉 𝖕𝖗𝖆𝖎𝖘𝖊 𝕲𝖔𝖉 𝖊𝖛𝖊𝖗𝖞 𝖉𝖆𝖞;
> 𝕿𝖍𝖊 𝕬𝖕𝖔𝖘𝖙𝖑𝖊𝖘 𝕮𝖗𝖊𝖊𝖉 𝖇𝖊𝖑𝖎𝖊𝖛𝖊 𝖆𝖑𝖘𝖔,
> 𝕯𝖔 𝖆𝖘 𝖞𝖔𝖚 𝖜𝖔𝖚𝖑𝖉 𝖇𝖊 𝖉𝖔𝖓𝖊 𝖚𝖓𝖙𝖔;
> 𝕽𝖊𝖈𝖊𝖎𝖛𝖊 𝖙𝖍𝖊 𝕾𝖆𝖈𝖗𝖆𝖒𝖊𝖓𝖙 𝖆𝖘 𝖜𝖊𝖑𝖑 𝖆𝖘 𝖞𝖔𝖚 𝖈𝖆𝖓:
> 𝕿𝖍𝖎𝖘 𝖎𝖘 𝖙𝖍𝖊 Whole Duty of Man.　　　　25

And maintain that this Catch *is to be preferr'd before all the Sermons
that have been preach'd for this six and thirty years by the Non conformists.*
Did she but see these very passages here, and how, under colour of
some particular Author that does not please you, you run down and
baffle that serious business of Regeneration, Justification, Sanctifi- 30
cation, Election, Vocation, Adoption, which the Apostle *Paul* hath,
beside others, with so much labour illustrated and distinguish'd;
and did she but perceive that you have done all this and worse, only
as a Horse to gain *Provender*, or *like a Hog*, to procure your self *Beans*,

4–5 *Learning*] *Learing* 74.　　20 daily] *learn to* Hicringill.　　24 Receive the
Sacrament] Sacraments *take* Hicringill.　　27 *six and thirty*] thirty Hicringill.
28 . Did 74; ; did 73.

I dare say the good old Woman (although she was not strait handed to her ability) would grudge all the Oat-meal that you spent her in Grewel, and with the Skillet had boyled over.

But for *your desiring for the present, though you could be very large upon*
5　*this Subject, that those who would be further satisfied in the Mysterie, would repair to* Pinne-makers-Hall, *every* Tuesday *about ten a clock in the forenoon*; it is not the first Conventicle in your life-time that you have invited men to, though I suppose this now was only meant as a better direction to Informers: but in return to the Wit of it, this being
10　one of your most happy rencounters, you should have consider'd that the best part of your own *Push-pin Divinity* was fetch'd as far as from *Aberford*, a Town in *Yorkshire* which subsists wholly on that Trade, and from whence you have furnish'd your self with Pins in abundance to set up with.

15　　Thus at last, as you mock at men for *passing through so many Stages of Regeneration*, I have clamber'd as well as I could over these six Stages of your Theology. And I cannot but upon reflexion wonder that so good a Cause as that of Conformity could not be managed by better Doctrine and Argument. But certainly if any thing more
20　material could have faln within the circuit of humane reason, or could that have been fitted up with a better stile or more polish'd language, we could not have failed of it. For you are it seems the last Resort of Theological Understanding, and a man deservedly chosen out of the whole Body of the Clergy for this glorious enter-
25　prize. A man that, while I am writing these lines, are proclaim'd, even under Doctor *Tomkins* his *Imprimatur*, by another Mascarade-Divine, to be *the Wonder of this Age*, and so you will be of the future. Give me leave therefore, Mr. *Bayes*, to sit in the Pit and clap my hands among the Herd of your humble Admirers.

30　　I have thus far made good my former charge against you, and submitted partly to make my self the Defendant out of my Service to the Readers, and Candor towards you, but henceforward I shall take my liberty. And now, when I look over the rest of your Book, it makes me very good sport to see you play more tricks then a
35　Dancing Bear for the recreation of the Spectators. But you were

25 are] is 74.　　26 *Imprimatur* 74; *Imptimatur* 73.　　27 *this*] his *A Free and Impartial Inquiry.*

afraid you should want Company, and therefore, instead of delivering Bills about, or being usher'd through the streets by the Bear-
ward and his Musick with the usual Ceremony, you have Printed
a Preface to the Reader even before my *Reproof*, *You have no other*
civility to request of the Reader, then only to desire him, that if he shall   5
think what you have written worth his perusal, to read it over with an
unprejudiced mind, and an ordinary attention. Ay, pray come in, pray
come in Gentlemen. You shall have the rarest sport that ever was
seen. Every man for his Five shillings, and welcom. Whether or no
a man can think it worth his perusal before he has read it over, it   10
had been more seasonable to advise men to an ordinary frugality,
and an unprejudiced Pocket. The remainder of my business here
with you is only to pick up and down your Flowers of the Bear-
Garden. But how to begin with you or where to end is unsearch-
able: for indeed there was never such a Book written, except those   15
of your other *Bayes*, of which 'tis excellently said;

> *If it be true that Monstrous Births presage*
> *The following mischiefs that afflict the Age,*
> *And sad disasters to the State proclaim;*
> *Playes without Head or Tail may do the same.*   20

The Empire of Atoms is more in order and Chance it self has a better method. Therefore I shall be obliged to write too at adventure
and sit by you, scumming off whatsoever comes uppermost, as it
rises.

You had deliberately discours'd from *p.* 47. to *p.* 54. of your   25
Ecclesiastical Politie, to which I refer, against all Trade and Traffick
in opposition to Non-conformity; and that, while it was not recti-
fied, *to erect and incourage trading Combinations was only to build so many*
nests of Faction and Sedition. and you had reckon'd that the Non-
conformists swarmed *most in great Cities and Corporations*; you had in-   30
structed men how Christ *whipp'd the Tradesmen out of the Temple.* Your
whole book was an Haloo to Princes and all mankind to fall upon
Tender Consciences with the severest rigour, and hereupon I said
'twas some sign of the Non-conformists peaceable temper that you were not
Deified, and well I might say so. But you hereupon are in a terrible   35
pelt that I have animated the Rabble against you; but *from me you*

fear no other weapon but a Spanish *Fig, or some more secret* Italian *dispatch.* No, no, set your heart at rest, Mr. *Bayes,* the very rabble are too judicious to meddle with you; and you need not apprehend or be jealous of any unless it be the *Cæcilian* Figs, or those others which
5 were used at the first institution of the ceremony of *il Fico,* which your obsequiousness would have digested, from what place soever you had suck'd 'm.

There was another fear upon you, lest, having been so liberal to the Prince in Ecclesiastical matters, the Church should sue you for
10 Dilapidations of its Power; wherein you have done just nothing, unless you had retracted the very words and things which I have justified upon you, and by one word of confession you might have saved your self and the Reader all this labour. But your proud heart would not come down. But *the Priestly and the Imperial Power,* you
15 now say, *are both Supream in their several kinds.* The Priestly *is in its kind Supream, Universal, and Uncontroulable. Our Saviour deputed the Apostolical order or succession of Apostles* (in which you have some Interest) *to super-intend the Affaires of the Holy Catholick Church.* These *may require obedience to their Constitutions, under pain of the Divine dis-*
20 *pleasure, and the lash of the Apostolical Rod.* I question it; if you will say *Christs* constitutions you say right, but yours are *Et-cætera* Constitutions. *When the exterminating sentence is passed upon the Offenders, it smites like the Sword of an Angel,* &c. *It cuts a man off from all the advantages of the Communion of Saints, and of our Saviours Incarnation:*
25 *and that is a Capital Execution.* Is it so? But at the Rates that our Excommunications are managed, and upon consideration for what matters they are inflicted, I doubt, and by what sort of persons they are issued, that there will be every day fewer men of your opinion. And many will think, if it be but an affair of *the Day of Judgment,*
30 that the Non-conformists may abide the Tryal. But these discourses of yours, Mr. *Bayes,* have been the occasion that I have read several books over, which otherwise I should never have thought of. And wondring with my self how it was possible that such a man as you should ever come to be intrusted with the Keys, I met, in
35 studying the point only as to your own particular, with some shrewd passages out of Arch-bishop *Cranmer,* subscribed by his own

16 *the*] his Parker.   24 *Incarnation* 74; *Inoarnation* 73.

hand. *In the Admission of Bishops, Parsons, Vicars, and other Priests, there are divers comely Ceremonies and Solemnities used, which be not of necessity, but only for good order and seemly fashion: for if they were committed without such Ceremonies, they were nevertheless truly committed. There is no more promise of God, that Grace is given in committing the Ecclesiastical Office, then it is in committing the Civil. In the Apostles time there was no appointing of Ministers, but only the uniform consent of Christian multitudes among themselves to follow the advice of such as God had most indued with the Spirit of Wisdom and Counsel. And when any were appointed or sent by the Apostles or others, the people did accept them, not for any Supremacy, impery, or dominion, that the Apostles had over them, but as good people ready to obey the advice of good Counsellours. The Bishops and Priests were at one time, and were not two things, but one and the same Office in the beginning of Christs Religion. Princes and Governours may make a Priest by the Scriptures, and that by the Authority of God committed to them, and so may the people also by their election. In the New Testament, he that is appointed to be a Bishop or a Priest needeth no Consecration by Scripture; for election or appointing thereto is sufficient. It is not against Gods Law, but contrary, they ought indeed so to do; and there be Histories that witnesseth that some Christian Princes and other Lay-men unconsecrate have done the same. They that be no Priests may Excommunicate also, if the Law allow thereunto.*

This from so excellent a Person, a most worthy Prelate, and most glorious Martyr, with other things of the like nature, from Authorities to you undeniable, have brought some odde thoughts into my head how you came to be a Clergyman, or what kind of Mungrel creature you are: which was the reason I told you, that you for your part ought to have stood fast to your Maxime, that the Magistrate may exercise the Priesthood in his own person; though you have thought fit again in this Book to disown it. And then withall, reflecting as to your particular, who do so studiously oblige the Clergy by qualifying them for Political and secular imployments, although there be many Constitutions (and I thought them Priviledges) against it; I begin to be of your mind, and that you are very capable of them great or small: and I acknowledge your humility, who being of so eminent parts, have not disdain'd, nevertheless at first to exercise the Office of the Scavinger: In good time you may make a further progress.

You are offended at me for using you with so much familiarity, for you perceive that we are so *intimately acquainted, as if we had either rob'd Orchards or Lampoond the Court together.* You best know what you are good at, but I have had so little Society with you, except in your Books, that my ignorance may be excusable. But I suppose you spoke figuratively, and by *robbing of Orchards* you understood *Baldwins-Garden*; and by *Lampooning the Court*, you meant *three-Crane-Court*; and you might have inlarged with *Bonds-Stables* and the *Pall-mall*, for I perceive you have had some conversation there which you would count it uncivil to commemorate, but neither do I remember that I was ever there in your Company.

In the same page you accuse me *with comparing his Majesty to a mad Horse, kicking and flinging most terribly.* 'Tis unkindly done of you, to say no worse: and to leave the Reader better possess'd against me, you quote not the place. The thing is below any answer, but to refer to the 110*th.* page of my former Book being *Horaces* of *Augustus*.

I cannot omit, lest some should take it for an expression of mine, what follows, for you seem to have couch'd it so on purpose. *This is too like the stubbornness of your Shrew, that when she was duck'd over head and ears, stretched up the Symbols, or, as your Pin-divines would have it, the Sacraments of Lowsiness and Cuckoldry.* I have heard of some that have impoysoned with the Sacrament, of another Emperour that had his Sirname from the Font, *Constantinus Copronymus*, having marr'd it at his Baptisme, as did also *Wenceslaus*; of Witches that have imployed the *Hostia* in their Sorceries; and of Hereticks who have administred the Sacrament in the impurest Elements: but I never read before of a Divine that had to such height improved the Invention. But, for the Sacrament of Lowsiness I have formerly reckoned with you; for the Sacrament of Cuckoldry cast up your own accounts. I cannot imagine where you took the rise too of this jump of Wit, unless either from a Secular; *Andronicus Comnenus*, who furnished an Horn-Gallery with a several Stags head for every mans Wife he had to doo with: or from an Ecclesiastick; who was in former times like you a

32 your 74; your your 73.

Penner of Declarations, and fill'd a whole Trunk with the single shooes of Women, such was his humour, with whom he had the same occasion; this man having chosen the measure of the Wives Foot, the other of the Husbands Head, to remain as the Trophies of their Lasciviousness. This is I know only a *Julianisme*, and you think, and are glad of the occasion, that as oft as you have to do with the Non conformists, you have a liberty to speak prophanely, like those that will on purpose, curse and swear the rather in Civil Company. For I suppose you make thus bold with the Sacraments, because I mention'd an argument not very weak on their part, that to institute and impose Ceremonies, was to make so many new Sacraments; forasmuch as our Church declares, *that they serve not only for decent order and Godly discipline, but they are apt to stir up the dull mind of man to the remembrance of his duty to God, by some special and notable significancy whereby they may be edified.* And further our Church defines a Sacrament *an outward visible Sign of an inward spiritual grace.* And I added, *Our Author besides makes them by his Principle, when commanded, a new part of the Divine Law.* But to this I do not find that in a very large and noisome discourse you give any tolerable answer, but this jeer of *Sacraments of Lowsiness and Cuckoldry,* as in your other book, that they cry *Sacraments Sacraments,* as if you had been swearing a *Dutch* Oath; save that you insist upon the old Answer still, that *Divine Institution is the only thing necessary to the Nature and Office of a Sacrament.* Whereas I think with submission, that by the same argument, there can be no Idolatry in the World. For Idolatry is either worshipping a False God; or else the worshipping of a true God after a false manner. Now may you not as well say, that because there is but one true God, therefore men cannot adore a false one; because there is but one true worship, men cannot practise superstition; as because there are but two true Sacraments men cannot devise new ones? And though the Church allows them not for Sacraments, You may remember the case of *Julians* Soldiers at the burning of Incense. It seems to me much the same, as if, because God made man upright, it were not possible for him to seek out many inventions. But enough of this, only I will furnish them with one argument more, though none of the weightiest, out of the

16 *visible* 74; *visiblc* 73.

Rationale of the *Common Prayer*, which you ought not to have been ignorant of, the Bishop instructing us, that the Collects are by some of the Ancients called *Sacramenta, either because their chief use was at the Communion, or because they were uttered* per Sacerdotem. At this
5 rate there would indeed be *Sacraments Sacraments*; I might pretend to be a shred of a Sacrament; the whole Liturgy would be so many Sacraments; nay your Reproof might bustle to be a Sacrament, as being uttered too *per Sacerdotem*.

In many places of your Book, and sure you think it a lucky hit,
10 you would fix upon me the old *Martin Mar-Prelate* (in one page you do it four times). Let me only desire you as often to remember *Martin Parker*, and your relation to him; for to my knowledge, if you do not make *Ballads to the Disgrace of Religion*, you are a Singer of such Ballads, and if you be curious I will at a more convenient time
15 Rehearse them to you.

You had said our Saviour in chasing the Sellers out of the Temple (Tradesmen you call them) had *put on, out of an hot fit of Zeal, a seeming fury and transport of Passion, and that he took upon him in that Action the Person and Priviledge of a* Jewish Zelote. This I found fault
20 with in my former book, and with good reason, if you would but consider that you say, *a well-meaning Zelote is the worst of all Villains.* You still defend it here by the examples of *Phinees* and *Elias*; and to have been *a Power or at least a license for private persons to execute by publick authority notorious malefactors, upon the place, without form and*
25 *process of Law.* This Priviledge is very far fetch'd, and long discontinued, if from the time of *Phinees* and *Elias* until our Saviour there were no new Claim enter'd. But really it seems to me, by this and some other passages, that you do not attribute much belief to the miracles of our Saviour, among which perhaps this was one of the
30 most remarkable. For, to omit other Authors, *Grotius* who ought to be of as much value with you as all the rest put together, interprets the Text thus: *Regni sui in hominum animos Specimen aliquod Christus dederat Asinorum accitu. Majus nunc & maxime admirabile edit in purganda æde paterna, nulla ui externa sola Divina virtute venerabilis.*
35 Our Saviour, saith he, *had given an experiment of his Kingdom over the*

8 *Sacerdotem* 74; *Saeerdotem* 73.   11 times). 74; ~ 73.   14 be 74; he 73.
23 *for private persons om.* Parker.

minds of men by his sending for the Asses. He gives now a greater and most
admirable proof thereof by this cleansing of his Fathers house, which he did
by the Majesty of his Divine Power, not of any external violence.
    I had quoted upon occasion Mr. *Hales* his Book of Schism, And
Doctor *Stillingfleet* (who though yet living, deserves the honour to   5
be already cited for good Authority) does the same, as I find since,
stiling him *as learned and judicious a Divine as most our Nation hath bred,
in his excellent though little Tract of Schisme;* and transcribes the same
Passages. You hereupon laugh at me, for having said in his commendation that he was a man *who had clear'd himself from froath and*   10
groons. Had I been the Author of that expression, it was not at all
ridiculous, but is very proper and significant, and founded upon a
Latine classical saying. But the best sport is 'tis Mr. *Hales* his own
words in that same book; and though Mr. *Hooker* were *so long winded
an Author* that you never could read him, methinks you might have   15
had the patience upon this occasion to have perused Mr. *Hales* his
book of eight pages. But to amend the matter you say, *the loftiest
thing that can be said of so great a man as Mr.* Hales *is, that he was neither
a Mad-man nor a Fanatick.* I yield, Mr. *Bayes,* and instead of admiring
that Majesty and Beauty which sits upon the Forehead of Masculine Truth   20
and generous Honesty, I will henceforward admire only the Maidenly
modesty and rosial blushes that bloom on your Cheeks and inhabit
your Forehead. But this will not suffice: Mr. *Hales* you say too was
a *Socinian.* I see you did not serve your Fanatick Prenticeship in
vain. No man can tell you truth but he must presently be a *Socinian.*   25
No more *Socinian* than *your* self, Sir. You have spent much paper in
your *Defence,* to decipher the Fanatick deportment toward all Adversaries: but, whether, it be theirs or no, I am sure you have learnt
it to the height. *He has drop'd,* you say, *some loose passages in that Treatise, for which himself was then censured and the Book is still, though the*   30
*Author be pardon'd, because as he did not first publish it, so he afterward
recanted it.* Most judicially said, and in the language of the Tribunal.
But who told you this fine Story? Doctor *Heylin* I warrant you; for
as for your self it appears you never read him. But if Mr. *Hales* of
Schisme be too loose for you, will you be pleas'd to admit my Lord   35

Arch-bishop of *Canterburies* authority; that the Schisme is alwayes
the Crime of those who give the occasion. But if neither Mr. *Hales,*
nor the late Lord Arch-bishop may be trusted in the matter, pray,
Sir, inquire in the Shops for *Copernicus of Schisme,* if there be any such
5 Treatise, for that Author would have been the most proper to have
salved the *Phænomena* either way.

You take occasion here and in very many other places of your
book, to tax me partly upon Bishop *Bramhall's* account (and more
of my Lord Arch-bishop *Laud, Hugo Grotius,* and others) as if I had
10 traduced him under a seeming commendation. To this once for all.
Had it not been for your Preface to Bishop *Bramhall* (which I will
never pardon, because it drew me out into publick to be a Writer)
I had never medled with him. But no man will fare the better or
gain reputation by keeping you company: whereas you intrude
15 your self upon men of the best authority, by their names to render
your self considerable. In that Preface you stuff'd out the Bishop
with such Bombast, you rung such an incessant peal of *In Laudem*
Thomæ *Bum, Bum, Bum, sine fine,* that it would have made an Horse
break his Halter. But now that I have wrought so good an effect,
20 as to rescue him in some sort from you, and that you have since
(which looks prettily) Printed your *Preface* without his Book, I will
not (though I have so fresh a temptation by your censure of Mr.
Hales) further molest his memory, but let his life and death be
buried together. And if I have in some historical passages writ too
25 distinctly, I cannot ascribe whatsoever errour of that kind I may
have committed, to any other cause then the reading of ill Books,
which have perhaps vitiated my stile as well as others. For ever
since you were to be sold at *Jo. Shirley's, Sam Thompson's, Rich.
Davis's, J. Martin's, James Collins's, Henry Hall's,* you have so per-
30 petually pester'd the Press with your own Books, and obstructed
better Authors, that men have scarce had any thing else to read,
and so your virulence has corrupted the Age you live in. For as I
instanced to you in my former Book, your malignant remark even
upon Bishop *Bramhall,* that, *as far as the prejudice of the Age would per-*
35 *mit him, he was an acute Philosopher;* I think it now pertinent to shew
in some few examples more how civil you are to your friends, and
of consequence how generous to your Adversaries. First, for friend

Galen. I confess that Galen *gave a kind of* Specimen *in his book* de usu
Partium, *which though it is indeed a famous work, yet it is not so Divine
as to be writ by Enthusiasme; but alwayes seem'd to me such a thing as might
either be very much amended, or much improved: which I do not say that I
may extenuate* Galen's *commendation.* No, I know you don't, just as 5
you did not publish your Preface *to impair* Mr. B's. *esteem in the least, but
to correct his scribling humour, and for a warning to the* Rat-Divines, *and
to show how the Bishop baffled him without condescending to his* Systematical *and* Push-pin *Divinity.* Then Friend *Harvy. In whatsoever manner
therefore Generation is performed, whether the Man do only,* &c. *(which 10
excellent Doctor* Harvy *guesses at, but not so ingeniously as he is wont.)*
And yet you were not acquainted with your *Comfortable Importance.*
Who next? *I wonder how* Mercurius Trismegistus *could Cousen those
great Counsellors of Criticisme,* Lipsius, *the* Scaligers, *&c. and I cannot
but admire that* Lipsius, Scaliger, Vossius, *nay, and* Grotius *too, so many 15
clear-sighted men should understand the thing wrong, as if they did it on set
purpose.* See more *our Countreymen* Sanford *or* Parker, *in a most learned
book of Christs descending into* Hell, *which begun by* Sanford, Parker
*finished, first attempted to accommodate, wrong and rashly, the Theological
History of the Gentiles to the Sacred History: but whoever was the first 20
Author, the venerable Names of* Scaliger, Selden, Bochart, Vossius, *ay
and* Grotius *again, brought it in reputation: so that every man that affects
to be accounted a prime Philologer, sets up forthwith to accommodate of any
fashion the* Greek *matters to the* Hebrew; *the Scabbado of which affecta-
tion does so break out every day,* &c. but they got the Itch it seems 25
first of *Grotius,* and those other Scoundrels. 'Tis to be consider'd
Mr. *Bayes,* that you are *the wonder of this Age,* so they must all subscribe to you, and carry your books after you. On: *I do not question
but that great and honorable Person* Picus Mirandula *was a person of stupendious parts and learning: yet I am sure that those notions wherewith he 30
made the greatest noise in the world, were but grand and pompous Futilities.*
For the School-Doctors you abuse them at every turn; and I could
away with it better but for one reason, which is, that you say in the
fifth Leaf of your *Preface*: It *was never any part of the Church of* Englands

3 *Enthusiasme* 74; *Enthasiasme* 73.   11 *ingeniously*] *ingenuously* 74.   16 *should*
74; *shouid* 73.   17 *Countreymen*] *Countreyman* 74.   19 *the* 74; *she* 73.   23 *accounted*
74; *ccounted* 73.

design to exchange the old School Doctors for Calvinian *Systemes and Syntagmes*; so that it is not so handsomly said of 'm therefore that *they are full of such stuff as makes fools stare, and wise men laugh.* But whereas I had hereupon said *p.* 213. that you had owned the School men for
5 Authors of the Church of *Englands* Divinity, you formally deny it, insulting with all your natural and acquired rudeness. It is not worth the Readers trouble to interess him in such a foolish brabble; but if any one please to take the pains to inspect your book again, as I have done and quoted the leaf on this occasion, the most he can
10 say will be that you have Cheated me; but if you have done it so cunningly that it cannot be made out evidently, I am content to go by the loss. Yet for a collateral proof, how far to rely either upon your good Faith or good Memory in what you your self write, let him take one instance where you quote me in my page 120. *Thus*
15 *when you cite for your own convenience that passage, that Rebellion is as the Sin of Witchcraft you are pleased to add too; that this Text will scarce admit my interpretation; and yet you know no more what my interpretation would be then you do what Witchcraft and Rebellion are.* You might have done me the favour instead of saying, *I cite it for mine own convenience,*
20 to have begun with my own words; *I will allow him that Rebellion is as the Sin of Witch-craft.* But that candor is not to be expected: Yet to show you that I know better what you write, and what your Interpretation would be then you do your self, pray read in your *Preface to Bishop* Bramhall, 32 leaf: where you say; *the Clergy of* Eng-
25 land *are as strongly principled against the hateful Sin of Rebellion as against Witch-craft or Idolatry.* Then see the Text 1 *Sam.* 15. 25. *For Rebellion is as the Sin of Witchcraft and Stubborness is as iniquity and Idolatry.* Now, Mr. *Bayes,* whether did I not at least guess shrowdly at your Interpretation? But you are excusable forasmuch as you con-
30 fess'd in that *Preface,* both at beginning and end, *that you knew not what it would prove, nor had leisure nor patience to examine whether it were Idle or not Idle.* Proceed, I *might have added to them the late grand Dogmatical Master of Modern Orthodoxy, whose rude Dogmatizing has occasion'd as many controversies in the Christian Church as ever* Manes *and*
35 Valentinus *did.* Had you told his name it had been fairer; but by

19 favour 74; favovr 73.   24–5 *Clergy of* England] *the People* Parker.
33 *Modern om.* Parker.

the Project of that whole book it seems to be *Calvine*. So, Mr. *Bayes*, he is sped: You have done his work that he shall never lift up his head again. Yet; Lucian *is every where so abusive and bitter in his Satyres against all sorts of Philosophers, that, if his mouth be any slander, they must have been a Pack of the vilest Villains that ever breathed.* Never- 5 theless you say, *some have slander'd* Plato *himself together with* Socrates *as guilty of that unnatural sin of the lustful* Sodomites; *which calumny had never gain'd any credit with us, had it not been reported by some of the ancient Fathers; and yet it is too notorious to dissemble, that those Fathers were not only very careless in their relations concerning them, being ap-* 10 *parently guilty of innumerable faults of memory, but also in many instances highly disingenious; Insomuch that I find no Prose-Writer agree so much with their reports as* Lucian, *whose main design it was to abuse every thing that was grave and sober.* Well spoke for your Clients, Mr. *Bayes*; ay, and for your self too. For, *while you*, forsooth, *take only that most* 15 *delightful prospect to behold others scrambling and aspiring to those things which you contemn and trample upon, and while your palate is not surfeited and cloy'd with the same repeated relishes;* (for you were but newly come from your Grewel) *nor your Eye quite weary of beholding the same repeated objects,* (you had not yet seen your *Comfortable Importance*); *yet* 20 *you could have been highly contented* (*upon the account of a Philosophick curiosity*) *to leave this present Theater, that you might enter upon the next for the delight of being entertain'd with a new Scene of things;* yet you handled it so, that by *p.* 242. you were *upon the very point of your departure to* (the Scene of) London, and to play *Bayes* his part upon this 25 present Theatre. Go on and prosper. But; *had the pristine learning of* Egypt *been the same it was in later ages, it had been as great a disparagement to* Moses, *as 'tis now justly reputed a commendation, that he was accomplished in all the* Egyptian *learning, and had amounted only to this, that he was a vain, trifling, superstitious fellow.* Why so? You put it, Mr. 30 *Bayes*, too hard upon *Moses*. For neither did you intend it as a disparagement to Bishop *Bramhall*, that *as far as the prejudice of the Age would permit him, he was an acute Philosopher.* Still: It *is not my design by representing those Primitive Sages as fools and dunces, to rob them of that*

8 *credit* 74; *eredit* 73.   13 *every thing*] everybody Parker.   20 (you . . .
Importance); 74; *om.* 73.   21 *account* 74; *account* 73.   25 (the . . . of) 74;
om. 73.   25–6 , and . . . Theatre 74; *om.* 73.

esteem and veneration with which they have been deservedly honoured in all succeeding ages. That is more gentle where you say, *you might give account too of the mean abilities of* Orpheus *and* Pythagoras, *but that you delight not to speak too hardly of any Virtuoso's Ashes.* Nevertheless you
5 tell Dr. Bathurst, You *had sufficiently convinced him how little the Vertue of* Cato, *and Honesty of* Regulus, *were to be valued.* But to conclude, whether do you handle our Saviour himself more softly? *And then if we look into our Saviours life, the unparallel'd civility and obligingness of his Deportment seems to be almost as high an Evidence of the truth and*
10 *Divinity of his Doctrine as his unparallel'd miracles were.* For it is altogether *unimaginable that so sweet-natur'd a person should be so base and profligate an Impostor, as he must have been if he had been one.* And yet your self must, and do, avow, that he was not so sweet-natur'd to the Scribes and Pharisees, *Mat.* 23. 15. *Woe unto you Scribes and*
15 *Pharisees, Hypocrites, for ye compass Sea and Land to make one Proselyte and when he is made, you make him twofold more the child of Hell then your selves,* &c. and so in many other places. You know too that he was once in a very *hot Fit of zeal, and a seeming Fury and Transport of Passion.* You say too, that, *whereas the gentle and sweet natur'd St.* John *was his*
20 *darling Disciple, you often find him checking* Peter's *rude and unmannerly zeal.*

But by the way; where is it that you find it so often? I cannot find it more then once, which was when he rebuked him for cutting off *Malchus* his ear: neither is he there so severe upon him as you are
25 to tax him of *rudeness and unmannerliness.* But once is not often. You, I doubt, trusted herein too much to your memory, and thought he had check'd his zeal four times, because the same thing is related by all the four Evangelists. I find indeed that our Saviour, *John* 21. 22. check'd *Peter* for inquiring what should be of *John;* and asked
30 him *what is that to thee?* But here he reproved not his zeal but his curiosity. And at another time, *Mat.* 14. 31. when *Peter,* walking on the water began to sink, he blamed his want of Faith. And *Mat.* 16. 23. Our Saviour said to him, *get thee behind me Satan, thou art an offence unto me, for thou savourest not the things that be of God, but the*

4–6 Nevertheless . . . *valued.* 74; *om.* 73.   17 that *om.* 74.   25 *unmannerliness* 74; *unmaneerliness* 73.   28–9 *John* 21. 22 Ed.; I *John* 22. 73, 74.   32–3 Mat. 16. 23. 74; 16 Mat. 23. 73.

things that be of men. But this was not neither because of *Peter's* zeal, but the unseasonable care he had of our Saviours preservation. And I do not at present remember that he was check'd oftner upon whatsoever occasion. This mistake arises from reading of *Plutarch*, when you should be at your Bible and Devotions: and *the ravishing delight* 5 *you take in labouring your periods, and framing your own thoughts and conceptions into words,* makes you forget the Text of Scripture. You were sure, and had some *Idea* remaining, that some-body was check'd; and so it were for zeal, (which was to your present purpose) it was not so much matter with you on whom it lighted. Whereas indeed 10 I doubt it was that very *John* whom you oppose to *Peter.* For, *Luke* 9. 54. he, because a Village of the *Samaritans* would not entertain our Saviour, would presently have *commanded fire from Heaven to consume them, as did Elias* (whom too you quoted for one of your *Zelotes.*) And him indeed our Saviour severely rebuked for that zeal, telling him, 15 *he knew not what manner of Spirit he was of.* And to this I might add *Mark* 10. 35. And *Matth.* 20. 20. Where the Mother of *Zebedees* Children, and the Sons *James* and this *John* would first have covenanted with our Saviour, that he should grant them whatsoever they desired, and then made it the request of their Family, *that they* 20 *two might sit, one at his right hand and the other at his left in his Kingdom*; for which he rebuked them, saying further, *Whosoever will be great among you shall be your Servant, and whoever will be the chief of you shall be the Servant of all.* So that indeed I doubt you have rob'd *John* to pay *Peter* with his *rudeness and unmannerliness*; and in making it *often,* 25 you have mistook thus the number of the persons for the frequency of the time. But you may perhaps object, that this last of *John* was not a fault of zeal, but of ambition; nevertheless, because some mens zeal is only for preeminence, and thereupon they are often rude and unmannerly to their Betters, I thought it not unseasonable to put 30 you in mind of it on this occasion, that you might apply it to your self, and learn that being the Arch-deacon you ought in stead of contending for Superiority over others *to be their Minister.* But I pray you reflect seriously upon this your mistake, and hereafter either read the *English Bible* more carefully and *the words* (but you will not 35

1 *Peter's* 74; *Petor's* 73.   5 *ravishing* 74; *ravisting* 73.   *delight*] *delights* 74.
17 *Mark* Ed.; *Matth.* 73, 74.   *Matth.* Ed.; *Luke* 73, 74.

allow them to be so) *of our Saviour and the Apostles*, or else, like a
Traditor, lay it by for good and all, as *a book in some places erroneous,
in some places scarce sense, and of dangerous consequences, when every pert,
bold, and conceited fellow takes upon himself to raise Doctrines and Opinions*
5 *thence, contrary to the meaning of God in his holy Word, and contrary to
the mind and meaning of the Holy Ghost*, &c.

But, to let these things be as they will, it is however too bold to
say (but you durst not adventure further) that *the Civility of our
Saviours deportment was almost as high an evidence of the Divinity of his*
10 *Doctrine, as his unparallel'd Miracles, otherwise he had been a base and
profligate Impostor.* You ought not to put such things as these upon
Cross and Pile so; for ill use may be made of it, though it should be
against your intention. And really, had you writ as much of
Mahomet as you have here done of *Christ* and *Moses*, you have put
15 fair to be, as you have been the second Author of *Ecclesiastical Politie*,
so now, of the *Tre Grandi Impostori*. So that you see I hope by this
time if my stile hath differently decipher'd the same person in different circumstances, where I learnt it, but have not yet attained
the height of your faculty.

20 You condemn me for having in my p. 309. mentioned the Reverend Bishop *Andrews* his form of Consecration of a Church or Chappel, which I might have done at large, and inserted something of
History that depends upon it: but I did not. Neither shall I now
say any thing further, but only refer you to Arch-bishop *Parker*
25 p. 85. of his *Antiquitates Ecclesiæ Britannicæ*, where you may find
what his judgment was in this case of things of the very same
nature.

I had said *p.* 166. of my book, that I could quote my Lord *Verulam*
to your confusion: hereupon you tell me the *Quotation of my Lord*
30 *Verulam would have been more to the purpose or the Story of Pork, which
you say I know, but I say I do not know, or however if I did you might have
had the manners to have told it for His Majesties sake, because he knows how
to make use of it,* you think you put me hard to it. I am sorry that
I must trouble the Reader with such stuff, and these mean contests
35 *de Lana Porcina.* But this is all the Fleece a man can hope for in
Sheering you. I had told you Sir, (there was not a word of His

12 so; 74; ∼. 73.

Majesty) in my *p*. 300. alluding to your Tautologies, *that all the variety of your Treat is Pork (you know the Story) but so little disguised by good Cookery, that it discovers the miserableness or rather the penury of the Host.* Now here have you brought my *p*. 166. into conjunction with my *p*. 300. that (which every man will discern) because my Lord *Verulam* was mentioned you might make a Quibble betwixt *Pork* and *Bacon*. Nor did I ever see a Quibble fetch'd at greater distance, or more cunningly carried. But in whatsoever you undertake, you are extraordinary, as (because I promis'd you before some instances in your *Ecclesiastical Politie*) where you are informing the world concerning some *Sects of men made up of sanctified Fury*, &c. *Tois gar Presbuteroisin*, &c. which was to make a Greek Quibble forsooth, upon the Presbyterians, and of so many ages ago. Whereas the good old Poet never dreamed of any such thing, or such a Nation and the Cronology and Geography of it varies as much as in the Play of *Moses* and *Julius Cæsar*. A third instance shall be in an Anagram you give us of *Calvin*, that is *Culina:* though it be in two Languages that understand not one another, and the man spent very little in his Kitchin, nor made provision for it, but all went to his Study, and yet his whole Inventory at his death mounted not to above Seventy pounds *sterling*. This may serve for a *Specimen* or scantling of your Wit, and to shew how well you spent your time at both Universities: *which I do not say by any means to diminish your just commendation,* for certainly none ever quibbled with greater *Enthusiasme*.

I shall upon this occasion take leave to digress a little further concerning *Calvin* and *Geneva* to which you are every where a declared Enemy. The Town you might have spared, if not for his, yet for *Sales* his sake, the Bishop of *Geneva*; whose Book was thought fit to be licensed by your Predecessor Doctor *Heywood*: though afterwards it was called in and burnt by Proclamation, but the Doctor was *punished with Preferment*. But as to *Calvin* himself, it had been well that you had rather imitated the incomparable modesty and candor of Reverend Mr. *Hooker* in all his Writings, and especially in this particular, but how should you imitate him whom, notwithstanding your challenging and defying the Non-conformists with

---

3 *Cookery*] *Cockery* 74.   *discovers* 74; *diseovers* 73.   6 betwixt] between 74.
10 *Politie*) 74; ~, 73.   21 pounds] pound 74.

his *Ecclesiastical Politie*, it seems you had never read. *I think*, saith he, *that* Calvin *was incomparably the wisest man that ever the* French *Church did enjoy, since it enjoyed him. Divine knowledge he gather'd not by hearing or reading so much, as by teaching others. For though thousands* were *debtors to him as touching knowledge in that kind, yet he to none, but only to God the Author of that most blessed fountain the Book of life; and of the admirable dexterity of Wit, together with the helps of other learning, which were his guids.* And I find the Reverend Bishop of *Durham,* Doctor *Morton* in his little Tract *de Pace Ecclesiastica,* had no less opinion of him. In that Tract the Bishop, as also Bishop *Davenant,* Bishop *Hall,* and others do with singular Wisdom and Piety treat concerning reconciliation of Protestants among themselves: a design much more probable and better timed then that which was set up by others for the accommodating of our Church with the *Roman.* There he saith, *Consulant illi si placet* Lutherum Melanchthonem Jac. Andream Brentium. *Nos* Calvinum *Nostrum,* Petrum Martyrum *&* Zanchium *proferemus* (we will produce saith he our *Calvin*) *qui singuli in Ecclesia Christi veluti primæ magnitudinis lumina fulserunt.* And he adds upon occasion in the next page, *Hæc* Calvinus *tam pacate tam placide tamque indulgenter ut jam non homo sed ipsa humanitas loqui videatur.* It were endless to cite the testimonies of all sorts of men, not only of the Protestant, but of the Romish perswasion, concerning that excellent person: but indeed he needs no more certain commendation then that he is traduced and accused by you. And whereas you tax him as pragmatical and intermedling with other mens matters; what could he do otherwise, all the Learned men of *Europe* solliciting his approved Judgment in the most weighty occasions. Nor therefore could he avoid that general correspondence by Letters, of another stile I am sure then your Letters are, who are therefore offended at him. Though you might have remember'd that there were some Letters too writ to him by Arch-bishop *Parker.* But the design of you and those of your Cast has been, and still it seems to continue, against all the forraign Churches: and you are but *Heylin* resuscitated, whose business it was by his scandalous

---

13 better 74; bettet 73.   15 *placet* Lutherum] placet, suum Lutherum Morton.
16 *Nostrum,* Petrum] Nostrum, Bucerum, Petrum Morton.   19 *pacate* 74,
Morton; *pacati* 73.   22 Romish perswasion, 74; ∼, ∼ 73.

Histories to blacken the whole Reformation, attributing (as Reverend Doctor *Moulin* well expresses it) and *imputing the excesses that happened by the ordinary course of humane business unto Religion.* And he did it to so good purpose, that I believe his Books have occasion'd among us the defection of more Protestants unto the *Romish* Religion, 5 then any thing that themselves have writ in the points of Controversie. And this distance from all other of the Reformed Churches hath been and is held up by you and your party so studiously, that beside what has been writ against them with all bitterness, they have even in cases of Extremity and Necessity refused to Com- 10 municate with them. Hence it is that you say in your *Preface*; *Therefore Reader I beg thy hearty prayers and endeavours for the Peace and Prosperity of the Church of* England (He had need when you do so dangerously interrupt it) *for when that is gone it will be very hard to find out another, with which, if thou art either honest or wise, thou wilt* 15 *be over-forward to joyn Communion.* And why so? Truly I know not unless it be for some more peculiar and Ceremonial perfection that our Church may have attain'd to above others. And this indeed hath been alwayes magnifyed and esteem'd to that height by those of your Bran and Leaven, that even our own Kings and Bishops have 20 all along been Characteriz'd by them well or ill, according as they promoted those matters or remitted them. As for *Henry* the *Eight*, he is a gone man, and his *Sacriledge* will never be pardon'd even in his Successors. For *Edward* the *Sixth*, that miracle of Princes, *yet his death was none of the Infelicities of the Church of* England. But might 25 he not have lived to be wiser and better? But in the blessed Reign of Queen *Mary* (as in the Preface of the *Oxford* Statutes compiled in the time of Arch-bishop *Laud*) *Potiunte rerum Maria, inter incerta vacillans Statuta viguit Academia, celebrantur studia, enituit disciplina, & optanda temporum fælicitate* (if it could be had again for wishing) 30 *Tabularum defectus resarcivit innatus Candor & quicquid legibus deerat moribus Suppletum est.* But then upon her death there came in an iron Age. *Terras Astrea reliquit.* For *Decurrente Temporum Serie* (that is in Queen *Elizabeth* and King *James* his times) *& Vitiis & Legibus pariter*

9 beside] besides 74.   29 *celebrantur*] colebantur Praefatio.   31 *deerat Ed.*; *decrat* 73; *deeret* 74.   33 *Terras . . . reliquit* om. Praefatio.   *Astrea*] *Austrea* 74. *Serie* 74; *Seric* 73.

8124228   X

laboratum est: all was quite spoyled; yet sometimes she was *Elizabeth*, and sometimes *old Elsibeth* with you, thereafter as she behaved her self in the matter of Conformity. There in her *Quinto* Eliz. *she was miserably out in her Divinity.* And then in *Decimo Tertio* She did no
5 better when she was contented the Puritans should only subscribe the Articles of Doctrine. But at other times she was pretty tolerable. King *James* was more busie then belong'd him, when he writ a Letter to her in behalf of the Nonconformists: but after he succeeded her in *England* he made amends. But he had a great fault
10 nevertheless, that he was so uncivil to the *Arminians*, even to such a degree, as to stile Arminius *the Enemy of God*, Arminianisme *Heresie*, the Arminians *Hereticks and Atheistical Sectaries.* For though in *England* he advanced the Episcopal Government, yet he had adhered to the Doctrine of *Calvin*, which you and your Tribe do so
15 detest, that though a King please you never so well in matter of Conformity, yet unless he humour you too in *Arminianisme* or such devices, he cannot be assured of your good graces. And so it is too even as to the Bishops. Arch-bishop *Cranmer* is subject to many exceptions. But Arch-bishop *Parker* was a *Prelate of great worth, and*
20 *no less eminent in the Churches cause.* But Arch-bishop *Grindall was a man of another Spirit, he having convers'd with* Calvin *and* Beza *abroad could not shake off their Acquaintance, or was as willing to continue it as they, when Bishop of* London, *he condescended to have a* French *Church set up in the City: when of* York *he entertain'd correspondence with* Zanchy *a*
25 *Divine of* Heidelberg. An hainous crime; *Nay, but when he was Archbishop of* Canterbury, *he not only conniv'd at the Lectures, which were newly set up by the Puritans, but even incouraged them.* A sad man was he! But then came Arch-bishop *Whitgift*, who repair'd all that had run to ruine *by the negligence and remissness of some great Bishops*, and by
30 the zeal of the *Grendalizing* Lecturers. And yet this truly venerable Bishop could not escape censure too among you; for, though he were right in Ceremonies, yet he was wrong in substance, and gave authority to the Articles of *Lambeth*, which run point-blank against the *Arminian* Tenets. Therefore notwithstanding all his merits, he

---

19 *worth*] parts Heylyn.   21 *convers'd* 74; *convers'd* 73.   24 *correspondence*]
a new Intelligence Heylyn.   28 he! 74; ~ 73.   29 *by the . . . Bishops*] by
the connivance of some Bishops Heylyn.   30 Lecturers] Lectures 74.

can scarce be forgiven. But Arch-bishop *Bancroft* was a man I trow
without exception. But then as misfortune would have it Arch-
bishop *Abbot* succeeds him, and *he was too facil and yielding in the
exercise of that great Office, and by his extraordinary remissness in exacting
strict Conformity to the prescribed orders of the Church in point of Ceremony,* 5
*he seemed to resolve those legal determinations to their first indifferency. And
he brought in such an habit of Non-conformity, that the future reduction of
those tender-Conscienced men to a long discontinued obedience was at the last
interpreted an Innovation.* This is out of your Doctor *Heylin*, who goes
down with you for Gospel, and is to you like meat, drink, and 10
cloathing. All this adoe must be made for things that profit nothing,
(save that to you indeed they are very profitable) and according as
great Princes or eminent Prelates are more or less ceremonious, so
must they be ranked in your Calendar. By how much a man is more
a Christian you account him the worse Bishop: and it is now grown, 15
instead of the requisites in Scripture to that sacred Office, a sufficient commendation to have been *an admirable Ritualist.*

'Tis now time to return to our Pork & *Bacon*; but because you cry
Pork Pork as often as any Raven, I will first to stay your Stomach,
give you the story of the Pork, and the rather to satisfie another 20
friend of mine, who did me the favour to interpret it of his Highness
the Duke of *York*, when he contented himself the former year with
the homely fare of the Marriners at the *Dogger-bank.* It was at an
Audience of the Embassadors of the *Ætoleans* and *Antiochus*, in the
Council of *Achæa*, *Quintius*, the *Roman* General, being present. 25
Antiochus his Embassadors boasted there very much of the potent
Armies of their King; thundring out the hard names of *Elymæans*,
Cadusians, *Medians*, &c. of which they consisted: whereupon *Quintius*, to take off the wonderment and terrour, replyed; (and I will
give you honest *Philemon Holland* for an Interpreter) *Now in faith this* 30
is mine Host of Chalcis *up and down, a friendly man I assure you and a good
fellow in his house, and one that knoweth how to entertain his Guests, and
make them very welcom. We went upon a time to make merry with him,
and I remember it was at Mid-summer, when the dayes are longest and the
Sun at the hottest. And as we wonder'd how, at such a season of the year,* 35
he met with that plenty of Venison, and such variety withall; the man

nothing so vain-glorious as these fellows are, smiled pleasantly upon us, and
said we were welcom to a Feast of good Swine and no better: But well fare
a good Cook my Masters, who by his cunning hand, what with seasoning it,
and what with serving it up with divers Sawces, has made all this fair shew
5 *of wild flesh, and the same of sundry sorts.* Thus, Mr. *Bayes*, have I
reveal'd to you this great mysterie of Pork, of which you were so
curious, and which tended only, as I told you, to show how jejune
you were, who in all your matters, and even in that of railing,
whereof you are most copious and the best furnished, yet are forced
10 to serve up to the Reader continually the cold Hashes of plain
repetitions, to stuff out your Books and fill your Table. I hope I
have with this stay'd your Stomach, and if you will but expect a
little, I will too in convenient time bring in your *Bacon.*

You had, to make the Ceremonies go down better with the Non-
15 conformists, said, *that 'twas no more for the Magistrate to impose them*
then to determine a new signification of words. For it is your great Art
to make the Ceremonies at once stupendiously necessary and at the
same time despicably little; both a Fly and a Whale,

In whose vast bulk, though store of Oyle doth lye,
20   *We find more shape, more beauty in a Fly.*

This I made merry with, as of good reason. For it would raise a
very great disorder in the world to boule-verse so, and overturn the
signification of all words: for even in the name of your Function,
if a man should but chance to lispe, it would make a dangerous
25 alteration; but however to impose such contrary significations with
the same penalties too would make wild work, and pester the
Nation with a whole swarm of Informers. But in that debate, I instanced in *Augustus Cæsar*, who was so shy of unusual words: and
this you will needs have to be a notable mistake, because *Julius*
30 *Cæsar* Compiled a book *de Analogia*, forgetting that *Suetonius* describes at large *Augustus* his hereditary exquisiteness in that particular. *Those which delighted in new words, and those which affected old*
(apply it to Ceremonies) *he equally dispised, both being alike contemptible:*
insomuch that it was reported, he displaced a Consular Lieutenant

---

1 *are*] here Holland.   2 *good swine*] good tame swine Holland.   31 *Augustus*
74; *Angustus* 73.

for a fault of Orthography. And if Orthography in Worship were now as strictly observed, perhaps your Spiritual Lieutenancy might run the same risk.

I had chanced in my Book to speak of *Huddibras*, with that esteem which an excellent piece of Wit upon whatsoever subject will always merit. But you hereupon fall into such a Fit and Rupture of railing at me, that you have exceeded not only all the Oyster-women and Butter-whores, but even your self, pretending that I have done him some dishonour. Should I study a suitable return to you I could not raise my self into more choler then to call you a *Jewel*, a *Glass-drop*, a *Tintinnabulum*, words that you with some sympathy delight in, and whose Heraldry is to be Pendant. As for you, I cannot restrain you of this liberty, who have wisely taken safe-guard in the Ecclesiastical Function, and, fore-seeing betimes what occasion you might have, thought fit to Post your self up in Print that *you are not Valiant*. Only I could have for your own sake wished you had not call'd me *Judas*, lest so eminent a Divine as you are should appear more concerned for *Huddibras* then for your Saviour. For the rest you may please to know, that, whatever you have here said to me, cannot either diminish or increase my esteem for that Author.

You foam again as in the Falling-Sickness, because I had said that I thought God never intended the Clergy for Political and Secular imployments, and you make it to be no less then Blasphemy. If they be so enamour'd of those drudgeries, and have deputed you to maintain it, much good may it do them and you. But why should you upon no more occasion tell me: *Fatuos & hujus Terræ filios quod attinet (saith a Jewish Zelote) non magis nostro judicio prophetare possunt quam Asinus & Rana. Asses and Todpoles may as soon expect the Impressions of the Divine Spirit as such Dunces and Sots as you?* But these words of yours I suppose you pretend to be dictated by that Spirit. And further you say, *The Ruac Hakodesh dwell in such a distemper'd and polluted mind as yours! It may as soon unite it self to a Swine.* Ruac Hakodesh, Mr. *Bayes*, this is as your other *Bayes* has it, *A Crust, a lasting Crust for your Rogue Critiques: I would fain see the proudest of them all but dare to nibble at this. If they do, this shall rub their gums for 'm, I*

1 Orthography. 74; ~: 73.   21 Author. 74; ~, 73.

promise you. I doubt your *Ruac Hakodesh* is but at best a *Bath col.*
But is not this of yours fine language think you for an *A. Sac. Dom?*
O Seytang Aurang Olanda bacalay Samatay. To show you, Mr. *Bayes,*
that I too have been sometimes conversant with the Jewish Zelotes,
I will tell you hereupon a Story out of one of them, that shall as
yours be nameless. There was among the *Jews* a certain kind of
people that were called *Proselytes,* which you may in *English* interpret *Turn-coats,* concerning whom was that expression that I quoted
you before of our Saviours, *Mat.* 23. 15. *Wo unto you Scribes and*
Pharisees, Hypocrites, for you compass Sea and Land to make a Proselyte, and
when he is made, you make him twofold more the child of Hell then you your
selves. Now what I shall tell you of these men, I would not have you
to misapply unto such Conscientious persons, as have re-united
themselves unto the Discipline of our Church; for I wish that all the
Non-conformists rather could find reason to do in like manner: but
it relates particularly to your self, who, abandoning all Modesty and
Christianity toward your former party, have defiled and dishonour'd
the Church that has receiv'd you into protection. But concerning
these *Proselytes* and Turn-coats it was that the *Jews* had that Maxime;
Proselyti & Pæderastæ impediunt adventum Messiæ: and again, *Proselyti*
sunt sicut Scabies Israeli; that they were like a Scab or Leprosie to
Israel. Therefore when a Proselyte was circumcised, they first
catechized him about the sincerity of his Conversion; whether
he did not do it, *ob adipiscendas Divitias,* to make his Fortune; *ob*
Timorem, for Fear of some inconvenience; or lastly, *ob Amorem erga*
aliquam Israeliticam, Whether there were not some woman in the
bottom of the business. For they had a shrowd suspicion of them,
Quod non periti essent Mandatorum, quodque inducerent Vindictas, atque
insuper quod forte eorum Opera imitarentur Israelitæ: and therefore it
was *quod Proselyti opus habebant Triumviratu,* and they would not
trust them until three men had examined and taken care that all
were right. And if it chanced that both the Man and the Wife came
together to be Proselytes, they were used to separate and keep them
apart for ninety dayes, *ut dijudicari possit interprolem in Sanctitate geni-*
tam. Nay, moreover there was a Baptisme peculiarly solemn before
they could be admitted. and a great ceremonial *Rationale* by which

9 Saviours] Saviour 74.   21 *sicut* 74; *sieut* 73.

it was to be administred. The whole body was to be dip'd *mersione una. Si, excepto apice minimi digiti, manebat adhuc in immunditia. Si quis capillosus admodum, omnem crinem capitis abluere necesse erat.* And there were many other scrupulous niceties in this washing. As for the Water; *homo Gonorrhæus non mundatur nisi in fonte: Sed Menstruosa & Proselytus in Collectione aquarum.* But put case the same man were *Proselytus* and *Gonorrhæus* too, though the Rabbies were very exact, I find not this decided; but it is easie to collect that he must have passed thorow both waters. They were so curious as to regulate what proportion too of water was sufficient, and the least quantity that could be allowed was, *Quatuor Seæ aquarum* and the dimension, *Cubitus quadratus,* &c. Now, Mr. *Bayes,* I would gladly be satisfyed whether you have been rightly and duly proselyted according to these Ceremonies, (for you know that the Jewish Ceremonies are not so abrogated but that the Proconsul may reestablish them) but particularly have you been drawn cross the River to *Lambeth?* has not so much as the top of your little finger escaped ducking? is there not one hair of your head but has been over head and ears in the River? All this ought to have been exactly observed, (especially considering how much filth you brought about you) else you are not a true Turn-coat but remain still in your uncleanness. And you might have had the advantage, in traversing thus the water, to have catched some of the prophecying *Todpoles* you speak of. But really, there is your self and some few more such Proselytes to our Church, that are so impure Creatures, that before you had been admitted into it, *'t had been absolutely necessary* for you to have passed thorow this cold Water Ordeal.

You do three times at least in your *Reproof,* and in your *Transproser Rehears'd* well nigh half the book thorow, run upon an Author *J. M.* which does not a little offend me. For why should any other mans reputation suffer in a contest betwixt you and me? But it is because you resolved to suspect that he had an hand in my former book, wherein, whether you deceive your self or no, you deceive others extreamly. For by chance I had not seen him of two years before; but after I undertook writing, I did more carefully avoid either visiting or sending to him, least I should any way involve

---

1 *mersione* Errata; *morsione* 73.   15 Proconsul 74; Procunsul 73.

him in my consequences. And you might have understood, or I am
sure your Friend the Author of the *Common Places* could have told
you, (he too had a slash at *J. M.* upon my account) that had he
took you in hand, you would have had cause to repent the occasion,
5 and not escap'd so easily as you did under my *Transprosal*. But I
take it moreover very ill that you should have so mean an opinion
of me, as not to think me competent to write such a simple book
as that without any assistance. It is a sign (however you upbraid
me often as your old acquaintance) that you did not know me well,
10 and that we had not much conversation together. But because
in your 125. *p.* you are so particular *you know a friend of ours*, &c.
intending that *J. M.* and his answer to *Salmasius*, I think it here
seasonable to acquit my promise to you in giving the Reader a short
trouble concerning my first acquaintance with you. *J. M.* was, and
15 is, a man of great Learning and Sharpness of wit as any man. It was
his misfortune, living in a tumultuous time, to be toss'd on the
wrong side, and he writ *Flagrante bello* certain dangerous Treatises.
His Books of *Divorce* I know not whether you may have use of; but
those upon which you take him at advantage were of no other
20 nature then that which I mentioned to you, writ by your own
father; only with this difference, that your Fathers, which I have
by me, was written with the same design, but with much less Wit
or Judgment, for which there was no remedy: unless you will supply his Judgment with his High Court of Justice. At His Majesties
25 happy Return, *J. M.* did partake, even as you your self did for all
your huffing, of his Regal Clemency and has ever since expiated
himself in a retired silence. It was after that, I well remember it,
that being one day at his house, I there first met you and acciden-
tally. Since that I have been scarce four or five times in your Com-
30 pany, but, whether it were my foresight or my good fortune, I
never contracted any friendship or confidence with you. But then
it was, when you, as I told you, wander'd up and down *Moor-fields*
Astrologizing upon the duration of His Majesties Government, that
you frequented *J. M.* incessantly and haunted his house day by
35 day. What discourses you there used he is too generous to remember. But he never having in the least provoked you, for you to

2 of 74; nf 73.   11 125 *Ed*; 115 73, 74.

insult thus over his old age, to traduce him by your *Scaramuccios*, and
in your own person, as a School-Master, who was born and hath lived
much more ingenuously and Liberally then your self; to have done
all this, and lay at last my simple book to his charge, without ever
taking care to inform your self better, which you had so easie oppor- 5
tunity to do; nay, when you your self too have said, to my knowledge, that you saw no such great matter in it but that I might be
the Author: it is inhumanely and inhospitably done, and will I hope
be a warning to all others as it is to me, to avoid (I will nor say such
a *Judas*,) but a man that creeps into all companies, to jeer, trepan, 10
and betray them.

   But after this fresh example of Romantick generosity, and your
John-like *Good nature*, you plunge over head and ears into History.
That of *Sibthorpe* and *Manwaring*, I had occasion before to speak of
in better method. I shall therefore only renew your own request in 15
your Epistle to the Reader, *that they would peruse it with an unprejudiced mind, and an ordinary attention*, and I shall leave the rest to their
judgments. For I do not know but that you may have some peculiar dispensation to determine those in 3° *Caroli* to have been *most
notorious Rebels*, notwithstanding that in the year 1667. this present 20
Parliament resolved in the most solemn and judicial manner, by a
concurrence of the Lords with the Commons, *that the Judgment
against them in 5 Caroli was illegal*. As to *Manwarings* particular,
whose cause you take up with a remarkable concernment, I cannot
but attribute it to some extraordinary correspondence of *Genius* 25
betwixt you. His very name hath more influence and power upon
you then Doctor *Bathursts* Talismans; and that very week that you
uttered this History of Doctor *Manwaring*, comes out in the Gazette
of the first of *May* (I know not by what sympathy) *The History and
Mystery of the Venereal* Lues, *being a more new and ample discovery of that* 30
*Disease, then yet hath been extant, with the Medicines and Methods of Cure
practised in* Italy, Spain, Germany, Holland, France, *and* England,
&c. by J. Manwaring, Doctor of Physick.

   You launch out into a Relation of the Conference too at *Worcester-
House*, betwixt the Episcopal and the Non-conformist Divines, by 35

12 Romantick *Errata*; Romanticks 73.   25 correspondence 74; cotrespondence
73.   30 *that*] this Gazette.   33 *J*] *E* Gazette.

His Majesties Commission. What is most to be taken notice of, is, that you say here and in several other places, that the Non-conformists had *nothing of Sin to object against those things from which they dissented.* I have heard to the contrary, that they did in eight,
5   if not ten several instances, but it is not my business to enumerate either for them or you. Only I admire, I confess, that upon such an occasion they could not in any one thing be gratifyed, not so much as in forbearing the Lessons of the Apocrypha. Insomuch that, as many remember very well, after a long tug at the Convocation
10 house about that matter, a good Doctor came out at last with great exultation, that *they had carried it for* Bel *and the* Dragon.

I cannot omit what it seems you thought necessary to be said in defence of your Cause, that *none are better qualifyed for State-affairs then Church men, and none have acquitted themselves with greater art and*
15 *success, and that things have rarely miscarried, but when their counsels have not been effectually follow'd (as you shall shew also in the cases of Cardinal* Granvile *and Arch-bishop* Laud.) Alas what needed you to have gone so far about, when your own Case all along, and even this your *Reproof* and this *Parallel,* are so pregnant a demonstration of their
20 abilities? And you acquit your promise, where you say, *that the wise and resolute Ministry of* Granvell *was render'd not only successless but odious to the People. For as he was a man of extraordinary wisdom, courage, and fidelity, that sincerely pursued his Masters interest, faithfully executed his commands, and kept up the height of his Authority; so being an* Im-
25 placable Divine *he saw to the bottom of the projects that were carryed on by the discontented Lords, and foresaw the tendency of Factions in Religion to Disorders and Seditions in the State.* I shall not suppose any one who reads this book to have so little convers'd with the modern History, as not to gather hence how ready you are to make good your word
30 to the Lady whom I mentioned, as to your Religion. But I have not yet heard of any Protestant, beside your self and the Recorder of *London,* who hath of late years so publickly avowed the Inquisition, of which that Cardinal *Granvell* was the chief Patron and Instrument. And instead of that honorable character you give him, I shall
35 refer you to *Grotius,* whom I chuse always to ply you with above

---

3 *which* 74; *whieh* 73.   11 exultation, 74; ~. 73.   28 convers'd 74;
covners'd 73.

all other Authors. *The Government of the Netherlands was in appearance in* Margaret, *but in effect, and as to the power, was only in* Granvell *in whom Industry, Vigilance, Ambition, Luxury, and Avarice, and all manner indeed of good and evil were remarkably visible*, &c. And therefore it is not the greatest instance of your prudence (whatsoever you thought in your *meer Conscience*) to take this publick *Liberty* of *dogmatizing*, and to pick out that Cardinal (whom I never thought of) to be the Precedent and Parallel of Arch-bishop *Lauds* administration.

I should after this do you injury, did I not take notice that whereas in your Preface to Bishop *Bramhall*, in the fifth leaf before you conclude, I told you that you spoke scandalously and with leering reflexion upon the Government and Ministers of State, you try with the best of your Skill to return it upon me. But so unfortunately, that, as always, you sink deeper and quag your self in your *Roman-Empire*, *were it possible*, say you (and I abhor to hear you) *that His Majesty should degenerate from the goodness of his nature, as much as they* say Nero *did*, and again, *these are the* Sejanus's *that you described.* It will not serve your turn, this evasion. 'Tis like mine Host in *France*, that when he swore *Jernie Dieu*, interpreted it of the *Dieu Bacchus*. You spoke not a word there of *Nero* or *Sejanus*, or that could be applyed to either; unless you can give us *Nero*'s *Coronation-Oath*, or *Sejanus* his *cases of Conscience*, or at least instance in that Emperours *being canonized for a Saint and Martyr*, so that for the Wit and Chronology of the business this too is calculated for the Play of *Moses* and *Julius Cæsar.* But for the discretion and loyalty of it, you might have long since answered, as for other passages, did either the *Rabble* or the *Statesmen* think you considerable; whereas indeed they reckon you it seems among that sort of men, who have a Priviledge to say any thing with impunity. But for the Long Parliament you have indeed an Ecclesiastical *Non obstante* to say what you will. I shall only take up at one Passage: *To deal plainly with you, I have read most of the Long Parliament Speeches over, and, though I know you will chide me for calling a whole Parliament Coxcombes, yet it is better to call them so then worse. Yet this censure I dare pass upon them, without any suspicion of arrogance within myself, that they were for the most part no*

better then School-boyes Declamations, &c. *all their discourses were much like yours, and accommodated to people that took Confidence for Reason, Nonsense for Mysteries, and Rudeness for Wit.* Ay, Mr. Bayes, *they wanted some certain helps, helps for wit, which you Man of Art have thought fit to make*
5   *use of. Ay, Sir, that's your position, and you do here aver, that no man yet the Sun ever shone upon, has parts sufficient to furnish out a Stage, except it be with the help of your Rules.* But I was misinform'd I perceive, who thought you might have call'd them all the names in the Rainbow but Coxcombes, and never heard them arraign'd of *want of Wit*, but
10 by your Abundance. But that you may not think altogether so meanly of them, (though indeed who is the man either in the former or this Age that is able to stand or appear before your profound Eloquence and piercing judgment) let me refer you, although many others might be cited, to two Speeches of the Lord *Falklands:* the
15 first concerning Episcopacy which begins, *He is a great Stranger to* Israel, *who knows not that this Kingdom hath long laboured under many and great oppressions*, &c. The second Speech was to the Lords, at the delivery of the Articles against the Lord Keeper, and begins, *These Articles against my Lord Keeper being read, I may be bold to apply*, &c.
20 And *if you think these worthy of perusal*, I shall expect your second opinion concerning the capacity and skill of those Gentlemen both in History and Oratory. But as for you, when Doctor *Heylin's* Divinity shall go for Orthodox, or his Prævarications pass for History, you may then, and not before, be reputed a Classical Author.
25 And all the *Canterbury* Tales you have told in the *Reproof* will be Chronicle. There was just such another *Italian* acquaintance of yours, one *Polydore, Virgil*, who coming into *England*, was dignifyed and distinguish'd like you, being made both a Prebend and an Arch-deacon; only you are not yet as he was come to be Collector
30 of the *Peter-pence*, but all in good time. This Gentleman did too, even as you, oblige this Nation with a piece of History, which after he had writ he used a notable invention, which if you would but imitate and burn all the Records of the times you write of, it were the only way imaginable to make you authentick.
35   As you are officious in your own Stories, so you are very inquisitive and critical upon some that I have told you; and for a great

27–8 dignifyed 74; signifyed 73.

space of your book you run out into such *Froath* and *Growns* and *Taplash* of Wit, that it deserves compassion. Insomuch that though men may perhaps believe that, as you your self affirm'd, *you are not valiant*, yet there is some reason to doubt the truth of what you say in the same place, *that you are not miserable.* But you are more par- 5 ticularly concern'd to know who that Queen was, and of what Country, that gave so ridiculous a Town Seal. For wheresoever you can suspect any thing smutty underneath, you are wonderful curious to be thorowly informed. But I have already gratifyed you in Pork, and am not bound to nauseate the Reader to comply with 10 your ignorance. I will tell you who that Tyrant was that demanded so many bushels of Fleas: It was *John Basiliwich* the great Duke of *Muscovy*, and it was of the Citizens of *Muskow* that he required it, fining them for Non-payment. But as for this Queen, it shall for certain reasons of State be a secret. Only, not to leave you wholly 15 in the dark, if you please to speak with your Fellow-Chaplain of the Copper-Mines, he will inform you, for it is in that Kingdom. And if he do not satisfie you, if you please to resort to me, I will shew you the Medal of the City with that Device upon the Reverse of it.

'Tis more then time that I left scumming you, for I perceive 'tis 20 all the same stuff: and, should I continue, I should leave you nothing in the bottom; therefore I shall only take notice of two things more very remarkable. The one is concerning the quotation out of St. *Austin*, which I speak of from *p.* 209. to *p.* 214. of my former book: *Signa quum ad res divinas pertinent Sacramenta appellantur.* You had said, 25 you would lay odds there was no such saying in S. *Austin*; and now, because your Answerer had said *sunt Sacramenta* in stead of *Sacramentæ appellantur* (which therefore you note in him as *a boldness with the Text for his own convenience, and an improvement beyond Modesty*) you think you are safe. But, good Mr. *Bayes*, whether or no doth an 30 Arch-deacon *pertinere ad res divinas?* And pray tell me what is the difference betwixt saying that you are an Arch-deacon, or you are called an Arch-deacon? But because I wonder'd you could not find it when I my self had met with it, *Ep. 5ta ad Marcellinum.* You say, *you will not laugh at me, no, for I rather deserve to be scourged for so gross* 35 *and impudent a falshood: whereas (as fortune would have it) the Fourth is*

27 *Sacramenta* 74; *Sacramentn* 73.

the last Epistle to Marcellinus *that St.* Austin *ever writ, and if you had search'd after a Fifth Epistle to him, you might have pored till the day of* Judgment. Let all ingenuous men judge this matter. I quoted it only in the order of the Epistles, where the first to *Marcellinus* is the
5 fifth Epistle. You say it should have been thus set down by me. *Ad Marcellinum: Epistola Quinta*: and that I quote it *Ep. Quinta ad Marcellinum.* I do not, but thus, *Ep.* 5ᵗᵃ *ad Marcellinum.* Mind first how falsely you have transcribed my quotation to fit it to your own turn; and then observe too upon what a frivolous and mistaken
10 ground, and about how slight a matter, you molest the Reader: for, beside what here, there runs a repetition of this matter of *Marcellinus*, and others of less consequence, through the whole *Reproof.* But, Mr. *Bayes*, this business is not yet ended thus: I will save your *poring till the day of* Judgment, and help you to a Fifth Epistle of St.
15 *Austin* too to *Marcellinus.* Take the Edition *Lugduni.* Anno 1561. and, whereas you say that (*as fortune would have it*) St. Austin *never writ but four Epistles to* Marcellinus; this is but your usual misfortune, to hamper your self worse when you would dis-intangle your own errours. For his 5th. 7th. 158th. and 159th. are his four Epi-
20 stles to *Marcellinus.* But you will find there *p.* 1080, a 222d Epistle, which is a fifth to the same person. It is noted so all along in the head of the pages, and the contents of it express before it begins: *Longa & docta est hæc Epistola, tractans de Baptismo parvulorum contra* Pelagium (Because it was against *Pelagius*, could you not or might
25 you not see it?) *quem tamen clementer in hac Epistola tractat. Hæc per examplaris vetustatem difficulter legi potuit, propter quod in aliquibus obscura est* (but not so obscure but you might have discerned it.) You say you find none of the *Non-Conformists dirty Thumb Nails in your Patrons Library.* But have not you, nor your poor *Leaf-turners* liberty
30 to peruse the Volumes? Or is there a peculiar Reverence due to the Books in that place that no man does or may touch them? Or have you lost all your credit too *apud* Jo. Shirley *in parva* Britannia, and is the *Pelican* grown hard-hearted? Could you but have reckon'd your five fingers you had not mistaken. But this proceeds from your
35 bragging of Books (so usual with you) which you have not the

patience to read over, no more then your own; or having cast your eye on the *Index* you imagine you have read the Author; for indeed here the *Index* points but at four Epistles, but the *Pollex* would have made them five.

The other passage of yours, and last which I purpose to recom- 5 mend to the Reader, is indeed accompanyed with many extra-ordinary circumstances. It is not that wherein you accuse your Answerer to have given their degrees to *Oliver* and *Ireton* at *Oxford*, though it is notoriously known that it was a Bishop yet living who performed that Ceremony. That is an untruth too slender to be 10 taken notice of in a Book so pregnant as the *Reproof*. But it is the whole hinge it seems whereupon your design of writing has turned. For upon occasion of a certain *Declaration published*, as you inform, *after the* Cheshire *insurrection*, which you affirm to have been sub-scribed by your Answerer, and which you have kept in deck until 15 this season; You pretend that you have dealt *so roundly*, as you call it, with him and the Party, and me too. Happy had it been for me that you had once understood how to speak truth. For had you not writ *so roundly*; I had never intermeddled in these matters, and so the *Reproof* too had been spared. However I have gain'd hereby 20 so much learning as to know what is the Figure of Falshood, It seems 'tis Circular, and in your phrase, to speak *roundly*; and you have stretch'd it so till it is *Unhoopable*. But I therefore shall answer you square. It is known and ready to be proved by thousands, that the Declaration mention'd was not writ by your Answerer, nor any 25 of his party; but by the Fifth-monarchy men, and its effect vented it self in that wild insurrection of *Vennor*. You your self, although you were not of so high a dispensation, yet were at that time of Age sufficient, and stirring enough in your little Sphere to have under-stood it rightly. But it is a grievous thing to forego a falshood that 30 is serviceable to the great design; and the *Ends of your publick Government will at least excuse if not hallow*, the most Orbicular un-truth. Hence it was that you were so forward to publish that book of *Baxter Baptized in Blood*. And hence now it is that, as your last reserve of Slander and Malice, as you had essayed in the *Preface to* 35

---

13 *Declaration* 74; *Deelaration* 73.   19 *roundly* 74; *ruundly* 73.   30 falshood 74; fashood 73.   32 least 74; last 73.

Bishop Bramhall, you throw this upon the body of the Non conformists, upon me too, and your Answerer. Yet neither is this Declaration so mad as that which you have penn'd, p. 64, 65, 66. of your
Reproof, in the stile and name of His Majesty, with a boldness of
5 which I think no Age can bring a Parallel. But seeing neither that
of *Baxter*, nor this attempt upon your Answerer and the Party, has
had that bad effect which probably you had proposed, I shall not
aggravate it further; but appeal to all Men, whether the world be
well used, when such railing books, grounded upon voluntary and
10 suborn'd suggestion and forgery, shall by publick License invade
mens quiet and disturb their Modesty, and stir up a tumult of writing; and yet, if any man shall but open his mouth to the contrary,
and in defence of common ingenuity, the same person that invented
or Licensed the falshood, shall have the priviledge likewise to pro-
15 hibit the Truth and the Discovery. Only, Mr. *Bayes*, forasmuch as
you do here avow that it was upon this occasion that you called for
Signal Marks, Acknowledgments, Recantations, &c. and seeing this occasion chances to be no occasion, pray learn hence forward to be
something more deliberate in your railing against the Non-confor-
20 mists. Perhaps if you would use your incomparable *Suada*, and move
them to Repentance in a Theological and Christian Language, they
might be prevailed with. For truly it do's befit all that have been
accessory to the late mischiefs and crimes, to walk with great innocence and modesty, though after the State has set them right, the
25 Church cannot of right, as you would have it, demand another
Allegiance. But to think, that Railing will do the work, or for men
to hear themselves called *Traytors, Villains, Schismaticks, Hereticks*, and
to have all mankind preach'd and harangu'd up to extirpate them,
for meer Non-conformity; and this by such a person as you (which
30 makes their suffering more infamous and odious to them) and for
you to perswade them that all this is wholsome for them and the
good of their Souls, and that therefore they should recant in your
hands, it is just as if *Rabshakeh* should pretend, when he threatned
the men of *Jerusalem* they should drink their own Piss, that he pre-
35 scribed them a remedy for the Scurvy. Pray do but try a little, Mr.
Bayes, for experiment how you your self could away with this Re-

27 *Schismaticks* 74; *Scismaticks* 73.

canting; if you were to disgorge all you had swallowed, and swallow all you had disgorged, it would make you I trow look very simply, and cast you into a Fit worse then of the *Miserere* or the Iliack Passion. Were you to recant all your false Doctrines, all your Profanations of Scripture, all your *Bear-Garden* and *Billingsgate* Railing 5 and Scolding; Nay, were you to recant (and in good Conscience you ought to refund) for your estate got by Plunder, and Sequestration and High-Court of Justice. Were you to recant for all the Circles, Semicircles, Complements, and Segments in the *Reproof*; Were you but to refund to your Book-seller, for all those books that you were 10 fain to give away to disperse them, and for that mutual *Gratification*, which you were not asham'd, notwithstanding all your Dignities, to pillage him of before he could pay his Printer: I doubt the least of these would come off with an ill grace, and 'twould go very hard and aukwardly with you. But, because this may be too severe, you 15 have here solemnly *protested that if your Answerer can convict you of any one Forgery, it shall not suffice to ask him forgiveness upon your knees, but you will make him a publick Recantation.* This thing of the Declaration, that it was subscribed by your Answerer, is a notorious and convict Forgery. Therefore do but now go to him, and kneel down on 20 your knees, and ask his blessing, & make but a private Recantation, and I will say you are so far an Honest man.

And now being so near a period I cannot but gratulate my good fortune, rather then my wisdom, that I have travelled such an Author through with no more extravagancy. 'Tis some kind of 25 deliverance to have found my way so well when I was to follow an *Ignis Fatuus*. Had he thought fit to make use of my admonition, there had been no occasion for this intercourse. But seeing he has chosen it, I hope there are few persons of Candor who need strain their invention to supply my excuse; it being more easie to justifie 30 to others, then to delight my self with this kind of writing. And among the most Eminent, I hope my Lord Arch-bishop will not (if this be the man I take him for) misinterpret me. But that as he was once pleased to *thank me, and acknowledge that I had done good service to the Church* in detecting to him another Doctor so effectually, that he 35

voluntarily subscribed never to come more within any Pulpit, although he is since *punished* with a Living of Three hundred pounds a year: so now his Grace will not take it ill that I have also discovered this man to him, the Tenure of whose Divinity is per
5 *Saltum, Sufflum, & Pettum*; and whose Purse and Conscience, being link'd with the same Tyes, do make together the perfect Character of an, *&c.*

What remains, Mr. *Bayes*, is to serve in your *Bacon*, but because I would do it to the best advantage, I shall add something else for
10 your better and more easie digestion. The first shall be your *Amminus Marcel.* whom if you had, as I advised you, bit off at both ends, he could not probably have molested you. But in the 27*th* book, having described the contention of *Damasus* and *Ursinus* for Ecclesiastical preeminence, he adds; *These kind of men ought indeed to be most*
15 *sharply reprehended, who, having obtained what they covet, are secure to be inriched with the offerings of the Ladies, and rowle about in Coaches, curiously drest up, and eat more delicately then Princes; whereas they might be truly happy, if neglecting the Grandeur and Ostentation of the City; which they make an excuse for their Vices, they would imitate, in their manner of*
20 *living, such Country Prelates, who eating and drinking moderately, cloathing themselves homely, and looking humbly, recommend themselves thereby to the everlasting Deity, and those that truly worship him, as modest and pure persons.* Again, in his 21. book, giving the Character of *Constantius,* among other things he saith that, *He did confound the Christian Reli-*
25 *gion, which is a perfect and plain thing,* Rem absolutam & simplicem, *with a Grannamish and doating Superstition, and instead of composing with gravity the perplexed questions which he excited, he promoted them further with a strife of words; so that the Prelates, trooping it up and down on the publick Post-horses, and canterburing from Synod, as they call it, to Synod,*
30 *whilest they indeavour to draw all Rites within their jurisdiction, there were scarce any Horses left to supply Travellers.* If this be for your service pray make use of it.

But lest you should say hereupon that your *Ammianus* was a *Socinian,* will you admit King *James* his judgment, who, after nineteen
35 teen years experience, tells the Parliament, *That the external Govern-*

13 *Damasus* Ammianus, 74; *Damascus* 73.   *Ursinus* Ammianus; *Ursicinus* 73, 74.
21 *themselves thereby* 74; *thcmselves thereby* 73.   34 *Socinian* 74; *Soeinian* 73.

ment appear'd well, Learned Judges, setled Peace, great Plenty, so that it was to be thought every man might have sat in safety under his own Vine and Fig tree; yet he was ashamed, and it made his hair to stand upright to consider, how his People have in this time been vexed and poll'd by the vile execution of Projects, Patents, Bills of Conformity, and such like; which, 5 *beside the trouble of his People, have more exhausted their Purses then Subsidies would have done.* You see that a *Bill of Conformity* (though it made not, in the phrase of your *Preface, an Archangel stare, yet it*) made a Kings hair stand an end.

But lest you should say King *James* was an *Arminian,* I shall now 10 bring in my Lord *Verulam,* whom you cannot refuse, having so often call'd for him. And I the rather quote him because a wise man is as it were eternal upon earth; and he speaks so judiciously and impartially, that it seems as if these very times which we now live in had been in his present prospect. There are two short Treatises of 15 these matters, one begins p. 129. the other p. 180. of his *Resuscitatio.* Pray, Mr. *Bayes,* let us both listen, for I assure you, before he has done, he will tell us many a wiser thing then is to be met with either in *Ecclesiastical Politie* or *Rehearsal.* 'The Controversies themselves (saith he) I will not enter into, as judging that the Disease 20 requires rather Rest then any other Cure. Neither are they concerning the great parts of the Worship of God, of which it is true; *Non servatur Unitas in Credendo nisi eadem sit in Colendo.* Not as betwixt the East and West Church, about Images, or between us and the Church of *Rome* about the Adoration of the Sacrament, *&c.* but we 25 contend about ceremonies, and things indifferent, about the extern Policy and Government of the Church. And as to these we ought to remember that the ancient and true Bounds of Unity are, one Faith, one Baptism, and not one Ceremony or Policy. *Differentiæ Rituum commendant Unitatem Doctrinæ.* The diversities of Cerimonies 30 do set forth the Unity of Doctrine, and *habet Religio quæ sunt Æternitatis, habet quæ sunt Temporis,* Religion hath parts which belong to Eternity, and parts which pertain to time. If we did but know the virtue of Silence and Slowness to speak, commended by St. *James,* and would leave the overweaning and turbulent humors of these 35 times, and revive the blessed proceeding of the Apostles and Primitive

10 *Arminian* 74B³⁻⁴; *Arnunian* 73; *Armenian* 74B¹⁻².   34 St. 74; St, 73.

Fathers, which was in the like cases, not to enter into Assertions and Positions, but to deliver Counsells and Advices we should need no other remedy at all. *Brother, there is Reverence due to your Counsel, but Faith is not due to your Affirmation.* St. *Paul* was content to say, *I and not the Lord,* but now men lightly say, *not I but the Lord,* nay and bind it with an heavy denunciation of his judgments to terrifie the simple, whereas saith that wise man, *the causless Curse shall not come.* The Remedies are first that there were an end made of this immodest and deformed manner of writing lately entertained, whereby matter of Religion is handled in the stile of the Stage. But to leave all reverence and religious compassion toward evils, or indignation toward faults, and to turn Religion into a Comedy or Satyre, to search and rip up wounds with a laughing Countenance, to intermix Scripture and Scurrility sometimes in one Sentence is a thing far from the devout reverence of a Christian, and scant beseeming the honest regard of a sober man. Two principal causes have I ever known of Atheism; Curious Controversie, and profane Scoffing. Now that these two are joyned in one, no doubt that Sect will make no small progression. *Job,* speaking of the Majesty and Gravity of a Judge, saith, *If I did smile they believed it not:* that is, if I glanced upon conceit of mirth, yet mens minds were so possessed with the Reverence of the Action in hand, as they could not receive it. Much more ought not this to be among Bishops and Divines, disputing about Holy things. Truly as I marvel that some of those Preachers which call for Reformation (whom I am far from wronging so far as to joyn them with these scoffers) do not publish some declaration, in dislike that their cause should be thus sollicited; so I hope assuredly that my Lords of the Clergy have no intelligence with this inter-libelling, but do altogether disallow that their Cause should be thus defended. For though I observe in one of them many glosses, whereby the Man would insinuate himself into their favours; yet I find it to be ordinary that many pressing and fawning persons do misconjecture of the humour of Men in Authority, and many times seek to gratifie them with that which they most dislike. Nevertheless, I note that there is not an indif-

9–10 entertained 74; enrertained 73.   20 Judge, 74; ~. 73.   35 Nevertheless 74; Neverrheless 73.

ferent hand carried to these Pamphlets as they deserve. For the one sort fly in the dark, and the other is uttered openly. Next I find certain indiscreet and dangerous amplifications as if the Civil Government,' &c. For it is impossible to omit any thing in those excellent discourses, without apparent injury to their Author, and to the Reader. And that which makes them more pertinent is, that he does not spare neither the Non-conformists but gives them too their just charge; for neither then certainly, nor now, are they to be excused: though the unequal dealing used towards them doth justifie them the more, and hath not allowed place or leisure in this Book for me to particularize their failings.

But least you should except against my Lord *Bacon*, as a Lay man, *not competent to judge of these Ecclesiastical matters in comparison with the Clergy, and who was but, as far as the prejudice of the Age he lived in would permit him, an acute Philosopher*; what say you to Doctor *Stillingfleet* in the Preface to his *Irenicon* from beginning to end? And in the Book it self from *p.* 117. to 123? I have made scruple to disguise the discourses of him and others, as some practise, to make them pass for mine own: and to quote them at length were unnecessary, being so easily found in the Author. But here in few pages you may find all that you have said with so many years labour, totally ruined.

But least you should reject Dr. *Stillingfleet*, as a Papist, may Bishop *Usher*, Dr. *Hammond*, Bishop *Taylor*, *Chillingworth* be allow'd of? I have them all ready at hand for you. But they are all I doubt *suspectæ Fidei*, and you will believe none but your self. This is that which hath seduced you, and, because you preach'd over your notes of *Ecclesiastical Politie* in a private Congregation, without being interrupted, you imagined the whole world had been of that mind, and 'twould pass for œcumenical Doctrine; Whereas I despair not of seeing yet by Gods goodness and the influence of his Majesty, upon the prudence and moderation of my Lords the Bishops, that if you still persist in your mischievous undertaking, you shall be but *Simon Magus* his sickle, to mow the whole field without any hand to manage it. It was in the latter end of Queen *Elizabeth*, after the long experiment of her Reign, that my Lord *Verulam* writ his first

---

5 their] the 74.   16 *Irenicon* 74; *Irenieon* 73.   18 others] other 74.
19 were 74; wete 73.

discourse I quoted, and his second at the coming in of King *James*, as Dr. *Stillingfleet* his at the restauration of His Majesty now reigning. But still at the beginning of the Reigns of our Princes, the proper seasons of redressing these Ecclesiastical matters, & of taking firm measures for their future government, some rub has been interposed unhappily that has thrown all of the Bias and so lost the Cast. Who is there that ever reads the Scriptures, unless he put on Ecclesiastical Spectacles, (and those too have a *Fly* ingraven upon them) but sees plainly what tenderness is due unto the scruples of Christians; that our Saviour hath taken Conscience into his immediate protection, and how conformable the Apostles were to his rule therein, both as to Doctrine and Practice? What *English*-man, reflecting seriously, but must think it hard that a man may be a Christian in *Turky* upon better conditions? that the *French*, *Dutch*, and the *Walloons*, even at *Canterbury*, may serve God here more freely then our own Natives? that it shall be a Priviledge among us to be an Alien, while an home-born Subject must pay the Double-duty (nay forfeit his whole estate) for the Protestant Religion? What Christian can conceive how a man should lose his right to the Sacraments for dissenting from the Ceremonies? I think I objected that to you once, but you have never deigned, as far as I can observe, once to answer it. But who especially that as a wise man weighs, what it is to impose things unnecessary upon people obedient to all other Laws, can advise the continuance of such Counsels? For a Prince to adventure all upon it, is like Duke *Charles* of *Burgundy*, that fought three Battels for an Imposition upon Sheep-skins. For a Clergy-man to offer at persecution upon this Ceremonial account, is (as is related of one of the Popes) to justifie his indignation for his Peacock, by the example of Gods anger for eating the forbidden fruit. But in you, Mr. *Bayes*, who are I know not well what, I look upon it as an effect of your madness, and only the *staring of an Arch-deacon*

You say, *that most wise men were of opinion you should not answer me, only desire the world to compare it with your discourses: yet others,* ('tis uncivilly said both as to your self and them) overpowr'd *you to this*

---

2 *Stillingfleet* his 74B³⁻⁴; *Stillingfleets* 73, 74B¹⁻². 3 still at 74B³⁻⁴; still is at 73, 74B¹⁻². 9 sees] set's 74. 21 deigned 74B³⁻⁴; designed 73, 74B¹⁻².

Reply, against the bent of your own inclinations. What *others* was it? Was the Devil in you? Or were there *certain tyes upon you,* as *Bayes* saith, *that you could not be disingaged from? and you writ for the sake of some ingenious persons and choice female Spirits, that have a value for you? otherwise you would see 'm all hang'd before you would ever more set Pen to Paper.* 5 If I might advise you, Mr. *Bayes,* do so no more: for *I verily believe you have writ a whole Cart-load of things, every whit as good as this, and yet the insolent Rascalls turn them all back upon your hands again.* But do as you please, I have not paid you the Tythe of what I owe you, but it lyes ready for you, when you please to send for it. You are a 10 Blatant Writer and a Latrant; and for lesser crimes, though of the same nature, was *Gnevoski,* the *Polander,* sentenc'd to lye barking underneath the Table. You put me in mind of the *Hollanders* in *Batavia,* who, having spent their other Ammunition, charged with Excrements; the purity of the Savage *Javaes* could not abide it, but 15 thereupon yielded them the Victory: neither does it become me to contend for it.

I will conclude in a short story, and more seasonable, because as your *Reproof,* it happen'd once at a Wedding. *Et vous avez passé Monsieur par la Baviere. Wenceslaus* the Emperour, Married the Duke of 20 *Bavaria*'s Daughter; the Duke, knowing the Emperours delights, brought along with him a Cart full of Jugling Conjurers, who playing their tricks, *Zytho* that was *Wenceslaus* his Magician, *accedens propius artificem* Bavarum *cum omni apparatu protinus devorat (ore ad aures dehiscente) calceos duntaxat, quia luto obsiti videbantur, expuens: secessumque* 25 *inde petens, ventrem insolita esca gravem in solium aqua plenum exonerat, Præstigiatoremque adhuc madidum Spectatoribus restituit, passim deridendum, adeo ut cæteri quoque ejus Socii a ludo abstinerent.* Whether I shall have the like success I know not (for truly our sport is much like it, and unfit for serious Spectators.) However I have spit out your dirty 30 Shoon.

THE END.

1 *own om.* 74.   8 *back om.* 74.   19–20 *Et . . . Baviere* 74; *om.* 73.
24 *ore ad*] ore usque ad Del Rio.   25 *calceos duntaxat*] solos duntaxat calceos
Del Rio.   28 *abstinerent*] desisterent Del Rio.   30 Spectators] Spectator
74B¹⁻².

NOTES

ACCORDING to the standards of the age, Marvell was scholarly in his quotation. He gives a page reference in most cases, and although he often paraphrases, he does not often distort. I have not indicated omissions, although misreadings are noted in the textual *apparatus*.

PART I

P. 3. 1. *The Author*] Samuel Parker.

4–7. *But if . . . Farewell*] Parker, *Defence*, 1671, 'Preface', A8ʳ.

8. *Dilemma*] *Defence*, p. 196.

21–2. *Chi . . . sapone*] Parker, *Discourse*, 1670, 'Preface', p. xii.

24–6. *S'il . . . offendi*] Spoken by Amarilli in Guarini, *Il Pastor Fido* (1590), III. iv. 19–24.

P. 4. 8–12. *The ensuing . . . Affairs*] Parker, *Preface*, 1672, A2ʳ.

9. *Bishop* Bramhall] John Bramhall (1594–1663), Archbishop of Armagh, Chaplain to Strafford in Ireland in 1633, bishop of Derry 1634. Presbyterians called him 'Bishop Bramble'. Parker's *Preface* was attached to his *Vindication of himself . . . from the Presbyterian Charge of Popery* (1672).

13. *Coif*] A close fitting cap covering the top, back and sides of the head.

13. *Bulls-head*] False frizzled hair, formerly much worn by women.

25. *none . . . Press*] Parker, *Preface*, A2ʳ.

P. 5. 3. *Imprimatur*] The formula ('Let it be printed') signed by an official licenser of the press, authorizing the printing of a book.

5–7. *fine . . . Conventicles*] 'A little before Dr. *Manton's* Meeting also was surprized, and he having notice of it before, was absent, and got Mr. *Bedford* to preach for him . . . he was fined according to the Act in 20 l. (and the place 40 l.) . . .' Baxter, *Reliquiae Baxterianae*, ed. Sylvester, 1696, Pt. III, p. 156. Conventicles—the meetings of dissenters for religious worship—had been forbidden by the Conventicles Act of 1664.

10. *sweaty Preaching*] Parker, *Defence*, p. 188.

15. *B.*] Sir John Birkenhead (1616–79), pamphleteer and satirist, authorized after the Restoration to search out unlicensed printers: *C.S.P.D.* 6 Jan. 1622, p. 237.

15. *L.*] Sir Roger L'Estrange (1616–1704), Tory journalist and from 1662 Surveyor of the Press; closely connected with the printing of *The Rehearsal Transpros'd*.

21. *Cadmus . . . Teeth*] 'I know they are as lively and as vigorously productive, [books] as those fabulous Dragons Teeth; and being sown up and down,

may chance to spring up armed men.' Milton, *Areopagitica*, in *Works*, 1697, p. 374.

   26. *bulky* Dutchman] Laurens Koster (*c.* 1370–1440), a Dutch printer, recognized as one of the inventors of the art.

   27–8. *Syntagmes*] Systematically arranged treatises.

   33–5. *as much . . . Affairs*] Parker, *Preface*, A2ʳ.

   33. De Wit] John De Wit (1625–72), Grand pensionary of Holland, Leader of the Republican party against the princes of the House of Orange. On 19 Aug. 1672, he and his brother Cornelius were murdered by the mob at the Hague.

P. 6. 3. J.O.] John Owen (1616–83), Leader of the Independents, Vice-Chancellor of the University of Oxford 1652–8, and prolific theological controversialist. In 1669, he answered Parker's *Discourse of Ecclesiastical Politie*, with *Truth and Innocence Vindicated*. Marvell mentions him many times and he seems to have read the proofs for *The Rehearsal Transpros'd*: see H.M.C., *Report on the MSS of A. G. Finch*, vol. ii, 1922, p. 10.

   11. Malmsbury] The town of Thomas Hobbes's birth. Parker's views on the necessity of 'absolute obedience' are not unlike those of Hobbes.

   19–21. *could not . . . Bookseller*] Parker, *Preface*, A2ʳ.

   25. *was . . . Courteous?*] cf. Virgil, *Eclogues*, viii. 49–50.

   26. Pink] The flower or finest example of excellence. See *Romeo and Juliet*, II. iv. 61.

   28–33. *hath brought . . . contrivance*] Parker, *Preface*, A2ʳ.

   35. *A.C.*] Andrew Clark, a printer in London in Aldersgate St., 1670–78.

P. 7. 1. *James Collins*] A bookseller in London whose shop was at the King's Head, Westminster Hall. For both these men, see H. R. Plomer, *A Dictionary of Booksellers and Printers, 1641–1667* (1907) and *1668–1725* (1922).

   6–8. *one of the . . . Throat*] Marvell may have been thinking of Tarquinus Priscus who died of a fish bone in the throat (Joannis Schenckii, *Observationum Medicarum Rariorum*, Lugduni, 1644, p. 202) or perhaps the death of the poet and gourmet Philoxenus who died as a result of eating a polyp a yard long (Atheneus, *Diepnosophistae*, viii, 341).

   8–9. *Put . . . Marquess*] 'Put up thy wife's trumpery, good noble Marquis', 'The Session of Poets', l. 90, *Poems on Affairs of State, 1660–1678*, ed. Lord (Yale 1963), p. 333. The Marquess is William Cavendish, Duke of Newcastle, who is represented as drawing the works of his wife (see below, p. 22 n.) from his posterior.

   19–20. *which way . . . thoughts*] Parker, *Preface*, A2ᵛ.

   20. Bayes] The main character of Buckingham's farce *The Rehearsal* (1672). Dryden, Sir Robert Howard, and Sir William Davenant were all supposedly satirized in this ridiculous figure.

   20–1. *The Intrigo . . . head*] George Villiers, Duke of Buckingham, *The Rehearsal*, 1672, I. i, p. 3.

21. *you'l . . . see't*] George Villiers, Duke of Buckingham, *The Rehearsal*, 1672, I. i, p. 6.

22–3. *could not . . . Love*] Ibid. I. i, p. 5.

24–5. *neither . . . foretel*] Parker, *Preface*, A2ᵛ.

31. *Volscius*] A character in *The Rehearsal*, III. ii, pp. 25 ff.

33. Parthenope . . . *Wall*] Ibid. p. 29.

35. *to head . . . Knightsbridge*] Ibid. p. 28.

P. 8. 1–3. *Go on . . . none.*] Ibid. p. 30.

6–9. *For as . . . neither*] Ibid. p. 30.

12–13. *his Majesties . . .*] 15 March 1672.

17–18. *the Season . . . undone*] Marvell is echoing Sir William Davenant's *Gondibert*, 1651, i. 2, 42.

> His Rivals that his fury us'd to fear
> For his lov'd Female, now his faintness Shunne;
> But were his season hot, and she but neer,
> (O mighty Love!) his Hunters were undone.

19. *Ephemerides*] A book of prognostications. Marvell seems to be jeering at *Gondibert*. The court wits also made fun of Davenant's epic, see *Certain Verses written by several of the Authors Friends; To be reprinted with the Second Edition of Gondibert*, 1653.

19–26. *heads . . . J.O.*] Parker, *Preface*, A2ᵛ.

21. Sidrophel] William Lilly (1602–81), a notorious astrologer. From 1644 to his death, he prepared an almanack each year. He appears as Sidrophel in Samuel Butler's *Hudibras*, Part II, Canto III. ll. 105 ff.

34–1 [P. 9]. *he had . . . Book*] Owen, *Truth and Innocence Vindicated*, p. 4.

P. 9. 7. Crooper] Crupper, the leather strap buckled to the back of the saddle and passing under the horse's tail.

8. *Push-Pin*] a child's game in which each player pushes or fillips his pin with the object of crossing that of the other player, hence a 'trivial occupation'. See Thomas Middleton, *The Changeling*, II. ii. 195.

9. *Procatarctical*] The immediate cause of any effect. *O.E.D.* cites Barlow's *Defence*, p. 92. 'The procatarcticall, or first mooving cause'.

P. 10. 4. *Roscius*] Quintus Roscius (*c.* 134–*c.* 62 B.C.) a Roman comedian who enjoyed the friendship of Cicero, who defended him in a lawsuit.

5. *Lacy's*] John Lacy (d. 1681) dramatist and comedian. A universal favourite as a comic actor in Charles II's reign, he was an enormous success as *Bayes* in *The Rehearsal*. Marvell may have been thinking here of a passage in John Humphry's *Case of Conscience*, 1669, where he cites a small boy as saying of *The Ecclesiastical Politie*: 'Lacy *hath confuted this Book; for he acting the Tyrant said in the Play, that Conscience was a greater King than he.*' (p. 9).

8. *tuant*] trenchant, cutting, or biting. Used in *The Rehearsal*, IV. i. p. 36.

8. Irrefragable Doctor] Alexander of Hales (d. 1245) the celebrated medieval theologian, styled *Doctor Irrefragabilis*.

P. 11. 1. jump] 'agree' or 'coincide' seems to be the meaning. See *O.E.D.*; cf. Butler, *Hudibras*, 1. iii. 1239–40:

> For all men live and judge amiss
> Whose talents jump not just with his.

10–11. *he was . . . Philosopher*] Parker, *Preface*, A3ʳ.

19. *Cyrus*] Monsieur de Scudèry, *Artamenes, or The Grand Cyrus*, englished by F.G., 1653.

19. *Cassandra*] Costes de Calprenède, *Cassandra, The Famed Romance*, 1652.

20. *Knight of the Sun*] Ortunez de Calahorra, *The First Part of the Mirrour of Princely deedes and knighthood. Wherein is shewed the Knight of the Sunne, and his brother Rosicleer*, trans., M. Tyler, [1579].

21. *King Arthur*] Caxton's edition of Sir Thomas Malory's *Morte Darthur* came out in 1485.

23–5. *Being . . . Designs*] Parker, *Preface*, A3ʳ.

26. Bishop of *Cullen*] Henry Maximilian (1621–88) Archbishop and Elector of Cologne.

27. Bishop of *Strasburg*] Franz Egon Fürstenberg (1625–82). Both men were aggressive supporters of Louis XIV; together with the Bishop of Munster they are frequently mentioned in the *London Gazettes* of 1672, see, for example, *London Gazette*, no. 665, 1–4 April 1672.

27–8. *He finished . . . undertook*] Parker, *Preface*, A3ᵛ.

28–9. Bishop of *Munster*] Christoph Bernard von Galen (1606–78), a warlike prelate who aided Charles II against the Dutch in 1665, and in 1672 was fighting for Louis XIV. He took numerous towns before laying siege to Groningen. He raised the siege on 27 Aug. (*London Gazette*, no. 707, 26–9 Aug.).

29–31. *As he . . . Bravery*] Parker, *Preface*, A3ᵛ.

34. *were both . . . Presbyterians*] Parker, *Preface*, A4ʳ.

34. *Toryes*] Dispossessed Irish outlaws; applied to any Irish papist or royalist in arms.

P. 12. 4–7. *Down by . . . Lice*] According to a manuscript note in Aubrey's copy of *The Rehearsal Transpros'd* in Bodley (Ashm. 1591) these lines are from John Ogilby's *Character of a Trooper*, a work written by him when he was in Ireland with Bramhall and Wentworth. Mentioned by Aubrey, *Brief Lives*, ed. Clark, vol. ii, 1898, p. 101 and Wood, *Athenae Oxonienses*, ed. Bliss, vol. iii, 1817, col. 741. I have been unable to trace a copy.

8–12. *'Tis true . . . extent*] Parker, *Preface*, A3ᵛ.

13. Pendets] *A pendet Brahmin* is a learned Hindu versed in Sanskrit.

13. History of the *Mogol*] François Bernier, *A Continuation of the Memories of Monsieur Bernier concerning the Empire of the Great Mogol*, Tomes III and IV, englished . . . by H.O., 1672. See p. 46 for the passage quoted.

14. *Dancehment Kan*] 'One of the most considerable *Omrahs* or Lords of that Court.'

33. Legend of Captain *Jones*] David Lloyd, *The Legend of Captain Jones*, 1648.

P. 13. 2-3. Legend of sixty-six . . . *Patricii*] Jocelyn, *Vita S. Patricii in Florilegium Insulae Sanctorum sev Vitae et Acta Sanctorum Hiberniae*, ed. T. Messingham, Paris, 1624, cap. clxxxvi, p. 81. Saint Patrick (373–463), the saint and bishop who brought Christianity to Ireland.

3-4. Ingenious Writer] Simon Patrick (1626–1707), Bishop of Ely, author of *A Friendly Debate between a Conformist and a Nonconformist*, 1669.

6. *Secundinus*] (*c.* 373–448) Bishop of Armagh, one of St. Patrick's chief assistants, he wrote a descriptive poem on the saint: 'Hymnus s. Secundini in laudem S. Patricii'. The story Marvell relates is from Jocelyn, *Vita S. Patricii*, cap. clxxvii, p. 77.

26. *Odo* Bishop of *Baieux*] Earl of Kent, half brother of William the Conqueror. Noted for his prowess in battle where he fought with a mace instead of a sword (d. 1097).

31. Earl of *Strafford*] Thomas Wentworth (1593–1641), Lord Deputy of Ireland. When Charles I became embroiled with the Scots, Strafford assured him 'You have an army here in Ireland you may employ to reduce this kingdom'. This was interpreted as meaning that he proposed the invasion of England by the Irish Army. As a result he was impeached and executed in 1641.

P. 14. 1. Bishop *Usher*] James Ussher (1581–1656), Archbishop of Armagh. His *Britanicarum Ecclesiarum Antiquitates . . . inserta est . . . a Pelagio . . . inductae Haereseos Historia* was published in Dublin in 1639.

6. *Pelagius*] The British theologian of the fifth century, author of the Pelagian heresy.

7. *Grubstreet*] The name of a street near Moorfields in London (now Milton St.) 'much inhabited by writers of small histories, dictionaries and temporary poems' (Johnson). Therefore, 'pertaining to the nature of literary hack work'.

9. *White Aprons*] Parker, *Preface*, a4^r.

9. *judicious Tankard-bearers*] Ibid., A7^v.

15. Irish Rebellion] on Sat. 23 Oct. 1641, a rebellion against English rule broke out all over Ulster. The leader of the insurgents was Owen Roe O'Neill.

16. *Publick . . . Abilities*] Parker, *Preface*, A3^r.

22. *Catholic . . . Christendom*] Ibid. A4^v.

23-4. *so vain . . . dayes*] Ibid. A4^v.

25. *Bishop . . . undertook*] Ibid. A3^v.

P. 15. 27. *Alexander's* Architect] Deinocrates, who proposed to fashion Mt. Athos (the 'Holy Mountain' terminating the most eastern of Macedonia's three peninsulas) into Alexander's likeness, representing him as pouring a libation from a kind of ewer into a broad bowl. Strabo, *Geography*, 14. 1. 23.

33. *Colossian*] Colossal, gigantic, of a vast size, *O.E.D.* Although St. Paul wrote his epistle to the *Colossians*, warning them against vain speculation (ii.

NOTES 333

8) and foolish ceremonies (ii. 16) Marvell does not seem to be referring to these people.

P. 16. 5. *Istmos of Peloponnesus*] The idea of cutting through the Isthmus of Corinth occurred to Periander (Diogenes Laërtes, i. 99), Julius Caesar (Suetonius, *Caesar*, 44) and Nero, among others. Only Nero commenced the project, to abandon it shortly after. (Suetonius, *Nero*, 19.)

6. *Red-Sea . . . Mediterranean*] The first attempt is credited to 'Sesostris' (Rameses ii. *fl.* 1333 B.C.): Strabo, *Geography*, 1. 2. 31. For the history of attempts see J. Charles-Roux, *L'Isthme et le canal de Suez*, 2 vols., Paris, 1901.

15. rebating] blunting, making dull, *O.E.D.*

26. *Austin*] St. Augustine (d. 604), first Archbishop of Canterbury. He wished to unite the Church he had already established in Kent with that in the West of England. At the meeting in 603 at Aust on the Severn, he refused to rise at the approach of the Bishops from Bangor. See Bede, *Historia Ecclesiastica*, II. ii.

P. 17. 25–6. *manage . . . extent*] Parker, *Preface*, A6ʳ.

27. p. 57] i.e. Bramhall, *Vindication*, p. 57.

33. *Garter*] The highest order of English knighthood.

33. *Clarencieux*] An English dukedom: the second King of Arms in England.

P. 18. 1. Commissioners of *Scotland*] See Marvell's letters to the Hull Corporation, 26 Feb. 1669/70, and to William Popple, 21 March 1670, *Poems and 'Letters'*, ed. Margoliouth, vol. ii.

24. Conference of *Worcester-House*] In the Summer and Fall of 1660 the Presbyterians requested the King to suspend proceedings upon the Act of Uniformity against Non-conformists to the Liturgy and ceremonies, until an agreement had been established. The King had a declaration on ecclesiastical matters drawn up, and together with several lords and bishops met Baxter and Calamy and other Presbyterian representatives at Chancellor Clarendon's lodgings in Worcester House on 23 Oct. 1660. Neal, *History of the Puritans*, vol. iv, 1822, pp. 259 ff.

30–1. *a zealous . . . Church*] Parker, *Preface*, A6ʳ.

34–5. Justice of Peace . . . Statue] Cf. Montaigne, *Essays*, trans. E. J. Trechman, vol. ii, 1927, p. 495.

35–6. *expunging . . . Cause*] Parker, *Preface*, A6ʳ.

P. 19. 1. *Arminian*] The doctrines of Jacob Arminius (1560–1609), a Dutch theologian. He opposed strict Calvinism, especially the decree of absolute reprobation and predestination. At this time Arminian views had gained considerable acceptance in the Church of England. In Holland Arminians were known as 'Remonstrants' and held republican opinions.

11–13. *if they . . . Security*] Bramhall here refers to the 'reading of Homilies': 'Or if it come short of Preaching . . .'

15–19. *maintains . . . people*] Bramhall, *Vindication*, pp. 155–7.

P. 20. 4. *Grotius*] Hugo Grotius (De Groot) (1583–1645), renowned Dutch scholar. He was a 'Remonstrant' who gradually moved toward the Catholic position.

7–8. *De Groot . . . Mombas*] '. . . the Pentionary *de Witt*, together with his brother *Ruwaert van Putten*, have by the Prince of Orange's orders been made prisoners; Monsieur *de Groot*, who else might have fallen into the same misfortune, being better forewarned, is privately retired with his whole family to Antwerp, where he hath had the trouble to hear that his Brother in law, Monsieur de Mombas is in great danger of losing his Head for his evil practises against the State.' *London Gazette*, no. 698, 25–9 July 1672; also *C.S.P.D.*, 20 July 1672.

P. 21. 9–10. *prefers . . . together*] *The Rehearsal*, IV. i. p. 35.

13. Draw-Can-Sir] '. . . a fierce *Hero*, that frights his Mistriss, snubs up Kings, baffles Armies, and does what he will, without regard to good manners, justice or numbers.' Ibid. IV. i. p. 34.

19. Simarre] *Cymar*: a loose robe or undergarment for women—also a bishop's gown.

23. Fifth Council] Protestants generally gave full acceptance to only four oecumenical synods: Nicaea I (A.D. 325); Constantinople (A.D. 381); Ephesus (A.D. 431) and Chalcedon (A.D. 451).

P. 22. 4. those two] *Sergius* and *Abdallah*: 'A Nestorian monk of Constantinople and a paynime Jew' Purchas, *Purchas his Pilgrimage*, 1613, p. 200.

9. *Huddibras*] Samuel Butler (1612–80) whose burlesque epic *Hudibras* satirizing the fanaticks appeared in three parts: 1663, 1664, 1678.

24. Modern Lady . . . *Latin*] In 1667, James Bristow of Corpus Christi, Oxford (1646?–67) '. . . began to translate into Latine some of the Philosophy of *Margaret* Dutchess of *NewCastle*, upon the desire of those whom she had appointed to enquire out a fit person for such a matter, but he finding great difficulties therein, through the confusedness of the subject, gave over, as being a matter not to be well performed by any'. Wood, *Athenae Oxonienses*, vol. ii, 1692, col. 835. Only the Duchess's life of her husband, William Cavendish (1667) was finally translated into Latin.

31–3. Complement . . . *Ecclesiæ*] Howell relates a similar story: '. . . I was told a Tale, that *Arminius* meeting *Baudius* one day disguis'd with Drink (wherewith he would be often) he told him, *Tu Baudi dedecoras nostram Academiam; et tu Armini nostram Religionem*: Thou Baudius disgracest our University, and thou *Arminius* our Religion.' James Howell, *Familiar Letters*, ed. Jacobs, 1890, p. 32. Dominick Baudius (1516–1613) was a Flemish scholar and poet.

35–6. they carry . . . *Imprimatur*] As chaplain to Gilbert Sheldon, Archbishop of Canterbury, Parker was empowered to license theological works.

36. *Mr. L.*] Sir Roger L'Estrange, see above, p. 5 n.

NOTES

P. 23. 26. Comet] Wood notes a comet, 16 Dec. 1664: 'In the next year followed a great plague in England . . .' A. Wood, *Life and Times*, ed. Clarke, vol. ii, 1892, p. 24.

33. Mr *Calvin*] Jean Calvin (1509–64), the Protestant reformer and theologian.

P. 24. 12. pag. 663] Actually pp. 662–3, Parker, *Defence.*

19. *Dodona's Grove*] A locality of ancient Greece near Epirus famed for its oracle, a seat of Zeus. James Howell had also written: *Dodona's Grove, or the Vocall Forest,* 1640.

24. Bp *Bramble*] Bishop Bramhall, see above, p. 4 n.

28–9. smiling . . . altered] Cf. Montaigne, *Essays,* trans. Trechman, vol. ii, p. 125.

32. Mistris *Mopsa*] See Philip Sidney's *Arcadia* (1590).

P. 25. 3. South-side] Marvell makes great play with this statement of Parker's though the latter may simply have followed Fynes Moryson in placing Geneva on the 'South side', see Moryson, *Itinerary* (1617), vol. i, 1907, p. 388, or P. Heylyn, *Cosmographie,* 1669, Bk. I, p. 136.

12–13. *Whether* . . . *in't*] Parker, *Defence,* p. 337.

15. *Helvetian* Passage] Caesar, *De Bello Gallico,* I. vi.

24. Altar-wise] In 1633 Laud ordained that the communion table should be placed in the East end of the church. The matter aroused considerable controversy, see Bishop Williams, *The Holy Table, Name and Thing,* 1636.

P. 26. 1–2. sold . . . *Earth*] *The Rehearsal,* v. i. p. 50.

7–8. *Calvinus* . . . *Lucianus*] Tallemant des Reaux relates of Rabelais '—Il fit l'anagramme de Calvin, *Calvinus—Lucianus* . . .' *Les Historiettes,* eds. De Monmerque et Paulin Paris, vol. vi, Paris 1862, p. 222. Marvell has another story from the same context, see below, Pt. II, p. 157 n.

14. *Reasons* . . . *Blackberries*] Shakespeare, *1 Henry IV,* II. iv. 242–3.

17. City of *roaring Lions*] Lyon in France.

27. *Lake perillous*] Perilous lakes and roaring lions, abound in romance literature, see Stith Thompson, *Motif Index of Folk Literature,* Copenhagen, 1958.

27–8. ran sheere . . . touching it] '. . . the River Rhodanus, which falls into this Lake, having so cleare a colour, as it seemes not at all to mingle with the standing water of the Lake'. Moryson, *Itinerary,* vol. i, p. 388. This had been noted earlier by Ammianus Marcellinus, xv. 11. 16.

P. 27. 9. Nuts] A source of pleasure or delight, *O.E.D.* 5a. The expression appears to be proverbial.

34. *exceeding* . . . *belief*] Preface, A3ᵛ.

P. 28. 4. 850 pages] There are actually 750 pages in Parker's *Defence.*

11. a *Mucke*] To run viciously mad, frenzied for blood. *O.E.D.* gives Marvell's as the earliest use.

18–19. *Sunt . . . ineptiae*] In a letter from Calvin to Francford, 15 Feb. 1555, there occurs the passage: 'In Anglicana liturgia, qualem discribitis, multas video fuisse tolerabiles ineptias.' Joannis Calvini, *Epistolae*, ed. T. Beza, 2nd ed., 1576, p. 158.

26. *Pall-mall*] A game practised in Europe from the sixteenth century, in which a boxwood ball was driven through an iron ring suspended at some height above the ground in a long alley. The player who, starting from one end of the alley, could drive the ball through the ring in the fewest strokes, or within a given number, winning.

26. *Arbalet*] The cross-bow.

27. *Court-boule*] *O.E.D.* suggests a form of bowls, perhaps played in a court. Grosart suggests 'short' as opposed to 'long' bowls.

28. Fort of St. *Katherine*] A fort erected by the Duke of Savoy two or three leagues south-east of Geneva. In 1600 Henry IV of France took the fort, and against the terms of the peace (1601), secretly allowed the Genevese to raze it. H. M. Baird, *The Huguenots and Henry of Navarre*, vol. ii, 1886, pp. 469–70.

29. *Escalade*] On the night of 11 Dec. 1602, the Duke of Savoy tried to gain possession of Geneva. The troops under Brunanlieu, scaled the walls, but were discovered and routed. The night of the *Escalade* is kept as a festival. Heinrich Zschokke, *The History of Switzerland*, trans. F. G. Shaw, 1875, p. 157.

32–3. *Switzerland . . . Savoy*] Marvell is doubtless thinking of the struggle between Philip II of Spain (1527–98) and Henry IV of France, after the latter's accession to the throne, in which parts of Switzerland were overrun and during which Charles Emmanuel, Duke of Savoy (1562–1630), tried to profit by the confusion and enlarge his dominions. See also P. Heylyn, *Cosmographie*, 1669, Bk. I, p. 138.

P. 29. 8. *Sancho . . . Island*] Cervantes, *Don Quixote*, trans. T. Shelton, 1620, Pt. II, ch. xlii: 'Of the advice that Don Quixote gave Sancho Pansa before he should go to governe the Island.'

14. *Bedlam*] The hospital of *St. Mary of Bethlehem*, used as an asylum for mentally deranged persons. It was originally situated in Bishopsgate.

14. *Hogsdon*] Hoxton, 'In the Seventeenth Century Hoxton was synonymous with Bedlam as a place for lunatics for whom there were three distinct asylums.' H. B. Wheatley, *London Past and Present*, vol. ii, 1891, p. 246. In Jonson's time a resort for citizens: *Alchemist*, V. ii. 19, and *Every Man in his Humour*, I. i. 47. See also Thomas Heywood's *The Wise Woman of Hogsdon*, 1638.

25–6. *Before . . . Hollow*] *The Rehearsal*, V. i. p. 45.

32–3. *Quadrature* of the *Circle*] The expression of the area of a circle by means of an equivalent square. This was regarded as very difficult. Hobbes wrote on the subject, see T. Hobbes, *Quadratura Circuli . . . demonstrata*, 1669.

P. 30. 7. Noble man] Gilbert Sheldon (1598–1677), Archbishop of Canterbury. Parker became his chaplain in 1667.

30. Tippet] A band of silk or other material worn round the neck with the two ends pendent from the shoulders in front; worn by ecclesiastics.

P. 31. 3. Bishop . . . Altar] The altar-piece of Magdalen College Chapel, Oxford, painted by Isaac Fuller (1606–72) described by Addison in his poem *Resurrection* (1718). The painting is reproduced as the frontispiece of T. Burnet's *Of the State of those that Rise* (1728) where the poem is reprinted. A small water-colour copy of the work hangs in the chapel. [E. D. J.]

3–4. *Maudlin de la Croix*] An abbess of Cordova supposedly in league with the devil, discovered *c.* 1545: '. . . she was raised from the ground in the presence of them all, above three Cubittes high.' S. Goulart, *Admirable and Memorable Histories Containing the Wonders of our Time*, tr. E. Grimeston, 1607, p. 550. She is called *Magdeline de la Croix* in Goulart, but Marvell could have read of her in J. Wier, *De Prestigiis*, 1577, Bk. VI, c. vi, col. 678, or in a work we know he possessed, Del Rio, *Disquisitionum Magicarum*, 1633, Bk. IV, c. 1, p. 509. [E. D. J.] According to a much earlier provençal legend, Mary Magdalen was also lifted up—Baring Gould, *Lives of the Saints*, vol. iii, Pt. II, 1914, pp. 611 ff.

10. speculate] *O.E.D.* suggests: inspect, examine closely, gaze at.

27. two Friends] Perhaps Simon Patrick and Thomas Tomkins. Patrick (1626–1707), later Bishop of Ely, was the author of the *Friendly Debate*, 1669, and was the man to whom Parker's *Defence* was addressed. Tomkins (1637–75) was Sheldon's other chaplain at this time, and wrote a number of works against toleration.

P. 32. 2–3. King of *France*] Charles VI (1368–1422). The story of the page who let his spear fall on his companion's helmet, so frightening the King out of his wits is to be found in Froissart's *Chronicle*, trans. Lord Berners, ed. W. P. Ker, vol. vi, 1903, p. 68.

16. *Lycanthropy*] A kind of insanity in which the sufferer imagines himself to be a wolf.

36. Cabal] Cabbala: The Jewish tradition of interpretation of the Old Testament, hence, any private or secret interpretation.

P. 33. 12–13. Bishop *Prideaux*] John Prideaux (1578–1650), Bishop of Worcester. He was Regius Professor of Divinity at Oxford 1615–41. On 24 April 1627 theologian Peter Heylyn (1600–2) took his B.D. before Prideaux, answering *pro forma* on these questions: '(1) *An Ecclesia unquam fuerit invisibilis?* (2) *An Ecclesia possit errare?* Both which he determined negatively contrary to the mind and judgement of *Prideaux* . . .' Wood, *Athenae*, vol. ii, 1692, cols. 181–2. In 1633 Heylyn proceeded to the D.D. answering affirmatively three questions: '(1) *An Ecclesia habeat authoritatem in determinandis fidei controversiis?* . . (2) *An Eccles. habeat authoritatem decernendi ritus et ceremonias?* . . . (3) *An Eccles. habeat authoritatem interpretandi Scripturas sacras?* . . . All which . . . were so displeasing to *Prideaux* the Professor, that he fell into very great heats and passion . . .' Wood, *Athenae*, vol. ii, 1962, col. 183.

17. *Rationale*] Anthony Sparrow (1612–85), Bishop of Norwich, wrote *A Rationale upon the Book of Common Prayer of the Church of England*, 1657.

18. *Holiness of Lent*] *The Paschal or Lent Fast, Apostolical and Perpetual*, 1662, was written by Peter Gunning (1614–84), Bishop of Ely, an ardent royalist, sometimes accused of leanings toward Popery.

30. *Mr. B.*] Richard Baxter (1615–91), the Presbyterian controversialist, one of the great figures among the dissenters. Bramhall replied to him in his *Vindication*.

35. *Bullice*] A wild plum, larger than the sloe. There are two varieties, black and white.

P. 34. 6. cryed *Peccavi*] In *The Cure of Church Divisions*, 1670, and *A Defence*, 1671, Baxter argues against schism and Church division.

16–17. *Art . . . miserie*] From an anonymous paraphrase of 1 Sam. 28:8–20, titled *In guilty Night* or *The Witch of Endor*. First published with a setting by Purcell in *Harmonia Sacra*, Pt. II, 1693, p. 45. The earliest manuscript version seems to be in a pre-1650 Song Book in Bodley: Don C.57, a setting by Robert Ramsay, organist of Trinity College, Cambridge, 1628–44. Marvell could have heard the work when a student at Trinity. Marvell is here seeing Parker in the role of Saul desperately conjuring up the ghost of Samuel (Bramhall).

18. *Hebrew Jew*] Shylock in *The Merchant of Venice*.

22–3. *being . . . Mercy*] Preface, C4^r.

25. the Proverb] 'Confess and be hanged', Stevenson, *Book of Quotations*, 1949, p. 399. Cf. *Othello*, IV. i. 38.

P. 35. 3–7. Now one . . . *Ghibilinus es*] The story is a familiar one, see G. Stella, 'Annales Genuenses', *Rerum Italicarum Scriptores*, ed. Muratori, Milan, vol. xvii, 1730, col. 1019; Platina, *Historia De Vitis Pontificum Romanorum*, 1610, p. 246, etc. The Pope was Benedict Caetani (1235?–1303) Boniface VIII, the unfortunate Ghibelline, Porchetus Spinola, Franciscan archbishop of Genoa. The incident took place on 22 Feb. 1300. I have not been able to trace Marvell's 'Historian' though 'La Raccolta di Romagna' notes that the difference between the two factions was apparent: '. . . nel tagliar del pane, nel cingersi, in portare il pennachio . . .' Von Ranke, *History of the Popes*, vol. i, 1908, p. 343.

9. the whole Stairs] Doubtless the flight of stairs in the chapel Sancta Sanctorum in the Piazza di San Giovanni, Rome. Leo IV granted an indulgence of nine years for every step climbed by the pilgrim on his knees while repeating the appropriate prayers. It is said that while performing this Luther recalled the verse 'The just shall live by faith', arose and descended. P. Smith, *The Life and Letters of Martin Luther*, 1911, pp. 18–19.

23. as *Gonsales . . . Gansas*] F. Godwin, *The Man in the Moone: or a discourse of a voyage thither by Domingo Gonsales the Speedy Messenger*, 1638. Gonsales trained a *certain kind of Wild Swan* to carry him and called them his *Gansas* (p. 25).

P. 36. 4–5. *Charms* . . . Heaven] Virgil, *Eclogues*, viii. 70.

5–6. never . . . *barking*] Proverbial: 'The moon does not heed the barking of dogs' (Ray).

14. *Ganteloop*] A military punishment in which the culprit had to run stripped to the waist between two rows of men who struck at him with knotted cords or sticks.

21–2. *candor* . . . *England*] Preface, A8ʳ.

25–7. *this Treatise* . . .*Writings*] Ibid. A8ʳ. Cf. Stillingfleet: '. . . the way that Ratts answer Books, by gnawing some of the leaves, for the body and design of it remains wholly untouched . . .', *A Discourse Concerning the Idolatry Practised in the Church of Rome*, 2nd ed., 1671, 'Preface', B1ᵛ.

P. 37. 2. Sow in *Arcadia*] Varro, *Rerum Rusticarum*, II. iv; tr. Storr-Best, 1912, p. 172. Also, Pliny, *Natural History*, xi. 85.

22. *Cris-cros-Row*] The Alphabet, from the figure of the Cross (Christ-cross-row) formerly attached to it in horn books.

28. Mr. *Bales*] Thomas Bales was one of the '. . . *Commissioners* about the reforming the buildings, wayes, streetes, & incumbrances & regulating the Hackny-Coaches in the Citty of London . . .' Evelyn, *Diary*, ed. De Beer, vol. iii, 1955, pp. 318–19. Wood refers to him as 'a drunken leache⟨r⟩ous Justice of Peace of Westminster; *Life and Times*, ed. Clark, vol. ii, 1892, p. 395.

P. 38. 13. *Syderal*] Coming from, caused by the stars.

18. *blew-John*] Brewer's after worts, i.e., the second run of beer.

23–4. Triumph . . . Victory] Cf. the proverb 'Ante victoriam ne canas triumphum', Bohn, *Handbook of Proverbs*, 1867, p. 81.

P. 39. 2–4. *such* . . . *impressions*] Discourse, 'Preface', p. i.

9. *Fayal*] An island belonging to Portugal, one of the Azores, formerly noted for volcanoes.

12. *Fellows diet*] Richardson, the famous fire-eater. Evelyn saw him at Lady Sunderland's 8 Oct. 1672: '. . . who before us devourd *Brimston* on glowing coales, chewing and swallowing them downe; he also mealted a beere glasse & eate it quite up: then taking a live Coale on his tongue, put on it a raw oyster, which coale was blown on with billows till it flam'd & sparkled in his mouth, & so remain'd til the Oyster gaped and was quite boiled . . .' Evelyn, *Diary*, ed. E. S. De Beer, vol. iii, 1955, pp. 626–7.

31–3. fed . . . Spiders] As the Prince of Cambay:

The *Prince* of *Cambays* dayly food
Is *Aspe* and *Basilisque* and *Toad* . . .

Hudibras, II, i, 753–4.

35. Mountebank . . . Antidote] Mountebanks have no 'more then three sorts of remedies; that is, the *Antidote* against poysons; the *Balsame* for wounds; and the Oynment for burnings.' J. Primrose, *Popular Errors*, trans. Wittie, 1651, p. 23.

P. 40. 2. *Cowitch*] Cowage: the stinging hairs of the pod of a tropical plant.

2. *Genial-bed*] Marriage or nuptial bed.

7. *Tom Triplet*] Dr. Thomas Triplet (1603–70). 'A very witty man of Ch. Ch.', prebend of Westminster and Tenton. Wood, *Fasti Oxonienses*, ed. Bliss, 1815, Pt. II, col. 255; and Aubrey, *Brief Lives*, ed. Clark, vol. ii, 1898, p. 263.

8. Dr *Gill*] Alexander Gill, the elder (1565–1635), High master of St. Pauls School. Aubrey tells the same story as Marvell, *Brief Lives*, vol. i, p. 262.

19. *Priscian*] The celebrated Roman grammarian of the latter half of the fifth century.

P. 41. 7. *Osbolton*] Lambert Osbolton (1594–1659), Master of Westminster School.

8. Dr *Busby*] Richard Busby (1606–95), Headmaster of Westminster School. His name was proverbial as a severe pedagogue. Nevertheless, many of the most distinguished men of the age received their schooling at his hands.

16. *Publick Rods*] *Preface*, d6ᵛ.

16. *Axes*] *Defence*, p. 219.

20. J.O.] Owen was Vice-Chancellor of the University of Oxford, 1652–8.

35. *Holy Brotherhood*] 'Santa Hermandad', in Spain the name of a combination formed to resist the exactions of the nobles, in 1476. It was subsequently given police functions. Marvell may also be referring to the Jesuits here.

P. 42. 1–3. *Instead . . . baggage*] Aubrey cites this poem of Triplet's. It is also to be found in *The Loves of Hero and Leander*, 1653, p. 56:

> For a piece of Beefe and Turnip
> Neglected with a Cabbage,
> He took up the Male *Pillion*
> Of his bouncing maid *Gillian*
> And sowc'd her like a Baggage . . .

23. Renegade] An apostate, esp. a Christian who becomes a Mohammedan.

31. formerly . . . Profession] Parker in fact belonged to a puritan sect when at Oxford, see *Introd.* I.

35. Politick Engine] Probably the notorious informer John Poulter (see *C.S.P.D.*, 1670). Dr. Mews the Vice-Chancellor wrote to Secretary Williamson, concerning him: '. . . John Poulter, who, from having mixed himself up with the fanatics, made some discoveries which it is hoped might have been improved upon. I have no doubt but that party is very angry with him, from a letter or libel sent me by post from London . . . here he cannot attempt anything, as the whole gang in Oxford have taken the alarm. I have several such instruments at work here . . .' 24 May 1670, *C.S.P.D.*, 1670, p. 235.

P. 43. 17–19. His Majesty . . . matters] *His Majesties most Gracious Declaration from his Court at Breda April 14. 1660*, 1660. 'We do declare a liberty to tender Consciences, and that no man shall be disquieted or called in question for differences of opinion in matters of Religion, which do not disturb the peace of the Kingdom.' (pp. 7–8).

34. Act . . . Indempnity] The Bill of Indemnity received the royal assent 29 Aug. 1660.

P. 44. 12. Minister of State] Edward Hyde (1609–74), Earl of Clarendon. Most dissenters regarded Clarendon as responsible for the Act of Uniformity, and the other statutes, named after him the 'Clarendon Code'. Marvell does not seem to have admired him (see 'Clarindons House Warming', *Poems & Letters*, ed. Margoliouth, vol. i, pp. 137–40). In 1667 he was deprived of the great Seal of Chancellorship and arraigned for high treason by Parliament. He escaped to Calais and lived the rest of his life in exile.

29. *quod Scripsi Scripsi*] Thus Pilate, John 19: 22.

P. 45. 1. pag. 10.] The following quotations are from Parker's *Discourse*. Marvell omits passages, and paraphrases freely.

30–2. *whilst . . . can*] *Discourse*, p. 91.

P. 46. 14. p. 80.] Actually p. 81.

23. enabled] authorized, sanctioned, and impowered.

25. P. 53.] *Discourse*, 'Preface', pp. lii–liii.

29. pag. 55.] Ibid., pp. liv–lv.

P. 47. 9. Pag. 54.] Ibid., pp. liii–liv.

27. *Gondibert*] Sir W. Davenant's epic poem *Gondibert*, 1651.

28. *Leviathan*] Thomas Hobbes, *Leviathan, or the Matter, Forme and Power of a Commonwealth, Ecclesiastical and Civil*, 1651.

28. fetch] A contrivance, stratagem, trick, *O.E.D.* 2.

P. 48. 5. *Premunire*] The writ for a person accused of asserting or maintaining papal jurisdiction in England, and therefore denying the ecclesiastical supremacy of the sovereign.

9. *Jejunium Cecilianum*] In Feb. 1562 William Cecil Lord Burghley drew up a paper to prove the necessity of restoring the English navy by a greater consumption of fish, and proposing to institute Wednesday as an extra day of abstinence (see H. N. Birt, *The Elizabethan Religious Settlement*, 1907, pp. 524–5). The result was an act for the observance of Wednesday as a fast day: W. Rastell, *A Collection in English of the Statutes now in force*, 1591, fol. 408ᵛ.

23. lightly] As may easily happen; probably, *O.E.D.* 6.

35. *Pushpin Divinity*] Preface, A8ᵛ.

P. 49. 8. *decorum*] In composition: that which is proper to person, place, time, or subject.

18–19. Ass in the Fable] The 24th fable of Aesop. See John Ogilby, *The Fables of Æsop Paraphrased in Verse*, 1651, p. 67. The plate opposite illustrates Marvell's reference.

20. ramp] To rear up; clutch widly at; trample with forelegs, *O.E.D.* 3.

24. 12th page] *Discourse*, 'Preface', p. xii.

27. pag. 82] *Discourse*, p. 82.

P. 50. 2. p. 18] Bramhall, *Vindication*, pp. 18–19.

2. *his Book*] Grotius, *De Imperio Summarum Potestatum circa Sacra*, Paris, 1647.

17–22. *old Pleas . . . old*] Owen, *Truth and Innocence Vindicated*, 1669, p. 108 [mispaginated as 208].

27–8. prophane *Ben. Johnson*] *Discourse*, 'Preface', p. xxiii.

28. gravest . . . Flatterers] Jonson, *The Alchemist*, II. ii. 59–60.

31. *Hunc . . . tutus*] Horace, *Satires*, II. i. 20.

P. 51. 11. Projectors for Concealed Lands] 'Concealed land' is that held privily from the King by a person having no title thereto: used especially of land that had been monastic property before the Reformation. 'Projectors' informed against the holders of such land. After the Restoration the same was done with state land taken or given away during Cromwell's regime.

17. prolling] Prowling: used in the sense 'to plunder' or 'to rob a person', *O.E.D.*

19. Lord Keeper] Sir Orlando Bridgeman (1606–74), Lord Keeper 1667–72.

28. *Charles the fifth*] The Emperor Charles V (1500–58); crowned Emperor 24 Feb. 1530 by Pope Clement VII in Bologna. Sandoval gives an account in which he notes: '. . . le vistieron una capa y roquet de canonigo de Santa Maria de Torres en Roma, y fue hecho canonigo de ella como era antigua costumbre de los emperadores en las ceremonias . . .' Prudencio de Sandoval, *Historia del Emperador Carlos V*, Tom. V, Madrid, 1847, p. 373. See also J. Sleidan, *A Famous Cronicle of oure time*, trans. J. Daus, 1560, fol. xxv^r.

P. 52. 2. Conversation] Manner of conducting oneself in society; behaviour or mode of life.

23. trepan] To lure, inveigle (into a course of action etc.).

24. peach] To give incriminating evidence against; inform against; to betray.

26. cuts] To shape one's discourse; trim; try not to commit oneself, *O.E.D.* 36. Grosart suggests 'falters' from the phrase 'to cut' used of horses: 'to strike the inside of the fetlock with the shoe or hoof of the opposite foot.', *O.E.D.* 27.

33. Casual Divinity] Casuistry: that part of ethics which resolves cases of conscience, applying the general rules of religion and morality to particular instances in which circumstances alter cases.

P. 53. 1–4. *tis better . . . disputable*] *Discourse*, p. 308.

11–15. *The Commands . . . error*] Ibid., p. 308.

P. 54. 2–3. *Ma tu . . . Nume*] Guarini, *Il Pastor Fido*, III. iv. 28–9.

8. *Quaesitum . . . verpos*] Juvenal, *Satires*, XIV. 104.

9. *Nullum . . . Prudentia*] The whole quotation, which Marvell continues below, is:

> nullum numen habes, si sit prudentia, nos te,
> nos facimus, Fortuna, deam, coeloque locamus.

Juvenal, Satires, X. 365–6.

25. the *Turk*] Evelyn saw the *Turk* on 15 Sep. 1657, he noted '. . . to see a famous *Rope-daunser* call'd the *Turk*, I saw even to astonishment the agilities he perform'd, one was his walking bare foote, & taking hold by his toes onely, of a rope almost perpendicular & without so much as touching it with his hands: also dauncing blindfold on the high-roope: & with a boy of 12 yeares old, tyed to one of his feete about 20 foote beneath him dangling as he daunced, & yet moved as nimbly as it had ben but a feather . . .', *Diary*, ed. De Beer, vol. iii, p. 197.

34–1. [P. 55.] *safer . . . Perswasions*] *Discourse*, 'Preface', pp. liv–lv.

P. 55. 2–3. *greater . . . Immoralities*] Ibid., pp. lii–liii.

14. *Rebellion . . . Witchcraft*] *Preface*, d1ʳ; 1 Sam. 15: 23.

29–30. those . . . complain of it] Marvell is no doubt thinking of the 'Court Wits'—Buckingham, Mulgrave, and Rochester.

35–6. *saevior . . . Orbem*] Juvenal, *Satires*, VI. 292.

P. 56. 20. *Sybarites*] The inhabitants of *Sybaris*, a Greek town noted for the luxury of its citizens. They were eventually destroyed by the people of Crotona. For Marvell's allusion to the dancing horses, see Athenaeus, *Diepnosophistae*, XII. 520.

32. *Julian*] 'The Apostate', Flavius Claudius Julianus (331–63) Roman Emperor. Educated as a Christian he was converted to paganism in 351. He became Emperor in 361 and endeavoured to restore pagan worship.

36–3 [P. 57.] *That whilst . . . Sedition*] *Discourse*, 'Preface', p. xlix.

P. 57. 10. *Bartlemew*-Register] The Act of Uniformity came into force on St. Bartholomew's Day, 24 Aug. 1662, when '. . . about two thousand relinquished their preferments in the church'. D. Neal, *The History of the Puritans*, vol. iv, 1822, p. 328.

10. *March*-Licences] The licenses to preach, applied for by non-conformists after the Declaration of Indulgence, 15 March 1672. Approximately 1,508 licenses were issued. Evelyn, *Diary*, ed. De Beer, vol. iii, p. 608 n.

13. *they live . . . men*] *Discourse*, 'Preface', p. xlix.

15–16. *but . . . number*] Ibid., p. 1.

16–17. *Country-Towns . . . twenty*] Ibid., p. xlix.

19. all . . . neck] The Emperor Caligula wished that all the Romans had only one neck, Suetonius, *Caligula*, 30.

23–4. set Crosses . . . occasion] The houses in which Protestants lodged were marked with a white cross for the 'Bartholomew massacre' of 1572 in Paris. H. M. Baird, *History of the Rise of the Huguenots of France*, vol. ii, New York, 1879, p. 455.

25–6. *wealthy Fanaticks*] *Discourse*, 'Preface', p. li.

28–9. *Pillories, Whipping-posts*] *Preface*, d4ᵛ.

29. *Galleys*] *Discourse*, p. 223.

29. *Rods, and Axes*] Ibid., p. 219.

P. 58. 4. *well-meaning Zelot*] Discourse, 'Preface', p. liii.

7–8. *Kingdoms . . . understood*] Discourse, p. 223.

14–15. *Religion . . . settlement*] Ibid., p. 12.

24. *Ciurma*] galley-slaves; the rowers in a galley.

32. *Sir John Baptist Dutel*] He is '. . . said to have been of French extraction and a knight of Malta. He was appointed Commander of the Fountain and Jersey, successively in 1665; and in 1671 of a galley in the streights'. (J. Charnock, *Biographia Navalis*, vol. vi, 1794, p. 254). There is a letter from Duteil to Arlington, *C.S.P.D.*, June (?) 1671: 'Requesting him to have letters despatched from the King to the Kings of France and Spain, the Viceroys of Sicily, Naples and Sardinia, the Grand Duke of Tuscany, the Republic of Genoa, and the Grand Master of Malta, asking leave for him to levy officers and soldiers and to buy slaves in their territories to arm the two galleys that the King has had built at Leghorn to serve against the common enemy of Christendom. . . .' *C.S.P.D.*, 1671, p. 351.

P. 59. 15–17. *the tyred . . . Suffering*] Tertullian, 'Ad Scapulam', 5, *Opera*, ed. Rigalti, Paris 1664, p. 71.

18. *Non tibi . . . Petro*] 'Alexander the third, pursuing the desperate course *of Gregory* the seventh, excommunicated the Emperor *Frederick* the First; and by raising War against him in every place, brought him to that exigent, that he was fain to prostrate himself at his feet: when the Pope treading on his neck, said aloud *Super Aspidem & Basiliscum* &c. profanely applying those words to the present occasion. And when the Emperor, to put the better colour on his disgrace, meekly replyed, *Non tibi sed Petro*; the Pope not willing to lose his part of so great a glory, subjoyned as angerly *Et mihi et Petro*.' Heylyn, *Cosmographie*, 1669, Bk. I, p. 93. The incident took place in 1177.

26–7. *Entremeses*] Something served between the courses of a banquet.

P. 60. 12. Saint *Dominick*] Dominic de Guzman (1170–1221), the founder of the Dominican order.

15. *Synesius*] A Greek writer, bishop of Ptolemais (d. *c.* 430). Marvell is here citing one of his letters, an encyclical document against Andronicus of Berenice: 'Not because of his instruments of torture to which I allude, that crush the fingers [*Dactylethrae*] and feet, [*Podostrabae*] compress the limbs, tweak the nose, [*Rhinolabides*] and deform the ears [*Otagrae*] and lips, [*Cheilostrophia*] of which things those who had forestalled the experience and the sight by perishing in the war were adjudged happy by such as had by ill fate survived.' *The Letters of Synesius of Cyrene*, trans. A. Fitzgerald, 1926, pp. 140–1. See also *Epistolographi Graeci*, ed. R. Hercher, 1873, p. 670, the letter is no. 58.

22. *Macassar*] 'In Macazar. . . . Their Arrow-heads are of Fish-bones, envenomed with incurable pyson.' S. Purchas, *Purchas his Pilgrimage*, 1613, p. 458. On 15 March 1665, Pepys notes 'Anon to Gresham College, where among other good discourse, there was tried the great poison of Macassa upon

a dog, but it had no effect all the time we sat there.' *Diary*, ed. G. Smith, 1906, p. 305; see also Butler, *Satires and Miscellaneous Prose*, ed. Lamar, 1929, p. 342.

30–1. *there cannot . . . totters*] *Discourse*, p. 166.

P. 61. 1. opiniastre] Stiff or stubborn in opinion.

7. Imp] A young shoot of a plant or tree; a sapling or sucker.

19. disvalise] < fr. *desvaliser*; to strip someone of his baggage; to rob or plunder.

23. scurvy disease] Syphilis: the disease first made its appearance in Europe following the siege of Naples in 1495. Opinion is still divided as to whether it was brought back by Columbus, or whether it existed in Europe prior to his journey to the West Indies, see R. R. Willcox, *A Textbook of Venereal Diseases*, 1950.

24. tell a story] The story may be found in George Sandys's *A Relation of a Journey*, 3rd ed., 1627, pp. 238–9. Marvell confuses two stories: one concerning certain merchants supplying the French army at the siege of Naples with flesh dressed as tunny—whence the source of syphilis. And the other, concerning the revenge of the Genoese on the Venetians, barrelling up the captured Venetian nobility as tunny, and sending it to Venice.

30. Nodes] Knotty swellings or concretions on some part of the body.

31. Buboes] Inflamed swellings or abscesses in glandular parts of the body. An ordinary symptom of the plague in the seventeenth century.

P. 62. 9. pag. 20] *Discourse*, p. 20.

13. *Mas Johns*] Presbyterian preachers. On 1 Jan. 1661 in the Scottish Estates, an Act Rescissory was passed, all the proceedings of the Scottish Parliaments since 1640 were cut away, and Charles I's Church was restored in its entirety.

16. Arch-Bishop] Alexander Burnet (1614–84), Archbishop of Glasgow. In 1669 he was forced to resign his see, being restored again in 1674. He was noted for his severity towards Presbyterians.

23. Book . . . of J.O.'s] Owen's *Truth and Innocence Vindicated*, 1669.

32. all the Teeth] An allusion to Richard III, born with 'all his teeth and haire to his shoulders.' W. Camden, *Remaines*, 1614, p. 282.

P. 63. 23. old excellent] i.e. 'excellent from of old'.

25. great Prelate] John Cosin (1594–1672), bishop of Durham.

26–7. *That . . . heels*] One of the articles of impeachment against Cosin read by Francis Rous (1579–1659) in the House of Commons 15 March 1640/1. Rushworth, *Collections*, Pt. III, vol. i, 1692, p. 209.

28. *Look . . . doo't*] Buckingham, *Rehearsal*, I. i, p. 10.

P. 64. 13. in *querpo*] Without clothes (Sp.).

14. p. 237] pp. 237–8, *Defence*.

22. *impulsion*] External influence exerted on mind or conduct.

P. 65. 7. p. 33] Not in fact p. 33, Marvell selects from a number of pages *round* p. 33.

    7–8. *Universal . . . Power*] *Discourse*, p. 27.

    8. *natural . . . Christ*] Ibid., p. 34.

    8–10. *firmly . . . Nations*] Ibid., p. 35.

    10–11. *Scripture . . . Princes*] Ibid., p. 35.

    30. Even . . . gray] 'One Palevizine an Italian Gentleman, and kinsman to Scaliger, had in one night all his haire chang'd from black to gray'. Scaliger, *de Subtil.*, p. 18, cited Fuller, *The Holy State*, 1642, p. 211.

P. 66. 4. *remonstrate* to] To raise an objection to; to state a grievance.

    5. Remonstrants] Alluding to the Arminian party at the Synod of Dort (1617).

P. 67. 17. *Sardanapalus*] According to fable, the last King of the Assyrian empire of Ninevah. See below.

    18. *Justine*] Marcus Junianus Justinus, a Latin historian of the Second Century. He wrote of Sardanapalus: 'When his lieutenant over the Medes, Arbactus by name, after great solicitation could hardly be admitted into his presence . . . he found him amongst a throng of Concubines spinning Purple on a distaff, and distributing their tasks unto them. . . . Which things observed, Arbactus being possessed with indignation . . . repairing to his companions, did communicate to them what he beheld. . . . A conspiracy therefore was plotted, and war was made on *Sardanapalus*. . . .' *The History of Justin, Taken out of the four and fourty Books of Trogus Pompeius*, trans. R. Codrington, 2nd ed., 1664, Bk. I, p. 4.

    22–4. *be . . . drugeries*] *Preface*, A6ʳ.

    34. p. 641] *Defence*, pp. 640–1.

P. 68. 6. tokens of Loyalty] The nonconformists lent large sums of money to Charles II, see Marvell's letter to Popple, 28 Nov. 1670, *Poems & Letters*, ed. Margoliouth, vol. ii, p. 304.

    24–5. 49th page] *Discourse*, 'Preface', p. xlix.

    35. march'd up *Holborn*] i.e. to Tyburn for execution.

P. 69. 2. Ear-mark] See above, note to p. 67.

    14. *p.* 85] J. Owen, *Truth and Innocence Vindicated*, p. 85.

    31–2. *I confess . . . occasion*] *Defence*, p. 229.

P. 70. 5. *Cecill*] Lord Burghley (1520–98), Elizabeth's famous minister of State. See above, note to p. 48.

    10. so eminent a Divine] See above, note to p. 33.

    14–16. *The matter . . . Consequence*] *Discourse*, p. 60.

    18–21. how preremptory . . . Supremacy] Ibid., p. 58.

    28–1 [P. 71.]. I may . . . Pleasure] *Defence*, p. 298.

P. 71. 19. *Sortes Virgilianæ*] A method of divination consisting in taking a passage from Virgil at random.

P. 72. 6. all but an Epistle] The full title of the book is: *A Defence and Continuation of the Ecclesiastical Politie: By way of a Letter to a Friend in London. Together with a Letter from the Author of the Friendly Debate,* 1671.

14. quetch] < O.E. *cweccan*: to quake; to utter a sound.

20. lock] A grapple or grip at wrestling; hence, 'a dilemna'.

26. *p* 69] *Discourse,* p. 69.

33. Counters-scarp] In fortification, the outer wall or slope of the ditch that supports the covered way.

34. incorrigible Scold] The story is related by Montaigne, *Essays,* II. xxxii, trans. Trechman, vol. ii, 1927, pp. 173–4.

P. 73. 34–3 [P. 74]. *many warm . . . examine*] *Preface,* e8ʳ.

P. 74. 5. *Dilemma*] See above, p. 3.

12. *Tiberius*] Suetonius cites Tiberius's letter: '. . . quid scribam vobis, p.c., aut quo modo scribam, aut quid omnino non scribam hoc tempore, dii me deaeque peius perdant quam cotidie perire sentio si scio.' Suetonius, *Tiberius,* 67.

19. *June . . . July*] Parker's *Preface* etc. was licensed 24 June 1672, and printed and published in Trinity term, 1672. See Arber, *Term Catalogues,* vol. i, p. 109.

P. 75. 7. *John a Nokes . . . John a Stiles*] Fictitious names for the parties in a legal action. Hence sometimes used indefinitely for any individual person.

11. Rencounters] Conflicts, skirmishes—including those of wit or argument.

22. Lord *Verulam*] Francis Bacon (1561–1626), Lord Chancellor, statesman, writer and philosopher.

25–7. *Arch-Bishop Whitgift . . . Bramhall*] The prelates Parker names here were notable more as pillars of the church than as 'wits'. Whitgift and Bancroft were, of course, vigorous opponents of puritanism. Montague aroused Marvell's ire as an 'Arminian', while Bilson was a conscientious churchman with a learned but commonplace mind, and Andrewes, though his sermons are full of word-play was hardly notable for any levity.

28. Mr *Tarlton*] Richard Tarlton (d. 1588). Fuller styled him 'The most famous jester to Queen Elizabeth'. See *D.N.B.*

29. The *Niches*] Describing the Old Exchange in 1708, Hatton noted: 'The intercolumns of the upper range are 24 Niches, 17 of which are replenished with the statues of our Kings and Queens.' E. Hatton, *A New View of London,* vol. ii, 1708, p. 615.

P. 76. 5–6. *hot fit of . . . Passion*] *Discourse,* 'Preface', p. vii.

25. Mum] An inarticulate sound made with closed lips, especially as an indication of unwillingness or inability to speak.

32. sleeps . . . Ears] A proverbial expression: 'enjoys undisturbed repose'. For other examples see B. Stevenson, *Book of Proverbs etc.*, 1949, p. 2135.

P. 77. 7–11. holy Brotherhood . . . Firebals] *Preface*, A8ᵛ. See also Marvell's letter to Popple, June 1672, *Poems & Letters*, ed. Margoliouth, vol. ii, p. 312.

13–14. *I am loud Thunder* . . . *doot*] *The Rehearsal*, I. i. p. 10.

21. burning . . . *Chatham*] In June 1667 the Dutch fleet sailed up the Medway and burned a number of English ships at Chatham. (Evelyn, *Diary*, ed. De Beer, vol. iii, pp. 484–7.) Marvell described the disaster in *Last Instructions to a Painter*, *Poems & Letters*, vol. i, pp. 154 ff.

28. Conflagration] The Great Fire of London 1666, see Evelyn, *Diary*, ed. De Beer, vol. iii, pp. 450 ff. The Jesuits were naturally suspected of having started the fire. Marvell actually examined witnesses concerning the origin of the fire for the House of Commons, see *A True and faithfull Account of the several Informations*, 1667, in *Somers Tracts*, ed. Scott, vol. vii, 1812.

30–1. yearly . . . Solemnity] On 10 Oct. 1666, '. . . was ordered a general Fast through the Nation, to humble us on the late dreadful conflagration, added to the plague and war, the most dismal judgements that could be inflicted. . . .' Evelyn, *Diary*, ed. Dobson, vol. ii, 1906, p. 261. See also *Journal of the House of Commons*, 24 Sep. 1666, vol. viii, p. 627.

34. *Diana's* Temple] According to a tradition of the time the first Church on the site of St. Pauls was erected on the site of a Temple dedicated to Diana. W. Dugdale, *The History of St. Pauls Cathedral in London*, 1658, p. 3.

36–1 [P. 78.] *We cannot* . . . *other*] J. Owen, *Discourse concerning Evangelical Love, Church-Peace and Unity*, 1672, p. 18.

P. 78. 1. *Socinianisme*] The doctrines of Faustus Socinus (1539–1604) from which modern Unitarianism springs.

6–7. *He might* . . . *Hittitism*] *Preface*, a1ʳ. The Perizzites, Hittites etc. were the various peoples in Canaan whom the Hebrews had subdued.

11. *tagging*] To supply prose or blank verse with rhymes.

13–15. *The Church of England* . . . *Communion*] *Preface*, a3ʳ.

24. Doctor *Thorndike*] Herbert Thorndike (1598–1672), Anglican divine. He died 11 July 1672. Marvell is probably thinking of his statement '. . . no Church can separate from the Church of *Rome*, but they must make themselves thereby *Schismaticks before God*'. H. Thorndike, *A Discourse of the Forbearance or the Penalties which a Due Reformation requires*, 1670, p. 19.

31. *Richard Montague*] (1577–1641) Bishop of Norwich. Archbishop Abbot complained of the work (see below, p. 129) and Commons voted that the book be burned and its author punished. Montague nevertheless received preferment. For the proclamation see *C.S.P.D.*, 17 Jan. 1629.

P. 79. 9. Mr. *Hooker*] Richard Hooker (1554–1600), the famous theologian. The first four books of *The Lawes of Ecclesiastical Politie* were published in 1594.

12. Mr. *Hales*] John Hales (1584–1656), theologian and philosopher. *A Tract Concerning Schisme and Schismatiques* (1642) was probably written in 1636.

20. best . . . brests] 'bene praeparatum pectus', Horace, *Odes*, II. x. 15.

P. 81. 13. *Cautissimi . . . feceris*] Pliny, *Epistles*, I. xviii. 5.

15. Second Council of *Nice*] A.D. 787, this Council dealt with the veneration of Holy Images.

P. 83. 3. *Cardinalism*] The institution or system of Cardinals.

3. *Nepotism*] The practise on the part of the Popes or other ecclesiastics of showing special favour to nephews or other relatives.

3. *Putanism*] 'The Trade and living of a Whore'. There is also a reference to three anti-clerical works by Gregorio Leti: *Il Puttanismo Romano*, Colonia, 1668; *Il Nipotismo di Roma: or The History of The Popes Nephews*, englished by W. A., 1669; *Il Cardinalismo di Santa Chiesa; or The History of the Cardinals of the Roman Church*, englished by G. H., 1670.

15–16. Christianity . . . Ambition] Hales, *A Tract Concerning Schisme*, 1642, p. 13.

32–3. *Dear Heart . . . Sweetness*] *Preface*, a2ʳ.

P. 84. 2. *Words . . . Sheets*] 'Modo sub lodice relictis uteris in turba.' Juvenal, *Satires*, VI. 195–6.

4–5. priviledg . . . Execution] Montaigne also notes this fact, *Essays*, trans. Trechman, vol. ii, p. 252. See Suetonius, *Tiberius*, 61.

9. *Wellfare . . . Fool*] *Preface*, a2ʳ. In 1672 an accusation was brought by Henry Mildmay, against Sir John Bramston, before the Council, of being a papist. The chief witness was a Portuguese, Ferdinand de Macedo, whose evidence showed umistakable signs of forgery. See Sir John Bramston, *Autobiography*, ed. Braybrooke, 1845, pp. 134 ff. There is a letter from Macedo in *C.S.P.D.*, 16 May 1672.

17–19. *without . . . Cause*] *Preface*, a2ᵛ.

29–30. to conquer . . . Armies] *The Rehearsal*, V. i, p. 35.

33–4. *Evangelical . . . Unity*] J. Owen, *A Discourse concerning Evangelical Love, Church-Peace and Unity*, 1672.

P. 85. 7–9. *one Syllable . . . ravings*] *Preface*, a2ᵛ.

20–1. *Sir John Falstaffe's . . . sinking*] *The Merry Wives of Windsor*, III. v. 9–11.

24–5. *Morality . . . Day*] *Preface*, a4ᵛ. John Owen, *Exercitations concerning the Name, Original Nature, Use and Continuance of a Day of Sacred Rest*, 1671.

25–6. *Septenary . . . Revolution*] *Preface*, a4ʳ.

26–7. *Self-evidencing . . . Scripture.*] Owen, *Of the Divine, Originall Authority, Self-Evidencing Light and Power of the Scriptures*, 1659.

33–5. *This is . . . Writings*] *Defence*, p. 274.

P. 86. 24. Collar of *Nesses*] The 'collar of ss' was worn at that time by the two chief justices and the chief baron of England. E. Foss, *The Judges of England*, vol. vii, 1864, pp. 17 ff.

P. 87. 9. p. 220] J. Owen, *Truth and Innocence Vindicated*, p. 220.
15. p. 337] *Defence*, p. 337.
27. p. 117] Bramhall, *Vindication*, pp. 116–17.

P. 88. 5–8. *Oh, what, . . . Rest*] *Preface*, a4ʳ.
20. *shall . . . Judgement*] Ibid., a7ʳ.
21–3. *Ah sweet . . . Enemies*] Ibid., a8ʳ.

26–8. *Barbers bason . . . Horse*] Cervantes, *Don Quixote*, trans. Shelton, Bk. III, ch. vii: 'Of the Higher Adventure and rich winning of the Helmet of Mambrino.' In this adventure Sancho changes the 'pannell' on the barbers ass, for that of his own.

P. 89. 13–14. *Governour . . . Subject*] *Acts*, 24: 25.
14. *Book of Martyrs*] *The Actes and Monuments of these latter and perillous dayes, touching matters of the Church*, by John Foxe, 1563.
18. *Scotch* History] In J. Foxe, *Actes and Monuments*, vol. ii, 1610. The section called 'Persecution in Scotland', pp. 1154 ff.
18–19. great Cardinal] David Beaton, Cardinal and archbishop of St. Andrews (1494–1546), a zealous persecutor, eventually brutally murdered.
19. Mr. *Guichard*] George Wishart (1513–46), Scottish reformer: '. . . suffered Martyrdome for the faith. . . .' 7 March 1546.
34. *Campanella*] Tommaso Campanella (1568–1639). The Italian philosopher.

> As Campanella used to screw and wrest
> His face like Theirs, to whom he then Addrest,
> And always found he had the best Success
> When best he did it, most of all to Please:
> So Famous Writers think their very Looks
> Will ad a great Advantage to their Books. . . .

Butler, *Satires and Miscellaneous Prose*, ed. Lamar, p. 183. Also Butler, *Two Letters*, 1672, p. 6.

P. 90. 3. *Superciliums*] eyebrows. Presumably Parker was a vain man who preened his eyebrows.
6–7. *Dunghill . . . Magazin*] *Preface*, a1ʳ.
20. Brothers of the Blade] There was an order of Knighthood known as the 'Brothers of the Sword', or 'Knights of the Sword' founded by Albert, third bishop of Riga, in 1201 (recognized by Pope Innocent III in 1204) to convert the Esths and Livs by the sword, and appropriate their land. In 1237 the Knights of the Sword were merged into the Teutonic Order.
21. down-right . . . Interpretation] 'If again it was not well cut, he would answer I spake not true: this is call'd the Reproof Valiant. If again it was not well cut, he would say I lie: this is call'd the Counter-check Quarrelsome: and so to the Lie Circumstantial and the Lie Direct'. *As You Like It*, v. iv. 78–83.

P. 91. 4–6. *Villain . . . trow*] *The Rehearsal*, v. i, p. 48.

5. *Valerio*] Marvell follows the original passage in Davenant's *The Sieg of Rhodes* (1656) 'The First Entry', *Dramatic Works*, ed. Maidment and Logan, vol. iii, 1873, p. 260.

8–9. *They . . . Lye*] *The Rehearsal*, v. i, p. 49.

11–12. *past . . . Mercy*] *Preface*, c4^r.

16. Rapper] An arrant lie, a downright falsehood.

18–26. *Symbolicalness . . . Spirits*] *Preface*, b3^v–b4^r.

21. *Scarlet Whore . . . Earth*] Rev. 17: 2.

21. Heliogabalus] Elagabalus (205–22), Roman Emperor, his short reign (218–22) was notable for its excesses.

22. *Bishop* Bonner] Edmund Bonner (1500–69), Bishop of London, notorious as a persecutor.

22. *Clary*] A sweet liquor consisting of a mixture of wine, clarified honey, and various spices.

24. *Vials of Wrath*] Rev. 15: 7.

27–8. Doctor *Baily's . . . Flower*] Thomas Bayly (d. 1657) was a royalist divine and afterwards a catholic controversialist. When in Newgate prison he wrote *Herba Parietis; or The Wall Flower*, 1650.

30–1. *Heliodorus* Bishop of *Trissa*] See Socrates, *Ecclesiastical History*, v, 22. The Greek romance *Aethiopica* (of which the two chief characters are Theagenes and Charriclea) is now generally attributed to a third-century sophist. Montaigne also cites the story: *Essays*, trans. Trechman, vol. ii, p. 391.

P. 92. 4. *Ordination . . . Nags Head*] A reference to the story (first put about by the Jesuit Christopher Holywood in 1604) that the Anglican succession originated at the Nags Head Tavern Cheapside. The fiction aroused some controversy and Bramhall wrote *The Consecration and Succession of Protestant Bishops Justified*, The Hague, 1658.

5. the *Cock*] A well known Inn in Suffolk St.: 'Dr. Guy Carleton consecrated bishop of Bristow at Westminster Feb. 11, Su.; kept his consecration dinner at a victualling house in Suffolk Street called "the Cock".' Wood, *Life and Times*, ed. Clark, vol. ii, 1892, p. 243.

6. porridge] A term used by the Dissenters of the Anglican service and prayer book—see *Absalom and Achitophel*, l. 576; and Dryden, *Poems*, ed. Kinsley, vol. iv, 1958, p. 1891 n.

6–11. I know . . . Salt-fish] The story that Marvell inserts in the 'Second Impression' concerning Thomas à Becket probably derives from Herbert Bosham's life of the saint. When a visiting monk noticed that Becket was eating pheasant, he smiled, and Becket said: '. . . frater ni fallor, cum aviditate majori tu tuam sumis fabam quam ego apositam mihi phasidem avem.' *Vita S. Thomae*, in *Materials for the History of Thomas Becket*, ed. J. C. Robertson, vol. iii, 1877, p. 233. *The Dog and Partridge*, perhaps Marvell means the

Dog and Duck a notorious inn in St. George's Fields, see H. B. Wheatley, *London Past and Present*, vol. i, 1891, pp. 509–10.

11. Mr *Cartwright*] The Actor who played *Thunder* in *The Rehearsal*, I. i, p. 10.

12. Nonconformist *Cartwright*] Thomas Cartwright (1535–1603), the famous puritan divine who engaged in a bitter controversy with Whitgift and was deprived of his post as Lady Margaret Professor at Cambridge, as a result of the latter's influence.

27. *Don Quixote*] Cervantes, *Don Quixote*, trans. Shelton, Bk. I, ch. vii: 'Of the good successe Don Quixote had in the dreadfull and never imagined adventure of the Windmils. . . .'

28. Whip a Gig] whip a top.

30. Lord Chief Justice] Sir Mathew Hale (1609–76) a noted judge. Lord Chief Justice 1671–5.

30. Sir *Edmond Godfrey*] Sir Edmond Berry Godfrey (1621–78), J.P. for Westminster. Burnet wrote of him that: 'He was esteemed the best justice of the Peace in England.' In 1678 his mysterious death precipitated the crisis known as the Popish Plot.

33–4. the Rack . . . dimension] An allusion to Procrustes, the famous robber in Attica. Plutarch, *Theseus*, XI.

P. 93. 12. *take care . . . evil*] *Preface*, b1^v.

19. run up . . . Angel] Num. 22: 25; referring to Balaam.

P. 94. 1–2. *Ratio ultima Cleri*] *Ultima ratio regum*, a motto engraved on cannon by 1613. Calderon referred to war as the *Ultima razon de regis*. Stevenson, *Book of Quotations*, 1934, p. 2117.

11. pudder] Disturbance; commotion; turmoil.

21. Answerer . . . Argument] Owen, *Truth and Innocence Vindicated*, p. 280. Owen uses the words 'Signa cum ad res Divinas pertinent, sunt Sacramenta'. The passage, as Marvell points out later, is from a letter of Augustine to Marcellinus, see Aurelii Augustini, *Opera*, Tom. II, 'Epistolae', Lugduni, 1561, Epistola, V, p. 19. In Migne's *Patrologiae Latinae*, vol. xxxiii, 1861, col. 527, it is Epistola, cxxxviii.

P. 95. 3–5. *Quum . . . emendes*] Horace, letter to Augustus, *Epistulae*, II. i. 1–3.

P. 96. 4. *Welch* . . . Proverb] Grosart cites 'Da yw'r main gyda't Efengel'.

13. *Fathers* opinion] Parker's father was John Parker (*fl.* 1655), a judge who prospered under Cromwell, becoming a baron of the exchequer and member of Parliament for Rochester. His views differed considerably from those of his son, as may be seen in his: *The Government of the People of England, precedent and present the same*, 1650, where it is maintained that: 'Kings and Governours are from the people, and are appointed for the peoples sakes.' (p. 1.) See also below Pt. II, pp. 180 ff.

15. *Symbolical*] *Preface*, b3^v ff.

P. 97. 16–17. Cartwright . . . Whitgift] Whitgift first replied to Cartwright's *A Second Admonition to the Parliament*, 1572, with *An Answere to a Certen Libel*, 1572.

32. *Trophies*] *Discourse*, p. 200.

33–4. *wrought . . . belief*] *Preface*, A3ᵛ.

36. *Curtana*] The pointless sword borne before the Kings of England at their coronation; emblematically considered the sword of mercy; also 'the sword of King Edward the Confessor'.

36. *Sir Salomon's*] The sword of Solomon: I Kgs. 3: 24. Marvell may also be referring to the foolish hero of John Caryll's *Sir Salomon; or the Cautious Coxcomb* (1671).

P. 98. 3. *Scanderbag*] George Castriot (1403–67), the national hero of Albania, famed for his victories against the Ottoman Turk. See J. de Lavardin, *The History of George Castriot, surnamed Scanderbeg, King of Albanie*, 1596.

8. a great Prelate] John Cosin (1594–1672) Bishop of Durham, whose *Collection of Private Devotions* (1627), mentioned seven sacraments rather than five, and was heavily criticised in Parliament. See below, p. 129.

24. *Roman* Emperour] Caligula, Suetonius, *Caligula*, 44.

34–1 [P. 99.] *could not . . . Ceremonies*] *Preface*, a2ᵛ.

P. 99. 27. Insana Laurus] Pliny notes the 'mad Lawrell' over-shadowing King Amycus's tomb. *The History of the World*, tr. Holland, 1601, I. xvi. 44, p. 495.

P. 100. 7. we . . . Porridge] 'Bishop *Bonner* having learnt that *Cranmer* and *Ridley* had retained some Ceremonies and Practises of the *Romish* Church, said, That he doubted not, since their Broath went down with them so well, but they would ere long come to feed upon their Beef too.' L. Du Moulin, *A Short and True Account*, 1680, p. 18. See also above, p. 92 n.

11. Transubstantiation] The term is not used till the twelfth century. Du Pin, *A New Ecclesiastical History*, vol. x, 1698, p. 156.

20–1. some . . . Rome] Marvell is doubtless thinking of 'Doctor Vane, and Doctor Goffe, and Doctor Bailey, and H. P. de Cressie' and others whom Baxter mentions in his *Grotian Religion Discovered*, 1658, p. 99. The names head a list of fifty-three converts to Romanism prefixed to a book entitled *Legenda Lignea*, 1653, by 'D.Y.' Bramhall takes up the charge in his *Vindication*, ch. iii.

25. Doctor *Thorndike*] See above, p. 78 n.

P. 102. 1–5. *Why . . . people*] *Preface*, b4ᵛ.

5. Tap-lash] The 'lashings' or washings of casks or glasses; the dregs of liquor.

6. p. 110] *Discourse*, p. 110.

14–17. The same . . . determined] Ibid., p. 108.

32. eight elephants] See above, p. 12 n.

P. 103. 12. *Augustus Caesar*] Suetonius, *Augustus*, 85.

17–18. *Homousians . . . Homoiousians*] The terms on which the great Arian heresy turned. A Homoiousian was one who held the Father and Son in the Godhead to be of like, but not the same essence or substance. A Homousian held that the three persons of the Trinity were of the same essence or substance (the orthodox *trinitarian* view). The first Council of Nicaea (325) established the orthodox view.

18. *Languedoc*] Dante distinguished between the languages of Latin derivation by means of the three affirmative particles *oc, oïl, si*. Hence the distinction between the *langued'oc* and the *langued'oui*.

19. *Faves . . . Haves*] The variants still exist in modern Gascon.

20–1. *Crabe . . . Cabre*] *Crabe* is the Languedoc variant, *cabre* the Gascon. La Curne de Sainte-Palaye, *Dictionaire historique de l'ancien langage françois*, Niort, N.D. I have been unable to trace this shibboleth.

P. 104. 6. *Let . . . order*] I Cor. 14: 40.

P. 105. 9. *Worster-House*-Conference] See above, p. 18 n.
19–20. *Wellfare . . . Fool*] Preface, a2ʳ.
20–1. *Oh how . . . this*] Ibid., a2ʳ.
27. *Rationale*] Sparrow, *Rationale upon the Book of Common Prayer*, 1657.
34–5. *Cloke . . . Parchments*] II Tim. 4: 13.

P. 106. 15. bran] Sort, class, quality.
21. *Unum . . . deesse*] Bramhall, *Vindication*, p. 20. A line from a fragment of a poem by Caesar on Terence, see Caesar, *Commentarii*, ed. Klotz, Lipsiae, 1927, p. 192. Marvell may have seen it in Suetonius's 'Life of Terence'; Terence, *Comoediae Sex*, Lugduni, 1644, 5ᵛ.
26–7. *Politick Would-be's*] As in Jonson's *Volpone*.

P. 107. 19. *Canibals*] Cf. Montaigne, *Essays*, i, 31. 'Of Cannibals'.

P. 108. 6. *His Father*] His adoptive father Julius Caesar (Suetonius, *Julius*, 83) not Gaius Octavius.
10–11. Predecessor] Henry III of France was assassinated by a Dominican friar Jacques Clement on 1 Aug. 1589.
15. latter] Charles II's mother, Henrietta Maria, was Henry IV's daughter.
25. perhaps two] See *Introd.* I.
32. p. 49] *Defence*, p. 49.

P. 109. 8. *Roman* Emperours] Caligula, Suetonius, *Caligula*, 58.
10. Parliament of *Poland*] The authority of the King was so limited by the General Diet in Poland at this time, that he was virtually helpless. Heylyn, *Cosmographie*, 1669, Bk. II, p. 150.
13–15. *Alexander . . . habit.*] *Quintus Curtius*, VI. ii. 2–4, and VI. vi. 7–9.
15–17. King of *Spain . . .* Retinue] Heylyn, *Cosmographie*, 1669, Bk. I, pp. 219.
20. Tyrant] Ivan IV ('the Terrible') tsar of Muscovy (1530–84). Heylyn repeats a story from Oderbornius's 'Life' of Johannes Basilides (1585) of how the tyrant sent to Moscow '. . . to provide a Coal-pack of live Fleas for a

Medicine: and when the Citizens returned answer that it was impossible, he fined them at 700 Rubbles for their Disobedience'. *Cosmographie*, 1669, Bk. II, p. 138.

24. certain Queen] Possibly Christina of Sweden (1626–89). She abdicated in 1654 and was converted to Roman Catholicism. A vast number of legends (mostly scurrilous) surround her life, though I have been unable to trace the source of the references.

P. 110. 1. Sturdy *Swiss*] William Tell, his legendary story is part of the history of the origin of the Swiss Confederation.

6. unhoopable] Not capable of being contained.

P. 112. 13. Rochet] A vestment of linen, of the nature of a surplice, usually worn by bishops and abbots.

P. 113. 4–6. *English* man . . . *ours*] Camden, *Remaines*, 1614, p. 279.

10. Peeks] Piques: fits of animosity or ill-feeling.

P. 114. 10. *Robert Parker*] (1564–1614) Puritan divine. His work, *A Scholasticall Discourse against symbolizing with Anti-Christ in ceremonies* (1607), aroused great opposition from the Church Party, the King was persuaded to issue a proclamation for his arrest, and he was forced to flee the country.

14. Archbishop of *Canterbury*, Parker] Mathew Parker (1504–75). *De Antiquitate Britannicae Ecclesiae* was first published in 1572. Marvell, from the page reference, seems to have used the edition of 1605, published in Hanover.

17. slaughter . . . *Bangor*] Bede, *Historia Ecclesiastica*, II. ii.

20. Romish Ceremonies] The Welsh Church differed from the Roman usage in the date of the celebration of Easter, the ritual of baptism, and a number of other points.

P. 116. 27. gird] Strike, cut at.

P. 117. 8. crimination] Severe accusation or censure.

P. 118. 3. *Mountagnes Essayes*] Montaigne himself notes that 'The headings of my chapters do not always embrace the matter of them'. (*Essays*, trans. Trechman, vol. ii, p. 464.) The 'Second Impression' reading *Mountague* may possibly be authoritative, but it seems unlikely. Marvell would then be referring to the very ordinary theological essays of Walter Montague (1603–77): *Miscellanea Spiritualia: or Devout Essaies*, 1648.

20. spreading false News] *C.S.P.D.* 12 June 1672, 'Proclamation forbidding the spreading of false news, and licentious talking of State and government. . . .' See also letter to Popple June, 1672, *Poems & Letters*, vol. ii, p. 312.

P. 119. 24–6. *To consider . . . none*] Preface, c4ᵛ.

36. beat up . . . Popery] 'And Pulpit, Drum Ecclesiastick,
Was beat with Fist, instead of a stick:'
S. Butler, *Hudibras*, ed. Z. Grey, vol. i, 1744, Pt. I, C.I, ll. 10–11, p. 4.

P. 120. 1–3. *poor . . . Security*] Bramhall, *Vindication*, pp. 160–1.

7–20. rusty . . . Parishes] Cf. Lucan, *Pharsalia*, trans. May, 1635, i. 240–3.

11. Habergeon] A sleeveless coat or jacket of mail or scale armour.

22. *Beza*] Theodore Beza (1519–1605) French theologian, friend, biographer and successor of Calvin.

22. Bandeleers] Bandoleer: a broad belt worn over the shoulder and across the breast by soldiers: it helped to support the musket and had 12 charges attached to it.

23. *Keckerman*] Bartholomeus Keckerman (1571–1609), German reformed theologian, author of *Systema Theologicum* (1602) translated as *A Manduction to Theology* (1620).

30. Train'd bands] See Tom Brown, *Amusements Serious and Comical*, ed. A. L. Hayward, 1927, p. 239: '. . . our holiday heroes and custard stormers of Cheapside. . . .'

P. 121. 3–4. *For my part . . . England*] Preface, c4^v.

17–18. *of . . . temper*] Ibid. A3^r.

18–19. *had a mind . . . extent*] Ibid. A3^v.

26–7. *Bassompierre*] François de Bassompierre (1599–1646), Marshal of France and favourite of Henry IV. His *Mémoires* were published in 1665.

27. *Aubigné*] Theodore Agrippa d'Aubigne (1552–1630), poet, historian and counsellor to Henry IV. I have been unable to trace the rhyme to either Bassompierre or Aubigné. However, the latter did use the word *chevauché*. 'Monsieur le Comte mon ami, voudriez-vous mettre vostre cousinet sur un here qu'on a chevauché à dos qui a les genoux tous eschorchez?' 'Confession catholique du Sieur de Sancy', *Œuvres*, 1877, ii, p. 258.

34. *Doctor Patrick*] Simon Patrick, author of *The Friendly Debate*.

34. *Father Patrick*] Father Patrick MaGinn, Abbot of Thuley (d. 1683) (see *H.M.C. report* 7, p. 410a.) One of the priests attendant on the Queen (*H.M.C. report* 7, p. 489a.). His name appears many times in *C.S.P.D.* 1668–70. He seems to have been a close friend of Arlington.

P. 122. 11–12. *First . . . State*] Preface, c6^r.

12. *By the . . . Irreligion*] Ibid. d7^v.

13. *By joyning . . . confederacy*] Ibid. e4^r.

25–6. *so little . . . Church*] Ibid. c6^r.

P. 123. 13. Leystall] Laystall, a place where refuse and dung is laid.

13. *Sambenitas*] San benito: under the Spanish Inquisition a garment of black colour, representing a scapular in shape, ornamented with flames, devils and other devices and worn by an impenitent confessed heretic at an *auto da fé*. '. . . you represent the Doctor [Dr. Owen] to the world; as *Romes* Inquisitors were wont to do Martyrs to the people; with Fiends and Devils painted on them; that so they might appear as hideous and frightful, as they would have them thought wicked and abominable.' *An Expostulatory Letter*, 1671, p. 5.

28–30. *The Power . . . Patronage*] *Preface*, c7^r.

36. *Petra . . . Rudolpho*] An allusion to Gregory VII's duplicity. Having humbled and absolved Henry IV in 1077, Gregory sent a crown to Rudolph of Swabia (d. 1080) inscribed with the words Marvell quotes. Matthew Paris, *Chronica Maiora*, ed. H. R. Luard, vol. ii, 1874, p. 16.

P. 124. 2. *Emperour . . . Ass*] The ceremony in which the Czar leads the Patriarch's ass after attending mass at Easter—Marvell saw this: as described by Guy Miege, *A Relation Of Three Embassies From His Sacred Majestie Charles II. To the Great Duke of Muscovie, The King of Sweden, and the King of Denmark*, 1669, p. 298.

3–7. *We may . . . Interest*] Parker, *Preface*, d7^r.

7. cokesing] i.e. 'coaxing'. Marvell also seems to have in mind the original meaning, 'to make a cokes of': befool; impose on; make a fool of.

15–17. *But should . . . Crown*] *Preface*, d7^r.

P. 125. 18. *Abbot*] George Abbot (1562–1633). He clashed bitterly with Laud in his effort to stamp out Arminianism—his disgrace at court (narrated below) occurred 1626–7.

23–4. learned . . . *Fisher*] W. Laud, *An Answere to Mr. Fisher's Relation of a third Conference*, 1624.

31. Impositions of Money] The 'Forced Loan' of 1626/7. L. N. Wall has suggested that this was a sore subject for Marvell, for he notes that Andrew Marvell (Grandfather of the poet?) refused to pay the loan without Parliamentary authority. *Notes and Queries*, vol. 5, no. 9, Sept. 1958. See also R. Leigh, *The Transproser Rehears'd*, 1673, p. 81.

P. 126. 6. Picket] Piquet, a card game played by two persons with a pack of 32 cards.

6–7. *Dignitary of Lincoln*] Mrs. Elsie Duncan-Jones has suggested to me that in all probability this is either Francis Drope (1629–71), Preb. of Lincoln 1669–70; or William Reresby (d. 1670), Preb. of Brampton.

9. *Pieces*] English gold coins; originally the *unite* of James I. In 1612 it equalled twenty-two shillings.

32–4. and are ready . . . bargain] In a letter to Popple 21 March 1670, Marvell remarks of the 'Bill against Conventicles': 'So the Fate of the Bill is uncertain, but must probably pass, being the Price of Money.' *Poems & Letters*, vol. ii, p. 301.

36. naked truth] Horace, *Odes*, I. 24. 7.

P. 127. 5. There was . . .] Abbot's *Narrative* may be found in J. Rushworth, *Historical Collections, 1618–1629*, 1659, pp. 434–57.

5–12. one *Sibthorp* . . . higher] *Historical Collections, 1618–1629*, p. 436. Robert Sibthorpe (d. 1662) published his sermon as *Apostolike Obedience. Shewing the Duty of Subjects to pay Tributes and Taxes to their Princes*, 1627.

6. Doctor *Pierce*] William Pierce (1580–1670), Bishop of Bath and Wells, an opponent of Calvinism, Vice-Chancellor of Oxford 1621–4.

14. he . . . Tribute] *Historical Collections*, p. 440.

14–18. Kings dutie . . . things] Ibid., pp. 439–40.

19. out . . . *Matthew*] Ibid., p. 439 (Matt. 22: 21).

20–1. *What . . . double*] Ibid., p. 438.

27–3 [P. 128]. His life . . . him] Ibid., p. 440.

29. Bishop of *Durham*] Richard Neile (1562–1640), partially responsible for Laud's advancement.

P. 128. 2. marrying . . . Lady R.] On 26 Dec. 1605, Laud, then chaplain to Charles Blount, Earl of Devonshire, married his patron to the divorced wife of Lord Rich.

5. Bishop *Williams*] John Williams (1582–1650), Chancellor and Archbishop of York.

7–11. Verily . . . We] *Historical Collections*, p. 440.

10. Rochester] John Buckeridge (1562–1631) Laud's tutor.

10. Oxford] John Howson (1557?–1632).

12–18. In my . . . live] *Historical Collections*, p. 442.

12. Doctor *Harsnet*] Samuel Harsnet (1561–1631), Archbishop of York: 'A zealous asserter of ceremonies.'

14. *Give . . . Cæsars*] Matt. 22: 21.

19–24. if . . . Divines] *Historical Collections*, p. 443.

26–9. sorry . . . Man] Ibid., p. 443.

30. Earl of *Essex* his divorce] Robert Devereux, third Earl of Essex (1591–1646). In 1613 his marriage to Frances Howard was nullified, and she married Sir Robert Carr, Earl of Somerset.

31. *was . . . Archbishop*] *Historical Collections*, p. 444.

P. 129. 1–6. it was . . . expunged] Ibid., p. 444.

1. Bishop of *London*] George Montaigne (1569–1628), an ardent ally of Laud.

6–14. Doctor*Woral . . . again*] *Historical Collections*, p. 444. Thomas Worral (*c.* 1589–1639), Canon of St. Pauls 1627–39. (Foster, *Alumni Oxoniensis*, vol. iv, 1892.)

11. Counsel at the *Temple*] John Selden (1584–1654), the great jurist.

15–18. Those . . . prison] *Historical Collections*, p. 455.

16. King of *Denmark*] Christian IV (1577–1648). In 1627 he was at war with the Emperor.

18–22. complained . . . *went*] *Historical Collections*, pp. 453–4.

19. *Mountagues* Arminian Book] Richard Montague, *Appello Caesarem*, 1625.

21. Bp of *Bath*] Then William Laud, translated to London in 1628.

P. 130. 2. Doctor *Manwaring*] Roger Manwaring (1590–1653), Bishop of St. David's. In 1626 he was appointed chaplain in ordinary to Charles I. In this capacity he preached before the King on 4 July 1627 at Oatlands on *Religion* and on 29 July at Alderton on *Allegiance*. The House of Commons urged that he be punished for his sermons; he was, however, given preferment.

5–16. That the . . . Princes] See *Religion and Allegiance*: 'The First Sermon', 1627, esp. pp. 24–33, Marvell paraphrases freely.

17–23. That . . . them] Ibid., pp. 19–20.

24–33. temporal . . . defence] Ibid., p. 49.

P. 131. 19–20. Gentry . . . *Abby Lands*] See P. Heylyn, *Ecclesia Restaurata*, 1661, 'To the Reader', a1ᵛ.

23. *Ecclesiastical Loan*] The King called on the clergy to help from the pulpits.

P. 132. 23–4. odious to King *James*] James I sent Bishop Carleton, Dr. Ward, Dr. Hall, and Bishop Davenant to join in the condemnation of the Arminian 'Remonstrants' at the Synod of Dort (1618).

24. *Barnevelt*] Johan van Olden Barneveldt (1547–1619), Grand pensionary of Holland, a republican, and supporter of the Arminians. Following the Synod of Dort, he was arrested and executed.

P. 133. 1–5. King . . . advanced] 'About the same time [July 1628], Mr *Montague* . . . was designed to the Bishoprick of *Chichester*. . . . Nevertheless his *Appello Caesarem* was thought fit to be called in, the King declaring, that out of his care to maintain the Church in the unity of true Religion, and the bond of peace, to prevent unnecessary disputes, he had lately caused the Articles of Religion to be reprinted, as a rule for avoiding diversities of opinions; and considering that a Book written by *Richard Montague*, now Bishop of *Chichester*, intituled, *Appello Caesarem*, was the first cause of those disputes and differences, which since have much troubled the quiet of the Church, he would take away occasion, by commanding all persons that had any of those Books in their hands to deliver them to the Bishop of the Diocess. . . .' Rushworth, *Collections*, 2nd ed., 1682, vol. i, pp. 634–5.

5–6. *Manwarings* Case] 'Doctor *Manwaring*, censured by the Lords in Parliament, and perpetually disabled from future Ecclesiastical Preferments in the Church of *England* was immediately presented to the Rectory of *Stamford Rivers*. . . .' Ibid., p. 635.

P. 134. 33–4. sent thither . . . them] On 23 July 1637, at St. Giles', Edinburgh, the attempt to read services from the English prayer book caused a riot. The Covenant followed, whereby the subscribers swore to resist the recent innovations to the death, and the two countries drifted into war.

P. 135. 7. *Arms* . . . *Tears*] 'They knew My chiefest Armes left Me, were those only, which the Ancient Christians were wont to use against their persecutors, Prayers and Teares.' Charles I, *Eikon Basilike*, ed. Almack, 1904, ch. 10, p. 70.

P. 136. 3. Declaration] The Declaration of Breda, 1660. See above, p. 43 n.

5. Conference] The Savoy Conference. On 25 March 1661, the King issued a commission to twelve bishops and twelve Puritan divines, and nine assessors on each side, requiring and authorizing them to meet together in the Master's lodgings at the Savoy or elsewhere from time to time during the next four months, to advise upon and review the Book of Common Prayer. See R. S. Bosher, *The Making of the Restoration Settlement*, 1951, pp. 226–30.

26. one memorable day] 24 Aug. 1662. See above, p. 57 n.

32–33. *all . . . Patronage*] *Preface*, c7ʳ.

P. 137. 3. Lease] Doubtless a case arising out of the sale of Bishops, Deans and Chapters' Lands, as the petition of one Alexander Baker noted: 'And whereas in these late Troubles the Lands belonging to all Deans and Chapters in *England*, were put to Sale by the then commanding though usurped Powers; and if the Tenants and Possessors of any such Lands did not come in and purchase the Reversion thereof within forty Days, that then they should lose their Tenants Right, and the said Lands might be sold to any other that would buy them.' White Kennet, *Register*, 1728, p. 628. There were many such cases, see *Journal of the House of Commons 1660–7*.

23–4. *Sold . . . Lane*] Published in 1672.

30. great Minister of State] Edward Hyde, Earl of Clarendon, see above, p. 44 n. '. . . the King is the most concerned in the world against the Chancellor and all people that do not appear against him, and therefore is angry with the Bishops, having said that he had one Bishop on his side, Crofts, and but one. . . .' Pepys, *Diary*, ed. Smith, 1906, p. 582, 16 Nov. 1667.

33. matter of *Divorce*] The bill to allow the divorced Lord Ross to remarry. See Marvell's letter to Popple, 21 March 1670, *Poems & Letters*, vol. ii, p. 301.

P. 138. 4. trinkle] To treat secretly, intrigue with.

23–4. *Union . . . resistance*] *Preface*, e4ʳ.

27. *jear the Parsons*] Ibid. e1ʳ.

P. 139. 15–16. *Pulpit-sweat . . . Ordinances*] Ibid. d1ᵛ.

20–1. *minding . . . Poetry*] Ibid. d8ʳ.

22–9. the Clergy . . . men] Ibid. e2ᵛ–e3ʳ.

P. 140. 1–2. *man . . . laughter*] Ibid. c5ᵛ.

5. Witches] See Joseph Glanvill, *A Blow at Modern Sadducism . . . with Reflections on Drollery and Atheism*, 1668.

27–8. *joyning . . . Confederacy*] *Preface*, e4ʳ.

32–8 [P. 141.] has at present . . . Guardians] Ibid. e7ʳ.

P. 141. 14–18. They . . . Martyr] Ibid. e5ᵛ.

28. *Infant*] Charles II had no legitimate heirs.

P. 142. 10–15. *by their . . . Discipline*] *Preface*, e8ʳ.

29–30. All . . . Pork] Livy, *The Romane Historie*, tr. Holland, 1600, p. 916. See below Pt. II, pp. 307–8.

34. *five mile Act*] Passed in 1665, the Act made it penal for any Nonconformist minister who had not taken the oath of non-resistance to teach in a school or go within five miles of any city, borough or corporate town where he had preached or taught before the Act of Uniformity.

P. 143. 1–2. *King Phys,* and *King Ush*] The two usurping Kings in *The Rehearsal,* II. i ff.

18. the *Poet*] Sir William Davenant (1605–1668).

19. *Bishop Davenant*] John Davenant (1576–1641), Bishop of Salisbury, a moderate Calvinist, he represented the Church of England at the Synod of Dort.

22–5. *For Prayer . . . lost*] Davenant, *Gondibert,* 1651, II. vi. 85, p. 197.

26. Union . . . Atheists] *Preface,* e4^r.

27. *Praise . . . minds*] Davenant, *Gondibert,* II. vi. 84, p. 197.

28–31. *Its utmost . . . tear*] Ibid. II. vi. 87, p. 197.

32. *Astragon*] Gondibert is being shown the temples of *Prayer, Praise,* and *Penitence,* by Astragon, the wise man who tends his wounds.

P. 144. 5–6. *Hum . . . Humble-Bee*] *The Rehearsal,* IV. i. pp. 35–6.

8–9. *hot fit . . . Passion*] *Discourse,* 'Preface', p. vii.

20–1. *spend most . . . God*] *Preface,* d1^v.

27. *Aretine*] Pietro Aretino (1492–1556), the Italian poet, notorious for his scurrilous satires.

28–30. *Qui . . . conobbe*] A legend attributes these lines to the famous historian and latinist Paolo Giovio (1483–1552). See Carlo Bertani, *Pietro Aretino e le sue opere,* Sondrio, 1901, p. 181 n.

PART II

T.P. 10. J. G.] John Gelson? A spy for Secretary of State Williamson in Holland 1672, brother of the Bishop of Oxford's secretary. *C.S.P.D. 1671–2.*

P. 149. 1. Doctor *Sermon*] William Sermon (1629–79), Physician-in-ordinary to the King. Wood calls him a 'forward vain and conceited person', *Fasti,* vol. ii, 1692, col. 874.

3. *lost . . . Understanding*] *Reproof,* 'Preface', A4^v.

6–8. *had . . . recruited*] Ibid., p. 1.

10–12. Mountains . . . produces] Parturient montes nascetur ridiculus mus. Horace, *Ars Poetica,* 139.

18. *Aytzema*] Lieuwe Van Aitzema (1600–9), Dutch historian and statesman.

19. *Prince of Orange*] William II (1626–50), died of small-pox 6 Nov. 1650. Marvell's details are from Aitzema, *Saken van Staet en Oorlogh 1645–56,* vol. iii, Graven-Haghe 1669, pp. 456–7.

22. having . . . Train] On 26 Nov. 1670, Parker 'had the degree of Doct.

of Div. confer'd on him at *Cambridg*, at which time *William* prince of *Aurange* or *Orange* was entertained there'. Wood, *Athenae*, vol. ii, 1692, col. 617.

23. *Juncture . . . Affairs*] Preface to *Bramhall*, A2ʳ.

P. 150. 1. *closer Importance*] Ibid. A2ʳ.

12. marryed?] Parker's wife was Rebecca Pheasant (Wood, *Life and Times*, vol. iii, p. 261). Marvell makes numerous references to the marriage which must have taken place immediately after the publication of *The Reproof* (see below, p. 174) which is advertised in the *Term Catalogue* for 6 May 1673, as being printed and published in Easter Term of that year. *Term Catalogue* ed. Arber, vol. i, p. 134. In a letter of 3 May 1673 Marvell notes that 'Dr. Parker will be out the next weeke'. *Poems & Letters*, vol. ii, p. 312.

15–16. *Pyramus . . . Wall*] *Mid-Summer Night's Dream*, I. ii; v. i.

18. own *Praecentor*] Suetonius, *Nero*, 24.

19–21. apprehended . . . Fidler] Ibid. 49.

P. 151. 13. Gazette] *London Gazette*, no. 781, 12–15 May 1673.

32–3. *some . . . Consequence*] E. Hickeringill, *Gregory, Father Greybeard*, 1673, p. 105.

P. 152. 17. *Abelteria*] ἀβελτερία: silliness, stupidity, fatuity.

29–30. *Distemper . . . Profession*] *Reproof*, p. 1.

31. *Clownish . . . Licentious*] Ibid., p. 1.

34–5. *Tentamina . . .*] Parker, *Tentamina Physico-Theologica de Deo*, 1665.

P. 153. 3–4. Aristotle . . . Goddess] Ibid., p. 2.

4–6. *Stilpo . . .* Shift] Ibid., p. 14.

16–18. how . . . Earth] Ibid., pp. 68–77 and 112.

21. *John Hinton*] Sir John Hinton M.D. (1603–82) royal physician, he attended the birth of Princess Henrietta in 1644.

21. Doctor *Chamberlain*] Peter Chamberlen M.D. (1601–83) celebrated *accoucheur*, supposed inventor of the short forceps.

23–4. of the Figure . . . Female] *Tentamina*, pp. 99–108.

25. Doctor *Harvy*] W. Harvey M.D. (1578–1657). The discoverer of the circulation of the blood. Marvell and Parker refer to his work: *Exercitationes de Generatione Animalium, quibus accedunt quaedam de Partu, de Membranis ac Tumoribus Uteri et de Conceptione*, 1651.

25–7. tells . . . business] *Tentamina*, p. 106.

27–8. blushing Gentleman] *Reproof*, p. 227.

28–9. undertakes . . . Procreation] *Tentamina*, p. 108.

31–2. dine . . . Goddess] Ibid., p. 262.

33–5. *Lucretius . . . Deities*] Ibid., p. 105. Lucretius, *De Rerum Natura*, I. i.

P. 154. 10–11. *out . . . ignemque*] *Tentamina*, p. 105.

12. *Pimples . . . Paracelsus*] Ibid., p. 73.

14–17. *that . . . desires*] Actually from *An Account of the Nature and Extent of the Divine Dominion and Goodnesse*, 1667, bound up with *A Free and Impartial*

Censure of the Platonick Philosophie, 1667, both by Parker; Marvell is using the second edition in which the pagination is continuous: pp. 210–11.

25–9. *being . . . Souls*] *A Free and Impartial Censure*, p. 19.

30–32. *tasted . . . seeing*] Ibid., p. 15.

P. 155. 1–2. *thinks . . . dearest*] *An Account*, p. 123, 'Preface'.

5. *Tridentine*] Pertaining to the Council of Trent.

20–1. *Phys . . . Kingdom*] *The Rehearsal*, II. i, pp. 17–18.

29. Italian Author] Aretino? (see above, Pt. I, p. 144). I have been unable to trace the phrase (*Fa tregua ma non mai pace*, quoted in the margin) but a similar idea is expressed in Aretino's *Marescalco*, V. vi: '. . . no fu mai uomo nè sarà che non resti avendo il male universale senza un duolmi un poco qui, et un duolmi un poco qua.' *Commedie*, ed. Sonzogno, Milan 1888, p. 72.

P. 156. 1. Asses Milk] Hickeringill, *Gregory, Father Greybeard*, p. 119.

27. *common drudgeries*] *Defence*, 'Preface', A6^r.

28. *innocent comforts*] Ibid. A6^r.

P. 157. 1–4. *so . . . him*] *Free and Impartial Censure*, p. 1.

6. importunity . . .] *Preface to Bramhall*, A2^r.

12. *sold . . . slavery*] *Free and Impartial Censure*, p. 1.

19. Louse . . . Jaundice] *Gregory, Father Greybeard*, p. 93. See also W. Sermon, *A Friend to the Sick*, 1673, p. 172.

20. *Sacrament . . .*] *Reproof*, p. 112.

22. Tribute of Fleas] See above, Pt. I, p. 109 and n.

24. Tartars . . .] '. . . one of them eatheth the lyce from another's head, sayinge, Thus will wee doe to our enemies. . . .' S. Munster, *A brief Collection . . . out of the Cosmographie*, 1574, p. 72.

28–31. Doctor . . . *Myrrhæ*] Tallement des Réaux, *Les Historiettes*, ed. Monmerque and Paris, vol. vi, Paris, 1862, p. 222. Also P. Legouis, 'La purge de Gargantua ou Marvell et Tallement des Réaux', *Études anglaises*, t. VI. N° 3, 1953.

34. *Beggars Bush*] A rendevous for beggars '. . . being a tree notoriously known on the left hand of the London road from Huntingdon to Caxton'. H. G. Bohn, *Handbook of Proverbs*, 1867, p. 206.

34. *Phthiriases*] Lousiness: a morbid condition of the body in which the lice multiply excessively. It afflicted the tyrants Herod and Sylla.

P. 158. 4–5. *Phthirophagi*] Louse eaters.

5–6. *Presidents . . . Rites*] *Preface*, e2^r.

10. St. *Francis*] St. Francis of Assisi (1181–1226). '. . . his mercy extended itself to lice and worms, which he would not suffer to be killed.' Jurieu, *Apologie pour les Reformateurs*, ch. i, p. 52. Cited Bayle, *Dictionary*, vol. v, 1737, p. 311, n[H].

14. *Succedaneum*] substitute.

15–16. renders . . . Louse] *Gregory, Father Greybeard*, p. 93.

17. his *Shop Divines*] *Reproof*, p. 21.

22–4. *So tame . . . impressions*] *A Discourse*, 'Preface', p. iii.

25–6. *them . . . all*] *Free and Impartial Censure*, p. 25.

26–7. *quanquam . . . indolis*] *Tentamina*, p. 109.

33. *Diaphoretick*] That which promotes perspiration.

35–2 [P. 159]. Turnep-tops . . . Choler] W. Sermon, *A Friend to the Sick*, 1673.

P. 159. 5. *Energumeni*] 'For the Church it self, it usually consisted of three parts; the first was the *Narthex* . . . it was that part of the Church that lay next to the great door by which they entred in: in the first part of it stood the *Catechumens*, or first learners of Christianity, in the middle the *Energumeni*, or those who were *possessed* by *Satan*. . . .' W. Cave, *Primitive Chritianity*, 1673, Pt. I, p. 138.

13–14. *asswaging . . . in-felicity*] Above, Pt. I, p. 11.

19–21. *cowardly . . . Profession*] *Reproof*, p. 1.

P. 160. 17–20. *if reward*] Ibid., 'Preface', A4ʳ.

22–3. *he must . . . Understanding*] Ibid., A4ᵛ.

P. 163. 29–30. wholsome usage] 'Before any person could regularly be elected or ordained to any clerical office in the Church, the electors and ordainers were obliged to make several inquiries concerning him . . . his faith, his morals, and his outward state and condition in the world.' J. Bingham, *Works*, ed. R. Bingham, vol. ii, 1855, p. 34.

P. 165. 20–2. *if . . . Security*] Bramhall, *Vindication*, p. 161 (mis-paginated as 159).

26–30. *taking . . . odious*] Preface to Bramhall, e1ᵛ–e2ʳ.

P. 166. 34. *Incognito*] *Marginal note:* '*Let the Author of the Friendly Debate be careful how he layes aside his Vizour.*' *Discourse*, 'Preface', p. xix.

P. 167. 5. Comedians] *Marginal note:* '*Many things are only design'd to set off his reasonings with a Comical humour and pleasantness*', Ibid., 'Preface', p. xvi.

19. *Nursery*] 23 July 1663 Killigrew and Davenant were granted a license: 'to erect a third playhouse, as a nursery for training actors. . . .' *C.S.P.D. 1663–4*, p. 214. Thomas Killigrew (1612–83) received a patent for the Kings Theatre 9 July 1660 (*C.S.P.D. 1660–1*, p. 114) and became Master of the Revels after the death of Sir Henry Herbert in April 1673.

35. *Bravo's* and *Filoux*] Villains and criminals.

36. *Venetian* Galleys] *Free and Impartial Censure*, p. 1.

P. 168. 2. supply . . . Slaves] *Discourse*, p. 223.

32. Letters of Mart] Letters of marque: A licence granted by a sovereign to a subject, authorizing him to make reprisals on the subjects of a hostile state for injuries done to him. Hence a licence to fit out an armed vessel or

privateer and employ it in the capture of the merchant shipping of the enemy's subjects.

34. *Bricolle*] Fr. 'On the rebound'.

36. Sir *John Falstaff*. . .] *I Henry IV*, II, ii.

P. 169. 20. *Onias*] Onias II, son of Simon the just, high priest of the Jewish people, he endangered them by refusing to pay the required 20 talents of silver to the King of Egypt. See Josephus, *Antiquities*, Bk. XII, ch. iv. Josephus does not relate Marvell's story.

21. *Simeon* the *Just*] A renowned high priest, identical either with Simon I (310–291 or 300–270 B.C.) son of Onias I, or with Simon (219–199 B.C.) son of Onias II.

P. 170. 8. *hominum* . . .] Lucretius, *De Rerum Natura*, I, i.

13–14. Wolves . . . Baboons] *Free and Impartial Censure*, pp. 34–5.

P. 171. 19. *Siquis*] A public notice requesting information: ecclesiastically, an inquiry concerning an intending ordinand.

P. 172. 23. Glass house] The Duke of Buckingham's 'Glass works', mentioned by Evelyn, 19 Sept. 1676. The works were established at Vauxhall *c.* 1670 where there is still a 'Glasshouse walk'. The buildings would have been visible from Lambeth Palace.

31. Weed] Seaweed, burned to make soda ash—sodium carbonate—for glass manufacture.

P. 173. 1–2. License . . . recalled] *Introd.* III.

5. degrade . . . crown] '. . . Caput degradandi cum eodem cultello aut vitro abradit degradator leniter dicendo: "Consecrationem et Benedictionem ac unctionem tibi traditam radendo delemus et te ab ordine pontificali cui inhabilis es redditus abdicamus." ' Foxe, *Acts and Monuments*, ed. Townsend, vol. viii, 1849, p. 78. Foxe gives 'the manner of disgrading all orders and degrees, as well archbishops as others, priests, deacons, sub-deacons, etc.' citing from the *Pontificale Romanum*.

13. Printed Catalogue] *The Term Catalogues 1668–1709*, ed. Arber, 1903.

24–5. Groat . . . Five Shillingsworth] *A Common Place Book*: 'price stitcht 6d.' (Arber, i, p. 128); *The Transproser Rehears'd*: 'Price Bound 1s.' (Arber, i, p. 135); *Gregory Father Greybeard*: 'Price bound 2.6d.' (Arber, i, p. 142).

P. 174. 15. clancular] Secret, clandestine.

25. *Sixiesme du valet*] In the game of *piquet*, a sequence of six cards of the same suit to the knave (strictly impossible since cards below seven are not included). A *sixième* counts for 16 points if 'good', i.e. better than the cards of the opponent.

27. *Quatorze*] Four Aces, Queens, Knaves or tens; if 'good' a *quatorze* reckons 14 points.

27. repiqued] If a player scores in hand alone 30 or more before his adversary reckons anything, he gains a *repique* and adds 60 to his score. Marvell notes that Parker could gain 90 points toward a game of 100 up.

28. him of *Lincoln*] See above, Pt. I, p. 126. 6–7 and note.

29. *Scaramuccio*] A cowardly boaster, stock figure of Italian farce; Marvell is doubtless thinking of the popular Scaramouch of his day, Tiberio Fiorilli (1608–94) whose Italian company was in England April–Sept. 1673. Evelyn saw him 29 May 1673. (*Diary*, ed. De Beer, vol. iv, p. 12) Marvell mentions his second visit in a letter to Popple 24 July 1675 (*Poems & Letters*, vol. ii, p. 320).

P. 175. 10. *Smectymnuus*] The title of a Presbyterian work published in 1641, made up from the initials of the authors: Stephen Marshall, Edmund Calamy, Thomas Young, Matthew Newcomen, and William Spurstow. The pamphlet was written in reply to Joseph Hall's *Humble Remonstrance to the High Court of Parliament* (1640).

14–15. learned Brothers of St. *Marthe*] Louis St. Marthe (1571–1655) and Gaucher St. Marthe (1571–1649). Twins noted through France for learning, piety and extraordinary likeness. P. Legouis, 'Marvell and the Brothers of St. Marthe', *Philological Quarterly*, 38, iv, Oct. 1959.

29. *Rosemary and Bayes* etc.] See *Introd.* I.

30. *S'too him Bayes*] Marvell notes in a letter to Sir Edward Harley that *S'too him Bayes* is 'writ by one Hodges' (*Poems & Letters*, vol. ii, p. 312). This may be Anthony Hodges (1614–86) rector of Wytham Berks., who delighted in 'buffooning and bantering' and was esteemed by the royalists their '*Terrae filius*'. (Wood, *Life*, vol. i, p. 152, and *Fasti Oxonienses*, ed. Bliss, 1815, Pt. I, col. 501.)

P. 176. 3–7. *This Great Soul . . . come*] Donne, 'The Progresse of the Soule', the first poem in the 1633 edition of the *Poems*. Stanza 7, p. 4. Marvell seems to be following a manuscript version, his variants are not in the printed texts.

9. Apple] Ibid., st. 9.

11–13. *To show . . . kill*] Ibid., st. 15, ll. 8–10.

17–18. *Already . . . Hen*] Ibid., st. 20, ll. 3–4.

19. little Fish] Ibid., st. 23.

20. another little Fish] Ibid., st. 25.

22. whale] Ibid., st. 31.

23. *Now . . . Seas*] Ibid., st. 34, l. 1.

24–5. *and . . . up*] Ibid., st. 32, ll. 8–9.

28–9. *being . . . address*] Ibid., st. 38, ll. 9–10.

31. *who . . . enemies*] Ibid., st. 39, l. 7.

P. 177. 5–7. Abel . . . *type*] Ibid., st. 41, ll. 4–6.

8–9. corrupted . . .] Ibid., st. 42.

9. taken . . .] Ibid., st. 43.

10. *Lycisca*] A dog engendered of a wolf and a bitch.

14–16. *He . . . trade*] Ibid., st. 45, ll. 4–6.

18–19. *from . . . perished*] Ibid., st. 45, ll. 9–10.

20. Ape . . .] Ibid., st. 46.

22–8. *Siphatecia . . . Thelemite . . . Themech*] Additions to the Biblical narrative, made sometime between the closing of the Old Testament narrative and the dispersal of the Jews under Titus and Vespasian. See Grierson's note in Donne, *Poems*, vol. ii, 1912, pp. 223–4.

22–3. making . . . *Apron*] *Progresse of the Soule*, st. 48.

23. stone . . .] Ibid., st. 49.

27. married . . .] Ibid., st. 51.

P. 178. 2–3. Gravity . . . Education] *Reproof*, p. 1.

12–13. *Arcadian* . . . Moon] Statius, *Thebaid*, iv, 275. Also Butler:

> From th'old Arcadians th'are believed
> To be before the Moon derived.
>
> ['The Elephant on the Moon', ll. 99–100]

Butler, *Satires and Miscellaneous Poetry and Prose*, ed. Lamar, 1928, p. 5.

19. Parentage of the *Nile*] Fresh discussion had been stirred up in 1669 by Sir Peter Wyche's publication of *A Short Relation of the River Nile*—accounts of the source of the Blue Nile by the Portuguese priests Paez and Lobo. Ptolemy had argued that the Nile had its source in two streams from two lakes fed by the melting snows on the Mountains of the Moon. See also Heylyn, *Cosmography*, 1669, Bk. IV, p. 58, and Parker, *Defence*, p. 19.

22. *Henry Parker*] d. 1470, a Carmelite friar of Doncaster, D.D. from Cambridge: '. . . Nam Anno Domini 1464, dum Londini ad D. Paulum è suggestu pro concione Christi paupertatem omnibus, & maximè personis Ecclesiasticis commendaret, nimis acerbè invectus est in clerum saecularem & Ecclesiae Praelatos, superbiae, fastus ambitionis magis audaciter quam prudenter accusavit . . . Quibus iniuriis irritati Episcopi omnes eos londini carceribus mancipari fecerunt et ex eodem suggestu palinodiam canere coegerunt.' J. Pits, *Relationum Historicarum de Rebus Anglicis*, Paris, 1619, p. 660.

31. *Robert Parker*] See above Pt. I, p. 114 and n.

36–7. *Humfrey Parker . . . Mr. Chancey*] 'Charles Chauncey, clerk, late vicar of Ware Co. Hertford, and Humphry Packer, yeoman' were brought before High Commission 26 Nov. 1635, for opposing the making of a rail about the Communion table at Ware. '. . . Packer after the setting up of the rail refused to come up to the rail to receive communion but made a journey to Marston [st.] Lawrence, Co. Northampton to Mr. Chauncey. . . .' *C.S.P.D.* 4 Feb. 1636. Both men made submission but had to pay costs. See *C.S.P.D.* 1634–6 and Rushworth, *Collections*, 1680, Pt. II, p. 316.

P. 179. 8. Petition] 'The Humble Petition of Many of His Majesty's Subjects in and about the City of *London*, and several Counties of the Kingdom.'

Presented to Parlt. 11 Dec. 1640. Rushworth, *Collections*, 1691, Pt. III, vol. i, pp. 93–6.

10–13. *Martin Parker . . . books*] Ibid., p. 94. The ballad writer Martin Parker (*c.* 1600–*c.* 1656), called the 'Prelats Poet', is known for his song 'When the King enjoys his own again'.

19. *peek*] pique: animosity, enmity.

24–5. *The Duke . . . Poet*] 'The Duke of *Muscovy* wrote Letters of late to the Q. of *Sweden* wherein he signified the cause of his Warr with the *Pole*. Two reasons he mentioned; one because a certain *Poland* Poet writing a Narration of former Warrs, wherein the *Pole* had the better, said they had beaten the *Muscovite*, without adding his Title, plain *Muscovite*. The other, because in quoting something touching the Genealogy of the *Muscovites* Ancestors, he named one as father which was the son; and for these two grand offences, he demanded of the *Pole* the offenders head; which being denied, he makes war upon them. . . .' *Mercurius Politicus*, no. 204, 4–11 May 1654, p. 3476. The Duke was Czar Alexius Mikhailovich (1629–76) and the war he precipitated lasted thirteen years (1654–67).

28. *Saffron-hill*] A street in the borough of Holborn running between Clerkenwell Rd. and Charterhouse St., formerly a notorious area.

28. *Pye-corner*] '. . . a place so called of such a signe, sometimes a faire Inne for receipte of travellers, but now divided into tenementes, and over against the said Pie Corner lyeth Cocke Lane which runneth down to Old-bourne Conduit.' Stow, *Survey of London*, ed. Kingsford, vol. ii, 1908, p. 22.

P. 180. 9–12. *What . . . hurl'd*] *The Rehearsal*, III. ii, p. 27.

13–19. *Bring . . . rather*] Ibid. III. ii, p. 26.

25. *ill Sire . . .*] John Parker, see above, Pt. I, p. 96 and n.

P. 181. 2. *Capel . . .*] Arthur Lord Capel (1610–49). The royalist primarily responsible for the renewal of the civil war, he joined with Henry Rich, Earl of Holland (1590–1649) and James, first Duke of Hamilton and Earl of Cambridge (1606–49) against Parliament. They were defeated and executed for treason 9 March 1649.

5. *Petition'd against*] 'John Parker and others' took possession of Fort-hampton, Gloucester, in 1648, when the owner, the Earl of Middlesex, was under the restraint of the Gentlemen Usher of the Black Rod. On 20 June 1648 the Earl petitioned the House of Lords and Parker and his companions were ordered to be brought before the House to answer their contempt in the breach of the privilege of the House. *Journal of the House of Lords*, vol. x, p. 338.

7–14. *The Government . . . dilabuntur*] The title-page of John Parker's *The Government of the People of England*, 1650.

21. *Graves*] Greaves, crackling: the fibrous matter in animal fat. Parker is presumably more ferocious than his fellow Grewellers because of his 'meat' eating.

24. *Elizabeth Hampton*] With Wm. Assheton (who also turned against his nonconformist beginnings) Parker attended 'the religious meetings in the house of Besse Hampton, an old decrepit laundress living in Halywell in the north suburb of Oxon.' Wood, *Athenae*, ed. Bliss, vol. iv, 1820, col. 606.

P. 182. 5. Warden of *Wadham*] Dr. Walter Blandford (1619–75), Bishop of Worcester, Warden of Wadham College, Oxford, 1659–65.

17–20. *Muleasses* ... Perfumes] Muleassis (*fl.* 1530) having fled from the Barbary pirate Khair-ed-Din Barbarossa, returned to Tunis to find his son ruling in his stead, he was defeated in the ensuing battle and '. . . soiled with his owne bloud and with the dust, flying among the rest, was knowne and taken: nothing more bewraying him than his odoriferous perfumes'. R. Knolles, *The General History of the Turkes*, 1638, p. 747. Just previously he had barely escaped with his life '. . . preserved by an old woman, who mooved with pitty, hid him from their fury under a great heap of garlicke. . . .' Ibid., p. 748.

P. 184. 4. Doctor *Bathurst*] Ralph Bathurst (1620–1704), physician, poet and theologian, President of Trinity College, Oxford, 1664–1704.

7–9. *to* . . . *Education*] *Free and Impartial Censure*, 'Dedication', B2ʳ.

20–1. *Plato* . . . *Calvin*] Parker gives 'good nature' as a quality of the Platonists not possessed by the Nonconformists. *Free and Impartial Censure*, pp. 25–8.

26. *Cambridge*] He was incorporated M.A. at Cambridge in 1667 and proceeded to D.D. in 1671.

P. 186. 19. Epidemical] universal.

33. *Crambe*] lit.: Cabbage, particularly *crambe repetita*: cabbage served up again; hence 'distasteful repetition'.

P. 187. 7–8. *Attack* . . . *Rear*] *Reproof*, p. 3.

10–15. *William the Conqueror* . . . *night*] Holinshed, *Chronicles*, vol. i, 1807 edn., p. 762. Also Milton: 'The Duke Arming, and his Corslet giv'n him on the wrong side, said pleasantly, *the strength of my Dukedom will be turn'd now into a kingdom.*' *The History of Britain* (1670) in *Works* vol. x, Col. U.P. 1932, p. 313.

30. same fate] The fable of the Eagle and the Arrow, in which the eagle is killed by an arrow feathered with one of it's own plumes. Esope, *Fables*, ed. Chambry, Paris, 1927, no. 7, pp. 6–7.

32–6. *Supreme* . . . *concerns*] *Discourse*, pp. 27–8.

P. 188. 1–3. Supream . . . so] Ibid., pp. 108–9.

7–8. *by* . . . *Nations*] Ibid., p. 35.

9. *Jewish* . . . *State*] Ibid., p. 32.

11. *antecedent to*] Ibid., p. 35.

13–14. *Scripture* . . . *Jurisdiction*] Ibid., p. 35.

15. *Posture* . . . *Affairs*] Ibid., p. 37.

15–16. *unhappy* . . . *Affairs*] Ibid., p. 38.

17–18. Antecedent Right of Sovereignty] *Discourse*, p. 40.

19–21. *Miracles . . . it*] Ibid., p. 48.

22–3. *Affairs . . . Emperors*] Ibid., p. 54.

30–1. *Wisdom . . . Power*] Ibid., p. 32.

31–2. *Governors . . . Extent*] Ibid., p. 58.

32–3. *Government . . . managed*] Ibid., p. 223.

33–4. *not . . . rights*] Ibid., p. 56.

P. 189. 2–3. *So . . . miscarriage*] Ibid., p. 19.

6. *Icterus*] 'A bird there is called in Greeke Icterus, of the yellow colour which the fethers carrie, which if one that hath the jaundise doe but looke upon, he or she shall presently be cured thereof; but the poore bird is sure to die for it. . . .' Pliny, *The Historie of the World*, tr. Holland, 1601, Tom. II, Bk. 30, ch. xi, p. 389.

8–10. *may . . . himself*] *Discourse*, p. 32.

25. Reincamerate] Re-annex to the Pope's domain.

26–7. *all . . . Patronage*] *Preface*, c7ʳ.

32–3. *if . . . labour*] *Discourse*, 'Preface', p. xlvi.

P. 190. 6. *Trumpet . . . Sheere-lane*] Shire (or Sheer) Lane entered Fleet Street a few paces east of Temple Bar and connected Fleet Street with Lincoln's Inn Fields, was known as Rogues Lane in the reign of James I (E. B. Chancellor, *Annals of Fleet Street*, New York, N.D., pp. 110–13). Midway along the lane from Fleet Street was the Trumpet tavern, one of the oldest licensed houses in London and later famous as the meeting place for the Tatler Club and the Kit-Kat Club. (Ibid., pp. 262–4.)

8. *Villains, Hypocrites*] *Discourse*, p. 273.

8. *Rebels, Schismaticks*] Ibid., p. 241.

8–9. *greatest . . . Hereticks*] Ibid., p. 319.

13. Tenters] Stretchers; i.e. in a position of strain or unease.

20–2. *must . . . Correction*] *Discourse*, p. 321.

23. *must . . . Villains*] Ibid., p. 272.

23–4. *must . . . Axes*] Ibid., p. 219.

30–1. eight times] Ibid., p. 271.

36. *Bridewell*] '. . . of olde time the kings house: for the kings of this realme have been there lodged, and till the ninth of *Henrie* the thirde, the Courtes were kept in the kings house wheresoever he was lodged. . . . But . . . this house became a house of correction . . . a Workehouse for the poore and idle persons of the Citie. . . .' Stow, *Survey of London*, ed. Kingsford, vol. ii, pp. 43–5.

P. 191. 5. *perish . . . Sardanapalus*] *Defence*, p. 656. See above Pt. I, p. 67 and n.

6. *King of the Night*] *Defence*, p. 641.

7–8. *Princes . . . Govern*] *Discourse*, p. 271.

12–14. *must . . . Government*] *Discourses*, p. 40.

24. insults] *Reproof*, p. 3.

29–33. *And . . .* Authority] Above, Pt. I, p. 97.

P. 192. 6–12. *'tis . . . determined*] *Discourse*, pp. 322–3.

14–18. *All . . . adoration*] Ibid., p. 99.

18–20. *All . . . Religion*] Ibid., p. 206.

25. next exception] *Reproof*, p. 6.

29. *turning . . . Leaves*] '. . . 'tis neither civil, nor ingenuous to trouble me with such Objections, that I cannot answer without reading over eight or ten large Volumes in Folio.' *Defence*, p. 452.

32. *Scandalous Plagiary*] *Reproof*, p. 6.

35. *indited*] Ibid., p. 6.

P. 193. 1. seriously . . .] Ibid., p. 7.

14–16. *the Fanaticks . . . Government*] *Discourse*, pp. 178–9.

32–2 [P. 194]. *We condemn . . . ours*] *Defence*, pp. 285–6.

P. 194. 13. Fellow-Prebend] Thomas Pierce (1622–91), prebendary of Langford Major at Lincoln, Dean of Salisbury, President of Magdalen College, Oxford (1661–72).

14–15. *he abhors . . . either*] Pierce, *The New Discoverer Discovered*, 1659, p. 167.

21–3. *making . . . Parliament*] *Reproof*, p. 7.

31. *Nequid . . . capiat*] Cf. the consular formula: 'Videant consules ne quid respublica detrimenti capiat.'

P. 195. 6–23. *should . . . impose*] *Discourse*, pp. 63–4.

27. Cardinal *Antonio . . .*] Antonio Barberini (1607–71) brother of Urban VIII; on 15 Sept. 1644 he was involved in the election of Giovanni Battista Pamfili (1574–1655) as Pope Innocent X. 'At length Cardinal *Pamphilio* being named by Cardinal *Barberino*, and his practises begun on all hands in his behalf, he refus'd with great moderation to be propos'd, if Cardinal *Anthonio* did not name him, who for some particular interests of his own, had procur'd his Exclusion by the *French*. *Anthonio* deny'd it, and declaim'd bitterly against his Brother *Francisco*; but at last laying aside all pretence of distast, or else seeing he could not secure his Exclusion, he consented to name *Pamphilio*, after an infinite number of perswasions and promises. . . .' G. Leti, *The History of the Cardinals*, tr. G. H., 1670, p. 283.

32–3. *any . . . Religion*] *Reproof*, p. 7.

34–5. *not . . . Anabaptists*] Ibid., p. 8.

P. 196. 2. a Book] *Mr. Baxter Baptiz'd in Bloud, or, A Sad History of the unparallel'd cruelty of the Anabaptists in New England. Faithfully Relating the Cruel, Barbarous and Bloudy Murther of Mr. Baxter an Orthodox Minister, who was kill'd by the Anabaptists, and his Skin most cruelly flead off from his Body*, Published by . . . Benjamin Baxter. With Allowance, 1673. This work was investigated in Council and found to be completely false (*C.S.P.D. 1673*, p. 312). Parker, who licensed the pamphlet, had to notify the public of its falsehood and his error (Bodley, *MS Tanner 290* f. 202, draft) and his testimonial, together with the exposure of the scandal was printed in a small pamphlet: *Forgery Detected and Innocency Vindicated* printed by J.D. [Marvell's printer, John Darby], 1673.

7–8. *reconcile . . . Age*] Preface to *Bramhall*, A2ʳ.

18. *Se . . . trovato*] A familiar phrase, supposedly a comment by Cardinal Ippolito D'Este on Ariosto's *Orlando Furioso*. Quoted by G. Bruno, *Degli Eroici Furori*, 1585. Stevenson, *Quotations*, 1934, p. 995.

24–8. *As . . . World*] Mr. *Baxter Baptiz'd in Bloud*, p. 1.

P. 197. 21–5. *had . . . Proposal*] *Discourse*, p. 76.

33. testimonial] *Forgery Detected and Innocence Vindicated*, pp. 12–13. See above.

P. 198. 10. *he falls . . .*] *Reproof*, p. 11.

12. *threw . . . amuze him*] 'Cete grandia ad instar montium prope Islandiam aliquando conspiciuntur, quae naues euertunt nisi sono turbarum absterreantur, aut missis in mare rotundis & uacuis uasis, quorum lusu delectantur, ludificentur.' Sebastian Münster, *Cosmographia Universalis*, Basel, 1559, p. 850. The accompanying illustration shows a whale playing with barrels (ibid., p. 852).

23. *de . . . Doliis*] Suetonius, *Claudius*, 16.

24–8. *the Church . . . confusion*] 'They cannot pluck a Pin out of the Church but the State immediately shakes and totters.' *Discourse*, p. 166.

31. *Cornelius his Tub*] A sweating-tub formerly used in the treatment of Venereal Disease. Also called (mother) 'Cornelius' tub'. 'Mother *Cornelius* tub why it was like hell, he that came into it never came out of it.' Nashe, *Unfortunate Traveller*, Everyman, 1949, p. 281.

35–1 [P. 199]. *though . . . land him*] And though it be a two foot *Trout*
'Tis with a single hair pull'd out.
Butler, *Hudibras*, II. iii. 13–14.

P. 199. 1–3. *he hath . . . Circle*] Above, Pt. I, p. 206.

11. Cardinal *Cusanus*] Nicolas Cusanus (1401–64). Marvell's reference is to: Nicolai de Cusa, *Opera*, Basel, 1565.

17. *all . . . Hoopable*] *Reproof*, p. 14.

21–2. *set off . . . pleasantness*] *Discourse*, 'Preface', p. xvi.

23. *Du Foy*] *Reproof*, p. 11. The valet in Etherege's comedy, *The Comical Revenge or Love in a Tub*, 1664 [E. D. J.]; Marvell must have known it.

24. *Conquest*] *Reproof*, p. 13. Parker cites:
Obey'd as Sovereign by thy Subjects be,
But know that I alone am King of me.
Dryden, *Conquest of Granada*, Pt. I. 1. i. 205–6.

24–5. *Archbishop of Granada*] Pedro Guerrero (d. 1576), Archbishop of Granada 1546–76, leader of the Spanish delegates to the Council of Trent, he was the chief opponent of the Pope and endeavoured to make the Episcopate and Council separate from the Pope. On 7 April 1562 at Trent he argued that *Residence* was a divine obligation. B. J. Kidd, *The Counter Reformation*, 1933, pp. 84 ff.

26. Kings of *Branford*] *Reproof*, p. 12.

P. 200. 15. *Colchester* . . .] An horrendous pun: Colchester was a notable centre for the manufacture of *baize*.

17. he objects . . .] *Reproof*, p. 20. *The Rehearsal* was first performed 7 December 1671 and published the following year about July. See Villiers, *The Rehearsal*, ed. Arber, 1927.

26–8. *before . . . contrivance*] Preface to *Bramhall*, A2ᵛ.

28–9. *either . . . it*] Ibid. e8ʳ.

30–1. *tired . . . Reader*] Ibid. e8ʳ.

32. *Emendatio temporum*] The title of a book by J. J. Scaliger, see below, p. 202.

35–2 [P. 201]. *must . . . labour*] *Gregory Father Greybeard*, p. 196.

P. 201. 12. I say] above, Pt. I, p. 109. The marginal note confuses the reference with *Gregory, Father Greybeard*.

13–17. *For which . . . Crown*] *Gregory, Father Greybeard*, pp. 195–6.

18–21. *This is . . . head*] *Reproof*, p. 498.

25–7. *first . . . drawn*] *Rehearsal*, I. i, p. 7.

29. *Prologue . . . Prologue*] Ibid., p. 7.

35. *which . . . first*] Ibid., III. ii, p. 30.

P. 202. 2. *Scaliger*] Joseph Justus Scaliger (1540–1609), scholar; his *De Emendatione temporum* (1583) is an analysis of ancient chronology. In *Thesaurus temporum* (1606) he collected, restored and arranged every chronological relic extant in Greek or Latin.

17–21. *to conclude . . . people*] *Rehearsal*, II. i, p. 12.

23–4. *Now . . . appear*] Ibid. V. i, p. 44.

28–9. loss of mine Ears . . .] *Reproof*, pp. 25, 31, 76.

P. 203. 2–5. Wisdom . . . Christians] Del Rio, *Disquisitionum Magicarum*, Cologne, 1633, p. 144.

8–9. running . . . Bishoprick] '. . . *Evagrius* (being chosen Bishop by *Theophilus* Bishop of Alexandria) had run away . . .' Socrates, *Historiae Ecclesiasticae*, Bk. IV, ch. 18, in *The Ancient Ecclesiastical Histories*, 4th ed. tr. Hanmer, 1636, p. 330.

9–10. *Ammonius . . . Office*] 'Ammonius . . . being urged with a Bishoprick, fled away secretly, cut off his right eare, that the deformity of his body might be a canonical impediment . . .' Ibid., p. 330.

14–15. *On the . . . David*] *Reproof*, p. 27, from, J. Denham and others, *Certain Verses Written by the Severall of the Authors Friends; To be Reprinted with the second Edition of Gondibert*, 1653, 'Gondibert', p. 17. Marvell identifies Denham as

the author (see below, p. 204). The 'alliance twixt Christ and David' refers
to the conjoined shields of the Cross of St. George and the Irish Harp on
the reverse of the coinage minted by the Commonwealth 1649–60. See H.
Grueber, *Handbook of the Coins of Great Britain and Ireland in the B.M.*, 1899,
plate 29.

27. 1657.] Marvell exaggerates his detachment, he was tutor to Cromwell's ward Wm. Dutton, 1653–6 and wrote several poems in praise of Cromwell. In 1657 he was made Latin Secretary. See Legouis, *Andrew Marvell*, 1965,
pp. 108–9.

34–5. my Father] Andrew Marvell snr. (*c.* 1586–1640) lecturer in Holy
Trinity Church, Hull, and master of the Charterhouse there: '. . . most
facetious in his *discourse*, yet *grave* in his *carriage*, a most excellent preacher . . .'
T. Fuller, *Worthies of England*, ed. Nichols, vol. i, 1811, p. 165.

P. 204. 8–10. homely . . . Eleventh] 'This *Oliver* was by Birth a *Fleming*, had
been Barber to King *Lewis*, and of greater Power and Authority with the
King, than any Nobleman in *France*. This Power and Influence which he had
over the King, was gain'd by vile and slavish Offices about his Royal Person,
too low to mention here; but among the rest, he generally us'd to suck his
Majesty's Piles . . .' Philip de Comines, *Memoirs*, trans. Uvedale, vol. ii, 1712,
p. 643.

17. the Author] Sir John Denham (1615–69), poet and satirist. He was
cuckolded by the Duke of York, went mad for a short time, and is supposed
to have revenged himself by transmitting the pox. Parker was remembered
as a cuckold, a manuscript epitaph in Bodley records: 'Double tongued he was
said to be, (that is) a knave, / But his Tongue, and his Horns both, are put
in the Grave.' (MS. Don. C55. fol. 18) Hearne gives a latin version, *Collections*, vol. ii, 1886, p. 158.

22. *Colossus of brass*] *Reproof*, p. 14.

23. *Brass . . . Heraldry*] Ibid., p. 17.

24. *Brazen Brow*] Ibid., p. 35.

24. *Out-brazen*] Ibid., p. 21.

32. *Scandalous plagiary*] *Reproof*, p. 6.

35–6. Multa . . . suggerit] I cannot find this passage in Cicero.

P. 205. 16–18. Doctor *Tomkins* . . . Negative] *Tomkins* proceeded to D.D.
15 May 1673.

19–20. the Professor] Richard Allestree (1619–81), Provost of Eton and
Regius Professor of Divinity at Oxford.

33–4. Ingagement . . . *Lords*] The *Engagement* was an oath of loyalty which,
on 12 Oct. 1649, Parliament made obligatory for all persons of responsibility
in England. *Journals of the House of Commons*, vol. vi, 1803, pp. 306–7.

P. 206. 1–3. *Populos . . . esse*] John Parker, *The Government of the People of England
precedent and present the same*, 1650, p. 1.

4–5. *Reges . . . Populi*] Ibid., p. 1. From S. Brutus (H. Languet?), *Vindiciae Contra Tyrannos*, Edinburgh 1579, Quaest. 3.

6–10. Kings . . . Spiritual] J. Parker, *The Government*, p. 6.

19–20. *spends . . . confutation*] *Reproof*, p. 3.

25. *perverting . . . Book*] Ibid., pp. 17 and 30.

31–3. *De privatis . . . Magistratus*] Calvin, *Institutio Christianae Religionis*, Geneva 1618, Bk. IV. xx. 31, fol. 540ᵛ.

33–4. dress'd . . . Princes] *Reproof*, p. 381.

P. 207. 25–6. affirm'd . . . Priesthood] Ibid., p. 22.

26–7. *things . . . Nature*] Ibid., p. 23.

28–30. *yet . . . confirms it*] Ibid., p. 28.

31–3. *The . . . person*] *Discourse*, p. 31.

33–3 [P. 208.] *because . . . practised*] Ibid., p. 32.

P. 208. 6–8. *Power . . . Nations*] Ibid., p. 35.

8–11. *though . . . other*] Ibid., p. 32.

12. *our Saviour . . . Princes*] Ibid., p. 33.

15–16. *for . . . Polity*] Ibid., p. 33.

16–18. *When . . . placed it*] Ibid., p. 48.

19–20. *the Divine . . . Church*] Ibid., p. 49.

22–3. *necessity . . . Prince*] Ibid., p. 49.

23–4. the *Pope*] Ibid., p. 54.

25–8. *though . . . Religion*] Ibid., p. 56.

29–31. *affirm'd . . . Institutions*] *Reproof*, p. 23.

35–6. *take . . . Correction*] Ibid., p. 1.

P. 209. 2–4. *To what . . . reason*] *Discourse*, pp. 34–5.

9–12. *though . . . Confirms it*] *Reproof*, p. 28.

26. *own . . . Superior*] *Discourse*, p. 34.

27–8. *All Power . . . Earth*] Matt. 28: 18.

29–30. *Scripture . . . asserts it*] *Discourse*, p. 35.

33–1 [P. 210]. *We derive . . . World*] Ibid., p. 40.

P. 210. 29. Doctor *Tomkins*] In *The Inconveniences of Toleration*, 1667, Tomkins argued against toleration on the grounds of reason and prudence.

P. 211. 3. here] *Reproof*, p. 22.

12. acuse me] Ibid., p. 24.

35. *Sacriledge . . .*] Ibid., p. 386.

P. 212. 12. Spiritual Deputy] 'Mr *Lee* of *Ickham*'? See below, p. 220.

17–18. *Works . . . Lasciviousness*] Galatians, 5, 19.

23. saunter . . . Countrey] Rochester has left a portrait of Parker in 'Tunbridge Wells'.

> Listning, I found the Cobb of all the Rabble,
> Was pert *Bayes*, with Importance comfortable:

He being rais'd to an Arch-deaconry:
By trampling on Religious Liberty;
Was grown so fat, and looked so big and jolly,
Not being disturb'd with care and melancholy;
Tho' *Marvel* has enough expos'd his Folly.

Poems, ed. De Sola Pinto, 1964, p. 89.

30–1. great Eater of *Kent*] Nicholas Wood. '. . . he would devour at one meal what was provided for twenty men . . . he . . . spent all his estate to provide Provant for his belly, and died very poor about the year 1630'. Fuller, *Worthies of England*, ed. Nichols, vol. i, 1811, p. 512.

P. 213. 11–12. *upbraided . . . Laws*] Reproof, p. 20.
13–15. *Ecclesiastical . . . Power*] Ibid., pp. 15–16.
17. *antecedent*] Discourse, p. 34.
17–18. *established . . . reason*] Ibid., p. 35.
18–19. *of Necessity . . . power*] Ibid., p. 40.
31–3. *hath . . . Tranquillity*] Ibid., p. 12.
36. *Christianity . . . Government*] Ibid., p. 178.

P. 214. 1–2. *asserted . . . God*] '. . . I only maintain it in defiance to the claims of any other humane power.' *Reproof*, p. 16.
5–11. *when . . . Uncontroulable*] Ibid., p. 16.
18–23. *there . . . Societies*] Ibid., pp. 20–1.

P. 215. 26–7. '*Tis . . . State*] Discourse, p. 215.
35–2 [P. 216]. If men . . . drawn] Suetonius, *Nero*, 32.

P. 216. 3–4. *though . . . Actions*] Ibid., 32.
6–7. *you . . . own*] Ibid., 32.
8–12. *he design'd . . . Fire*] Ibid., 43.
12–14. *A blazing . . . Rome*] Ibid., 36.
14–19. *He did . . . Engines*] Ibid., 38.
20–2. *He Sacrilegiously . . . money*] Ibid., 32.
24. *Persecutor of Christianity*] Ibid., 16.
25. *that . . . Power*] Ibid., 37.
27–8. *Governours . . . Power*] Discourse, p. 58.
28–30. *no Nation . . . Galleys*] Ibid., p. 223.
31–4. *by the Senate . . . Death*] Suetonius, *Nero*, 49.

P. 217. 6–7. *wishing . . . Neck*] Suetonius, *Caligula*, 30.
7–15. *lament . . . forgotten*] Ibid., 31.
16–18. *He was . . . equitable*] Ibid., 34.
21–2. *that he . . . pleas'd*] Ibid., 29.
23–8. *The Priest . . . Knife*] Ibid., 32.
31–4 [P. 218.] *He commanded . . . rarity*] Ibid., 22.

P. 218. 4–8. He took . . . *Apollo*] Ibid., 52.

8–9. He made . . . imbraces] Ibid., 22.

10. his Image . . . *Jerusalem*] Josephus, *Jewish War*, II. x. i.

17–18. *Son of Perdition* . . . afterwards] Hugo Grotius, *Annotationes in Novum Testamentum*, vol. ii, Paris, 1646, p. 678.

18–19. the *Adversary* . . . *God*] Ibid., p. 678.

19–21. *sitting* . . . *done*] Ibid., p. 679.

23–4. made . . . them] *Discourse*, p. 21 and p. 271.

25–8. *Cassius* . . . death] Suetonius, *Caligula*, 56.

31–4. it shall . . . *Church*] Heylyn, *Ecclesia Restaurata*, 1661, p. 132.

34–6. *King* . . . *Counsells*] Ibid., preface a2ᵛ.

P. 219. 3–12. took so . . . Consul] Suetonius, *Caligula*, 55.

26. Neighbour Prebend] There were twelve prebends at Canterbury; they were, in 1673, in order by stalls: 1. John Castilion (1613–88). 2. Parker. 3. W. Belk (1602–76). 4. Peter Du Moulin Jnr. (1600–84). 5. John Bargrave (1610–80). 6. John Aucher (1619–1701). 7. T. Pierce (1622–91). 8. E. Castle (d. 1685). 9. L. Herault (d. 1682). 10. Peter Hardress (d. 1678). 11. T. Blomer (installed Aug. 1673, d. 1706). 12. E. Stillingfleet (1635–99). [J. Le Neve, *Fasti Ecclesiae Anglicanae*, 1712.] Marvell's informant in matters of Canterbury gossip might have been Peter Du Moulin whose brother Lewis admired Marvell: J. Daillé, *The Living Picture of Lewis Du Moulin*, 1680, p. 88.

31. *Simon Magus*] 'Simon called *Magus*, because he was a Witch; a *Samaritan* by birth and a Christian by profession; he would have bought the gifts of the Holy Ghost for money. . . . He denied the Trinity and affirmed himself to be the true God.' [A. Ross, *Pansebia: or, a View of all Religions in the World*, 4th ed., 1672, p. 184.] According to Eusebius he lived at the time of the Emperor Claudius [*Ecclesiastical History*, ii. 13, trans. Crusé, 1903, p. 50]. However, the apocryphal *Acts of the Holy Apostles Peter and Paul* asserts that he lived under Nero. [*The Ante Nicene Fathers*, ed. Roberts and Donaldson, vol. viii, Buffalo, 1886, pp. 481–4.]

33–4. *Hactenus* . . . *Doctorem*] Grotius, *Annotationes in Novum Testamentum*, vol. ii, p. 681. Commenting on 2 Thess. 2: 8 and 9. He identifies Simon as 'Even him whose coming is after the working of Satan . . .'

P. 220. 3. *ut homines . . . detineres*] Grotius, *Annotationes*, ii, p. 682, on 2 Thess. 2: 10.

4. your attempting to fly] Simon claimed before Nero that he would fly with the assistance of his 'angels'—which he did—but Peter called upon the 'angels of Satan' to let him go, and he fell to his death. *The Acts of the Holy Apostles Peter and Paul* [*Ante Nicene Fathers*, vol. viii, p. 484].

20. Dean and Senior Prebend] John Tillotson (1630–94) was installed Dean on 4 Nov. 1672. The senior Prebend was John Castilion (see above, p. 219 n.).

26. *publick . . . Government*] *Discourse*, p. 12.

28–9. *no better . . . Authority*] Ibid., p. 12.

32–3. *Don Sebastian*] King of Portugal (b. 1554), supposedly killed at the battle of Alcacerquivir (1578). There were a number of accounts of his re-appearance, notably by the historian José Teixeira. This last was translated by A. Munday as *The Strangest Adventure that Ever Happened* (1601). He was supposed to be recognized by some 'secret marks and tokens'. [*A Continuation of the lamentable and Admirable Adventures of Don Sebastian* (1603); *Harleian Miscellany*, ed. Oldys, vol. v, 1810, pp. 489–92.]

34–5. imposed . . . *Nero*] Suetonius, *Nero*, 57.

P. 221. 1. *Adiatrepsia*] Suetonius, *Caligula*, 29.

8–9. made . . . occasion] Ibid. 50.

11. mentioned . . .] Above, Pt. I, p. 103.

13. accuse . . . Rebellion] *Reproof*, p. 210.

15–17. *Where* . . . Vesuvio] *Rehearsal*, v. i, p. 51 (mispaginated 53).

19. *Selene*] Greek goddess of the Moon.

23–4. *betraying* . . . *conversation*] *Reproof*, pp. 243–4.

26–7. your . . . *Pheasant*] Presumably Simon Patrick married Parker and Miss Pheasant. [See above, p. 150 n.]

36–3 [P. 222]. He condemned . . . River] Suetonius, *Caligula*, 20.

P. 222. 10. Doctor *Sibthorpe*] Above, Pt. I, pp. 127–9.

16. Here . . . *Reproof*] *Reproof*, pp. 366–76.

19. justifie it . . .] Ibid., p. 371.

27–32. *Impudence . . . at all*] Ibid., pp. 372–3.

34–6. *they had . . . Parliaments*] Ibid., p. 374.

P. 223. 2–5. *Punctilios . . . Custom*] Ibid., p. 375.

6–8. *whatever . . . Gospel*] Ibid., pp. 375–6.

15. *Petition of Right*] Passed by Parliament in 1628 forbidding the King to impose: taxation without consent of Parlt.; arbitrary and illegal imprisonment; compulsory billeting in private houses; and martial law.

19. *dare . . . determine*] *Reproof*, p. 375.

21–2. *You . . . dare*] *Rehearsal*, iv. i, p. 38.

23–4. *Ecclesiastical . . . Constitutions*] *Discourse*, p. 174.

29–31. *if Doctor . . . Commission*] *Reproof*, p. 370.

34–5. *Zeal . . . Pragmaticalness*] Ibid., p. 374.

P. 224. 9–11. *such as . . . Law*] 'The Humble Petition of . . . the City of London', Rushworth, *Historical Collections*, Pt. III, vol. i, p. 94, no. 10.

14–15. dash'd out . . . Clergy] The Petition notes: 'A Particular of the manifold Evils, Pressures and Grievances caused, practised and occasioned by the Prelates and their Dependants.'

21–4. *so granted . . . Kingdomes*] *Reproof*, p. 9.

24–32. *when beside . . . necessary*] Ibid., pp. 17–18.

NOTES

379

P. 225. 5–7. *He may . . . Deity*] *Discourse*, p. 66.

19. *a Guardian . . . Nature*] Is this a reference to Parker's mention of ἐπίτροπος δαίμων, *Reproof*, p. 12?

P. 226. 4. *Uilenspiegeled*] 'Duped' from Till Eulenspiegel the fourteenth-century German folk-hero noted for his roguery and practical jokes.

9. *I quoted you*] Above, Pt. I, pp. 99–100.

10–14. *if there . . . Errour*] *Discourse*, p. 308.

15–18. *Publick . . . attainment*] Ibid., p. 317.

P. 227. 1–3. *The same . . . Government*] Ibid., p. 40.

16. *Admensuration . . .*] 'And following Phoebus men are wont to measure out cities. For Phoebus ever delights in founding cities, and Phoebus himself lays their foundations.' Callimachus, 'Hymn to Apollo', *The Works of Hesiod, Callimachus and Theognis*, trans. Banks, 1856, p. 130.

30–1. *there is . . . Fanatick*] *Discourse*, 'Preface', p. li.

P. 228. 6. *Callimelanos*] Calomel: mercurous chloride, a drug used from the sixteenth century in the treatment of syphilis.

20–1. *Governours . . . of—*] *Free and Impartial Censure*, p. 219.

22–3. *those . . . dearest*] Ibid., p. 123. [Actually in the preface to the 2nd part: *An Account*.]

23–6. *for the . . . Rebellion*] Ibid., pp. 219–20.

28. Rogation week] The Monday, Tuesday, and Wednesday preceding Ascension Day.

29–30. *so easie . . . transgressed*] *Reproof*, pp. 17–18.

33. *blamed me*] Ibid., p. 11.

33–5. *You . . . Circle*] Above, Pt. I, p. 206.

P. 229. 24–6. *there are . . . nature*] *Discourse*, p. 317.

31. Brumall] < brevima: shortest day of winter. A quiet lull as T. Browne: 'About the brumall Solstice . . . the sea is calme and the winds do cease.'

P. 230. 3–8. *necessity . . . Nature*] Necessitas (Gr. Ἀνάγκη), in Orphic theology, the personification of absolute necessity. She appears as the mother of the Moirai (Fates), as the wife of Demiurgus (Fashioner of the world) and mother of Heimarmene (Destiny). Her power is even greater than that of the Gods, and the world revolves round the spindle she holds in her lap (see Plato, *Republic*, 616c). Horace represents her as grasping huge nails (*Odes*, I, 35).

33. common Maxime] Mendacem memorem esse oportere (a liar needs a good memory). Quintilian, *De Institutione Oratoria*, IV. ii. 91.

P. 232. 8–10. *The Jews . . . Enemy*] Josephus, *The Jewish War*, II. xix. 2.

P. 235. 30–1. *Blessed . . . them*] Matt. 5: 10–11.

34–1 [P. 236]. *Merciful . . . Mercy*] Ibid. 5: 7.

P. 236. 1–2. blessed . . . Earth] Matt. 5: 5.
    5. *terrour . . . evil*] Rom. 13: 3.
    11–13. *Woe . . . Sea*] Mark 9: 42.
    15–16. *tribulation . . . Christianity*] 2 Thess. 1: 6.

P. 237. 27–8. *Venenum . . . infusum est Ecclesiae*] According to legend, Pope Sylvester I (d. 335) heard these words spoken from Heaven on the occasion of the suppositious donation of Constantine—a reference to the secularizing of the Church. Neander, *General History of the Christian Religion and Church*, tr. Torry, vol. ix, 1858, Pt. I, p. 61.

P. 238. 22–3. Concubines . . . Magistrate] Sarpi, *Historie of the Council of Trent*, tr. Brent, 1620, p. 82; Du Pin, *Ecclesiastical History*, vol. xiv, 1710, p. 7.

P. 239. 6–7. set . . . Temple] Matt. 5: 5.
    7–10. showing . . . them] Ibid. 5: 8–9.

P. 240. 35–3 [P. 241]. The instances . . . nothing] At the Council of Trent: 'The Emperour *Ferdinand* by his Ambassadours . . . desired *a reformation both of the Pope and Court of Rome; to have the Cardinals reduced to the number of twelve or twenty-six at most; an abrogation of scandalous dispensations; a calling in of immunities granted against common right; a reducing of Monasteries under the jurisdiction of the Bishops of the Dioces where they stand; an abatement of the multitude of Canons and Decrees; a repeal of many that are superstitious; a reducing of Ecclesiastical constitutions to the rule of Gods law; prohibition against proceeding to excommunication, unlesse it be in case of mortall sin, or publique scandall; a purging of Masse-books and Breviaries, and expunction of that which is not taken out of the Scripture; a joyning of certain prayers and orisons in the vulgar tongue, together with the latine hymnes: communion under both kinds: a mitigation of that extreme rigour of fasting and licence for eating flesh: a permission for the marriage of Priests: a razing out of diverse glosses upon the Gospels, and a making of some new oaths by the most learned men, which all Curats should be bound upon great penalties to receive.'* The demands of the King of France were similar but neither were acted upon: '. . . this Councell made no conscience of satisfying the requests and demands of *Christian* Princes . . . The Emperour, the King of *France*, the Duke of *Bavaria*. . . .' *A Review of the Council of Trent*, trans. G. L., Oxford 1638, pp. 61–2. The Emperor concerned was Ferdinand I (1503–64), the King of France: Charles IX (1550–74). Pedro Guerrero, Archbishop of Granada, led the Bishops' party against the Pope.

P. 241. 28–35. Insomuch . . . celebrated] Paulo Sarpi, *The Historie of the Council of Trent*, trans. N. Brent, 1620, pp. 548–9.
    30. *Mosarabe* Ceremonies] Mozarab [< an Arabic word meaning 'would be Arab']: A Christian in Moorish-ruled Spain who was allowed to exercise his own religion provided he acknowledged the Moorish King and conformed to certain Moorish customs. The Mozarabic Liturgy was the national liturgy of the Spanish Church till the Roman liturgy was forced upon it at the close

of the 11th century; it still survives in Toledo. The mozarab breviary is one of the primary sources for the Book of Common Prayer.

32. *Antonius of Valtellina*] Antonio da Grossupto [in Valtellina] (d. 1570), Dominican, professor of *Materia Teologica* at the University of Vienna. He came to Trent in 1562 as theologue of the Bishop of Vigevano, Maurizio Petra. On 1 Aug. 1562 he spoke in favour of the concession of the communion *sub utraque specie* for the German-speaking areas. On 1 Oct. he spoke on the origins of Episcopal power. Marvell's account is from Sarpi.

P. 242. 31. *Kings . . . Church*] Isa. 49: 23.

P. 243. 16–18. *Most . . . Principles*] *Discourse*, p. 7.
  19. *some . . . within them*] *Reproof*, p. 12.
  19. *Pope . . . Bellies*] Ibid., p. 86.
  20–1. *Conscience . . . fancies*] Ibid., p. 86.
  22–3. *As the . . . tinks*] Proverbial: 'As the fool thinks so the bell tinks.' W. C. Hazlitt, *English Proverbs and Proverbial Phrases*, 1869, p. 73.
  33–4. *confined . . . perswasions*] *Reproof*, p. 29.

P. 244. 2. *meer Conscience*] *Discourse*, pp. 89–90.
  3–4. *Mankind . . . Practises*] Ibid., p. 92.
  5. *Thoughts . . . Actions*] Ibid., p. 89.
  5–7. *Christian . . . Law*] Ibid., pp. 95–6.
  27–32. *if the . . . Liberty*] *Defence*, p. 413.
  37–3 [P. 245]. *Mosaical . . . direct*] *Discourse*, p. 96.

P. 246. 34. Subalternals] Subalterns: inferiors.

P. 247. 14. *in Turky . . . Inspiration*] 'And they have an Order of Monkes, who are called Dervises, whom I have often seene to dance in their Mosques, on Tuesdayes and Fridayes, many together, to the sound of barbarous musicke; dances that consist of continuall turnings, untill at a certayne stroke they fall upon the earth, and lying along like beasts, are thought to be rapt in spirit into celestial conversations.' George Sandys, 'A Relation of a Journey' (1610) in *Purchas His Pilgrimes*, vol. viii of the Glasgow edn., 1905, pp. 132–3.
  20–1. *you quote . . .*] *Defence*, p. 413.

P. 248. 6–7. *Necessity . . . Gospel*] 1 Cor. 9: 16.
  24–5. *hath . . . so*] *Discourse*, p. 80.
  28–9. *all Laws . . . Conscience*] *Reproof*, p. 34.
  33–4. *transgresses . . . Horses*] 'Proclamation for restraint of excessive carriages to the destruction of highways. In partial conformity with a proclamation of the late King of 6 August 1622, it was commanded that no common carrier or other person should travel with any wain or cart which should have above two wheels, nor that upon any wain or cart there be laden above 20 cwt., or be used above five horses.' 9 March 1630, *C.S.P.D. Charles I 1629–31*, p. 208.

34. buries not in Flannel] On 16 Nov. 1666, a bill was introduced into the House of Commons: 'That no dead Person, or Persons whatsoever be dressed or wrapped up for Burial, or buried in any sort of Stuff or Things made of, or mingled with, Hemp, Flax, Silk, or Cotton; or in any Sort or Kind of Stuff whatsoever, except Flannel, or other Stuff made of Wool only.' *Journals of the House of Commons*, vol. viii, p. 650.

P. 249. 19–20. that *Italian*] Possibly Pope Innocent III (Lotario de' Conti di Segni) (*c.* 1160–1216) who assimilated the crime of high treason against God to that of high treason against temporal rulers.

35. *I will . . . Sacrifice*] Matt. 9: 13.

P. 252. 20–2. *whatsoever . . . Gospel*] *Reproof,* pp. 375–6.

26–8. *Order . . . Assembly*] In Locris '. . . the people are so strongly of opinion that it is right to observe old-established laws, to preserve the institutions of their forefathers, and never to legislate for the gratification of whims, or for a compromise with transgression, that if a man wishes to propose a new law, he legislates with a halter round his neck. If the law is accepted as good and beneficial, the proposer departs with his life, but if not, the halter is drawn tight, and he is a dead man'. *Demosthenes*, XXIV, 'Against Timocrates', 139, tr. Vince, Loeb Classics, 1935, p. 463. Marvell had heard the idea repeated in the House of Commons. '. . . it was moved in the House that, if any people had a mind to bring any new laws into the House, about religion, they might come as a proposer of new laws did in Athens, with ropes about their necks.' 10 Feb. 1668; Pepys, *Diary*, ed. G. Smith, 1906, p. 614.

P. 253. 2–3. *whether . . . Humano*] An issue raised at the Council of Trent. The Archbishop of Granada (see above) held that bishops were *Jure Divino* and therefore independant of the Pope. Sarpi, *Historie of the Council of Trent*, 1620, p. 597.

3–4. *Whether . . . Law*] Ibid., pp. 218–19.

6. *determined . . . Obligation*] Ibid., p. 487.

6. Pope] Pius IV (Giovanni Medici 1499–1565), Pope from 1559–65.

7–9. *declare . . . effectual*] Sarpi, *Historie*, p. 505.

22–31. *And because . . . News*] W. Rastell, *A Collection in English of the Statutes now in Force*, 1611, f. 378ʳ. See above, Pt. I, p. 48 n.

P. 254. 1–3. *Then . . . duty*] *Discourse,* p. 59.

4–9. *I will . . . Divinity*] *Reproof,* pp. 33–4.

32. Archbishop *Parker*] Matthew Parker (1504–75).

P. 255. 2–3. *have . . . Conscience*] *Rehearsal,* I. i, p. 8.

6. *Celsa . . . ridens*] *Free and Impartial Censure,* p. 18. Statius, *Silvae,* II, ii, 131–2; 'Villa Surrentina Pollii Felicis.' Marvell has inserted 'Senacula' for 'gaudia'.

11. *Sossiego*] Sp.: tranquillity.

15–17. *God . . . own*] *Discourse*, p. 60.

P. 256. 17–20. *Disobedience . . . out*] Hooker, *Works*, ed. Gauden, 1662, p. 224.

23–5. *in cases . . . Conscience*] *Discourse*, p. 308.

29–32. *if there . . . Errour*] Ibid., p. 308.

33. *render . . . themselves*] Ibid., p. 331.

34–2 [P. 257]. *a Doubting . . . Law*] Ibid., p. 287.

P. 257. 3. Bulbegger] A 'bogy', 'That which operates as a terror', *O.E.D.*

9–10. a Horse . . . Hay-cocks] 'Buridan's dilemma'—from its supposed inventor, the French philosopher, J. Buridan (*c.* 1297–*c.* 1358). It is not, however, found in his works.

11–13. *if we . . . Conscience*] *Discourse*, p. 287.

14. *He . . . eat*] Rom. 14: 23.

P. 258. 7. *their Heresie*] Gnosticism was at its strongest in the middle of the second century A.D. It was a mystical religion, characterized by the conviction of possession of secret and mysterious knowledge 'revealed' to the initiated.

P. 259. 3–5. *no passage . . . scatches*] He '. . . hath learn'd one lesson very well which the great Orator teaches his Scholar, viz. *to slide over those arguments which are hard, and take no notice of them*'. *Defence*, p. 745. *scatches:* Stilts.

7–8. *if it . . . Existence*] Above, Pt. I, p. 117.

15. Lord Archbishop] Gilbert Sheldon (1598–1677).

22. Doctor *Grigg*] Thomas Grigg, the licenser of Parker's *Tentamina Physico-Theologica*, he matriculated at Trinity College, Oxford, 1653, became Canon of St. Paul's in 1666, died in 1670.

26. *Typis A. M.*] Anne Maxwell, London, printer 1665–75, seems likely. The following details are from the title-page and unpaginated 'Epistle Dedicatory' of Parker's work.

35. *Shop divine*] *Reproof*, p. 21.

P. 260. 6–7. *Heylin . . . Leman*] Heylyn, *Cosmographie*, 1657, p. 159; see above, Pt. I, p. 25 n.

9–10. *Buckworths Lozengis*] 'Take notice that Mr. *Theophilus Buckworth*, the true Operator of the famous and long experienced Lozenges . . . hath now removed his dwelling . . . quantities of them [Lozenges] . . . are constantly to be had at Mr. *Tho. Rooks* . . . Mr. *William Milwards* . . . M. *Place* . . . Mr. *Magnus* . . . Mr. *Walter Hayes* . . . *Christopher Wilkinson* . . . Mr. *Hope* . . . *Thomas Palmer* . . . Mr. *Thomas Proudlove* . . . Mr. *Billingsly* . . . Mr. *Thomas Wright* . . . Mrs. *Elizabeth Bayley* . . . Mr. *Groves* . . .' *B.M.* Handbill, N.D., L.R.404.a4. no. 42.

30–1. *Clerus . . . mundi*] Proverbial. Gregory, *Father Greybeard*, p. 45.

31–2. *Suppose . . . quoth a*] *Rehearsal*, I. i, p. 7.

P. 261. 8–9. *the Chains . . . Education*] The 'Dedicatory Epistle' to Ralph Bathurst of *A Free and Impartial Censure.*

P. 262. 13. Sir *Francis Vere*] (1560–1609) General of the English troops in the service of the United Netherlands, the greatest English soldier of his generation.

19. *secular . . . Poet*] Horace on Augustus, *Odes*, i. 2. 45. Marvell adapted the poem himself in praise of Charles I: *Ad Regem Carolum Parodia*, and used the very line he notes: '*serus in coelum redeas diuque.*'

21. *Mr. Croxton*] James Croxton, born 1606, matriculated St. John's College, Oxford, 17 Jan. 1622/3, B.A. 1626, M.A. 1630. A favourite of Archbishop Laud, who recommended him to the Earl of Strafford for preferment. He was prebendary of Ferns 1637 or 1639. H. Cotton, *Fasti Ecclesiae Hibernicae*, vol. vi, 1850, pp. 137–8.

22–4. *sanctissime . . . Religio*] One of Prynne's charges against Laud was that he '. . . suffered the Popes own Titles of, *Sanctitatis Vestrae, Sanctissime Pater, Spiritus Sancti effusissime plenus; Optimus Maximusque in terris: Ille quo rectior non stat Regula, quo Prior est corrigenda Religio*; to be attributed to him in sundry Letters from the University of *Oxford*, Master *Croxton* and others without controll . . .' Prynne, *Canterburies Doome*, 1646, p. 441, also pp. 154, 194.

27–8. *it was . . . in't*] *Free and Impartial Censure*, p. 1.

34. *exceedingly . . . time*] Ibid., p. 123.

P. 263. 1. *upon . . . Coz*] Ibid., p. 242.

1–2. *dearest Coz . . . buz*] *Rehearsal*, IV. i, p. 36.

2–3. *From . . . May 2*] *Free and Impartial Censure*, p. 242.

15–20. *From all . . . interfiere*] Ibid., p. 164.

21. *Pinners hall*] In Old Broad St., London; in 1672, 'Some Merchants set up a *Tuesday's* Lecture in *London*, to be kept by six Ministers at *Pinner's*-Hall, allowing them 20s. a piece each Sermon; of whom they chose me to be one.' Richard Baxter, *Reliquiae Baxterianae*, ed. Sylvester, Pt. III, 1696, p. 103.

24–5. *not only . . . it self*] *Free and Impartial Censure*, p. 164.

P. 264. 6–9. *make . . . Christ*] *Reproof*, p. 56.

13. *Salvator Winter*] A notable mountebank, he claimed to have made up an elixir which would cure anything: 'In the Schools and in the Books not only of men but of Nature, by the means of long Travels, incessant works, dayly experiences, and continual speculations, we found out the key for to open the door of Natures Cabinet . . .' Handbill, *Nothing Without God*, bought by Wood in Oxford, 11 June 1664. See also *A Handbill extolling the virtues of a Medicine called Elixir, or Vegetable Spirit*, 1664, and *A Pretious Treasury or a New Dispensatory, contayning 70 approved physicall rare receits*, 1649.

14–20. *are not . . . Manners*] *Discourse*, 'Preface', p. xxxiii (actually p. 25).

26. *Don Belianis*] G. Fernandez, *Don Belianis*, trans. L. A., 1598.

27. *Grand Cyrus*] M. de Scudery, *Artamenes or the Grand Cyrus*, trans. F. G., 1653.

28. *Cleopatra*] G. de Costes de la Calprenède, *Cleopatra*, trans. R. Loveday, 1652. Three immensely popular romances.

30–2. *the Recreation . . . Discoveries*] *Free and Impartial Censure*, p. 3.

P. 265. 3–4. *before expounded . . .*] *Discourse*, p. 72; *Defence*, pp. 327–9; *Reproof*, pp. 116 ff.

17–19. *other . . . Gnosticks*] *Reproof*, p. 121.

22–4. *Faith . . . Fidelity*] Ibid., p. 121.

34. *Du-Foy*] The Pox afflicted french servant in Etherege's *The Comical Revenge; or, Love in a Tub* (1664).

P. 266. 4–5. *Aperta . . . Hæresibus*] Grotius on Gal. 5: 22, *Annotationes in Novum Testamentum*, vol. ii, 1646, p. 544. 5: 23 in the Greek text that Grotius is following.

11–16. *If you . . . Virtues*] *Reproof*, p. 118.

34–5. *Simon Magus . . . you*] *Free and Impartial Censure*, pp. 91–2.

36–1 [P. 267]. *men . . . did*] '. . . he makes statues walk . . . he rolls himself on the fire, and is not burnt; and sometimes he flies; and he makes loaves of stones; he becomes a serpent; he transforms himself into a goat; he becomes two faced; he changes himself into gold; he opens lockfast gates; he melts iron; at banquets he produces images of all manner of forms. In his house he makes dishes be seen as born of themselves to wait upon him, no bearers being seen.' *The Clementine Homilies*, I. 32, *The Ante Nicene Fathers*, vol. viii, p. 235.

P. 267. 1. *two Devils*] 'And indeed he was carried up into the air by demons . . .' *Constitutions of the Holy Apostles*, VI. ii. 9, *The Ante Nicene Fathers*, vol. vii, p. 453.

11. *Glandula Pinealis*] *Reproof*, p. 87. Descartes believed that the *pineal gland* in the middle of the substance of the brain was the seat of the soul. *Passiones Animae*, Amsterdam, 1650, Art. xxxi ff.

12–21. *It were . . . motion*] *Defence*, p. 342.

24–5. *vehemens . . . voluptas*] *Tentamina*, p. 105.

26–7. *Omne . . . fornicantem*] This commonplace is difficult to track to its exact source; a version exists in Aristotle's *Problemata*: '*Quare animal post coitum tristatur?* Respondetur, quia actus luxuriae est in se turpis et immundus, et sic animal abhorret talem actum, quia homines cum super hoc cogitant, erubescunt et tristantur.' *Problemata*, 1583, p. 129. See John Donne, *The Elegies and the Songs and Sonnets*, ed. Helen Gardner, Oxford, 1965, p. 213, note on 'Farewell to Love'.

31–3. *not be . . . ours*] *Defence*, p. 198.

P. 268. 4. *Flacius Illyricus*] Matthias Flacius (1520–75). A controversial and prolific Lutheran reformer.

4. *Bona . . . Salutem*] *Discourse*, p. 74. Owen pointed out that this was not

maintained by *Illyricus*: '. . . I do not remember that any such thing was maintained by *Illyricus*, though it was so by *Amsdorfius* against *Georgius Major*.' *Truth and Innocence Vindicated*, 1669, p. 55. Both Nicholas Amsdorf (1483–1565) and Flacius Illyricus attacked the view of George Major (1502–74) that 'Bona opera sunt necessaria ad salutem', Illyricus maintaining that 'non bonum sed malum praemium merentur' [*Clavis Scripturae*, Basel, 1617, Pt. II, col. 545] while Amsdorf declared 'Bona Opera sunt ad salutem noxia et perniciosa' (Melchior Adam, *Vitae Germanorum Theologorum*, Heidelberg, 1620, p. 70.)

22. one] John Owen.

23–5. *to . . . done*] *Reproof*, p. 53.

26. complyed with] Baxter contemplated answering Parker but was prevented by threats, *Reliquiae Baxterianae*, Pt. III, p. 102.

P. 269. 19. *comply with it*] Wood quotes a letter from the Jesuit Father Petre: 'the Bishop of *Oxon* has not yet declared himself openly: the great obstacle is his wife, whom he cannot rid himself of . . .' Wood, *Athenae Oxonienses*, vol. ii, col. 618.

20–1. *edifying . . . aprons*] Preface, a4ᵛ.

P. 270. 5–12. *exhibited . . . smother'd it*] *Reproof*, p. 66.

16–23. *Having . . . Consciences*] Above Pt. I, p. 46.

25–9. *So . . . Villany*] Ibid., p. 47.

29–30. *p. 54 . . . Politie*] *Discourse*, 'Preface', p. liii [mis-paginated: actually (c3)ʳ].

33. that *p. 55*] Ibid., 'Preface', pp. liv–lv.

P. 271. 5–13. *you are . . . Zelot*] Above Pt. I, pp. 57–8.

27. Tongue . . . Bone] Proverbial, Bohn, *Handbook of Proverbs*, 1867, p. 21. When a king of Java 'had broke promise with the *Hollanders*, and was challenged for it, he answered that *his tongue was not made of bone*', Heylyn, *Cosmographie*, 1669, Bk. III, p. 224.

28. other Slave] 'Wee that . . . print Books, sell ourselves into the greatest *Slavery* in the world . . .' *Free and Impartial Censure*, p. 1.

31–4. '*Tis demonstrable . . . Clergy*] See above, Pt. I, p. 56. *Reproof*, pp. 69–70.

P. 272. 1–2. *but . . . Debauchery*] Above, Pt. I, p. 56.

3–4. *if this . . . Invasions*] *Reproof*, pp. 69–70.

9–10. confound my terms . . .] *Reproof*, p. 70.

17–19. *if an hundred . . . last*] Ibid., p. 70.

20–2. '*tis easie . . . ruined*] *Discourse*, p. 216.

26–7. *comparisons . . . dangerous*] Above, Pt. I, p. 55.

27–8. *jumps . . . equal*] *Reproof*, p. 71.

32–3. *that . . . Conscience*] Ibid., p. 34.

P. 273. 1–2. *Debauchery . . . Religion*] Ibid., p. 68.

18. King *James*] Doubtless Marvell refers to James's *Basilikon Doron* (1599), a strongly protestant work which was placed on the *Index*.

32–4. throw in . . . *Divinity*] *Reproof*, pp. 33–4.

P. 274. 8–10. *tender . . . Villany*] *Discourse*, pp. 271–2.

10–14. *if Governours . . . state*] Ibid., p. 18.

16–18. *to judge . . . Immorality*] Ibid., p. 18.

19. *Gondomar*] Diego Sarmiento De Acuna, Count of Gondomar (1567–1626) Spanish ambassador to England. He was regarded in England as chiefly responsible for Raleigh's death: 'The *Conde Gondomar* an active subtil Instrument, to serve his Masters ends, neglected no occasion tending thereunto, which he mainly shewed in the particular of Sir *Walter Rawleigh*. . . . He first did underwork his Voyage to Guienna . . . and after his return with misfortune, he pursued him to death.' Rushworth, *Collections*, vol. i, 1659, p. 4.

P. 275. 18–19. *Clergy . . . Seculars*] *Reproof*, pp. 345–6.

31–2. here . . . *Reproof*] Ibid., p. 339.

P. 276. 8–10. *It is . . . else*] Ibid., p. 335.

14. good Doctor . . . *Tuesday*] Dr. Lake (1624–89) then prebend of York, later Bishop of Chichester. He objected to the noise of servants and apprentices interrupting divine service at York Minster on Shrove Tuesday 1673. In reaction they rioted and broke the windows of his house. *C.S.P.D. 1673*, 12 March, p. 36. [E.D.J.]

P. 277. 10–5 [P. 278]. Whereas . . . Subjects &c.] *Reproof*, pp. 64–6. Marvell has simply provided Parker's presumably ironic text with a Title, Colophon, and black letter type.

P. 278. 11. *James Collins*] Parker's printer.

15. *Etcaetera* Oath] On 29 May 1640, Convocation established an oath to be taken by all clergy and many of the laity in England: 'That I A.B. doe sweare that I do approve the Doctrine and Discipline or Government established in the Church of *England*, as containing all things necessary to salvation. . . . Nor will I ever give my consent to alter the Government of this Church by Archbishops, Bishops, Deanes, and Archdeacons, *&c.* as it stands now established . . .' Prynne, *Canterburies Doome*, 1646, p. 40. Rushworth, *Collections*, Pt. II, 1680, p. 1187. In his Impeachment, Laud was accused of being responsible for the oath.

16. another Dignitary] William Laud. '. . . this Archbishop in the year of our Lord 1633 by a Declaration compiled by himselfe, but published in his Majesties Name . . .' *Canterburies Doome*, p. 128. Prynne constantly accuses Laud of unlawfully penning Declarations.

26. *p. 55.*] *Discourse*, 'Preface', pp. liv–lv.

P. 279. 23. *his Son*] i.e., a son of Constantine.

P. 280. 1. *that Book*] Juliani Imperatoris, *Caesares*; pp. 98–101 of a parallel Latin/Greek edition of Julian's *Opera* (Paris, 1583) with separately paginated sections. Flavius Claudius Julianus (331–63) the 'Apostate' was Emperor 361–63.

11. *Constantine*] Flavius Valerius Constantinus (288–337) Roman emperor. He favoured the Christians and was converted to Christianity on his death bed. He presided over the Council of Nicaea in 325.

22–4. Julian *himself . . . Cruelty*] Above, Pt. I, p. 56.

26–30. *you bring . . . Hildebrand*] *Reproof*, p. 73.

P. 281. 5–11. *he . . . Toleration*] Ibid., p. 73.

14. *Ammianus*] Ammianus Marcellinus (*c.* 327–*c.* 392) Roman historian and soldier, he accompanied Julian in his campaigns against the Alamanni and the Persians.

14–26. *But when . . . another*] From his page reference, Marvell's edition is Ammianus Marcellinus, *Rerum Gestarum*, Hamburg, 1609, p. 225.

34–2 [P. 282]. *most . . . Christian*] Ibid., pp. 239 and 316. Bks. 22 and 25.

P. 282. 3–7. *Apollo's . . . thenceforward*] Ibid., p. 243. Bk. 22.

7–9. *left . . . handled*] Ibid., p. 257. Bk. 23.

18. *St. Austin* 18° *de Civitate Dei*] '. . . why are not *Julians* villanies reckned amongst the ten? was he not a persecutor that forbad to teach the Christians the liberall arts?' Augustine, *The Citie of God*, trans. J.H., 1640, Bk. XVIII, ch. 52, p. 744.

20. *Gregory Nazianzen*] Saint, one of the four great fathers of the Eastern Church (329–89). He wrote two *Invectives* against Julian, the first begins (in Latin translation) '. . . quorum opera tyrannus exstinctus ac deletus est, non Seon ille rex Amorrhæorum, neque Og, rex Basan, exigui principes atque Israelem, hoc est, parvam orbis partem vexantes; verum draco ille, apostata ille, magna illa mens, Assyrius ille, ille communis omnium inimicus atque hostis, qui et multum fuorem, multasque minas in terra profudit, et multam iniquitatem in excelsum locutus ac molitus est'. In *Patrologia Graeca*, ed. Migne, Tom. 35, 1857, col. 531.

20. *Chrysostome*] Saint John Chrysostom (*c.* 345–407), most notable of the Greek Fathers. His *Liber in Sanctum Babylam contra Julianum et Contra Gentiles* has a long attack on Julian; see *Patrologia Graeca*, ed. Migne, Tom. 50, 1862, col. 527 ff.

21. *Nectarius*] Patriarch of Constantinople following Gregory Nazianzen (d. 397). In his sermon on the martyr Theodore, he exclaimed of Julian '. . . una fuit etiam vesania et rabies contra divinam fidem nostram. Juliani, inquam, qui locutus est in excelsum Dei blasphemiam, et elevavit manum Deo inimicam adversus piissimam fidem nostram'. *Patrologia Graeca*, ed. Migne, Tom. 39, 1863, col. 1826.

28–9. ten Persecutions] The fifth-century historian Orosius numbered ten periods of Christian persecution under the following Emperors: 1. Nero (64–8). 2. Domitian (95). 3. Trajan (106). 4. Marcus Aurelius (166–77). 5. Septimus Severus (199–204). 6. Maximus (235–8). 7. Decius (250–2). 8. Valerian (258–60). 9. Aurelian (275). 10. Diocletian (303–13).

P. 283. 1–2. Cardinal *Granvell*] Antoine Perrenot, Cardinal de Granvella (1517–86), Spanish diplomat and churchman, noted for his savage repression of protestants, particularly as Archbishop of Maline, 1560–4.

2–6. The ripping . . . Frying-pans] Gregory Nazianzen, *Contra Julianum I*, *Patrologia Graeca*, ed. Migne, Tom. 35, col. 615.

10. *Mazarines*] Dishes for setting out *ragousts*, *O.E.D.*

13–18. his Malice . . . torments] Nazianzen, *Contra Julianum I*, *Patrologia Graeca*, Tom. 35, col. 630.

24. *Galileans*] Ibid., col. 599 ff.

P. 284. 6–12. *Julians* . . . them] Ibid., col. 631.

17–19. *some . . . Manufacture*] Discourse, 'Preface', p. xlviii.

22–3. *little . . . Conscience*] Ibid., p. 269.

23–4. *weakness . . . Wit*] Ibid., p. 279.

25–6. *they . . . them*] Ibid., p. 279.

27. *lash'd . . . peevishness*] Ibid., p. 305.

P. 285. 2. *Tintinnabulum*] Defence, pp. 461–2. A small tinkling bell, as hung on the neck of a bell-weather.

3. Bell . . . *Spain*] Juan de Quinones, *Discurso de la campan de Vililla* (Madrid 1625), gives the history of the miraculous bell of Vililla, which sounded of its own accord every time that religion was threatened by some danger. [E. D. J.] Marvell's knowledge of it could have come from Del Rio's account: *Disquisitionem Magicarum*, 1633, Lib. IV, cap. III, Q. ii, p. 579.

6–8. *spoke . . . Cymbal*] 1 Cor. 13: 1.

10. *Stentoro-Phonick*] A speaking trumpet invented by Sir Samuel Morland (1625–95) described by him in: *A Description of the Tuba Stentorophonica an Instrument of excellent Use as well by Sea as by Land*, 1671. Hudibras exclaims:

> I heard a formidable Noise,
> Loud as the *Stentrophonick Voice* . . .
>
> Butler, *Hudibras*, III. i. 251–2, ed. Gray, 1744, p. 130.

14–18. *when . . . peevishness*] Discourse, p. 321.

23. reaks] Pranks, wanton or riotous tricks, *O.E.D.*

25. Law] The 'Julian Law' or *Lex Julia de adulteriis et de fundo dotali* (18 B.C.) recognized the power of divorce in both husband and wife; not connected in any way with the Emperor Julian.

32–6. *whereas . . . forgot it*] The Rehearsal, IV. i, p. 33.

P. 286. 4–11. *Whether . . . Sanctification* &c.] Reproof, p. 97.

25. Mr. *Hooker's* Life] '*There is no meritous cause for our Justification, but*

Christ; no effectual but his Mercy. . . . We deny the Grace of our Lord Jesus Christ, we abuse, disannul and annihilate the benefit of his Passion. . . .' Hooker, *Works*, ed. Gauden, Life by Izaak Walton, 1666, p. 17.

25. his Sermon . . .] 'If here it be demanded, which of these we do first receive: I answer, that the Spirit, the vertue of the spirit, the habitual justice, which is ingrafted, the external justice of Jesus Christ, which is imputed; these we receive all at one and the same time . . . sith no man is justified except he believe, and no man believeth except he hath Faith, and no man except he hath received the Spirit of Adoption, hath Faith: for as much as they do necessarily infer justification . . .' Ibid., p. 520.

28–30. *Whether . . . beans*] *Reproof*, p. 98.

31–5. *Blessed . . . Gamaliel*] Ibid., p. 99. Rabbi Gamaliel I was a grandson of Rabbi Hillel, and president of the great Sanhedrin of Jerusalem. The Apostle Paul boasted of having sat at his feet. Acts 22: 3.

P. 287. 3. fighting . . . *Ephesus*] 1 Cor. 15: 32.

4–5. *much . . . mad*] Acts 26: 24.

6. *Elizabeth Hampton*] See above, p. 181 n. She died in 1661 and Wood records her epitaph made by the nonconformist Henry Hickman.

. . . .

She needs not us, but dearly miss shall wee
Our shee-professor of Divinity.

Survey of the Antiquities of the City of Oxford, ed. Clark, vol. iii, 1899, p. 191. The house in Holywell where she held her conventicles 'is commonly called the *ninth house* belonging to Mert. Coll.' *Athenae Oxonienses*, ed. Bliss, vol. iv, 1820, col. 226.

10–12. trample . . . Day] *Gregory Father Greybeard*, pp. 95–103.

12–14. *not . . . Apostles*] Ibid., p. 104.

14–15. *in some . . . consequences*] Ibid., p. 105.

17. whole duty of Man] *The Practice of Christian Graces Or the Whole Duty of Man Laid down In a Plaine and Familiar Way for the Use of All, but especially the Meanest Reader*, 1658. By Richard Allestree (1619–81), Regius Professor of Divinity at Oxford.

20–5. *By . . . Man*] *Gregory Father Greybeard*, p. 262.

26–7. *to be . . . Nonconformists*] Ibid., p. 261.

30–1. *baffle . . . Adoption*] *Reproof*, pp. 97–8.

P. 288. 4–7. *desiring . . . forenoon*] Ibid., p. 102.

12. *Aberford*] 'Situate in the West Riding, and 188 miles from London. . . . This town has been many years noted for its manufactory of pins; but other wise it is a place of no trade.' *The Universal British Directory*, vol. ii, 1790, p. 5.

26–7. Mascarade-Divine . . . *Age*] The author of *A Free and Impartial Inquiry*, 1673, refers to: '(that wonder of his Age) Dr. Parker.' p. 33. John Eachard is suggested as the author but this seems unlikely.

P. 289. 4–7. *have . . . attention*] *Reproof*, 'Preface', A4ᵛ.

17–20. *If it . . . same*] *Rehearsal*, 'Epilogue', H4ᵛ.

25. p. 47 to p. 54] *Discourse*, 'Preface', pp. xlvii–liv.

28–9. *to erect . . . Sedition*] Ibid., 'Preface', p. xlix.

31. *Christ . . . Temple*] Ibid., 'Preface', p. vii.

34–5. *'twas some . . . Deified*] See above, Pt. I, p. 59.

35–6. *Terrible pelt . . .*] *Reproof*, p. 82.

36–2 [P. 290]. *from me . . . dispatch*] Ibid., pp. 109–10.

P. 290. 1. Spanish *Fig*] poison. Also an 'Italian Fig': 'Some report he [Boniface VIII] was poyson'd with an *Italian* Fig', Leti, *Il Cardinalismo di Santa Chiesa*, tr. G.H., 1670, p. 233.

5. *first . . . Il Fico*] In 1161 Milan revolted from Frederick Barbarossa and insulted his wife Beatrix. 'To revenge this horrible affront, the Emperor besieged and forced the Town; adjudging all the people to die without mercy, but such as would undergo this ransome. Between the Buttocks of a skittish and kicking Mule, there was fastned a bunch of figs; one or more of which, such as desired to live must snatch out with their teeth, their hands bound behind them, as the Mule was pacing through the streets. A condition which most of them accepted; and thereupon gave occasion to the custome used among the *Italians*: who when they intend to scoff or disgrace a man, are wont to put their thumb betwixt two of their fingers, saying *Ecco la Fico . . .*' Heylyn, *Cosmographie*, 1669, Bk. I, p. 124.

8. *another fear . . .*] *Reproof*, pp. 164–80. A defence against charges of Erastianism.

14–15. *the Priestley . . . kinds*] Ibid., p. 178.

15–16. *is in . . . Uncontroulable*] Ibid., p. 176.

16–18. *Our . . . Church*] Ibid., p. 167.

19–20. *may . . . Rod*] Ibid., p. 168.

22–3. *When . . . Angel*] Ibid., p. 169.

23–5. *It cuts . . . Execution*] Ibid., p. 176.

P. 291. 1–21. *In the . . . thereunto*] Cranmer, 'Seventeen Questions concerning the Sacraments', *Remains*, ed. Jenkyns, vol. ii, 1833, pp. 101–3. Marvell probably took this passage from manuscript, for the 'Questions' were not printed before Burnett; they are found in the Lambeth and Cottonian collections.

29. *disown it*] *Reproof*, pp. 22–3; pp. 164–80.

P. 292. 5–6. *intimately . . . together*] Ibid., pp. 105–6.

10. *Baldwins-Garden*] An area running between Leather Lane and Grays Inn Lane. As the site of a former religious building it had the privilege of sanctuary in civil processes and consequently was a haunt of criminals who there resisted arrest. In 1697 an act of William III, 'The Escape from Prison Act', abolished all such alleged privileges.

10–11. *three-Crane-Court*] Three Cranes Lane runs off Upper Thames St., and possessed a tavern—The Three Crane Tavern—that Pepys mentions (23 Jan. 1662).

11. *Bonds-Stables*] By Fetter Lane: *London Directory*, 1790.

15–16. *comparing . . . terribly*] *Reproof*, p. 106.

19. 110*th*. page] part I, p. 50.

21–4. *This is . . . Cuckoldry*] Ibid. p. 112.

25. impoysoned . . . sacrament] Henry VII, German king and Roman Emperor (1269–1313). '. . . supposed to be poisoned in the Chalice by a Frier at *Benevent*, a town of the Pope's.' Heylyn, *Cosmographie*, Bk. II, 1669, p. 41.

25. another Emperour] Constantine V (719–75) Emperor. Called *Copronymus* (<κόπρος: dung, manure) '. . . for that when he was baptized he bewrayed the Font . . .' *Cosmographie*, Bk. II, p. 222.

27. *Wenceslaus*] Holy Roman Emperor (1361–1419). 'This emperor, for his beastliness, was deprived of the imperial dignity by the princes electors, A.D. 1399.' Wanley, *The Wonders of the Little World*, ed. Johnston, vol. ii, 1806, p. 186.

27–8. imployed the *Hostia*] 'And, most hateful of all, at the bidding of the aforesaid Serpent thrust from Paradise, you did keep in your mouths the most Holy Sacrament of the Eucharist received by you in the sacred Church of God, and did execrably spit It out upon the ground that you might with the greatest of all contumely, contempt and blasphemy dishonour God, our true and sacred Hope, and promote the glory, honour, triumph and kingdom of the devil himself . . .' 'A Summary . . . of All the Crimes of Witches', F. M. Guazzo, *Compendium Maleficarum*, ed. Summers, 1929, Bk. II, ch. xv, p. 136. See also p. 21, where the Eucharist placed in the mouth of an ass is used to produce rain.

28. Hereticks . . .] 'The *Nicholaitans*, so called from *Nicholas* one of the seven Deacons, *Act* 6 . . . gave themselves to all uncleanness. . . . Mans seed and menstruous blood were with them sacred, and used by the *Gnosticks* in their divine service . . .' A. Ross, *Pansebeia*, 4th ed., 1672, p. 188. The *Cataphrygians* were equally unclean: 'In the *Eucharist*, these wretches mingled the Bread with Infants Blood . . .' Ibid., p. 197.

34. *Andronicus Comnenus*] (1110–85), An emperor notorious for profligacy and excess.

P. 293. 10. I mentioned] Above, Pt. I, p. 97.

12–15. *that . . . edified*] *The Book of Common Prayer*, 'Of Ceremonies'.

16. *an outward . . . grace*] Ibid., 'A Catechism'.

17–18. *Our . . . Law*] Above, Pt. I, p. 215.

19. very large . . . discourse] *Reproof*, pp. 180–204.

21. *Sacraments Sacraments*] *Defence*, p. 447.

23–4. *Divine . . . Sacrament*] *Reproof*, p. 186.

32–3. *Julians . . . Incense*] Burning incense to Jupiter was imposed by Julian as a test of conformity to paganism: 'Each was obliged to throw incense upon the fire, and so receive gold from the emperor, pay for perdition, small

price for so dear a thing—for entire souls of men, and for sin against God.'
Gregory Nazianzen, 'First Invective against Julian', *Julian the Emperor*, trans.
King, 1888, pp. 50–1. *Patrologia Graeca*, Tom. 35, col. 610.

P. 294. 2–4. Collects . . . Sacerdotem] A. Sparrow, *A Rationale upon the Book
of Common Prayer*, 1672, p. 68.

    11. . . . four times] *Reproof*, p. 113.

    17–18. *an hot . . . Passion*] *Discourse*, 'Preface', p. vii.

    18–19. *he took . . . Zelote*] *Defence*, p. 152.

    19–20. found fault with] See above, Pt. I, p. 144.

    21. *a wellmeaning . . . Villains*] *Discourse*, 'Preface', p. liii.

    23–5. *a Power . . . Law*] *Reproof*, p. 134. *Phinees*: Num. 25: 11. *Elias*: 1 Kgs.
18, and 2 Kgs. 1: 10 etc.

    32. the Text] Matt. 21: 12.

    32–4. *Regni . . . venerabilis*] Grotius, *Annotationes in Libros Evangeliorum*,
Amsterdam, 1641, p. 353.

P. 295. 5. Doctor *Stillingfleet*] Edward Stillingfleet (1635–99) bishop of
Worcester. At the time of Marvell's writing, he was a royal chaplain, canon
of the 12th prebend of Canterbury.

    7–8. *as learned . . . Schisme*] Stillingfleet, *Irenicum*, 1661, p. 120.

    9. laugh at me] *Reproof*, p. 143.

    10–11. *who . . . groans*] See above, Pt. I, p. 83. Hales, *A Tract Concerning
Schisme*, 1642, p. 4.

    13. Latine classical saying] 'Omnem spumam musti cum faecibus expur-
gare', Columella, *De Re Rustica*, 12, 20, 8.

    17–19. *the loftiest . . . Fanatick*] *Reproof*, pp. 143–4.

    20–1. *that . . . Honesty*] Ibid., p. 143 and above, Pt. I, p. 83.

    23–4. Mr. *Hales . . . Socinian*] *Reproof*, p. 136.

    27. Fanatick Deportment . . .] *Defence*, ch. i, pp. 14 ff.

    29–32. *He has . . . recanted it*] *Reproof*, p. 136.

    33. Doctor *Heylin*] Heylyn, *Cyprianus Anglicus*, 1668, pp. 361–2.

P. 296. 1–2. Schisme . . . occasion] W. Laud, *A Relation of the Conference between
William Lawd . . . And Mr. Fisher*, 1639, sect. 21, p. 133.

    8. tax me . . .] *Reproof*, p. 140 etc.

    28–9. *To Shirley's . . . Halls*] Parker's booksellers: *J. Shirley* (d. 1666) London
bookseller at the Golden Pelican, Little Britain, published the *Tentamina*. *S.
Thompson* (d. 1668), London bookseller at the Bishops Head in Duck Lane.
R. Davis (1646–88), Oxford bookseller. *J. Martin*, London bookseller at the
Bell in St. Pauls Churchyard 1649–80. *James Collins*, London bookseller 1664–
81 at a number of places. *Henry Hall*, printer at Oxford 1642–79, printer to the
University from 1644.

    32–3. I instanced . . .] See above, Pt. I, p. 11.

    34–5. *as far as . . . Philosopher*] *Preface*, A3^r.

P. 297. 1. *Galen*] Claudius Galenus (*c.* 130–*c.* 200), the celebrated physician and medical writer.

1–5. *I confess . . . commendation*] *Tentamina*, p. 77.

6–9. *did not . . . Divinity*] *Preface*, A8ʳ⁻ᵛ.

9–11. *In whatsoever . . . wont*] *Tentamina*, p. 106.

13–14. *I wonder . . . Scaligers*] Ibid., p. 189.

13. Mercurius Trismegistus] 'But of all other which this age brought forth among the Heathen, *Mercurius* was the most famous and renowned; the same which was also called *Trismegistus*, or *Termaximus*; and of the *Greekes Hermes*.' Raleigh, *Historie of the World*, I. i, p. 318. Originally the Egyptian god *Thoth*, who, according to Diodorus Siculus invented almost all arts and sciences. A great number of Astrological and Philosophical works attributed to *Hermes Trismegistus* were in circulation in the early Christian era.

14. Lipsius] Justus Lipsius (1547–1606), Belgian scholar noted for his study of Roman History and Antiquities.

14–17. *I cannot . . . purpose*] *Temtamina*, p. 188.

15. Vossius] Gerhard Johann Vossius (1577–1649) German scholar and theologian, friend of Grotius, one of the first to treat theological dogmas and heathen religions from the historical point of view.

17–25. *our . . . day*] *Tentamina*, p. 269.

17. Sanford] Hugh Sandford began an answer to Bilson on the Apostles' Creed relating to Christ's descent into Hell; he died after two years and Robert Parker finished the work: *De Descensu Domini nostri Jesu Christi ad inferos libri quatuor ab auctore doctissimo Hugone Sanfordo Coomflorio Anglo inchoati, opera vero et studio Roberto Parkeri, ad umbilicum perducti, ac jam tandem in lucem editi*, Amsterdam, 1611.

17. Parker] Robert Parker, puritan divine; see above, Pt. I, p. 114 n.

21. Bochart] Samuel Bochart (1599–1667) French scholar, protestant pastor at Caen, author of *Geographia Sacra*, 1646.

28–31. *I do . . . Futilities*] *Free and Impartial Censure*, p. 100.

29. Picus Mirandula] Giovanni Count Pico della Mirandola (1463–94), Italian philosopher and writer. Among other studies Pico endeavoured to find a proof of the Christian mysteries in the Kabbalah.

32. abuse them . . .] *Free and Impartial Censure*, pp. 68 and 93; *Reproof*, p. 201.

34–2 [P. 298]. *It was . . . Syntagmes*] *Preface*, A6ʳ.

P. 298. 3. *such . . . laugh*] *Free and Impartial Censure*, p. 68.

5. you formally deny it] *Reproof*, pp. 200–1.

14–18. *Thus . . . are*] Ibid., pp. 124–5.

24–6. *the Clergy . . . Idolatry*] *Preface*, d1ʳ.

30–1. *you . . . prove*] Ibid., A2ᵛ.

31–2. *nor . . . Idle*] Ibid., e8ʳ.

32–5. *I might . . . did*] *Free and Impartial Censure*, p. 93.

34. Manes] Mani (*c.* 215–*c.* 277) '. . . a *Persian* by birth, and a Servant by

condition, was Father of the *Manichean* Sect; which was the sink of almost all the former Heresies, for from the *Marcionites* they derived their opinion of two Principles, or gods; one good, the other bad.' Ross, *Pansebeia*, 1672, p. 203.

35. Valentinus] 'The *Valentinians*, who from their whimsical knowledge were called *Gnosticks*, had for their master *Valentinus* an *Egyptian*, who lived in the time of *Antoninus Pius* Emperour, about 110 years after Christ. He taught that there were 30 *Æones*, Ages, or Worlds, who had their beginning from *Profundity* and *Silence*; that being the Male, this the Female. Of the Marriage or Copulation of these two, were begot *Understanding* and *Truth* . . .' Ibid., p. 190.

P. 299. 3–5. Lucian . . . *breathed*] *Free and Impartial Censure*, p. 6.

   6–7. *some have* . . . Sodomites] Ibid., p. 19.

   7–14. *which* . . . *sober*] Ibid., p. 20.

   15–17. *most* . . . *upon*] Ibid., p. 18.

   17–23. *palate* . . . *things*] Ibid., pp. 15–16.

   26–30. *had* . . . *fellow*] Ibid., p. 101.

   32–3. *as far* . . . *Philosopher*] Preface, A3^r.

   33–2 [P. 300]. *it is* . . . *ages*] *Free and Impartial Censure*, pp. 102–3.

P. 300. 2–4. *might* . . . *Ashes*] Ibid., p. 102.

   7–12. *And* . . . *one*] Ibid., pp. 24–5.

   18. *hot Fit* . . . *Passion*] Discourse, 'Preface', p. vii.

   19–21. *gentle* . . . *zeal*] *Free and Impartial Censure*, p. 25.

   23. rebuked him . . .] Matt. 26: 52 etc.

P. 301. 5–7. *ravishing* . . . *words*] *Free and Impartial Censure*, p. 3.

   17. *Mark* 10.35 . . . *Matth.* 20.20] The editions print *Matth.* 10.35. and *Luke* 20.20., which is erronious. Marvell's wording corresponds to Tomson's translation of Beza's version of the New Testament (1576), Mark 10: 35–44. The King James version has 'Minister' for 'servant'.

   33. *their Minister*] Matt. 20: 26, Mark 10: 43.

   35–1 [P. 302]. *words* . . . *Apostles*] Gregory Father Greybeard, p. 104.

P. 302. 2–6. *in some* . . . *Ghost*] Ibid., p. 105.

   8–11. *Civility* . . . *Impostor*] *Free and Impartial Censure*, pp. 24–5.

   12. Cross and Pile] < Fr.: *croix et pile* the obverse and reverse side of a coin. Marvell may mean—'a position and its opposite' or he may mean 'making these matters as a mere "toss up" '.

   15. second Author] Richard Hooker, *Of The Lawes of Ecclesiastical Politie* (1594–1662) was the first.

   16. *Tre Grandi Impostori*] An apparently suppositious work mentioned by many seventeenth-century writers and ascribed to men like Aretino, Bruno, and Campanella. 'That villain and Secretary of Hell, that composed that miscreant piece of the three Impostors, though divided from all Religions, and

was neither Jew, Turk, nor Christian, was not a positive Atheist.' T. Browne, *Religio Medici*, ed. Martin, Oxford 1964, p. 21 and n.

20. condemn me . . .] *Reproof*, p. 138.

29–33. *Quotation* . . . *of it*] *Reproof*, p. 155.

35. *de Lana Porcina*] After Horace: 'Alter rixatur de lana saepe caprina', *Epistolae*, I. xviii. 15. A proverbial expression for 'wrangles of no importance' —'mere wars of words'.

P. 303. 11–12. *Sects . . . Presbuteroisin*] *Discourse*, p. 150. A pun on the Greek word for 'elder': πρεσβυτέροισιν. By the 'good old Poet', Marvell doubtless refers to Homer who uses the word, *Iliad*, XV. 204.

20–1. not . . . *sterling*] '—he, whose whole effects, including the proceeds of his library which was well sold, scarcely amounted to 300 gold pieces . . . observed, not less shrewdly than truly, "If some will not be persuaded while I am alive, my death at all events, will show that I have not been a money-making man." ' T. Beza, *Life of Calvin*, in *Tracts*, by J. Calvin, trans. Beveridge, Edinburgh, vol. i, 1844, pp. xvix–c.

21. scantling] a specimen or sample.

28. *Sales*] St. Francis of Sales (1567–1622) Bishop of Geneva. His *Introduction to a Devout Life* (first published in 1609) was licensed by Heywood and withdrawn. Prynne urged the licensing as a charge against Laud.

29. Doctor *Heywood*] William Heywood (1600–63) fellow of St. Johns College, Oxford, and chaplain to Archbishop Laud and Charles I. He was petitioned against by his parishioners and attacked by Prynne as a 'licenser of Popish Books' and 'a constant practiser of these Ceremonious incurvations; directly derived from Popish Bishops, Priests, Munks, Missalls.' *Canterburies Doome*, p. 63.

P. 304. 1–8. *I think . . . guids*] R. Hooker, *Of The Lawes of Ecclesiastical Politie*, 1662. 'A Preface To them that seeke (as they terme it) the *Reformation of Lawes and Orders* Ecclesiastical in the Church of England.' n.p.: B1ʳ.

9–11. Doctor . . . *Hall*] Thomas Morton (1564–1659), Bishop of Durham; John Davenant (1576–1641) Bishop of Salisbury, Master of Queens' College, Cambridge; Joseph Hall (1574–1656) Bishop of Norwich. Their opinions are set forth in *De Pacis Ecclesiasticae Rationibus inter Evangelicos usurpandis Et de Theologorum fundamentali consensu*, first published 1634. Marvell is using the edition of 1636 published at Amsterdam.

15–18. *Consulant . . . fulserunt*] Morton, *De Pacis Ecclesiasticae*, 1636, p. 3.

15. Melanchthonem] Philipp Melanchthon (1497–1560), German theologian and reformer, close friend of Luther.

15–16. Jac. Andream Brentium] Johann Brenz (1499–1570), Lutheran divine.

16. Petrum Martyrum] Pietro Martire Vermigli (1500–62). An Augustinian abbot who rejected Roman Catholicism, fled to Strassburg, was invited to England by Cranmer and in 1548 was appointed Regius Professor of

Divinity at Oxford. He returned to Strassburg on the accession of Mary, eventually taking the chair of Hebrew at Zürich. He maintained a constant correspondence with Jewel and other English reformers.

17. Zanchium] Girolamo Zanchi (1516–90). Brought to protestantism by Peter Martyr, taught at the universities of Strassburg and Heidelburg.

31. some Letters] There are no letters to Calvin in Parker's *Correspondence*, ed. Perowne and Bruce, 1853. Strype notes a letter to Parker from Calvin in 1560, to which Parker apparently did not reply, *Life of Parker*, 1711, p. 69.

P. 305. 24–5. *his . . . England*] Heylyn, *Ecclesia Restaurata*, 2nd ed. 1670, a2ᵛ.

28–32. *Potiunte . . . est*] *Corpus Statutorum Universitatis Oxon*, 1634, Siv. 'Praefatio ad Lectorem.'

33. *Terras . . . reliquit*] Ovid, *Metamorphoses*, I, 150. The goddess Astraea was the last of the deities to leave the earth.

33–1 [P. 306]. *Decurrente . . . est*] *Corpus Statutorum*, S1ᵛ.

P. 306. 7. *King James . . .*] James wrote to Elizabeth on behalf of the puritan John Udal (d. 1592), and Thomas Cartwright (see above, Pt. I, p. 92 n.) and his brethren in 1591. Neal, *History of the Puritans*, vol. i, 1822, pp. 414, 418.

11–12. *the Enemy . . . Sectaries*] James I, *The Workes*, 1616, p. 355, 'A declaration against Vorstius'.

19–20. *Prelate . . . cause*] Heylyn, *Aërius Redivivus: Or The History of the Presbyterians*, 2nd ed., 1672, p. 244.

20–5. *Grindall . . . Heidelberg*] Ibid., pp. 244–5. Edmund Grindal (1519–83), Archbishop of Canterbury, suspended by Elizabeth because he would not carry out her policy of suppressing the puritan lectures and discussions. The French protestants were restored to their church in Threadneedle St. in 1559. Neal, *History of the Puritans*, i, p. 137.

26–7. *connived . . . them*] Heylyn, *Aërius Redivivus*, p. 246.

29. *by the . . . Bishops*] Ibid., p. 262.

30. *Grendalizing*] Ibid., p. 261.

32–1 [P. 307]. *wrong . . . forgiven*] Ibid., pp. 341–2.

33. Articles of *Lambeth*] Nine calvinist propositions maintaining the doctrines of Grace and Predestination compiled at Lambeth in 1595 by a committee under Whitgift. They were never authorized, and strongly opposed by Elizabeth.

P. 307. 1. *Bancroft*] Heylyn, *Aërius Redivivus*, pp. 371–2.

3–9. *he was . . . Innovation*] Ibid., pp. 383–4.

17. *admirable Ritualist*] Parker notes of Bramhall that he was 'a resolute Assertor of the Publick Rites and Solemnities of the Church', *Preface*, A6ʳ.

22–3. Duke of *York . . . Dogger-bank*] This doubtless refers to the crucial shortage of victuals in the English fleet commanded by the Duke of York in the North Sea, May 1665, which forced the fleet to return to Harwich for provisioning. D. Hannay, *A Short History of the Royal Navy 1217–1688*, 1898, p. 338.

24–5. *Ætolians . . . Quintius*] In 192 B.C. the Aetolians invited the Seleucid King, Antiochus III (242–187 B.C.) to join them in overrunning the rest of Greece, following the withdrawal of Roman troops. The Roman general and statesman Titus Quinctius Flamininus (*c.* 228–174 B.C.) was the civil representative of Rome in negotiations at Aegium in Achaea. Livy, *The Roman Historie*, tr. Holland, 1600, Bk. XXXV.

30–5 [P. 308]. *Now in . . . sundry sorts*] Ibid., p. 916. Philemon Holland (1551–1636), physician, school headmaster, and the 'Translator-general of the age'.

P. 308. 15–16. *that 'twas . . . words*] Discourse, p. 108.

19–20. *In whose . . . Fly*] The Rehearsal, IV. ii, p. 40.

22. boule-verse] < F. bouleverser: to disrupt, turn upside down.

31. *de Analogia*] Suetonius, *Julius Caesar*, 56.

32–3. *Those . . . contemptible*] Suetonius, *Augustus*, 86.

34. he displaced . . .] Ibid. 88.

P. 309. 11. *Jewel . . . Tintinnabulum*] Jewel, *Glass-drop: Defence*, p. 445. *Tintinnabulum:* Ibid., p. 461: a small tinkling bell.

16. *you . . . Valiant*] Free and Impartial Censure, p. 15.

22–4. You foam . . . Blasphemy] Reproof, p. 326.

27–30. *Fatuos . . . as you*] Ibid., p. 326.

32–3. *The* Ruac . . . *Swine*] Ibid., p. 326. Ruac Hakodesh: *Heb.*: 'Divine Spirit'.

34–1 [P. 310]. *A Crust . . . you*] Rehearsal, II. ii, p. 14.

P. 310. 1. *Bath col.*] *Heb.*: 'Daughter of a Voice': the supernatural method of communicating God's will. It can also mean simply a 'rumour'.

20–1. *Proselyti . . . Israeli*] The Talmud, 'Yebamoth', 47b and 109b. *The Babylonian Talmud*, ed. Epstein, 1936. It is apparent that Marvell is using a work containing passages originally from the *Talmud*.

23. catechized . . . Conversion] Ibid., 'Yebamoth' 47a.

31. three men . . .] Ibid., 'Yebamoth' 47b.

34. apart . . . ninety days] Ibid., 'Yebamoth' 42a.

P. 311. 1–12. *mersione una . . . quadratus*] The strict requirements for ritual purification may be found in the *Talmud*, Tohoroth II, 'Zabim'.

5–6. *Sed Menstruosa . . . aquarum*] Ibid., 'Yebamoth' 47b.

28. three times . . .] Reproof, pp. 125, 191, 212.

28–9. *Transproser Rehears'd*] By Richard Leigh (Wood, *Athenae*, vol. ii, 1692, col. 619).

30. *J.M.*] John Milton.

P. 312. 3. a slash] '. . . I refer . . . to blind *M*. who teaches School about *Morefields.' A Common-Place-Book Out of the Rehearsal Transpros'd*, 1673, p. 36.

18. Books *of Divorce*] Milton's: *The Doctrine and Discipline of Divorce*, 1643; *The Judgement of Martin Bucer Concerning Divorce*, 1644; *Tetrachordon*, 1645; *Colasterion*, 1645.

28. his house] From 1661–4 Milton lived in a house in Jewin St. near Moor-fields, doubtless this was where Parker and Marvell met visiting him. See D. Masson, *The Life of John Milton*, vol. vi, 1880, pp. 452–3.

P. 313. 13. *John*-like *Good nature*] 'John' is a generic name for a footman. Marvell presumably means to indicate a back-biting servility.

13. you plunge . . .] *Reproof*, pp. 366 ff.

16–17. *that . . . attention*] Ibid., 'Preface', A4ʳ.

19–20. *most notorious Rebels*] Ibid., p. 376.

20–1. this present Parliament resolved] On 23 Nov. 1667 the House of Commons resolved that the judgement against Elliott, Holles, and Valentine was illegal and on 15 Apr. 1668 the Lords followed suit: 'Upon due Consideration had of what hath been offered on both Parts thereupon, the Lords Spiritual and Temporal in Parliament assembled do order and adjudge, That the said Judgement given in the Court of Kings Bench in 5ᵗᵒ *Caroli* Primi, against the said *Denzell Holles* and others, she [*sic*] be reversed.' *Journal of the House of Lords*. For the Judgement of the Kings Bench concerning these men, when it was pronounced that they had raised a sedition against the King, were not in receipt of Parliamentary Privilege, and would be imprisoned and fined, see Rushworth, *Historical Collections*, Pt. I, 2nd ed. 1682, pp. 690–1.

27. Doctor *Bathursts* Talismans] *Free and Impartial Censure*, 'Epistle Dedicatory', B2ᵛ.

29–33. *The History* . . . Physick] *The London Gazette*, no. 777, 28 Apr.– 1 May 1673.

34. a Relation . . .] *Reproof*, pp. 457 ff.

P. 314. 3–4. *nothing . . . dissented*] Ibid., p. 458. For the Worcester House Conference, see above, Pt. I, p. 18 n. Marvell seems to be confusing this with the 'Savoy Conference', in which an assembly of presbyterians and bishops endeavoured to revise the Book of Common Prayer in a series of meetings at the Bishop of London's lodgings at the Savoy, beginning on 15 April 1661. The presbyterians asked: 'that no lessons should be taken out of the apocryphal books' (Burnett, *History of My Own Time*, ed. Airy, vol. i, 1897, p. 319) and towards the end of the conference: 'Charged the rubric and injunctions of the Church with eight things flatly sinful.' (Neal, *History of the Puritans*, vol. iv, 1822, p. 298.) The conference ended without success, so the King sent a letter to Convocation on 20 Nov. 1661 commanding them to review the Book of Common Prayer. The result was a prayer book more exceptionable to the presbyterians, for Burnett notes: 'it was resolved to gratify them in nothing' (*History*, i, p. 324). Convocation even took in more lessons out of the Apocrypha, 'in particular the Bel and the Dragon' (Ibid., p. 325).

10. a good Doctor] In the copy of the *Rehearsal Transpros'd*, Pt. II, in Magdalen College, Oxford (N.18.26) there is a contemporary annotation: 'Dr. Crowther Principall of St. Mary Hall, Oxford: and preb. of Worcester'. Dr. Joseph Crowther (1610–89) Praecentor of St. Paul's and Chaplain to James Duke of York, became Principal of St. Mary Hall in 1664. He died a prisoner in the Fleet in 1689. (See Wood, *Fasti*, ed. Bliss, Pt. II, 1820, cols. 236–7; Kennet, *A Register*, 1728, p. 640.)

13–17. *none . . . Laud*] *Reproof*, p. 330.

17. Granvile] Antoine Perrenot Granvella (1517–86), Cardinal, diplomat, Secretary of State for Charles V, and Philip II; notorious for his persecution of protestants in the Netherlands. See above, p. 283 n.

20–7. *the wise . . . State*] *Reproof*, pp. 511–12.

31–2. the Recorder of *London*] Sir John Howell, Sergeant at Law, Recorder of London 1668–76; on 23 Feb. 1677, the King issued a Royal Warrant granting him a pension of £400 *per an.* (*Calendar of Treasury Books, 1676–9*, vol. v, Pt. I.)

32. Inquisition] At the trial of the quakers William Penn (1644–1718) and William Mead for unlawful and tumultuous assembly, the jury although under immense pressure finding them not guilty, 'The Recorder, among the rest, commended the *Spanish* Inquisition, saying it would never be well till we had something like it.' (Marvell, letter to Popple, 28 Nov. 1670, *Poems & Letters*, vol. ii, p. 304.)

P. 315. 1–4. *The Government . . . visible*] Grotius, *De Rebus Belgicis: or, The Annals and History of the Low Country Warrs*, tr. T.M., 1665, p. 23.

2. Margaret] '*Margaret*, base daughter of the said *Charles*, [V], first married to *Alexander Medices*, afterwards to *Octavius Farnese* Duke of *Parma*.' Ibid., p. 21.

11. I told you . . .] Above, Pt. I, pp. 140–1.

15–17. *were . . . did*] *Reproof*, p. 288.

17. *these . . . described*] Ibid., p. 288. Sejanus: Favourite and minister of Tiberius, who endeavoured to gain absolute power by eliminating members of the royal family. Tiberius had him put to death A.D. 31.

19–20. *Jernie . . . Bacchus*] The first edition has *Je venie* corrected to *Je renie*. The meaning is clearly 'I abjure God', but the second edition is more likely to be Marvell's version since it was a popular oath:

> While those, with which he idly plays,
> Have no regard to what he says;
> Although he *Jernie* and blaspheme,
> When they miscarry, Heav'n and them;
> And damn his Soul and swear and curse,
> And crucify his Saviour worse . . .

Butler, *Satires and Miscellaneous Poetry and Prose*, ed. Lamarr, Cambridge, 1928, 'Satire upon Gaming', p. 47.

23. *being . . . Martyr*] Preface, e5ᵛ.

24–5. *Play . . . Caesar*] See above, Pt. I, pp. 141–2.

31–3 [P. 316]. *To deal . . . Wit*] Reproof, p. 400.

P. 316. 3–7. *some . . . Rules*] The Rehearsal, I. i, pp. 23–4.

14. Lord *Falkland*] Lucius Cary, 2nd Viscount Falkland (*c.* 1610–43) poet and patron of poets, advocate of reason in religion and friend of Hales and Chillingworth, he supported reformation of the Church, but opposed the abolition of episcopacy. He died fighting for the King.

15–17. *He is . . . oppressions*] Speeches and Passages of this Great and Happy Parliament, 1641, p. 188. This powerful speech against the bishops was delivered on 8 Feb. 1641.

18. Lord *keeper*] John Finch, Baron Finch of Fordwick (1584–1660), Speaker of the House of Commons 1628–9, Chief justice 1634, noted for his brutality and the decision that ship money was constitutional. Appointed lord keeper in 1640, he was impeached by the Long Parliament of the same year. Falkland led the attack on him.

18–19. *These . . . apply*] Speeches and Passages, p. 83. Speech of 14 Jan. 1641 urging the speedy dispatch of the proceedings against Lord Finch.

27. *Polydore Virgil*] (*c.* 1470–1555) Writer and historian, he came to England from Italy in 1501 as deputy collector of Peter's pence. In 1508 he was appointed archdeacon of Wells, and in 1513 prebendary of Oxgate in St. Paul's Cathedral. He published his *Historia Anglica* in 1534. In *de Antiquitate Cantabrigiae* (1574) Caius charges that Polydore Virgil: 'committed as many of our ancient and manuscript historians to the flames as would have filled a waggon, that the faults of his own work might pass undiscovered.' (cited, H. Ellis, ed., *Three Books of Polydore Vergil's English History*, Camden Soc. 1844, Preface, p. xxiii.

36. *critical . . .*] Reproof, pp. 500 ff.

P. 317. 3–4. *you . . . valiant*] Free and Impartial Censure, p. 15.

5–6. *more . . . concerned*] Reproof, p. 503.

6. that *Queen*] Christina of Sweden, see above, Pt. I, p. 109 n.

11. *Tyrant*] Above, Pt. I, p. 109 n.

16. *Fellow-Chaplain*] Thomas Tomkins (1637–75) prebendary of Exeter and rector of Lambeth, zealous churchman, author of *The Inconveniences of Toleration*.

17. *Copper-Mines*] Sweden was famed for its copper mines, particularly those of the town of Fahlun. See Outhier's 'Journal of a Voyage to the North in the Years 1736–7' in Pinkerton (ed.) *Voyages*, vol. i, 1808, pp. 326 ff. and Fortia's 'Travels in Sweden', Pinkerton, *Voyages*, vol. vi, pp. 461 ff.

25–6. *You . . . Austin*] Defence, p. 452.

27. *sunt Sacramenta*] Owen, Truth and Innocence Vindicated, p. 280.

28–9. *a boldness . . . Modesty*] Reproof, p. 198.

35–1 [P. 318]. *you . . . writ*] Ibid., p. 196.

P. 318. 1–3. *and if . . . Judgment*] *Reproof*, p. 197.

5–7. it should . . . *Marcellinum*] Ibid., p. 196.

15. Edition *Lugduni* . . .] Augustini, *Omnium Operum*, Tomus secundus, 'Epistolae', Lugduni, 1561.

28–9. you . . . *Library*] *Reproof*, p. 195.

P. 319. 3. *Pollex*] Thumb: i.e. actually reading the work.

5. The other passage . . .] *Reproof*, pp. 422–6.

7–8. you accuse . . . *Oxford*] Ibid., p. 292. Owen was Vice-Chancellor of Oxford 1652–8.

9. a Bishop] Edward Reynolds (1599–1676), Bishop of Norwich, Vice-Chancellor 1648–9. On 19 May 1649, Cromwell and Thomas Lord Fairfax were created Doctors of Civil Law. Wood, *Fasti*, ed. Bliss, 1820, ii, col. 152. Henry Ireton (1611–51), parliamentary general and son-in-law of Cromwell, was not, as far as I can ascertain, a recipient of an honorary degree.

13–15. certain . . . Answerer] *Reproof*, p. 424.

13. *Declaration*] *An Essay toward Settlement upon a sure foundation, being a testimony for God in this perillous time by a few who have been bewailing their own abominations*, 19 Sept. 1659 [Thomason, 669.f.21(73)]. John Owen's name headed the petitioners but it was not, as was soon pointed out (Johnson, *Examination of the Essay*, 1659), Parker's well known answerer. It seems to have been written by the Fifth Monarchists. L. F. Brown, *The Political Activities of the Baptists and Fifth Monarchy Men In England During the Interregnum*, 1912, pp. 189–90.

14. Cheshire *insurrection*] A royalist uprising in Cheshire during August 1659 led by Sir George Booth (1622–84). It was to have been part of a general insurrection on behalf of the King, which failed. Booth was eventually defeated by the Rump Parliament general, Lambert, and imprisoned. Clarendon, *History of the Rebellion*, vol. iii, 1720, Pt. II, pp. 672–4.

19. *so roundly*] *Reproof*, p. 425.

26. Fifth-monarchy men] A fanatical sect who wished to bring about the 'Fifth Monarchy' (Dan. 2: 44) which would succeed the four empires of Assyria, Persia, Greece and Rome. During it, Christ and his saints were to rule for one thousand years (Rev. 20: 4).

27. *Vennor*] Thomas Venner (d. 1661) a cooper by trade and Fifth Monarchy preacher, he was involved in a plot against Cromwell's government in 1657 and on 6 January 1661 he again urged his followers to overthrow the government and set up the Fifth Monarchy. After some fighting he was captured and executed.

32. Orbicular] complete, *O.E.D.*

P. 320. 17. *Signal . . . Recantations*] *Reproof*, p. 424.

20. *Suada*] persuasive eloquence, *O.E.D.*

33–4. *Rabshakeh . . . Piss*] 2 Kgs. 18: 27.

P. 321. 3–4. Iliack Passion] Also called *Miserere*: a painful affection due to intestinal obstruction, especially in the ileum—the third portion of the small intestine.

16–18. *protested . . . Recantation*] *Reproof*, p. 426.

32. Lord Archbishop] Gilbert Sheldon (1598–1677), Archbishop of Canterbury 1663–77.

P. 322. 5. *Saltum, Sufflum, & Pettum*] 'Dancing, whistling, and farting': a servile act of vassalage for one's Lord. See *Du Cange*, 'Suffletus' where he cites a usage: 'Usus est quotannis ut aliquis ex vassallis Dom *de Belhomme de Graulay* prope Sagium ad vesperam vigiliae Natalis Domini stipitem ad ejus Coquinae focum deferat; statimque tenetur saltare, crepitum edere et sibilum quod vulgo dicitur *un sault, un pet et un Sifflet . . .*'

14–23. *These . . . persons*] Ammianus Marcellinus, *Rerum Gestarum*, Hamburg 1609, p. 362. [Bk. XXVII, 3, 14–15.] Ammianus does not mention reprehension. Gibbon quotes the same passage, *Decline and Fall*, ch. XXV. In the first edition Marvell, or the compositor, has *Damascus* for *Damasus*, and *Ursicinus* for *Ursinus*. Ursicinus was governor of Nisbis.

24–31. *He did . . . Travellers*] Ibid. pp. 218–19 [Bk. XXI, 16, 18].

35–7 [P. 323]. *the . . . done*] Speech of James I in 1621 to the House of Lords; Rushworth, *Historical Collections*, 2nd ed., 1682, Pt. I, p. 26. Marvell paraphrases.

P. 323. 16. one begins] 'An Advertisement touching the Controversies of the Church of England.' Written 1589, printed 1640. Bacon, *Works*, ed. Spedding, vol. viii, 1862, pp. 72 ff.

16. the other] 'Certain considerations touching the better Pacification and Edification of the Church of England.' 'Presented to the King at his first coming in', printed 1604. Bacon, *Works*, ed. Spedding, vol. x, pp. 102 ff.

16. *Resuscitatio*] The 3rd Edition, 1671, ed. W. Rawley.

19–8 [P. 324]. The Controversies . . . *come*] Bacon, *Resuscitatio*, 1671, p. 129.

34. Slowness to speak] *James*, i, 19.

P. 324. 5. *I and not the Lord*] 1 Cor. 7: 10.

7–8. *the . . . come*] Prov. 26: 2.

8–24. The Remedies . . . Holy things] Bacon, *Resuscitatio*, p. 130.

20. *If . . . not*] Job 29: 24.

24–4 [P. 325]. Truly . . . Government] *Resuscitatio*, p. 131 [mispaginated as 133].

P. 325. 14–15. *as far . . . Philosopher*] Preface, A3ʳ.

23. Dr. *Hammond*] Henry Hammond (1605–60), distinguished English divine; on his death bed he is supposed to have exhorted his anglican colleagues not to persecute for any matter of religious difference [W. Penn, *The Great Case of Liberty of Conscience*, 1670, p. 42], a fact which immediately became ammunition for the dissenters.

23. Bishop *Taylor*] Jeremy Taylor (1613–67), Bishop of Down; his *Discourse of the Liberty of Prophesying*, 1646, is used as the central apology for toleration in the Restoration.

23. *Chillingworth*] William Chillingworth (1602–44). One of the foremost expositors of reason in religion in the century, in his *Religion of Protestants*, 1638: 'Take away this *Persecuting, Burning, Cursing, Damning* of men for not subscribing to the *words of men*, as the words of God . . .' [p. 198].

33–4. *Simon Magus . . .* it] 'Clemens Romanus saith of Simon Magus . . . That he commanded a scythe to mow of its own accord, and that it mowed down ten times more than any other.' N. Wanley, *The Wonders of the Little World*, ed. Johnston, vol. ii, 1806, p. 270.

P. 326. 14–15. *French . . . Canterbury*] 'Together with the exiles, the Dutch and German Protestants, who in the reign of King Edward VI had the Church in Austin-friars assigned them for a place of worship, returned to England. . . . They petitioned the queen to restore them to their church and privileges . . . the queen confirmed their charter, which they still enjoy. . . . The French Protestants were also restored to their church in Threadneedle-street, which they yet enjoy.' Neal, *History of the Puritans*, vol. i, 1822, pp. 136–7. The chapel of St. John or St. Gabriel, beneath Anselm's tower in Canterbury Cathedral is still used for services in which the French language is used; it was devoted to this purpose in 1561 on behalf of French protestant refugees.

18. Double-duty . . . estate] An act of 2 & 3 Edward VI, made any person refusing to set out tithes liable to pay double the value in the ecclesiastical court or treble in a common law court. This act was enforced with great vigour, in particular against the Quakers, often leading to the seizure of estates. [See A. Pearson, *The Great Case of Tithes*, 1732]. Estates were also seized upon inability to pay fines under the various enactments of the Clarendon Code. [See Neal, *History of the Puritans*, vol. iv, 1822, chs. vi–ix.]

25–7. Duke *Charles . . .* Sheep-skins] Charles the Bold, Duke of Burgundy (1433–77) was defeated by the Swiss in successive battles at: Granson [2 March 1476], Morat [23 June 1476], and Nancy [5 Jan. 1477] in which he was killed. The occasion of the expedition was '. . . truly a poor Cartload of Sheepskins that the Count de *Romont* had taken from a *Swiss* in his Passage through his Territories'. [de Comines, *Memoirs*, tr. Uvedale, 1712, Bk. V, ch. i, p. 408.]

28–30. justifie . . . fruit] Julius III (Giovanni Maria del Monte, 1487–1555). '*Vergerius* writes . . . when he missed a dish of cold peacock, which he had commanded to keep to him, having other new rosted peacocks, he vomit out most horrible blasphemy against God. And when one of his Cardinals answered, *Let not your Holinesse be offended at so light a matter*. He replyed, *If God was so angry for the eating of one apple, that he cast out our first parents out of Paradise; wherefore shal it not be lawful to me who is his Vicar, to be angry for a peacock, seeing it is far greater then an apple?'* J. Welsch, *Popery Anatomized*, 2nd ed., Glasgow, 1672, pp. 382–3.

33–1 [P. 327]. *most . . . inclinations*] *Reproof,* p. 527.

P. 327. 2–5. *certain . . . Paper*] *The Rehearsal*, I. i, p. 8.

6–8. *I verily . . . again*] Ibid., I. ii, p. 15.

11. Blatant] < The epithet for the thousand-tongued monster begotten of Cerberus and Chimaera by which Spenser symbolized calumny. Also 'vulgarly clamouring', *O.E.D.*

11. Latrant] Barking, *O.E.D.*

12–13. *Gnevoski . . . Table*] The word *Gniew* means 'wrath' or 'indignation' in Polish, this story would then refer to the 'angry one'; I have been unable to trace it, however. The Pope treated a Venetian nobleman, Francis Dandalo in this manner: '. . . he was enforced by way of Penance, to, *lie like a Dog with a Collar of Iron about his Neck under the Pope's Table.*' Care, *History of Popery*, vol. ii, 1735, p. 97.

13–16. *Hollanders . . . Victory*] The events took place on the establishment of Batavia by the Dutch in 1619. Stamford Raffles cites a 'Javan historian': 'When the fort was finished, the mud wall was removed; batteries were unexpectedly displayed, and under their protection the Dutch refused to pay a *doit*. War then commenced, in which the Dutch were reduced to such an extremity, as to be obliged to use stones in lieu of balls, which were expended. Even this resource failed; and, as a last expedient, bags of the filthiest ordure were fired upon the Javans, whence the fort has ever since borne the name of *Kota tai.*' T. S. Raffles, *The History of Java* (1817), Oxford Historical Reprints, vol. ii, Japan 1965, p. 154.

19–20. *Et . . . Baviere*] A suggestion that Parker had been through the stage of excessive salivation that characterizes the mercury treatment of syphilis. See Littre, *Dictionaire*, 'Supplement', under *Baviere*.

20. *Wenceslaus*] Wenceslaus IV (1361–1419) King of Bohemia and of the Romans. He married Joanna (d. 1386) daughter of Albert I duke of Bavaria (d. 1404) in September 1370.

23–8. *accedens . . . abstinerent*] Del Rio, *Disquisitionum Magicarum*, 1633, Bk. II, Q. xxx. i, p. 317.

INDEX

PRINTED IN GREAT BRITAIN
AT THE UNIVERSITY PRESS, OXFORD
BY VIVIAN RIDLER
PRINTER TO THE UNIVERSITY

	DATE DUE		